# Social Security

## PROGRAMS,
## PROBLEMS,
## and
## POLICIES

# THE IRWIN SERIES IN INSURANCE

## EDITORS

**EDISON L. BOWERS**
*The Ohio State University*

**DAVIS W. GREGG**
*The American College of Life Underwriters*

# SOCIAL SECURITY
## Programs, Problems, and Policies

Selected Readings

by **WILLIAM HABER**
*Professor of Economics*

and

**WILBUR J. COHEN**
*Professor of Public Welfare Administration*

*Both of The University of Michigan*

**RICHARD D. IRWIN,** Inc.

Homewood, Illinois · 1960

First Printing, September, 1960

Library of Congress Catalogue Card No. 60–15870

PRINTED IN THE UNITED STATES OF AMERICA

# Preface

IN THE TWENTY-FIVE YEARS which have passed since the Social Security Act was enacted by the Congress, numerous articles, research studies, speeches and voluminous legislative hearings have been published. Unfortunately, there is not available at the present time a comprehensive book on either the old-age, survivors and disability insurance or our unemployment insurance programs, nor is there available a good up-to-date general treatment of the entire field, summarizing and coordinating the whole area.

Social security is a controversial and dynamic topic with many aspects —philosophical, theoretical and humanitarian; financial, administrative, social, economic and political; statistical, actuarial, medical and legal. Frequent changes in federal or state legislation and administrative practices have made it difficult, if not impossible, for the average person to keep up with current developments.

This book of selected readings is aimed, therefore, at meeting the need which exists among many students, teachers, legislators, and personnel officers, controllers, and other management and union officials, and many of the more than 100,000 persons engaged in the administration of social security. The pioneering volumes of Rubinow, Epstein, Armstrong, Douglas, Burns, and Stewart are still useful but not up to date. Textbooks on social security by Burns, Gagliardo, and the more recent volume by Turnbull, Williams, and Cheit necessarily abbreviate the treatment of some of the controversial and significant issues. Various labor economics textbooks such as those by Millis, Lester, Daugherty, Taft, Reynolds, and Gitlow are necessarily brief on social security and do not discuss many topics, some of which are not solely within the field of labor economics. Likewise, textbooks used in sociology or social work also omit specialized social security subjects such as "experience rating" in unemployment insurance.

This compilation of readings is not intended as a substitute for a definitive text on social security or specialized textbooks for different courses. It is intended, however, to provide more comprehensive treatment of significant developments and critical issues in social security material on particular aspects of the topic. At the same time it can be used by the busy student, teacher, legislator, and management or labor executive to locate material quickly on particular programs or issues.

The selection of a very limited number of readings out of the hundreds of excellent possibilities was no easy task. The editors do not pretend that they have made the only possible selections. They are conscious of the fact that many outstanding publications had to be omitted for lack of

space, but they have attempted to list many of these in the selected bibli-
ography following each section.

The readings in this volume were selected not in terms of whether the
editors agreed or disagreed with the point of view taken or the validity
of the arguments or facts presented. They have attempted to select, as in
a case book on law, the important viewpoints which bring out major lines
of reasoning that should help the reader develop his own point of view.

The many issues and problems in social security and the newness of
some of the programs account, in large part, for the fact that much of the
important information and opinion is buried deep in Congressional hearings, government bulletins, and professional journals of economists, social
workers, statisticians, lawyers, actuaries, and the medical profession. Most
of this material is not readily available to the average person. Much of the
interesting and important material which throws valuable light on current
developments is available only in the mimeographed material published
by the various organiziations, or other organized groups supporting or
opposing legislative changes in the program in Congress or state legislatures. This volume of selected readings makes available some of these
which are not easily accessible.

Students may wish to refer to the authors' *Readings in Social Security*
published in 1948 by Prentice-Hall, Inc., which contains many historically important readings not reproduced in this volume.

Keeping up to date on social security developments is a task of sizable
proportions. For those who attempt the task the best single source of current information is the section on "recent publications" which appears in
the *Social Security Bulletin* published monthly by the Social Security
Administration, Department of Health, Education, and Welfare. The
August, 1960 *Bulletin* contains an excellent historical and statistical survey
of the first quarter century of the Social Security Act. A collection of the
most significant bibliographical items is found in *Basic Readings in Social
Security*, published by the Department of Health, Education, and Welfare
in August, 1960.

Professor J. Douglas Brown of Princeton University, one of the outstanding authorities in the United States in the field of social security,
has stated that experience indicates that the survival of democratic capitalism will depend upon the genius of man in combining three ingredients
—individual incentive, mutual responsibility, and an effective framework
of protection against the corroding fear of insecurity. He urges the need
for renewed study and effective action of the basic question "How can
we establish an effective framework against the fear of insecurity in order
to sustain capitalism?" The editors hope that in some small way this volume will contribute to further study and effective action of the basic
question raised by Professor Brown.

The University of Michigan                        WILLIAM HABER
September, 1960                                   WILBUR J. COHEN

# Acknowledgments

WE WISH to express our gratitude to the many authors and publishers who have given us permission to reprint their publications.

We are indebted to the following for the use of articles or materials appearing in government publications or other documents which were not copyrighted: ARTHUR J. ALTMEYER, HERMAN M. and ANNE R. SOMERS, MARGARET S. GORDON, VICTOR CHRISTGAU, ALFRED M. SKOLNIK, JOSEPH ZISMAN, ROBERT M. BALL, EDWIN E. WITTE, HARRY S. TRUMAN, AIME J. FORAND, and IDA C. MERRIAM.

We are also grateful to our research assistant, HUGH J. CROSSLAND, JR., who in addition to assisting us in the preparation of our articles on employment security, read and checked galleys and page proof and prepared the index and the background of contributors.

Special permission was obtained by the editors for those selections which are copyrighted. These are:

American Assembly, Columbia University, for permission to reprint FREDERICK LEWIS ALLEN, "A Look Back and a Look Ahead" and "The Role of Individual Thrift, Private Enterprise and Government."

Society of Actuaries for permission to reprint R. A. HOHAUS, "Equity, Adequacy, and Related Factors in Old Age Security."

The University of Chicago Press for permission to reprint from the *Social Service Review*, J. D. BROWN, "The American Philosophy of Social Insurance" and WILBUR J. COHEN, "Needed Changes in Social Welfare Programs and Objectives."

Columbia University Press for permission to reprint R. A. HOHAUS's comments on "Income Security for a Free Society," from *National Policies for Education, Health and Social Services*, JULIUS HOCHMAN, "The Retirement Myth," and J. M. BECKER, "The Problem of Abuse in Unemployment Benefits."

*California Law Review*, for permission to reprint HERMAN M. and ANNE R. SOMERS, "Private Health Insurance" and CHARLES I. SCHOTTLAND, "Basic Characteristics of OASDI."

*Fortune Magazine* for permission to reprint, "The Steady Push for Pensions."

*Industrial and Labor Relations Review* for permission to reprint WILBUR J. COHEN, "Some Issues and Goals in Social Security."

The University of California for permission to reprint from MARGARET S. GORDON and RALPH W. AMERSON, *Unemployment Insurance*.

The University of Illinois, Bureau of Business Research, for permission to reprint from CLINTON SPIVEY, *Objectives and Appraisal of Experience Rating*.

*The Reader's Digest* and KENNETH O. GILMORE for permission to reprint KENNETH O. GILMORE, "The Scandal of Unemployment Compensation."

*Yale Law Journal* for permission to reprint "AMA Attitudes toward Compulsory Health Insurance."

*The New Republic* for permission to reprint ANNE TAYLOR MOORE, "Medical Care in Great Britain."

New York University for permission to reprint ROBERT TILOVE, *Experience under State Disability Benefit Laws*.

The University of Miami Press for permission to reprint from JAMES C. VADA-KIN's *Family Allowances.*

*American Economic Review* for permission to reprint J. DOUGLAS BROWN, "Social Insurance: A Problem in Institutional Economics."

American Public Health Association for permission to reprint WILBUR J. COHEN, "Trends and Issues in Social Welfare Expenditures and Programs.

American Management Association for permission to reprint J. DOUGLAS BROWN, "Management's Stake in the Survival of Contributory Social Insurance."

*Commentary* and DILLARD STOKES for permission to reprint "Does Our Social Security System Make Sense."

*Barron's* for permission to reprint the editorial, "What Price Welfare?"

American Public Welfare Association for permission to reprint EVELINE BURNS, "A Salute to 25 Years of Social Security," and WILLIAM M. HABER, "Why Financial Need in an Expanding Economy."

## SOME BACKGROUND NOTES ABOUT THE AUTHORS

ARTHUR J. ALTMEYER was Chairman of the Technical Board of the Committee on Economic Security which drafted the original Social Security Act; Chairman of the Social Security Board; and Commissioner for Social Security in the Department of Health, Education, and Welfare.

FREDERICK LEWIS ALLEN was editor of *Harper's* Magazine and the author of *Only Yesterday* and *The Big Change.*

HERMAN M. SOMERS is Chairman of the Department of Political Science, Haverford College, and co-author of *Workmen's Compensation: Prevention, Insurance, and Rehabilitation of Occupational Disability.*

ANNE R. SOMERS is co-author with her husband, Herman M. Somers, of books and articles on social security and of their forthcoming volume, *Doctors, Patients, and Third Parties: The Organization and Financing of Medical Care.*

REINHARD A. HOHAUS is Vice President and Actuary of the Metropolitan Life Insurance Company and has been a member of governmental, business, and insurance advisory committees on social security.

J. DOUGLAS BROWN is Dean of Faculty of Princeton University; Chairman of the Advisory Council on Social Security of 1938; principal advisor on the formulation of the old-age insurance program to the Committee on Economic Security; and member of other governmental advisory committees; and is widely recognized as a student of social insurance philosophy.

JULIUS HOCHMAN is Vice President of the International Ladies Garment Workers Union; a discerning student of the labor movement and social problems.

MARGARET S. GORDON is Associate Director of the Industrial Relations Institute of the University of California at Berkeley.

CHARLES I. SCHOTTLAND is Dean of the Florence Heller School of Graduate Studies in Social Welfare at Brandeis University; formerly Commissioner of Social Security, Department of Health, Education, and Welfare; and formerly the Director of the California Department of Welfare.

VICTOR CHRISTGAU is Director of the Bureau of Old-Age and Survivors Insurance in the Social Security Administration, Department of Health, Education, and Welfare; and was formerly the Director of the Minnesota Department of Employment Security.

ALFRED M. SKOLNIK is a member of the staff of the Division of Program Research, Social Security Administration, Department of Health, Education, and Welfare.

JOSEPH ZISMAN was formerly a member of the staff of the Department of Program Research, Social Security Administration, Department of Health, Education, and Welfare.

ROBERT M. BALL is Deputy Director of the Bureau of Old-Age and Survivors Insurance, Social Security Administration, Department of Health, Education, and Welfare.

JOSEPH M. BECKER, S.J., is on the faculty of the Institute of the Social Order at St. Louis University; author of two important books on unemployment insurance.

KENNETH O. GILMORE is a staff member of *Reader's Digest.*

FEDELE F. FAURI is Dean of the School of Social Work, The University of Michigan; Chairman of the Federal Advisory Council on Employment Security; formerly Director of the Michigan Social Welfare Department; and a consultant to the congressional committees handling social security matters.

EDWIN E. WITTE was Professor of Economics at the University of Wisconsin; Executive Director of the Committee on Economic Security; former President of the American Economic Association and the Industrial Relations Research Association; and was primarily responsible for the research and formulation of the original Social Security Act.

HARRY S. TRUMAN, Independence, Missouri.

DAVID R. HYDE and PAYSON WOLFF were students at the Yale Law School who participated in the preparation of an extensive report of the organization of the American Medical Association.

ANNE TAYLOR MOORE wrote the article on "Medical Care in Great Britain" for the *New Republic.*

ROBERT TILOVE is Vice President of Martin Segal and Co., Inc., New York City, specialists in pension and welfare funds.

AIME J. FORAND was a Representative in Congress from Rhode Island; a ranking member of the House Committee on Ways and Means which handles social security matters; and the congressional sponsor of the much-discussed Forand Bill to provide medical care to the aged under the social security system.

IDA C. MERRIAM is Director, Division of Program Research, Social Security Administration, Department of Health, Education, and Welfare; formerly an Assistant Editor of the *Encyclopedia of the Social Sciences;* and the author of *Financing Social Security.*

DILLARD STOKES is a journalist and writer.

EVELINE M. BURNS is Professor at the New York School of Social Work, Columbia University; the author of four books on social security; the author and Research Director of the report on *Security, Work, and Relief Policies* of the National Resources Planning Board; and member of the Federal Advisory Council on Employment Security.

# Table of Contents

## CHAPTER IV. THE EMPLOYMENT SECURITY PROGRAM: UNEMPLOYMENT INSURANCE AND THE EMPLOYMENT SERVICE

### CHAPTER V. MEDICAL CARE AND HEALTH INSURANCE

### CHAPTER VI. RELATED SOCIAL SECURITY PROGRAMS

## CHAPTER VII. THE ECONOMIC AND SOCIAL IMPLICATIONS OF SOCIAL SECURITY

## CHAPTER VIII. APPRAISAL AND CRITICISM

## CHAPTER IX. RECENT DEVELOPMENTS: 1960 SOCIAL SECURITY LEGISLATION

# I       Some Persistent Issues in Social Security

## INTRODUCTION

THERE ARE NOT just two points of view on social security; there can be several points of view. Differences arise over such matters as the level of benefits to be provided, the methods of financing the costs, the methods of administration, the relationship of public to private plans, and numerous other problems. But basic to any consideration of how any program of social security should be formulated and administered are the extent and importance of the problem of insecurity. The solutions recommended by many persons and groups are, in large part, determined by the weight given to the seriousness and ramifications of the problem of insecurity and the available alternatives.

In the health field, for instance, the major issue still being debated in this country is whether the inadequacies in health and medical care warrant the establishment of a compulsory health insurance program or whether the problem can be satisfactorily handled by private and local or state public resources with little or no additional aid from the federal government.

Even if there is general agreement that the extent of the need warrants action, there are differences in the ways suggested to meet the need. At the present time there is general agreement that the need of the aged warrants some national program for old-age security. But there are still differences of opinions on what elements in a program best meet this need.

The problems of insecurity are much more apparent during periods of recession or depression than during periods of high employment and full production. But even in periods of good business activity there remain many factors which produce serious social problems. Inequalities in income distribution; local, state, and regional differences in employment, housing, educational, and health opportunities; and racial and other bars to full utilization of the productive skills of minority groups result in dependency and want. Physical or mental inadequacies, delinquency, crime, and similar human failings result in want for some families. In good times or bad, people become aged or disabled, become unemployed or die, leaving dependents unable to buy the necessities of life in a money economy.

All through the consideration of specific issues in social security the reader will have to weigh in his own mind the seriousness of the problem of insecurity. Is the remedy appropriate to the evil to be remedied? What are the consequences of one remedy as against another? The answers to these and similar questions will depend, in large part, upon detailed and accurate knowledge about the character and extent of insecurity in our society.

Insecurity is a changing problem. It varies with the business cycle, the character of the economy, and the life cycle of the family. It varies as our social and economic institutions provide new protections. It varies as the standards of living change.

Methods of dealing with the problems of insecurity also vary. As our society becomes more complex, the methods of dealing with insecurity also tend to become more complex. The recent spurt in the development of health, welfare, and retirement plans through collective bargaining raises many new problems. It will be interesting to watch what the effect of such private plans will be on the public provisions for social security and how such plans will be coordinated with other social security programs.

The relationship between public and private responsibility is still fluid in the United States. The respective roles of social security and private action are still evolving. No one can see far enough ahead to visualize the framework of the programs in the future.

# 1. SOME ASSUMPTIONS AND OBJECTIVES IN SOCIAL SECURITY

Arthur J. Altmeyer,
*Survey Graphic,*
September, 1945.

. . . It is a good time to re-examine some fundamental assumptions made in setting out on that course since the bill became law with President Roosevelt's signature on August 14, 1935—and to do this in the light not only of the road we have come, but of the road we still have to travel.

Clearly, social security substitutes hopes for fears. There are those among us who trust neither human nature nor democratic government; and who ten years ago believed that to cut down fear of losing a job as a motive force among men would lead to a nation of loafers. There are those of us who do trust both human nature and democracy and hence believed that it is hope, not fear, that leads to high endeavor.

Now, as then, what you and I and Americans generally assume about man and his world tends to set our approach to social security—an approach which a decade of experience should modify if we take it to heart.

In formulating any philosophy of social security for ourselves, we must get our bearings by starting not ten but 500,000 years ago. I mean this seriously, because such a philosophy harks back to those age-old assumptions which have come down to us concerning the nature of man. Next, it depends on the relatively modern views we hold, one way or another, about the nature of government.

If we get that far and our heads are still above water, we shall have to clarify our thinking on the economic order in which we believe human beings can be happiest; the forces we count on to make it tick, how they affect one another, how and whether social security fits into the pattern. And finally, for practical purposes, we have to decide what fiscal policies are likely to make ends meet.

Let us begin by briefly taking these bearings together.

## Some Basic Perspectives

On the *nature of man*, we have a choice of several theories. I pin my faith to man's infinite perfectibility—the only theory which to my mind has kept us sane in a world at war. Even with the devastating and terrible things men have done to each other in the 1940's the vast majority have not sunk to the lowest levels set down in recorded history. Rather, the outcome has hung on matching courage and force with high hopes and human feeling. Certainly the GI is a very different person from the warrior of ancient times. Insofar as we can piece together the story written first in fossil remains, then on tablets of clay and finally on paper, mankind has progressed.

On the *nature of human society*, we have to make up our minds whether the impulse to cooperate is stronger than the urge to combat. Here I choose the affirmative, despite two world wars since the turn of the century. The United Nations have demonstrated that their ability to cooperate is strong enough not only to survive but to unite against future aggression while the fight is still on.

On the *nature of government*, our view here in the United States was projected by Rousseau, Jefferson, Paine and others, when the prevailing theory was still the divine right of kings. These insurgents of 175 years ago said in essence: "No, each man has within him the capacity of infinite perfectibility, and government has developed out of a social compact entered into voluntarily by ordinary people who join together for a common purpose."

Their thesis was that government exists for the governed and can endure only so long as it serves individuals reasonably well; that to survive, a democratic society must rely on hope and incentive, rather than fear and compulsion, to influence the conduct and aspirations of its citizens. In this perspective, social security has a place beside the civil liberties which safeguard our freedom.

On the *nature of our economic order*, my assumption is that in this country we believe in a competitive economy with differential rewards. But that is not to say that we want one in which some people get more simply because other people get less. Over a century ago, Saint-Simon laid down the dictum: From each according to his ability and to each according to his need. A society successfully built on that foundation would be a rather fine one in which to live. Nor does a competitive economy necessarily have to reject Saint-Simon.

Progressive taxation, which takes from each according to his ability to pay, is fully accepted as equitable in the U.S. Social security itself can, and, in this country, does pay benefits in differing amounts to take account of differences in lost earnings. Yet at the same time it recognizes the actual or presumptive needs of beneficiaries.

If we can agree on the kind of economic order we want, we still have the difficult job of reckoning with the forces on which its success depends. From their output of goods and services must come a people's standard of living. Thus we must consider the nation's productivity in deciding what social security benefits will be paid and under what conditions. Consider, also, in a competitive society their effect on wage rates, on mobility of workers, on the business cycle and full employment.

## Fiscal Bearings

Then very practically, because benefits cost money, we must consider how to finance social security within the whole framework of modern government. Here several basic questions arise.

Is it a definite goal of a social security system to redistribute income? If so, is this to be done vertically or horizontally, or both? When this term is used, most people think of the vertical process—as between large and small incomes—through which common public services are sustained by a graduated income tax. But there also can be horizontal redistribution among people at the same general economic level—for example, among workers who are earning and those who are not because they lack jobs or are disabled or old. Social security thus has an obvious bearing on the question of how far, and in what direction, and for what justification, sharing wealth shall be carried on in a modern democracy.

Next, to what extent should contributions called for by social security take the form of incentive taxation and be employed for purposes other than to obtain funds necessary to meet the cost of benefits? For example, employers generally are now very strongly in favor of "experience rating" under state unemployment insurance laws. They maintain that if an employer's payroll contributions are lowered when he has a record of steady employment, it will be to his interest to continue that record.

Some employers would say that the main purpose of unemployment insurance is not to pay benefits to people who are involuntarily unemployed, but thus to stabilize employment. Regular and dependable wages are of course better than out-of-work benefits.

Others recognize that major factors which cause unemployment are outside the control of employers individually or as a group. They hold that one basic purpose of an insurance program in the interests of the community as a whole is to spread the burden between inherently good "employment risks" (such as the public utilities) and industries that are subject to seasonal and other swings in employment (such as building construction).

Whatever our views, we should, of course, be sure that any incentive taxation can and does actually provide an effective spur to employment. Even more important, we must be sure that no secondary considerations defeat the primary purpose of giving workers everywhere adequate protection. We must make sure, for example, that competition between the states to reduce contributions for their employers does not result in such low rates that the amount of benefits is inadequate and their duration cut short when hard times come.

We must consider also how such benefits fit into what is usually called "compensatory spending"—how they help maintain household consumption through various phases of the business cycle and hence promote a steady stream of purchasing power on which workers and business alike, and the nation as a whole, must depend.

## Basic Objectives

All these fundamental questions must be borne in mind when we are asked what we are aiming at through social security. My answer would be, we are aiming at a minimum level of well-being for the people of this nation. Because we live in a money economy, that means the minimum of income and services essential to decent human existence.

What is sufficient for that decent level varies from person to person, from community to community, from nation to nation. It varies with the relationship of population to national resources, with the ability of a nation to maintain a sufficient output of goods and services. If the United States were an overpopulated country with meager resources, our idea of a decent level of human existence would be very different from what it is today.

As a corollary—or as a modification of this fundamental concept of a minimum of income and services for all—social security involves the principle that persons similarly situated shall be treated alike. In public assistance, this means that people with equal needs shall receive equal assistance; that needy children in a particular family should receive neither more nor less than those in any other family or any other community or state—whose needs are the same.

This principle also encompasses the idea that people with the same wage history, the same wage loss, and the same record of contributions shall receive the same amount of social insurance benefits. To illustrate: Under the *federal* old-age and survivors insurance system, an old mill worker who has worked for thirty years at from $20 to $30 a week in Rhode Island gets exactly the same benefit when he retires as any other wage earner who has worked as long, at like wages, in any other covered job anywhere in the country—whether in a factory or store or office or mine; whether in North or South, East or West.

Under the *federal-state* unemployment compensation system, on the other hand, an unemployed worker in one state, where benefit standards are high, may be eligible for two or three times as much in the aggregate if he remains unemployed, as a worker with exactly the same record of past employment and past earnings who happens to live in a state where benefit standards are low.

However, the principle of maintaining a minimum level of well-being need not exclude differentials *above* that minimum which take into account differences both in wage loss and in social insurance contributions on behalf of the persons entitled to benefit. The argument can be made that wage earners who have been able to achieve higher earnings build up greater obligations and that their wants are enhanced. Thus, both payroll deductions and old-age insurance benefits of the $20-a-week worker are lower than those of one who has averaged twice that, and still lower than those of the worker who had customarily brought home $50 a week in his pay envelope.

But because this is social insurance, there is a minimum benefit below which no insured worker can fall. Also a maximum benefit, . . .

### Rights to Social Security

We say that social insurance benefits are paid as a matter of right. What does this mean? We are really talking about rights enforceable through due process of law. But while these rights presume definite procedures to qualify for benefits, the benefits themselves may be conditioned on many things.

The federal Social Security Act provides two kinds of programs—public assistance and social insurance. In the one, rights are conditioned on need; in the other, on wage loss. Yet they are of the same kind, although people sometimes hold that those arising out of contributions paid by a person, or on his behalf, are the more valid. I do not believe that such a distinction can be made. We do not say that the right of parents to send a youngster to public school depends on whether or not they pay direct taxes.

But contributions do affect the attitudes of beneficiaries, of legislators and the public generally. In our kind of economic society, the belief prevails that people should not only get what they earn but pay for what they get. It follows that the closer the connection between premiums and benefits, the more clearly are social security rights recognized. This explains the stigma often attached to receipt of public assistance. Often the applicant himself feels that somehow or other he has failed to make the grade.

Given our competitive system, I don't know how we can avoid this dilemma. However, there is growing realization that an individual's need is usually due not to his own inadequacy, but to his economic and social environment, to bad luck or other fortuitous circumstances.

To me, it seems impossible to draw hard and fast lines between social insurance and public assistance. When people say that social insurance is something you get because you have paid for it, they forget that no social insurance program provides precisely what you have paid for it. Social insurance benefits are weighted in favor of the low wage earner, in favor of the short-time, intermittent wage earner, in favor of persons with dependents.

Moreover, it is universally true that the structure of any social insurance system must be erected on the base of presumptive social needs rather than of exact private equities. The system cannot ignore individual equity but the primary consideration is social adequacy.

## Human Equations

People say, also, that social insurance is governed by objective provisions; that it does not require "snooping around and prying into" personal matters such as come up in administering public assistance. Such a distinction, too, is not valid.

Take questions necessary in determining dependents' benefits under old-age and survivors insurance: whether the wage earner's wife and children are living with him; whether or not aged parents were wholly dependent on a deceased worker. Surely these are personal questions.

Or take questions that must be asked under an unemployment compensation act to make sure that claimants for benefits are genuinely unemployed and had good cause to quit their last job; whether or not they refuse to accept suitable work; whether they are available for work.

By way of more detailed illustration, take those last two questions which come up in infinite variety when workers claim unemployment benefits. Here is Mrs. Jones who, when cutbacks come, loses her job on a day shift in a big plant in Detroit. She has three children, and protests she cannot get anyone to stay with them at night. So she says she cannot take a third-shift job offered in another plant. That calls for night work which, as she sees it, isn't "suitable" under the circumstances, but she is "available" during the hours she has always worked.

Someone in the local office must appraise both Mrs. Jones' household situation and her work history. Perhaps she is a widow and has long supported her children; they depend wholly on her earnings. Should she be ruled "unavailable" for work because she feels she can't take the night job? Or should she get, for at least a time, the benefits to which her past wage record would entitle her; and thus have a chance to look for day work which will permit her both to earn and to fulfill her responsibilities?

Or perhaps day work is available but only as a scrubwoman, making no use of the mother's skills. She says the job would be too hard for her physically, and points to its meager wage. Against this she weighs the money value of the laundry, sewing, careful marketing and other services she could perform for her family. All in all, if unemployment benefits can't be paid to her, she concludes she would do better to devote herself to her home and apply for aid to her dependent children.

Does Mrs. Jones refuse "suitable work" if she turns down the scrubwoman's job?

Such factors as these and many others must be sifted and evaluated by an unemployment compensation agency in determining whether or not an insured worker is able to work, available for work, has not refused suitable work. Surely these, too, are personal questions!

\*　\*　\*　\*　\*

### Insurance and Assistance

In the years of transition immediately ahead, both social insurance and public assistance are bound to confront not only such difficult judgments on personal situations but mass strains on their resources and flexibility.

It is good, therefore, to report that public assistance is moving toward greater simplicity, objectivity and adequacy than in the past. Benefits are no longer paid in kind, such as grocery orders and bushels of coal, but in cash. The recipient therefore has money, as other people do, to spend as he thinks best. If an applicant disagrees with the action taken in his case, he has a right to a hearing. The Social Security Act requires that the personal information he gives the public assistance agency be held confidential. Many states are abolishing what is known as "relatives' responsibility," that is, an old legal requirement that aid cannot be given to a needy person who has relatives considered able to help him, even though in fact they fail to do so.

Such developments are rubbing out some of the old distinctions between public assistance and social insurance so far as kinds of benefits and administrative procedures go. What are the children's allowances that Canada has just begun to pay to all families with children—out of general revenues and without a showing of need? Are they public assistance or social insurance or something else?

I am not arguing that we should abolish public assistance and turn everything into social insurance; much less that we should abolish social insurance and turn everything into public assistance. We should go on adapting these programs to achieve the common objective of social security—a minimum level of well-being. If we do that, their future will take care of itself. The program which proves more effective, more in harmony with the conscience of the people, will become dominant.

In the meantime—in peace years as in war years—it is vitally important to proceed on the assumption that social insurance should be our first line of domestic defense against want and fear. Its practical and hopeful values are time-tested and world-tested. Social insurance has the unique advantage that it automatically relates benefits to loss of earnings, automatically protects benefit rights, automatically provides the funds to pay benefits and automatically controls costs.

Public assistance is our essential second line of defense against misery and defeat among people who lack social insurance protection—or whose needs transcend the benefits that an insurance system provides.

In the United States, as in all other countries that have developed social legislation, the first step has been to recognize the needs of particular groups whose special plight has won wide public attention—the blind, the aged, widows and orphans, and so on. A law is passed to deal with a particular group, and in time there come to be several measures dealing with various parts of a problem. Next comes a time—which I think we are now entering—when we can draw aside and try to look at our experience as a whole over a ten-year span; to iron out discrepancies, strengthen weak spots, and fill in gaps.

\* \* \* \* \*

General recommendations for strengthening and rounding out the social security program in the United States have been made by the Social Security Board to Congress. These call for extending social insurance to protect all gainfully employed persons everywhere—and their dependents. They call for covering the other major risks of involuntary wage loss to which a worker is liable—those from sickness and disability no less than unemployment and old age. They call for insurance against costs of medical care.

They call, also, for expanding federal-state public assistance programs to meet the needs not merely of the special groups now covered, but of any person who lacks the basic minimum for subsistence. And they hew to the line that insurance benefits and assistance payments alike shall be more adequate; that inequities in the protection available to persons whose circumstances are similar but who live in different parts of the country can and should be removed.

I am optimistic enough to believe that progress in this second decade of social security in the United States will at least equal the progress we have made in the first. But I am also confident that when the next ten years have rolled by, we shall still be talking about the inadequacy of the program in achieving minimum well-being.

Social security will always be a goal, never a finished thing, because human aspirations are infinitely expansible—just as human nature is infinitely perfectible.

# 2. SOME MAJOR ISSUES IN SOCIAL SECURITY

WILBUR J. COHEN and
WILLIAM HABER, 1960.

*"For all the defects of the [Social Security] Act, it still meant a tremendous break with the inhibitions of the past. The federal government was at last charged with the obligation to provide its citizens a measure of protection from the hazards and vicissitudes of life. One hundred and ten years earlier, John Quincy Adams had declared that 'the great object of the institution of civil government' was 'the progressive improvement of the condition of the governed.' With the Social Security Act, the constitutional dedication of federal power to the general welfare began a new phase of national history."*—Arthur M. Schlesinger, Jr.

FEW PERSONS question the need for some kind of social security for themselves or their children and their neighbors or even the Nation as a whole. But there are major differences of opinion on how such security can best be attained, while accomplishing other objectives simultaneously.

The timeless quest for social security has resulted in many different ways and means to achieve that goal. The modern development of social security began in the 1880's when Chancellor Bismarck in Germany inaugurated a social insurance program. Since that time every major industrial nation has established some type of social security program. Regardless of political or economic philosophy, whether democratic or totalitarian, governments throughout the world have instituted, retained, or expanded social security programs.

In the United States, the general principle of social security is now supported by all political parties. Employers' organizations, insurance companies, labor unions, and numerous civic and professional groups have endorsed the basic idea.

The explanation of this wide acceptance of the general principle lies in the character of our modern industrial society—interdependent, complex, international—based on money incomes, a high degree of occupational specialization, and a growing, dynamic economy.

Some form of social security, therefore, is an indispensable institution in our modern economic life. But how should such social security programs as may be necessary or desirable be organized within our complex economic system? Here is where reasonable people can begin to differ.

A review of the social security programs in operation throughout the world indicates there is no "best" program in an absolute sense. Each country has tried to develop its social security institutions in terms of its own constitutional and political history, the psychological factors of importance to its people, the extent of private methods of security, the economic conditions of the country, and related institutional factors. There are in existence as many different social security programs as there are countries. Moreover, these programs in the different countries are amended from time to time. Social security is thus a process rather than a single fixed idea or institution.

## Some Issues in Social Security

It is not surprising, therefore, that specific issues in formulating or revising social security programs should become intertwined with so many other fundamental and complex problems. The wide range of issues and related problems can be illustrated by mentioning just a few of the issues.

How does a specific social security program or proposal affect individual initiative, self-reliance, thrift, and incentive?

Does a particular program or proposal lead to bureaucracy, to restriction of individual freedom, to increasing government controls?

What is the desirable level of cash benefits to be paid under different social security programs? Should different standards apply to different programs?

Should everyone receive the same benefit or should the benefits vary in relation to previous wages, contributions, the number of dependents, or the length of time in the program, or should they be based upon need or other factors?

What is the relation of a governmental system of social security to voluntary social security institutions? Can they work together? How?

Can voluntary health insurance plans handle the problem of prepayment of medical costs? What is the future of union health and welfare funds? What effect will they have on a comprehensive social security system?

Are payments to the aged a "burden" on the economy? Are reserves necessary or desirable in old-age insurance? Are private pension plans desirable? Who should bear the costs of pensions? What effect do pension programs have on investments, incentives, and the general progress of the economy?

How much would a comprehensive system of social security cost? Could we afford it? Can we afford not to have such a system? What are the effects of these costs on employment, business, the economy?

How should social security be financed—through payroll taxes, general revenue, or earmarked income taxes? Should costs be divided equally between the employer and employee, or in some other way?

How would such a comprehensive system be administered? How would it be related to our federal-state system? How can national standards and decentralized administration be assured?

What should be the administrative relationship between the employment service and unemployment insurance?

What are the economic and social implications of a social security program, to business, labor, the family, and the nation as a whole?

Is there need in the United States for a system of children's allowances? What effect would it have on wages, prices, collective bargaining, and the size and welfare of the family?

These are only some of the major questions which must be kept in mind. While they are difficult, they are not insoluble. These and similar questions are being studied in numerous countries; they are key issues in the United States today and are likely to continue to be for some time. Many of the fears concerning the original Social Security Act of 1935 proved groundless. Many of the administrative problems which were believed to be insuperable, have been solved. Is there any reason to doubt that the American genius for innovation can be applied in the further evolution of our social security program?

Any review of the social security institutions and policies in the United States leads to the inescapable conclusion that social security is an important social invention—it is here to stay—and that it can and will evolve along with our other institutions so that it will always remain a program adapted to American experience and ideals.

A major argument against compulsory social insurance is that "once it has been accepted that compulsion may be laid upon the individual to improve his life, on the ground that his voluntary efforts to improve it himself are unsatisfactory, there is no logical place to stop short of minding his life from birth to death."[1]

The American Life Convention, the Life Insurance Association of America, and the National Association of Life Underwriters issued a joint report on social security in 1945 which took an opposite point of view. This report stated:

> There should be neither conflict nor confusion between social security, properly defined, and that type of security which comes from the exercise of personal industry and thrift. While the one represents the basic protection which can safely be provided through Government programs set up by society at large, the other gives the individual the right and the opportunity to raise himself and his family to such level of security as his industry and thrift dictate. They complement each other rather than conflict with each other.

A basic problem of our time is how to maintain maximum freedom in our economic life and also provide security for the individual and his family. On the one hand, there are those who believe that in relieving and protecting the individual against economic hazards we discourage individual initiative and responsibility, and thereby increase dependency.

---

[1] National Industrial Conference Board, April, 1946. Published in *Congressional Record*, May 23, 1946, p. A-3081.

But there is also ample evidence to support the belief that destitution feeds upon itself and carries in its train evils that increase already existing complex social and economic problems. Social security is designed to set up certain protections to those in distress and thus restore their hope and their faith and make them self-respecting, self-sustaining, and valuable members of society. In achieving this goal, many controversial problems are encountered.

To understand and appraise critically past and present developments in social security as well as any future changes, familiarity with many different forces in our society is vitally necessary. The historical factors involved in the establishment and growth of our nation, social and political institutions, economic institutions, and economic conditions—all these and many more are part of the picture.

Over one hundred years ago a leading writer said, "Misery generates hate." This brief but penetrating statement indicates that there are many ramifications of the problem of insecurity. Beveridge stated the same issue very clearly: "The greatest evil of unemployment is not physical but moral, not the want which it may bring but the hatred and fear which it breeds."[2] If misery and unemployment breed hate, hate also breeds war. So what first appears to be the problem of an individual is discovered, on analysis, to be the problem of the family, the church, the community, the state, the nation, and the entire world.

The immediate problem in meeting insecurity is to make possible a more equitable distribution of available goods and services; the broader task is to see to it that there are more goods and services for everyone, and that they are equitably distributed. These are large tasks. They cannot be accomplished by any single person or group of persons working alone; they require social engineering of the highest order. Social security is a part of the larger problem of distribution of goods, services, and incomes, and of the larger task of social engineering.

Lewis Meriam, in his book *Relief and Social Security*, has stated that "social security and relief are not in and of themselves directly productive." While some people will not believe that this statement is a complete or accurate picture, it is a provocative one requiring serious consideration and analysis. Is it fair to say that individual methods of assuring security—life insurance, savings banks, purchase of homes—are not directly productive? Are employer pension plans, Blue Cross and Blue Shield medical insurance plans, and accident and health insurance not directly productive?

An employer buys insurance for his business plant or inventory because it gives him freedom from the uncertainty of a great loss which may bankrupt him. Bankruptcy would mean a loss of capital, unemployment

---

[2] William H. Beveridge, *Full Employment in a Free Society* (New York: W. W. Norton, 1945), p. 15.

for his employees, and the waste of his skills and the skills of his employees. A sound and effective system of unemployment insurance and employment services can reduce the lost time between jobs, preserve skills, and give employees, employers, and society the advantage of having individuals employed at jobs at their maximum skills.

Life or survivors' insurance enables fatherless children to continue their education, thus assuring that the children will be able to make their greatest productive contribution to society. Aid to dependent children helps to keep families together so that children may grow up with the sense of security and well-being that makes for productive citizens. Old-age insurance enables employers to regularize the costs of retirement of superannuated employees.

Health insurance encourages persons to seek a doctor early because of the absence of the financial barrier at the time of sickness. In general, any insurance or benefit plan which enables persons to avoid large losses frees such persons from the worry or uncertainty which detracts from their maximum productivity. Assistance or relief programs which prevent the breakup of the family, minimize deterioration of the skills, and sustain the hopes of individuals, contributes to the national welfare and the national security. In the last analysis, national production depends upon human beings; consequently, the conservation of human resources is the best investment for national production, national welfare, and national security.

Are security and freedom incompatible? Perhaps theoretically when each concept is carried to an extreme and illogical conclusion. But when tempered by reason and practical considerations, they do not appear to be incompatible. Security and freedom are part of the very same problem. Freedom without security is the freedom to starve, the freedom to be homeless, dependent, or sick. Security without freedom is the security of the prison and the concentration camp.

A properly designed social security program can assure both freedom and security. But to achieve this desired objective there is much hard work to be done. To design a sound social security program, account must be taken of all the diverse and complicated issues noted above. There are eligibility provisions, coverage determinations, contribution rates, methods of collecting contributions and paying benefits, fair hearings in cases of disputed claims, and a host of similar problems to be handled.

## Equity and Adequacy in Old-Age Programs

One of the persistent problems in income maintenance programs is the application of the two principles of "equity" and "adequacy" in the construction and modification of specific benefit provisions. These principles apply primarily to the formulation of policy in contributory programs but, to some degree, they also are applicable to noncontributory and general pension programs. Those persons responsible for designing an old-age benefit program have wrestled with the conflict between these principles and the innumerable problems involved in combining or separating them in the same program.

The concept of "equity" derives from private insurance, which has played an important role in influencing the evolution of "social" insurance. This concept conceives of the individual's benefit as the annuity which would be purchasable by the contributions made on the individual's behalf. A strict construction of this concept would be incompatible with the fundamental purposes of social insurance, since it would preclude the payment of any except the most inconsequential benefits in the initial operation of the plan.

All countries, however, are faced with the task of defining and redefining "adequacy" of benefits. Some concept of "social adequacy" is explicitly or implicitly behind every benefit structure. The objective may be to keep most persons off poor relief, or to pay a "minimum subsistence," or to provide a "basic floor of protection," or to provide a level of living compatible with a standard of "health and decency." There may be many other expressions of the objective. They may vary from country to country and from time to time in a particular country. This is one of the basic problems of an old-age benefit program which has a tie-in with many other factors, such as costs, incentives, cultural patterns, the standard of living of the economy, and the relationship to other institutional arrangements, such as private insurance, private pension plans, and savings —just to mention a few.

Reinhard Hohaus, Vice President and Actuary of the Metropolitan Life Insurance Company, was the first to point up the implications of these two principles in his stimulating article on "Equity, Adequacy and Related Factors in Old-Age Security" published in *The Record* of the American Institute of Actuaries in June, 1938. He showed that private insurance, being voluntary in character, must be built upon the equity between the various classes insured or people would drop their insurance in one group for another. Social insurance, on the other hand, being compulsory in character (as far as contributions are concerned) aims primarily at providing society with some protection against major hazards which are widespread and far-reaching enough to become "social" in scope and complexion.

Private insurance, then, is adapted to the individual's need for, and his ability to afford, protection against a risk. Social insurance, on the other hand, is molded to society's needs. Hohaus claims that society's need is for a minimum of protection and thus introduces a controversial element as to what is meant by "minimum." He concludes that "private insurance would collapse if it stressed considerations of adequacy more than those of equity, so will social insurance fail to remain undisturbed if considerations of equity are allowed to predominate over those of adequacy."

He says that this "need not necessarily imply that all considerations of equity should be discarded from a social insurance plan; rather the point is that, of the two principles, adequacy is the more essential and less dispensable."

No neat generalizations can be drawn from the experience as to the changing emphasis on "equity" and "social adequacy." Too many other factors come into play to make observations or decisions on only two elements in the equation.

Benefits in various social security programs are a compromise between adequacy, motivation, equity, and many other factors. Among these other factors are costs, methods of sharing the costs, the desirability of having minimum and maximum benefits, and administrative considerations related to prompt and efficient payment of benefits.

In the legislative evolution of any program, consideration must be given to the fact that not all elements are of equal importance in improving the benefit adequacy of a program. In terms of adequacy of any program as a whole, there are a number of factors to be given consideration in addition to the level of benefits. Among these factors are the eligibility for benefits, duration of benefits, classes of beneficiaries, types of benefits, and similar elements. Value judgments enter into decisions of priorities and there is no substitute for judgment in this connection.

One conjecture may be tentatively drawn from both the experience of Western Europe and of the United States. If productivity and, hence, the general level of living continue to rise, then it may become necessary to re-examine the concept of "social adequacy" incorporated in the social security program. The "minimum" concept may rise as the level of living rises for the economy as a whole. A decline in the standard of living through war, inflation, or population increases would raise still other issues. Thus, the question of "social adequacy" of the benefit amount, and the scope of the program, may be a changing one which each generation in each country will have to decide for itself, in relation to many variables.

### The Uniform versus the Wage-Related Benefit

A major issue which has resulted in basic differences in the way programs have operated in various countries is whether the old-age benefit should be uniform or wage-related. Expressed in general terms, this may be stated as the question whether the payment should be the same amount for everyone or whether it should vary for each person in relation to an individual's earnings.

Old-age benefit programs developed out of a concern by society for the large number of persons who became aged without any independent source of income. Wages were low, and it was difficult, if not impossible, for most individuals to save a sufficient amount for their old age. Without some method of providing some regular income for aged persons, there would be much social and political discontent.

An old-age benefit program involves, however, a matter of redistribution of income within any nation, as among old and young, the retired and the employed, and the higher-income with the lower-income receivers. Thus, a major matter of economic and social policy had to be decided as to how much income was to be redistributed and how. This question thus touched on philosophical, economic, social, and humanitarian objectives.

A major factor in this situation was the decision of the British social security system in 1911 to pay disability and unemployment benefits on a uniform basis irrespective of wage levels. This same principle was embodied in the British old-age insurance program of 1925 and has become a major distinguishing characteristic of the British programs for nearly fifty years. Although now under serious criticism in Great Britain by advocates of the wage-related philosophy, the British approach adopted in most of the British Commonwealth has exerted a major influence on many programs throughout the world.

The British approach of paying a uniform benefit each week was born in a period when old-age pensions were designed primarily to help keep persons off poor relief. There was not much variation in wage levels; thus, a uniform amount was quite satisfactory for a very substantial proportion of persons. It was simple and understandable to large numbers of persons, and relatively easy to administer in an era when business machines and mechanized procedures for handling administrative matters were unknown. But, more basic than even these factors, was the egalitarian belief which grew out of the socialist movement that all persons should be treated equally when in need. Groups of workmen, both in small groups in their local "friendly societies" and in their large national unions and political associations, ardently advocated "equal shares for all" as a method of sharing their scarcity. There was no general recognition of a society where productivity would be increasing, wages would rise, the standard of living would improve, or in which inflation would be a major factor. These elements did not begin to play any major role in reshaping social security policy in most countries until after World War I, and only became a matter of general recognition after World War II.

In an era of scarcity, low wage levels, and the influence of a strong socialist movement, uniform benefits were rationalized as the most effective method of redistributing the available amount of income to the benefit of the lowest-income groups. The public responsibility for the aged was thus expressed in terms of achieving the maximum social result by assuring a "basic minimum subsistence" to the aged and leaving the individual free to supplement this meager amount from whatever other source he could. The philosophy thus developed that the sole and best method of carrying out public responsibility with the minimum cost and interference with other objectives in society was to have a uniform benefit for all.

Several problems began to arise. If a country wished to have an insurance or pension program with benefits not related to an individual's need, but as a matter of statutory right, it seemed necessary to finance a major share of the cost from payroll contributions. If there was also to be a uniform benefit, then it was only reasonable to have a uniform contribution, irrespective of earnings. In order that a uniform contribution would not be burdensome on the lowest wage earners, it must necessarily be geared to, and limited by, the income of the low-income receivers. Hence, there was a very restricted limit to the amount which could be derived from the payroll contributions. As the standard of living rose over the years, it was necessary to either raise the uniform contributions, which would bear most heavily on the smallest earners, raise a larger proportion of the costs from other kinds of revenues, or keep the level of old-age benefits down, or some combination of these three elements.

This is the dilemma of uniform benefit programs. In Great Britain, serious consideration has been given to modification of their uniform benefit program. The Trades Union Congress and the British Labor Party reversed a long-standing policy in 1956 as did the government in 1958 by advocating building on to the uniform benefit program a supplemental wage-related program.

### Simplification of Social Security

Anyone who reads for the first time the federal old-age and survivors insurance law or the federal or a state law relating to unemployment insurance is amazed and depressed at the complexity of the legislation. Neither is it easy to grasp immediately why some programs are exclusively federal, why others are on a federal-state cooperative basis, and why still others are exclusively state. Nor is it immediately apparent why one program is financed exclusively by employer payroll taxes, another exclusively by employee payroll taxes, and still others jointly.

Is a simple social security system the answer to the complexities of our present and any proposed program? Each person must answer this question for himself. But it should be kept in mind that a complex society may result in a complex social security system—not necessarily, of course. But there is reasonable presumption that the complexities of a social security program are derived from the complexities of our social and economic system.

There is much to be said for and against a simple social security system. The Townsend Plan for old-age pensions is predicated on a simple idea. A concept or a plan that is simple, however, does not necessarily assure that the concept or plan is valid. The British social security plan is relatively simple compared to the social security systems of many other countries. But can we transplant the British model in United States' soil without numerous modifications?

Perhaps we can simplify our social security program in the United

States. This is a desirable objective. It is difficult, however, to see just how this simplification process can occur in any important respects at the present time when some important risks are still not covered by social security programs. If programs in the health and disability field are ultimately enacted, it is very likely that they may be more complex than even our present programs. The number and complexity of our private and public health institutions would seem to indicate that they will be related to any governmental medical care insurance program, thus creating a system which will be built upon present arrangements.

It would be foolhardy to predict the character of our future social security system. But it is safe to say that the future system may be vastly different from that which we have today. Yet, the future will be inextricably tied in with the past. This is the history of all social legislation and institutions. It is especially true of the development of social security institutions.

Yet new times do bring important breaks with the past. In Great Britain, as a result of the Beveridge Plan, the system of flat-rate contributions collected by stamp books and flat benefits was retained in the new social security plan. But the "friendly societies" were eliminated after thirty-five years of use in the social security program; a comprehensive national medical service was established instead of a very limited health insurance system; and family allowances were established.

The order and timing of establishing various social security programs in different countries also indicates that different institutional factors affect the pattern of social security development. Germany, for instance, the first country to establish a social insurance program, enacted health insurance in 1883, old-age and permanent disability insurance in 1889, survivors' insurance in 1911, and unemployment insurance in 1927. Great Britain enacted health, unemployment, and temporary and permanent disability insurance in 1911, old-age and survivors' insurance in 1925, family allowances in 1945, and substituted a national medical care service for its health insurance program in 1946.

Canada enacted a national unemployment insurance program in 1940 and family allowances in 1944. It has no survivors' or disability insurance system.

Mexico enacted a comprehensive social insurance program in 1942 covering old age, survivors, temporary and permanent disability, health insurance, and workmen's compensation. It does not have unemployment insurance or family allowances.

New Zealand enacted a comprehensive social security plan in 1938, covering all programs.

Do these chronologies throw any light on what may evolve here in the United States? Will the United States adopt a comprehensive disability and health insurance program? It would appear that any comprehensive health insurance program most likely would evolve from our present voluntary plans and thus present a greatly different plan than those in operation in other countries. Because of American wage levels, it may not now appear that we shall adopt a national system of family allowances in the immediate future.

There are some persons who believe that ultimately our federal-state unemployment insurance program will be superceded by a single national system, that "experience rating" (the system of varying employers' contributions) will eventually be eliminated from unemployment insurance; others believe that our federal old-age and survivors' insurance benefit will be paid in a flat amount instead of varying with wages and the years of contributions; others, that instead of payroll taxes, the costs of social insurance will be financed out of general revenues.

The ultimate decision on these and similar questions will depend upon not only economic and financial considerations but the psychological reaction of people responding to changing economic developments and to changing political developments, domestic and international.

The social security system in the United States is quite unique in a number of different ways. The United States has developed the most comprehensive system of private social security protection of any country in the world by means of private insurance, supplementary company pension plans, union health and welfare plans, and similar programs. It also has one of the most extensive programs of veterans' pensions and related social security programs for veterans and their families of any country in the world. Cash assistance payments to needy individuals based upon an individual determination of need are very extensive in the United States as compared with other countries. Finally, the United States is the only important English-speaking country in the world which does not provide for some sort of cash allowances for children.

In order to appraise the total social security protection available to individuals and their families in this country it is therefore necessary to look at all of the arrangements that exist for the purpose of providing such security whether they are public or private, comprehensive or piecemeal, or voluntary or compulsory. The social security system of the United States may be compared to a mosaic—or perhaps better still a jigsaw puzzle—which one must view in its entirety and in perspective if one is to see the whole picture. There are striking gaps and overlaps which will become apparent when the entire picture is studied. In addition, differing and sometimes conflicting principles are apparent in different programs. It becomes a more difficult, although perhaps not an impossible, task to rationalize the principles and objectives of the various programs as well as to insure maximum protection at a minimum cost, economic and efficient administration, and sound results advantageous to the individual and his family and at the same time to the Nation as a whole.

**Economic and Financial Issues**

Social security is a big enterprise that has many economic, financial, and social ramifications. It warrants, therefore, very careful consideration with respect to its impact on the economy in general, and on communities, individuals, and families. Because of the special provisions in law or in private plans, the impact on particular industries, states, and income levels is also of special importance.

In studying these matters, attention must be paid to the fact that social security contributions and disbursements do not necessarily involve increased contributions or disbursements to the economy as a whole. They do, however, involve shifting of the burden of initial payment of costs, some adjustment of income yields and disbursements in relation to the business cycle, and modification of the eventual incidence of costs. While precise effects are difficult to ascertain, the effect of social security plans may be that the young pay for the old, the well for the sick, the employed for the unemployed, the high-income person for the low. Yet such a statement is obviously an oversimplification because of the multitude of factors involved. The character of the taxes and premiums used to finance the programs, the nature and level of the benefits provided, and the relationship of both factors to employment, income levels, and numerous other factors in the economy, make it impossible to make a flat statement which will stand for all programs under all circumstances.

Although, as pointed out above, social security finances may be viewed from many points of view, two most important points of view—although not the only ones—are those of the individual and the nation. The individual may see his problem of financing his social security in the simple form of paying his costs. Such problems as investment of the funds, their effect on enterprise, and their inflationary or deflationary effects, may not be very apparent to him. As an individual or as the breadwinner of a family, his concern is with paying his share when he can, and having the assurance of receiving the benefits promptly when they are needed. This is equally the concern of the nation. Yet broader economic and financial matters must concern the nation's lawmakers and the administrators of social security. Their task must be to meet the needs of the individual and his family, taking into account the psychological and political factors which affect the individual and the over-all national needs and circumstances.

From time to time various proposals have been made to provide old-age and other social security benefits, not primarily to encourage retirement, but to insure adequate purchasing power necessary for a full employment economy. One view is that if we have full employment we can and should provide generous social security benefits as a part of a program of high living standards, humanitarianism, and assurance of continued full employment. Another view, however, is that without substantial disbursements under governmental programs such as social security continued full employment cannot be assured, and it is necessary, therefore, that social security payments substantially exceed the income specifically levied for that purpose in order that any deflationary tendencies in our economy may be offset.

These views affect both the problems relating to financing the benefits and to the amount and character of the benefits. Some persons have advocated that old-age (and survivors' and permanent disability) benefits are "universal" and should be provided to all persons who meet a simple test, that the benefits should be a flat amount which would not vary with the previous wage of the individual or the length of time in the insurance system, and that the cost of such benefits would be financed out of general revenues. On the other hand there are those who advocate that insurance benefits should be paid to individuals who meet such risks only in relation to their contributions. There are, of course, variations and combinations of these two points of view.

It is sometimes stated that social security plans would be unnecessary if arrangements could be worked out to assure all workers a living wage, an annual wage, or guaranteed employment. It is extremely doubtful, however, that the problem of needy individuals and families could be eliminated entirely even under conditions of full employment in a free enterprise economy. While steady jobs at high incomes would help greatly in reducing the amount of need and destitution, the incomes of many families would still be reduced or cut off entirely by the premature death of the worker, permanent disability, sickness, old age, and unemployment.

Even when job opportunities are plentiful, many aged persons are unable to continue working because of infirmities. Sickness and disability may strike unexpectedly, leaving an entire family dependent after other savings and income are used up. The unexpected death of the breadwinner may find a family without adequate security.

Some wage loss from unemployment occurs even during periods of full employment. For a variety of reasons, it is inevitable that even under the most favorable conditions a certain number of persons at any given time are temporarily without a job. For example, there will be shutting down of individual plants and businesses for such operations as retooling and the taking of inventory. Similarly, there is always a certain amount of movement of workers from one job to another which frequently involves short periods of unemployment for the individuals changing jobs. More important still in causing spells of unemployment are technological changes, changes in tastes and fashions, and the movement of industries and workers to new locations.

A comprehensive social security program could contribute to achieving full employment in a number of ways. It could assist particularly through unemployment insurance in assuring labor mobility, which is necessary to full employment. It could reduce or remove the economic barrier to withdrawal from the labor market of groups such as the aged, the disabled, and women with young children in their care. It could increase job opportunities in the fields of public and private health. It might also aid in maintaining full employment by sustaining the total demand for goods and services.

The payment of social security benefits to persons whose income has been cut off or who are in need has the effect of placing purchasing power in the hands of families many of whom might otherwise lack it. This purchasing power will normally be spent promptly for consumers' goods. Such additions to consumer demand will give employment in turn to many persons who otherwise might not have jobs.

The effects of social security payments upon purchasing power will be of especial significance in periods when there is a tendency for consumer demand and employment to decline. It is inherent in the very nature of the social security program that total income exceeds disbursements in periods of high employment and that disbursements to individuals and families increase in periods when economic activity slackens. Thus, social security benefits serve to provide something in the nature of a floor under purchasing power if a shrinkage in the latter threatens. A comprehensive system of social security provisions, therefore, can contribute a great deal toward stabilization of consumer demand and, in turn, toward minimizing rapid and wide fluctuations in national income and employment.

Whether or not social security can produce a permanent increase in the effective demand for consumer goods would depend upon the relationship at any time between total payments to individuals and the total amount of and sources of revenues of the social security system. In periods when a part of the payments are financed from the reserves or out of general revenues which do not themselves curtail consumption, the net effect of the payments will be to increase the total amount of consumer purchasing power. To the extent, however, that the contributions and taxes used to finance benefits themselves curtail consumption, they serve to offset the stimulating effects of the payments. The net over-all economic effect of the program on consumer demand will depend, therefore, upon the relationship existing at particular times between payments adding to purchasing power and contributions and taxes subtracting from it.

The frequency and effects of the common economic hazards would be less under full employment and, in turn, the cost of providing protection against these hazards would be lower than otherwise. The cost of social security would be lower both absolutely and in relation to the income out of which social security is financed. Hence, under a full-employment economy, the Nation can afford a better and more comprehensive system of social security than might otherwise be possible.

## Looking Ahead

We know a good deal more today about the practical problems involved in formulating and administering social security than we knew in 1934 when the original plan was being drafted. We have had over twenty years' experience in administering and perfecting the largest insurance program in the world—federal old-age, survivors and disability insurance. Every state has an unemployment insurance law which has been in effect some twenty years or more. The public assistance and maternal and child health and welfare programs of the Social Security Act are in operation throughout the country. Workmen's compensation exists now in every state in the union. Private employer, union, and consumer health and welfare plans have been increasing.

This mosaic of social security programs in the United States represents what is perhaps the most complex system in effect in any country in the world. This in itself is not a criticism of our system, if it can be called a system. It is a fact that we have such a complex system. The explanation for this fact undoubtedly is due to the complexity of our economy and the piecemeal way in which we have allowed our social security program to grow. Yet, we must recognize the result is intentional—a single, simple social security plan for the entire Nation covering all risks from the cradle to the grave has never been recommended or advocated by any responsible person or group in the United States. It has been recognized that the American scene requires a bundle of programs to carry out the purposes of social security and that these programs must be individual and group, private and public, all fitted together to meet a multitude of needs.

There is general recognition, however, that our present public and private programs are inadequate and need improvement. The coverage and the benefits of existing programs must be expanded and liberalized. While there is general agreement with this objective, innumerable specific problems are involved in determining how such extension of coverage can be achieved and to what extent the benefits can be liberalized. Some persons and groups have suggested radical departures in the methods of financing and administering old-age benefits. On the other hand, there has been very strong advocacy for continuation of the existing administrative structure and relationships in the field of unemployment insurance in opposition to various proposals for basic changes in the unemployment insurance program. This volume contains selections dealing with these suggestions with the hope that they will offer a basis for further consideration of changes in our present programs.

In the conflict of ideas which takes place in the intellectual market place, extreme statements may be made by proponents and opponents of particular plans or proposals. It is necessary therefore to weigh very carefully the validity of the arguments that are used and the relevancy of the information brought to bear in support of or in opposition to any particular point of view. A critical mind supplied with adequate information is essential for the appraisal and criticism of existing and proposed programs and the formulation of revised and expanded programs adjusted to changing economic and social needs.

To approach the problems of social security solely through intellectual means and factual information, however, is not sufficient. Social security, although it has many aspects and ramifications, has basically a social purpose; consequently, social objectives must be kept foremost in mind in weighing economic, fiscal, and administrative implications of any proposal. In short, it is necessary to weigh many factors simultaneously when one evaluates any concrete proposal in the social security field.

Social security legislation, like all other legislation, cannot be evaluated apart from actual administration. It has been said that a bad law well administered can be of greater good and greater significance than a good law badly administered. The way in which social security laws are administered is therefore as important as the provisions of the law itself. For instance, the maintenance of such intangible, but very real values, as the dignity of the individual, incentive for employment and rehabilitation, and encouragement of thrift, self-reliance, and initiative are the result of the interaction of both law and administration. It becomes more difficult, of course, to appraise and evaluate the intangibles. Here is where facts and figures by themselves are not always available, or when they are available, are the sole determinants of policy. In the last analysis, perhaps the intangible elements are the most real and the most important. Constant appraisal of all of these factors in social legislation is essential.

It is not always easy to adjust the different approaches of the individual, the lawmaker, the administrator, the economist, and the social worker to issues in the social security field. Each may come to the problem of social security policy with the same general purpose, but with a different emphasis. Where multiple purposes must be achieved, a simple single formula is not the likely solution. It may be difficult to tell how to weigh the various elements in a social security issue except in particular setting. Even then there are reasonable differences of opinion among reasonable people.

One conclusion may be drawn from the last twenty-five years of discussions on social security; conditions change and so do people's ideas. So, we may expect changes in theories and judgments on economic, social, financial, and administrative issues. Constant reappraisal of experience and future expectations, therefore, is essential.

No doubt the complexity of the many factors involved in social security makes it difficult to predict the way a particular provision will operate. Where incentives and ideals are involved, the economist, the insurance expert, the lawyer, and the social worker must join with other professions in attempting to analyze and influence possible future trends. Here is the challenging task—how the many varied skills can join together to adapt an important program such as social security to the changing needs of our American economy.

# DISCUSSION QUESTIONS

1. Winston Churchill has characterized social insurance as "bringing the magic of averages to the rescue of the millions."
Explain the meaning of this. Is it more true of social insurance than private insurance?

2. Why is social security necessary in a nation with relatively high and increasing standard of living?

3. Should social security be considered a "radical" or a "conservative" idea? Explain your reasons.

4. In what way did the Great Depression of 1929 change the views in the United States on public responsibility for social welfare?

5. In what ways does the social security system in the United States differ from programs in other countries?

# SELECTED REFERENCES

THE AMERICAN ASSEMBLY. *Economic Security for Americans: An Appraisal of the Progress During the Last 50 Years.* New York: Graduate School of Business, Columbia University, 1954.

BURNS, EVELINE M. *Social Security and Public Policy.* New York: McGraw-Hill Book Co., Inc., 1956.

DEWHURST, J. FREDERIC, and others. *America's Needs and Resources: A New Survey.* New York: The Twentieth Century Fund, 1955.

FARMAN, CARL H. "World Trends in Social Security Benefits," *Social Security Bulletin,* XX (August, 1957), pp. 3–14.

GAGLIARDO, DOMENICO. *American Social Insurance.* New York: Harper and Brothers, 1955.

HOUSE COMMITTEE ON WAYS AND MEANS, SUBCOMMITTEE ON SOCIAL SECURITY. *Analysis of the Social Security System. Hearings* (83d Cong., 1st sess.), 6 parts and appendix I and II. Washington, D.C.: U.S. Government Printing Office, 1953 and 1954.

——— *Social Security After 18 Years: A Staff Report* (83d Cong., 2d sess.). Washington, D.C.: U.S. Government Printing Office, 1954.

House Committee on Ways and Means, Subcommittee on Social Security. *Social Security After 18 Years: Statement of the Democratic Members of the Subcommittee on Social Security* (83d Cong., 2d sess.). Washington, D.C.: U.S. Government Printing Office, 1955.

International Labour Office. International Labour Conference.
Report IV (1): *Objectives and Minimum Standards of Social Security.* Geneva, 1950.
Report IV (2): *Objectives and Minimum Standards of Social Security.* Geneva, 1951.
Report V (a) (1): *Minimum Standards of Social Security.* Geneva, 1951.
Report V (a) (2): *Minimum Standards of Social Security.* Geneva, 1952.
Report V (b): *Objectives and Advanced Standards of Social Security.* Geneva, 1952.

Joint Committee on the Economic Report, Subcommittee on Low-Income Families. *Characteristics of the Low-Income Population and Related Federal Programs* (84th Cong., 1st sess.). Washington, D.C.: U.S. Government Printing Office, 1955.

Meriam, Lewis, and Schlotterbeck, Karl. *The Cost and Financing of Social Security.* Washington, D.C.: The Brookings Institution, 1950.

Merriam, Ida C. *Social Security Financing.* Social Security Administration, Division of Reserach and Statistics, Bureau Report No. 17, 1952.

Russell, J. E. (ed.). *National Policies for Education, Health and Social Services.* Garden City, N.Y.: Doubleday and Co., Inc., 1955.

U.S. Department of Health, Education, and Welfare, Social Security Administration. *Annual Report of the Social Security Administration.* Washington, D.C.: U.S. Government Printing Office, 1936 to date.

—— *Basic Readings in Social Security.* Washington, D.C.: U.S. Government Printing Office, 1956.

—— *Social Security Programs Throughout the World.* Washington, D.C.: U.S. Government Printing Office, 1958.

Woytinsky, W. S., and others. *Employment and Wages in the United States.* New York: The Twentieth Century Fund, 1953.

# II

# Historical Developments and Emerging Concepts in Social Security

## INTRODUCTION

THE SOCIAL SECURITY ACT of 1935 was the immediate outgrowth of President Roosevelt's message to Congress on June 8, 1934, in which he painted in broad, bold strokes a picture of existing needs and forthcoming developments, saying: ". . . we are compelled to employ the active interest of the nation as a whole through government in order to encourage a greater security for each individual who composes it."

The President created the Committee on Economic Security to study the entire problem of social and economic security and make recommendations to him. This Committee made its report early in 1935 and its basic recommendations were embodied in the Social Security Act of 1935.

In signing the Social Security Act, President Roosevelt said:

[The Act] represents a cornerstone in a structure which is being built but is by no means complete—a structure intended to lessen the force of possible future depressions, to act as a protection to future administrations of the government against the necessity of going deeply into debt to furnish relief to the needy—a law to flatten out the peaks and valleys of deflation and of inflation —in other words, a law that will take care of human needs and at the same time provide for the United States an economic structure of vastly greater soundness.

The 1935 Act provided federal grants to the states for three forms of public assistance; to the needy aged, blind, and dependent children. Second, it enabled states to enact unemployment insurance laws and expand their employment services. Third, it set up a federal system of old-age insurance for persons working in industry and commerce. Fourth, it provided additional federal funds for the extension of state public health and rehabilitation facilities under the supervision of the United States Public Health Service and the Federal Vocational Rehabilitation Service and for the development of state maternal and child health and welfare programs under the supervision of the Federal Children's Bureau.

The only program in the legislation solely administered by the federal government was federal old-age insurance. All other programs provided for the states to administer them with financial aid from the federal government.

On November 23, 1936, the U.S. Supreme Court upheld in a 4 to 4 tie decision the constitutionality of the New York state unemployment insurance provisions of the federal law. It was not until nearly two years after the passage of the Social Security Act that the Supreme Court upheld the constitutionality of the insurance provisions of the federal act. On May 24, 1937, the Supreme Court, in two separate decisions written by Justice Cardozo, upheld the constitutionality of the provisions of the federal law relating to both old-age insurance and unemployment insurance.

In 1939, survivors' insurance was added to the old-age insurance program. In 1956, disability insurance was included as a third risk. During the period 1942–49, four states and the railroad program provided cash sickness benefits.

There is no universally accepted definition of social security. Different definitions of the term stress different elements. Some definitions are very broad; others are narrow.

The term "social security" is broader than "social insurance" and has been used to cover a wide range of governmental and even private voluntary arrangements. The term "social security" originated in the United States and has spread throughout the world. Although the term has been used in such a variety of ways and so broadly as to sometimes lose any value as a term of precise meaning, it does have the advantage of describing a number of different programs which are related in their general purpose. Since private and public plans are in different stages of evolution in the United States, and there are many variations of these plans throughout the world, social security is a more general term to cover all programs both in the United States and abroad.

While the major elements in the social security program in the United States differ but little from those contained in the original legislation, some modifications are beginning to emerge. These are still relatively minor and do not represent any basic departure from the original philosophy. On the other hand, some major philosophical and program departures have been made in the British system of social security since 1945. Changes in the American system will undoubtedly be the byproduct of our unique American experience and will be influenced by the economic, social, governmental, and cultural climate of the American community.

# 3. ECONOMIC SECURITY: A LOOK BACK AND A LOOK AHEAD

FREDERICK LEWIS ALLEN,
*Economic Security for Americans:
An Appraisal of the Progress
during the Last 50 Years,*
Columbia University, 1954.

WHAT HAVE BEEN the key dates in modern American history?

Ask this question of a number of reflective citizens and you will probably get a number of answers. Henry Steele Commager has argued that the eighteen-nineties constituted a great watershed—a time during which modern American life and thought began to take shape. Others might mark down 1914 as a prime turning-point, because it was then that we began to discover what it was like to live in a warlike world; or 1941–45, because it was then that we learned that in such a world the role of a great power was inescapable for us. Others might possibly try to pick out some date symbolic of the arrival of the automobile, that transformer of communities and of our daily lives.

I for one hope that our natural impulse to try to forget the miseries of a time of anxiety and frustration will not blind us to the fact that a very significant turning-point was the Great Depression which followed the stock-market crash of 1929. For it was during those years—and especially during the early nineteen-thirties, when the survival of American capitalism seemed almost a matter of touch-and-go—that a lasting change took place in the attitude of the American people toward their economic and political institutions.

I have been wondering what any of us would have thought if before the crash—let us say in 1928—he had received an invitation to a large and imposing meeting to discuss Economic Security for Americans. I think he might have wondered whether he was being coaxed to a meeting of visionary social workers, or radicals, or cranks, or all three. For although we thought a lot about securities in those days—that was when the Bull Market was headed for the roof—we thought very little about Security with a capital S.

Our Social Security system was then unborn; if you had proposed such a scheme in 1928 most of your neighbors would have thought you wildly unrealistic; it was not enacted into law until 1935. Most of our other schemes, public and private, for giving organized financial protection to the potential victims of infirmity and adversity, are even younger. And indeed the very concept of Economic Security . . . is a product of the Great Depression and of its prolonged and immense psychological impact upon the nation.

## Europe and the U.S.

Social insurance, was, of course, an old story in Europe long before that.

In Germany, Bismarck inaugurated compulsory insurance against accidents, sickness, widowhood, and old age in the long-ago eighteen-eighties. Later on, Britain adopted a system of old-age pensions; set up an unemployment system in which the employee, the employer, and the government each paid a part of the premium; and subsequently an old-age insurance system to which the government likewise contributed. But there was almost no such social experimentation here in the United States until after the onset of the Depression. The general American opinion was that all this sort of thing was socialistic nonsense and that American citizens ought to be able to look after themselves.

We had had federal pensions for military veterans ever since the heyday of the G.A.R., but these were expression of special national gratitude, not of any general federal concern for economic security. The responsibility for looking after the aged, the infirm, and the victims of economic disaster fell almost wholly upon the states and cities and towns—and of course upon private charity, which bore a heavy share of the load. (In Muncie, Indiana, when Robert and Helen Lynd were gathering material in the mid-twenties for their intensive study of an American city, *Middletown*, they found that a private welfare organization, the newly-set-up Community Fund, was spending eight dollars for every dollar spent in public poor-relief from tax sources.) The first state to pass an old-age pension law had done so in 1923, and by 1929 only four other states had followed suit. Otherwise, as Leo Wolman and Gustav Peck put it in *Recent Social Trends*, "the superannuated were left to their own devices or were supported in the public almshouses and the privately endowed homes for the aged."

## Compensation, Pensions, Insurance

In one respect a striking advance in social legislation had been made in the United States.

The first state system of workmen's compensation had gone into effect as far back as 1911, and by 1929 there were workmen's compensation laws in all but four states. Also there were various pension systems for civil service employees, for men in the military services, and for special groups such as the clergy, who were considered to have done such praiseworthy work for so little cash return that they deserved special protection after their retirement. A good many corporations had set up pension plans—although Frank V. Whiting, chairman of the board of pensions of the New York Central Lines, made the melancholy observation in 1928 that "a large majority of industrial pension plans are insolvent," having been adopted "without knowledge as to the ultimate cost." And there had been, during the nineteen-twenties, a rapid growth of group life insurance, so rapid that in October 1928 an official of the Equitable Life Assurance Society estimated that 5,800,000 employees were already covered by seven and a half billion dollars of insurance. But by and large the individual and his family were supposed to attend to their own security.

"Against the risks of industry for the wage earner," wrote Wolman and Peck, "employers have made little voluntary provision. The pension plans of private industry still cover only a small fraction of the wage earners of the country. Insurance against sickness and the provision of medical care is made adequately in isolated cases only."

## A Positive Philosophy

The shortage of such plans, public and private, before 1929 did not reflect a callous or neglectful attitude on the part of Americans. It reflected a positive philosophy: that personal prosperity was a matter of personal responsibility; that it was up to the individual to work, save, and succeed; and that the inventiveness of America, its vitality, and its strength, lay in the self-reliance of Americans. Already the onrush of industrialism had somewhat battered this conviction, for when a factory laid off men by the hundreds there was little that individual resourcefulness could do to enable a man to feed his family; but the majority still clung to it firmly.

A man was supposed to do his own saving for a rainy day—to stash money in a savings bank—to take out life insurance on his own—and, if he could rake together more than a few hundred dollars, to buy stocks and bonds. Men were especially urged to buy stock in the company which employed them. And in the heady atmosphere of the Big Bull Market there were even sage and respected financiers who declared, as did John J. Raskob, that "everybody ought to be rich," and could become so by buying common stocks and saving and reinvesting the dividends. If a man's savings were exhausted by a series of rainy days, then it was up to his family to help him; or, if they failed, to his neighbors, or, at worst, to some local charity or the local poor-relief bureau.

The prevalent credo of those days has been aptly, if tartly, outlined by the Lynds in their second volume, *Middletown in Transition:*

> This is a country of boundless prosperity which guarantees an equal chance to everybody. If people don't get ahead it isn't the fault of society.
> Unfortunately there has always been in this and every other society a fringe of "unfortunates." Things like this just happen.
> But these things "happen" usually in part because the people involved have violated the gospel of "hard work and thrift."
> Therefore society should not do much for them because such extra help "weakens the character" of the recipient.

President Hoover put it clearly in a statement to the press in February 1931, when unemployment was mounting, and there were loud calls for the federal government to take part in the provision of relief, and he was engaged in a last-ditch resistance to these appeals as a matter of profound principle:

This is not an issue as to whether people shall go hungry or cold in the United States. It is solely a question of the best method by which hunger and cold shall be prevented. It is a question as to whether the American people, on the one hand, will maintain the spirit of charity and mutual self-help through voluntary giving and the responsibility of local government as distinguished, on the other hand, from appropriations out of the Federal Treasury for such purposes. My own conviction is strongly that . . . if we start appropriations of this character we have not only impaired something infinitely valuable in the life of the American people but have struck at the roots of self-government.

The same sort of feeling was manifest in American reactions to the British "dole." In the years immediately following 1929, when the economy of the United States was going into a convulsive and agonizing decline, and breadlines were lengthening on the streets, Americans noted with dismay what was happening in Britain, where the Depression was likewise severe.

When unemployed British workmen had run through all the unemployment insurance money to which they were entitled, and still couldn't find jobs, the British government decided to continue payments to them, even if it had to foot the whole bill. Whereupon American conservatives had nightmare visions of an impending time when the cries of anguish from the American jobless might cause them, too, to become wards of government. Would these idle workmen be dependent thereafter for their fortunes, not upon their own resourcefulness, but upon their ability to persuade the government that they should be paid for doing nothing? "The dole," said the New York *Herald Tribune* in 1931, "has persuaded millions that the government owes them a living . . ." Essentially the same note reverberated through the columns of newspaper after newspaper: it must not happen here!

## The Effects of Depression

What happened thereafter was terrifying.

The Depression defeated the hopes of those who had thought of it as a mere dip in the business cycle; it went on and on and got worse and worse. I remember, in the winter of 1930–31, visiting a friend whose plans for his future career had been smashed by the collapse of the value of his investments. He told me that a shrewd economist of his acquaintance had told him that the Depression might continue for another two or three years. The idea struck me as unbelievable and appalling. But the Depression was actually destined to continue, in varying degrees of intensity, for almost a decade. And in so doing it ate away relentlessly at the comfortable economic assumptions of the American people.

Men and women who had saved diligently for a rainy day saw their savings engulfed in the torrent of rain which fell on all investments. Men and women who had believed that hard work and ability are rewarded in this world found that hard work and ability didn't make much difference to a man whose company had decided to liquidate his whole department. Men and women who had believed, with Herbert Hoover, that "the spirit of charity and mutual self-help" in each community should look after the needs of those who were in trouble, found that there were whole communities without enough cash to meet the situation. Economic events seemed to move with a savage disregard for all the virtues on which millions of people had built their hopes. "Depression," as Peter F. Drucker has written, "shows man as a senseless cog in a senselessly whirling machine which is beyond human understanding and has ceased to serve any purpose but its own."

Hoover went down to defeat in the election of 1932; Franklin D. Roosevelt entered the White House with his lively program for recovery and reform; and for a time business perked up. Soon Washington came to the aid of the all-too-numerous unemployed with a series of measures which developed into the WPA—not quite a dole, but an elaborate system of federally-managed work relief which kept starvation at bay. But bewilderment and fear had settled down in millions of American homes, and remained there. Grim experience had taught people that America's economic life no longer followed the simple patterns which had been expounded by the *laissez-faire* economists; and had persuaded them that if they and their neighbors were to have nourishment and hope, things must be differently organized and the organization would have to be undertaken on a national scale.

And this bewilderment and fear did not possess only the fathers and mothers of the American family. It affected the children too, as the climate in which they were growing up altered. "The present day college generation," wrote the editors of *Fortune* in 1936, "is fatalistic . . . the investigator is struck by the dominant and pervasive color of a generation that will not stick its neck out. It keeps its shirt on, its pants buttoned, its chin up, and its mouth shut. If we take the mean average to be the truth, it is a cautious, unadventurous generation, unwilling to storm heaven, afraid to make a fool of itself. . . . Security is the *summum bonum* of the present college generation."

The youths of whom the editors of *Fortune* were speaking in 1936 have now, in 1953, reached an average age of about thirty-six. Since many of their juniors must have gathered, however indirectly, some sense of their parents' apprehensions, or of their friends' parents' apprehensions, one might hazard the guess that today in the United States there are few men and women of thirty and over who have not been affected in some degree, in their subsequent life, by their recollection of a day when economic trouble could strike without apparent reason, and by their resolve, as they grew older, not to trust wholly to their own capacities, but to see that they had some sort of shelter ready against the buffetings of economic chance.

## Two New Political Principles

It was in this atmosphere that two principles gradually won such general acceptance during the nineteen-thirties that neither of our major political parties has subsequently seen fit to question them.

One principle is that the fortunes of individual Americans are inextricably interlocked; that we are "all in the same boat"; and that if any of us fall into deep trouble it is the job of the rest of us—not simply family and friends and neighbors, or even the local community, but the federal government itself if need be—to help them.

The other principle is that it is the job of the federal government, through whatever means, to see that there shall not be another Great Depression. Most of us want to keep as much economic liberty as possible for ourselves as individuals; most of us hate to see the powers of the federal government extended; but we realize that it is the only instrument on which we can rely, in a severe economic emergency, to provide us with a measure of security.

It was in this atmosphere, likewise, that a long series of federal guarantees and insurance devices were adopted in Washington during the nineteen-thirties to protect various groups of Americans against the vagaries of economic chance. One might cite as examples the federal underwriting of farm prices, the federal guaranteeing of housing mortgages, the federal insuring of bank deposits. If the workings of what the old-time economists called "economic law" threatened to hurt a lot of people, Washington would step in and stop the damage.

And it was in this atmosphere that Congress passed the Social Security Act of 1935, which offered a nationally adminstered compulsory system of old-age insurance, a system of unemployment insurance which was to be operated by the states under federally prescribed standards and with federal aid, and a system of federal grants to the states to help them look after various other kinds of needy people.

## U.S. Social Security

It is a curious fact of American political history that sometimes the measures which as time has gone on have proved to be most significant were not those that originally aroused the fiercest partisanship, but those which were adopted with little debate, because there was implicit agreement that the time for them had come. During the first fifteen years of this century, for example, the issues on which people got most choleric were such things as the initiative, referendum, and recall of judicial decisions; but the measure which proved to have the most lasting impact on the country was the federal income tax amendment, which was passed almost by common consent at the behest of the conservative President Taft.

Similarly, Social Security was not one of the New Deal measures which caused the most apoplectic uproar. It might almost be described as a New Deal afterthought. During the earliest years of the Roosevelt Administration there had been a committee at work on it, headed by Secretary of Labor Frances Perkins; but the bill might not have seen the light of day until much later than 1935, if ever, had not President Roosevelt been worried about the offensive against his Administration, not from those who thought it was doing too much, but from those who thought it was doing too little—from Huey Long with his "share-the-wealth" slogan, and more especially from Dr. Francis E. Townsend with his extraordinary proposal for putting old people on the federal payroll. Yet when the Social Security Bill came before Congress, it swept toward passage on a broad tide of acceptance.

There were routine objections, of course.

A representative of the A.F. of L. said that employees ought not to have to pay their half of the premiums; a representative of the N.A.M. said that employers ought not to have to pay their half; and a representative of the Communist party said that the rich ought to pay everything. The bill was so extraordinarily complex that few legislators had more than the haziest notion of what it would do; a member of the House Committee on Ways and Means, Representative Samuel B. Hill, said at one point: "I want to confess it is difficult for members of the Ways and Means Committee, who have studied it for weeks and weeks, to get the full purport and understanding of all its provisions and ramifications." But pass it did, with ease; for by general agreement the time for it had come.

No other New Deal measure—at least after the first hundred days—drew so few fulminations from the business community and so many encomiums from so many groups.

A series of public opinion polls conducted by the American Institute of Public Opinion at intervals from 1935—the year when the Act was passed—until 1941, which asked (with slight differences in wording), "Are you in favor of government old-age pensions?" drew assenting answers, time after time, from an overwhelming majority of those questioned: 89 per cent in December 1935, 91 per cent in August 1938, 94 per cent in January 1939, 90 per cent in November 1939, and 91 per cent in July 1941. As a measure for providing as much protection for the future as Americans felt they could afford to buy, the Act was at least a great popular success.

The old-age pension part of the Social Security Act went into effect at the beginning of 1937. No longer would any wage or salary earner receive a check for the full amount of his or her salary. All over the country, squads of bookkeepers began computing deductions for each employee and setting aside similar amounts on behalf of their companies, while in the offices of the government, legions of bookkeepers began the endless entries and computations which would result in the building up of a vast reserve for future federal payments to the old people of the land.

## We Are Still Striving for Security

As the nineteen-thirties drew to a close, and the international skies darkened, the economic skies began to brighten. Defense spending was gradually soaking up our unemployment—though it was not until about 1943, when we had been at war with Germany and Japan for over a year, that one could definitely say that a surplus of labor had been converted into a shortage of labor.

During the nineteen-forties and early nineteen-fifties we Americans have had plenty of cause for worry as to our national survival, for we have gone through the ordeal of a World War, a Cold War, and a Limited War in Korea; and during most of this time we have been contemplating the horrible possibility of atomic annihilation. But we have had few new causes for *economic* worry. For we have enjoyed almost uninterrupted prosperity—a prosperity whose duration and vitality have been almost incredible to those of us who remembered well the long semi-paralysis of the nineteen-thirties.

Miraculously, we have achieved in the United States a per capita income more than 40 per cent larger than that of the golden year 1929, even after full allowance is made for rising prices. And we have seen new industries burgeon, old ones transformed by a new efficiency, new opportunities for ambition multiplying.

Yet we have *not* seen what one might have anticipated under such reassuring circumstances; we have *not* seen a noticeable relaxation of the popular desire to achieve economic security. Why not?

One reason, as I have suggested above, is that the memory of the Depression remains with us, earnestly though most of us have tried to wipe it from our minds. Every time anybody even suggests that a "recession" may be imminent, a perceptible shiver goes down the national spine, and in business conversations one hears such curious phrases as "peace threat," as men wonder whether a slackening of military spending would bring an economic convulsion.

Another reason may possibly be that throughout these years of booming trade we have been constantly reminded that our individual lives and fortunes may hang upon decisions made in Washington, in Moscow, or elsewhere, decisions over which we as individuals have no immediate control. We have witnessed the triumph of a reformed, disciplined, and democratized capitalism; we have emphatically *not* seen the triumph of the individual as a person who can look after himself under all circumstances.

### Increasing Reliance on Institutions

Furthermore, the individual during these years has become used to an increasing degree of dependence upon institutions, governmental or private. Take, for instance, what has happened to his salary check, which, as we have noted, usually covered the full amount of his earnings as recently as 1936. I am looking now at the stub which accompanied my own latest salary check. It shows a big deduction for "W.H. Tax"—that's withholding—and one for "F.O.A.B."—that's federal old-age benefit— and one for "HOSP."—that's for hospital insurance, a privately managed enterprise devised for my further security—and another for "INS." —that's for group life insurance, which again is non-governmental. (There is still another space on the stub for "DUES" which is empty in my case because I don't belong to a union.) Nearly all these deductions represent the institutionalizing of something that in earlier years I might have expected to look after by myself. Today I am glad to have a private institution—the corporation that employs me—take care of these payments on my behalf, and of all the bookkeeping they involve, whether they represent arrangements made with the federal government, or with a state, or with other private institutions.

This is a very small and limited example of a massive face of our times; that we all of us have come to take it for granted that we shall trade off some of our personal independence for the protection of our security by institutions. Not only have we become used to having a big government which intervenes in our affairs in many ways; we have become used to having all manner of private organizations similarly look after things for us. One might sum up the change by saying that for the rugged American individualism of tradition we have been substituting a rugged American associationism.

Still another reason why the desire for security has not appreciably slackened may be that any personal savings that we may have been able to accumulate since the Depression have been under attack by inflation, and unless they were invested with preternatural foresight have probably diminished in future value to us. And also that with the high taxes of today, windfalls for the fortunate aren't what they would have been in the old days.

I remember, during World War II, asking an author who was so lucky as to have a best-selling novel and a sell-out play going simultaneously whether he would like to receive an extra five hundred dollars for the manuscript of a serial. After careful calculation he said yes, he thought he could buy a case of scotch with it after the government got through with it. The tax would not be quite so high today, but it would be high enough to cut his windfall to shreds.

There are other reasons of a very different nature.

## The Urbanization of the Population

As fewer and fewer families live on self-sufficient farms—either because they have left farming altogether for city jobs, or because they make their living from cash crops—fewer and fewer old people can live out their years at small cash expense. And in our urbanized and suburbanized communities of today there are fewer and fewer of the large houses in which there was room in the first-story back room for Grandma, or the ell for simple-minded old Uncle Ezra.

One thing our magnificent prosperity has not brought us is *space*—space for the members of different generations to live together without getting in one another's way (one might almost say getting in one another's hair); space to put up the indigent relative. And with the change in the size of our living quarters has come a change in the American *mores:* to an increasing number of people it no longer seems right and proper—it seems, rather, a hardship—for the members of different adult generations to live under the same roof. And when most unemployed people and most old people must live as separate economic units instead of eating a little of a family supply of food and taking up a little of the family living space, the problem of security looms larger.

## An Aging Population

And finally, there is the overwhelming fact that there are, proportionately, more and more old people. The life expectation of Americans has increased since 1900 from 49 years to over 68 years. It has been said that for every problem that is solved, a new problem is created by its solution; the triumph of medicine over the savage diseases of yesteryear has created the problem of what to do with the aged.

One might say that the American men and women of money-earning age are caught in a pinch. Their parents and grandparents had more children to help look after them in their old age, for the birth-rate was much higher in those remote days. In 1890, married women who had reached the age at which they could no longer have children had had an average of 5.1 children apiece; in 1910, 4.1 children; in 1920, 3.6 children; by 1940 the figure had come down to 2.6. Now the birth rate has gone up again, and the schools are jammed with children; and our money-earners have to support these children and also worry about the financial status of their long-lived elders!

And all this has happened, ironically enough, in an era when it has become increasingly the fashion, among business concerns and other institutions, to set for their older employees a definite retiring age of sixty-five or even sixty. They have done this in a laudable desire to maintain the vigor of their enterprises and to provide opportunities for youth (and also to reduce, for executives, the anguish of having to decide which older employees to retain and which to dismiss); but they have certainly made more painful the pinch in which the middle generations are now caught. Under such circumstances, any system for providing economic security for old people looks like a godsend, not only to them, but to their apprehensive sons and daughters and nephews and nieces.

Perhaps it is not so strange after all that the popular interest in security devices did not decline when the Great Depression came to an end, but pressed with vigor on.

### What the Individual Is Doing for Himself

Some people might have guessed that, with the Social Security Act on the statute books and with the way open for other organized measures for security, at least the impulse toward private, unorganized saving would wane. People would think that the government and their employers and unions would take care of their future and that there was no further need for piling up personal reserves. This does not seem to have happened.

When the "defense boom" got under way in 1939 and 1940, observers in many American communities noted that the workers who were getting high wages in the defense plants were not tossing their money around, but were putting it away. They had learned a profound lesson during the Depression and were taking advantage of it now; they were paying off their debts, painting the house, making long-delayed repairs, sending the children belatedly to the dentist, and so forth.

During World War II, personal saving was made almost obligatory— for those above the minimal income levels—by rationing and shortages of goods, and the rate of saving was especially impressive: there were years when close to 25 cents out of every dollar of personal income (after taxes) was being saved. Much of this money, of course, went into war savings bonds. And even since the end of the war the rate of saving has been by no means negligible, despite the enormous sales of automobiles, tractors, refrigerators, washing machines, television sets, and other popular goods.

Look, for instance, at home ownership. (The buying of a home may or may not be regarded as strictly a form of saving—but usually it is at least a step toward economic security.) During the years from 1900 through 1940, there had consistently been more renters than owners in the United States: to put the fact more precisely, only from 43 to 48 per cent of the "occupied dwelling units" in the country had been occupied by owners. But during the nineteen-forties a great change took place, and when the figures were in for 1950, they showed that the percentage had jumped to 55—a remarkable gain, even though a lot of the owners were living in heavily mortgaged homes.

And there were other impressive figures.

Between 1940 and 1950, the amount of life insurance in force had more than doubled. The amount of money in mutual savings banks had nearly doubled. The amount of postal savings had more than doubled. The amount in savings and loan associations had gone up more than three times. And the amount in U.S. savings bonds—thanks to heavy buying during the war—had gone up nearly 18 times. It is true that the total of installment loans to consumers had gone up very sharply too. But even making allowances for this fact—and for the shrinkage in the value of the dollar—it became pretty clear that the American people are still mindful, even in a time of protracted and dazzling prosperity, of the need for husbanding their personal resources.

*   *   *   *   *

And meanwhile we have seen, too, what we might more reasonably have anticipated—a great expansion of the Social Security system and a striking growth of private pension systems and other organized safeguards against old age and adversity.

*   *   *   *   *

Altogether, one may reasonably say that we have moved fast since 1935.

### Where Do We Stand Today?

The historical record is pretty clear. The road ahead is anything but clear. I think that certain generalizations as to the situation we face are plainly warranted; but even as I write those words "plainly warranted" I realize how much easier it is for a historian to plot our past course than to plot our present position, and I proceed warily. At any rate, here are the generalizations:

1. *Even today, our Social Security and pension systems are inadequate.* This is not necessarily to say that they should be promptly expanded, for the question of expanding them must be considered against the background of a variety of other economic and social questions, as we shall presently see. But at least it is a cold fact that nobody should be deluded into thinking that Social Security alone will support him in his old age, even on the meagerest basis, without some other source of income or aid. Even with an industrial pension to supplement it, the aging worker will be faced with a very sharp contraction of his income. The necessity for personal saving continues. Indeed you and I and the rest of us, facing our own individual futures, had better behave almost exactly as if the American credo of the nineteen-twenties, as I quoted it above from *Middletown in Transition,* had never been modified. Social Security may pay for the soup course in our old age, and an industrial pension added to it may cover the vegetables, but we had better do our own saving if we want any meat.

2. *Our various systems for economic security are a hodgepodge.* Who is covered, and for how much, and who isn't covered at all, is less a matter of merit than of accident: it is likely to depend on where you live, and what sort of a job you have—and on whether the authors of any of

the plans now in existence happen to think of anybody situated as you are. Some of the plans overlap unreasonably. Yet even so, perhaps we are better off than if we had one magnificent and symmetrical system. There are advantages in having our economic security in a number of baskets. It is characteristically American to depend on a mixture of public and private institutions to take care of our problems, and I think healthily so.

3. *The expense of any social insurance or pension system of reasonable adequacy is very great,* for the simple reason that widowhood and old age are likely to be protracted, many illnesses are dismayingly expensive, and unemployment is epidemic and may be protracted. It takes an unconscionable time to build up adequate reserves for a pension fund, and it is all too easy to underestimate the amount of money which will be necessary. We must expect some of our new corporate pension systems to break down, as did so many of the old schemes, from having faced the future too blithely. And even our public systems, inadequate though they are to satisfy the needs they try to meet, take a good deal of money out of people's pockets.

4. *And the question of how much money we are willing to invest in security plans cannot be considered in a vacuum.* It is easy to focus our attention on some one plan and say that it should be enlarged. But look at some of the broader problems involved.

How much money are we willing to obligate ourselves to take out of the stream of current spending year after year, to invest in our future? If there should be a sharp economic downturn, this question might loom large.

If any contemplated plan involves a contribution by the government, can we be sure, in the first place, how large this will have to be, and can we be sure, in the second place, that the taxpayers will be able to afford it? Are we sure that the time will not come when the taxpayers' money had better not be expended, instead, on something of more immediate urgency, such as national defense?

It is a comfortable thing to back guarantees to various groups of citizens with the credit of the government; but might a time come when the credit of the government overloaded with obligations, would be in jeopardy?

How shall the reserves of our private pension funds be invested? And if the total of such reserves should be greatly increased, can they be invested in ways which will combine reasonable safety with a dynamic effect upon the national economy?

### Some Major Issues

These are only a few of the questions which come to mind; but at least they may serve to suggest that the problems of economic security are interlocked with other problems of possible consequence, and that the person who considers them is in a position something like that of the man who is deciding whether to buy an automobile on the installment plan: it is a good car, but how sure is he that when some future payment comes due he may not have a more pressing need for his money?

Some other questions of a somewhat different order suggest themselves.

Does not the adoption of a fixed age for retirement—say sixty-five—add unnecessarily to the load which our old-age security must carry? I am not speaking of upper executives, who presumably should be required to step aside in order to assure the continuance of an energetic leadership in the corporation or other institution; but of the general run of employees. Might not the discovery of methods for keeping our senior employees self-respectingly self-supporting well into their old age make for an easing of this whole problem—and also make for the happiness of the senior employees themselves? To put a man on shorter hours at reduced pay, or to put him on less critical or wearing work, might be less of a shock to his pride than to send him home to draw a pension—and would relieve the pension fund of a heavy burden.

How much security is too much? At what point does a security system begin to dampen initiative? My own hunch is that today in the United States we are, by and large, far from any such danger; that so long as our national advertising continues to whet the appetite for more and better goods, and so long as the roads to advancement are not blocked, and we persist in our national zest for doing new things and big things (a zest which has many other bases than the hope of economic security), the impulse to live lazily on a small bounty will not be widespread. But one can hardly say that the danger is non-existent.

And finally, when we look at our security arrangements as a whole, must we not realize that we face an especially knotty problem in the predicament of our lowest income group—let us say that 24 per cent, or thereabouts, of the American people who have personal or family incomes of less than $2000 a year? As I have written elsewhere, these people are not "the masses"; they are not a proletariat. They are, rather, a great number of very widely scattered people who for one reason or another are out of luck, such as small business men whose ventures have foundered; farmers who have had a bad year or series of years; lone widows, deserted wives and children; migratory laborers; workers of marginal ability; and invalids and defectives. Among them will be found the largest proportion of people unconnected with any money-making venture, who are least likely to be eligible under any carefully drawn insurance or pension plan, and who are least likely to have other resources to supplement their insurance or pension benefits, or to have friends or relatives who can come to their aid in time of need. As Robert Heilbroner has said, the condition of these people is not really an economic problem; it is a social problem. Yet their ability to live decently and self-respectingly is a test of the adequacy of our American system.

How far can we expect insurance and pension plans to meet the needs of many of them? Take medical insurance, for instance; apparently our present voluntary systems can go far to meet the general run of medical needs for the rest of the population, but cannot expect to serve many of this lowest income group. Shall the federal government carry this part of the load, or shall we say that these people are uninsurable, and leave their care to federally-aided local assistance and to private charity, more or less as at present? To ask this apparently simple question is to raise a host of others—that of big government, that of federal solvency, that of the character of the medical profession, that of the general public health, that of local ability to meet local needs, and so forth.

I have said that the need for personal saving still persists, no matter what security plans we devise. So also does the need for private generosity, no matter how cunningly the plans are drawn. And so does the need, on the part of experts who gravely weigh the problems of economic security for the American people, to remember that it is the men and women on the lower rungs of the economic ladder whom these problems concern most pressingly and acutely.

# 4. RECENT DEVELOPMENTS AND EMERGING CONCEPTS

HERMAN M. and ANNE R. SOMERS,
*Bulletin of the International
Social Security Association,*
March–April, 1957.

YOUR EDITOR originally invited us to review the "philosophical basis" of social security in the United States. The only practical way of performing such a task is to undertake a theoretical interpretation of American practice and experience. In the United States theory rarely comes first. It evolves from a series of responses to needs and circumstances. When these responses fall into a pattern or trend, they may then be translated into concepts.

Even such a task is not simple. No one philosophy or coherent set of objectives runs through our social security legislation and practice. We are a nation of continental dimensions with highly diversified ethnic, cultural, economic and social influences. We have learned to live together with reasonable success, under a federal government, through continuous compromise and accommodation. Many contradictory and often clashing influences have participated in and affected our institutions. During the past 25 years we have known extremes of depression and prosperity and both have left their mark on American social security. Through trial and error there emerges what is workable and what renders maximum satisfaction in a conglomerate nation. The workability and satisfactory results are the basis of acceptable theory.

Therefore we must examine the dominant trends in the evolution of American social security practice if we are to explain the dominant viewpoints. Readers of this journal need no general description of social security institutions in the United States.[1] We confine our discussion to an identification of several major trends and an estimate of their meaning. These are not all the significant trends, by any means, but only a selection of those which appear to us to have particular interest.

In reviewing these developments, readers from other countries will undoubtedly find much that is familiar as well as much that appears strange. This is as it should be. There are basic elements of social security which are universal in purpose and requirements. A common humanitarian concern and basic methodology bind together *bona fide* social security systems wherever they may be found. Much of the initial approach to social security in the United States had its origins in the older European systems.

On the other hand, there is much in American social security which is indigenous, as is also the case in other nations.[2] Social security techniques are best evaluated with reference to their appropriateness to the community they are designed to serve. No particular technique or approach has inherent or universal superiority. As problems and characteristics of one nation differ from another, so the instruments of social security will be differently adjusted and applied. The stressing of similarities or differences is usually arbitrary; both are naturally present in ample degree, as the reader will readily recognise in the eight points which follow.

**I**

*Social security, with social insurance as its keystone, has become accepted as an established part of American institutional life. Nineteenth-century views alleging a basic conflict between security and freedom have declined rapidly as evidence of the contrary truth unfolds.*

Calling attention to the general acceptance of social security is largely a form of reminder that by European standards the organised system of social security in the United States is a phenomenon only 20 years old. As the nation itself is very young, the timing is not as disproportionate as may appear. It is easily forgotten how recently we emerged from a predominantly rural society.

Following considerable debate and challenge, social security has been

---

[1] For a good summary description, see A. J. Altmeyer, "The Development of Social Security in the U.S.A.," this *Bulletin*, Vol. VII, No. 12 (December, 1954).

[2] Our travels through six European countries last year revealed not only that the frequent emphasis on differences between European and American "systems" was often greatly exaggerated, but also that the differences among the various European systems were often as great as between any European country and the United States.

endorsed by virtually all segments of the population and has ceased to be an issue between our major political parties which now vie for credit in strengthening the programmes. There is, of course, and will continue to be, wide and healthy disagreement on the precise character, objectives, and extent of these programmes.

But amidst the continuing debate and experimentation there stands a solid framework of consensus on the desirability of a basic system of social security programmes designed to provide income-maintenance and protection against certain serious economic and social hazards associated with modern industrial society.

Americans are pragmatists in behaviour, even if traditionalists in vocabulary. While old slogans die hard and phrases like "free enterprise" still hold a hallowed place in our lexicon, we in fact exercise a higher degree of governmental control or regulation of business and industry than do many countries whose political vocabulary permits a greater acknowledgement of socialisation.

Similarly, we have accepted the weight of evidence that security does not destroy freedom. During the entire period of social insurance expansion in the United States, Americans have seen productivity steadily rise at rates and to heights which would have been regarded as fantasy had anyone been bold enough to predict them as recently as 1940. To make these technological advances effective required a highly ambitious labour force as well as inventive and adventurous management. We have observed labour's traditional resistance to technological change converted to co-operative acceptance. We have seen full employment accompanied by expansion of the number of persons available for work in relation to total population. We have observed workers' reluctance to accept the post-war reduction in overtime hours at a time when earnings and security were greater than ever before. We have seen that in an environment of high earnings and increased security malingering has become a progressively less significant phenomenon, generally confined to identifiable groups, compared with the days of low earnings and insecurity of the 'thirties. In short, the data suggest that it is insecurity rather than security which threatens enterprise and freedom.

The American business-minded community is now finding justification for social security not only in its traditional function of providing for individual and family welfare but also because it serves certain broad economic functions simultaneously: for example, the maintenance of adequate levels of purchasing power is now sought not only for contra-cyclical purposes but also to insure, in normal times, the confidence of buyer and seller in the practicability of instalment buying by wage-earners through assured continuity of income. We are recognising that just as security and freedom underpin one another, so business welfare and human welfare can be mutually supporting. Both are aided by high levels of social security.

Most Americans today would accept the following description by a French authority of the proper goals of a social security system in a free society: "The real problem is to promote income security policies giving the largest possible room to individual and family freedom, to individual and family responsibilities. Many examples show that this is possible. And if this is possible, this must be the goal of all free countries, for freedom by security, and income security with freedom, are the best way, if not the only way, to allow every man and woman to make the best use of his own potentialities."[3]

## II

*While the American system emphasises social insurance, it is accepted that comprehensive social security includes public assistance and welfare services.*

There was a brief early period when some Americans talked as if a fully developed social insurance system might obviate the necessity for public assistance and perhaps even other welfare services. If any such expectation really existed, it receives no attention anywhere now. Public assistance is now recognised as an essential supplementation of social insurance which, by definition, cannot be designed to meet individual needs.

Today about 5.5 million persons are receiving public assistance as compared to over 11 millions receiving social insurance payments. Throughout the period of expanding social insurance in the United States, provisions for public assistance and welfare services have been simultaneously liberalised and expanded at least as rapidly. The Federal Government has steadily increased its share of the costs of public assistance as compared to the states and local governments, from 22 per cent in 1938 to 50 per cent in 1955. A new category of public assistance was added in 1956: aid to the permanently and totally disabled. Federal grants to state and local governments for maternal and child health services, public health services, vocational rehabilitation, and similar welfare services increased almost 14-fold from 1938 to 1955. The annual cost of welfare services, exclusive of special ex-servicemen's programmes, is over $4,000 million and of public assistance almost $3,000 million, as compared to about $10,000 million for social insurance.

During one stage of social insurance, before it had achieved general acceptance or understanding, there was some danger that an imbalance in favour of assistance might occur. It was during the period when old-age assistance payments were averaging better than old-age insurance benefits that the latter's integrity was threatened. If that should occur again, or if any substantial proportion of insurance beneficiaries should

[3] Pierre Laroque, "Major Issues Raised by Contemporary Trends in Income Security Policies," in J. E. Russell (ed.), *National Policies for Education, Health and Social Services* (New York: Doubleday & Co., 1955), p. 284.

simultaneously require assistance, the social insurance structure would be endangered. It appears that the two types of programmes serve as a discipline upon each other. A competitive co-existence has tended to elevate the standards of each.

While we will continue to emphasise the desirability of maximum utilisation of the technique of social insurance, wherever feasible, as compared to public assistance, it does appear that we are accepting the implications of the European phrase, "from social insurance to social security" —that is, the need for a comprehensive nationwide approach to the problem of income security.

### III

*Our programmes have developed along a pluralistic pattern characteristic of other American institutions. However, it is fully recognised that social security is primarily a governmental responsibility.*

There has been much deserved attention to the dramatic development of private income-security plans through industrial, usually collectively bargained, pension programmes, health and welfare plans, and supplementary unemployment benefits (originally publicised as "guaranteed annual wage"). This has caused some people to overlook the fact that the basis of American social security remains public and that private employee benefit plans, important as they are, remain supplementary and secondary.

The public programmes have been the major stimulus of private programmes. The American experience is similar to that described by M. Laroque: "Contrary to what could have been expected, the development of public income security schemes has generally given a new impulse to voluntary schemes and institutions, as if the fractional security automatically guaranteed induced the people concerned to seek a fuller security by their own effort."[4]

When the initial great drive for retirement pensions in industry took place, more than a decade after the national public programme went into effect, the typical pattern was to inter-relate the private pension with the public one, making the former a supplement to the latter in order to reach a pre-determined total. Similarly, supplementary unemployment benefits are additions to the pre-existing state unemployment insurance systems and are dependent on such systems.

Despite the striking growth of private plans in these areas, at the moment only a fraction of the numbers receiving public benefits are receiving similar types of private payments. Also there is no support for the view that the coming of private benefits lowers the standards of the pub-

---

[4] Pierre Laroque, *op. cit.*, p. 280.

lic programmes. On the contrary, the frequently more generous levels established in private plans has stimulated, and made politically feasible, the raising of public standards.

Private programmes have achieved their most significant advances in fields where public programmes have been only spottily and inadequately established, primarily in medical care and temporary disability (cash sickness) insurance. Public policy in these fields has not yet taken clear shape. There is no doubt that the experience of the private programmes will have an influence on the ultimate public policy. Already, for example, the successful development of private health insurance plans has led to almost universal acceptance of the insurance principle for medical care, once strongly opposed by the American Medical Association even in the private sphere. A very important question is whether the expansion of private programmes will retard or advance the development of public programmes for medical care and temporary disability insurance. Informed opinions differ on this point, but it appears more likely that the long-run effects will be helpful to governmental programmes.

Our experience underlies our belief that the interaction of public and private programmes offers more advantages than disadvantages, that the relationship is mutually beneficial and serves the general public interest. While the basic programmes must be public and should be available without discrimination, we have found in many fields of activity that the prod and example of private activity often stimulate or hasten progress in public spheres. An example can be found in the field of education. About 75–80 per cent of all expenditures for education in the United States comes from public funds. But this quantitative measure gives no indication of the pervasive qualitative influence of such private institutions as Harvard or Notre Dame Universities, Haverford College, or the New York School of Social Work. Sometimes the picture is reversed. The government's relatively small share of costs in the medical field equally understates its role and influence.

Another form of pluralism results from the American federal constitution. The states retain some sovereign authority and a vast amount of sovereign psychology. Each of the states has its own unemployment insurance and workmen's compensation laws. There are widely varying benefit levels, eligibility standards, and administrative procedures. Whether the local advantages of such decentralisation outweigh the disadvantages is widely argued in our country. It is, however, clear that the important advances in social security in recent years have relatively enlarged the role and influence of the national government, and its leadership is dominant. The federally operated old-age, survivors, and disability programme has become far the largest and most significant. In the nature of our economy and in keeping with other trends in public affairs, it seems inevitable that this tendency will increase in the future.

## IV

*There has been a slow but steady expansion in the risks covered by social insurance as well as an increase in persons covered.*

American social insurance, as an organised system, started recently and modestly. The Social Security Act of 1935 made provision for only two income-loss risks: old age (retirement) and unemployment. Workmen's compensation laws already existed in all but four states, which have since added such laws. The number of persons originally covered by the 1935 laws was relatively moderate, caution being caused largely by fear of administrative difficulties.

The two most significant advances in risk coverage have been incorporated into the original old-age insurance structure, now called OASDI (Old-Age, Survivors, and Disability Insurance). In 1939, a survivorship insurance programme was created to pay monthly benefits to surviving dependants of an insured worker. In 1956 there was added insurance for permanent and total disability. Payments for the latter programme, now limited to workers 50 years old or over, begin July 1957. They will receive the same benefit as for retirement except that there are no increments for dependants (until the beneficiary reaches 65 and is transferred to the old-age programme with all its rights). It can be predicted that after some experience with this programme, the customary pattern will be followed. The age requirement will be lowered or eliminated and dependants' benefits will be added.[5]

Since the war, four of our most industrial states have passed temporary disability laws which, together with the special law for railroad workers, cover more than one-fifth of the nation's employees.

Coverage within programmes has also been expanded. The OASDI programme now covers 9 out of 10 gainfully occupied persons, plus their dependants. Today 50 millions of the nation's 56 million children and 9 out of 10 married women with children are protected against death of the breadwinner. The only significant groups now omitted from coverage are self-employed doctors (by their own choice) and certain state and local government employees, covered by other public programmes. As the programme is still "maturing," the full effects of the extended coverage are not yet reflected in old-age benefit eligibility. In 1960, about 65 per cent of all persons in the population 65 years of age will be eligible. Before the year 2000 the figure will reach 94 per cent.

Social insurances now provide support for more than half the aged population and 17 per cent receive public assistance. Most of the remain-

---

[5] A portion of the gap in protection of those permanently disabled before having an opportunity to acquire an attachment to the labour force, and thus social insurance coverage, is being closed through a 1956 extension of benefits for permanently disabled children, incapable of self-support, after age 18, provided they were disabled at an earlier age.

der support themselves by earnings. In 1956, virtually all the aged men and four-fifths of the aged women in the country either had earnings or received payments from a public income-maintenance programme.

Coverage in unemployment insurance, as in workmen's compensation, is far more restricted, although it too has expanded. About 80 per cent of wage and salary earners are now under unemployment insurance programmes. About 40 per cent of the excluded are state and local government employees; others are employees of very small firms and agricultural, domestic, and casual workers. Resistance is particularly strong against extending coverage to the last category because of the feeling that unemployment insurance is not feasible except for workers with regular labour market attachment, else the administrative problem of dealing with malingering becomes too difficult. This has also led to an increasingly severe interpretation of eligibility and harsher disqualifications. There is evidence that the latter trend has been unnecessarily aggravated by the effects of inter-state cost competition and the "experience-rating" method of financing, one of the gravest points of contention in the social security system.

American social insurance is still far from comprehensive either in risk coverage or coverage of persons. Nor is the fact that the public assistances catch most of the omissions any cause for complacency on this score. Yet the direction in which we are moving is clear. Take into account that the system has been operating for only 20 years, that during one-fourth of that time the nation was absorbed in a world war, and, during all but the first few years, we have had almost continuous high levels of employment and income—the kind of period which normally does not generate much pressure towards extending social insurance—and the progress towards a fully developed system may be regarded as generally commendable.

## V

*There is increasingly widespread activity, lively experimentation and public debate in the area of medical care insurance. Rapid changes are taking place in both the organisation and financing of medical care, but the eventual pattern is still uncertain.*

Medical care is the most conspicuous, and controversial, gap in the American social security structure. The gap is somewhat less extreme than is often represented. Many special groups are provided with total or partial government health services: ex-servicemen, military personnel, occupationally injured workers, persons with tuberculosis, mental illness, and others. Merchant seamen have enjoyed free public medical care for 150 years. The large and growing programme of medical care for public assistance recipients already includes, in some states, the "medically indigent"—i.e., those with income sufficient to meet all other costs but medical care. Altogether, in 1955, state, local and national governments spent approximately $5,000 million for health services, almost one-third of all public and private expenditures. Considering personal health services only (excluding general public health activities) the government's share of the total was 23 per cent.

In part the gap is met by private health insurance which has witnessed a phenomenal rise during the past decade. It is estimated that over two-thirds of the population now have some form of medical care insurance, although often for limited hospital expenses only; about 57 per cent are insured for some surgical expense; a little over one-third for some portion of other medical expense.

A large part of this development has resulted from collective bargaining, in which health insurance is now a standard item. About 78 per cent of employees have some form of coverage. Employers and unions are co-operating in establishment of health clinics for workers and their families.[6] Many insurance companies, hospitals, medical schools and dedicated groups of doctors are designing imaginative schemes to make modern medical care available to people at prices they can afford. There is increased recognition of the advantages and feasibility of comprehensive health services and group practice clinics such as those operated by the Health Insurance Plan of Greater New York, with its 500,000 members, the Kaiser Foundation Health Plan of California, Group Health Association of Washington, D.C., and others. While these now reach only about 4 per cent of the population, they are vastly significant as examples of this modern approach to medical care.

The degree of protection provided by private health insurance varies enormously, however, and it is estimated that, as a whole, it meets only about 22 per cent of the total private medical bill, or about 17 per cent of total public and private outlay for civilian personal health services, as compared with the government's 23 per cent. In recent years, the private plan expenditures have increased more rapidly than the government share.

While the actual picture is thus better than is often presented, Americans are generally agreed that all this is not enough. The present government is committed to some sort of additional action in the area of public medical insurance. It will again propose to Congress a plan for federal "reinsurance" of private programmes, mainly intended to help insure the aged, low-income groups, and other so-called "poor risks." It is probable

---

[6] "The outlook that many industrial leaders have toward medicine and health is exemplified by recent remarks of Benson Ford, a grandson of the man who played an important part in making it possible for a working-man to buy the automobiles he helped produce:

"'Inclusive health care,' he said, 'should provide to every American citizen, at a cost that he can reasonably meet, all of the services necessary to keep him healthy and productive . . . I for one am not in the least worried about the so-called threat of "socialised medicine." '" R. K. Plumb, "Medicine Faces Challenge," *New York Times,* January 7, 1957.

that special provisions will be made for purchasing medical care insurance for aged beneficiaries of OASDI with the programme's funds. The government last year provided for the purchase of health insurance for dependants of servicemen. It has proposed a programme of health insurance for the 2.5 million federal employees.

Clearly this is a period of ferment. The next few years will be replete with lively experimentation in various directions to find means, short of a comprehensive national insurance scheme, to deal satisfactorily with this difficult problem. Underlying all the surface tensions and controversies are two profound recent developments common, in greater or less degree, to all the western nations: the "technical revolution in medicine"[7] and the change in popular expectations with regard to medicine.

Both of these are phenomena with roots going back to the beginning of scientific medical research and the Renaissance rejection of mediæval fatalism with regard to man's personal fate. But it is only within the past half-century, more especially the past 30 years, that the two movements have accelerated and converged with revolutionary impact on existing medical institutions. The challenge to prevailing patterns of professional organisation is as great as to current medical economics.

Not unnaturally, resistance has also been great. One result is conflict between those institutions which embody the new trends—the leading medical schools, the great teaching hospitals[8] and group practice clinics in all of which individual specialization can be combined with an over-all co-ordinated approach to the "whole man" uncomplicated by economic considerations—and those medical doctors who still prefer to practice

---

[7] Included are the tremendous advances in medical and related research, the great improvement in medical training, the development of new and far more accurate diagnostic techniques, the discovery of predictable and effective methods of treatment such as insulin and the antibiotics, the remarkable advances in surgery, the gradual opening up of knowledge with regard to emotional and mental health, and a greater appreciation of the complex etiology of disease and liability.

[8] For a striking example of parallel thinking on both sides of the Atlantic with regard to one of the basic problems—the evolving role of the modern community hospital—compare the following British and American statements. ". . . it is possible to see the centre of gravity in hospital work shifting from in-patient treatment to community service. With the out-patient deparment becoming . . . 'the focus of health services which promote health,' and thus helping to mobilise diagnostic facilities, observation units, specialised therapeutic services, domiciliary consultant work and much else besides, the hospital will, in effect, be *servicing* the community's health and welfare agencies—and not least . . . the general practitioner—with a battery of scientific and technological aids. It will no longer be predominantly and primarily a hospital in the traditional sense." B. Abel-Smith and R. M. Titmuss, *The Cost of the National Health Service* (Cambridge University Press, 1956), pp. 153–54.

The *New York Times*, in a special series on health insurance, writes January 11, 1957: "Some plans for reorganisation of hospitals . . . are being considered . . . plans for setting up community service centres to provide diagnostic and counselling services, health education, training and programmes to teach the afflicted how to care for themselves at home are under way. These changes, if they come, will further alter the pattern of medical service from the conventional pattern set up largely on economic lines."

"solo" medicine on a "fee-for-service" basis, whether general practitioners or unattached specialists. In the field of medical economics the basic problem is how to make this wonderful but frightfully expensive modern medicine available at a price acceptable to both producers and consumers, while maintaining maximum freedom for both.

The United States is engaged in painstaking, and somewhat painful, introspection and research. In July 1956, President Eisenhower and the Congress authorised a national health survey programme—the first since 1935—to include continuing surveys and special studies to determine the extent of illness and disability in the nation and to study related health problems. We are also evaluating the experience of the great variety of existing medical care programmes.

Many people feel that future public health insurance policy is being written today in prevailing private insurance practices. For this reason they advocate the establishment, as soon as possible, of minimal national standards, possibly in conjunction with the proposed federal reinsurance programme or with public subsidies for those private plans which are really trying to cope with the basic problems of modern medical care and modern medical economics. In the formulation of such standards we would have to devote intensive study to the many-faceted experience of European countries.

### VI

*Benefits have become increasingly directed towards the family unit rather than the individual insured.*

Originally, both the old-age insurance and unemployment insurance benefits were paid exclusively to the individual insured worker. In 1939, dependents' allowances were added to retirement benefits, and a survivorship programme was added to provide benefits for the widows and surviving children of insured workers. Since then dependency has been more broadly defined and family benefit levels liberalised. The OASDI programme is now primarily a family benefit programme. A similar trend has taken place in the special programme for railway workers.

The maximum individual retirement benefit under OASDI is $108.50 per month. The maximum family benefit is $200, but the surviving family of a deceased worker with 3 dependent children may get $200 a month even when the father's individual benefit was only $80. In June 1956, aged widows alone were averaging $49 a month; widows with one dependent child $109; widows with 3 dependent children $136. In retirement benefits, the average individual benefit was $60 (males, $66; females, $51), but beneficiaries with eligible wives averaged $105, and those with wives and dependent children about $123.

This trend has also been evident in the Aid to Dependent Children (public assistance) programme. Originally, federal funds were available only for payments to the children themselves. Since 1950 such funds may also be used for mothers or other relatives caring for the children, which raised the family total significantly. Family benefits under this programme now average over $90 a month. In 1956, the Congress, in liberalising the law and adding new services, explicitly stated as the aim of the programme to help maintain and strengthen family life and to help keep children in their own homes.

American social insurance theory and law have always stressed the importance of variable benefit levels proportionately related to individual wage loss, qualified by a monetary maximum. In the long-term insurance programmes, the principle of wage-loss compensation has been significantly modified by considerations of presumptive need indicated by family composition. Some find the spread of family benefits disturbing because it appears to represent a threat to the basic principle of differential wage-related benefits. They point out that family-related benefits tend towards flat rates.

This represents an ancient problem in social insurance, the problem of reconciling equity with adequacy. The wage-loss principle has become entrenched in American theory because of its apparent equity in a contributory system, and because it is an essential basis for justifying high average benefit levels. However, wage-loss alone is not always an adequate gauge of presumptive need, and presumptive need must be given some account if social insurance benefits are going to prove adequate for the preponderant majority of recipients.

In programmes with long periods of average benefit duration previous earnings are less significant as an index than in the short-term programmes which fill gaps between normal periods of wage-earning. The OASDI pattern actually represents a reconciliation of the two principles. Despite the heavy weighting for dependants in the benefit formula the basic amount to which the family allowances are attached is proportionate to an index of wage loss, although the proportion is heavily skewed in favour of the lower income worker. And the allowances are also expressed as a proportion of the basic benefit, not as flat sums.

In the short-term programmes, family composition has not had such a significant development. Only eleven states allow increments for dependent children of the unemployed, and these are generally meagre. In the short run, the wage-loss is generally considered a pretty good index of presumptive needs. Also, the drive to raise short-term benefits as close to actual wages as possible reduces the margin for dependency allowances. While the need for allowances is therefore less in these programmes, there are signs that they may continue to spread slowly, chiefly as a means of selectively breaking through the otherwise rigid weekly maxima.

The trend towards supplementary family benefits does not, however, indicate that we are approaching a general programme of family allowances. This is a high wage economy. By October 1956, average wages in manufacturing had reached $82 a week and average hourly earnings exceeded $2. Generally speaking, there is little problem of adequacy of family income during periods of employment. The real problems centre upon periods of interrupted income and emergencies. In programmes designed for such periods there has been a significant modification of principle.

## VII

*There has been a significant and constructive movement in the direction of adding service benefits to cash income maintenance.*

As a healthy reaction to the indignities of relief "in kind," still common in the early days of the Great Depression, Americans confined their reformed income-maintenance programmes strictly to money payment plans. Service programmes such as public health, child welfare and maternal health services, were continued and expanded. But these were distinct from the income-maintenance programmes—public assistance and social insurance.

With the firm institutionalisation of the cash programmes and the rapid advance in social and scientific technology, there had come about a realisation that a great deal could be done within such programmes to increase the well-being of beneficiaries through means which they themselves could not purchase, and that intelligent direction could make a great many of them self-supporting again. The suspicion that service benefits were a threat to cash benefits has been allayed. Moreover the categorical structure of the public assistances (as well as social insurances) causes an identification of particular groups with particular problems and leads to the development of special programmes to assist them.

There has followed a tendency to strengthen all income-maintenance programmes by adding appropriate direct services. This is especially pronounced in the assistances but is also developing in the insurances. In workmen's compensation, medical care and rehabilitation benefits have been receiving increasing emphasis. The new federal disability programme stresses rehabilitation and establishes both negative and positive incentives. Deductions are to be made from monthly benefits if the individual refuses rehabilitation without good cause. A worker engaging in gainful activity under an approved state rehabilitation plan will be officially considered totally disabled and entitled to disability benefits for a full year after the beginning of such employment.

The state employment services are placing increasing emphasis on vocational counselling, labour market analysis, and other aids to improving job placement for the unemployed. Family counselling and other social work techniques have been introduced in the Aid to Dependent Children programme (the major cause of dependency is no longer orphanhood, a disappearing phenomenon, but desertion by the father). Provision of medical services has been augmented in all assistance programmes. It is highly probable that within the next few years some OASDI funds will be used to purchase health insurance for aged beneficiaries.

In 1956, Congress amended the statements of purpose for all the assistance programmes to make it explicit that, in addition to giving financial aid to needy persons, the intention is to provide services to help assistance recipients toward independent living.

For this purpose, more knowledge is needed. Congress therefore has authorised a programme of co-operative research and demonstration projects by public and private welfare agencies to learn more about the causes of dependency and the most effective means of dealing with it. Five million dollars has been authorised for the first year of the programme.

This broadened approach will also require the services of additional specialised personnel. This has been acknowledged by an appropriation of federal funds to assist the states in increasing the number of trained public welfare personnel. The new funds are to be used by the states to make training grants to institutions of higher learning and to establish fellowships.

These new goals and additional means represent one of the great advances in our social security evolution. It offers a great opportunity for "humanising" and "personalising" our huge social security programmes, as well as an opportunity to take advantage of the vast quantity of new specialised knowledge, especially in the medical care and social work fields. At the present stage of our history, there need be no fear that these new channels will become substitutes for the basic cash income-maintenance functions. They should be added sources of strength.

## VIII

*The social insurance principle of differential benefits has faced a sharp challenge as a result of the rapid rise of real wages. From this experience there appears to be emerging a reaffirmation of the concept of high benefit levels as a needed support for a dynamic economy as well as for individual and family welfare.*

As already noted, the principle of differential benefits was adopted in American social insurance programmes partly because it was essential for maintaining relatively high benefits. Furthermore, the insurance system was regarded as an extension of the wage and salary system for periods of cessation of normal earnings. Labour has regarded the employers' contributions to the insurance system as a form of deferred wages. In workmen's compensation the basic benefit-wage ratio is generally 66⅔ per cent; in unemployment compensation it is 50 per cent. While based on a similar principle, the OASDI formula is more complex and, as indicated, modified by additional considerations. The basic benefit for a single retired worker is 55 per cent of the first $110 of average monthly wages, plus 20 per cent of the next $240. A percentage of the basic benefit is added for each dependant or survivor.

The programmes all have a maximum statutory limit, originally established to keep the highest-paid workers from drawing exceptionally high benefits. In 1939 only a small proportion of workers received wages or benefits high enough to be affected by the maxima. However, wages have been rising rapidly and steadily. As might be expected, the required legislative action to adjust the statutory maxima has lagged considerably. As a result, an increasing number of beneficiaries receive the maximum which has taken on some of the characteristics of a flat rate. The intended benefit-wage ratio has been nullified for a large number of workers.

Yet, the interesting point is that the maxima have been steadily increased, and actual benefit levels have gone up more rapidly than the cost of living. But wages have risen far more than the cost of living and the benefit levels have failed to keep up with wages. For example, most unemployment insurance laws in 1939 had a maximum of $15 a week; by 1955 most states had raised the maximum to $30. The average weekly benefits for total unemployment more than doubled, rising from $10.66 to $25.04, and more than kept up with prices, which increased about 93 per cent. But average weekly earnings in manufacturing industries rose in that period about 320 per cent.

Clearly this type of development could not be quarrelled with if the objective were only to keep up with the cost of living. Nor could it be challenged if the objective were the maintenance of a minimum subsistence level. The challenge arises in terms of a violation of the principle of differential benefits. In 1939 when the weekly maximum was $15, only one-fourth of weekly payments were at that level. But by 1955 when the maximum was typically $30, the number of payments made at the maximum was almost 60 per cent. This also meant that the intended benefit-wage relationship of 50 per cent had ceased to be a reality for most workers, and this too was a basis for challenge. But such a challenge is persuasive, and the "principles" supportable, only if compatible with more fundamental views regarding the role of social security.

It requires the view that benefits must reflect the steadily rising *standard of living*, as reflected by wage levels, not merely changes in the *cost of living*. The justification for wage-related benefits at this high level of earnings, is now increasingly related to the economy's need to maintain consumer purchasing power and to allow both consumers and sellers to anticipate that a worker will be able to maintain instalment payments even during interruptions of employment. The American economy is geared to mass production and mass consumption. Social security benefits, as well as wages, must be adapted to this fact. Furthermore, in an economy marked by a rapid rate of technological change, high social security payments during adjustment periods help to minimise labour resistance to the new technology. Many additional points of a broad economic character are made. The interests of social security beneficiaries have thus become closely identified with the welfare of the general economy.

The outcome of this ferment is not yet certain. There is and will continue to be resistance to the implications of such a view. Yet it does appear that the tide is clearly in favour of this new conception of the role of social security. In 1954, President Eisenhower told Congress, "Because the floor of security to the individual has been built primarily on welfare considerations, its contribution to the economic progress of the United States has not been adequately appreciated." The President and the Secretary of Labor have been urging upon the states immediate increases in unemployment insurance benefits to reach the intended 50 per cent earnings ratio. Many proposals are being made to prevent the cumbersome maxima from interfering with established levels by providing for automatic adjustments. It is significant that the Republican Party of New York State has proposed that statutory maxima be abolished and that the figure be administratively established every six months to represent 50 per cent of average wages in covered employment so that the rapid wage rises which are currently characteristic of the economy may be quickly reflected in benefits. It was the conspicuousness of the lapse from the criteria of differential benefit levels in percentage terms which made it possible to obtain liberalisation of benefit provisions in both workmen's compensation and unemployment insurance in most states in 1955.

The main reasons for optimism that this view will continue to be effective are the facts of high prosperity, steadily rising productivity, and labour scarcity. High employment levels and high wages have made the social security programmes less expensive than anticipated, in proportion to the national income and in relation to payrolls. In 1956 the total costs of public social insurance programmes in the United States approximated 6 per cent of payroll, with employers contributing about two-thirds and employees about a third. Benefit levels of public assistances have also been rising liberally, but together with social insurance costs they represent a lower percentage of the growing national income than in 1940. Opportunities for generous benefits and liberal interpretation of objectives will continue as long as costs appear easily manageable. An expanding economy will ensure that costs remain proportionately moderate, even as the programmes grow. In turn, the view is taking hold that social security can help to make the economy, which sustains it, dynamic and expanding.

\* \* \* \* \*

What may one conclude from these trends regarding the American view of social security? No sensible American would wish to say with assurance. We are conscious of the fact that we are in the process of a great social and economic transformation, whose full significance we cannot yet see. We are well aware of our good fortune in having been spared the scourge of war and bombing in our own land. We have had no major depressions since our social security programme took shape, and we are not yet certain whether we have found the magic formula for avoiding such depressions, or whether we have just been lucky. About basic doctrines, we feel highly tentative; in our actions we are highly experimental.

We have been actively altering, adjusting, and expanding our social security programmes during the past 20 years. As the reader will have recognised, many of the changes have brought our programmes in closer conformity with traditional views of social security as they are, for example, known in Europe. In some degree, as the reader will also have seen, we have explored paths dictated by the special requirements of our own situation. Regarding the latter no American would maintain that we have developed an exportable product. We find few institutions or theories which are of universal applicability. Each of us must choose that which fits best our own needs and experiences.

In no instance, however, would we maintain that differences in institutional arrangements necessarily reflect divergent values. We know from personal association with leaders in this field in many lands that the basic morality underlying these programmes is essentially the same everywhere. Particular concepts do and will vary: for example, the concept discussed in section VIII above is probably peculiarly relevant to the United States. This is not a question of philosophical or ethical values, but rather of economic reality: How far is it true that social insurance can serve additional economic functions as there described? The answer will be different for different economic orders.

An eminent European scholar with wide experience of United States life wrote the following not long ago: "We know . . . that no new world can be discovered by mapping it in advance or proving its existence beforehand. What is more, one may not even suspect its existence, and having discovered the continent of new welfare, may die believing that it was only the old continent of wealth, the fabulous Indies."[9]

Whether we are indeed on the verge of such a discovery, whether we are actually in sight of the goal of abolishing poverty,[10] requires more capacity to foretell the future than we can claim. But while we would not express it as prediction, we would identify it as American aspiration and faith. We share with all free peoples the vision of abolition of privation

---

[9] Alexander Pekelis, *Law and Social Action* (Cornell University Press, 1950), p. 41.

[10] Professor Wilbur J. Cohen, . . . has said, "We can—and I believe we will—abolish poverty in our country in our lifetime." In part he bases this expectation on the exhaustive studies of the Twentieth Century Fund (*America's Needs and Resources*, 1955) which estimates that, by 1960, expenditures for consumption goods would have to be increased only 4 per cent to permit "the small minority of substandard families and individuals to achieve a 'health and decency' standard of living without any modification in the living standards of the vast majority whose incomes are more than adequate to maintain such standards." At the rate the American economy is expanding this appears feasible.

and the provision of security with liberty. And we share the conviction that in these and other hopes our futures are all bound together in interdependence upon the preservation of peace. With mutual regard for our differences and sensitivity to our larger common ground, we can share "the will to discover, the will to enlarge the tiny segment of the world we know, the will to learn and do better, the firm and deep-seated conviction that men may, again and again, in everyone's lifetime, see

> . . . thin with distance, thin but dead ahead,
> The line of unimaginable coasts."

# 5. EQUITY, ADEQUACY, AND RELATED FACTORS IN OLD AGE SECURITY

REINHARD A. HOHAUS, *The Record,*
American Institute of Actuaries,
June, 1938.

PRIVATE INSURANCE offers protection against a wide variety of risks pertaining to life, health, and property. As a rule, it is entirely voluntary. An individual decides whether he wishes to have any one, or a number, of the various types of protection offered; and, if so, how much of it he wants or can afford, regardless of the extent to which this may meet his needs. Private insurance exists for those who feel the need for protection against certain contingencies sufficiently to join voluntarily with others, exposed to a similar risk, in maintaining a fund from which will be paid the risks that occur within the group.

Because of its voluntary nature, then, private insurance must be built on principles which assure the greatest practicable degree of equity between the various classes insured. Not only would the very nature of the case make it basically unfair to have one homogeneous group of insured designedly pay for part of the costs of providing insurance for another group for which the actuarial measure of the risk is quite different, but such a practice would lead to a cessation of insurance soon after the former group came to understand that it could save money by being treated as an independent, financially self-contained unit.

Social insurance, on the other hand, is of vastly different character and is generally assigned a considerably different function. It aims primarily at providing society with some protection against one or more major hazards which are sufficiently widespread throughout the population and far-reaching in effect to become "social" in scope and complexion. Usually these risks are not many in number. Yet, if not guarded against through some organized means, they produce large dependency problems that take their toll in terms not only of financial but of human values as well.

Directed against a dependency problem, social insurance is generally compulsory—not voluntary—giving the individual for whom it is intended no choice as to membership. Nor can he as a rule select the kind and amount of protection or the price to be paid for it. All this is specified in the plan, and little, if any, latitude is left for individual treatment. Indeed, social insurance views society as a whole and deals with the individual only in so far as he constitutes one small element of that whole. Consistent with this philosophy, its first objective in the matter of benefits should, therefore, be that those covered by it will, so far as possible, be assured of that minimum income which in most cases will prevent their becoming a charge on society. Not until this is accomplished should financial resources (whatever, if anything, may remain of them) be considered as available to provide individual differentiation aiming at equity.

Private insurance, then, is adapted to the individual's need for, and his ability to afford, protection against one or more of a large variety of risks. Social insurance, on the other hand, is molded to society's need for a minimum of protection against one or more of a limited number of recognized social hazards. The minimum may be considered as that income which society feels is necessary and economically practicable for the subsistence of individuals comprising it. These payments, it is held, must be met in one form or another anyway, and social insurance endeavors to organize the budgeting therefor and dispensing thereof through systematic governmental processes. Hence, just as considerations of equity of benefits form a natural and vital part of operating private insurance, so should considerations of adequacy of benefits control the pattern of social insurance. Likewise, as private insurance would collapse if it stressed considerations of adequacy more than those of equity, so will social insurance fail to remain undisturbed if considerations of equity are allowed to predominate over those of adequacy.

Social adequacy, of course, concerns not only the size of the benefits but also the proportion of the population covered under a social insurance plan. The latter phase obviously has a substantial influence on the value of a plan to society. But its bearing on the relationship between equity and adequacy is perhaps even more important. The smaller the proportion covered by a plan, the less it represents that national commonness of purpose which, by transcending the importance of the individual, justifies a necessary modification of strict individual equity. The smaller the relative coverage, therefore, the more do practical influences impede the rationalization of adequacy in a benefit formula.

The foregoing need not necessarily imply that all considerations of equity should be discarded from a social insurance plan; rather the point is that, of the two principles, adequacy is the more essential and less dispensable. Entirely aside from the question of introducing a degree of equity for its own sake are other reasons that have been advanced for its recognition in some form. Among these are (a) that it provides some measure of individualistic treatment; (b) that it acts as an impetus for the proper payment of the prescribed contributions; and (c) that it causes the benefits to reflect automatically (though to a limited extent only) some of the differences among individuals and as between geographic regions in costs and standards of living—differences that, in a country of the size of the United States whose population consists of many types and races of people, are naturally so great, and indeed so fundamental, as to command acknowledgment.

Just exactly what is meant by equity in social old age insurance, however, is not a clear-cut matter. There seem to exist many interpretations of this principle. The precise (private insurance) construction conceives of the individual's benefit as the annuity produced by the accumulation, at interest and with appropriate adjustment for mortality during any period in which that factor is involved, of specified contributions previously made directly in his behalf. Quite different in its effect on the range of benefits is the concept that the amount of benefit should bear merely a very limited relationship to some base reflecting the individual's membership record. The former construction is, of course, quite incompatible with the fundamental purposes of social insurance, since it completely precludes the role of adequacy in the initial stages of the operation of a plan. Whatever equity is injected into a social insurance benefit formula, therefore, must take a form tending toward the latter position.

Applying this discussion to the Federal old age benefits system, it would appear that, though already embodying a combination of the principles of equity and adequacy, it unduly stresses the former. In the early years the benefits would be small, forcing many of the annuitants to resort to other assistance for maintenance, while in later years, as contribution records grew, the pensions would reach relatively large amounts. Hence, the plan in its effort to provide some equity appears in a substantial measure to neglect considerations of adequacy for early beneficiaries. Moreover, it excludes a large proportion of the working population—comprising several classes that are in need of protection probably as much as, if not more than, some of those now included. This too seems a limitation of the scheme contrary to the social conception of adequacy. It would appear, therefore, that both the particular distribution of emphasis as between equity and adequacy in the benefit formula and the limited coverage of the plan—more perhaps than any other factors—presage the likelihood of a modification of the present old age benefits system after the nation at large becomes more conversant with its provisions and their implications.

# 6. THE AMERICAN PHILOSOPHY OF SOCIAL INSURANCE

J. Douglas Brown,
*The Social Service Review,*
March, 1956.

THE DEPRESSION which had its trough in 1932 shook the United States out of a quarter of a century of lethargy in solving the problem of human want and distress arising out of the free play of business activity under a *laissez faire* system. Earlier attempts at alleviating this problem had been indirect and had been centered upon such efforts as the reform of the banking system. That men should be thrown out of work by periodic "bad times" was considered inevitable and an occasion for charity rather than statesmanship. That banks should fail and businesses go bankrupt was a more practical challenge to the limited economic understanding of our political leaders, and the result was the Federal Reserve Act of 1913. It was an ex-college professor, Woodrow Wilson, who secured the passage of this limited but constructive approach to the prevention of depressional unemployment. He may have helped the bankers and the businessmen over the smaller bumps in the road, but the worker was still the first man off the tailboard when the going got rough.

Our first attempts at social insurance in this country were strongly influenced by our hesitancy to deal *directly* with the problem of human want and distress arising out of business activity. To move against the pitiful effects of industrial accidents, we felt we must proceed by the circuitous route of replacing employers' liability. The burdens of the legal superstructure imposed upon the state systems of workmen's compensation because they were fathered by lawyers and mothered by judges have impaired their effectiveness to this day. This parentage imbedded the concept of blame so deeply in social insurance thinking that even a great depression failed to uproot it. In all fairness it must be admitted that the emphasis on prevention in workmen's compensation programs through variable insurance costs did stimulate a continuing safety movement which later proved to be good industrial relations practice in any case.

The depression of 1932, however, proved to even the conservative elements in America that the forces of economic competition and change were too inherent in our system of political economy to rely upon prevention alone for the protection of our citizens against distress caused by loss of earnings. At long last, it was realized by many that the emphasis must shift, so far as the worker was concerned, to a system of benefits payable as a matter of right regardless of the degree to which the employer or the government succeeded in eliminating disastrous economic or physical hazards along the way. So many able, willing, and thrifty workers faced want and distress that the older concept of personal responsibility or blame for one's dependency was no longer tenable, at least as a general principle.

In post-dated national introspection we can now see that we came by this older concept honestly, if not too wisely. We were a people who drew many of our economic virtues from the mores of an agricultural economy. On the farm and in the village the sources of minimal living were ever present and usually cheap. Thrift was closely reflected in physical action and tangible resources—a well-kept farm and house, and a cellar well stocked with food. The man who faced want had failed to exercise thrift and, labour being always scarce, he could trade work for food with those who were more foresighted.

But not all of our inheritance of economic philosophy came to us from the pleasant farms and villages of America. A tough and stubborn overlay of thought came from across the Atlantic, from the smoke and soot of British industrialism. The best British minds had solved the problem of separating competition and conscience. One was for weekdays and the other for Sunday. It was left to God to resolve the two and Adam Smith had helped God out of his predicament. The individual worker was primarily a factor in production. The emphasis was placed heavily on "worker," and "individual" had but statistical significance. America had few economists who could challenge the authority of their British colleagues, and what did they know about political economy compared to the successful businessman?

It would be a satisfying conclusion for one in the profession to be able to say that it was the economists who finally persuaded the American businessman that the doctrine of economic harmonies was out of date. But that would be far from fact. It was rather the people through the power of the universal franchise who demanded that government do what neither private industry nor private charity could do, provide a solid and respectable floor of protection between the loss of a job and the loss of personal dignity. It was the resurgence of the recognition of the individual and of his rights within a civilized society that became the political dynamite that blasted away the barriers to making our government more fully a government *for* the people rather than merely a framework for regulating the free play of economic forces. While many organized groups—labor, farmers, and the aged—spearheaded the drive for governmental intervention, it was the people who gave the irresistible weight. Fortunately our political leaders, and especially our President, were quick to reflect the will of the people.

It was out of this resurgence of recognition of individual rights that the American approach to social insurance got its start. We were not a people to be bought off by a Bismarck seeking to perpetuate an empire. Nor were we a class-divided society that sought a levelling kind of wholesale relief. Rather we wanted our government to provide a mechanism whereby the individual could prevent dependency through his own efforts. We wanted to keep the individual in the picture as a person and not merely as a statistic. To us social security was a social mechanism for the preservation of individual dignity, not for the insurance of a political *status quo*.

Twenty years is far too short a time to permit the development of mature historical perspective concerning any significant development in human affairs. We are still too close to the mountain to distinguish the higher peaks from the closer foothills. Further, anyone who participated in such a development is likely to emphasize aspects that were important in his mind during the heat of the campaign rather than those results that may have come about almost unconsciously by general acceptance and without stirring debate. But it *is* an interesting exercise to attempt to outline an American philosophy of social insurance and to suggest how that philosophy originated. Like most ideological phenomena, it will not be accepted as either universal or orthodox by anyone, including the writer. We are a nation of dissenting pragmatists who indulge in inductive processes only under the mild compulsions of academia.

I

The first and foremost element in our philosophy of social insurance has already been suggested. Without that element social insurance does not exist. It is that the system must provide protection as a matter of right and not as a benevolence of a government, an institution, or an employer. In establishing social insurance, our federal and state governments discarded the presumption that a payment to an eligible individual was a generous act of mercy by a sovereign, in favor of the presumption that such a payment, under social insurance, was the honest fulfilment of a contract between citizen and State. The right of the eligible beneficiary is protected, in general, by the conscience of the electorate and, in particular, by an established appeals machinery.

It is unnecessary to repeat that this concept of individual right in social insurance is peculiarly compatible to the American mores. We have fought for our rights more than once and our ancestors came here to preserve them. We are not given to the acceptance of wholesale assurances. We deeply prefer individual rights. We may on occasion crowd into great halls and stadia but we prefer to hold our own tickets.

II

A second element in our philosophy of social insurance entered into our legislation, state and federal, almost without conscious recognition or debate. It is that all citizens should be eligible to coverage under a system regardless of class or level of income, and that, in principle, exceptions to coverage were to be made only for constitutional or administrative reasons. Unlike European systems, American programs arose in a classless society in which individual economic status, and with it social position, was ever in a state of flux. The wage-earner of yesterday was the manager of today, and, if luck failed, the unemployed wage-earner of tomorrow. Why should not the first segment of his earnings be protected under social insurance since as a citizen he should be able to enjoy the advantages of an individual "contract" under a universal system?

This concept of citizen-wide coverage under a social insurance system has been a powerful factor in the expansion of our old-age and survivors insurance system. It has, of course, been reinforced by the obvious fact that all men grow old and die, even though they may avoid unemployment. The concept has influenced the removal of constitutional obstacles by legal devices in the case of state employees. It has had sufficient vitality to overcome in large measure the hesitancy of fiscal administrators. A tough and unyielding barrier has been the pride in profession of a limited group who have made independence of government in their economic activity a political religion reminiscent of that of our Victorian grandfathers.

### III

A third element in our philosophy of social insurance also arises out of the essential emphasis upon the individual in the American mind. Under our approach, the individual worker establishes, within limits, the level of his protection by his individual contribution to our economy. The limits to this principle are important, but the concept is central. Benefits, in general, in the American system are firmly related to the wage system. Differentials in wages resulting from the efforts of the worker are reflected to a degree in differentials in benefits. The relative continuity of earnings under the wage system is also reflected to some degree in the level of protection. The simple device of averaging wages over a period in the determination of benefits has important significance in adding a factor related to contribution through time to that of the economic worth of such contribution in a single period of time.

The concept of differential benefits related to wages and duration of earnings is essentially a conservative element in our social insurance philosophy. In America, we still believe that a man should be rewarded for his own efforts. An established differential in one's earning and living standards is a precious asset, not only to the individual but to society in its progress toward a better world. The motivation of the individual from within himself is a primary and essential source of power in a free society. It can be attenuated by external measures only at the peril of an accumulating loss of momentum. It should be set aside as a primary determinant of a benefit structure at the outside margins of that structure only when other considerations, also stemming in the last analysis from the necessity for motivation, become paramount.

The degree to which differential benefits should reflect differential earnings or contribution has been one of the most thoroughly debated issues in our social insurance philosophy. Our old-age and survivors insurance system went through a radical change in this respect early in its existence. The relation of benefits and contributions has continued to be an issue in repeated revisions. Our state unemployment insurance programmes have also reflected a restless rethinking of the problem. The issue has been summed up in the expression "equity versus adequacy." The dangers of shortsighted action are still with us.

As a social mechanism it is not incumbent upon social insurance to reflect in full proportion the differentials of the wage system either at the lower and upper limits or in the gradations within these limits. Differentials, as a factor in motivation, must be measured by the response they receive, not by their arithmetic. The response of university professors to a thousand-dollar differential is very different from the response of big league ball players. Given the principle of differential benefits, the slope of the gradations can be tested in their effect only by the response of those coming under the system. At the lower limit, an obviously inadequate benefit reduces the over-all attractiveness of coming under the system and securing its benefits rather than relief. This is, of itself, a deterrent to motivation. At the upper limit, there is a zone where individual effort, undergirded but not measured by any social mechanism, should be largely responsible for the extra degree of personal security attained. Our greatest danger at present appears to be that lagging benefit structures will dangerously foreshorten the spread of differentials by low ceilings justified only by legislative inertia.

Fortunately, in America the differential concept in social insurance has been reinforced by the need of our systems to reflect wide geographical differentials in our wage structure. We had two good reasons for building our systems on this foundation: to preserve motivation and to relate earnings and benefits in diverse economic situations. If another reason were needed, it was our predisposition for accounting machinery which made percentage computations of wages both easy and convenient in the payroll offices of the country.

## IV

A fourth element of our philosophy of social insurance is in the process of evolution. Its desirability is still debatable in certain areas of protection. This is the concept of protection of the family unit as such by social insurance against all the hazards which that unit might face. On the one hand, old-age and survivors insurance, covering a lifetime risk, has been extended to prevent dependency of both man and wife in old age and also to prevent dependency in the family through the premature death of the head of the family. Steps are under consideration to protect the wage-earner where permanent and total disability deprives him of earnings in his later years. On the other hand, state unemployment insurance systems are moving but slowly toward providing supplemental benefits related to the needs of the wage-earners' family. The protection of the family against the losses and costs of illness is a great unknown country in which the explorer, and even more the philosopher, faces a vast, unmapped wilderness.

That the family is a distinct and cherished unit in American society is almost an axiom. The farm was operated as a family economy. The drift toward the city has had its unfortunate effects, but the return ebb to suburbia has tended to re-establish the vigour of the family tradition. One need but scan magazine advertisements or television guides to be convinced that the family is here to stay. Even the airlines and the railroads reflect this fact.

But why has the concept of the family unit been slow in entering fully into our philosophy of social insurance? It seems again to be a reflection of the essential individualism of the American citizen. There is still the tradition that a man's family is his business, not the government's. So long as he can support himself, it is not the concern of the state how many children (not wives) he has. Granted that death and old age may terminate his ability to support his family, and social insurance protection is welcome against these contingencies, he is not sure that he wants his children counted during temporary periods of unemployment and would prefer, perhaps, a differential benefit more fully proportional to his earnings.

## V

I have left until last an element in the American philosophy of social insurance which I hope will grow from strength to strength despite severe limitations put upon it by what are to me shortsighted theoretical and political considerations. This is the concept of joint contributions by employer and employee. In the development of our old-age and survivors insurance system, this concept was adopted almost without debate. In the state-by-state development of unemployment insurance it was introduced in a minority of states and has been gradually withdrawn even in most of these. The argument that the employer was primarily responsible for lay-offs and therefore should pay for benefits was too strong to resist, even where the soundness of this argument was questioned. The loss of employee contributions was the price we paid for so-called "merit rating." I still think that the price was greater than the gain.

The soundness of the concept of joint contributions in an American system of social insurance does not arise out of economics. It stems from our political and social traditions. Of course, arguments can be made about shifting and incidence, as with all taxes or costs, but the fact remains that the first incidence of any contribution to government or to any other recipient—church, family, or trade union—is of great psychological importance. Out of such incidence political influence arises, loyalty and responsibility are encouraged, and personal satisfaction and dignity are gained. Why would a church prefer the contributions of the many to the largesse of the few if it did not realise the tremendous psychological value of contribution as a stimulus to individual responsibility and dignity?

Social insurance systems must be *within* the state but *separate* from the state. To be strong, responsible, and alive, they must have the interest and attention of the citizen, not as voter alone, but as contributor and beneficiary. In America we have a wholesome suspicion of big government. And now we have given government the tremendous task of providing a floor for our individual security. I for one would feel more certain that our leaders in government would continue to respect the sanctity of the trust we have imposed upon them if every potential beneficiary who is gainfully employed were both a voter and a contributor to all social insurance systems.

These five elements appearing in American social insurance systems seem to have sufficient definition to make them anchor-points of an American philosophy. Perhaps this is all we can expect to discern in the experience of two decades. There are, however, other aspects of social insurance policy which arise out of our system of government or out of diverse and changing political philosophies which might be mentioned. They are, perhaps, not so much elements of an American philosophy of social insurance as examples of necessary accommodation in such systems to the environment in which they have developed.

First is the fact that our social insurance program contains a mixture of federal and state elements. This arises in part out of a strong urge toward decentralised state initiative and responsibility in our federal system of government and in part out of the historical accident that some states, such as Wisconsin and Ohio, were already active in respect to unemployment insurance legislation at the time the national government entered the field. Although the national government in 1935 established a compelling and controlling framework for the separate state systems, the continued resistance to any further federal encroachment upon the states' domain has been a dominant characteristic. This is, however, less an element in our social insurance philosophy than an introduction into another important field of American social policy of our persistent defence of state prerogatives.

In economic and actuarial terms, a social insurance system would be most efficient if it covered the area of a national economy. Insurance administration is basically a routine operation for which unit costs decline with increasing size. Even in the more complex field of private life insurance, companies of great size have been outstandingly successful. The risks of old age, death, survivorship, disability, and unemployment can be better averaged over a wider area. In a limited reserve system in which mutually offsetting flows of contributions and benefit payments are depended upon heavily for current financing, a wider averaging of risks is important. Apart from the political environment, the only justification for decentralisation is the more complete adjustment of administrative methods to varying local conditions. But this is a normal problem in all national activities having impact upon local situations, such as the postal system, the forest and park services, the internal revenue service, and rivers and harbour work. The administration of old-age and survivors insurance on a national basis with regional and local offices appears to be effective.

Attempts to secure through reinsurance the advantage of sharing the risk of unemployment on a nation-wide basis have proved unsuccessful. What might appear to be a sound social insurance philosophy is counterpoised against a philosophy of government which has great vitality. Perhaps only a severe and protracted business depression will break down the resistance to nationalising our state systems of unemployment insurance.

A second feature of American social insurance systems which arises out of our pragmatic political philosophy, as opposed to any distinct philosophy of social insurance, is the lack of definition in respect to reserve policies, state or federal. Early in the development of our old-age insurance system, the size of the reserve to be accumulated was a burning question. To avoid a large reserve, the scale of contributions was held down. The question of eventual governmental contributions to the system to compensate for these low rates during the early years of the system has been shelved for our children and grandchildren to answer. With a vast national debt, there is a plethora of government securities for social insurance trust funds. Reserves have risen to impressive levels but no one seems worried. The early issue between "pay-as-you-go" and "large reserves" seems to have faded into the background. In old-age and survivors insurance, we have let the actuaries worry about the problem of balancing income and outgo over time. Perhaps this is a mark of financial sophistication. We trust specialists in most aspects of life, why not in the planning of the financial aspects of social insurance? In any case, the essential security of the national system rests upon the taxing power of the United States Government and the willingness of the people to have it exercised.

The degree of accumulation of reserves in state unemployment insurance systems has also been the result of pragmatic political considerations rather than of any reasoned philosophy. The predominant determinants of such reserves have been the various formulas for merit rating, rather than the probable drain on reserves in time of heavy unemployment. Built-in controls on merit rating related to the size of reserves have been a limited concession to the need for planning, but otherwise the practical politician has had more influence than the actuary or the economist specialising in social insurance. The notion that the state government should contribute to the unemployment insurance reserve in time of heavy drains has yet to shock the unbelieving ears of state legislators. We have schooled them all too well that the employer pays the bill for unemployment insurance.

A third feature of American social insurance systems which is more a matter of practice than a theory is also a reflection of our persistent faith in the capacity of employers to assume a heavy share of the cost of worker security. This is the strong and growing acceptance of the concept of supplementation of social insurance benefits by employer-financed benefits. The early battle in old-age insurance to make that system a universal floor of protection upon which company pension plans could build has been more successful than was thought possible. And now both supplementary retirement benefits and supplementary unemployment benefits are common goals in collective bargaining. Instead of a two-layer system of protection, social and individual, we have a three-layer system with a juicy slice of supplementary protection inserted into the sandwich as a result of vigorous collective bargaining. Perhaps it was too much to hope that the ceiling on benefit differentials would be raised soon enough to parallel the differentials in earnings in our most prosperous and most strongly organized industries. Since even the trade-union leaders who have won supplementary benefits remain uncertain of their proper relation to social insurance systems, it is understandable if such supplementation is not yet made an amendment to our philosophy of social insurance.

It is well to end this discourse with this reference to amendment. I have found in lecturing on social insurance for many years that such lectures have a high rate of obsolescence. Facts change rapidly, philosophies more slowly but inevitably in the light of individual and public understanding. This lecture is no exception. But it is far more fun to try to understand a rapidly evolving social mechanism in a dynamic America, even at the expense of rewriting one's lectures every year, than to add a few footnotes to the completed history of an ancient state. A lecture bearing the name of a leader who added so much impetus to both change and understanding in the America he loved should bear the imprint, "Subject to change without notice." He would understand this fully because he himself rewrote repeatedly many pages in the history of labor in this country.

# 7. INCOME SECURITY FOR A FREE SOCIETY

REINHARD A. HOHAUS, comments on paper by RICHARD A. LESTER, *National Policies for Education, Health and Social Services, 1955.*

THIS INSTITUTION we have come to know as Social Security reaches out into almost every area of life—social, economic, political, scientific, psychological, and even moral and religious. It derives its being and inspiration from many different disciplines, and calls on the talents of many professions. The intricate network of relationships with which we are concerned involves not only various technical aspects, but also broader social and economic questions. These general questions are such that there will always be room for differences of opinion as to the degree of emphasis to be placed on one or another of the numerous factors they embrace. Yet analysis may naturally develop certain broad concepts, which in turn lend themselves to the formulation of a basis of policy.

Professor Lester considers some of the interdependent social and economic questions involved in the benefit-level phases of our social insurance plans, with emphasis on the interplay between them. He provocatively discusses a subject that has many facets. It covers with brevity and clarity many of the questions which suggest themselves—consciously or unconsciously—to a diligent student of social insurance.

Especially stimulating is the way in which he stresses, and documents, this excellent statement:

Unfortunately one cannot arrive at the determination of the proper level of social insurance benefits by mathematical means, or by scientific tests, or even by pure logic. The answer depends upon one's economic and social philosphy— the sympathy he has for human misfortune, the stress he places on preserving individual dignity, and the kind of society he envisions as desirable. The answer will also vary with the kind of economy in which the level is to apply (the general standard of living, the distribution of personal income, and the division between market and governmental determination of economic affairs) and with the traditions, history, and culture of the society in question. Consequently, the appropriate level of assured income under a social insurance program cannot be discussed *in vacuo* or in abstract terms. Its fitness must be judged in relation to a particular society and economy.

The following considerations, which are particularly pertinent to the United States scene, might be added:

1. The appropriate roles of local, state, and Federal governments in a nation's political organization. Related thereto, of course, is the extent to which a nation's structure is homogeneous or heterogeneous.

2. The nature and degree of interest which various major segments of a nation's society take in the nation's social insurance programs and the influence they exercise. Related to this is the nation's religious atmosphere and the concerns various church organizations have as to social insurance matters.

As an aside, whether the author intended it or not, his analysis strengthens my feeling that the activities of the International Labor Office in the social insurance field should be reappraised. Instead of aiming at international conventions embodying specific detailed proposals for eligibility, benefit levels, and the like, that body should content itself with furnishing an international channel for exchange of ideas and experience. The object would be to make clear to nations contemplating adoption of social insurance plans, or reconstruction of existing plans, that there is a variety of social instruments and approaches available, from which measures appropriate to their particular economies and social structures can be developed.

A major point in Professor Lester's analysis is the distinction made between "temporary" risks, such as unemployment, and "lifetime" risks, such as old-age retirement. He brings out clearly how various considerations apply differently in these fields, and how important it is that these two kinds of risks be studied separately. Conclusions which may be reasonable for one area may be quite inappropriate in the other. The discussion also suggests to this reader added reasons for continuing our present setup under which our different types of social insurance are handled through separate programs and by different agencies and levels of government.

Among the points which Professor Lester's paper raises, and which we might profitably discuss, are the following:

1. Benefit levels are part of a trinity consisting of benefits, coverage, and financing. No one of these can be considered independently of the others.
2. There are disadvantages in our national government providing benefits, directly or indirectly, on a means test basis.
3. "Lifetime" risks involve a special problem because of the implied long-range commitments.
4. Coverage of self-employed under OASI also raises special problems.
5. Separate administration of OASI, U.I., and W.C. programs need not rule out a provision that a person will not be entitled to draw benefits concurrently from more than one program.
6. Should social insurance benefits be taxable?
7. Malingering is a problem under private as well as public programs. Under sickness benefit plans managements are often troubled about adverse effects of wage-loss compensation close to normal earnings.
8. Economic conditions have an important effect on the questions of (a) malingering, through the relation of benefit to normal pay, and (b) attitudes on a compulsory retirement policy.
9. Financial experience with eligibility requirements, waiting period, and quantity of administration under both public and private plans requires careful study.

10. A controlling factor in setting the level of benefits is, or should be, the productive capacity of the nation. While there can be work without income security, we cannot have income security without work.

In his concluding section, Professor Lester comments that "in the absence of adequate research studies, one is forced to put on the hat of a social philosopher and pose as a wise man." In that spirit, I should like to outline my philosophy regarding old-age benefits under the Federal program, the objectives of which have been stated as inclusion of all workers, employed and self-employed; payment of benefits related to prior earnings and as matters of right without a needs test; and financing on a contributory basis. I am in full agreement with these objectives.

For us the individual by his very nature is a free man, and the democratic form of society is a community of free people banded together in the spirit of mutual respect and self-discipline. We have faith in the ability of the common man, together with his fellow-citizens, to direct and mold the future of his country. But we know—the impacts of war and defense have brought it home to us even more clearly than before—that with freedom and power goes responsibility, and much is expected of the individual if he is to be worthy of the rights with which he is born.

We recognize that definite obligations rest on the individual in at least three directions: to himself and his family; to those for whom and with whom he works; and to society as represented by his fellow-citizens and himself, and by the agencies they have set up for the common good.

We know that in the forefront of these obligations is the provision of a measure of protection against loss of earnings due to death, old age, disability, and unemployment. As a people we have accepted the challenge in each of the three foregoing directions by the development over the years of three different classes of insurance.

The first class of insurance, in order of time, is *individual insurance*— protection the individual secures for himself and his family; the second, a variety of employee benefit plans, of which group insurance is an outstanding American contribution; and the third, social insurance—designed for the well-being of our fellow-citizens in times of adversity. Each has a special function to perform and need not, and should not, compete with or overlap the others. When soundly conceived, each class of insurance should in fact derive mutual support from the others and perform its role better because of their existence. Properly integrated, they may be pictured as a three-legged stool affording firm and well-rounded support for the citizen.

In thus focusing attention on insurance I recognize, of course, that there are other approaches to loss of income protection and I do not belittle them. However, America perhaps more than any other nation has come to appreciate the special merits of the insurance approach.

The success of democratic processes depends largely on the extent to which the individual assumes his responsibilities as a citizen and as a family man. Among the responsibilities he naturally feels most keenly are such as concern the security and welfare of those dependent upon him. He will wish to set his own level of protection and *individual insurance* programs give him the opportunity to do so. Indeed, individual insurance is an institution essential and characteristic of that innate spirit of self-reliance which is and must continue to be traditionally American. The very large volume in force expresses more eloquently than words the real value of this insurance to our people.

*Group insurance* is historically a much later development than individual insurance. The idea may be traced to the more or less natural feeling of responsibility on the part of the employees in an organization and their employer for the welfare of the individual worker and his family in times of stress.

Various types of employee benefit plans, aiming to give a more definite measure of protection in a manner suited to preserve the beneficiaries' self-respect and dignity, were therefore developed. In some cases those plans were initiated solely by the employer, in others by the employee, and in still others by the joint action of employer and employees, who shared the cost between them.

Recent years have seen a great expansion of soundly conceived and operated plans. They have expanded both in the scope of the benefits provided and in the number of employees covered, and we may expect this to continue. By providing a measure of security on a basis designed to preserve or bolster the dignity of the individual employee, such plans have become an important element in maintaining not only good industrial relations, but also that faith and confidence in the existing order on which the democratic spirit relies and thrives.

In this country *social insurance* is the newest but by no means the least of the three branches of insurance to which we have referred. Without proper preventive or protective safeguards against loss of income, the individual is naturally exposed to certain economic risks which may take such large tolls in terms of human and financial values as to warrant their description as social hazards. For a social hazard that lends itself to this form of treatment, social insurance generally aims to fulfill in a more orderly and systematic manner—better adapted to the existing social and economic environment—a responsibility society had to a large extent assumed in the past through other channels.

Though differing in important respects from individual and group insurances, social insurance has borrowed the name "insurance" from them because of certain important broad resemblances. It provides benefits specifically determined by formula, payable upon the fulfillment of specified conditions, which do not, however, include subjection to a means test. This permits the beneficiary to accept them without any sense of incurring the stigma of charity, especially if a "consideration" in the form of contributions or ear-marked taxation has been required of him.

Important, however, as the contributory principle may be, its limitations should be clearly understood. It should not mislead a contributor into misapprehending the social nature of the plan and the financial realities behind it. It should not, for example, lead him into feeling that he has paid in full for a protection to which actually his contribution has been only nominal, or into thinking that because funds are on hand, the nature and purpose of which he does not comprehend, therefore larger benefits are in order.

The fundamental objective of social insurance, it may be said, is to serve society and its constituent individuals. By providing for as large a proportion of its citizens as is practicable a measure of economic security on a self-respecting basis, the state may be relieved of a potentially serious burden of dependency. For benefit levels to be socially adequate for this purpose, a major factor in determining them would be the probable minimum requirements to keep the family from becoming public charges. This in turn suggests that consideration be given to variation in the amount of benefits by the number of dependents of the insured. However, while that basis has wide acceptance for lifetime risks, its appropriateness for temporary risks is very much of a controversial issue.

Under such a philosophy the level of protection and the formula for arriving at it are usually quite different from what is appropriate to either individual or group insurance. By reason of its social adequacy objective and its compulsory character, social insurance cannot and need not pursue individual equity in the sense of a mathematical adjustment between the benefit and the risk as measured by an appropriate premium—an adjustment which, in voluntary insurance, must on the average effect a long-range equivalence between costs and charges, if insolvency is to be avoided.

This does not imply, however, that all considerations of equity should be excluded from a social insurance plan. Rather the point is that, of the two principles, adequacy takes first place. Entirely aside from the question of introducing a degree of equity for its own sake are other reasons that have been advanced for admitting it in some form. Among these are that it acts as an incentive for the proper payment of the prescribed contributions; that it automatically provides some measure of individualistic treatment on the basis of earnings, and that it causes the benefits to reflect automatically (though to a limited extent only) some of the differences in costs and standards of living between geographic regions and other groupings of people.

Just exactly what is meant by equity in social old-age insurance, however, is not a clear-cut matter. The precise construction adopted in private insurance conceives of the individual's benefit as the annuity produced by the accumulation, at interest and with appropriate allowance for mortality gains during any period in which that factor is involved, of specified contributions previously made by him or in his behalf. This construction is, of course, quite incompatible with the fundamental purposes of social insurance, since it completely precludes the role of adequacy in the initial stages of the operation of a plan. Quite different in its effect on the range of benefits is the concept that the amount of benefit should bear merely a limited relationship to some base (such as average earnings) reflecting the individual's economic status. Whatever equity is injected into a social insurance benefit formula, therefore, should be based on this concept.

Having concluded that both social adequacy and equity should be reflected in the old-age insurance benefit formula, the next question is how to blend the two elements. Here the analogy of the best formula for a dry martini is helpful. While it seems to be generally agreed that much more gin (adequacy) should be used than vermouth (equity), there are decided differences of opinion as to what ratio of adequacy to equity should be. Also a given person's ideas as to the blend and even the kinds of adequacy and equity may be quite different for lifetime than for temporary risks.

This question cannot be divorced from the scope of average coverage and the financing of the plan. The closer coverage is to being universal, the less weight need be given to equity, although some equity should always be included under a plan which is financed in part by contributions of potential beneficiaries. A review of the developments over the last twenty years in our Federal old-age plan indicates clearly that it would be unrealistic to consider benefits (conditions of eligibility as well as level of payment) apart from coverage, or from financing. Furthermore, a good case can be made that this applies to the "temporary" as well as the "lifetime" risks.

Without passing judgment on either the present or proposed numerical factors in the benefit formula for OASI, the type of formula now in effect is a simple and effective one for blending adequacy and equity. It permits ready adjustment in the amounts of benefits when this is desired because of changed conditions.

However, it does introduce anomalies and abuses as long as the plan does not cover substantially all employed and self-employed persons. For that and other reasons Congress should enact the proposals recommended by the President for extension of coverage and the recommendations it has received for inclusion of the Federal Civil Service employees and armed forces under OASI.

In conclusion I should like to refer to an area in which research and study are greatly needed. I have long been deeply concerned by developments over the years whereby the Federal Treasury absorbs more and more of the costs of old-age assistance.

Public assistance and social insurance represent entirely different approaches, which, like oil and water, do not naturally mix. That, however, does not mean that conflict or even competition must necessarily result between them. After all, they have a common purpose as defenses against want, and there is no reason why they could not function harmoniously in achieving that end. But, if this is to happen, it is necessary that each be assigned its proper place and keep to that place without encroaching on the preserves of the other.

Hence the first step is to define these proper places. When that has been determined, it is the task of the legislators to devise a working plan in the light of what is possible and desirable within the framework of the definition and of the administrators to see that neither the assistance nor the insurance concept oversteps its proper bounds.

It is my conviction—and I judge it to have also been the philosophy of those who planned our original Federal Social Security legislation of 1935—that old-age assistance should play a definitely subordinate role. It was clearly the intent of the President's Committee on Economic Security, and of the legislators who followed the main outlines of their blueprint, that public assistance, though necessarily large at first, should decline as social old-age insurance grew stronger, and should eventually retain no more than a residual function.

When the OASI benefits were liberalized in 1950 and 1952, one might have expected the Congress to amend the Old Age Assistance provisions so as to reverse the trend of more and more Federal grants. Instead, over the years, Congress greatly liberalized the formula for the Federal government's share of the assistance grants. The present outlook is that OASI benefits will again be liberalized substantially this year, but with no retrenchment in the assistance field.

The issue of the Federal government's withdrawal from the old-age assistance field and various proposals for accomplishing that, in whole or in part, have been the subject of extensive debate for well over a year. This debate generated so much heat that it probably deferred rather than advanced the day when the issue may be resolved on a sound basis.

There is in my opinion no other issue as important as this in the old-age field. It calls for an early solution mutually satisfactory to all concerned. While complicated and controversial questions are involved, I am confident that a study of them by a representative group of individuals determined to explore them as objectively as possible will result in proposals which will be generally acceptable and will call a halt to the race between social insurance and assistance. I do hope that through the sponsorship of a public or private agency or group that such a study project will be undertaken in the very near future. Unless the great weaknesses of the present old-age assistance arrangements are removed by one method or another, we cannot consider the Federal government's role in old-age security is on a sound basis.

# 8. TWENTY—FIVE YEARS OF PROGRESS IN SOCIAL SECURITY

WILBUR J. COHEN,
1960.

PERHAPS NO OTHER single piece of legislation concerned with domestic policy adopted in the last twenty-five years has been more effective than the Social Security Act in helping to promote the well-being and happiness of the American people. Under this one Act, we now have a system of old-age, survivors and disability insurance, unemployment insurance, federal grants to the states for the needy aged, blind, dependent children, the needy permanently and totally disabled, as well as federal grants for maternal and child health, crippled children, and child welfare services. It can now be said unequivocally that our social security system of nationwide social insurance and federal grant-in-aid programs for public welfare has become a permanent part of the basic fabric of our social institutions and that these programs have the support of both major political parties.

Twenty-five momentous years of social security now have been completed. Much has been accomplished in this time, more than many people expected when the limited program initially was established in 1935. The vision of the framers of our social security system has provided us with a sound basic structure. Yet there are important gaps and inadequacies which still demand attention. As we enter the second quarter century, what does our social security balance sheet show in terms of assets and liabilities? What changes in program emphasis are required to meet the challenges and trends ahead of us? What are the problems and prospects which face us in the decade ahead?

Many questions such as these come to mind as we commemorate the twenty-fifty anniversary of the enactment of the Social Security Act. What is past is prologue to the future. As we look ahead and try to fathom the future we can gain reassurance in the substantial achievements of the Act.

## Social Security Objectives

The Social Security Act of 1935 was passed by the Congress and became law on August 14, 1935 with the objective of meeting certain immediate needs and helping to prevent future want and dependency. Through the federal-state partnership implemented by federal grants-in-aid, assistance became available in February, 1936 under the federal-state program for needy persons in three groups of the population that, in good times as well as bad, have little or no capacity to earn their own living— the aged, the blind, and children deprived of parental support or care through the death, absence from the home, or physical or mental incapacity of a parent. Longer-range provisions of the Act were designed to provide insurance benefits for employees in commerce and industry that would furnish a basic income in old-age retirement and during limited periods of involuntary unemployment.

The popular idea of "social security" has often given exclusive emphasis to the provisions in the legislation for the aged and to income maintenance. This is not correct. It is highly significant that the original law also included grants-in-aid to states for maternal and child health and welfare services, public health services for the whole community, vocational rehabilitation services, and financial support for the expansion and maintenance of a nationwide employment service. The Aid to Dependent Children and Child Health and Welfare provisions of 1935, the survivors' insurance provisions of 1939, and the social service amendments of 1956 illustrate the important role that family welfare has had in the original and subsequent development of the law.

During the twenty-five years many important and far-reaching changes in the social security law and administrative organization have been made. These changes reflect not only amendments to keep the program in line with rising levels in earnings and living costs and administrative experience but also reflect a broadening in the character, scope, and concept of "social security."

### Integrity of the Family

Over the years the social security program has given increasing recognition to the significance of the family as a unit and the importance of family welfare. This trend is becoming more apparent in various programs, but there are also serious blocks to further progress in this area which require removal.

The public assistance provisions in the original law affirmed the importance of family life by limiting the use of federal funds for needy aged or blind persons to those who were not inmates of public institutions and funds for needy children to those who were living in family homes in the care of one of a number of specified relatives. Moreover, the Act affirmed the dignity and responsibility of recipients by specifying that aid was to be given in the form of money, which the receiver was free to spend as he or she deemed best, rather than as aid in kind, such as orders for groceries or fuel, which too often reflected condescension and unwarranted suspicion in past relief administration.

The emphasis in old-age insurance was shifted from the individual to the family by the legislative changes made in 1939. Benefits were added for the aged wife and minor children of a retired insured worker and for family dependents of insured workers who die either before or after retirement. Insurance benefits to dependents and survivors were broadened and increased by the amendments of 1950, 1954, 1956, and 1958, and disability insurance benefits added in 1956.

The capacity of Aid to Dependent Children to safeguard family life was strengthened in 1939 when Congress increased the federal matching share from one third to one half and again in 1950, when Congress provided that federal grants could be used in payments that include the needs of the mother or other relative who cares for the children as well as the children themselves. The Social Security Amendments of 1956 gave concrete expression to the need for services to preserve and maintain family life through the ADC program. Such services, however, are still limited and only developing very slowly.

The original appropriations authorized for Maternal and Child Health, Crippled Children, and Child-Welfare Services were increased in 1939, 1946 and 1950, 1956 (child welfare only), and 1958. The transfer of the Children's Bureau to the Social Security Administration in 1946 made it possible to try to more closely relate child welfare with the insurance and assistance programs dealing with children and families. However, much more remains to be done to develop an effective and coordinated program at the federal, state, and local levels to strengthen family life. Survivors' insurance benefits, Aid to Dependent Children, and Child-Welfare Services all are parts of the social security program designed to aid in preserving and strengthening family life.

State unemployment insurance laws are an important part of the social security program that helps to maintain family income. Unemployment insurance benefits not only keep families from reducing their standard of living but reduce the anxiety and friction which inevitably result when no money is coming in to pay the grocery and rent bills, insurance, and medical expenses. About one fourth of the states recognize the importance of providing additional benefits where the unemployed individual has family dependents, but the movement for making dependents benefits is not likely to make much further progress in view of the fact that unemployment insurance is currently financed entirely by employers.

As a result of the social security programs, therefore, in countless homes, insurance or assistance payments mean that an old couple can live out their remaining years together in a familiar setting, near their relatives and friends and with their cherished possessions; that children in families broken by death or separation or impoverished by the breadwinner's disability can continue to receive their mothers' care instead of being parceled out among relatives or left without supervision while the mother takes outside work; that in many families in which earned income has been cut down or cut off by unemployment, disability, or old age have an assured income that they can use just as others in the community use their money, continuing to plan and manage their own family affairs.

The millions of dollars paid out under programs established under the Social Security Act can be added, and so can the number of persons—old, young, and in the working ages—to whom these payments have gone. What cannot be computed is the self-respect and peace of mind made possible by these programs in homes into which pay envelopes no longer come, the strain and worry and humiliation averted from parents and from children whose lives otherwise might have been scarred by the anxieties of their elders or by separation from home and parents. In the midst of just concern about the social maladjustments in American homes, it is well to remember the far greater number of homes where high standards of conduct have been upheld in the face of adverse circumstances, frequently with the aid of modest social security payments and inadequate social services provided during the past twenty-five years.

While the social security program has done much to help in strengthening family life, there are vast problems still unmet and unsolved. There are still many families with children and with low incomes. There is still a substantial amount of wage loss caused by sickness, disability, and unemployment which is not compensated. There are still delinquent and neglected children. There are many areas without trained public assistance and full-time child welfare workers. Aid to Dependent Children is still grossly inadequate. Health, welfare, and recreation services are not available to all families in every community. Social insurance benefits are inadequate in many cases. Medical care of high quality is not actually available to all who need it. These are some of the unfilled needs to be dealt with in the decade ahead.

### Extension of Insurance Coverage

The studies by the Committee on Economic Security preceding the establishment of the social security program recognized that the risk of loss of livelihood in old age was so nearly universal that the coverage of the old-age insurance program should be as broad as possible. Administrative considerations, however, dictated the decision to cover only employees in commerce and industry at the start. These were groups for which wage reporting and collection of contributions could be organized with less difficulty than in such excluded areas as agricultural employment, domestic service, and self-employment, even though workers in these and other excluded fields also needed protection because of their generally low earnings and irregular employment.

Administrative considerations were of particular importance at the start of the program because the Old-Age and Survivors Insurance system relates benefits to individual earnings and hence keeps an individual record of covered earnings for each of millions of workers throughout their working lives. Some persons predicted that such a system could not be maintained at all or, if so, only at exorbitant cost. Despite those predictions, payment of benefits, including the added benefit for dependents and survivors, was started at an earlier date than had been scheduled initially, and the system has continued to operate efficiently and economically as coverage has been widened, demonstrating the feasibility of operating a vast public program efficiently and economically and, at the same time, with courtesy and individualization.

In 1950, coverage was extended to most urban self-employed persons (except certain classes of the professional self-employed), to regularly employed agricultural and domestic workers and, on a voluntary group basis, to lay employees of nonprofit organizations and to many state and local government employees. In 1954, Congress further amended the Act, making it possible for coverage to be extended to some 10 million persons who, at some time during a year, have earnings as farmers or in previously excluded jobs in agriculture, or in domestic service, and to additional groups of state and local governmental employees, and persons in other employments. In 1956, military service was covered under the program on a permanent contributory basis and 850,000 additional jobs in other groups were included. With these major extensions, coverage of substantially all gainful work in the United States is within sight— a goal that seemed politically and administratively unattainable twenty-five years ago. There are still some hurdles to overcome. With universal coverage, the possibility of examining "blanketing-in" of the uninsured aged again may be examined for legislative consideration.

## The Human Element

Program developments in social security have been the product of many complex social, economic, financial, and legislative changes. But these factors operated only through the medium of human beings who took responsibility and leadership for conceiving, achieving, and administering these changes. We must never forget the important role in the evolution of social legislation played by responsible and dedicated men and women, politicians, social workers, social reformers, and administrators. Justice Holmes expressed the thought that the inevitable only comes to pass through the effort of human beings.

The roster is long of those whose ideas and energy made a significant contribution to the progress of social security in the past twenty-five years. The list would be long and impressive.

Young men and women today in state and federal programs, in schools of social work, in local employment security and welfare agencies, all have an opportunity to contribute to building a structure which, in the words of President Roosevelt when he signed the 1935 law, "is being built but is by no means complete."

Social legislation is the product of the consciousness of social needs, conflicting points of view, cooperation among various groups, compromise, and timing. The original Social Security Act and its Amendments illustrate these forces at work in the crucible of hard reality. Many persons will find fault with particular provisions of the legislation. But, as a whole, they are a blending of many points of view represented in our complex, diverse, and changing economy.

No one in the spring of 1955 or 1958 would have predicted that social security legislation would have been enacted in 1956 and 1958, respectively, of such scope and importance. Many persons felt that additional time was necessary to "digest" the 1954 legislation. However, when control of Congress changed in 1955, the whole situation changed; but this alone did not guarantee the passage of the 1956 or 1958 legislation.

What is possible in social legislation at one moment of time is not always possible at another. Disability insurance, for instance, probably could have been enacted in 1935 along with the original law. But it wasn't. The disability insurance provisions passed by the House of Representatives in 1949 might have passed in 1950 if Senator George had supported it. But he didn't. But it passed in 1956 with an age limitation of 50 years because it was coupled with a proposal to reduce the age for women to 62 and because Senator George changed his mind and, as his last major act as a Senator, made it a major policy issue, with the help of Senators Lyndon Johnson and Robert Kerr. Thus, it finally passed with the help of many persons and groups who had to oppose one of the strongest coalition of forces in the history of social security legislation.

The record of the first twenty-five years of social security is a proud heritage for the many thousands of persons engaged in the administration of public welfare. There are, however, still frontiers to be conquered in social security. The remainder of this article attempts to summarize the present status of the social security program and to indicate some of the possible frontiers which need attention.

## Changing Emphases

The importance of the recent changes in the social security program indicates the extent of public interest in the program and the growing national concern with problems of social legislation.

A steady series of periodic legislative changes in 1946, 1948, 1950, 1951, 1952, 1954, 1956, and 1958 followed the war years 1940–45 when social security legislation was inactive. At the present time far-reaching social security amendments are pending in the U.S. Congress and in some state legislatures. Thus, further changes in the social security program seem probable in the immediate future.

During the past two decades, both the insurance and assistance provisions have been broadened and strengthened by the extension to additional groups of the population and additional risks, and by improving the scope and adequacy of benefits. The improvements have not followed any simple formula or pattern. Various provisions were adopted at different times to meet emergent situations or the specific needs of groups whose insecurity had gained public recognition. In addition total payments under the programs have changed as programs matured and the needs of the economy changed. During the early years of the program, public assistance payments were by far the most important expenditures. During the immediate postwar years, and in the recent recessions, unemployment insurance benefits were of importance.

In June, 1959, there were over 13 million persons drawing OASDI benefits. About 7 million persons were receiving public assistance, although about 700,000 of the aged persons drawing assistance were also receiving an OASDI benefit. About 2 million persons were drawing unemployment insurance benefits.

In mid-1959, all social security and related payments were being made at a rate of $25 billion a year, equivalent to about 7 per cent of all personal income. Of this amount over $3 billion was for unemployment and cash sickness benefits. Over $17 billion annually was being spent under public programs for old-age, survivors', disability, and workmen's compensation benefits. Total payments are continuing to rise as the programs mature, expand in coverage, and the benefits are improved.

Social security operations began in 1936. At that time public expenditures to counter want and dependency were heavily weighted by the demands resulting from long-continued mass unemployment and the exhaustion of personal and community resources in earlier years of the depression. Workers already old or then unemployed could not benefit immediately, if at all, from the social insurance programs to be initiated under the Social Security Act. It took time for old-age insurance and unemployment insurance to accumulate contributions and to establish wage records on which to base workers' rights to the benefits to be paid in later years.

The benefit provisions of social insurance programs got under way in 1938–40. As jobs opened up before and during World War II for practically everyone who could work, the balance in social security payments shifted. Since the end of 1943 the total amount paid out under social insurance and related programs, not including veterans' programs, has outrun the total for public assistance by an increasing margin.

Social insurance in the United States does not now cover all major income risks that threaten the economic independence of families. Nor can any social insurance system provide protection that will suffice for persons who suffer extraordinary catastrophe or a series of misfortunes. Some individuals, moreover, because of incapacity or other circumstances, do not participate in the labor force to a sufficient extent to acquire rights to any benefits at all or to benefits in an amount sufficient to meet their minimum needs. Because important groups were excluded from the system prior to 1950 and 1954, many persons were not covered by the insurance program. For these reasons, public assistance will continue to be a necessary supplement to social insurance, but the aggregate of social security payments will continue to be made up increasingly of the payments made under social insurance programs and decreasingly of payments under public assistance.

## Broken Families

The addition of survivor benefits to the federal old-age insurance program in 1939 gave the system new meaning for American families during, as well as after, the breadwinner's working years. At the present time the face value of all the survivors' insurance protection is equivalent to the face value of all the private life insurance protection in the United States—in total about a trillion dollars! Together private life insurance and the survivors' insurance provisions of OASDI protect American families against a risk which 50 years ago was the major cause of dependency and want in the United States.

The survivor benefits brought an important and needed protection for aged women who commonly outlive the husbands whose earnings have been the chief source of family livelihood. Even more important in terms of the numbers of persons concerned and the social potentialities, survivor benefits assured continuing income for the children of insured workers and the mothers of these children in the event of the worker's death. This protection of childhood is especially important in that it is ordinarily established in the early years of family life, when parents have had little time or opportunity to build up other resources against the catastrophe of loss of family support by the breadwinner's death.

Within a few years after the survivors' insurance benefits were established, the number of fatherless children receiving insurance benefits began to exceed the number of fatherless children receiving Aid to Dependent Children. At the end of 1957, there were about seven times as many fatherless children receiving insurance benefits as compared with the number of fatherless children receiving Aid to Dependent Children.

In December, 1934, there were about 2.8 million fatherless children under age 18, 7 per cent of all children under that age. By the end of 1957, about 70 per cent of all paternal orphans—their total number then down to about 1.9 million, and to about 3 per cent of all children—were receiving monthly insurance benefits as survivors of insured men, and about another 5 per cent were receiving benefits under the ADC program. Over 90 per cent of the nation's children under age 18 are insured now by public programs against loss of support by the parent's death.

While orphans were declining in number and insurance payments were reaching an increasing proportion of them, the number of families broken by marital difficulties has been on the rise. In consequence, the need for assistance to such families was increasing and a progressively larger proportion of the caseload of Aid to Dependent Children comprised those who had been deprived of normal support or care because of the continued absence from home or the incapacity of either parent. This trend is expected to continue and to present a serious problem requiring increased attention of welfare personnel, public and private. In mid-1959, there were 2.3 million children receiving Aid to Dependent Children, of whom less than 15 per cent received aid due to the death of the father, nearly 25 per cent due to the disability of the father, and over 60 per cent due to the absence of the father from the home.

Two important trends are evident in our public assistance programs: caseloads in Old-Age Assistance are declining but increasing in Aid to Dependent Children. The total number of recipients on the ADC rolls (including adult caretakers) already exceeds the number on the OAA rolls. If present trends continue, within a few years the number of dependent children will exceed the Old-Age Assistance caseload.

## Old-Age Security

At the end of 1934, about half of all persons aged 64 or over were estimated to be mainly or wholly dependent on relatives and friends for their support. Except for the development of the public income-maintenance programs for the aged, the burden of such dependency would have increased rapidly as the aged population grew at the average rate of 3 per cent a year, twice as rapidly as the total population. In December, 1958, however, more than 80 per cent of the aged had income under social insurance and related programs and/or public assistance, in contrast to a little more than 10 per cent with such income 25 years earlier.

The great gain over the 25 years in assured old-age income has been through the development of social insurance and related programs. In December, 1934, only about 5 per cent of the aged received payments under the programs of these types then in existence—public employees' retirement systems and veterans' pension and compensation programs. Twenty-five years later, social insurance and related payments went to almost 70 per cent of the aged population; OASDI alone benefiting about 60 per cent.

Public assistance provided the principal support for a little less than two million aged persons (about 12.6 per cent of the total number) at the end of 1958 and supplemented Old-Age and Survivors' Insurance payments for another 700,000 (about 4 per cent of the total number). Since the autumn of 1950, the number of Old-Age Assistance recipients has declined steadily in relation to the aged population, as progressively more persons 65 and over have been able to establish eligibility for OASDI.

The expansion of OASDI has not adversely affected private insurance for old age, survivorship (life insurance), or disability. Private provisions for old-age retirement have grown particularly in the last ten years. The postwar expansion of private group pension plans brought the number of aged beneficiaries of such plans in December, 1957 to 1,250,000, the majority of whom also received Old-Age and Survivors' Insurance. Twenty-five years earlier there were perhaps 150,000 or 200,000 private pensioners, many of them under plans operated by the railroads and later transferred to the rolls of the federally operated Railroad Retirement Act.

Income from personal investments and payments under individual annuities and supplementary life insurance contracts provide support for comparatively few of today's older persons—possibly 10 per cent of the over 15 million aged in the population. This proportion is, however, probably larger than in December, 1934 when extensive unemployment had already eaten up the savings of the great majority. Home ownership was likewise less common twenty-five years ago than now and in consequence relatively fewer aged persons in the mid-1930's had this resource as a supplement to cash income.

While much remains to be done, substantial progress has been made in securing for old people the independence of some income of their own. At the end of 1958, it is estimated, all but 10 per cent of the aged had income from employment, social insurance and related programs, and/or public assistance in contrast to the 60 per cent who were without such sources of livelihood twenty-five years earlier. In another ten years OASDI alone probably will be providing lifetime benefits for close to four fifths of the retired persons 65 and over in the United States.

Despite the progress made, there is still need for many improvements in the OASDI and OAA programs. Benefit amounts are still too low in many instances. Some persons are still uninsured. Medical needs of many older persons are unmet. These problems remain to be solved in the years ahead.

## Unemployment Insurance

To replace part of the earnings lost by jobless workers, the Social Security Act established a federal-state system of unemployment insurance in 1935. A tax-offset device in the federal act effectively encouraged the individual states to set up their own systems under broad federal standards. Whereas only Wisconsin had an unemployment insurance law at the beginning of 1935, all jurisdictions had such legislation by the middle of 1937. Employer contributions began in 1936 in half the states, and benefits first became payable in all states by the summer of 1939.

The protection of the program grew rapidly as employment expanded and many states extended coverage beyond the federal requirement (establishments employing eight or more). But as the economy swung into an all-out war effort, the role of unemployment insurance changed. Unemployment dropped to an unprecedented low in 1944, and benefit payments served to tide workers over during short periods of unemployment resulting from conversion from civilian to military production and from one type of war goods to another. In contrast to five million beneficiaries in 1940, only 500,000 persons drew benefits in 1944.

When the war ended, unemployment insurance contributed immeasurably in smoothing the transition to peacetime production, cushioning the impact of mass layoffs from war plants in 1945 and 1946 for the individual and also for the economy.

The federal-state unemployment insurance program did not have to bear the full brunt of the postwar economic readjustment. In anticipation of the effect of mass demobilization in adding millions of returning servicemen to the already expanded labor force, Congress enacted the Servicemen's Readjustment Act in 1944. Of the 15 million World War II veterans, more than 9.5 million filed unemployment claims for "readjustment allowances" under that act in the five years ended August, 1949. Their benefits during that period totaled $3.8 billion paid out of general revenues. More than $1.5 billion was paid in servicemen's readjustment allowances from general revenues in 1946, while $1.1 billion in benefits was financed under the regular state unemployment insurance program.

The recessions of 1949–50, 1953–54, and 1957–58 again tested the ability of the program to cope with widespread unemployment. Again unemployment insurance played a constructive role as it had in a variety of economic climates in recent years.

As employment rose in the years following the recession, claims and payments under the program diminished markedly. By the end of 1953, total state unemployment reserves of almost $9 billion had been built up. Benefit payments hit a new high of $4.3 billion. Despite these heavy benefit drains, the state unemployment insurance reserves still had $7 billion at the end of 1958.

Both the coverage and duration of unemployment benefits have been improved by the states during recent years. State unemployment laws have been broadened to include smaller concerns. In 1954, Congress amended the federal law to extend coverage to covered employers with four or more employees and to federal government employees. Provision was also made for a loan fund of $200 million to assist states whose funds run low. Not all states, however, provide benefits for a uniform duration of 26 weeks, as recommended by President Eisenhower, nor have weekly benefits in all states reached the goal of at least 50 per cent of the workers' gross earnings in covered employment. A number of states, however, improved their laws in the face of a threat of federal standards, and it is likely that continued progress will be made in improving the benefit structure of the program in the next decade. Whether the states can and will achieve satisfactory protection without additional federal standards remains a challenging and controversial issue.

### Disability Protection

From the outset, the social security program has recognized the individual and social importance of meeting risks of sickness and disability, both in the provisions for services for maternal and child health and for crippled children and for assistance to the needy blind and to children whose need arose from the parent's physical or mental incapacity. In 1950, resources to counter need arising from disability were augmented by the establishment of federal grants for assistance for needy adults who are totally and permanently disabled. In 1952, Congress enacted a "disability freeze" provision in the insurance program but it never became operative. Then, in 1954, Congress made the provision effective. This was an important addition to the law in recognition of the impact of disability on benefits being paid under the existing program. Periods in which a worker has been totally disabled, as defined in the law, are omitted in computing his insured status and the average earnings on which his eventual old-age benefit and benefits to his dependents or survivors are based. Previously such a period without covered earnings lowered benefits subsequently payable, and it sometimes resulted in loss of insured status so that neither the worker nor his survivors could qualify for any payments under the system.

A program of cash benefits for periods of extended total disability passed the House of Representatives in 1949 but failed of enactment. Again the House passed it in 1955. Legislation to provide cash benefits, as part of the Old-Age and Survivors' Insurance system, to insured persons totally disabled for an extended period of time beginning at age 50 was enacted into law in 1956. This was an important step in the development of social insurance. The disability insurance provisions were adopted in the Senate by a close vote of 47 to 45 after a vigorous debate and controversy. Disability insurance had been discussed in Congress for 17 years. In 1956, it became a reality. What originally began as a limited old-age insurance system in 1935 became a broad social insurance program by 1956 covering three major risks. A new dimension had been added to social institutions in the United States.

In December, 1958, there were about 5.7 million persons in the United States with disabilities lasting six months or more. Of these an estimated 3.1 million were in the age group 14–64 and, hence, would have been at work or seeking work except for their disability. With the rise in the proportion of the aged in the population, and the ability of modern medicine to prolong the life of many disabled persons, the number of persons with long-term disabilities (more than 6 months' duration) appears to have been increasing both absolutely and relatively.

Public provisions to offset the actual or potential wage loss among disabled persons and their dependents have been extended in recent years. In 1935, protection through public programs was confined to work-connected disabilities under state and federal workmen's compensation laws, to service-connected and nonservice-connected disabilities under the veterans' and armed services programs, to sickness and disability under programs for employees of federal, state, and local governments, and to special programs for the blind in about half the states.

Since that time, in addition to disability insurance in OASDI, both permanent and temporary disability benefits have been provided under the railroad retirement system, and temporary disability insurance programs have been adopted for industrial and commercial workers in four states (1942–49). Assistance to the needy blind is now provided in all states. Aid to the needy permanently and totally disabled in mid-1959 was being paid in all but five states.

The number of persons in the ages 14–64 with long-term total disabilities who are receiving some support from public programs designed to provide income maintenance—insurance, pension, or assistance—in case of disability has increased from something less than 200,000 in 1934 to nearly 1.2 million in 1958, or from about one in ten in 1934 to about 38 per cent in 1958.

Disability insurance benefits to persons age 14–64 were paid in December, 1958 to about 290,000 persons under OASDI and to about 285,-000 under the railroad retirement and public employee retirement and workmen's compensation systems. There were 320,000 persons receiving assistance under the program of Aid to the Permanently and Totally Disabled and 60,000 receiving Aid to the Blind. There has also been a large increase in the number of persons receiving veteran's compensation. About 340,000 totally disabled veterans under age 65 are now receiving veteran's benefits as compared with 100,000 in 1934. (The large number of veterans receiving benefits for partial disabilities are not included in these figures). With the aging of the veteran population of World War I, the growth in the number of recipients of nonservice-connected disability pensions has been particularly striking. As a result of the delay in enacting a general social insurance program providing cash disability benefits to persons of any age, and the restrictions in disability protection under private pension plans, the veterans' and public assistance programs still are bearing the brunt of the public burden of income maintenance for the long-term totally disabled.

Private provisions against the risk of extended disability have expanded in recent years, especially in connection with private pension plans under collective bargaining, but the number of workers with such protection is still relatively small. More extensive has been the growth of private protection against the risk of temporary disability, the development of voluntary cash sickness plans, and the widespread purchase of individual and group disability insurance. This has resulted in strong and continued opposition to public legislation for temporary disability.

### Social Security and the National Welfare

Social security has become an accepted institution in our economy. Contributory, wage-related social insurance programs now give to most workers and their families the assurance of a continuing income in retirement, in the event of the death of the breadwinner and during temporary periods of unemployment. Most employees also have protection in the event of work-connected disabilities and some in the event of sickness or disability of nonwork-connected origin. With this assurance, individuals can plan to build up additional security through private arrangements and individual savings. During this 25-year period, private health, pension, and insurance protection has increased as has individual savings. For those whose total resources are inadequate to meet their current needs, public assistance is available for the aged, the permanently and totally disabled, the blind, dependent children, and in some localities other needy persons.

The protection afforded and the benefits paid under these programs represent not only a source of support for the individuals and families who receive them, but also a stabilizing influence on the economy. Social security payments make up only a small part of total income payments to individuals, but they go to groups who cannot at the time earn the means to buy goods and services they need and should have, and which the economy is able to produce and distribute. Social security payments provide a steady base of income for these groups in good times and in bad. They also provide an automatic adjustment to changing economic conditions. They are part and parcel of our American way of life. We can look forward to making progress during the next twenty-five years just as we have in the past twenty-five years.

# DISCUSSION QUESTIONS

1. Distinguish between the concepts "social security," "social insurance," "private insurance," "public assistance," and "public welfare."

2. Max Lerner states in his *America as a Civilization* (1957, page 131): "Americans . . . have responded piecemeal and in irregular fashion to the need . . . [and] what has emerged in each area of welfare is the acceptance of the principle of responsibility but with the least challenge to private enterprise, the least burden on the tax structure, and the greatest reliance on the voluntary principle." Discuss and illustrate.

3. Appraise the relative importance of "equity" and "adequacy" in a social insurance program.

4. Explain the tardy development of social security in the United States compared to other countries.

5. "The American social security program appears to have an individualistic rather than a collectivistic philosophy and direction."
Suggest some elements of the U.S. program which emphasize the individual approach. Do you observe any reversal in this emphasis?

6. "Social Security is the product of its environment—technological, cultural, social."

Explain this in relation to the influence upon social security of the following: age distribution of the population, degree of industrialization and urbanization.

7. "Some foreign social insurance programs generally provide uniform benefit levels for all eligible claimants. In American programs, on the other hand, benefit levels are usually related to the wage experience of the insured person." Suggest the relative advantages and disadvantages of the two approaches.

# SELECTED REFERENCES

ALTMEYER, ARTHUR J. "Dependents' Allowances in Social Insurance," *Social Security Bulletin* (April, 1947), pp. 3–6.

BALL, ROBERT M. "Social Insurance and the Right to Assistance," *Social Service Review* (September, 1947), pp. 331–44.

BEVERIDGE, WILLIAM. *The Pillars of Security.* New York: The Macmillan Co., 1943.

———. *Social Insurance and Allied Services.* New York: The Macmillan Co., 1942.

HAYEK, FRIEDRICH A. *The Road to Serfdom.* University of Chicago Press, 1944.

HOPKINS, HARRY L. *Spending to Save.* New York: W. W. Norton & Co., Inc., 1936.

INSTITUTE OF LIFE INSURANCE. *Life Insurance Fact Book.* New York, 1959.

INTERNATIONAL LABOUR OFFICE. *Approaches to Social Security: An International Survey.* Montreal, 1942.

LAROQUE, PIERRE. "Major Issues Raised by Contemporary Trends in Income Security Policies," in James E. Russell (ed.), *National Policies for Education, Health, and Social Services*, pp. 256–84. Garden City, N.Y.: Doubleday & Co., Inc., 1955.

LARSON, ARTHUR. *Know Your Social Security.* New York: Harper & Brothers, 1955.

LESTER, RICHARD A. "The Nature and Level of Income Security for a Free Society," in James E. Russell (ed.), *National Policies for Education, Health, and Social Services*, pp. 392–422. Garden City, N.Y.: Doubleday & Co., Inc., 1955.

MERIAM, LEWIS. *Relief and Social Security.* Washington, D.C.: The Brookings Institution, 1946.

MILLIS, HARRY A., and MONTGOMERY, ROYAL E. *Labor's Progress and Some Basic Labor Problems*, chaps. ii, iii, and v. New York: McGraw-Hill Book Co., 1938.

ROHRLICH, GEORGE F. "Social Security: Freedom from Want without Want of Freedom," in Conference on Science, Philosophy, and Religion in Their Relation to the Democratic Way of Life, *Freedom and Authority in Our Time*, pp. 95–102. New York, 1953.

RUBINOW, I. M. *The Quest for Security.* New York: Henry Holt & Co., Inc., 1934.

NATIONAL RESOURCES PLANNING BOARD. "The Problem of Economic Security," *Security Work and Relief Policies,* chap. ii. Washington, D.C.: U.S. Government Printing Office, 1943.

SMITH, A. DELAFIELD. "Community Prerogative and the Legal Rights and Freedom of the Individual," *Social Security Bulletin* (August, 1946).

U.S. COMMITTEE ON ECONOMIC SECURITY. *Report to the President.* Washington, D.C.: U.S. Government Printing Office, 1935.

————. *Social Security in America: The Factual Background of the Social Security Act as Summarized from Staff Reports to the Committee on Economic Security.* Washington, D.C.: Social Security Board, 1937.

WILLCOX, ALANSON W. "The Contributory Principle and the Integrity of OASI," *Industrial and Labor Relations Review* (April, 1955), pp. 331–46.

WITTE, EDWIN E. *Five Lectures on Social Security.* University of Puerto Rico, 1951.

# Problems and Policies in Old-Age, Survivors, and Disability Insurance

## INTRODUCTION

WHAT IS TODAY the old-age, survivors, and disability insurance program (OASDI) was originally established by titles II and VIII of the Social Security Act of 1935. The program was held to be constitutional by the U.S. Supreme Court in 1937.

Old-age insurance was the only type of monthly insurance benefit provided in the original law. Survivors' insurance benefits were added in 1939, and disability insurance benefits in 1956. In addition, the program has been broadened in the scope of jobs covered and in the adequacy of benefits provided.

Monthly benefits first became payable under the program in 1940. Since that time the number of beneficiaries and benefit payments has grown markedly. Today, OASDI is the largest and dominating influence in social insurance or social welfare institutions in the nation. Moreover, it is the only general program which is administered on a single, national basis. Other general programs, such as unemployment insurance and public assistance, are administered on a state basis with federal funds and some standards. Other programs, such as state workmen's compensation and cash sickness benefits, are administered on a state basis without any federal tie-in.

The gigantic scope and far-reaching implication of the OASDI system raise many questions of public policy.

The OASDI system in the United States is still in the early stages of development. Present-day costs are below those which will eventually evolve as the program matures and the number of beneficiaries increases. Cost may also increase as the level and scope of benefits change, although relative costs may be stabilized or decline if the gross national product continues to increase.

Obviously, old-age programs cost money. And different groups in society have different ideas as to how these funds can best be raised. The concepts of equity and adequacy of financing and benefits vary. There is no single formula to appraise these differences or developments.

Are payments to the aged a "burden" on the economy? Are reserves necessary or desirable in old-age insurance? Are private pension plans desirable? Who should bear the costs of pensions? What effect do pension programs have on investments, incentives, and the general progress of the economy?

The problems involved in determining the adequacy of OASDI benefits will probably become more complex as the various forms of private benefits expand. The level of living enjoyed by OASDI beneficiaries more and more will be provided from more than one source of income.

A very important factor in determining the adequacy of OASDI benefits depends upon the availability and adequacy of medical care financed on a prepayment basis (that is, not out of pocket). If comprehensive medical care is afforded, the adequacy of cash benefits will be improved. For instance, aged persons ordinarily must allocate a substantial portion of their retirement incomes for possible out-of-pocket medical expenses. To the extent that a larger portion of medical costs are met by prepayment arrangements, the more adequate will be their cash benefits. It is likely that, with the passage of time, more comprehensive medical care protection on an insurance basis will develop.

Another important factor is the extent of home ownership. To the extent that beneficiaries own their own homes, or are paying for their own homes, or have substantial rental commitments, the adequacy of their benefits may be affected. Housing costs are a substantial and variable factor in the adequacy equation.

A very challenging problem is whether the long-run improvement in the adequacy of OASDI benefits depends more upon relating and justifying changes to productivity increases and earnings levels rather than to price changes or family budget figures.

As the standard of living and productivity rise for the community as a whole, will the level of OASDI benefits also rise? In Germany, Great Britain, and Sweden proposals have been advanced for dealing with this question. No one in the United States has yet devised a satisfactory formula to do this automatically. We might be able to accomplish such improvements in benefits through the legislative process on an *ad hoc* basis, but, based upon past experience, we may not do so as promptly as would be desirable. Is it possible to do so more promptly?

These are some of the current questions which are of importance in the evaluation of the OASDI program.

# 9. THE RETIREMENT MYTH

Julius Hochman in *The Social and Biological Challenge of Our Aging Population,* Columbia University Press, 1950.

The "old man" is in the limelight. Discussion and debate center around him. He is analyzed from many angles by learned societies, magazines, and newspapers. Library shelves bulge with books about him. He has made the grade and has become a regular feature on our leading radio networks.

Geriatricians, through scientific research, are working hard to prolong his life and ease the painful process of aging. Indeed they now promise him a life span of a hundred years. As the average life in the United States in 1900 was nearly 50 years and in 1947 almost 65, this goal does not seem so implausible.

Psychologists and social workers are determined to make the aging years the beginning of a happy life in which the "old man" will learn to play, will develop new interests and hobbies, and will release hitherto untapped creative powers.

Demographers emphasize that the ratio of the aged—65 years and over—to the rest of the population is increasing rapidly. It rose from 1,000,000, or 3 per cent of the population in 1870, to 9,000,000, or 6.8 per cent in 1940. By 1980, it is estimated, 20,000,000, or 9 per cent of the population, will be 65 years and older.

It is the accepted attitude of our time that men of 65 and over are incapable of providing for themselves and must therefore be supported by society. Sociologists and economists are deeply concerned. They point out that the increased burden of the support of this fast-growing group by a proportionately decreasing number of the working population will tend to reduce our standards of living and drive our economic system to bankruptcy, with dire consequences to our national life.

The "old man" himself is bewildered. He appreciates the fact that his span of life has been increased. But it is difficult for him to understand why the powerful forces of society that shape and control economic life have marked him a useless man to be discarded. He does not like it even when it is labeled "retirement." He wonders. Retire on what? Retire to what? To what in terms of life's content? To what in terms of that vague and yet so meaningful word "happiness"? He is disturbed and depressed. He wonders why he should have to retire at all. Would it not be better for him to follow the injunction laid down by God to the first man: "In the sweat of thy face shalt thou eat bread till thou return unto the ground"?

## AGED
## POPULATION
## OF UNITED STATES

Number and Percentage of
Total Population
1900–1970

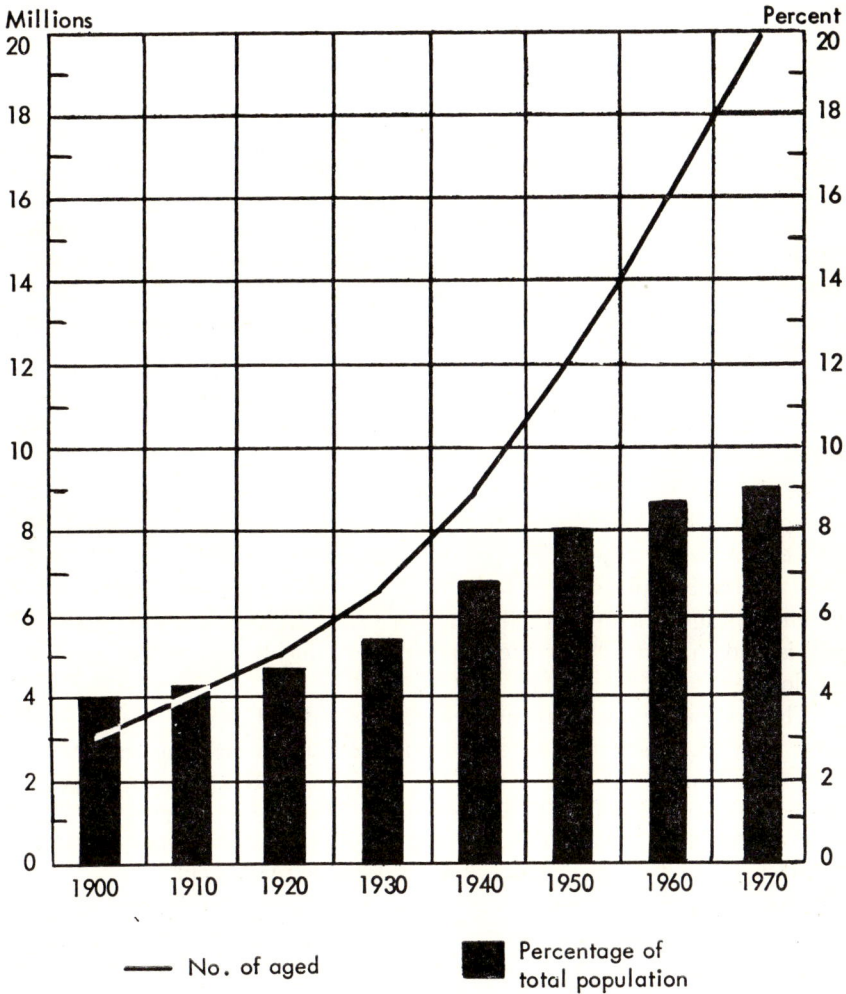

Millions                                Percent

(chart: horizontal axis years 1900–1970, line "No. of aged" rising; bars "Percentage of total population")

—— No. of aged      ■ Percentage of total population

As a matter of fact there are still large sections of our people who continue to live by that injunction. This is particularly true of our rural population. The small independent farmer rarely thinks of retirement unless he is actually incapacitated. Normally, in the process of aging, he does not withdraw to idleness as his physical capacities begin to wane. He merely sheds those tasks that are beyond his strength. He gives up plowing and other hard work, and with the help of a son or a hired man, continues to run his farm. Then, one day, the neighbors hear that John Smith has passed away. As they gather to say their farewells, they whisper to one another, "Why I talked to him only the other day. He looked hale and hearty. He died in harness, as he always hoped he would."

The industrial worker is denied this privilege. Modern industry has whittled away his skills and separated him from control over his work and its product. Often, he may spend a lifetime simply attaching bolts, in a process that requires many hundreds of operations to complete. His employment depends upon the vicissitudes of economic life and upon other people's decisions. When the demand for labor is great, as it is in wartime, his value to the community is high and industry competes for his services; but when the demand for his labor drops, unemployment is his lot. And the old are the first to go.

It is the belief of business and industry—a belief amounting to an obsession—that when a worker reaches the age of 65, he is useless and must be discarded. His continued employment is not only considered unprofitable but is regarded as a hindrance to the success and efficiency of the enterprise.

Workers are not the only group that feel the brunt of this practice. Even the executive-management class is affected, and so are the employees of educational institutions and "white-collar" salaried persons. No group except the self-employed is exempt.

In the not too remote past, the older worker was unceremoniously dumped to shift for himself. But public resentment has compelled employers to devise new techniques to dispose of the "old man." Compulsory retirement plans have been initiated, by which the "old man" is given a meager income, hardly enough to keep body and soul together, and is told to start a "new life" and do the things he has "always wanted to do."

The compulsory retirement plan idea has spread rapidly. Today, millions of workers are committed to retirement at the fixed age of 65. The monetary benefits of these plans are discouragingly small—in some instances, a mere pittance. The New York *Times* recently told the story of a worker in the steel industry who received his first monthly retirement check with a note wishing him "a long and happy life." The check was for $5.82.

Most compulsory retirement plans were introduced and are administered for industry by insurance companies, who have turned them into lucrative business. Experts employed by insurance companies have developed a technique to promote the sale of retirement policies to industry as well as to individuals. To the employers, these experts present statistics and charts proving that the compulsory retirement of their employees at a stated age is absolutely necessary to the success of their enterprise. The public, on the other hand, are incessantly told that compulsory retirement plans are instituted for the benefit of the workers out of purely humanitarian considerations. And to the worker the idea is recommended as offering a great opportunity for a new life and the realization of all his youthful dreams.

On June 16, 1947, the *Journal of Commerce* published a special supplement devoted to employee-pension welfare programs. In this supplement two insurance executives describe and extol the idea of compulsory retirement insurance. They frankly advocate it as the means for employers to rid themselves of their older employees. They state:

> Undoubtedly the primary reason for the adoption of the greater percentage of pension plans is the desire to remove older employees from the payroll at a time when their retention is no longer economically justified. . . . It is approved accounting procedure to determine the effective life of mechanical equipment, and to provide for its replacement when its retention in use is no longer profitable. The retirement of over-age machinery is compulsory in every well-managed business. It is likewise good business practice to determine the effective productive life of employees, and to provide for their compulsory retirement when their retention on the payroll is no longer profitable for the employer. . . . There appears to be a general agreement that, in most businesses and on most jobs, age 65 marks the end of the most productive period of life.

Thus speak the philosophers of the insurance companies to industry. It is all a question of accounting. The worker is in the same class with the machine. You use him just so long; then he gets old and you throw him on the scrap heap and get yourself a younger worker. That is what retirement is for. It should be noted that this compulsory retirement policy affects not only the worker who has reached the age of 65 but millions of middle-aged workers as well. To meet the calculations of the actuaries, many industrial corporations set a hiring age limit. That limit ranges from 30 to 55, the age of 45 being probably the most common. At times, when employment is not plentiful, it becomes extremely difficult for workers near the age limit to find jobs. What this does to the lives of millions of Americans should be obvious.

To the worker retirement is presented in an entirely different light. He is assured that it is to be the beginning of a new and happy life for him, an opportunity at last to go places and do things—the very things he has always dreamed of doing but couldn't quite manage. Pick up almost any popular magazine or, on occasion, even newspaper and you will be sure to find at least one display picture with the appropriate text showing John Smith retired, puttering away in a neat flower garden in front of a colorful little cottage, or else walking up the gangplank of a luxury liner about to start on a trip around the world. Hobbies and sports are not neglected. Every emotion, every yearning and aspiration, is exploited. Baseball naturally gets special attention.

The following advertisement was obviously written to catch the baseball fan. It is a unique item of Americana. I certainly hope future historians will not consider it a true picture of our time. Yet, because it was sponsored by "the life insurance companies and their agents" it has appeared in 375 daily newspapers, even that could very well happen. At any rate, it reached the public as one of a "series of messages from the nation's foremost authorities," a true-to-life story signed by Dr. Lloyd E. Dewey, Professor of Finance, New York University, and it read as follows:

> Very few people are ever able to quit work in time to enjoy life, and yet all of us dream of doing it.
> Today the average child at birth can expect to live eighteen years longer than his grandfather lived. Are these years to be some of the best of your life, as they are for my friend, Joe Thomas, or will you miss your chance to have your dream come true?
> Joe used to be in a machine shop at Steward and Brown. (I am changing real names, of course.) A great sports fan, Joe's ambition was to retire and see every home game of the St. Louis Cardinals, his favourite team. . . .
> Go to the ball park any day now, and you'll see Joe cheering in the stands!

> Joe will tell anyone he owes it all to a man he met by chance in his early thirties, a life insurance agent named Ed Barrow, who became one of the best friends he ever had. It was Barrow who sold him the idea of planning for the future—a hard job when most of us are interested only in the present. . . .

Accompanying this "true story" is a picture of Joe cheering in the grandstand. He drinks pop! It's most exciting.

Why couldn't Joe have gotten to all the night games and the Saturday and Sunday games when he was working? What does Joe do when the Cardinals are on the road? What does he do during the winter? What will Joe do with his life between baseball seasons? On all this the professor is silent.

What is the attitude of the real Joe who reaches 65? Does he want to retire? No one has ever asked him. The recently developed collective bargaining plans permitting voluntary retirement offer the first opportunity to gauge the worker's feelings in this matter. The first collective bargaining retirement plan in this country was introduced in the New York coat and suit industry. It was, like all similar programs, established on a voluntary basis, as far as the obligation to retire is concerned. Contributions to the fund began in 1944, and actual retirement in June, 1947. At first, retirement benefits were $50 a month, and all workers reaching 65 were eligible for retirement. Of these, 1,500 have retired—only 24 per cent of those entitled to the privilege.

The Amalgamated Clothing Workers Union Retirement System in New York City, matching social security benefits, has been taken advantage of by only 3,000 members, or about one-third of 9,000 eligibles.

The New York *Times* of May 29, 1949, reporting on the functioning of the retirement plan of the United Mine Workers welfare fund, stated:

> Miss Josephine Roche, former assistant secretary of the Treasury, who is now director of the UMW welfare and retirement fund reports: Fifteen thousand

miners past the age of 62 and with twenty years or more of mine work behind them are receiving retirement payments of $100 a month. The average age of those who have retired is 66. Miss Roche said that most of them were suffering from permanent disabilities resulting from mine accidents or mine-contracted illnesses.

"Even though the UMW benefits are added to federal old-age insurance payments, which average about $30 a month for miners leaving the pits at 65, only 'a negligible percentage' of the able-bodied miners past retirement age have taken advantage of the pension provisions," Miss Roche said.

"Even with only two or three days' work in the mines, most of our people would rather keep working as long as they can," she noted. "We know of several past 80 who are still at work."

In the New York Dressmakers Union of the I.L.G.W.U., where a retirement fund was recently inaugurated, a record was kept by an interviewer of some of the reactions of workers who applied for retirement but finally decided to continue working. Here is a typical case. A worker of 69 sat for half an hour pondering the question and finally said: "If I don't go on working, tell me, what will I do with all my time?" Another worker declared: "If I work, I'll stay healthy longer mentally and physically."

It is obvious that instinctively the worker has deep inner resistance to withdrawal from work. The evidence accumulated by geriatricians and psychiatrists amply indicates that retirement is frequently followed by crisis and severe emotional disturbance, sometimes even by death.

Why this resistance, why this inner conflict? Why the reluctance to accept benefits offered? Unfortunately, modern psychology has not given adequate attention to this question. Perhaps some suggestions of the answer can be found in a footnote in Sigmund Freud's *Civilization and Its Discontents*. Freud writes:

When there is no special disposition in a man imperatively prescribing the direction of his life-interest, the ordinary work all can do for a livelihood can play the part which Voltaire wisely advocated it should do in our lives. It is not possible to discuss the significance of work for the economics of the libido adequately within the limits of a short survey. Laying stress upon importance of work has a greater effect than any other technique of living in the direction of binding the individual more closely to reality; in his work he is at least securely attached to a part of reality, the human community. Work is no less valuable for the opportunity it and the human relations connected with it provide for a very considerable discharge of libidinal component impulses, narcissitic, aggressive and even erotic, than because it is indispensable for subsistence and justifies existence in a society. . . . And yet, as a path to happiness, work is not valued very highly by men. They do not run after it as they do after other opportunities for gratification.

Let us first consider Freud's remark in the earlier part of this passage: "Laying stress upon the importance of work has a greater effect than any other technique of living in the direction of binding the individual more closely to reality; in his work, he is at least securely attached to a part of reality, to the human community." To the economist, work may be only a way of earning a living, but to Freud it is more, much more. It is also a way of life. For the average man, it is the bond with reality, the means of communal contact and participation. It serves to identify the individual with society, past, present and future. Its functions as a high form of sublimation, helping to make out of a man a social, civilized being. That is why forced retirement usually precipitates such a severe emotional crisis: it is nothing less than the rupture of the pattern that has hitherto given meaning and value to life.

With the rise of trade unionism, millions of workers have been able to achieve a wider sense of belonging than even their work has succeeded in conferring upon them. The union gives the worker added stature in the community. Through his union he asserts himself as a person. Through collective bargaining, he becomes a partner in industry. From time to time, he demonstrates his power by using his collective strength to improve his lot in life. As a union member, he becomes a major contributor to philanthropy at home and abroad. He exercises influence in his community. He becomes an important factor in politics. The newspapers note his actions and make him part of history. Forced retirement means isolation from the labor collectivity and a collapse into individual insignificance. No wonder it is felt to be so dreadful by most workers threatened with it.

It will be noted that, in the passage I have cited, Freud observes that "as a path to happiness, work is not valued very highly by men. They do not run after it as they do after other opportunities for gratification." This conclusion is of course based on European experiences and does not altogether represent the attitude towards work in our culture. I have, however, found a distinct difference in attitude toward work between the older and the younger worker. In my own rather amateurish survey of the attitude of workers to forced retirement, I have found two quite contradictory reactions: older people want to continue working and shy away from retirement; but strangely enough it is the young to whom retirement appeals. Why this curious difference in attitude? I venture the following as a possible explanation. Every young person starts life with illusions about himself. He believes he can, and hopes he will, do something great. Usually, he does not admit to himself the illusory element in these dreams, but as he gets on in life, he necessarily adapts himself to reality and goes about earning his living as best he can. Yet he does not give up the hope of obtaining his secret aims. Some day, he tells himself, he will get the chance, and when anyone comes to him with a scheme by which he will some day be able to retire and do the things he has always wanted to do, he welcomes it. As he grows older, however, and begins to approach his retirement age, he begins to realize that what he hadn't been able to accomplish at 25 or 30, he is not likely to do at 65; and the very hope that once led him to look forward to it now makes the prospect of retirement quite distressing—because he knows that once he retires he will have to admit to himself that his great expectations were always largely illusory. Thus, the paradoxical attitude of the young man, if examined a little more closely, really confirms the analysis I have been trying to develop.

It is generally recognized that the happiest people are those fortunate few, who, through a combination of special faculties, and inner drives, become the great creative artists, scientists, philosophers, and statesmen of their time. These men do not retire; their work is their life. They frequently live to a ripe old age and remain active to their very last breath. The great mass of people are not quite so fortunate. Most of them are forced to accept work not to their liking, but, even so, work becomes the bond between them and the community, between them and social reality. It constitutes their main social function and creates that sense of belonging without which life is hardly livable.

This is especially true of our American culture. Our entire educational and social pattern emphasizes a man's place in the working community. It is dinned into us from the start that we must be useful citizens, that we must do our share of the work, that we must make our contribution to society. The conventions of our civilization demand that a man either make money or earn money. He does not truly "belong" unless he is usefully employed, in the broad sense in which our civilization views usefulness. The playboy is looked upon with contempt because he is a stranger to man's normal activities. Yet the forced retirement idea is based on the conception that a man who has been taught all his life that he must be socially useful through work can make a sudden transition to idleness and still retain his self-respect. This notion is dangerously false. His very youthful hopes, as we have seen, now operate to intensify the fear of forced retirement. The realization that the things one had always dreamed of doing to establish oneself in the eyes of society are nothing but illusions tends suddenly to deflate one's self-esteem and to precipitate a serious emotional crisis.

I think it can now be seen why the myth of retirement, as it has been popularized and glamorized by the insurance companies, is dangerous. I am not decrying the various plans and programs devised to provide for old age. Most emphatically, I am not. It is natural for us to try to provide for ourselves against all the hazards of life. We all want to be protected against the dreadful threat of indigence in old age. Those who can afford it lay aside part of their earnings for this purpose. For those who cannot, adequate old-age pensions should be made available. I do not begrudge the insurance companies their lucrative retirement and annuity business, but are we not entitled to ask them to rise above the morality of the ordinary hawker? Do they really have a right to play fast and loose with human welfare? Why can't they sell annuity retirement policies on an honest basis? Why can't they present their case in ads like this:

> Some day you will be an old man. The chances are you will live to a ripe old age, continue in good health and be able to follow your accustomed profession, business or occupation to the very end of your life. On the other hand, you may fall victim to any of the illnesses or incapacities that sometimes afflict people of advanced age. If it comes to that, you may be deprived of the ability to provide for yourself. Why not give some thought to it now while you are still young and begin saving for that possible emergency? Insurance is the best way to do it.

There is nothing quixotic in an ad like this, however little it may appeal to the insurance companies. We have accident insurance and workmen's compensation laws; do we therefore encourage accidents and mishaps, or teach people to look forward to collecting? We have unemployment insurance; do we therefore carry on propaganda about the beauties of living on unemployment insurance? No; we try to reduce accidents to a minimum, and we are searching for ways and means of achieving full employment. In other words, in these and so many other cases, we regard insurance as a provision against unfortunate contingencies which we try to prevent from happening. Why should it be any different with retirement in old age?

The entire philosophy of old-age insurance as part of social security has been rather confused. In the depression of 1935, when the Old-Age Insurance and Survivors Act was passed, it was no secret that the intent of the act was to remove older workers from the market. This was in line with the general practice prevailing in industry and business enterprise at the time. It is this philosophy of forcing or encouraging retirement that I am arguing against. It stands in gross contradiction to the very meaning of the word "security" in the name of which it is justified. For security means freedom from care, and, while it is necessary to one's well being to feel that one is safely provided for should he be unable to earn his living in advanced years, freedom from care is largely nullified by the dread of being forced to retire at a fixed age, even though at that age one may still be productive and capable of doing useful work in the community. There is no fear equal to the terror of being relegated to the scrap heap as a useless, worn-out "old man."

Of course, there are many who have to retire, and not exactly at the age of 65 either. Some may be unable to work long before reaching that age. It is conceded by all authorities that old age is by no means chronological. People in such condition should be provided for—and adequately—even if retirement is forced upon them before they reach the magic age of 65. There may be some who, though in a position to continue working, will want to retire or at least try retirement at a stipulated age. They too should be given that opportunity. But the great mass of people will most likely want to continue to work, feeling, as indeed they have a right to feel, that forced retirement at any age cuts them off from the stream of life. These people must be given the opportunity to live their lives out to the end. For that, our entire philosophy of retirement will have to be reconstructed.

## LIFE EXPECTANCY IN THE UNITED STATES

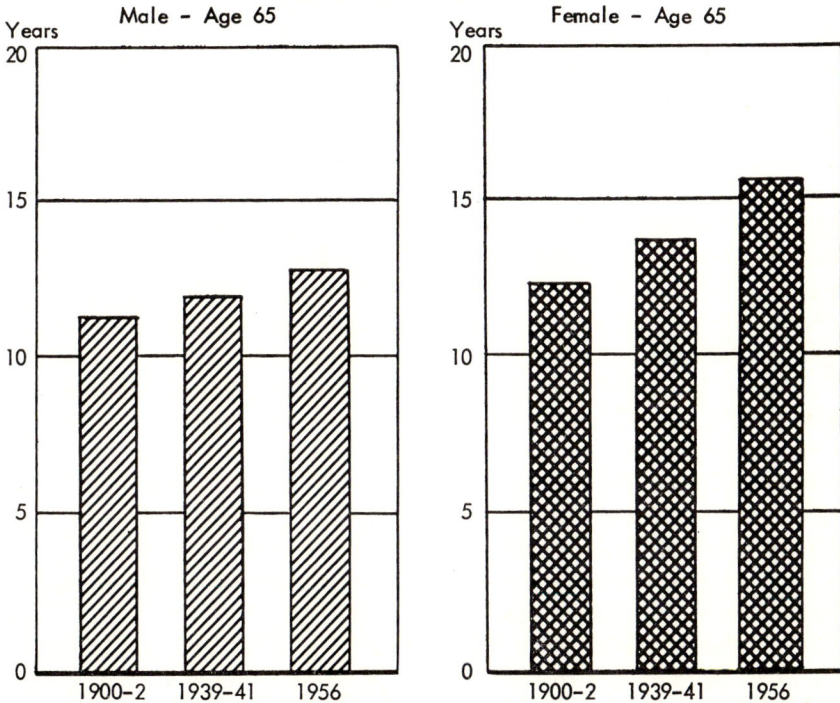

Male – Age 65

Years

1900-2   1939-41   1956

Female – Age 65

Years

1900-2   1939-41   1956

The retirement myth must be destroyed. Our program should be directed not toward getting rid of the "old man" but toward helping him age usefully and gracefully. Retirement plans should be conceived and administered not to make retirement compulsory at any age but, like all other forms of social security, to provide means of life should retirement become necessary. The collective bargaining plans we mentioned before are showing the way in this respect. They are all voluntary plans, offering pensions to those who want to retire. Some of them, such as the plan in effect in the New York coat and suit industry, even provide for a kind of trial period, permitting the worker to retire at the stated age with the understanding that if he finds retirement unbearable he can go back to work. These plans are also more flexible as to age of retirement. Although the official age laid down in its rules is 65, the coat and suit industry plan permits retirement in a limited number of cases at 60, if health demands it. And the benefits offered in collective bargaining plans are considerably less inadequate than those offered in any other type.

The "old man" should be encouraged to remain at work as long as he wishes and is able to do so. The advantages of medical science should be made more readily accessible to him. Longer and more frequent vacations for the older workers, perhaps subsidized from the retirement funds, could be very helpful. In order to enable him to continue working, arrangements should be devised to permit the older worker to shift to part-time or to easier tasks when necessary. Social security payments might be used to supplement incomes should the latter prove inadequate because of the reduction of hours or intensity of work. Programs to retain older workers would be very useful, and in such a program, industry, labor and government could cooperate.

Old-age security is increasingly becoming a part of standard collective bargaining. Unions will have to rethink many of their problems in terms of the "old man." They have a real responsibility to keep older workers usefully employed so long as health permits.

But above all, it is necessary to destroy the superstition that old age is simply a chronological matter and that a date can be fixed when a man ceases to be useful to society. The problem is especially acute in industry. Age as a barrier to employment must be abolished. The attitude of management must be radically changed. The conscience of the nation, as expressed in the Clayton Act, has condemned the doctrine that labor is a commodity. Workers are not machines to be thrown on the scrap heap the moment they can be profitably replaced by a newer piece of machinery. They are human beings and their work is their life. The gates of factory, mine or mill must not be shut upon those who are able to work, simply because they have reached a certain age.

It is a mistake to think that the "old man" presents only a special problem of concern merely to himself. The problem of the "old man" is the problem of our entire society. All of us, we hope, will ultimately be old, and the fate we prepare for the old people today will be ours tomorrow. Moreover, the attitude of a society to its older people is one of the most significant aspects of its spiritual culture. The relationship between the generations is a measure by which civilization is tested. We do not want to emulate the Oriental pattern, in which age is worshipped to the point where progress is stifled. But we cannot, in our civilization, grounded as it is in the Judeo-Christian ethic, long permit an attitude that is, at bottom, little better than the savage practice of killing off the old people as soon as they become a burden on the tribe. If we are to be true to the ethical ideals of our civilization, we must learn to overcome the fateful antagonism which manifests itself in the impulse to shove the "old man" out of sight. Children do it by sending parents to an old-people's home or institution. Industry does it by "retirement." To ease our conscience, we arrange for a meager maintenance. We think we have settled the matter and gotten rid of the trouble, but we have not. With the passing of time, the youth of today becomes the old man of tomorrow, and he in his turn must pay the price of neglect and rejection.

We must accept the "old man" and help him live out his life as he was meant to do. This is a basic moral imperative, which we can defy only at utmost peril to our society. And, as in so many cases, it is quite possible that if we adopt an attitude in line with our moral responsibilities, it may prove to be of great utility to our social economy. If we permit the "old man" to work and help him to work in ways that are best suited to his age, he may well become a positive economic asset, instead of a liability, as he is regarded today. Decency and moral responsibility may yet pay off economically.

# 10. THE INCOME STATUS OF OLDER PERSONS

MARGARET S. GORDON, before
the Senate Subcommittee on Aging,
June 18, 1959.

### Factors Affecting the Income of Older Persons

DURING THE LAST quarter of a century, the United States has made substantial progress toward the development of a comprehensive system of economic security for older persons. Yet poverty among the aged remains one of our most persistent and difficult economic and social problems. As recently as 1957—the last year for which nationwide income data are available—more than a sixth of all persons aged 65 and over in the nation had no income, and about three-fifths had incomes of less than $1,000 a year.[1]

Elderly men fared substantially better than elderly women. Only 5 per cent of the men aged 65 or over had no income, as compared with 28 per cent of the women. Furthermore, while half of the elderly men with income received less than $1,421 in 1957, half of the elderly women with income received less than $741.

Not only is the problem of poverty in the aged population more serious among women than among men, but there are marked variations in the income status of elderly persons that are associated with their labor force status, marital status, urban or rural residence, and other factors.

From middle age onward, there is a persistent tendency for the proportion of persons in the labor force to decline with advancing age. This means that, within the population of those aged 65 and over, the older an individual is, the less likely he or she is to be in the labor force. Further-

---

[1] U.S. Bureau of the Census, *Current Population Reports: Consumer Income.* Series P-60, No. 30 (December, 1958).

more, those who *are* in the labor force are more likely to be engaged in part-time work as they grow older.

A striking indication of the influence of labor force status on the incomes of aged men is provided by Census Bureau income data for 1957. Although the median income of all men aged 65 and over was $1,421, those who were year-round full-time workers (about a fifth of the total) had a median income of $3,427.[2]

What is less generally recognized is that the occupation in which a male worker has been engaged during his working life has an important influence on whether he is likely to be in the labor force after age 65. As the Steiner-Dorfman study, which was based on a nationwide survey conducted in 1952, indicated, nonmanual workers were more likely to be in the labor force after age 65 than manual workers.[3] Careful analysis indicated that this difference was chiefly attributable to differences in the proportions who felt well enough to work. Although the great majority of elderly men who were out of the labor force reported that they did not consider themselves well enough to work, this was more likely to be true of the men who had been engaged in manual work than of those who had been in nonmanual occupations. Also of considerable interest was the fact that the great majority of these elderly men who were out of the labor force said that they had retired because of ill health rather than because of formal retirement systems, and this, too, was more likely to be true of those who had been manual workers.

Among aged women, only about 9 per cent were in the labor force in 1952, and most of those who were not had either had no work experience since before age 50 or did not consider themselves well enough to work.

Partly because married men in the 65 and older group are more likely to be in the labor force than nonmarried men, the income status of elderly couples tends to be superior to that of elderly persons without a spouse. There are no recent income data that bring out these relationships clearly for the entire aged population, but Census income data indicate that the median income of families headed by an individual aged 65 or more—most of whom are elderly couples—was $2,490 in 1957, as compared with a median income of only $918 for elderly unrelated individuals. Median income would be substantially lower for both groups, if employed persons were excluded. Data from the 1957 National Survey of Old-Age and Survivors Insurance Beneficiaries indicate that half the beneficiary couples had an annual income of less than $2,190 while a fourth had less than $1,500. However, income included appreciable amounts of part-time earnings in some cases. If we exclude earnings and other temporary sources of income, the picture is considerably less fa-

---

[2] *Ibid.*

[3] Peter O. Steiner and Robert Dorfman, *The Economic Status of the Aged* (Berkeley: University of California Press, 1957), chap. iv.

vorable, with half the couples receiving less than $1,700 and a fourth receiving less than $1,200.[4]

### Persistence of Low Incomes in the Aged Population

Why do so many elderly people continue to have low incomes, despite the substantial liberalization of the social security program that has occurred during the 1950's? There are many reasons for this, and we shall mention only a few of the more important ones.

One factor of considerable importance has been the marked decline in the proportion of elderly men in the labor force since 1950. This represents a continuation of a long-run trend that has been greatly accelerated during the last decade. According to the Current Population Survey of the Bureau of the Census, only 34.5 per cent of all men aged 65 and over were in the labor force in April 1959, as compared with 46.1 per cent in April 1950.[5] Whether and to what extent this sharp drop has been attributable to the rapid growth of private pension plans, with their compulsory retirement provisions, is not entirely clear. What *is* clear is that the rise in the average income of elderly couples and aged men has been held back by this decline in the proportion of earners among elderly men.

Another important explanation of the persistence of poverty among older persons is that, although more than half of all persons aged 65 and over now receive old-age and survivors insurance benefits, there are many beneficiaries, particularly among those who retired some years ago, whose benefits are based on earnings received when wages were very much below their present levels. This factor tends to hold down the average benefits received under OASDI, which amounted to only $71.40 for a retired worker in January, 1959. Although the maximum benefit is now $127, it will be several years before any retired workers can receive this maximum. It must be kept in mind, in this connection, that each time the maximum monthly benefit and the related ceiling on annual taxable earnings have been increased, the new maxima have applied only to earnings received after the effective date of the amendment.

Although about 18 million workers are covered by private pension and deferred profit-sharing plans, many of these plans are relatively new and comparatively few workers have retired under them. The 1957 National Survey of Old-Age and Survivors Insurance Beneficiaries showed that only a fourth of the aged beneficiary couples were receiving income from employer or union pensions. The proportion of single retired workers receiving pension income was substantially smaller (15 per cent),

---

[4] U.S. Bureau of Old-Age and Survivors Insurance, *National Survey of Old-Age and Survivors Insurance Beneficiaries, 1957, Highlights from Preliminary Tabulations—Income* (Washington, D.C., 1958).

[5] U.S. Bureau of the Census, *Current Population Reports: Labor Force*, Series P-57, Nos. 94 and 202 (May, 1950 and May, 1959).

while only a negligible fraction of aged beneficiary widows received any income from this source.[6]

Among older persons in the aged population, there are a good many who are not eligible for either old-age and survivors insurance or private pension benefits. This is the group that is dependent primarily on old-age assistance or on support from relatives. Although monthly old-age assistance payments are comparatively generous in a few of the states, they were below $70 a month in the majority of states in January, 1959 and below $50 a month in 11 states, chiefly in the South. For the nation as a whole, the average monthly payment was $64.54, but it ranged from a low of $29.54 in Mississippi to a high of $107.74 in Connecticut.[7]

### Living Costs for Elderly People

The mere fact that the incomes of elderly people are comparatively low does not in itself prove that they are seriously inadequate. The critical problem in appraising the adequacy of the incomes of the aged is to determine what percentage of elderly couples and individuals have incomes that fall below those required for carefully defined levels of living.

Unfortunately, we do not have adequate or up-to-date information on the budgetary requirements of elderly people. The most recent attempt at careful appraisal of the income status of the entire aged population was the Steiner-Dorfman study, which related to the income status of the aged in 1951.[8] The authors of this study made various adjustments, on the basis of a budget for an elderly couple that had been developed by the Social Security Administration in 1948, in order to determine what the budgetary requirements of various types of aged economic units would have been in 1951. They found that 44 per cent of the elderly couples and a substantially larger proportion of the men and women without a spouse had total receipts that were below the amounts needed to maintain a "modest but adequate" level of living. More serious was the fact that more than a quarter of the couples, about a third of the men without a spouse, and approximately half of the women without a spouse had less than the amounts required for a "bare subsistence" level of living.

Although the proportions with inadequate incomes have undoubtedly declined since 1951, it seems apparent, on the basis of the available income data, that there are still many elderly couples and individuals with seriously deficient incomes. It is virtually impossible, however, to arrive at even approximate estimates of the proportions with inadequate incomes at the present time, in view of the fact that neither income nor budgetary data are available in sufficient detail.

The best we can do is to develop some rough estimates of current

---

[6] U.S. Bureau of Old-Age and Survivors Insurance, *op. cit.*

[7] *Social Security Bulletin*, 22, No. 4 (April, 1959), p. 34.

[8] Steiner and Dorfman, *op. cit.*, chap. vi.

living costs for elderly couples and individuals in urban areas, where the majority of elderly persons live, recognizing that costs are substantially lower in rural farm areas. Adjusting the Steiner-Dorfman budgets for the 11.4 per cent increase in the BLS consumer price index since 1951, we find that an elderly home-owning couple in an average urban community would probably require annual cash receipts of well over $1,900 a year for a "modest but adequate" level of living in the spring of 1959. However, this is an average figure, and the costs would be considerably higher for couples living in rented quarters in some of the largest cities. On the basis of budget data prepared by the Welfare and Health Council of New York City, for example, we may estimate that in the spring of 1959 an elderly couple living in rented quarters in New York City would require approximately $2,300 if the husband and wife were both retired, and substantially more than this if the husband were still working.[9]

There is little doubt that aged widows are still the most seriously impoverished sector of the aged population. The Steiner-Dorfman budgets, adjusted to a 1959 basis, suggest that an elderly woman living in rented quarters in an average urban area would require about $1,200 a year, for a "modest but adequate" level of living, while the required amount would be about $850 to $900 if she were living in the household of one of her children. The budget prepared by the Welfare and Health Council of New York City, adjusted to 1959 consumer prive levels, suggests that a nonworking elderly woman living alone in rented quarters in New York City would require about $1,600 a year, or about $133 a month. Yet the average widow's or widower's benefit under OASDI in January, 1959 was only about $56 a month.[10]

It should be emphasized that all these budgetary estimates are extremely rough. It is probable that living costs for elderly couples and individuals have risen more sharply since the early 1950's than the movements of the BLS consumer price index suggest. The index is designed to measure changes in living costs for city wage-earner and clerical-worker families, but elderly couples and individuals have somewhat different needs from those of families with younger heads and are affected differently by changes in living costs. Families with aged heads, for example, spend relatively more on food, housing, heat and medical care and relatively less on clothing, furniture, transportation, personal care, and recreation than families with younger heads.[11] Their comparatively higher expenditures for medical care are related to the fact

---

[9] Welfare and Health Council of New York City, Research Department, *A Family Budget Standard for the Use of Social and Health Agencies in New York City* (New York, 1955).

[10] Computed from data in *Social Security Bulletin*, 22, No. 2 (April, 1959), p. 28.

[11] See Wharton School of Finance and Commerce, *Study of Consumer Expenditures, Incomes, and Savings*, Vol. XVIII (Philadelphia: University of Pennsylvania, 1957).

that they are more likely to be ill. The California Health Survey, for example, indicated that those 65 years of age and over experienced nearly three times as many days of disability in a year, on the average, as the general population and were twice as likely to be suffering from chronic conditions.[12] Between 1951 and the early months of 1959, medical care costs increased 34 per cent—more than any other component of the consumer price index—while housing costs also increased relatively sharply. On the other hand, the cost of clothing, on which elderly persons spend relatively little, scarcely changed during this period.[13]

Nor does this comparison tell the whole story. Families with younger heads are much more likely to have some type of health insurance and are therefore more adequately protected against the unusual medical costs that may strike a particular family in a particular year than are those in the 65 and older bracket. A nationwide survey by the Census Bureau in September, 1956 indicated that only 36.5 per cent of all persons aged 65 and over had some type of health insurance protection, as compared with 63.6 per cent of the population as a whole.[14] The 1957 National Survey of Old-Age and Survivors Insurance Beneficiaries indicated that about a third of the aged beneficiary couples and nearly a fourth of the nonmarried beneficiaries had coverage for hospitalization and surgery, while an additional seventh of the couples and nearly a sixth of the nonmarried beneficiaries had coverage for hospitalization only.[15] The survey also showed that annual medical costs were as high as $500 or more for about a sixth of the couples and about 8 per cent of the nonmarried beneficiaries.

### How High Should OASDI Benefit Levels Be?

The 1957 National Survey of Old-Age and Survivors Insurance Beneficiaries indicated clearly that the majority of aged beneficiaries had very little independent retirement income other than their OASDI benefits.[16] With more than half of the aged population receiving benefits under the program, and the proportion affected steadily increasing, it is clear that the level of OASDI benefits is the major determinant of the income status of the retired sectors of the aged population as well as of many who are earning small amounts on a part-time basis while receiving benefits. Thus the most important single policy issue in relation to the income of the aged has to do with the determination of OASDI benefit levels.

It is clear that no single criterion can be used in the determination of

---

[12] California Department of Public Health, *Health in California* (Berkeley, 1957).

[13] U.S. Bureau of Labor Statistics, *Consumer Price Index for March 1959,* and earlier issues of the same publication.

[14] U.S. Social Security Administration, *Health Insurance Coverage by Age and Sex, September, 1956* (Washington, D.C., 1958).

[15] *Social Security Bulletin,* 22, No. 4 (April, 1959), p. 5.

[16] U.S. Bureau of Old-Age and Survivors Insurance, *op. cit.*

appropriate benefit levels. In this country we have been applying, and probably will continue to apply in the future, a combination of criteria in seeking to resolve the complex issues involved. The most important of these criteria are: (1) the relation of benefits to a retired worker's earnings under the system, (2) the budgetary needs of elderly couples and individuals, (3) the extent to which these needs should be met through other sources of income, and (4) the capacity of the economy to meet the costs of the program.

The basic principle underlying our OASDI program, and of most old-age insurance programs throughout the world, is that a retired worker's benefits, and those of his dependents and survivors, should be *related to his earnings* under the system. Indeed, this is the only one of our four criteria that is explicitly recognized in the law. Since contributions are based on earnings, this means that benefits are also related to contributions. Adherence to this general principle, however, does not necessarily mean that a retired worker's benefits must be strictly proportional to his average earnings throughout his period of coverage. In fact, virtually every country has found it necessary to modify the principle of strict proportionality to actual covered earnings because of (1) long-term inflationary pressures, (2) the desirability of providing benefits for those covered only a short time before retirement, and (3) the need to provide some minimum level of benefits for those with particularly low earnings. Some countries relate benefits to earnings in the last few years before retirement or adjust them on the basis of a formula which takes account of the upward trend of wage levels.

Although OASDI benefit levels have been increased a number of times, they have not much more than kept pace with the rise in earnings. The average monthly benefit of $71.40 received by a retired worker in January, 1959 represented about 23 per cent of average net spendable monthly earnings in manufacturing for a worker with no dependents, as compared with about 21 per cent in 1940. What is particularly striking about this comparison, of course, is not that benefit levels have risen so little as a percentage of average monthly factory earnings, but that they represented such a small percentage at both the beginning and end of the period.

To the extent that we have departed from the principle of strict proportionality to covered earnings in this country, we have done so with a view to giving recognition to *need*. Even the provision of benefits for dependents and survivors, which was not a feature of the original social security act, involves recognition of the differing needs of individuals with varying numbers of dependents. The setting of maximum and minimum benefit amounts is likewise based on a criterion of need, as is the slanting of the benefit formula to provide a larger proportion of average monthly wages to those with low earnings. So are the provisions permitting newly covered workers to acquire insured status in a relatively short period, the provision for dropping out periods of low earnings, and peri-

odic adjustments of the entire benefit structures in response to changes in the cost of living.

Once the criterion of need is given explicit or implicit recognition, a number of questions arise. Should need be defined in terms of a bare subsistence level of living, or some higher level? Given the desired level of living, should the aim be to set minimum, average, or maximum benefits at a high enough level to meet such a standard? These are just two among the many questions that might be mentioned.

It is impossible to resolve these questions without considering the third criterion, *the extent to which the needs of aged beneficiaries* should be met through other sources of income. In his social security message of January, 1954, the President pointed out that the "system is not intended as a substitute for private savings, pension plans, and insurance protection. It is, rather, intended as a foundation upon which these other forms of protection can be soundly built."[17]

Although most people would agree with this broad statement of objectives, there are wide differences of opinion as to just what constitutes an "adequate foundation upon which other forms of protection can be soundly built." When we leave the realm of broad philosophical debate and take a close look at the facts, we find that it is the lowest income groups in the aged population who are least likely to have accumulated savings or private pension income in amounts sufficient to make an appreciable contribution toward living costs. Furthermore, although income from private pensions makes an appreciable contribution to total income for some retired people, only a relatively small percentage of aged couples and individuals receiving OASDI benefits, as we have seen, receive such pension income. The proportion receiving some income from assets is substantially higher, but the amounts received are typically small. The 1957 survey indicated that the median amount of asset income for single male retired beneficiaries receiving such income, for example, was $96, while for beneficiary couples it was $180.[18]

There is no evidence that the expansion and liberalization of the social security program has discouraged saving. Annual personal saving represented a higher proportion of personal disposable income in 1957 than in 1940,[19] while life insurance holdings have been increasing at a substantially more rapid rate than disposable income.[20] But it remains true that it is difficult for the average wage-earner to accumulate enough savings to contribute substantially toward his retirement income. As Ewan Clague has pointed out, "to buy from an insurance company a modest annuity of say $75 a month beginning with age 65 requires for a man an accumula-

---

[17] *Social Security Bulletin*, 18, No. 8 (August, 1955), p. 12.

[18] U.S. Bureau of Old-Age and Survivors Insurance, *op. cit.*

[19] Computed from data in *Survey of Current Business*, July, 1958, pp. 6–7.

[20] See Institute of Life Insurance, *Life Insurance Fact Book*, annual.

tion of about $11,900, and for a woman, since women live longer than men, about $13,900."[21]

We come now to our fourth criterion, *the capacity of the economy to provide retirement income* for aged persons. Total old-age retirement and survivorship benefits and old-age assistance payments under government programs in 1957 amounted to 11.8 billion dollars, or 3.3 per cent of the national income.[22] This included payments under railroad retirement, civil service, and other federal, state, and local government retirement programs, as well as OAA payments and old-age and survivorship benefits under OASDI. Although most of these payments went to persons aged 65 and older, the total included payments to female beneficiaries aged 62 to 64 and to younger widowed mothers and dependent children. Adding retirement payments under private pension plans, amounting to $1,150 million in 1957, we arrive at a grand total of $13 billion, or 3.6 per cent of the national income.[23] If we consider that persons aged 65 and over represent 8.6 per cent of the population, this seems a modest percentage of the national income to be devoted to these programs. Although comparable data are not readily available for other countries, a report issued by the International Labor Office indicates that total social security expenditures of all types, including expenditures for such systems as unemployment insurance and workmen's compensation as well as old-age programs, amounted to only 5.4 per cent of the national income in this country in 1954, as compared with 10.7 per cent in the United Kingdom, 18.5 per cent in France, 19.2 per cent in Germany, and 9.1 per cent in Canada.[24]

Although the percentage of the national income represented by payments under retirement and old-age assistance programs has increased somewhat as the retirement programs have matured, it has not increased as much as was anticipated when the Social Security Act was enacted. Indeed, increasing income levels and productivity have made it possible to expand and improve the OASDI program without increasing the taxes imposed under the program as much as was originally expected. Furthermore, it has been estimated that, with a $4,800 ceiling on annual taxable earnings, only 75 per cent of all covered workers and 50 per cent of the regularly employed men will have their full earnings taxed for both contributions and benefits in 1959. By contrast, in 1938, when the ceiling was $3,000, 97 per cent of all covered employees and 94 per cent of

---

[21] Ewan Clague, "Do American Workers Save for Retirement?" in G. B. Hurff (ed.), *Economic Problems of Retirement* (Gainesville: University of Florida Press, 1954), p. 22.

[22] Computed from data in *Social Security Bulletin—Annual Statistical Supplement, 1957*, pp. 14 and 74, and *Survey of Current Business* (July, 1958), p. 7.

[23] *Ibid.*, and *Social Security Bulletin*, 22, No. 3 (March, 1959), p. 10.

[24] International Labor Office, *The Cost of Social Security* (Geneva, 1958), pp. 161–64.

regularly employed men, had their full earnings covered.[25] Thus, total tax payments as a percentage of total earnings in covered types of employment have not risen as much as tax rates on employers and employees.

Assuming the present provisions of the law, it will be necessary to raise tax rates somewhat as the program continues to mature. However, past experience suggests that tax rates may not have to be raised as much as is now contemplated to maintain the present program. Meanwhile, many Americans would undoubtedly agree that, given the current low level of average OASDI benefits, we can afford to increase somewhat the proportion of the national income represented by OASDI expenditures. At the same time, a strong case can be made for making improvements in the program gradually, much as we have been doing in each congressional session since 1950. There is little doubt that the economy can absorb a series of slight increases in payroll taxes more readily than a single, sharp increase.

In appraising the capacity of the economy to improve our social income-maintenance programs for older people, it is important to bear in mind the fact that additional expenditures under these programs do not necessarily mean an equivalent additional social cost. To some extent, the effect is to remove some of the burden of support from individual families, who in many cases can ill afford it. It is appropriate to remind ourselves in this connection that a middle-aged couple relieved of the burden of supporting an aged parent may be in a better position to provide higher education for teen-age sons and daughters.

### Policy Implications

On the basis of all the criteria we have discussed, some increase in OASDI benefits would seem to be in order. Yet it is clear that there is no simple or clearcut answer to the question as to what constitutes an appropriate increase. Taking into account all four criteria, I would suggest that a reasonable long-run goal would be minimum benefit levels which would provide a subsistence level of living and average benefit levels which would provide a "modest but adequate" level comparable to that described in connection with the Social Security Administration's 1948 budget for an elderly couple.[26] Given a continued rise in productivity, this goal should be attainable without undue strain on the economy in the near future.

However, since minimum and average benefit levels would appear to be substantially below these levels at present, it might be well to provide for adjusting the benefit structure in several steps. In addition, there is much to be said for certain other selective adjustments, which would cor-

[25] *Social Security Bulletin,* 22, No. 2 (February, 1959), p. 6.
[26] *Social Security Bulletin,* 11, No. 2 (February, 1948), p. 7.

rect some of the more serious inadequacies in the present benefit program, while retaining the link to previous earnings. In the absence of access to all the relevant cost estimates, I hesitate to establish priorities, but I would suggest the following adjustments as deserving of serious consideration, not necessarily in the order mentioned:

1. *Raising the ceiling on annual taxable earnings to cover the full earnings of perhaps 90 to 95 per cent of all covered workers.* This might be accomplished in several steps, but it would have the effect of both substantially increasing the related maximum benefits and strengthening the financial base of the program.

2. *Raising widow's benefits from 75 per cent to 100 per cent of the primary benefit amount.* This change would be designed to improve the relative income position of the most impoverished group in the aged population. The cost would be partially offset through a decline in the number of widows partly dependent on old-age assistance.

3. *Introducing some type of provision for health insurance under the OASDI program,* providing, at a minimum, hospital and nursing home services for aged beneficiaries. It should be emphasized, however, that *adequate* protection should include provision for surgical expenses and for medical care outside hospitals and nursing homes.

4. *Lengthening the permissible drop-out period for persons with long periods of covered earnings.* This would be a step in the direction of relating benefits to the five or ten years of highest earnings. There is a good deal to be said for this method of meeting the problem of the long-run upward trend in wages, as opposed to the method, used in many private pension plans and some foreign programs, of relating benefits to earnings in the last few years before retirement.

5. *Expanding the program of disability benefits to protect persons permanently and totally disabled before age 50.* Other changes that might be considered in the disability program are liberalizing the definition of disability to provide for serious permanent partial disability among older persons and perhaps, as Wilbur Cohen has suggested, paying the cost of rehabilitating disabled persons under the program.[27] Indeed, a more effective rehabilitation program. as has been demonstrated by a number of studies, would materially reduce the costs of institutional care for older persons.

6. *Liberalizing the retirement test,* to permit beneficiaries to supplement their retirement income more effectively through part-time earnings.

Along with these changes in OASDI, there is a need for changes in the OAA program. Here the most critical problem continues to be the low level of average monthly payments in some of the states. The new formula for federal financial contributions, adopted under the 1958 amendments, which provides a basis for slightly higher proportional payments to states with relatively low per capita incomes, represented a step toward meeting the need for greater uniformity. This formula might well be liberalized somewhat.

---

[27] Wilbur J. Cohen, "Some Issues in OASDI," in *Proceedings of the Social Security Conference, November 18–19, 1958,* Labor and Industrial Relations Center, Michigan State University, and Institute of Labor and Industrial Relations, University of Michigan and Wayne State University (East Lansing: Michigan State University, 1959), p. 8.

Another problem which should be considered in any broad examination of our income-maintenance programs for older persons, is the question of equity arising out of the multiplicity of government and private programs existing side by side. At one extreme there are the aged individuals who have never qualified for OASDI and live in states with unusually low monthly OAA payments, or those who barely qualify for minimal OASDI benefits. At the other extreme—leaving out of consideration elderly persons with ample private assets—are those fortunate individuals who can qualify for benefits under each of three or four retirement programs. In between are large numbers who may at one time have been covered by both OASDI and a second retirement program, public or private, but who shifted jobs either voluntarily or involuntarily before serving long enough to be eligible for benefits under the second program.

Although we are undoubtedly committed to a complex system of multiple programs for the indefinite future, some of the inequities could be removed through closer integration of certain programs with OASDI, as recommended by the Bradley Commission in the case of veterans' pensions. On the whole, however, the most effective way of meeting the problem of inequity is to improve the basic protection offered under OASDI.

### The Need for a Preventive Approach

In the long run, the goal of economic security for older people must be sought, not merely through income security measures for the aged, but also through greater emphasis on the preventive approach in attacking the sources of economic distress in old age. Adoption of the preventive approach implies directing attention at the *social and economic adjustments associated with aging* rather than at the *social and economic problems of old age*. It implies analyzing the sources of economic distress in old age in relation to their antecedents in an individual's earlier career.

If widowhood, illness, and obsolescence of skills are the major sources of economic distress in old age, as Steiner and Dorfman have cogently argued, we are provided with a set of clues as to where to direct at least part of our attention in developing a preventive approach.

Measures to improve employment opportunities for older men and women would be consistent with this approach. So would emphasis on research especially designed to shed light on the reasons for the relatively high incidence of ill health among aging manual workers. The problem of obsolescence of skills is likely to become even more serious in the future than it has been in the past, as a result of the current rapid pace of technological change. The preventive approach would emphasize training programs for older persons, as well as educational policies designed to equip a young man or woman to meet the shifting skill requirements of a dynamic economy throughout his or her working career.

The preventive approach to the problem of old-age security would also give explicit recognition to the interdependence of all social security programs. The individual who has received adequate unemployment insurance benefits during periods of unemployment is likely to approach retirement with more assets, including at least a mortgage-free house, than one who has experienced serious loss of income through unemployment. The disabled person who has received disability benefits is also likely to approach old age in a less weakened financial position than the victim of disability who has been unprotected by any form of social insurance. Thus, though we may not swing over to Britain's "cradle-to-grave" approach to social security, we need to take more explicit account of the impact of each program on all the others, and, specifically, on the social and economic adjustments associated with aging.

# 11. LEGISLATIVE PROVISIONS OF THE OASDI LAW

Social Security
Administration, 1959.

THE BASIC IDEA of old-age, survivors, and disability insurance under the social security law is a simple one.

*During working years employers, their employees, and self-employed people pay social security taxes which go into special funds; and*

*When earnings have stopped because the worker has retired, or died, or is disabled and is 50 years of age or over, benefit payments are made from the funds to replace part of the earnings the family has lost.*

Nine out of ten working people are building protection for themselves and their families under the social security law. If your work comes under the law, you need to know what protection it provides for you and your family.

This . . . will tell you what your social security rights and responsibilities are. It includes the changes made in the social security law by the amendments of 1958.

### Retirement Payments

When you have worked long enough to be "insured" under the social security law and have reached "retirement age," you can be paid monthly social security payments for any months in which you are "retired." Retirement age is 65 for men and 62 for women. However, if a woman decides to take the payments before she reaches age 65, she will get a permanently reduced amount.

### How Much Work Is Required to Be Insured?

The amount of work required to be "insured" depends on when you reach retirement age. A person who reached this age in June, 1954 or earlier needs about 1½ years of work; one who reaches retirement age in the first half of 1959 needs about 4 years of work; and one who reaches retirement age in the first half of 1961 about 5 years. A person who reaches retirement age in 1971 or later will need ten years.

### The Amount of Your Payments

The amount of your payments is figured from your average earnings in covered employment and self-employment up to the time you reach retirement age or up to the time you actually retire, depending on which will give you the higher benefit. The more regularly you work under social security before retirement and the higher your earnings, the higher the amount of your benefit will be. The exact amount cannot be figured until you retire and apply for the payments, but you can estimate the amount from Table 1.

TABLE 1

*Examples of Monthly Payments Beginning after 1958*

| Average monthly earnings after 1950[1] | $50 or less | $75 | $100 | $150 | $200 | $250 | $300 | $350[2] | $400[3] |
|---|---|---|---|---|---|---|---|---|---|
| Retirement at 65........⎫ Disability at 50.........⎭ | $33.00 | $45.00 | $59.00 | $73.00 | $84.00 | $95.00 | $105.00 | $116.00 | $127.00 |
| Retired woman worker starting at: | | | | | | | | | |
| 62[4]................. | 26.40 | 36.00 | 47.20 | 58.40 | 67.20 | 76.00 | 84.00 | 92.80 | 101.60 |
| 63................. | 28.60 | 39.00 | 51.20 | 63.30 | 72.80 | 82.40 | 91.00 | 100.60 | 110.10 |
| 64................. | 30.80 | 42.00 | 55.10 | 68.20 | 78.40 | 88.70 | 98.00 | 108.30 | 118.60 |
| Retired couple—wife starting at: | | | | | | | | | |
| 62[4]................. | 45.40 | 61.90 | 81.20 | 100.40 | 115.50 | 130.70 | 144.40 | 159.50 | 174.70 |
| 63................. | 46.80 | 63.80 | 83.60 | 103.50 | 119.00 | 134.60 | 148.80 | 164.40 | 180.00 |
| 64................. | 48.20 | 65.70 | 86.10 | 106.50 | 122.50 | 138.60 | 153.20 | 169.20 | 185.30 |
| 65................. | 49.50 | 67.50 | 88.50 | 109.50 | 126.00 | 142.50 | 157.50 | 174.00 | 190.50 |
| Widow, surviving child, or dependent parent....... | 33.00 | 33.80 | 44.30 | 54.80 | 63.00 | 71.30 | 78.80 | 87.00 | 95.30 |
| Widow and 1 child or 2 dependent parents....... | 49.60 | 67.60 | 88.60 | 109.60 | 126.00 | 142.60 | 157.60 | 174.00 | 190.60 |
| Widow and 2 children..... | 53.10 | 67.60 | 88.60 | 120.00 | 161.60 | 190.10 | 210.20 | 232.00 | 254.10 |
| Usual maximum family payment[5]................. | 53.00 | 67.50 | 88.50 | 120.00 | 161.60 | 202.40 | 240.00 | 254.00 | 254.00 |
| Single lump-sum death payment................. | 99.00 | 135.00 | 177.00 | 219.00 | 252.00 | 255.00 | 255.00 | 255.00 | 255.00 |

[1] In figuring your average, you may omit up to 5 years of lowest earnings, and any period your record was frozen because you were disabled.

[2] Average monthly earnings over $350 will not be possible before 1960 in most cases.

[3] A $400 monthly average will generally not be possible for anyone who has reached the age of 27 before 1959.

[4] Retirement payments to women are permanently reduced if started before age 65.

[5] In some cases, payments to a family will be a few cents higher than the amounts shown in this line because each person's benefit is rounded to the next higher 10 cents.

If you are a woman, your retirement payments can start when you reach age 62. But if you decide to take the payments before you reach age 65, you will get a permanently reduced amount.

### The Meaning of "Retired"

You do not need to stop work entirely to be considered "retired" under the social security law.

You can earn up to $1,200 a year and still get all your social security payments for that year.

You can earn up to $2,080 and still get some payments.

Even if you earn over $2,080, you can still get payments for months you don't work. You can get a payment for any month you neither work for wages of more than $100 nor render substantial services in self-employment.

Any income you may have from insurance or investments is not counted as earnings for social security purposes.

After age 72 you may receive payments regardless of how much you earn.

### Your Application for Payments

When you receive old-age or disability benefits, payments can also be made to certain of your dependents:

Your unmarried children under 18 years of age;

Your children over 18 who were disabled before they reached 18 and have remained so since;

Your wife, regardless of her age, if she is caring for a child who is getting payments based on your social security account;

Your wife at age 62 or over whether or not there are children entitled to payments;

Your dependent husband at age 65 or over.

If a wife chooses to start getting payments before she is 65 she gets a reduced amount for as long as she receives wife's benefits, unless she is caring for a child who is getting payments on her husband's account.

Benefits may be paid to the husband of a woman receiving retirement benefits if the husband is 65 or over and was receiving at least half his support from his wife at the time she started receiving retirement payments.

Monthly payments to the aged wife or dependent husband of a person entitled to old-age insurance payments can be made after the marriage has been in effect at least 3 years.

If the couple are parents of a child, or if the wife or dependent husband was entitled to social security payments on the account of another person at the time of the marriage (or could have become entitled by filing an application), the 3-year waiting period is not required.

### Increasing Payments by Additional Work

If it will result in higher benefits, you may have your benefit refigured *after the end of the year in which you applied* to include your earnings for that year. Also, if you have earnings over $1,200 covered by the law in *any later year*, you may have your benefit refigured by filing application 6 months after that year.

### Survivors' Payments

In case of your death certain members of your family can get monthly payments if you have worked long enough under the law.

In addition, a single lump-sum payment can be made to your widow or widower if she or he was living with you in the same household. Otherwise, the lump-sum payment can go to repay the person who paid your burial expenses. The lump-sum is three times the amount of your monthly retirement benefit, but it cannot exceed $255.

### Who Can Get Survivors' Payments

Survivors' insurance payments can go to:

Your unmarried children under 18 years of age.
Your children 18 or over if they were disabled before reaching 18 and have remained so since.
Your widow at age 62 whether or not there is a child entitled to payments.
Your dependent widower at age 65.
Your dependent parents (father 65, mother 62).
Your divorced wife, if she has in her care your child who is also entitled to payments.

For an aged widow or widower to get benefits the marriage must have been in effect for at least 1 year.

### Benefit Amounts

A person who becomes entitled to more than one benefit payment in effect receives only the largest of the amounts.

#### Amount of Your Family's Benefits

| The monthly payment to your— | Is this part of your monthly amount:* |
|---|---|
| Wife† | One-half |
| Child (when you have retired) | One-half |
| Dependent husband | One-half |
| Widow | Three-fourths |
| Each child (after your death) | One-half (plus an additional one-fourth divided equally among all your children) |
| Dependent widower | Three-fourths |
| Dependent parent | Three-fourths |

* Except where dependents' or survivors' benefits must be reduced to keep the total family payments within the maximum provided in the law.
† See special reduction provisions in effect between age 62 and 65.

If either the deceased worker or the widow were married to someone else before they married one another, the widow should bring along a death certificate for the former spouse, or divorce papers if the marriage ended in divorce, family letters or other documents, or even newspaper clippings reporting the death or divorce. However, a widow should not delay filing her application because she does not have some of these papers available.

### How Much Work Is Required?

Payments may be made to a widow with a child in her care, and to the child, if at the time of death the worker was either "fully insured" or "currently insured." Benefits for parents and widows aged 62 or over without children require a fully insured status; a widower's payments require both fully and currently insured status.

The amount of work needed to be fully insured at death is always at least 1½ years and never more than 10 years. Within these limits the exact amount required depends on the date of death and on the person's age at death.

A person is currently insured at death if he has credit for at least 1½ years' work in the 3 years before his death.

### The Retirement Test Applies to Both Dependents and Survivors

Monthly survivors' insurance benefits under the law are intended to replace, in part, the earnings lost to the family because of the death of the family breadwinner. These payments are subject to the same earnings test as the one for retired workers: payments to a survivor are withheld for one or more months of the year if he or she works and earns more than $1,200 in the year.

### An Application Is Necessary

Survivors' insurance payments cannot start until an application has been made. In case of the death of a person who has worked under the social security law, some member of the family should get in touch with the social security office promptly.

Back payments can be made if the application is not filed in the first month for which benefits are payable, but back payments cannot be made for more than 12 months.

The application for a lump-sum payment must be made within 2 years after the worker's death unless good cause can be shown.

### DISABILITY PROTECTION

### Disabled Workers

If you become disabled after working long enough under social security and are 50 years old but less than age 65, you may qualify for monthly disability benefits, and certain members of your family may also be paid monthly benefits, just as if you were a retired worker.

If you are disabled after working long enough under social security, and are not yet 50, you should apply to have your earnings record "frozen." This "freeze" will protect your future benefits (at age 50 or retirement age) from being lowered or forfeited. A freeze also protects benefit rights for members of your family.

### Disabled Children

A disabled child of a retired insured worker, or of an insured worker who has died, may receive child's benefits even after reaching 18 years of age if he or she—

Is disabled according to the terms of the social security law;

Became disabled before reaching 18 years of age and has remained so ever since; and

Is unmarried at the time of application.

A disabled child needs no work credits to be eligible for payments.

The mother of a disabled child entitled to benefits may also be entitled to monthly payments if the child is in her care.

### How Disabled Must You Be?

To be found disabled under the social security law, you must have a condition so severe that, in the words of the law, it makes you unable to "engage in any substantial gainful activity."

Your disability must be the kind of physical or mental condition which will show up in medical examinations or tests. It must have lasted for at least 6 months, and be expected to continue for a long and indefinite time.

If your handicap is poor eyesight, the decision as to whether you are "disabled" under the law will depend on whether you are able to do substantial work. There is, however, a special provision which entitles people who are totally blind (as defined in the law) to have their social security records frozen even if they are able to work.

### How Much Work Is Required?

To have your social security earnings record frozen or to get disability insurance payments at age 50 or over, you must have social security credits for at least 5 years of work out of the 10 years before you became disabled. (In addition you must be fully insured, but since everyone who has credit for 5 years of work is fully insured until June 30, 1961, this requirement will not affect anyone until then.)

### Proof of Your Disability

When you apply for the disability "freeze" or for disability insurance benefits your social security office will give you a medical report form which you should have filled in by your doctor or by a hospital or clinic where you have had treatment. You are responsible for whatever charges the doctors or hospital may make for their services.

*Your doctors are not asked to decide whether or not you are "disabled" under the social security law.* That decision is made by an agency of your state under an agreement between the state and the federal government. A team of trained people in the state agency (doctors and others who have had experience in seeing the effects of disabling conditions upon people's ability to work) will make the decision after considering the medical evidence and other information as to whether you can do any substantial gainful work—your education, your training, the kinds of work you have done in the past, and your other abilities.

### Vocational Rehabilitation and Special Employment Services

When you apply for disability benefits or for a disability "freeze," your state vocational rehabilitation agency will be notified. That agency will decide whether you can benefit from rehabilitation services, and if so, what kinds of services will be most helpful to you.

By contacting the local office of your state employment service, you may also get employment counseling and selective employment services.

People found eligible for disability insurance benefits (or for disabled child's benefits) will not be paid those benefits if, without good cause, they refuse rehabilitation services offered to them by their state vocational rehabilitation agencies.

### The Amount of Your Disability Benefit

The amount of your monthly disability insurance payments depends on your average monthly earnings as shown in your social security record. It is the same as the amount of the old-age insurance benefit you would get if you were already 65. You can estimate the amount of the payment to yourself and your dependents from Table 1.

### When Disability Stops

When you apply for disability benefits you will be given a post card form which should be completed and mailed if you return to work.

If you become able to engage in substantial gainful activity and are therefore no longer "disabled" under the law, your benefits, as well as the payments to your dependents, will be stopped.

If you should go to work as part of the rehabilitation program given by your state vocational rehabilitation agency, your disability benefits (and any payments to your dependents) may be paid for as long as a year while you are testing out your work capacity.

If you take a job or go into a business, not as a part of a planned rehabilitation program of your state vocational rehabilitation agency, benefit payments can sometimes be continued for a trial period of 3 months.

When you reach age 65, if you are still receiving disability benefits, your payments will automatically be changed from disability payments to retirement payments.

When a disabled worker's benefits are not payable, his dependents' benefits also stop. Benefits paid to a mother because she has a disabled child in her care are stopped when the disabled child's benefits are no longer payable.

If a person receiving benefits as the dependent of a disability insurance beneficiary works and earns more than $1,200 a year, he will not be due one or more of the monthly benefit checks.

## Amount of Work Required

To get monthly payments for yourself and your family, or if your survivors are to get payments in case of your death, you must have been in work covered by the social security law for a certain length of time.

The amount of work required is measured in "quarters of coverage." A quarter of coverage corresponds in a general way with a calendar quarter of work.

A calendar quarter is a 3-month period beginning January 1, April 1, July 1, or October 1 of any year. The exact meaning of a quarter of coverage is different, however, for certain different kinds of work.

For most kinds of employment you get one quarter of coverage for each calendar quarter in which you are paid $50 or more in wages.

If you are self-employed and have net earnings of $400 or more in a year, you get four quarters of coverage for that year. (If your earnings from self-employment are less than $400 in a year, they do not count toward social security benefits.)

If you are a farm worker you get one quarter of coverage for each $100 of cash wages covered by the law paid to you in a year.

However, no matter how much or little you earn in any single calendar quarter, you get four quarters of coverage for any year from 1951 through 1954 in which your total earnings were $3,600 or more, and for any year from 1955 through 1958 in which your total earnings were $4,200 or more. Beginning with 1959, you get four quarters of coverage for any year in which your earnings are $4,800 or more.

No matter how much you earn, you cannot get more than four quarters of coverage for any one year.

You may have earned quarters of coverage by working in an employment covered by the law at any time after 1936 and in self-employment covered by the law after 1950.

The number of quarters of coverage you have is used only in figuring whether or not you are insured. Your quarters of coverage do not determine the amount of your payments. The amount of your payments depends on the amount of your average earnings.

## Fully Insured

Just how many quarters of coverage you must have to be fully insured depends upon the date you reach retirement age, or if you die or become disabled before reaching retirement age, upon the date of your death or disability.

You will be fully insured on reaching retirement age if you have the number of quarters of coverage shown in Table 2. (Retirement age is

65 for men, 62 for women; if you do not have enough quarters of coverage when you reach retirement age, you may earn them after that time.) Look in the fourth column if you reach retirement age in the first half of the year and in the fifth column if you reach retirement age in the last half.

TABLE 2

*Quarters of Coverage Needed*

| Year in which you were born | | Year in which you | | |
|---|---|---|---|---|
| Men | Women | reach retirement age | Jan.–June | July–Dec. |
| 1888 or earlier..... | 1891 or earlier..... | 1953 or earlier..... | 6 | 6 |
| 1889............. | 1892............. | 1954............. | 6 | 7 |
| 1890............. | 1893............. | 1955............. | 8 | 9 |
| 1891............. | 1894............. | 1956............. | 10 | 11 |
| 1892............. | 1895............. | 1957............. | 12 | 13 |
| 1893............. | 1896............. | 1958............. | 14 | 15 |
| 1894............. | 1897............. | 1959............. | 16 | 17 |
| 1895............. | 1898............. | 1960............. | 18 | 19 |
| 1896............. | 1899............. | 1961............. | 20 | 21 |
| 1897............. | 1900............. | 1962............. | 22 | 23 |
| 1898............. | 1901............. | 1963............. | 24 | 25 |
| 1899............. | 1902............. | 1964............. | 26 | 27 |
| 1900............. | 1903............. | 1965............. | 28 | 29 |
| 1901............. | 1904............. | 1966............. | 30 | 31 |
| 1902............. | 1905............. | 1967............. | 32 | 33 |
| 1903............. | 1906............. | 1968............. | 34 | 35 |
| 1904............. | 1907............. | 1969............. | 36 | 37 |
| 1905............. | 1908............. | 1970............. | 38 | 39 |
| 1906 or later...... | 1909 or later...... | 1971 or later...... | 40 | 40 |

You will be fully insured at the time you become disabled or die if at that time you have one quarter of coverage (earned at any time after 1936) for each two full calendar quarters after 1950. In counting the number of calendar quarters after 1950, omit:

Quarters in which you were under 21 years of age.
Quarters during which your earnings record was frozen because you were disabled.

In no case can you become fully insured with less than six quarters of coverage; and no matter what your date of birth, you will never need more than 40 quarters of coverage to be fully insured. A fully insured status, however, affects only your eligibility for benefits, not the amount.

## Currently Insured

You will be currently insured if you have at least six quarters of coverage within the 3 years before you die or become eligible for retirement benefits. (Not all kinds of benefits are payable when the worker is only currently insured.)

Table 3 shows for each type of social security benefit whether the worker must be fully insured, currently insured, or both.

## TABLE 3

### Retirement Payments

| Monthly payments to— | If you are— |
|---|---|
| You as a retired worker.................... | Fully insured |
| *And monthly payments to your—* | |
| Wife 62 or over........................... | Fully insured |
| Dependent child (under 18)................. | Fully insured |
| Dependent child 18 or over who became totally disabled before that age................... | Fully insured |
| Wife (regardless of age) if caring for child..... | Fully insured |
| Dependent husband 65 or over.............. | *Both* fully and currently insured |

### Survivors' Payments

| Monthly payments to your— | If at death you are— |
|---|---|
| Widow 62 or over......................... | Fully insured |
| Widow or dependent divorced wife (regardless of age) if caring for your child who is entitled to benefits............................. | Either fully or currently insured |
| Dependent child (under 18)................. | Either fully or currently insured |
| Dependent child 18 or over who became disabled before that age..................... | Either fully or currently insured |
| Dependent widower 65 or over.............. | *Both* fully and currently insured |
| Dependent parent (mother 62 or father 65).... | Fully insured |
| *Lump-sum payment to your—* | |
| Widow or widower, if living with you in the same household, or if he or she paid your burial expenses. Otherwise, the lump-sum can go to the person who paid your burial expenses................................ | Either fully or currently insured |

### Disability Payments

| Monthly payments to— | If you are fully insured and have— |
|---|---|
| You and your dependents* when you are aged 50–64 if you are totally disabled for work.... | 20 quarters of coverage in the 40 calendar quarters before the beginning date of your disability |

\* By dependents is meant the same members of a family listed as dependents of a retired worker.

## Social Security Taxes

Federal old-age, survivors', and disability insurance benefits are paid for by a tax based on the worker's earnings.

If you are employed, you and your employer share the tax equally. If you are self-employed, you pay the tax at a lower rate than the combined rate for an employee and his employer.

As long as you have earnings that are covered by the law, you continue to pay the social security tax regardless of your age and even though you may be receiving social security benefits.

*How Taxes Are Paid.* If you are employed, your tax is deducted from your wages each payday. Your employer sends it, with an equal amount as his own share of the tax, to the District Director of Internal Revenue.

If you are self-employed and your net earnings are $400 or more in a year, you must report your earnings and pay your social security self-employment tax even if you are not required to pay any income tax.

The tax does not apply to earnings in excess of $4,200 for 1958; beginning with 1959, earnings up to $4,800 in a year will be taxable for social security purposes. Self-employed persons will first pay at this increased rate for 1959 with the income tax return they make early in 1960.

If you have earnings from both employment and self-employment, your employers deduct from your pay the tax on your wages; if your wages amount to less than the maximum creditable in a year, you must pay the self-employment tax on your net earnings from self-employment. If your combined earnings for a year from self-employment and wages exceed the maximum creditable for social security purposes, you pay only on the part of your net earnings from self-employment necessary to bring the total up to the maximum.

Your wages and self-employment income are entered on your individual record by the Social Security Administration. This record of your earnings will be used to determine your eligibility for benefits and the amount you will receive.

The law does not provide for a refund of the social security taxes paid except when more than the required amount of contributions has been paid.

### The Trust Funds

The social security taxes collected by the Internal Revenue Service are deposited in the Federal Old-Age and Survivors' Insurance Trust Fund and the Federal Disability Insurance Trust Fund and are used to pay the benefits and administrative expenses of the program. They may be used for no other purpose. The portion of the trust funds not required for current disbursement is invested in interest-bearing United States Government securities.

This table shows the present tax rates and scheduled increases:

| Calendar Year | Employee | Employer | Self-Employed |
|---|---|---|---|
| 1960–62 | 3 | 3 | 4½ |
| 1963–65 | 3½ | 3½ | 5¼ |
| 1966–68 | 4 | 4 | 6 |
| 1969 and after | 4½ | 4½ | 6¾ |

This schedule of tax rates is designed to meet the future obligations of the program and keep it on a self-supporting basis.

### If You Work after Payments Start

When you apply for old-age or survivors' insurance benefits, your social security office will give you complete information on how your earnings will affect your benefit payments and will tell you when and how to make reports to the Social Security Administration. The explanation that follows is intended to give you a general idea of the conditions under which benefits may be paid to people who are still working.

### Beneficiaries Who Earn $1,200 or Less in a Year

A retired worker, a dependent of a retired or disabled worker, or a survivor who does not earn more than $1,200 in a year can get benefit checks for all 12 months of the year.

### Beneficiaries Who Earn More than $1,200 in a Year

If in a year before you reach 72 you earn more than $1,200, the number of monthly benefit checks due you for that year will depend on the amount of your total earnings and on how much work you did in each month. The following table shows how earnings of more than $1,200 for a year may reduce the number of monthly benefits payable to you.

| Annual Earnings | Reduces Number of Monthly Checks Payable by | Annual Earnings | Reduces Number of Monthly Checks Payable by |
|---|---|---|---|
| $1,200.01–$1,280 | 1 | $1,680.01–$1,760 | 7 |
| 1,280.01– 1,360 | 2 | 1,760.01– 1,840 | 8 |
| 1,360.01– 1,440 | 3 | 1,840.01– 1,920 | 9 |
| 1,440.01– 1,520 | 4 | 1,920.01– 2,000 | 10 |
| 1,520.01– 1,600 | 5 | 2,000.01– 2,080 | 11 |
| 1,600.01– 1,680 | 6 | 2,080.01–or more | 12 |

BUT regardless of the above:

*Beginning in 1959, no matter how much you earn in a year, you can get the monthly payment for any month in which you neither earn wages of more than $100 nor render substantial services in self-employment.*

If you are a self-employed person, the decision as to whether you are rendering "substantial services" will be based on the facts in your particular case.

When a retired or disabled worker is not due a benefit check for a certain month, no checks are payable for that month to his dependents whose benefits are based on his account.

The earnings of a person who is receiving benefits as a dependent or as a survivor affect only his own benefits and will not stop payments to other members of his family.

*Earnings from work of any kind,* whether or not it is covered by the social security law, *must be counted* in deciding the number of monthly benefit checks due a beneficiary for a year. Total wages (not just take-home pay) and any net earnings from self-employment must ordinarily be added together in figuring up your earnings for the year. However, income from savings, investments, pensions, and insurance does not affect your old-age or survivors' insurance benefits and should not be counted in your earnings.

*In the year in which you first become entitled to benefits,* your total earnings for the year including months before and after age 65 must be counted in determining how many benefit checks can be paid to you. For example, if you reach 65 and apply for old-age benefits in June, and if your total earnings for the year amount to $1,440, the number of checks payable to you for the 7-month period, June through December, would, according to the table, be reduced by three checks. This assumes there were at least 3 months during the June-December period in which you earned more than $100 each month. Of course, a benefit could be paid for all of these months if you earned $100 or less each month.

After you reach age 72 your benefits are payable to you no matter how much you earn from then on. But your earnings for the entire taxable year in which you reach 72 must be counted in determining whether payments can be made to you for the months in that year before your 72d birthday.

## Beneficiaries Outside the United States

Special rules affect the payment of old-age, survivors' and disability benefits to people outside the United States. If you intend to leave the United States while you are receiving benefits, get more information about these rules from your social security office.

## Events That Stop Payments

If one of the events listed below occurs, payments are stopped. The last check due is the one for the month before the event.

Generally, if a person receiving monthly benefit payments as a dependent or as a survivor marries a person who is not also a beneficiary, his or her right to payments stops. However, if the beneficiary marries another adult beneficiary, payments to both may continue. Moreover, if a widow remarries and her second husband dies within a year after their marriage and is not fully insured, she may regain her right to any benefits payable to her at age 62 under the social security account of her first husband.

Payments to a wife or dependent husband are ended if a divorce is granted.

Payments to a wife or widow under 62, or the divorced wife of a deceased insured person, will stop when she no longer has in her care a child who is also entitled to monthly payments.

Payments to a child under 18 stop when the child marries.

When a child entitled to benefits reaches age 18, his payments are stopped unless he is disabled. When the child of a deceased insured person is adopted, his payments end unless the adopting person is the child's stepparent, grandparent, aunt, or uncle.

When any person receiving monthly benefit dies, his or her payments are ended. If a person receiving disability benefits recovers or returns to work, his payments (and any payments to his dependents) will stop.

If a person is convicted of treason, espionage, sabotage, sedition, or other subversive activities, the court may revoke his right to any old-age, survivors', or disability insurance benefits based on earnings before the conviction. Benefits to his dependents and survivors are not affected.

If a person receiving payments is deported from the United States, his benefits are stopped. Benefits to his dependents and survivors who are citizens of the United States or who are in the United States are not affected.

## KINDS OF WORK COVERED

### Military Service

*For Active Duty in 1957 or Later.*  If you perform active duty or active duty for training as a member of the uniformed services of the United States after 1956, your service counts toward social security protection for you and your family. Your base pay is credited to your social security record.

Your share of the social security tax for your old-age, survivors', and disability insurance protection will be deducted from your military base pay just as the social security tax of a civilian employee is deducted from his wages. The government, as your employer, will pay an equal amount.

*For Active Duty before 1957.*  If you were on active duty in the military or naval forces of the United States during the World War II period (September 16, 1940, through July 24, 1947) or the post–World War II period (July 25, 1947, through December 31, 1956), you may be eligible for social security wage credits of $160 for each month of this active duty, provided your discharge or release was under conditions other than dishonorable. (Ninety days of active service are required unless discharge or release was because of disability or injury incurred or aggravated in line of duty.) These wage credits may be granted to those who died in service as well as to those who died after discharge.

In general, you do not get social security wage credits for one of these periods if monthly payments based in whole or in part on the same period are payable by the military organization or by another federal agency (except the Veterans Administration). The World War II period and the post–World War II period are treated separately. However, if you have active military service after 1956, you will receive wage credits for any active service after 1950 and before 1957 even though you get retired pay from your service department based on that service.

Wage credits of $160 a month are also provided for certain American citizens who before December 9, 1941, entered the military service of a foreign country which was, on September 16, 1940, at war with a country that became an enemy of the United States during World War II.

Credits for military service before January 1, 1957, count the same as wages in civilian employment. These credits are not actually listed on your social security earnings record until you apply for retirement or disability benefits, or when an application is made for survivors' benefits in the event of your death. At that time proof of your military service will be needed.

## Farming

Your net earnings from self-employment as the operator of a farm or ranch count toward benefits for you and your family if (alone or combined with your earnings from any other self-employment covered by social security) they amount to $400 or more in a year.

*Figuring Self-Employment Earnings from Farming.* If you are a self-employed farmer you must report your net earnings from self-employment as a part of your income tax return. You may be able to use either your actual net earnings or an amount figured under an optional method.

For taxable years ending on or after December 31, 1956,

If your gross income from farming is $1,800 or less, you may count as your net earnings from farming either your actual net earnings or two-thirds of your gross farm income.

If your gross farm income is more than $1,800 and your net farm earnings are less than $1,200 you may count as your net earnings from farming either your actual net earnings or $1,200.

If your gross farm income is more than $1,800 and your net farm earnings are $1,200 or more you must use the actual amount of your net earnings.

*Farm Rentals.* The cash or crop shares you receive from a tenant or share-farmer will count for social security purposes if under your arrangements with the tenant or share-farmer you "participate materially" in the production of the crops or livestock or in the management of the production.

In order to "participate materially" you must take an important part in the management decisions or in the actual production.

*Share Farmers.* If you farm land owned by someone else and the crops or livestock you produce are divided between you and the landlord under an ordinary crop-sharing arrangement, with your share depending on the total amount produced, then you are considered a self-employed farmer for social security purposes. This is true even if the landlord takes an active part in the farm operations.

*Farmworkers.* If you worked for a farmer or ranch operator in 1955 or 1956 you are entitled to social security credit if the farmer paid you $100 or more in cash wages in the calendar year.

Beginning with 1957 your cash wages from farmwork count toward social security benefits under either of these conditions:

If an employer pays you $150 or more in cash during the year for farmwork, *or*

If you do farmwork for an employer on 20 or more days during the year for cash wages figured on a time basis (rather than on a piece-rate basis).

For the $150-a-year test, the cash wages for both piece-rate and time-rate work counts. The total number of days worked does not matter so long as you are paid $150 in cash by the employer in the year.

For the 20-day test, the total amount of your wages does not matter so long as you work for one employer on 20 days or more for cash wages based on some unit of time such as an hour, a day, or a week.

Household workers employed on a farm or ranch operated for profit are covered under the same rules as other farm employees.

*Farm Labor Crews and Crew Leaders.* Cash wages paid to members of a farm labor crew are covered by the social security law under the same rules that apply to other farmworkers.

The crew leader is the employer of the crew members if he both furnishes them to the farmer and pays them (regardless of whether he pays them on his own behalf or for the farmer), *unless* the crew leader and the farmer have a written agreement which shows that the crew leader is the farmer's employee.

If the farm operator and the crew leader have a written agreement which shows that the crew leader is the farmer's employee, then the crew members are also the farmer's employees.

*If there is no such written agreement and the crew leader does not pay the crew members, then whoever has the final right to control the work is the employer.*

### American Citizens Working Abroad

United States citizens employed by American employers in foreign countries or aboard vessels or aircraft of foreign registry are covered by social security. (Seamen and airmen employed on American vessels or aircraft are ordinarily covered regardless of citizenship.)

United States citizens working abroad for a foreign subsidiary of a United States corporation may be covered by the law if the parent corporation makes an agreement with the Secretary of the Treasury to see that social security taxes are paid for all United States citizens employed abroad by the foreign subsidiary.

### Household Workers

A domestic worker's cash wages (including carfare if paid in cash) from an employer for work in a private household are covered by the law if they amount to $50 or more in a calendar quarter regardless of the number of days on which the employee worked in that quarter.

If you employ a household worker who will come under the law and you are not receiving the forms for making the tax reports, ask your social security office or your Internal Revenue Service office for a copy of Leaflet OASI-21, "Do You Have a Maid?" This leaflet explains how to get the forms and make the reports.

A person employed to do industrial work at home—piecework, quilting, needlework products, etc.—is covered by the law if the cash wages paid by his employer amount to $50 or more in a calendar quarter.

### Employees of Nonprofit Organizations

Some organizations are exempt from payment of income tax because none of their earnings goes to the benefit of any private shareholder or individual. These are referred to as "nonprofit" organizations, and their employees are covered by social security under certain conditions.

Employees of nonprofit organizations are covered by the law only if they earn $50 or more in wages in a calendar quarter. Employees of nonprofit organizations operated exclusively for religious, charitable, scientific, literary, educational, or humane purposes, or for testing for public safety may be covered by the law only if—

The organization files with the Director of Internal Revenue a certificate (Form SS-15) waiving its exemption from the payment of social security taxes, and

At least two-thirds of the employees indicate their desire to participate in social security by signing the Form SS-15a that goes with the certificate.

If these conditions are met, the employees who signed will come under social security, but the employees who did not sign will not be covered.

### Employees of State and Local Governments

Since the beginning of 1951 the law has provided for covering state and local government employees who are not under a state or local retirement system under voluntary agreements between the individual state and the federal government.

Since January 1, 1955, a state has been permitted to bring employees (except policemen or firemen) who are under a state or local retirement system under its old-age and survivors' insurance agreement with the federal government. This can be done if a referendum is held among the members of the system and a majority of the members eligible to vote in the referendum vote in favor of old-age and survivors' insurance coverage.

The Social Security Act provides for the coverage of certain state and local government employees, including policemen and firemen, under special provisions which apply only to certain states.

The law states it is the policy of Congress, in making coverage available to retirement system members, that coverage under old-age and survivors' insurance shall not impair the protection of members and beneficiaries under the existing retirement system.

### Federal Employment

Most employees of the federal government *not* covered by another federal retirement system are covered by social security.

## Ministers and Members of Religious Orders

Ordained, commissioned, or licensed ministers performing services in the exercise of their ministry, Christian Science practitioners, and members of religious orders who have not taken a vow of poverty can secure social security coverage by filing with the Internal Revenue Service a certificate (Form 2031) indicating their desire to be covered as self-employed persons.

In general, the certificate must be filed by the due date of the clergyman's income tax return for his second taxable year ending after 1954 in which he has net earnings from self-employment of at least $400, some part of which was derived from the exercise of his ministry. A clergyman who had such earnings in any two of the years 1955 through 1958 must have filed his waiver on or before April 15, 1959. If a waiver certificate is not filed within the appropriate time limit, the clergyman will be permanently barred from obtaining social security coverage as a self-employed minister, Christian Science practitioner, or member of a religious order.

Beginning with taxable years ending on and after December 31, 1957, net earnings from self-employment include, for social security tax purposes, the rental value of a parsonage (or rental allowance) and the value of meals and lodging furnished to the clergyman (but not to a Christian Science practitioner) for the convenience of his employer. These amounts, however, continue to be exempt for federal income tax purposes.

## Railroad Employment

A retired worker who has at least 120 months (10 years) of railroad service and who has also done enough work under social security to qualify for social security payments may receive retirement benefits under both the railroad retirement and old-age, survivors', and disability insurance systems. When a railroad worker retires with fewer than 120 months of railroad service, no railroad retirement annuity is payable and his railroad earnings after 1936 are considered in determining his disability or old-age payments under social security.

Survivors of a worker can be entitled under one system only, either railroad retirement or old-age, survivors', and disability insurance, even though the worker may have been entitled during his lifetime under both. Regardless of which program pays, records of the deceased worker's railroad earnings after 1936 and his earnings under social security will be combined to determine whether he is insured and the amount of any payments to survivors.

If the worker was receiving a railroad retirement pension or annuity at the time of his death, any payment to his survivor is ordinarily made by the Railroad Retirement Board. Also, the Railroad Retirement Board usually makes payment to the survivor if the deceased railroad worker had 120 months or more of railroad service and no substantial amount of regular employment after his last 12 months of railroad service.

If the deceased worker did not have as many as 120 months of railroad service, and under certain other circumstances, the Social Security Administration makes payment to the survivor.

Railroad workers or their survivors may get further information from the nearest social security or railroad retirement office, or they may write to the Railroad Retirement Board, 844 Rush Street, Chicago 11, Ill.

### Work Not Covered

The principal kinds of work not covered are self-employment as a doctor of medicine and employment in most federal jobs covered by a federal retirement system.

Any work performed as an employee by a parent for his son or daughter, by a child under 21 for his parent, by a husband for his wife, or by a wife for her husband is not covered by social security. This applies also to foster or step-relationships. Services performed as an employee of a partnership are not covered if any of the family relationships mentioned above exists between the employee and each of the partners. Services performed by or for "in-laws" and relatives other than those named above are covered provided a genuine employment relationship exists.

Work for an organization which is registered or has received a final order to register under the Internal Security Act of 1950 as a Communist-front, Communist-action, or Communist-infiltrated organization is not covered by the law beginning with the effective date of the final order or July 1, 1956, whichever is later.

### Right of Appeal

If you are not satisfied with the action taken on your claim, you may ask the Bureau of Old-Age and Survivors Insurance to reconsider it. If you wish to have a hearing on your claim, you may ask for a hearing by a referee of the Appeals Council regardless of whether or not it has been reconsidered by the Bureau. There is no charge for reconsidering your claim or for review or hearing by the referee.

Your social security office will explain how you may appeal and will help you to get your claim reconsidered or reviewed.

After you receive notice of the referee's decision, if you are not satisfied with it you may ask for a review by the Appeals Council of the Social Security Administration in Washington.

If you are not satisfied with the decision of the Appeals Council, you may wish to take your case to the federal courts.

### Account Number Cards

If your work is covered by the Social Security Act, you must have a social security account number. This account number, which is shown on your social security card, is used to keep a record of your earnings. You should use the same account number all your life.

There are more than 160 million names in the social security records, and some of them may be names exactly like yours. Your social security account number keeps your account from being confused with the social security account of anyone else.

Both your name and account number are needed to make sure you get full credit for your earnings. If you are employed, show your card to each employer so that he may use your name and account number exactly as they appear on the card when he reports your wages. If you are self-employed, copy your name and account number on the form you use to report your net earnings for social security credit.

Your nearest social security office will issue you a social security card or a duplicate card to replace one that has been lost. If there is no social security office in your town, ask at the post office for an application blank.

If your name has been changed, ask your social security office for a new card showing the same account number and your new name.

### Checking Your Account

Each employer is required by law to give you receipts for the social security taxes he has deducted from your pay. He must do this at the end of each year and also when you stop working for him. These receipts (Form W-2) will help you check on your social security account because they show not only the amount deducted from your pay but also the wages paid you. For some kinds of work, this includes your wages paid in forms other than cash—for instance, the value of meals or living quarters must generally be included. For work in a private household or on a farm, however, only cash wages count.

You should keep a record of the amount of self-employment income you have reported. In figuring your earnings, do not include income from investments, pensions, or insurance policies.

You may check the official social security record of wages and self-employment income credited to you by writing to the Social Security Administration, Baltimore 2, Md., and asking for a statement of your account. You can get an addressed post-card form at your social security office for use in requesting this information.

If an error has been made in your account, the social security office will help you get it corrected. You should check on your account at least once in 3 years, since there is a limit to the period within which certain corrections can be made.

### Social Security Offices

The Social Security Administration has district offices conveniently located throughout the country. These offices have representatives who go regularly to other communities to serve the public.

If you have any questions about social security, call at one of these district offices or get in touch with it by telephone or mail. The people who work there will be glad to answer questions and to explain your rights. They will:

Issue you a social security account number card.
Help you get a statement of the earnings credited to your social security account.
Assist you in correcting any errors in your account.
Help you with your application to have your earnings record "frozen" if you are disabled.
Assist you in filing a claim for old-age, survivors', or disability insurance benefits.
Assist you in reporting events that might affect your benefit payments if you are already a beneficiary.
Give you general information or booklets about your rights and responsibilities under the program.
Assist groups or organizations to inform their members about social security through talks, films, and other activities.

To find the address of the social security office in your locality, ask at your post office or look in the telephone directory under United States Government, Department of Health, Education, and Welfare, Social Security Administration.

# 12. BASIC CHARACTERISTICS OF OASDI

CHARLES I. SCHOTTLAND, "Where Are We in This Business of Social Security?" *California Law Review,* August, 1958.

THE PROGRAM TODAY may best be described by nine main characteristics.

## 1. Coverage Is Almost Universal

A basic premise of the system is that all persons, regardless of income level or type of employment, should be covered by the system.

Limited in its original coverage to wage earners in industry and commerce, the old-age, survivors, and disability insurance program has been expanded until it now covers, or makes eligible for coverage, nine-tenths of all gainfully employed workers, including the self-employed. For some years now, as many as 90 per cent of the nation's children and their mothers have had survivorship protection that assures them of a monthly income if the family breadwinner were to die.

The background studies of the Committee on Economic Security recognized that the risk of loss of livelihood in old age was so nearly universal that the coverage of the old-age benefits program should be as broad as possible. Nevertheless, administrative, constitutional and other special considerations dictated the congressional decision to cover only employment in industry and commerce, where accurate wage reporting could be obtained through relatively simple additions to employers' regular book-keeping practices.

The 1950 amendments brought in categories of work for which coverage had appeared too difficult administratively in the beginning—regularly employed agricultural and domestic workers and most self-employed persons other than farmers. While continuing in general to apply the principles of compulsory coverage, these amendments provided elective coverage on a group basis for state and local government employees who were not already covered by retirement systems—elective because constitutional barriers generally preclude taxation of state and local governments. The amendments also provided elective coverage on a group basis for employees of nonprofit organizations; these organizations objected to compulsory coverage as a threat to their traditionally tax exempt status.

The 1954 amendments extended coverage to self-employed farmers, to ministers (on an individual election basis, because of special considerations), and to most state and local government employees covered by retirement systems. Also, more agricultural and domestic workers were covered by broadening the definition of regularly employed.

Lawyers were covered through the 1956 amendments, on the same basis as other self-employed persons, after the Congress had been convinced that a majority of the members of the profession wished to be included in the system. Similarly, coverage was extended in 1956 to other self-employed professional groups—dentists, chiropractors, veterinarians, naturopaths, osteopaths, and optometrists—but not to doctors of medicine, who have, through the American Medical Association, opposed coverage of physicians.

Amendments in 1956 also extended coverage to members of the armed forces on the regular compulsory, contributory basis used for civilian employment.

Thus, the scope of the program has gradually been broadened until more than nine-tenths of all gainfully employed persons are covered or could be covered by election. The only major exclusions from coverage today are self-employed physicians, many policemen and firemen with their own retirement systems, federal employees under the Civil Service Retirement system, very low-income self-employed persons, and farm and domestic workers with irregular employment.

As to geographical coverage, the 1935 act applied only to the continental United States and to Alaska and Hawaii. Now coverage also applies to Puerto Rico and the Virgin Islands and to American citizens working abroad for American employers.

The insurance program has thus gone a long way toward meeting the goal of universal coverage envisaged by the Committee on Economic Security when it formulated our social security measures.

### 2. Benefits Are Paid as a Matter of Right

A fundamental element in the old-age, survivors, and disability insurance program is that benefits are paid as a matter of "right." Benefits are not paid as a gratuity, nor do they depend upon the discretion of administrators. The right to benefits is a statutory right which can be enforced by court action. The rights of persons who have met certain specified conditions are detailed by the Social Security Act and protected by an appeals machinery. Where benefits are denied or the individual is dissatisfied with the determination of the Bureau of Old-Age and Survivors Insurance, he may either request a reconsideration by the Bureau of Old-Age and Survivors Insurance or file an appeal with an "Appeals Council" for a review of the decision by a referee. The Appeals Council may render the final decision subject only to judicial review; appeal may be taken to the federal district court.

Thus, a person's rights to benefits are protected by provision for both an administrative appeal and judicial review.

### 3. Integrated Protection Is Provided against Three Major Risks

A person who has attained "insured" status is protected against the risks of old age, disability, and death. The old-age, survivors, and disability benefits are administered as a single program. The same wage records are used as a basis for all types of benefits.

A person is "currently insured" if he has at least six quarters of coverage within three years of death or eligibility for benefits. A quarter of coverage is a calendar quarter in which the individual has been paid wages of at least $50.00 in covered, nonfarm employment or for which he has been credited with at least $100.00 from farm employment or from self-employment. A person is "fully insured" when he has forty quarters of coverage or at least one quarter of coverage for each two calendar quarters since 1950. He is insured for disability purposes if he is fully and currently insured and, in addition, has twenty quarters of coverage out of the last forty calendar quarters.

(*a*) *Old-Age Insurance Benefits.* The 1935 act provided monthly old-age benefits for the worker himself. In 1939, before any monthly benefits had been paid, the law was amended to also provide benefits for the worker's dependents. Additional categories of dependents were added in subsequent amendments. Under present law monthly benefits are payable to fully insured retired people—to men at age 65, and women at age 62—and to the following dependents: a wife age 62 or over, a dependent husband age 65 or over, a child under 18 or disabled before age 18, and a wife of any age caring for a child entitled to benefits.

(*b*) *Survivors Insurance Benefits.* Benefits for the survivors of a deceased worker were introduced by the 1939 amendments. Upon the death of a fully insured worker, benefits are payable to a surviving widow age 62 or over, a surviving dependent widower age 65 or over, a child under 18 or disabled before age 18, a mother who has such child in her care, or a dependent parent (a mother must be age 62 or over and a father must be at least 65). The survivor benefits for children and their widowed mothers are also payable even if the worker was only currently insured. A lump-sum payment is payable at death if the deceased worker was either fully or currently insured.

(*c*) *Disability Insurance Benefits.* The recommendations of the Committee on Economic Security, designed as they were as a "piecemeal approach, dictated by practical considerations," did not include provisions to maintain income during disability. Recognition of the importance to the individual and to society of measures to cope with this risk was limited, in the original Social Security Act, to the provisions for services for maternal and child health and crippled children, and for assistance to the needy blind and to children whose needs arose from the parent's incapacity. In 1950, a further attack on need arising from disability was made through the provision of federal grants to the states for assistance for needy adults who are totally and permanently disabled.

In its 1948 report, the Advisory Council on Social Security to the Senate Committee on Finance had stated: "Income loss from permanent and total disability is a major economic hazard to which, like old age and death, all gainful workers are exposed. The Advisory Council believes that the time has come to extend the nation's social-insurance system to afford protection against this loss." In amending the program shortly thereafter, however, the Congress rejected the social insurance approach and chose instead the public assistance method, establishing the above-mentioned assistance program.

Prior to 1954 the basic insurance program not only provided no cash benefits for the disabled; it afforded no protection against the impairment of the disabled worker's old-age and survivors insurance protection. A period of disability without covered earnings at best lowered the old-age and survivors insurance benefits subsequently payable and at worst could result in a loss of insured status so that neither the worker nor his survivors could qualify for any payments under the system. Amendments in 1954 removed this disadvantage by providing for "freezing" old-age and survivors insurance status during extended total disability.

Congress significantly changed the basic insurance system in 1956 by enacting—after much controversy—provisions for monthly insurance benefits beginning at age 50 for workers who are permanently and totally disabled. Disability insurance benefits are payable, after a waiting period of six months, to totally disabled workers between the ages of 50 and 65 who qualify both as to work requirements and degree of disability. The amount of the disability benefit is the same as the amount the worker would receive if he became entitled to old-age insurance benefits in the first month of his waiting period. No additional amounts, however, are paid for family dependents.

## 4. The System Is Contributory

In contradistinction to some foreign social insurance programs that are financed in whole or in part by general revenues of the government, our program is financed through contributions by workers and employers, or the self-employed where there is no employer. The contributions are a tax upon payrolls or self-employment income. The tax is on the first $4,200 of earnings. The law provides for an increase in taxes until 1975, when the maximum tax will be reached.

The contributory principle has many advantages, but of utmost importance is the effect in encouraging a responsible attitude among those covered. The taxpayer knows that the benefits for himself and his family are made possible by the payment of social security taxes and this knowledge gives him a personal interest and stake in the adequacy and soundness of the program. It is believed that this principle has been a major factor in the growing support and acceptance of the program.

## 5. The System Is Soundly Financed

From the beginning of the program, the methods of financing have been controversial. Should the program be on a "pay as you go" basis? That is, should current taxes be sufficient, and no more than sufficient, at all times to pay for current expenditures? Should taxes be fixed so that they equal the "level premium cost" as in many forms of private insurance? How should funds be invested? These and other questions have been debated in public print—frequently with more heat than light.

Without detailing the various controversies, suffice it to say that the appropriate committees of Congress and numerous students of the problem have concluded that, in general, the present system, as it has evolved, is a satisfactory one. This system involves several features.

(*a*) *A Self-supporting System.* It is agreed that the system shall be self-supporting; *i.e.,* that the special social security taxes and interest earnings of the trust funds must be sufficient to finance all expenditures. Contributions received under the schedule described above, when added to income from interest on the trust funds, are expected to be sufficient to meet the cost of benefits indefinitely into the future, as far as can be foreseen.

(*b*) *Actuarial Soundness.* It is generally agreed that the program must be financed on an actuarially sound basis. This does not mean, however, that a government program must establish reserves similar to private life insurance. Actuarial soundness implies that, in the long run, the total income must be sufficient to match total outlay.

(*c*) **Trust Funds.** The Social Security Act creates two trust funds—a "Federal Old-Age and Survivors Insurance Trust Fund," and a "Federal Disability Insurance Trust Fund." Into these funds are deposited the taxes collected from the employees, employers, and self-employed. A Board of Trustees is established by the act consisting of the Secretary of the Treasury, who is the "Managing Trustee," the Secretary of Labor, and the Secretary of Health, Education, and Welfare. The Commissioner of Social Security serves as Secretary of the Board of Trustees. The trustees are required to report to Congress annually on the actuarial status of the trust funds and on estimated income and disbursements for the ensuing five years. These reports have assumed great importance in view of the fact that the figures and statistics presented therein are relied upon by congressional committees as a basis for congressional action.

The monies in the trust funds are invested in government securities, and interest earned is added to the funds. Assets in the funds now total approximately 23 billion dollars.

(*d*) **Advisory Council on Social Security Financing.** The concern of Congress regarding social security financing and its desire to assure financing on a sound basis led to an amendment to the Social Security Act in 1956 establishing an "Advisory Council on Social Security Financing." This council is established for the purpose of "reviewing the status of the Federal Old-Age and Survivors Insurance Trust Fund and of the Federal Disability Insurance Trust Fund in relation to the long-term commitments of the old-age, survivors, and disability insurance program."

The council must be appointed by the Secretary of Health, Education, and Welfare at least two years prior to the scheduled tax increase and consists of the Commissioner of Social Security as chairman and 12 other members.

It is anticipated that the council will review the actuarial cost estimates, investment policies of the trust funds, and related fiscal matters to determine whether the program requires changes to maintain it on a financially sound basis.

### 6. Participation Is Compulsory

Another feature of the system is that coverage is compulsory, with very few exceptions. This principle has been adhered to since the beginning of the system in order to protect it from adverse selection of risks as well as to protect the country as a whole against widespread destitution due to the very risks insured against, namely old age, disability, and death of the wage earner.

The 1950 and 1954 amendments which provided for elective coverage did not represent a reversal in the intent of Congress to preserve the compulsory character of the system. On occasions when voluntary coverage on an individual basis was proposed, Congress has recognized that it involved grave dangers with respect to the financing of the system—those most likely to elect would be persons who could expect the largest return for a relatively small contribution. Furthermore, persons who could most easily spare the money, rather than those who most needed the protection, would be more likely to elect to participate. Overriding considerations of a special character, however, entered into the decisions to introduce certain voluntary elements into the coverage. Constitutional barriers generally preclude the federal government from imposing the employer tax upon state and local governments and, traditionally, certain nonprofit institutions have been tax-exempt. These groups were therefore brought into coverage on an elective basis. Because, generally speaking, coverage is not optional for individual employees of states or localities or of nonprofit institutions, but rather is on a group basis with new employees compulsorily covered, it does not involve the financial risk to the system inherent in an individual election.

In providing coverage for ministers through individual election in the 1954 amendments, the Committee on Finance of the Senate stated: "A provision for coverage on an individual election basis, while not generally desirable, is considered by your committee to be justified in this area because of the special circumstances. Many churches have expressed the fear that their participation in the old-age and survivors insurance program as employers of ministers might interfere with the well-established principle of separation of church and state. Many church representatives also believe that individual ministers who do not wish to be covered on grounds of conscience should not be required to participate in the program."

Significantly, although proposals for coverage on an individual election basis have been made over the years in connection with several other groups—such as farm operators and self-employed professional persons— clergymen have been the only group for which this basis of coverage was acceptable to Congress. Even then strict provisions as to coverage are included—a limited period to make election and irrevocability of election once made.

## 7. Benefits Are Wage Related

Again in contradistinction to some European systems, our social security program emphasizes the relation of the economic status of the worker to the benefits he receives. Thus, the worker himself establishes his level of benefits by his earnings on which he pays contributions. The tax is on wages up to $4,200 of earnings per year. A person who earns $4,200 or more per year during his potential working life—and there are provisions for dropping out years of low earnings in determining the average wage —will receive the maximum monthly retirement benefit of $108.50 at age 65 or later retirement. A person who averages only $3,000 will receive $88.50 per month.

The scale of benefits, ranging from a monthly payment of $30 minimum to $108.50 for the individual worker and $200 for a family, although wage related, is weighted in favor of the low-income worker.

The provision of differential benefits related to wages has several objectives: preserving the worker's motivation for making the maximum contribution to the economy, relating benefits to diverse economic situations, and relating benefits to differing standards of living. It is interesting to note that several countries which originally rejected the wage-related principle are now veering in the direction of this type of program.

### 8. Emphasis Is Placed on Family

Many children in the United States are in homes where family income is low or only moderate. Rural areas where income levels are low have more than their proportionate share of the nation's children. In many families with young children, the father has not yet reached his full earning power and the mother is needed at home. The parents have had to meet the extra expenses of setting up the home and starting the family, so they often have not been able to save much money.

For these reasons, it is especially important that families with children have some assured means of support when the breadwinner's earnings stop or are greatly reduced. Because of the survivor protection under the federal insurance system, nine out of ten of the mothers and young children in the nation now have the assurance that they can receive monthly benefits if the father of the family dies.

At the beginning of 1957 there were more than 1.9 million children under age eighteen whose fathers had died and almost 700,000 widows with children in their care. Over half of these mothers were working and more than two-fifths were receiving monthly survivor benefits from the old-age and survivors insurance program. More than 1.1 million of the children whose fathers were dead received such benefits. Almost 400,000 children in families in which the father had died were benefiting from other social insurance and related programs, especially the veterans' programs.

Thus, the old-age, survivors, and disability insurance program contributes to strengthening and maintaining family life by providing income upon death of the breadwinner. This reduces the necessity for mothers to place children in foster care in order to be free to accept a job. Most families can now rest assured that death of the breadwinner does not mean a complete stoppage of income.

### 9. Benefits Replace Earnings Lost

A basic principle of the old-age, survivors, and disability insurance system is that the benefits are paid only when earnings are *lost* because of these three occurrences—old age, death of the wage earner, and disability. The program is not an annuity system and, in general, benefits are not paid to persons whose income from earnings continues. This concept gives rise to one of the most controversial aspects of the program, namely, the "retirement test."

A worker who reaches retirement age is considered "retired" if his earnings do not exceed $1,200 per year; after he reaches age 72 he is "retired" regardless of his earnings. For each $80 (or fraction thereof) which a person under 72 earns above $1,200, he loses one month's benefit, except that he never loses a benefit for a month in which he earns wages of $80 or less or does not engage in substantial self-employment. Therefore, a worker earning $2,080 in a year—with over $80 each month—would lose all benefits for the year.

Although controversial, this retirement test feature is an essential part of the program. To abolish it, changing the character of the program from insurance against wage loss to an annuity arrangement, would permit persons who continued to work full time at their regular jobs to receive full benefits.

There are about 10 million people age 65 or over who could initially qualify for benefits. Almost 2 million have not applied for them, presumably because they are not substantially retired. About 7.5 million are receiving their checks each month, and 300,000 are receiving checks for some months of the year. Only 200,000 applicants have all 12 monthly checks withheld.

These two groups of people who are not drawing full benefits because they have substantial earnings from work—the 500,000 who have applied and almost 2 million who have not yet applied—are the ones who would benefit if the retirement test were eliminated.

To abolish the test would involve a combined increase of the employer-employee tax of 1¼ per cent of covered wages—a tax that would be paid by all workers for the benefit of persons beyond retirement age who have substantial income from their own earnings. Whenever the retirement test provision has been examined it has generally been concluded that the test should be retained—that for the best use of available funds, benefits should be paid to persons who most need them rather than to those who have not substantially retired.

# 13. FINANCING OLD-AGE, SURVIVORS, AND DISABILITY INSURANCE

*A Report of the Advisory Council on Social Security Financing, 1959.*

## I. INTRODUCTION

THE OLD-AGE, SURVIVORS, and disability insurance program provides a continuing income for individuals and families who have lost income from work on account of death, retirement in old age, or permanent and total disability after age 50. Under the program, employees (with matching contributions from employers) and self-employed people, while they are working, pay a percentage of their earnings into a fund. Payments are made from the fund to the contributors and their families to replace a portion of the income lost when these risks materialize.

About 12½ million people are now drawing monthly benefits under the program, with payments for 1959 estimated at $10 billion; more than 72 million people are insured under the program; and some 75 million workers are currently contributing toward future benefits. About 9 out of 10 of the Nation's workers are covered, and about 9 out of 10 of its mothers and children can look to the program for continuing income if the family earner dies.

The financing of this program is the largest financial trusteeship in history. It involves in varying degree the personal security of practically all Americans—not only those who have retired or are nearing retirement age but those just starting to work, those who are children today, and the generations of the future. For millions of Americans the social security benefit will spell the difference between deprivation, on the one hand, and an assured income provided on a basis consistent with self-respect and dignity, on the other. Involving practically all the people, as old-age, survivors, and disability insurance does, the program's financial operations are large. It is very important that the program be adequately financed and that orderly provision be made to assure the discharge of its obligations.

The social security system has created for millions of Americans expectations regarding their future place in economic society. These expectations could be defeated by discharging the system's obligations in dollars having a substantially lesser command of goods and services than the beneficiaries have come to count upon in their personal planning. The Council believes that the trusteeship is so large and the number of people involved so great that the defeat of beneficiaries' expectations through inflation would gravely imperil the stability of our social, political, and economic institutions.

Although the security of the individual depends in part on programs such as old-age, survivors, and disability insurance that assure a source of income when earnings stop, security depends even more fundamentally on the continued ability of our society to produce a large volume of goods and services under conditions of economic stability. The Council has not considered it part of its task to evaluate in detail the effect of this system of social insurance on the stability and productivity of the economy. Our judgment is, however, that the program, if maintained on a sound basis, can be of great benefit to the economy as well as to the individual citizen. We believe that the almost universal acceptance of this program of social insurance is well-deserved and that it is a permanent institution in American life.

## II. THE MAJOR FINDING

*The method of financing the old-age, survivors, and disability insurance program is sound, and, based on the best estimates available, the contribution schedule now in the law makes adequate provision for meeting both short-range and long-range costs.*

The Council finds that the present method of financing the old-age, survivors, and disability insurance program is sound, practical, and appropriate for this program. It is our judgment, based on the best available cost estimates, that the contribution schedule enacted into law in the last session of Congress makes adequate provision for financing the program on a sound actuarial basis.

The Council has studied the estimates of the short-range and long-range costs of the old-age and survivors insurance program, the various demographic and other assumptions on which they are based, and the basic techniques used in deriving the estimates.[1] The Council believes that the assumptions are a reasonable basis for forecasts extending into the distant future, and that the estimating techniques are appropriate and sound. The Council endorses the present practice under which both the estimating techniques and the assumptions are re-examined periodically to take account of emerging experience and changing conditions.

It is our judgment that the program is in close actuarial balance since the level-premium equivalent of the contribution rates varies from the estimated level-premium cost by no more than one-quarter of 1 percent of covered payroll.[2] There is no advantage in trying to achieve a closer

---

[1] See sec. VII B for a discussion of the estimates. The estimates referred to throughout this report are the official estimates of the Social Security Administration. The latest estimates are contained in *Actuarial Cost Estimates and Summary of Provisions of the Old-Age, Survivors, and Disability Insurance System as Modified by the Social Security Amendments of 1958* (Washington, D.C.: U.S. Government Printing Office, 1958). The Report of the Board of Trustees for the fiscal year 1958 will be submitted to the Congress by March 1, 1959, and will contain both the detail of the cost estimates and a reprint of this report of the Advisory Council.

[2] The "level-premium cost" is the percent of covered payroll that, if charged from now on indefinitely into the future, would produce enough contribution and interest income to the fund to meet the cost of the benefit payments and administrative expenses. The "level-premium equivalent of the contribution rates" is the percent of covered payroll that, if charged from now on indefinitely into the future, would produce the same amount of income to the fund over the long-range future as will be produced by the graded schedule of contribution rates. The level-premium cost of the OASI part of the program is 8.27 percent of payroll on the basis of the intermediate cost estimates; the level-premium equivalent of the contributions is 8.02 percent of payroll. The level-premium cost of the disability insurance part of the program is 0.49 percent of payroll; the level-premium equivalent of the contributions is 0.50 percent of payroll.

balance between estimated long-range income and outgo, especially since those estimates are subject to periodic review and such review encompasses the testing of the adequacy of the schedule of contribution rates. If earnings should continue to rise in the future as they have in the past, the level-premium cost of the present benefits, expressed as a percentage of payroll, would be lower than shown in the cost estimates we have used.

The Council is also pleased to report that under the new schedule of contributions and benefits not only is the system in close actuarial balance for the long run, but also after 1959 the income to the system is estimated to exceed the outgo in every year for many years into the future. We believe that it is important that income exceed outgo during the early years of development of the system as well as that the system be in close actuarial balance over the long range.

We have no suggestions for basic changes in the present plan of financing. We do, however, have certain specific recommendations which we believe will strengthen the plan.

## III. SUMMARY OF OTHER FINDINGS AND CONCLUSIONS

The Council's recommendations are designed to supplement, not to alter, the basic provisions of the existing financing plan. Specifically, the Council endorses the contributory principle, an interest-earning fund on a limited basis, investment of the funds solely in United States Government obligations, and the other major features of the present financial arrangements.

The Council anticipates that further changes in the social security program will be needed as changes occur in the labor force, wage levels, and doubtless in other factors that in a dynamic economy will affect the appropriateness of the program. Because of these changes and such changes as may occur in the factors which enter into the actuarial cost estimates, we believe there is a need for periodic scrutiny of all factors which in any way affect the financing of the program. These factors include the maximum earnings base for determining benefits and contributions. This maximum determines the proportion of the Nation's payrolls available to finance the program and is a major factor in determining the extent to which the program pays benefits reasonably related to the past earnings of the individual. As a whole, our recommendations look toward a continuing review of the financial arrangements so that they, along with the other provisions of the program, can be kept sound and workable in a changing economy.

At this time we recommend no change in the contribution schedule. It is not certain, however, that the ultimate rate should go into effect in 1969, as provided in the present law. A sound decision on whether there should be a change in the amount or timing of the increase scheduled for

1969 can best be made in the period just before 1969 after the advisory council then serving has evaluated the question.

The Council suggests that greater emphasis be given in the future to estimates of the probable course of the income and outgo of the system over the then ensuing 15 or 20 years. As the program reaches a greater degree of maturity and the contribution rate approaches the level of a reasonable minimum estimate of the costs over a period of many decades into the future, it will be appropriate, as it has not been in the past, to base financial decisions largely on what may be expected to take place during the period of 15 to 20 years thereafter. Estimates showing the relationship of income and outgo over the very long-range future have been and will continue to be important as a guide to policy and necessary as a brake against making commitments which, though inexpensive today, may have substantially greater costs in the long-run future. As the system matures, however, forecasts of what will happen during the shorter run will become progressively more significant and useful.

The Council recommends certain changes in the provisions governing the interest rate on the special obligations issued for purchase by the trust funds, and also certain other changes in the management of the funds that are designed to bring their earnings more nearly into line with earnings of private investors in long-term Government bonds.

## IV. THE PLAN OF FINANCING OLD-AGE, SURVIVORS, AND DISABILITY INSURANCE

The plan of financing the old-age, survivors, and disability insurance program is as follows: Employees pay taxes on their annual earnings up to a maximum amount—$4,800 beginning in 1959. Each employer pays taxes at the same rate on the first $4,800 paid to each of his employees in the year. Year-by-year costs will grow for many years, and the law provides that tax rates will gradually increase from a combined employer and employee rate of 5 percent in 1959 to an ultimate rate of 9 percent, to be reached in 1969. The self-employed pay at a rate equal to one and one-half times the rate paid by the employee.

The contribution rates now scheduled are intended to provide enough income to meet all of the costs of the system into the indefinite future. Funds collected in the early years of the program and not needed for immediate benefit payments are invested in United States Government obligations. The interest earnings on these obligations are available to help pay for the larger cost of the system in later years. The scheduled contribution rates include a fixed one-half of 1 percent combined employer-employee contribution for disability benefits for workers and their dependents (three-eighths of 1 percent for the self-employed) and the proceeds of this tax are held in a separate fund. The administrative expenses of the system, as well as the benefits, are paid from the taxes established to finance the system.

In the following pages the Council reports on each aspect of the financing plan described above: Contributions by Employees, Employers, and the Self-Employed; The Earnings Base for Contributions and Benefits; The Schedule of Contribution Rates; The Role of the Trust Funds; and The Management and Investment of the Trust Funds.

## V. CONTRIBUTIONS BY EMPLOYEES, EMPLOYERS, AND THE SELF-EMPLOYED

**A.** *The Council believes that, as provided in present law, a substantial part of the cost of this program should be borne directly by those who benefit from it.*

The fact that the worker pays a substantial share of the cost of the benefits provided, in a way visible to all, is his assurance that he and his dependents will receive the scheduled benefits and that they will be paid as a matter of right without the necessity of establishing need. The contribution sets the tone of the program and its administration by making clear that this is not a program of government aid given to the individual, but rather a cooperative program in which the people use the instrument of government to provide protection for themselves and their families against loss of earnings resulting from old age, death, and disability. The Council also believes that the direct earmarked tax on prospective beneficiaries promotes a sense of financial responsibility. It is very important that people see clearly that increases in protection necessarily involve increases in costs and contributions.

We believe that the experience of the last 22 years has shown the advantages of contributory social insurance over grants from general tax funds. It is true that, up to the present time, workers as a group have not contributed a large share of the cost of their own protection. Most workers covered in the early years of the program will contribute during only a part of their working lifetime, and, under the graduated schedule in the law, contribution rates have been low relative to the value of the protection provided. But this situation is changing. Young workers starting out under the system in recent years will contribute a substantial part of the cost of their protection.

**B.** *The Council believes that it is also appropriate for a substantial part of the cost of the program to be borne by an employer contribution and for the self-employed to pay a rate equal to one and one-half times the employee rate.*

Protecting the members of the labor force and their dependents against loss of income from the hazards of old-age retirement, permanent and total disability, and death is, at least in part, a proper charge on the cost of production. Moreover, business enterprises have a significant stake in assuring that orderly provision is made to meet the needs of their employees and their families for income when their working lives are over. The earmarked contribution for social security is a recognition of this stake. The direct contribution gives employers status in the program and a clear right to participate in the development of the program and in the formation of policy.

The rate for the self-employed—one and one-half times the rate paid by the employee—is a recognition of the fact that the self-employed person, in respect to his own employment, has some of the characteristics both of employee and employer. The Council has found no reason for a change in this rate.

## VI. THE EARNINGS BASE FOR CONTRIBUTIONS AND BENEFITS

*In an economy characterized by rising wages and salaries it is necessary to give periodic review to the maximum amount of earnings subject to contributions and credited toward benefits, since this maximum determines the proportion of the covered payrolls available to finance the program and is a major factor in determining the extent to which the program pays benefits reasonably related to the past earnings of the individual.*

The Council believes that it is an essential part of the contributory concept to have the worker pay contributions on the same amount of earnings as the amount that is credited to him for benefit purposes. Since, under a plan designed for broad social protection, it has not been considered appropriate to cover the full earnings of very high-paid employees and self-employed persons and to pay correspondingly high benefits, there has always been a maximum on the amount of earnings subject to tax and creditable toward benefits. Exactly where this maximum should be set is a difficult question. It is complicated by the fact that over the years wages and living levels tend to rise, so that any particular maximum set in the law may be soon outdated.

When the old-age and survivors insurance program first went into operation in 1937 the maximum earnings base was $3,000, and it remained at that level until 1951. In 1938, the first year for which adequate data are available, the full earnings of 97 percent of all covered employees, and of 94 percent of regularly employed men, were included under that maximum. As wage levels rose, the percentage of workers who had all their wages credited under the program declined; thus, by 1950, instead of the highest-paid 6 percent of regularly employed men having a part of their wages excluded, 57 percent had some of their wages excluded.

The maximum earnings base was raised to $3,600, effective in 1951; to

$4,200, effective in 1955; and to $4,800, effective in 1959. In 1959, it is estimated, 75 percent of the workers covered under the program, and 50 percent of the regularly employed men, will have their full earnings covered for both contributions and benefits.

Insofar as the maximum contribution and benefit base is not increased as earnings rise, the proportion of payrolls in covered employment that is taxed declines. For example, between 1938 and 1950 the proportion dropped from 92 percent to 80 percent. The proportion taxed in 1951 after the increase in the maximum to $3,600 was 84 percent. It is estimated that the proportion taxed in 1959 will be about 83 percent.

Benefits are a higher proportion of earnings at lower earnings levels than at the higher levels. Hence raising the maximum contribution and benefit base without change in the benefit formula results in a reduction in the percentage of covered payroll needed to meet the long-range cost of the system. The cost estimates underlying the contribution schedule can be interpreted to imply that if earnings rise there will be an upward adjustment of benefits and of the earnings base. However, the tax rates required for the support of the adjusted benefits would be higher than those in the present contribution schedule if the earnings base is not increased as earnings rise.

The Council is of the opinion that there should be a maximum on earnings taxed and credited toward benefits; that the contribution should be levied on the same amount of earnings as the amount that is credited for benefits; and that the maximum should be increased from time to time as wages rise.[3]

Although there is no definitive logic supporting $4,800 as the correct amount—i. e., neither too high nor too low—for the maximum contribution and benefit base, we do not recommend any further change in the base at this time, since the change to $4,800 is just going into effect in 1959. We assume that further consideration will be given to this maximum after the effect of the $4,800 figure has been evaluated.

### VII. THE SCHEDULE OF CONTRIBUTION RATES

A. *The Council endorses the contribution schedule in present law on the basis of the cost estimates we have reviewed. We believe that the 1959, 1960, and 1963 rate increases should go into effect as scheduled and that conditions will probably warrant the 1966 rate increase as well. The last increase—that scheduled for 1969—will need to be evaluated*

---

[3] The Council believes it desirable to call specific attention to the fact that in the relation between the tax on earnings and the benefits paid under the old-age, survivors, and disability insurance system there is an element of progressive income taxation. Covered workers who, together with their employers, pay taxes on the higher ranges of the creditable earnings base receive less than proportionate benefit rights. This serves to make possible more than proportionate benefits for those paying taxes on the lower range of the creditable earnings base.

*in the light of the conditions current at that time and in the light of the cost estimates then available.*

As a result of the amendments of 1958, the contribution schedule in the law has been speeded up and the rates increased. The present schedule, covering both old-age and survivors insurance and disability insurance, is as follows:[4]

| Year | Contribution Rate | | |
|------|-----------|-----------|-----------------|
|      | Employers | Employees | Self-employed |
|      | *Percent* | *Percent* | *Percent* |
| 1959 | 2½ | 2½ | 3¾ |
| 1960–62 | 3 | 3 | 4½ |
| 1963–65 | 3½ | 3½ | 5¼ |
| 1966–68 | 4 | 4 | 6 |
| 1969 and thereafter | 4½ | 4½ | 6¾ |

The Council is agreed that a graded contribution schedule is sound policy. It is true that the ultimate rate is somewhat increased by the loss of interest on funds which would otherwise have been accumulated by the application of an earlier high, level rate. We believe, however, that this loss is of far less significance than would be the effect of the sudden imposition of the full rate necessary to support the program.

The Council is also agreed that the rates should be high enough in the early years of the program to cover at least year-by-year disbursements. Disbursements will ultimately be substantially greater than they are now, and we believe there is no justification for current contributors paying less than enough to cover current disbursements. Moreover, many people were disturbed to have the outgo from the Old-Age and Survivors Insurance Trust Fund greater than the income in 1957 and 1958, and in prospect in 1959. We are therefore in complete accord with the action taken by the Congress to increase the rates in 1959 and 1960. These changes are necessary to avoid an excess of outgo over income in 1960 and in the next several years.

The Council also believes that the rate increase provided by the new schedule for 1963 is justified by all the evidence now available. Although it might prove possible to postpone the 1963 increase for a year or two, it is nevertheless clear that a rate increase will be needed soon after 1963, if not in that year, to prevent outgo from again exceeding income. We be-

---

[4] As indicated in the description of the financing plan, the scheduled contribution rates include a fixed one-half of 1 percent combined employer-employee contribution for disability benefits for workers and their dependents (three-eighths of 1 percent for the self-employed). The questions discussed in the next several pages relate largely to the old-age and survivors insurance program only and grow out of the gradual imposition of the ultimate rate for that program.

lieve that there is merit in maintaining the schedule in the law unless and until there is a strong case for change.

Probably the increase scheduled for 1966 will not be necessary at that time to provide income in excess of outgo. Its effect, unless significant changes occur, will be to increase fund accumulation.[5] Although the Council does not regard building of a large fund as a primary goal, we nevertheless believe that it will prove desirable to have the 1966 rate go into effect. It will further the objective that the person who gets the protection should pay a substantial part of the cost of the protection. It will hasten the approach to the payment of the full rate necessary to support the system and will increase public understanding of its costs. It will reduce the shifting of costs to future members of the system. Before the 1966 rate is scheduled to go into effect, however, other advisory councils will have the opportunity to consider the timing of the introduction of this rate in the light of cost estimates and conditions current at that time.

Under the set of cost estimates we used for evaluating the contribution rate schedule, if the employer-employee contribution rate of 8 percent for the combined old-age, survivors, and disability insurance system scheduled for 1966 goes into effect in that year the income to the Old-Age and Survivors Insurance Trust Fund will exceed outgo until 1982. Under other sets of estimates that we examined, such income will exceed outgo for a period of from 12 years after 1965 (under estimates showing high costs) to about 80 years (under estimates showing low costs). In view of the likelihood that an increase above the 1966 rate will not be needed to cover the year-by-year costs of the program for a considerable period of time, we are doubtful whether the 9 percent rate should go into effect, as scheduled, in 1969.[6] However, we are not recommending that any change be made now in the schedule of contribution rates in present law. Instead, we recommend that future advisory councils, in the light of conditions current at the time of their inquiries, give study to the timing level of any contribution rate increase to be made after the one bringing the rate to 8 percent.

---

[5] Some have argued that an excess of income over outgo may have bad economic effects. Whether the economic effects are good or bad will depend on the general economic situation at the time and on the fiscal policies of the Government. In any event, the amounts by which the fund is increased in any year would in all probability be too small to have any effects on the economy that would be serious or that could not be readily compensated through other governmental action.

[6] It is recognized, of course, that if the long-range estimates were to remain unchanged but the imposition of the ultimate rate were postponed beyond 1969, a contribution schedule showing the system in actuarial balance would, because of this delay, have an ultimate employer-employee rate above the 9 percent in present law for the combined old-age, survivors, and disability insurance system. For example, if the 1969 rate increase were postponed until 1982, when, according to the cost estimates we have used for evaluating the contribution schedule, an increase would be needed to prevent disbursements from exceeding income, then a 9.89 percent rate would be needed in 2025 and thereafter to produce the same degree of long-range actuarial balance as the schedule in present law.

Once the rate currently charged approaches the level of a reasonable minimum estimate of the costs over a period of many decades into the future, decisions about the imposition of further rate increases should be guided, in our judgment, largely by conditions expected in the 15- or 20-year period immediately ahead, including the size of the trust fund. Under such a plan a judgment of whether the last step-up in the contribution schedule should go into effect in 1969 can be best made just prior to that time.

**B. *The Council believes that the establishment of a contribution schedule in the law based on the concept of long-range actuarial balance is sound policy and should be continued. However, future decisions concerning the financing of the program should increasingly take into account estimates of trust fund income and outgo over the ensuing 15 or 20 years based on expected earnings and employment levels and on demographic developments.***

The Council endorses the long-standing practice adopted by Congress of including in the law a contribution schedule which according to the cost estimates places the system substantially in actuarial balance into the indefinite future. We believe this procedure to be the best way of making people conscious of the long-range cost of the current provisions of the program and of the cost of proposals to modify the present program.

The long-range estimates of the cost of the program are presented in the form of a range, showing the effect of assumptions resulting in high costs, and other assumptions resulting in low costs. Reflecting the great uncertainties attached to costs that may develop in the more distant future, these estimates indicate a broad spread in the possible range of program costs toward the end of the present century and in the first half of the next century. For purposes of financial planning, the practice has been to take an average of the high-cost and low-cost estimates to obtain so-called intermediate cost estimates. On the basis of these intermediate cost estimates a schedule of contribution rates is developed to provide contribution income sufficient to meet the costs of the system as they fall due from the present into the long-range future. The Council has examined these estimates and believes that the assumptions on which they are based are reasonable and that the methods used in making them are sound.

The long-range cost estimates, based as they are on assumptions reflecting the possible variations in long-range trends in such cost factors as fertility, mortality, retirement rates, and family composition, while producing a wide range in possible costs several decades ahead, show a fairly narrow range in possible costs in the shorter-run future. This is because the economic factors which may show significant ups and downs in the short run are assumed in the long-range estimates to have a smooth trend. Thus, for example, the estimates assume that the volume of employment will average out over the long run somewhat below full employment.

The estimates also assume that average annual earnings will remain level.[7] However reasonable these assumptions may be for the long-range estimates, they cannot be used for estimates designed to show expected operations over a short-run period. Here the possible variations arising from the economic factors will be very significant, and the Council believes that there is need for cost estimates that take these economic factors into account.

As stated above, the Council believes that when the contribution rate approaches the level of a reasonable minimum estimate of the costs over a period of many decades into the future, decisions about the imposition of further rate increases, if needed, should be guided largely by estimates covering a period of 15 or 20 years. Like the estimates covering the period of 5 future years that are presented in the Annual Reports of the Board of Trustees, these 15- or 20-year forecasts should be based on assumptions which take into account future developments with respect to economic as well as population changes.

## VIII. THE ROLE OF THE TRUST FUNDS

A. *The Council approves of the accumulation of funds that are more than sufficient to meet all foreseeable short-range contingencies, and that will therefore earn interest in somewhat larger amounts than would be earned if the funds served only a contingency purpose. The Council concludes, however, that a "full" reserve is unnecessary and does not believe that interest earnings should be expected to meet a major part of the long-range benefit costs.*

Income not currently needed for benefits is held in two trust funds— the Old-Age and Survivors Insurance Trust Fund and the Disability Insurance Trust Fund. These trust funds serve two primary purposes: (1) they are contingency reserves for use in temporary situations when current income is less than current outgo; and (2) they are a source of investment income which helps pay the benefits and administrative costs of the program.

As contingency reserves, the assets of the trust funds are available,

---

[7] The assumption that average earnings will remain level is not, of course, in accord with what has been happening in this country throughout its history. If average earnings do in fact continue to rise and if no changes are made in benefit levels, the costs of the program, expressed as a percentage of payroll, will be lower than those shown in the estimates. In this sense it can be said that the estimates overstate the costs of the benefit provisions now in the law. As a practical matter, however, it may be expected that, as average earnings continue to rise, there will be an upward adjustment of benefits. If the added cost resulting from such adjustment is sufficient to balance the reduction in the cost of the program that results from rising average earnings, the level-premium cost of the program, expressed as a percentage of payroll, will be the same as is shown in the estimates.

when needed, to supplement current receipts in periods when disbursements may temporarily rise above income. The Council believes the trust funds are and will continue to be larger than would be required for contingency purposes alone. Both the trust funds are expected to grow for many years and should remain well in excess of foreseeable contingency needs.

Although larger than needed for contingency purposes, the trust funds will continue to be considerably less than would be required under "full reserve" financing, often used for private pension plans. The "full reserve" basis contemplates the accumulation during an initial period of very substantial funds which, if the pension plan were to cease operating, would be available to discharge existing liabilities. These are liabilities to the then current beneficiaries and the liabilities accrued to date for those still in active employment. In a national compulsory social insurance program it can properly be assumed that the program will continue to collect contributions and to pay benefits indefinitely into the future. The old-age, survivors, and disability insurance program therefore does not need a full reserve. It may be considered to be in actuarial balance when estimated future income from contributions and from interest on the investments of the accumulated trust funds will, over the long run, support the estimated disbursements for benefits and administrative expenses.

Although the Old-Age and Survivors Insurance Trust Fund will be only a fraction of the "full reserve," as defined above, it will grow to considerable size and play a significant role as an interest-earning fund. Interest will, of course, be available to help pay benefit costs and to some extent will make later contribution rates lower than they would otherwise have to be. Interest earnings since the program began, in 1937, have already totaled over $5 billion.

In a dynamic system of social insurance, the significance of the role played by an interest-earning fund is quite different from what it would be under a static system. If benefits are adjusted upward as earnings levels rise, then the interest earnings on a fund of any given size will meet a decreasing proportion of benefit costs. In the light of potential increases in earnings and benefits as decades pass, we believe it unwise to count on interest to meet a major part of the costs of the program in the far-distant future.

We see no merit in the provision of present law which requires the Trustees to report to the Congress whenever, in the course of the next 5 years, it is expected that either of the trust funds will exceed three times expenditures in any one year. The implication of the provision is that the trust funds should not be allowed to exceed the result of this formula. We do not believe that the trust funds should be held to any arbitrary relationship to expected annual expenditures, and we recommend that the provision be repealed.

**B.** *The investment of the trust funds in United States Government obligations is a proper use of the excess of income over outgo for the benefit of the contributors to the funds. The trust funds are properly kept separate from the general fund of the Treasury and have the same lender status as other investors in Federal securities.*

The Council is aware that there is some misunderstanding concerning the nature of the trust funds of the program and their distinct separation from the general Treasury account. The members are in unanimous agreement with the advisory councils of 1938 and 1948 that the present provisions regarding the investment of the moneys in these trust funds do not involve any misuse of these moneys or endanger the funds in any way, nor is there any "double taxation" for social security purposes by reason of the investment of these funds in Government obligations.

Each of these trust funds is kept completely separate from all other funds in the Treasury. The income and disbursements of the Old-Age and Survivors Insurance Trust Fund and the Disability Insurance Trust Fund are not included in the administrative budget of the Government. Instead, the President reports their operations separately in his Budget Message to Congress. The debt obligations held by the trust funds are shown in Treasury reports as part of the Federal debt, and interest payments on these obligations are regularly made by the Treasury to the trust funds. The securities are sold or redeemed whenever necessary to obtain cash for disbursement by these funds.

When the trust fund receipts not needed for current disbursements are invested in Government securities, the funds are lenders and the United States Treasury is the borrower. The trustees of the funds receive and hold Federal securities as evidence of these loans. These Government obligations are assets of the funds, and they are liabilities of the United States Government, which must pay interest on the money borrowed and must repay the principal when the securities are redeemed or mature.

The marketable securities held by the funds are identical in every way with Federal bonds bought and sold on the open market by other investors in Federal securities. The special obligations issued directly to the funds are public debt obligations backed by the full faith and credit of the United States. Interest on, and the proceeds from the sale or redemption of, securities held by each of the two trust funds are credited to and form a part of each fund. Thus the trust funds are completely separate from the general fund of the Treasury and have the same status as lenders that other investors in Federal securities have.

The confusion that there is "double taxation" for social security purposes arises because, in addition to paying social security taxes, people must also pay taxes to pay interest on, and repay the principal amount of, the obligations held by the trust funds. But the taxes that must be raised to pay interest on these obligations, or to repay the principal, are not levied for social security purposes. They are levied to meet the costs of the defense program and the other purposes for which the borrowed money was expended by the Treasury in accordance with congressional appropriations. If the trust funds did not exist, money for these purposes would have been borrowed from other sources, and in this case, too, taxes would have to be raised to pay interest and principal on the borrowings. The purchase of Government obligations by the trust funds is financially sound in relation to both the social security program and the fiscal operations of the Federal Government.

## IX. THE MANAGEMENT AND INVESTMENT OF THE TRUST FUNDS

**A.** *The investment of the trust funds should continue to be restricted to interest-bearing obligations of the United States Government or to obligations guaranteed as to principal and interest by the United States.*

The Council recommends that investment of the trust funds should, as in the past, be restricted to obligations of the United States Government. Departure from this principle would put trust fund operations into direct involvement in the operation of the private economy or the affairs of State and local governments. Investment in private business corporations could have unfortunate consequences for the social security system—both financial and political—and would constitute an unnecessary interference with our free enterprise economy. Similarly, investment in the securities of State and local governments would unnecessarily involve the trust funds in affairs which are entirely apart from the social security system.

**B.** *The investment of the trust funds should be in obligations having maturities which reasonably reflect the long-term character of the funds.*

The bulk of the assets of the trust funds will be on continuous loan to the Federal Treasury, and therefore the funds' investments are essentially long-term in character. The maturities of special issues should reflect this fact. Before the 1956 amendments to the Social Security Act, the law included no provision regarding the maturities of special obligations issued for purchase by the trust funds. Up to that time, special issues had been 5-year notes or 1-year (or less) certificates of indebtedness. The 1956 amendments added the provision that special issues shall have ". . . maturities fixed with due regard for the needs of the trust funds. . . ." This requirement has been interpreted by the Managing Trustee to to mean maturities of 5 years or longer. Accordingly, he inaugurated a program to lengthen gradually the maturities of special obligations issued to the trust funds. The special issues held by the funds on June 30, 1958, consisted of 1-year certificates, 2- to 5-year notes, and 6- to 10-year bonds.

**C.** *Each special obligation issued for purchase by the trust funds should carry a rate of interest that, in principle, equals the rate of re-*

*turn being realized by investors who purchase long-term Government
securities in the open market at the time the special obligation is issued.*[8]

The Council believes the rate of return on trust fund investments in
special issues should be comparable to what the Treasury would have to
pay for long-term money if borrowed from other investors. Such a rate
of return seems to us the way to avoid either a financial advantage or disadvantage to the funds. Such a rate on special issues would go a long
way toward eliminating any conflict of interest that might be encountered by the Secretary of the Treasury, acting both as the principal fiscal
officer of the Government and as manager of the trust funds, in deciding
whether to invest trust fund assets in marketable obligations or in special
issues.

The provision in the present law for setting the interest rate on the
special issues needs revision in order to make possible the attainment of
this policy. The present law requires that special obligations issued for
purchase by the trust funds bear interest at a rate equal to the average rate
of interest, computed as of the end of the month preceding the date of
issue, on all marketable interest-bearing public debt obligations that are
not due or callable until after the expiration of 5 years from date of original issue. The interest rate on special obligations issued to the trust funds
at the beginning of fiscal year 1959 was 2⅝ percent. During recent years
about nine-tenths of the Old-Age and Survivors Insurance Trust Fund
investments have been in special obligations; on June 30, 1958, about 95
percent of the Disability Insurance Trust Fund investments were in special obligations.

The Council endorses the policy in present law which relates the interest rate on special obligations to the interest rate on long-term marketable obligations. This policy correctly identifies the special obligations
as being primarily long-term investments.

We recommend, however, that two changes be made in the law in order
that the rate of return on special obligations be as nearly as possible equal
to the rate being realized by investors who purchase long-term Government securities in the open market at the time such a special obligation is
issued. The rate on each special obligation should be made equal to the
average *market yield* on long-term marketable Federal obligations outstanding when the special obligation is issued, rather than to the average
*coupon rate* of such marketable obligations. This change would cause the
interest rate on the obligations issued for purchase by the trust funds to
reflect the market rate of return prevailing at the time of issuing any
given block of securities to the trust funds. The average yield should be
computed on the basis of market quotations in a recent past period, such

---

[8] It is recognized that the Managing Trustee may need to keep a minor part of
the funds in short-term securities, at an interest rate appropriate thereto, to meet immediate prospective needs.

as the month preceding the special issue, and, as at present, the average so computed should be rounded to the nearest one-eighth of 1 percent.

The second change we recommend is that the interest rate fixed for a special obligation should be based on the average rate of return on all outstanding marketable Federal obligations that will mature more than, say, 5 years after the date of the special issue, rather than on all bonds that are not due or callable until after 5 years from the date when they were originally issued.[9] This change is necessary to eliminate from the computation those bonds which have in fact become short-term obligations.

In adjusting to the proposed new statutory formula, we believe a gradual and orderly transition over a period of several years would be desirable. We recommend, therefore, that before the new formula becomes effective the present maturity distribution of the special obligations held in the funds be reviewed and, if need be, adjusted to carry out this broad objective.

**D. *Investment of the trust funds, as at present, should be either in special issues or in public issues, but the statute should be amended to provide that public issues may be acquired only when they will provide currently a yield equal to or greater than the yield that would be provided by the alternative of investing in special issues.***

With the adoption of a statutory formula giving to the trust funds a return based on market rates of interest, we believe it is proper for the bulk of the funds to be invested in special obligations. Investment in special issues has the great advantage of avoiding disturbances of the capital market. At the same time, the Council believes that it would be desirable to continue to allow the Managing Trustee to invest in public issues when he finds that it is in the public interest to do so, provided such investment would involve no sacrifice of income to the funds.

From time to time, circumstances arise in which investment of trust fund assets in public obligations may be in the public interest. At a time of declining bond prices, for example, purchase of public issues on the open market may help preserve the asset value of Federal securities held by private investors. It may also assist the Treasury Department in the sale of new issues of Federal securities at a time when the market for Government bonds is unfavorable.

We recognize that it has been the practice of the Managing Trustee to purchase marketable obligations for the trust funds only if the current yields on the marketable obligations exceed what would be obtained by purchasing special obligations. The Council believes, however, that it would be desirable to make this practice a statutory obligation. The Council therefore recommends adoption of a provision allowing purchase of marketable securities only when such purchase is in the public interest

---

[9] See footnote 8.

and would provide currently a yield equal to or greater than the alternative of investing in special issues. This provision would supersede the present statutory provision that special issues shall be purchased only if it is not in the public interest for the trust funds to purchase other Federal securities.

   **E.** *The law should be amended to state that the Board of Trustees as a whole has the responsibility to review the general policies followed in managing the trust funds, and to recommend changes, as needed, in the provisions of the law that govern the way in which the trust funds are to be managed. In keeping with the nature of its responsibilities, the intervals between meetings of the Board should be not more than 6 months.*

   The Council believes that the present statutory provision giving full authority for management of the operations and investments of the trust funds to the Secretary of the Treasury as Managing Trustee is sound. Generally the Secretary of the Treasury, by reason of his position and experience, is the person in the Government who is best equipped for this responsibility. However, the Council believes that all members of the Board of Trustees should participate in the review of the general policies followed in the management of the trust funds. We, therefore, recommend an amendment to the law to give more specific recognition to the responsibility of trusteeship of all members of the Board and to require that the intervals between meetings be not more than 6 months.

   **F.** *The Council has examined broadly the way administrative expenses are charged to the trust funds and the financial provisions relating to the Railroad Retirement Account and to the coverage of the members of the armed forces and believes that the arrangements are fair.*

   The Council believes that the trust funds should be treated in all respects as funds held in trust, bearing their proper share of expense but not operating so as to subsidize other activities of government.

   The Council did not look, in great detail, into the question of the charging of administrative expenses, but we believe that with relatively minor exceptions all administrative costs are being charged to the trust funds. These include the administrative expenses of the Bureau of Old-Age and Survivors Insurance, the expenses incurred by the Internal Revenue Service in the collection of social security taxes, and expenses incurred by other units of the Department of Health, Education, and Welfare and of the Treasury Department in connection with old-age, survivors, and disability insurance. The administrative expenses of the total program, although charged to the respective trust funds, are subject to the regular appropriation procedures of Congress.

   Under the 1951 amendments to the Railroad Retirement Act, wage credits accumulated under the railroad retirement system by workers who die or retire with less than 10 years of railroad employment are transferred to the workers' accounts under the old-age, survivors, and disability insurance program. Benefit payments are made by the old-age, survivors, and disability insurance program on the basis of the combined earnings records. Retirement and disability benefits are payable under both programs to workers with 10 or more years of railroad service who also qualify under old-age, survivors, and disability insurance. The survivors of workers with 10 or more years of railroad service receive benefits under one program or the other based on combined wage records. Each year the two agencies jointly determine the amount of money which, if transferred from the Railroad Retirement Account to the Old-Age and Survivors Insurance Trust Fund or vice versa, would place the trust fund in the same position it would have been in if railroad employment had always been covered under the Social Security Act. The amount so determined is transferred. There is provision for similar annual interchanges between the Railroad Retirement Account and the Disability Insurance Trust Fund beginning with the fiscal year 1958. This is an arrangement which seems to us to be fair to both programs.

Beginning January 1, 1957, contributory coverage was extended to members of the uniformed services. Noncontributory wage credits of $160 a month have been provided to persons who served in the armed forces from September 16, 1940, through December 31, 1956. In addition, provision had been made for noncontributory survivors insurance protection for certain World War II veterans for a period of 3 years following their discharge from the armed forces. The Old-Age and Survivors Insurance Trust Fund received reimbursements from the general fund of the Treasury for the additional costs of these survivor benefits paid before September 1, 1950. Under the 1956 amendments, the additional costs of the survivor benefits after August 31, 1950, and all past and future expenditures arising from the noncontributory military wage credits, will be met by reimbursements from the general fund to the appropriate trust funds. These reimbursements should not be regarded as a Government contribution or as a departure from the policy of self-support. Instead, these contributions are made by the United States Government from general funds in its capacity as employer of the members of the armed forces.

## X. CONCLUSION

In conclusion, the Council would reiterate what we have said earlier in this report: In a dynamic society a program of old-age, survivors, and disability insurance requires periodic review of its operations to assure that its effectiveness is maintained. The Council is pleased to report that according to the best cost estimates available the contribution schedule now in the law makes adequate provision for meeting the cost of the benefits provided. We have found that the method of financing is sound and that no fundamental changes are required or desirable. Our recom-

mendations are intended to strengthen the measures necessary to carry
out the basic principles inherent in the program.

# 14. OLD-AGE AND SURVIVORS INSURANCE AFTER TWENTY YEARS

Victor Christgau,
*Social Security Bulletin,*
**August, 1955.**

THE PURPOSE of the old-age and survivors insurance program is to provide
protection against economic insecurity for the worker and his family
when the earnings upon which they have depended for support are cut
off by his retirement or death. This basic purpose was reaffirmed by
President Eisenhower in his social security message of January 1954.
The President pointed out that the old-age and survivors insurance system had been developed in response to the need "arising from the complexities of our modern society. . . . The system is not intended as a
substitute for private savings, pension plans, and insurance protection. It
is, rather, intended as the foundation upon which these other forms of
protection can be soundly built. Thus, the individual's own work, his
planning and his thrift will bring him a higher standard of living upon
his retirement, or his family a higher standard of living in the event of his
death, than would otherwise be the case. Hence the system both encourages thrift and self-reliance, and helps to prevent destitution in our national life."

That the old-age and survivors insurance system, established by Congress in 1935, has moved toward its goal by relatively rapid stages is clear
when the program's accomplishments are viewed against the backdrop
of the years.

The old-age insurance program was designed as an expression of the
Nation's conviction that older retired persons should have a continuing
income, to which their rights would be established by law on the basis of
their earnings and contributions and which would be available without a
means test. The proportion of aged men and women in the Nation's population had been increasing. In the 1930's their plight had become particularly difficult. These were depression years, when even young persons found it increasingly hard to get or keep jobs and family savings
evaporated.

Later, in 1939, survivor insurance provisions were added to the Social
Security Act in recognition of the problem encountered by families

when the breadwinner died. The resulting legislation was basically the old-age and survivors insurance program as it is today, although it has been expanded by the comprehensive amendments of 1950 and 1954.

The test of whether the new program was constitutional came early. This issue was resolved in 1937 by the U.S. Supreme Court in an 8-to-1 decision, in which Justice Cardozo wrote:

> Needs that were narrow or parochial a century ago may be interwoven in our day with the well-being of the Nation. What is critical or urgent changes with the times. . . . Congress did not improvise a judgment when it found that the award of old-age benefits would be conducive to the general welfare. . . . The number of persons in the United States 65 years of age and over is increasing proportionately as well as absolutely. What is even more important the number of such persons unable to take care of themselves is growing at a threatening pace. . . . The problem is plainly national in area and dimensions.

* * * * *

In 1953, at the invitation of Mrs. Oveta Culp Hobby, Secretary of Health, Education, and Welfare, a group of men and women from business, labor, agriculture, education, and professional organizations took a look at the question of extending the program's coverage. They recommended that coverage be made as universal as possible. Congressional committees later held public hearings at which representatives of organizations reflecting a cross section of American life presented their views on what changes should be made in the program.

The 1954 amendments, strengthening the principle of a contributory system with benefits varying according to past earnings and paid without a test of financial need, grew out of these deliberations. The revisions were in many respects the most significant since the 1939 amendments. They provided almost universal coverage, increased benefits, and provided for protecting the benefit rights of individuals out of work for extended periods because of physical or mental disability.

Maturity for the old-age and survivors insurance program is by no means an accomplished fact. No worker has yet been under the system for a full working lifetime, and beneficiary rolls are smaller than they will be in the future, when practically everyone who works will have had the opportunity to gain protection under the program.

### Coverage

Questions of coverage were particularly troublesome for the architects of old-age insurance 20 years ago. Was it possible from an administrative standpoint to include in the program every type of employment? Could self-employment be covered? Could a workable system of tax collection and a sound method of reporting earnings be devised for all sorts of employment? Progress was destined to come gradually. At first, coverage was limited to employment in commerce and industry in the continental United States, Alaska, and Hawaii, where accurate and relatively simple wage reporting could be adapted to employers' regular bookkeeping practices.

\* \* \* \* \*

Thus today most of the gaps in coverage have been closed. About 90 percent of all paid jobs are covered by old-age and survivors insurance. As a result of amendments to the Railroad Retirement Act in 1946 and 1951, the railroad retirement and old-age and survivors insurance programs are so closely coordinated that railroad employment can be considered to be covered by old-age and survivors insurance.

The bulk of those still not included are Federal employees covered by Federal employee retirement systems, both civilian and military. Others not covered by the program are self-employed physicians, lawyers, dentists, naturopaths, osteopaths, chiropractors, veterinarians, and optometrists, as well as domestic and farm workers earning less than a specified amount and self-employed persons with net earnings of less than $400 a year.

### Benefits

During the 1940's, when the Nation's attention was focused on the war, old-age and survivors insurance benefits failed to keep pace with prices and earnings levels, which had increased dramatically. The industrial employee who in 1939 earned $100 a month was earning an average of $249 in 1950. The cost of living had risen 73 percent. Benefits, however, continued to be determined by the formula established under the 1939 amendments and within the $3,000 annual wage ceiling in effect since the program's start. As a result, maximum monthly benefits in 1950 were $45.60 for the retired worker and $68.40 for an aged couple. During the 1940's many States had higher average old-age assistance grants than the maximum benefit that could be paid to a retired worker under old-age and survivors insurance, and more of the aged population were drawing old-age assistance payments than insurance benefits.

To remain effective, the old-age and survivors insurance program must keep pace with the social and economic changes that take place in a dynamic society like that of the United States. In 1950, benefits were increased in recognition of the rise in living costs and the increase in wage levels. The 1950 benefit formula resulted in maximum monthly benefits of $80 for the retired worker and $120 for the aged retired couple. These amounts represented substantial percentage increases from the maximums possible under the 1939 law. In 1952 the maximums were raised to $85 and $127.50 through adoption of a formula providing 55 percent of the first $100 of average monthly earnings and 15 percent of the next $200.

In her testimony before congressional committees during their consideration of the 1954 amendments, the Secretary of Health, Education, and Welfare said:

Old-age and survivors insurance benefit levels were originally fixed in the mid-1930's, during a depression economy. Benefit increases enacted by Congress since then have done little more than keep pace with the inflationary trend our Nation has heretofore experienced. In my opinion, a readjustment of benefits to take into account the improved standard of the basic elements of living for the American worker is necessary. . . . These old-age and survivors insurance benefits are too low, under today's conditions, for old-age and survivors insurance to fulfill its purpose of providing basic retirement and survivorship protection and reducing the need for public assistance to the lowest possible level.

The new 1954 benefit formula kept the percentage of the first step at 55 but increased to $110 the amount of average monthly earnings to which it applied. At the same time, the second step of the formula was raised from 15 percent to 20 percent. Since annual earnings to be considered under old-age and survivors insurance were increased to $4,200 beginning with 1955, this new percentage applied to the next $240 of average monthly earnings.

The top benefit for a retired worker under the 1954 revisions ($108.-50) is equal to 31 percent of $350, the maximum monthly earnings that can be counted. The first step of the benefit formula, however, calls for 55 percent of the first $110 of earnings. The program has thus continued to recognize that the lower-paid worker needs a higher percentage replacement of his previous earnings than do men and women with higher earnings.

When in 1951 coverage was extended by the 1950 amendments to about 10 million additional workers, these workers faced at retirement the prospect of having 14 years (1937 through 1950) during which they had no covered earnings included in computing their average monthly earnings for benefit purposes. To avoid this result, provision was made for a new "starting date" that put the newly covered workers in the same position as those first covered in 1937. The amendments specified that if a worker has 1 quarter of coverage (whenever earned) for each 2 calendar quarters elapsing after 1950 up to the time he reaches age 65 or dies, he is insured, provided he has worked at least 6 calendar quarters in covered employment. Any worker who has 6 quarters of coverage after 1950 can have his average wage figured by using only years after 1950. While this action was taken primarily for the newly covered workers, it also was advantageous for workers who had entered coverage in 1937 and continued to work after 1950. For them, the provision meant that their benefits could be based on relatively current earnings and did not have to include earnings in the years preceding the rapid rise in wages during the war.

When another 10 million persons were brought into the system by the 1954 changes, provision was made to eliminate, in calculating their benefits, the 4 or 5 years of lowest or no earnings. This provision was of particular help to the newly covered, who could drop out the 4 years (1951–

54) when the opportunity for coverage was not open to them. For those workers who are already covered, short periods of unemployment, sickness, or absence from work for other reasons will not reduce the average.

One of the principal causes of low average monthly earnings is long periods out of work because of extended disability. A section of the 1952 amendments would have preserved the old-age and survivors insurance rights of those who became totally and permanently disabled before reaching retirement age. That provision expired before it could become effective, and in 1954 the present "disability freeze" provision was adopted. Under it, periods of time during which a worker or self-employed person is out of work because of extended disability may be eliminated in computing benefits. This provision will also bring to the attention of State vocational rehabilitation agencies disabled men and women who might be restored to gainful work.

As an outgrowth of these changes, low benefit payments in the future will generally reflect the earnings of men and women who are part-time or intermittent workers—only marginally a part of the Nation's working population and not primarily dependent on their earnings for their support.

### Retirement Test

Since 1940, when benefits first were paid on a monthly basis, the Social Security Act has prescribed the test to be used in determining when an individual is retired—that is, substantially out of gainful employment. The test has been revised with the changing times through which the program has passed since 1935. From 1940 through August 1950, benefits were intended to be paid only when the beneficiary was for all practical purposes completely retired from covered employment, and the law therefore provided that earnings of $15 or more in a month in covered employment would result in benefit suspension for that month. By 1950 a new philosophy was emerging: that it would be better if the older worker were able to retire more gradually and that therefore he should be able to receive his monthly benefits while engaging in some intermittent or part-time work. The 1950 amendments took cognizance of this philosophy. The revisions increased the permitted earnings amount to $50 monthly for beneficiaries under age 75 who worked in covered jobs and allowed earnings of $600 annually for those who had covered self-employment. In 1952, these amounts were raised to $75 and $900 respectively.

Today, under the 1954 amendments, beneficiaries are subject to a test based on earnings over the period of a year. Effective January, 1955, they may earn $1,200 annually without loss of benefits. One month's benefit is suspended for each $80 above that amount, except that no benefit is suspended for any month in which the beneficiary does not do substantial work in self-employment or earn wages that exceed $80. With almost universal coverage, it became administratively feasible as well as logical to apply the earnings test to noncovered as well as covered employment.

In recognition of the fact that some persons covered by the system might work throughout their lifetime, never retiring to a degree sufficient to make possible receipt of monthly benefits toward which they had contributed, payments were authorized in 1950 to beneficiaries aged 75 or older regardless of the extent of their current employment. The 1954 amendments reduced the age to 72.

Payment of benefits as annuities at age 65 regardless of earnings has been consistently rejected as too expensive for the program to support. The purpose of old-age and survivors insurance benefits is to help prevent dependency by providing a regular income to breadwinners and their families when wages or self-employment income stops at retirement or death. If there were no retirement test, benefits would be payable not only to those who had retired but also to those older workers who are still employed and have substantial earnings. The additional benefits that would be paid out to employed workers and their dependents would add substantially to the cost of the system and would not increase the security of the beneficiaries unable to work or unable to find employment.

### Financing the Program

Money to pay benefits comes from taxes paid by employees, their employers, and the self-employed men and women covered by the program. Congress has made clear its intent that the old-age and survivors insurance program be self-supporting and actuarially sound. The tax schedule for the program is designed to accomplish this purpose.

From 1937 through 1949 the tax for employees and employers was 1 percent each on taxable earnings. In 1950 the rate went up to 1½ percent. The rate for the self-employed, who were first covered in 1951, was set at one and one-half times the employee rate. The rates increased in 1954 to 2 percent for employees and employers and 3 percent for the self-employed. Tax rates are scheduled to increase gradually until 1975, when they will be 4 percent each for employees and employers and 6 percent for the self-employed.

All taxes collected under the program go into the Federal old-age and survivors insurance trust fund, a special fund in the U.S. Treasury. Money in the fund can be used only to pay benefits and the costs of administering the program. Amounts not required for current expenditures are invested in interest-bearing U.S. Government bonds.

### Relationship to Old-Age Assistance

Program growth during the past two decades is reflected in the relationship of old-age and survivors insurance to old-age assistance. From the beginning, old-age and survivors insurance was intended to maintain a basic income for retired workers and thereby reduce the need for public assistance. During the early years of program operation, more aged persons received old-age assistance than insurance. By January, 1955, however, more than twice as many aged persons were receiving insurance—5.5 million—as were receiving assistance—2.5 million. The turning point was reached when the requirements for insured status were liberalized and benefits increased by the 1950 amendments.

OASI AGED BENEFICIARIES AND OAA RECIPIENTS

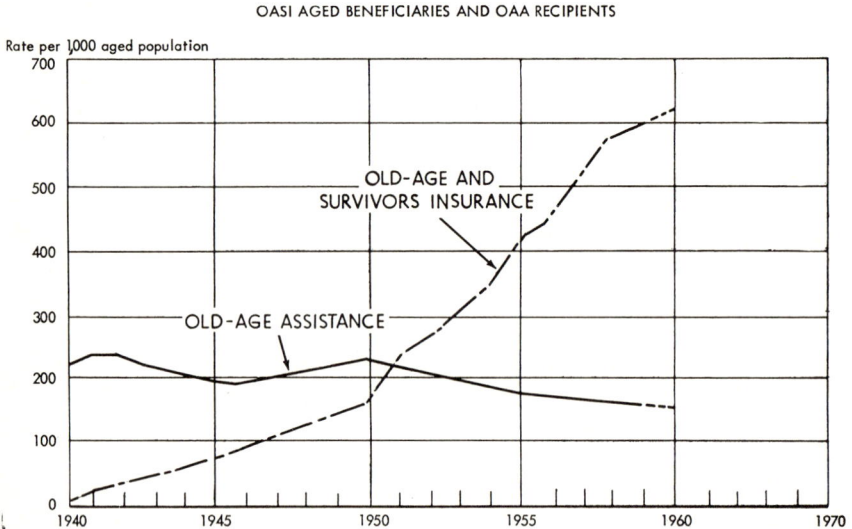

* * * * *

*Disability-Freeze Operations.* Late in 1954, a fourth operating division—the Division of Disability Operations—was created within the Bureau. The disability-freeze operation brought a new element into Bureau administration, involving a Federal-State partnership. Under the terms of the 1954 amendments, a State may designate one of its agencies to make determinations of disability on applications taken by old-age and survivors insurance district offices. Agreements for this purpose are worked out between the State agency and the Department of Health, Education, and Welfare. The Bureau's newest division has four major tasks—laying the groundwork for negotiations with the State agencies, reviewing State agency decisions on disability, making original decisions for those cases not covered by State agreements, and establishing standards and procedures for paying the State agencies, as well as developing medical guides, policies, and training materials for use by Bureau personnel and the State agencies.

*Staff Services.* In Baltimore there are, in addition to the operating divisions, the central headquarters staff. There about 500 employees provide personnel and administrative management services for the entire Bureau, train new employees and conduct refresher courses for older employees, prepare informational material, and develop policy to assure uniformity in the decisions made in applying program provisions to specific situations. There, too, the Bureau's research program is conducted to see how well the program is serving the people.

*Systematic Planning.* Careful and precise planning is a keystone of Bureau administration. A Bureau-wide system of work planning is one tool that is used.

The budget process is another planning tool. By 1942 the Bureau had moved into performance budgeting—where estimated costs and the activities planned for are brought together.

Administrative costs have been kept to a minimum by constant attention to improving ways of doing business, in small procedural details and in large-scale changes alike. Since 1941 the volume of the Bureau's work has increased about four times; the staff required to handle it has increased less than one-fourth as much as the workload. The administrative cost of about $112 million for this fiscal year will be about 1.8 percent of the income during the year to the old-age and survivors insurance trust fund. This percentage can be taken as a crude index of operational effectiveness. When the program was established, it was estimated that administrative costs would run to about 10 percent of trust fund income in the early years of the program and then drop to about 5 percent. Costs actually have never exceeded 3.6 percent since passage of the 1939 amendments.

### Summary

Old-age and survivors insurance over the years has provided an increasing measure of protection for the individual and his family against destitution and want resulting from loss of income when the breadwinner retires or dies. To the extent that the individual has been protected, society and the Nation's economy as a whole have been strengthened. The program has become identified with the economic welfare of the country within the framework outlined in 1948 by the Advisory Council in its report to the Senate Committee on Finance:

> In the last analysis the security of the individual depends on the success of industry and agriculture in producing an increasing flow of goods and services. However, the very success of the economy in making progress, while creating opportunities, also increases risks. Hence, the more progressive the economy, the greater is the need for protection against economic hazards. This protection should be made available on terms which reinforce the interest of the individual in helping himself. A properly designed social-security system will reinforce the drive of the individual toward greater production and greater efficiency, and will make for an environment conducive to the maximum of economic progress.

Old-age and survivors insurance is not a static program. Having met many of the challenges of the past, it must constantly turn its attention to the future. For, as President Eisenhower has said, "To help individuals provide for . . . security—to reduce both the fear and the incidence of destitution to the minimum—to promote the confidence of every individual in the future—these are proper aims of all levels of government, including the Federal Government."

# 15. RECENT TRENDS IN PRIVATE RETIREMENT PLANS

Alfred M. Skolnik and Joseph Zisman, "Growth in Employee-Benefit Plans, 1954–57," *Social Security Bulletin,* March, 1959.

Private retirement programs continued in 1957 the rapid growth they had experienced since World War II. By the end of 1957, 17.7 million employees were covered. Total contributions to finance the plans rose to almost $4.6 billion, reserves to $34.8 billion, the number of beneficiaries to 1¼ million, and benefits to almost $1.2 billion. Since 1950 coverage has increased more than 80 percent, contributions 120 percent, the number of beneficiaries 178 percent, and reserves and benefits have trebled (table 1). The data presented in table 1 have been considerably revised for the current article. Data on pension plans operated by trade unions and to which employers made no contributions are included for the first time; additional data with respect to multi-employer plans have made possible improved estimates of coverage, resources, benefits, and number of beneficiaries under such plans; and revised reports by the insurance industry and by the Securities and Exchange Commission have been taken into account. The revised estimates, prepared by the Division of the Actuary, reflect the same trends shown in the data presented last year.

## Coverage

In 1957, 1.4 million employees were added to the coverage of private pension and deferred profit-sharing plans, bringing the total to an estimated 17.7 million. Nearly all these employees were also covered under the Federal old-age, survivors, and disability insurance program. Almost 3 out of 4 of those protected by private plans were under noninsured plans, and the remainder were under insured programs underwritten by insurance companies. Though coverage under noninsured programs has gone up since 1951 at a somewhat faster rate (65 percent) than that under insured plans (55 percent), the difference was not sufficiently great to alter appreciably the proportion of employees covered by each type. The increase in coverage in insured plans has been accompanied by a marked growth in deposit administration plans. In 1951, there were only 445,000 employees covered by such plans. By the end of 1957, the number had

## TABLE 1

### Private Pension and Deferred Profit-Sharing Plans: Estimated Coverage, Contributions, Reserves, Beneficiaries, and Benefit Payments, 1930–57[1]

| Year | Coverage,[2] end of year (in thousands) | | | Employer contributions (in millions) | | | Employee contributions (in millions) | | | Reserves, end of year (in billions) | | | Number of beneficiaries, end of year (in thousands) | | | Amount of benefit payments (in millions) | | |
|---|---|---|---|---|---|---|---|---|---|---|---|---|---|---|---|---|---|---|
| | Total | Insured plans | Noninsured plans | Total | Insured plans | Noninsured plans | Total | Insured plans | Noninsured plans | Total | Insured plans | Noninsured plans | Total | Insured plans | Noninsured plans | Total | Insured plans | Noninsured plans[3] |
| 1957 | 17,700 | 4,500 | 13,200 | $3,900 | $1,230 | $2,670 | $680 | $300 | $380 | $34.8 | $14.0 | $20.8 | 1,250 | 370 | 880 | $1,150 | $260 | $890 |
| 1956 | 16,300 | 4,100 | 12,200 | 3,490 | 1,110 | 2,380 | 610 | 290 | 320 | 30.3 | 12.4 | 17.9 | 1,130 | 330 | 800 | 1,010 | 230 | 780 |
| 1955 | 15,200 | 3,900 | 11,300 | 3,190 | 1,100 | 2,090 | 550 | 280 | 270 | 26.5 | 11.2 | 15.3 | 990 | 290 | 700 | 860 | 200 | 660 |
| 1954 | 14,100 | 3,700 | 10,400 | 2,930 | 1,030 | 1,900 | 510 | 270 | 240 | 23.0 | 9.9 | 13.1 | 870 | 260 | 610 | 720 | 170 | 550 |
| 1953 | 13,100 | 3,500 | 9,600 | 2,930 | 1,010 | 1,920 | 480 | 260 | 220 | 19.8 | 8.8 | 11.0 | 740 | 220 | 520 | 620 | 150 | 470 |
| 1952 | 11,600 | 3,200 | 8,400 | 2,510 | 910 | 1,600 | 430 | 240 | 190 | 16.9 | 7.7 | 9.2 | 640 | 190 | 450 | 540 | 130 | 410 |
| 1951 | 10,900 | 2,900 | 8,000 | 2,260 | 820 | 1,440 | 380 | 210 | 170 | 14.2 | 6.6 | 7.6 | 540 | 170 | 370 | 460 | 110 | 350 |
| 1950 | 9,800 | 2,600 | 7,200 | 1,750 | 720 | 1,030 | 330 | 200 | 130 | 11.7 | 5.6 | 6.1 | 450 | 150 | 300 | 380 | 90 | 290 |
| 1945 | 6,400 | ..... | ..... | 830 | ..... | ..... | 160 | ..... | ..... | 5.4 | ..... | ..... | 310 | ..... | ..... | 220 | ..... | ..... |
| 1940 | 4,100 | ..... | ..... | 180 | ..... | ..... | 130 | ..... | ..... | 2.4 | ..... | ..... | 160 | ..... | ..... | 140 | ..... | ..... |
| 1935 | 2,700 | ..... | ..... | 140 | ..... | ..... | 90 | ..... | ..... | 1.3 | ..... | ..... | 110 | ..... | ..... | 100 | ..... | ..... |
| 1930 | 2,700 | ..... | ..... | 130 | ..... | ..... | 70 | ..... | ..... | .8 | ..... | ..... | 100 | ..... | ..... | 90 | ..... | ..... |

[1] Includes pay-as-you-go, nonprofit organizations, and union pension plans and deferred profit-sharing plans. Excludes railroad plans, except those supplementing the Federal railroad retirement program. In 1930, private railroad plans covered an average of 1.3 million employees and paid about $30 million in benefits to about 50,000 beneficiaries. In 1935 they covered an average of 1.1 million workers and paid about $40 million to about 60,000 beneficiaries.

[2] Excludes pensioners.

[3] Includes refunds to employees; also lump sums under deferred profit-sharing plans.

Source: Social Security Administration, Division of the Actuary.

increased to 1,415,000—a rise of 27 percent from the preceding year and of 70 percent from 1954.

Part of the expansion in coverage is the result of the natural growth resulting from increased employment in some establishments with plans and from the fulfillment by employees of eligibility requirements for coverage. Much of it results from the creation of new plans and the addition of new participating employers to existing multi-employer plans. Trade unions in industries consisting largely of small employers have continued their drive for the establishment of jointly administered multi-employer plans. The International Brotherhood of Teamsters, for example, early in the year reached an agreement with 2,000 food companies in Delaware, southern New Jersey, and Pennsylvania, establishing a new employer-financed pension plan covering 25,000 employees. The International Alliance of Theatrical Stage Employees signed an agreement with 13 motion picture exchanges that provides for the establishment of an industry-wide pension plan covering 6,000 employees working in 34 cities.

Coverage by industry and by area is somewhat uneven, as shown by studies of the Bureau of Labor Statistics. Retirement plans in 1957 covered practically all the nonsupervisory workers in privately operated electric and gas utility systems employing 100 or more workers. In the motor-vehicle-parts manufacturing industry such plans were found in establishments (with 100 or more employees) that employed 85 percent of the production workers and 88 percent of the office workers. On the other hand, only one-sixth of the production workers in footwear manufacturing were employed in establishments (with eight or more employees) that had retirement plans. In the nonelectrical machinery industry, employment in establishments with retirement plans ranged from 20 percent in the Portland (Oregon) area to 91 percent in the Hartford area.

### Employer and Employee Contributions

Almost $4.6 billion was contributed in 1957 by employers and employees to insured and noninsured pension plans—an increase of 12 percent from the preceding year and of 73 percent from 1951. A growing proportion of these sums was contributed to noninsured pension plans during the period—67 percent in 1957, 61 percent in 1951—although, as already pointed out, the total proportion of coverage by such plans has not changed.

The proportion contributed by employers to both insured and noninsured plans has been virtually the same—about 85 percent—from 1951 to 1957. Their contributions averaged about 80 percent of the total for insured plans and about 88 percent for noninsured plans throughout the period.

An average of $269 per employee was contributed by employers and employees in 1957, an increase of only $9 from 1956 and of $14 from

1951, or less than 6 percent for the period. Employer contributions in 1957 averaged $229 per employee, only 5 percent greater than in 1951, and employee contributions, which averaged $40 per employee in 1957, had increased somewhat faster—about 9 percent. In insured plans the average contribution experienced a slow but steady decline (4 percent for employers and 9 percent for employees), and in noninsured plans it increased noticeably (11 percent for employer contributions and 34 percent for employees).

The average employee contributions cited above are obtained by dividing the total annual employee contributions by the average number of employees covered during the year. Actually, only a small proportion of the covered employees make contributions. In its analysis of provisions in effect in the winter of 1957–58, out of 100 plans under collective bargaining the Bureau of Labor Statistics found only 14 contributory plans —that is, plans requiring employee contributions. The 14 plans included only 12 percent of the 3.3 million covered workers. As already noted, unpublished data from community wage surveys conducted by the Bureau in 1957 and early 1958, covering both union and nonunion manufacturing establishments, reveal that 80 percent of the 2.1 million workers employed by firms with pension plans were in establishments reporting noncontributory plans. A study of provisions in effect in January 1957 in 290 large pension plans in New York State (plans covering at least 1,500 employees in that State) shows that one-fourth of the plans were contributory and an additional 4 percent contained both contributory and noncontributory features. In contributory plans, employee contributions generally ranged from 1.5–3.0 percent of the first $3,000, $3,600, or $4,200 of annual wages (depending on when the plans were established or last amended) plus 3–5 percent of the excess.

Employer contributions to pension plans vary, of course, from plan to plan. In employer-administered plans the employer contributes the amount (over and above employee contributions) necessary to provide the benefits contemplated. The cost of past-service credits (credit for service before the plan was established) is almost always financed entirely by the employer. The type of funding, the composition of the covered group, and the benefit provisions determine the cost. The Bureau of Labor Statistics study shows that, in plans jointly administered by employers and trade unions, employer contributions generally range from 5 cents to 15 cents per man hour, or from 2 percent to 5 percent of payroll.

The Chamber of Commerce of the United States in its study of 1957 fringe costs illustrates the wide variations by industry in the expenditures for pension plans. In the 827 firms studied, employer payments ranged from an average of 2.6 percent of payroll in the wholesale and retail trade to 8.6 percent in the petroleum industry. An illustration of how employer costs vary within a single industry is found in the experience of plans negotiated by employers in the steel industry and the United

Steel Workers of America. These plans covered more than 950,000 members in 1956, almost 78 percent of whom were in bargaining units with 1,000 or more members. All the plans are noncontributory. Although the plans vary somewhat, 75–80 percent of the covered workers are under the "typical plan" that provides standard benefits. Some employers have complete discretion as to the method of funding. The vast majority, however, make contributions in amounts necessary to pay current pensions and to provide (in various degrees) advance funding of future pensions. Contributions for 83 percent of the covered members are paid into pension trusts. Insured plans and the partly insured and partly trusteed plans cover 11 percent, and the remainder are in unfunded plans. The average employer contribution per employee for the most recent fiscal year (usually the year ended December 31, 1957) was more than $258. The average was less than $50 for about 6 percent of the members; they were in the small nonfunded plans, some of which had no pensioners. More than $400 per employee was contributed with respect to almost one-third of the workers covered, $100–$200 for almost 35 percent, and $200–$300 for about 38 percent.

### Reserves

As of the end of 1957, $34.8 billion was accumulated in reserves maintained by insured and noninsured private retirement programs—an increase of $4.5 billion from 1956. Since 1951 the reserves had more than doubled.

Approximately 54 percent of the 1951 reserves, compared with 60 percent in 1957, was accumulated by noninsured plans. During the same period the average reserve per covered employee rose from about $1,000 to $1,638 for noninsured plans and from $2,400 to $3,255 for insured plans. These increases reflect not only the additions to reserves resulting from liberalization of benefits, maturing of the plans, and improved funding arrangements but also to efforts—especially in noninsured plans—to improve the earnings of the funds held in reserve. A recent Securities and Exchange Commission report indicates, for example, that the proportion of the total of corporate pension fund assets that is invested in U.S. Government securities dropped from 30 percent in 1951 to 10 percent in 1957. The proportion held in corporate bonds increased only from 45 percent to 54 percent and fluctuated between 52 and 54 percent in the period 1954–57. Preferred stocks, which constituted less than 4 percent of the total assets in 1951, amounted to about 3 percent in 1957. Common stocks, on the other hand, rose from less than 12 percent of the total assets in 1951 and from about 19 percent in 1954 to almost 25 percent in 1957. In dollar amounts, their book value rose from $812 million to $4,770 million. While the total assets of the funds trebled from 1951 to 1957, common stock holdings went up to almost six times what they had been. The Commission states that the increase in the average rate of earnings of corporate pension funds, from 3.58 percent in 1955 to 3.84 percent in 1957, reflects the shift to higher-yielding investments and the generally upward trend in interest rates.

## Beneficiaries and Benefits

At the end of 1957, about 1¼ million pensioners were on the rolls of private plans—an increase of 131 percent from 1951. By far the largest number were beneficiaries of noninsured programs. Since 1951 there has been an increase of 138 percent in the number of beneficiaries under such programs. In insured plans the increase was 118 percent.

Benefit payments in 1957 amounted to $1,150 million, compared with $1,010 million in 1956 and $460 million in 1951. The bulk of these sums —more than three-fourths—was paid under noninsured programs in all 3 years. For almost nine-tenths of the 1957 beneficiaries, these benefits supplemented the benefits they received under the Federal old-age, survivors, and disability insurance program. An estimated 165,000 had worked in noncovered employment or retired before they had met the age or work requirements to qualify under the Federal program. The benefits under noninsured plans include refunds of employee contributions to individuals who withdraw from the plans before retirement and before accumulating vested deferred rights, payments of the excess of employee contributions to survivors of pensioners who died before they had received in retirement benefits an amount equal to their contributions, and lump-sum payments made under deferred profit-sharing plans. The nature of the available data does not permit the separation of these lump-sum payments from the amounts representing monthly retirement benefits. The average monthly retirement benefit, therefore, cannot be derived.

Few private pension plans appear to have been modified as a result of the 1956 amendments to the Social Security Act providing benefits to totally and permanently disabled employees aged 50 or over, according to a 1957 study of the National Industrial Conference Board. Of 98 companies with pension plans without disability benefit provisions in 1955, only four added such a provision after the enactment of the 1956 amendments and another nine were planning to do so. Most of these 13 companies had negotiated plans. Of 66 companies with plans that had disability provisions in 1955, practically none had changed or planned to change them to conform with the amended law. Almost half of the 66 companies had provisions for offsetting the Federal disability benefits against their disability benefits, although only one-third had such provisions with respect to age-retirement benefits.

Provisions for retirement before the "normal" retirement age at the option of the employee seem to be increasing—especially in negotiated plans. Thus the Bankers Trust Company in its 1956 survey of 240 employer-administered retirement plans reported that, of the plans with early retirement provisions, only 43 percent of the 43 "pattern plans" (all negotiated plans) and about 33 percent of the other 175 plans with such provisions permitted early retirement at the employee's option. The Bureau of Labor Statistics study reports that in 75 percent of the plans with early retirement provisions such retirement was at the employee's option.

Few instances are known in which retirement age for women was lowered following the 1956 amendment to the Social Security Act providing optional retirement at age 62 for women in covered employment. In the spring of 1957, the Executive Board of the International Ladies' Garment Workers Union proposed to its locals, joint boards, and departments that negotiations be undertaken to lower the retirement age for women from 65 to 62 in pension plans covering their members. In March, 1957, the pension plan negotiated by the Textile Workers Union and the Berkshire-Hathaway Mills was amended to make such a reduction in the retirement age for women.

# 16. THE STEADY PUSH FOR PENSIONS

*Fortune* Magazine,
June, 1959.

IT IS NOW ten years since organized labor began to bargain for pensions in a big way, and there is every indication that the pension issue will grow in importance during the decade ahead. Pension-plan improvements have figured prominently in recent settlements in autos, farm machinery, and rubber. In the steel negotiations now under way, the union is demanding "adequate" pensions for its members, a sizable proportion of whom, according to a survey undertaken recently by Samuel Lubell, want pension improvements more than wage increases. Lubell found that many steelworkers have become disillusioned about wage increases that are eaten away by taxes and inflation. Pension payments are partially tax-exempt and furthermore the great spread of pension plans has given many workers a new interest in a stable price level.

The union's first real breakthrough on pensions came in 1949. Early in that year the Supreme Court upheld a ruling by the National Labor Relations Board that the terms of pension plans were bargainable issues—even if the plans had been set up voluntarily by the companies. Late in 1949 the Steelworkers struck for six weeks and finally won a program, financed entirely by the companies, which provided minimum payments of $100 a month, including social security, for all workers over sixty-five with twenty-five years of service. Within a year similar benefits had been secured by more than a dozen unions; by mid-1950, more than five million workers—in steel, auto, rubber, mining, electrical, paper, and the garment trades—were covered by negotiated pension plans. In the past decade this number has grown to at least ten million. Including workers *not* in a collective-bargaining unit, the total of Americans now covered by group pension plans comes to about 18 million.

The plans that emerged from the first round of pension bargaining were almost all linked to social-security payments, i.e., employers were obligated to provide the difference between these payments and some fixed amount (ordinarily $100 a month). In 1950, an unmarried, retired worker was entitled to about $36 a month from social security, and so the company share was about $64. Many companies suddenly discovered that social-security payments were inadequate. When the auto workers won their first pension plan, Ernest Breech of the Ford Motor Co. came out for increased social-security benefits. With industry and labor largely united on the issue, Congress increased the benefits in 1950—to around $65 for an average unmarried worker. This brought the companies' own obligation down to $35. A 1954 increase in social-security benefits brought them up to an average of $85 and a maximum of $98.50, and for a short time the steel companies, among others, were paying next to nothing for pensions.

### Breaking the Link

But that same year the Steelworkers finally broke the link between social security and their own pension plan. The union won acceptance of a formula providing for a minimum company payment of $2 a month for each year of service, with $5 subtracted from the total monthly benefit. In the past few years this kind of plan has become typical, at least in heavy industry, and $2.50 is now the prevailing figure for company payments—though the pattern may rise with the steel settlement. Retired workers with thirty years of service in steel, auto, rubber, and farm machinery are now receiving payments of $75 a month. Since social-security payments have been increasing every two years, the retirement income of millions of blue-collar workers is beginning to look fairly substantial. A single man receiving the maximum benefits would get $116 a month upon retirement, and a married couple would get $174. With the private pension payments added to these, the total retirement income of thirty-year workers is moving rapidly to a "norm" of some $250 a month. The Auto Workers currently estimate that a retired couple needs at least $237 a month. The U.A.W. agrees that most of their thirty-year men are now getting this much, but points to the difficulty that most retired workers have not spent thirty years on the job. The average income of U.A.W. members who are now retiring is only $220—little more than 50 per cent of the average after-tax pay of working members.

In some industries, however, retired workers are getting a much higher proportion of their working pay. The National Maritime Union and the American Radio Association have pensions which, together with social security, can leave the worker and his wife with about 70 per cent of his pre-retirement income. The highest pension possible under any collective-bargaining agreement is around $25,000 a year—which could be received by some elite "workers" represented by the American Federation of Television and Radio Artists. Even in heavy industry some highly paid skilled workers are given pensions outside the equalitarian $2.50-per-month-per-year pattern. About 10 per cent of steelworkers have their pension figured on a so-called "1 per cent formula."* A rolling-mill operator, for example, who earns $10,000 a year, would retire in thirty years with $165 a month (rather than $75), plus social security.

If any limit to organized labor's pension ambitions is in sight, it appears to be around the point at which total retirement income is 70 per cent of working income. An Auto Workers' specialist in the field, James Brindle, doubts "that U.A.W. members would hit the bricks for pension increases over 70 per cent."

### The Vested Interest

Even before the dollar amount of pension benefits reaches the 70 per cent level, the unions are likely to pay increased attention to vesting rules, i.e., to the rules that set a minimum number of years a man must work to have an equity in the pension fund. The first pension plans in steel required a worker to have twenty-five years of service with his company and be sixty-five in order to receive any benefits. If he left the company for two years and then returned, he had to start all over again accumulating pension credits. Later contracts whittled the eligibility period down to fifteen years in steel, but a worker who quits before his sixty-fifth birthday still gets nothing. In most of the auto industry there is full vesting after a man has worked ten years and passed his fortieth birthday, but most of the steel pensions are still underwritten by workers who never get them. Jones & Laughlin estimates that only three out of ten workers on its payroll will actually collect their pensions.

In some industries, where employers are small and labor turnover is high, pension credits are transferable. A Teamster member can switch jobs almost anywhere within the union's Western Conference and continue amassing credits. A few plans, in fact, are nationwide, e.g., those covering members of the Garment Workers, the National Maritime Union, and the American Radio Association. The Steelworkers have demanded transferable pension credits in the past, and will renew the demand in the current negotiations.

---

* The monthly benefit is 1 per cent of average monthly earnings for the ten years preceding retirement, multiplied by total years of service, less $85.

# 17. MAJOR QUESTIONS OF PUBLIC POLICY

ROBERT M. BALL,
*Pensions in the United States,*
National Planning Association,
1952.

. . . MAJOR QUESTIONS of public policy will be raised which are not necessarily in the area of general agreement and which seem to require further research and consideration. To give definitive answers to some of the questions raised will require a great deal of additional experience, study, and discussion.

Before intelligent action can be taken on some of the problems, more facts are needed. At the present time, many elementary facts about private pension plans—the level of protection afforded, the number of persons protected, the coverage of various types of plans, the amount of money being put into the plans, the number of pensioners, and so forth—are uncertain. Policy formation cannot, however, always await the completion of research and, moreover, the solutions of some of the problems hinge largely on value judgments which can be made now as well as later. In some areas action should be immediate.

## THE INTERRELATIONSHIP OF THE VARIOUS PENSION PLANS AND OTHER PROGRAMS FOR INCOME MAINTENANCE OF OLDER PERSONS

In making sure that our commitments for the future are adequate but not excessive, perhaps the most important goal is to develop a rational relationship among the various programs. Will veterans be granted a general pension payable regardless of employment and regardless of other retirement income? What is to be the relationship of old-age and survivors insurance to the other public retirement programs operated by the Federal, State, and local governments? How much of the job of supplying retirement income is to be done by old-age and survivors insurance and how much by the private supplementary plans? What are the factors which will determine the need for old-age assistance in the future?

Under present arrangements, some people now working will not get any pension at all when they retire, the great majority will get the pension of the general public program alone, some will get the pension of the public program and a supplementary pension; a few will get several pensions from various sources. What is the best way to improve this situation?

### The Veterans Program and Social Security

There are now about 19 million veterans in the United States. A major question of public policy is the extent to which these veterans are to be granted special benefits in addition to the protection which they share with others under social security. For our present investigation the issue in this area is primarily whether aged veterans will be granted a general pension without regard to other income and without regard to service-connected disabilities.

The present veterans' legislation does not provide a general pension to aged veterans. It provides compensation to those with service-connected disabilities, and for other veterans it, in effect, guarantees a minimum level of living in old age; as indicated previously, the nonservice-connected program pays a benefit only if income from other sources is below $1,400 for the single veteran and $2,700 if he is married.

There is general acceptance of the program for service-connected disability. Moreover, the present program for cases not service-connected may not be unduly expensive if the availability of other types of protection is taken into account in considering modifications in the future. For example, if the present income tests and benefit levels are retained for the veterans program and old-age and survivors insurance is liberalized as the community standard of living rises, a large proportion of veterans would have from other sources the minimum level of living now guaranteed and would not be eligible for the special veterans' benefit. Under these conditions, veterans' pensions for the aged in 1975 would amount to about $600 million in terms of 1951 prices. If, on the other hand, in planning the nonservice-connected disability pensions and in considering proposals for general veterans pensions, the Congress does not recognize that most of the same people will be entitled to old-age and survivors insurance benefits and that many will still be working after age 65, high costs will result. If the income limitation and the amount of benefit under the veterans program, as well as benefit amounts under the old-age and survivors insurance program, are adjusted as the standard of living increases,[1] the cost of veterans' pensions to persons over 65 would in 1975 be about $3 billion in terms of 1951 prices. A general pension for aged veterans adjusted to a rising standard of living and paid without regard to other income, including income from work, would cost about $5 billion in 1975 (1951 prices). These additional costs would be incurred largely to pay additional benefits to persons who were either still at work or already drawing OASI benefits. In some instances, of course, the retired veteran would also be drawing a private pension.

---

[1] Adjustments were made to provide the same level of relative adequacy as when the current amounts were established.

### Old-Age and Survivors Insurance and the Other Government Programs

. . . There is very substantial support for the extension of old-age and survivors insurance to the more than 10 percent of the labor force not now protected by any plan. In addition, it would be highly desirable to work out a more rational relationship among the various public programs. Private plans are usually designed with the benefits of the public program taken into account so that they represent a planned supplementation. This is not true of the various public programs for special groups. The Civil Service Retirement System, the systems of the Armed Forces, and the systems of the State and local governments are designed, not as supplements to old-age and survivors insurance, but as if the benefit paid by the special system were the only one which an individual receives. Because so many Americans move from one job to another during the course of a lifetime, some workers fail to qualify under any system while a large number of others, contrary to the assumption on which these special plans are based, will also receive benefits from old-age and survivors insurance. Indeed, if present arrangements are continued, it will not be uncommon for a person to qualify, for example, under the Federal Civil Service System, old-age and survivors insurance, and some other program such as the Reserve Officers System of the Armed Forces.

This type of duplication and multiplication of benefits is inequitable and results in higher than necessary costs because these independent systems do not take special account of those cases where their beneficiary also receives an old-age and survivors insurance benefit weighted in favor of the low-paid worker and the worker who is under the system for relatively short periods. A person who is under Federal civil service for part of his working lifetime, for example, receives a civil-service benefit directly related to his years of service and no account is taken of the likelihood that he will also be receiving an old-age and survivors insurance benefit based on the rest of his working lifetime and weighted favorably in relation to his years of service in employment covered by old-age and survivors insurance.

There is not the same objection to a person receiving old-age and survivors insurance benefits plus a supplementary private pension based on 15 years' service with one company and another pension based on 15 years' service with a different company. Service with both companies is counted for old-age and survivors insurance purposes so there is no weighting as a result of short service under old-age and survivors insurance. Moreover, both private plans will have taken into account the fact that the pensioner will receive an old-age and survivors insurance benefit.

Various groups are engaged in studying the relationship of old-age and survivors insurance to the other public programs and in attempting to work out the best method of providing protection at the lowest possible cost. During 1952, a special joint committee of the House and Senate was concerned with the relationship of the Railroad Retirement program to old-age and survivors insurance. Between these two systems coordination has already progressed to a considerable degree.

At the same time, under Public Law 555 the executive branch of the Government has been directed to conduct a special study of the inter-relationship of the various pension systems covering Federal employees and old-age and survivors insurance. The Senate Finance Committee has also indicated its desire to hold hearings early in 1953 on the relationship of the State and local retirement systems to old-age and survivors insurance. Some action in this whole area may be expected over the next few years.

Coordination between old-age and survivors insurance and the other Government programs will probably be accomplished, in some cases, by extending old-age and survivors insurance to the employments now covered by special plans with the special plans being redesigned to make them similar to the supplementary plans of private industry and the non-profit area. In other areas, coordination may take different forms.

### Private Plans and the Basic Public Program

The pension plans of private industry and the nonprofit area are de-signed to provide benefits supplementary to OASI. It follows, therefore, that their character is greatly influenced by the nature of the OASI system.

Old-age and survivors insurance is a variable benefit system. There is an absolute minimum of $25 a month payable to any retired worker who meets the minimum service requirements ($37.50 for a couple when the wife is 65 or over). The worker who spends full time under the system will in the future ordinarily receive at least $55 a month ($80 for a couple). These are the amounts payable on an average wage of $100 a month. The benefits increase as the average wage earned under the system increases until they reach a maximum of $85 for the single man and $127.-50 for man and wife, payable to all those who average $300 a month or more. The $200 a month worker will get $70 and, when married, $105.

For workers who are under the system full time and who earn more than a minimum wage, benefits are a decreasing percentage of the wage, although they are higher in amount than for those who earn only minimum wages. At a $300 average wage (the maximum counted under the program), the benefits for a man and wife are 43 percent of the wage instead of 80 percent as at a $100 average wage. Because of the program's maximum wage base, the benefit for man and wife is only 26 percent for the $500-a-month worker. Even if the present benefit formula were applied up to $500 a month, the benefits for husband and wife at this wage level would be only 35 percent of the wage.

Old-age and survivors insurance, then, is not geared to a budget concept of minimum subsistence as is the British system, but is geared rather to individual circumstances. It pays to many of those who are under the System only part time less than old-age assistance would pay. To the worker who is under the System full time and who has earned only minimum or near-minimum wages, it aims to pay amounts which will make recourse to assistance unnecessary except in cases of special need.[2] (It cannot be assumed that retired workers who earned only minimum wages have significant income from other sources; the benefit for such workers must in itself supply minimum subsistence.) To the worker above minimum wages, the system will pay benefits which are somewhat above the assistance level in most States.

In considering this benefit philosophy, the first question which arises is: How reasonable is it to pay benefits below subsistence to many of those who spend only part of their working lives under the program? People are under the system less than full time for a variety of reasons. One large group of those not under the system for a lifetime is made up of women workers who work in covered employment in their younger years but do not work after marriage. Another sizable group consists of workers who spend a part of their lives working in noncovered employment, such as Government service or farming. It seems reasonable that both of these groups should get lower retirement benefits from old-age and survivors insurance than those who stay in OASI full time and contribute throughout their working lives. Nor is there any particular reason why their old-age and survivors insurance benefit should be enough to support them even at minimum subsistence levels.

The reduction in benefit that now takes place because of a worker's disability is in a different category. Congress has indicated its intention of considering this question in 1953. The present formula also proves unduly harsh in its treatment of the individual who suffers involuntary unemployment. One way of meeting this problem would be to pay full rate benefits to those who were in the system say 30 years out of the possible 45 working years between the ages of 20 and 65, with reductions only for those with less than 30 years. This would make it possible for an individual to secure maximum benefits even though out of the system for part of his working life.

There is little quarrel with the idea of paying the minimum-wage worker an amount at least equal to a low subsistence level if he is under the program full time. The major controversy on benefit philosophy in old-age and survivors insurance arises in determining how much above this amount should be paid to workers who earn more than minimum wages.

---

[2] The limitation on paying an adequate subsistence benefit to the full-time worker at minimum wages is the wage itself. The old-age and survivors insurance system now pays to a couple 80 percent of the average wage up to $100.

There is substantial agreement among labor, management, and experts that the benefit should vary with wages and that those who earn more than minimum wages should receive more. But how much more? Should the second step in the old-age and survivors insurance formula be 15 percent as at present or should it be raised to 20 or 25 percent? Should only the first $3,600 of wages earned in a year be counted toward the benefit as at present or should the maximum amount be raised to a higher figure?[3] Should the weighted part of the benefit formula be applied to more of the average monthly wage? As indicated in part II, there is little likelihood that old-age and survivors insurance benefits for workers at more than minimum wages would be made so high that they would be considered sufficient retirement income in themselves. The issue concerning the proper relationship of OASI and the private supplementary plans therefore is largely one of degree.

Decision on points such as these regarding old-age and survivors insurance will have a considerable effect on the character of the job which the private pension movement will be expected to do. If old-age and survivors insurance is improved for workers with more than minimum wages it is likely that the standards for total retirement income will be raised and the goals of joint old-age and survivors insurance and private supple-

---

[3] One of the most controversial issues growing out of the need to adjust benefits to the long-range trend of increasing wages has been the timing of increases in the wage-base maximum. Some have favored raising this maximum now in order to include the total wages of workers to the same extent that the $3,000 maximum included total wages in 1939. This would now require about a $6,000 maximum instead of $3,-600. Where only a part of a worker's earnings can be credited toward benefits, the benefit amount necessarily represents a smaller proportion of the total wage loss upon retirement. Moreover, the fact that only earnings of $3,600 or less may be included in the average means that the individual whose customary earnings are at or above the taxable maximum, but who in some years receives below that amount because of sickness or unemployment, suffers a permanent reduction of his average monthly wage and hence his benefit amount; earnings above $3,600 in other years cannot be used to restore his average for benefit purposes even back to the maximum level allowed by law. While this situation will occur no matter what limit is set, it is argued that the maximum should be high enough so that all earnings of nearly all workers can usually be credited.

Others have argued that wages have not yet increased sufficiently above the 1939 level to require a further increase in the maximum wage and contribution base. This group recognizes that at some point the wage-base maximum should be raised, but they favor moving in this direction very slowly because such increases raise the benefits for higher-paid workers retiring in the early years of the program more than it increases their contributions. See *Recommendations for Social Security Legislation,* the Reports of the Advisory Council on Social Security to the Senate Committee on Finance, Appendix 1-F "Résumé of Minority Opinions on Changes in Benefit and Contribution Base," p. 64 (80th Cong., 2d sess.), Document No. 208 (Washington, D.C.: U.S. Government Printing Office, 1949). A few seem to favor holding the wage base to the lowest possible point indefinitely. This course would, in time, transform the system from a variable-benefit program related to wages to virtually a flat-benefit system. With a long-range trend of increasing wages, sooner or later most full-time workers under the program would be getting close to the maximum-benefit amount because most of them would be earning maximum wages throughout most of their working lifetime.

mentary plans enlarged. Moreover, in the long run it may be that the sponsors of private plans will want to put less money into pensions and more into disability benefits or health protection if the public pension program is significantly improved and present arrangements for health and disability are still inadequate.

It is, of course, possible to provide for pensions which are too high when compared with other things people want to do with their money. Pensions are expensive. . . . Coverage is usually an automatic accompaniment of the job; the worker gets the amount of protection provided by the plan whether he wants it or not. Thus, the pension limits the right of individuals to spend as they wish. In a free economy such limitations should be approached with caution. Moreover, there are social needs other than the protection of the aged which must be provided for by limiting the right of the individual to spend as he wishes.

The task is to leave as high a proportion of income as is compatible with adequate social protection to the free choice of individual spending. Failure to provide adequate protection on an automatic basis results in the ills arising from poverty and dependence. On the other hand, if we go too far in allocating the income of individuals for specific purposes, either through Government programs or private institutions, we will have traded economic freedom for a new paternalism.

The dynamic character of the pension problem resulting from price, wage, and standard of living changes is also an important factor in determining the relationship between old-age and survivors insurance and the various other programs. If old-age and survivors insurance benefits are raised as wages rise, then the problem of adjusting to economic change for private plans is very much reduced.[4] If old-age and survivors insurance benefits are not increased as wages rise, then much greater increases are necessary in the private plans.

Many of the larger industrial companies are developing well-rounded retirement programs which include preparation for retirement, post-retirement counseling and service programs, and a pension plan which when combined with old-age and survivors insurance aims at providing an adequate income for a satisfactory old age. It may be expected that such plans will spread and that more and more persons will be covered by them. In our estimates we have assumed that roughly half the labor force will be covered by some type of private plan in 25 years.

---

[4] While there is agreement that old-age and survivors insurance benefit liberalizations will be needed from time to time, there are differences of opinion concerning the extent to which the program should be designed to adjust automatically to increasing wages. One proposal that would go a long way toward accomplishing an automatic adjustment to increasing wages would be to base benefits on an average wage figured over a limited period, such as the five or ten consecutive years of highest earnings, rather than the span of a working lifetime. The long-term rise in wage levels, it is argued, cannot be sufficiently taken into account if wages must be averaged over a 30- or 40-year period, inclusive of a past period of lower wage levels.

However, only slightly over 5 percent of the 9 million aged not now working are drawing private pensions or are the wives of persons drawing such pensions. Thus it has not been possible to plan the public program on the assumption that most people will also have protection under supplementary plans. In all likelihood it will not be possible to do so in the future. Ten years from now this 5-percent figure might be as high as 10 or 15 percent. It takes time for pension coverage to be translated into pension payments, and even in the long run, coverage under private plans will tend to have serious limitations. To a very considerable extent, the problem of income maintenance for the aged is not a matter of retirement benefits, strictly defined, but a matter of survivorship protection for aged widows. Of the 9 million nonworking persons under discussion, well over a third are not retired workers or retired workers' wives, but are aged widows. Private plans do practically nothing for this group.

Furthermore, private plans tend to be confined to the long-term employees of relatively large industrial employers. Coverage is likely to continue to be inadequate or largely nonexistent for persons who work for relatively small employers, for agricultural and domestic workers, for the self-employed, and for older workers who change their jobs and thus fail to meet service requirements.

It is to be hoped that protection furnished by the private plans will be greatly extended and improved, but, realistically, the benefit level in old-age and survivors insurance must be set in recognition of the fact that in the foreseeable future it will continue to be the only form of regular retirement pay for the great majority of retired workers, their wives, and aged widows.

### Public Assistance

Public assistance is the residual method of meeting the income needs of the aged. To the extent that retirement systems, veterans programs, individual savings, and help from relatives do not meet need, public assistance must pay enough to bring the individual up to the minimum level of living that the community considers acceptable. The future of old-age assistance depends, then, in the first instance on the extent to which other arrangements meet total need. This means most importantly the extent to which old-age and survivors insurance will meet total need.

Will the old-age and survivors insurance program be extended to those who do not now have any organized kind of retirement protection? Coverage is now very inadequate in rural areas and unless it is further extended to farm workers and farm operators the assistance burden will continue to be heavy in rural States. In studying why old-age assistance recipients were not entitled to old-age and survivors insurance, the Social Security Administration found in a sample survey that approximately one-half the assistance recipients who had worked after 1936, and who were not entitled to old-age and survivors insurance, had worked in agriculture.[5]

If the price level continues to rise, will insurance payments be adjusted promptly or will assistance have to step in and do a big job of supplementation? Payments under old-age and survivors insurance are now at such a level for most beneficiaries that supplementation under assistance could easily become very large. About 14 percent of old-age and survivors insurance aged beneficiaries are now receiving old-age assistance and this percentage would be even higher if many people were not reluctant to ask for assistance.

Will assistance standards be raised faster than benefit amounts under old-age and survivors insurance? That is, leaving aside the question of prices, will old-age and survivors insurance benefits be liberalized as the concept of adequate minimum standards is liberalized, or will there be a big need for assistance supplementation on this score?

Another factor is that the present low benefits of old-age and survivors insurance can for a short time after retirement be combined with even meager assets to supply a minimum standard of living. The chances are, however, that as assets are exhausted many more old-age and survivors insurance beneficiaries will have to turn for supplementary help to assistance unless their old-age and survivors insurance benefits are raised. As the average length of time that old-age and survivors insurance beneficiaries have been on the rolls increases, therefore, there will be a tendency for the overlap to increase.

Will arrangements with other public systems be worked out so that an individual reaching old age will be sure of protection under some system? At present an individual who changes jobs may fail to qualify under the plans of the Federal Civil Service, the Armed Forces, State and local governments, or old-age and survivors insurance. Moreover, under some plans he may get a refund of contribution when he leaves his job and arrive at old age without retirement protection.

Will the benefit formula be adjusted so that periods of disability and unemployment will have a less severe effect on benefit amount than they have now?

Will large numbers of widows continue to arrive at age 65 without insurance protection by reason of the fact that they themselves did not work and their husbands died before gaining coverage under old-age and survivors insurance?

One of the great uncertainties concerning the future of old-age assistance arises from the fact that the amount of "need" for assistance is a matter of definition, and the individual States have considerable freedom

---

[5] See Charles E. Hawkins, *Old-Age Assistance Recipients: Reasons for Nonentitlement to Old-Age and Survivors Insurance Benefits*, Social Security Bulletin (July, 1952).

in making their own definition. It is probable that some States will continue to liberalize their definition of need by exempting higher amounts of assets from consideration, possibly by changing their policy so as to ignore the income and assets of relatives, and in other ways liberalizing the definition of the minimum level of living to be supplied by assistance. Although the Federal Government pays a large part of the bill, Congress has given the control of the assistance situation largely to the States. The Federal Security Agency must approve a State plan before Federal money is made available and an administrative limit on the amount of property a recipient may have and still be eligible for assistance has been established. No administrative limits, however, have been established for other aspects of need. Under present policy, if a State wanted to define the need of an individual in terms of $100 a month and the individual's income from old-age and survivors insurance was $75, the State could grant a $25 supplementary assistance payment and have 80 percent of the cost paid by the Federal Government. When practically all aged people are getting old-age and survivors insurance, will the States respond by liberalizing the definition of need under assistance? It may be that in the long run the Federal Government will either have to get out of old-age assistance entirely or establish a more detailed Federal definition of need in order to control the amount of matching it is willing to do.

The amount of assistance to be supplied in the future will be affected not only by the adequacy of alternative methods but by the political power of the aged in the various States. In some places the amount of assistance will probably remain high even though other arrangements are reasonably satisfactory.

These are some of the imponderable questions which will determine the amount of old-age assistance in the future. . . . There is general agreement that insofar as possible the income maintenance needs of the aged should be met on a nonmeans-test basis and that old-age assistances should be reduced to the lowest possible extent consistent with the goal of meeting the reasonable needs of the aged population. Nevertheless, unless there is a basic change in old-age and survivors insurance, assistance will remain large for some time to come. This is true because of the immaturity of our various retirement systems.

### THE PROBLEM OF IMMATURITY

Substantial coverage under private plans is new and thus, as previously indicated, those persons drawing private pensions together with their wives make up perhaps 10 percent of the group of 5.5 million persons over 65 which consists of retired men, their wives, and single and divorced women. Very few of the 3.5 million nonworking widows are drawing private pensions. Most persons already retired will never work again and will consequently not earn a pension, and although a higher percentage of those retiring in the future will be eligible for payments it will be at least 25 years or more before even greatly improved coverage and eligibility provisions would result in the payment of private pensions to as much as 20 or 25 percent of the retired group living at that time. The present extremely low figure is a problem of immaturity—a result of the fact that a private retirement plan cannot be expected to do anything about those who had already retired when the plan was inaugurated.

The public programs, by and large, are much more mature. The Civil Service Retirement System was started in 1920, the Armed Forces system about 1860, many State and local systems in the 1920's, and the railroad retirement program in 1935. The old-age and survivors insurance program has been operating for 15 years. Moreover, under old-age and survivors insurance, the eligibility requirements for older workers are very liberal. Consequently, . . . the public programs today are paying pensions to about two-thirds of the nonworking group over 65 made up of retired men and their wives, and single and divorced women. Even the public programs, however, are paying less than one-fourth of the nonworking aged widows.

Under present arrangements, a larger and larger percentage of aged persons will be eligible in the future for pensions from the public programs. This process would be considerably speeded up by universal coverage under old-age and survivors insurance, by coordination arrangements between old-age and survivors insurance and the other public systems, and by the exclusion of periods of disability from determination of eligibility for old-age and survivors insurance. Nevertheless, most of those who have already stopped work and are not now eligible for old-age and survivors insurance will never become eligible so long as eligibility for benefits is based on demonstrated work in covered employment. By and large, they must continue to be cared for, at least in part, by public assistance or by friends and relatives, for few of them have enough in the way of savings to completely support themselves throughout the period of their life expectancy.

Some persons have advocated maturing the old-age and survivors insurance system immediately. They have argued that it is inequitable to exclude any aged person from old-age and survivors insurance benefits because his participation in the labor force, or the participation of the person on whose earnings a widow was dependent, took place before the effective date of the program or because his occupation was excluded at the time he worked. Those in favor of maturing the system now would establish universal coverage for current workers and at the same time pay all those over 65 who had retired with a minimum old-age and survivors insurance benefit, whether or not the individual or a husband demonstrated any recent attachment to covered employment.

The old-age and survivors insurance system has already made substantial concessions to the present aged by giving full-rate benefits to those about to retire and yet requiring from them very little in the way of contribution. The theory under old-age and survivors insurance has been that with a test of recent employment, a worker might be given the equivalent of past service credits on the presumption that he undoubtedly had many other years of covered employment over a working lifetime. Under the 1950 amendments, workers already retired were made eligible for at least minimum benefits if they had a year and a half of covered employment at any time after 1936. Those who argue for maturing old-age and survivors insurance immediately argue that this very liberal treatment of some of the present aged makes the exclusion of those who do not qualify seem all the more inequitable; they favor, in effect, granting past service credits to all the present aged.

There is, however, no general agreement on the wisdom of paying benefits under old-age and survivors insurance to all the present aged. It would mean that for the first time eligibility to benefits would be separated from a record of wages and contributions and it might consequently have a more serious impact on the public's conception of the program than perhaps it logically should. Many hesitate to advocate further temporary concessions in meeting the problem of the present aged if those concessions tend to weaken public understanding of the long-run principles of the program.

It is true that the concessions already made to the present aged, or even paying benefits to all nonworking aged widows and retired workers, would not necessarily mean any change in the long-run nature of the program. The principles of the system could be the same for those reaching the age of 65 a generation from now regardless of what is done about the present aged. The question raised by proposals for covering all the aged now is whether a wage-related contributory system could be preserved for the long run under conditions where large numbers of people in the early years of the program were paid flat-rate benefits without establishing eligibility on the basis of a contribution or a work record.

If the present aged were to be blanketed into the system, some feel it would be desirable to have the income tax apply to that part of the old-age and survivors insurance benefit which exceeds the value of the employees contribution. (A tax is paid currently on the contribution.) One objection to paying benefits without a needs test to those who have not paid a significant part of the cost of the benefit they receive is that those retired persons over 65 with substantial incomes are given a tax-free bonus based solely on their age and retired status. Making that part of the benefit which exceeds the contribution subject to income tax would recover a portion of this "windfall." Those largely dependent on the old-age and survivors insurance benefit would not be hurt by such a proposal for they are seldom subject to income tax.

The objections to the proposal in this form are largely administrative, but they are substantial. Could an individual after retirement really be expected to know how much he had paid toward his benefit over a period of many years? There would be no inexpensive way of checking the accuracy of his claim. It could be done, of course, from the old-age and survivors insurance records, but at considerable cost. Another possibility would be to exempt the employee contribution from taxation when paid and then tax the entire benefit during retirement.

Under most proposals for paying benefits to all the present aged under old-age and survivors insurance, the Federal Government would withdraw entirely from old-age assistance and would instead pay from general taxation (although not necessarily currently) the cost of the old-age and survivors insurance benefits going to noncontributors.[6] Some feel that this might result in less adequate care of the present aged in some States. The basic old-age and survivors insurance payment would probably not be enough to meet need alone, and yet, without the inducement of Federal matching, some States undoubtedly would reduce what they now put into old-age assistance. Moreover, it is possible that in the absence of Federal standards there would be a tendency in some State administrations to turn in the direction of the practices of the old poor law. On the other hand, it is possible that in the absence of Federal standards requiring that only "needy" persons be paid, some States would remove the test of need, transforming their old-age assistance programs into universal flat pension plans and adding greatly to the cost of caring for the retired aged.

The reaction of the various States to the new situation which would be created by maturing old-age and survivors insurance immediately would depend on the amount of the minimum Federal benefit. It is difficult to decide on the correct amount. It should be high enough to reduce substantially the need for assistance. Yet it must not be too high or it would threaten the very existence of the wage-related contributory program. It is important that there be a substantial difference between the amounts paid on the basis of contributions and the basic guaranty paid without contribution if those covered by the contributory program are going to continue to support it. On the other hand, there are also substantial advantages in maturing the OASI program as rapidly as possible. Whether there would be a net gain for the aged and for the Nation in these proposals for paying old-age and survivors insurance benefits to all of the present retired group is now a matter of debate.

The Federal matching offer in old-age assistance is now a maximum of $35 per month. If all of the retired aged over 65 were guaranteed this amount, additional expenditures would come to about $1,400,000,000 in 1953. This figure takes into account the cost of raising to $35 those old-age and survivors insurance and old-age assistance benefits now below this amount and paying $35 to all those not receiving either old-age and sur-

---

[6] In Referendum No. 93, however, the U.S. Chamber of Commerce committee on social legislation proposed paying benefits to all the present aged without a Government contribution.

vivors insurance or old-age assistance.[7] The estimated Federal share of old-age assistance for 1953 and the estimated income-tax yield on the additional payments (on the assumption the OASI benefit is made taxable) has been subtracted from the amount of the increased costs to arrive at the figure for additional expenditures. If the $35 were payable at age 70 rather than 65, the additional expenditures for 1953 would be about $950,000,000 (assuming old-age assistance continued for those aged 65–69).

## A UNIVERSAL PAY-AS-YOU-GO SYSTEM

If the old-age and survivors insurance program were to be matured immediately by blanketing-in the present aged, certain other changes should be considered at the same time. Coverage of all current workers, desirable at any time, would be essential. Yet, one danger in these maturity plans is that the presently excluded groups might consider it advantageous to stay out and collect the "free" benefit without making direct contributions and reports to the program. A system which always gave contributors something more than noncontributors, though somewhat costlier than the estimates for the minimum-guaranty plan indicated above, would have a better chance of protecting the contributory principle. In any event there would have to be a considerable difference between the free and the contributory benefit to make coverage attractive to those now excluded.

If the present aged were blanketed into the insurance program, the financing method should be reexamined at the same time. Pay-as-you-go financing would then be a realistic alternative to the present approach. Whether desirable or not, and opinions differ, pay-as-you-go financing on the basis of earmarked contributions is hardly possible unless the system is substantially mature. The pay-as-you-go method, which equates income from contributions and short-term expenditures, is not compatible with a self-financed system which does not cover the group already retired. Under such a system, pay-as-you-go would require present contribution rates to be cut by one-third. Later on, rates might have to be three times as high as the rates now being charged. This is true because benefit costs will rise gradually from now until the end of the century. As the program matures, a larger and larger proportion of those retiring will have had an opportunity to earn wage credits and a larger and larger proportion of aged widows will also qualify for benefits.

With the present program, employee contribution rates on a pay-as-you-go basis would look like this (including protection for survivors) if the low-cost estimates were taken: 1953, 0.9; 1960, 1.4; 1970, 2.0; 1980, 2.5; 1990 and thereafter, 2.9. If the high-cost estimates were taken, the

---

[7] Federal retirement systems other than old-age and survivors insurance have been included in this estimate of additional cost. The $35 has been assumed to be a minimum guaranty rather than an additional payment.

rates would be like this: 1953, 1.0; 1960, 1.9; 1970, 2.7; 1980, 3.5; 1990, 4.5; 2000 and thereafter, 5.0.

From the standpoint of persons who spend a working lifetime under the program, it seems somewhat absurd to charge first a rate of only 1 percent and then gradually to increase the rate to perhaps as much as 4 or 5 percent. For social insurance just as for private insurance, it is much easier for workers to pay a more or less level rate over a working lifetime.

If the program were to be matured by blanketing-in the present aged it would be possible, however, on a pay-as-you-go basis to charge rates in the early years which would be much closer to the ultimate rates. With the payment of at least $35 per month to all of the nonworking aged, benefit disbursements including lump-sum and younger survivor benefits in 1953 would be about $5,300,000,000 or almost 4 percent of covered payrolls, an increase of $2,600,000,000 over expected benefit disbursements under present law. Thus a contribution rate of 2 percent on employers and 2 percent on employees could be charged immediately without increasing the reserve.

Under such a plan, many consider it desirable that as the population ages the ultimate contribution rates should be held down by having the Government contribute as well. It seems inequitable to put the cost of the "free" benefits on the contributor. The pay-roll tax is regressive in nature —a flat-rate tax on only the first $3,600 of wages and self-employment income—and in effect these benefits would be substituting for the Federal share of old-age assistance which is raised on a much more progressive basis. Even if one were to consider the employer tax as the sole source of revenue for the "free" benefits, there would be a substantial shift to a less progressive form of taxation.[8] Moreover, a shift to pay-as-you-go means

---

[8] Many persons feel that it would be desirable to have an eventual Government contribution to the old-age and survivors insurance program even if the other provisions of the program are kept as they are now. The payments of full-rate benefits to those retiring in the early years of the program has created a situation similar to "blanketing in." A level premium rate to finance the benefits presently promised for a generation of workers under the program for a working lifetime is slightly more than 4 percent on the basis of the intermediate cost estimates; that is, a contribution rate of 2 percent on employer and 2 percent on employee under the assumption of reserve financing would just about meet the full cost of benefits for this group in perpetuity. A combined contribution rate of 4 percent would not be enough, however, to pay full-rate benefits to the workers now old, since they will be contributing for relatively short periods of time. The deficit of contribution which arises from this fact is the equivalent of nearly another 2 percent of payroll on a level premium basis, making the level premium rate for the whole system about 6 percent. The case under reserve financing for meeting the deficit of contribution of older workers through a Government contribution is strong; this is an accrued liability unrelated to the value of the protection for those who come afterward. Nevertheless, there are some advantages in financing the system entirely from payroll contributions. There is always the possibility that a contribution from general taxation might not be forthcoming, and that benefits might have to be reduced accordingly. Although the Government contribution might be designed to make up for the deficit of contributions of older workers, it is not unlikely that it would be thought of as a general subsidy to the program and obscure the fact that younger workers and their employers would have paid their own way.

that the ultimate rates must be considerably more than under a reserve system. Under pay-as-you-go, unless a Government contribution is substituted for the interest payments, the contributor who has paid throughout his lifetime has lost the advantage of interest. A contribution schedule showing the percentage of pay roll required on a pay-as-you-go basis with a Government contribution and a blanketing-in of the currently retired group might be as follows:

| | Employer | Employee | Government | | Employer | Employee | Government |
|---|---|---|---|---|---|---|---|
| 1953...... | 2 | 2 | ......... | 1980.... | 2.5 | 2.5 | 2 |
| 1960..... | 2 | 2 | 1 | 1990.... | 3 | 3 | 2 |
| 1970..... | 2 | 2 | 2 | 2000.... | 3 | 3 | 3 |

If a pay-as-you-go system were established without a Government contribution to make up for interest earnings on a reserve, it would be particularly important that the benefits be adjusted to keep up with any increases in prices or the level of living. Otherwise, as the system matures the combined employer-employee contribution rate will exceed the value of the protection for those contributing. On the other hand, if the long-range trend of rising wages continues, adjustment of the benefits so that they remain reasonably related to the wage level current at the time of retirement would probably more than make up for the loss of the interest earnings which would have resulted from a system geared to a reserve.

Benefits may be related to current levels of living by periodic legislative action or by more or less automatic devices such as relating benefits to a high 5- or 10-year average monthly wage and tying the benefits of those on the rolls to various kinds of cost-of-living or wage indexes. Another approach which can be used in a pay-as-you-go system is illustrated by the so-called apportionment plans in France and the plan recommended in Sweden in 1950 by the Pension Investigation Committee.[9] These plans relate benefits to the past earnings of the individual but in such a way as to give him the advantage of price rises or productivity increases as reflected in current wage levels. Specifically, under such plans an individual would receive each year a credit under the system which would express in "points" the relation of his covered earnings to average covered earnings for that year. On retirement his points would be averaged and his benefit each year would be based on the relationship of his lifetime average to average earnings under the system for the year in which the benefit is

---

[9] See proposal for a General Pension Insurance in Sweden. A summary of investigations made by the Pension Committee 1950. Published by the Swedish Government. The Swedish proposals do not bring in the present aged. In fact, the plan would be a slowly maturing one, paying much lower benefits to older workers. Moreover, there is no weighting in the benefit formula for lower paid workers. However, the point system described in the proposal could be used in combination with various specifications.

paid. Other types of pay-as-you-go plans are illustrated by the new Canadian system which pays a flat $40 to all persons at age 70, and the system adopted in Switzerland in 1947 which included those in the retired group who could meet an income test.

Financially, a universal pay-as-you-go system would operate more or less on this theory—a given percentage of covered earnings is collected now from current earners and their employers, and possibly from the Government, and apportioned among the present retired group. The current earners, in turn, have the expectation of a given percentage of future earnings when they retire. In a successful economy, the pensioners participate in the gain; in the event of a general decline in the level of living over time, pensions drop as well as the income going to other groups in the population. A contingency fund could be used, however, to prevent the need for benefit reductions in periods of unemployment; the financing might well be designed to balance over the business cycle.

The aging of the population creates a special problem. As the proportion of aged grows it takes a larger percentage of total pay rolls to supply benefits which bear the same relation to wages as at the beginning of the plan. Thus, to fulfill the goal of the plan, a larger percentage of future earnings must be reserved for later pensioners than is needed at the beginning.

Although there are enough apparent advantages in this kind of an approach to deserve careful study, it is possible that this way of designing a retirement system would give less security to the potential beneficiary than the more familiar pattern of building up an individual reserve. Would it, for example, be more likely under such a plan than under the more orthodox present system that benefits would be subject to change because of political pressures? In this kind of system would the pension be secure?

## PROTECTION FOR THE PERMANENTLY AND TOTALLY DISABLED

Retirement pay is important not only for those of 65 and over, but for all persons who are more or less permanently out of the labor market. The most serious gap in this respect is the failure of present arrangements to give adequate protection to workers who are out of the labor market because of permanent and total disability.

Of all the risks to economic security, total disability is perhaps the most devastating. Disability is more of an economic burden than old age for it may come at a time when children are not yet grown and the responsibility for their support is greatest. Moreover, it adds a dependent to be taken care of—a dependent who may need special care and incur extra expenses. Few persons, even those receiving high salaries, accumulate enough savings to support their families during long years of disability.

Adequate permanent and total disability protection is now largely unavailable. Individual insurance against permanent and total disability is offered by many private companies but under restricted conditions and at rates which are prohibitive for many. Under private pension plans, many years of service are typically required for disability protection and often the protection is only the actuarially discounted retirement benefit. Workmen's compensation protects workers only in case of work-connected disabilities, usually accidents, and even then does not usually assure an income for the entire period of the disability. Probably only about 5 percent of all permanent and total disability cases are of work-connected origin.

To a considerable extent, benefit compensation for retirement in old age rests on a general presumption of the likelihood of serious disabilities in later life. In fact, unless provision is made for disability insurance, there will be increasing pressure for a general reduction in the qualifying age for old-age benefits, so that disabled persons will not have to wait so long for their insurance income. It would not seem wise, however, to make retirement benefits generally available at younger ages.

Rehabilitation, where it is possible, is the most economical method of providing for disabled persons and is, of course, the most satisfactory for the individual. Some people fear that disability benefits payable on an insurance basis would hinder rehabilitation; that the disabled person would cling to the security of the benefit in preference to the uncertainty of a work situation. This is not only a fear of deliberate malingering but, even more importantly, a fear that the benefit would foster psychosomatic illnesses by making them attractive in terms of financial security. There is no doubt that these are serious problems which must be taken into full account in the development of a disability program. There is a great deal we do not know about the motivation of the disabled person. How can we encourage his desire to be independent and foster his drive once again to be a free, fully functioning person? How can we help him to move away from the relative "safety" of helplessness?

In spite of these difficulties, however, it is clear that we must give the disabled financial support while being rehabilitated if rehabilitation is feasible—for the rest of their lives if rehabilitation is not feasible. We have no intention in this country of allowing the disabled to go without the necessities of life. That is why in 1950 we adopted a Federal-State program of assistance for the permanently and totally disabled. The issue is now quite clearly one of method. Should the means test be retained for the disabled or should their support be put on an insurance basis?

There is no general agreement on this issue. Two compromise proposals have been suggested. One approach is to design a disability insurance program with very strict eligibility and benefit provisions so as to make certain that only persons with long records of employment become eligible for benefits, that the benefits paid are low in comparison with the accustomed standard of living of the individual, and that they are paid only after a long waiting period and after every effort at rehabilitation has been exhausted. Another possibility is to pay the benefits only after the attainment of a given age—say, 50 or 55. Most of the arguments made against disability insurance, even if generally valid, have little application to proposals for lowering the retirement age for those with total disabilities.

## PRIVATE PLANS AND GOVERNMENT REGULATION

The recent rapid spread of private pension plans and the expectation of further rapid growth in the near future has led to concern about the security of some of the plans now being established. Will they be able to continue under less favorable conditions? If not, will Government be under pressure to assume the obligations of some of these plans in order to protect the expectations of the workers?

It is true that the continued existence of a private plan depends on the financial position of its sponsors. Plans established in prosperity and under favorable tax conditions may be discontinued under less favorable circumstances. Even during prosperous times, many plans are discontinued. About 15 percent of the plans (covering, however, a relatively small percentage of employees) approved by the Bureau of Internal Revenue since 1942 have been dropped. In our economy, individual businesses are continually being replaced by other enterprises and whole industries become outmoded.

It is a very serious matter to promise security which does not materialize. It is quite likely that the inability of any big collective bargaining plan to continue would result in pressure for Government to assume the liabilities of the plan. Some argue, therefore, that it would be desirable to require strict funding of private plans as a condition of tax offset under Federal law. Others hold that the Government should offer to operate supplementary plans by allowing employers and employees to buy additional protection under the Government system on an actuarial basis and with all rights vested in the individual so that he would receive some protection in spite of the failure of an individual business or the discontinuance of a plan.

Both of these suggestions require much more thorough study and discussion before they are given legislative consideration. Additional regulation of funding by Government would be a very complicated administrative task. Criteria are difficult to establish and, moreover, real control would involve the Government in a determination of the most likely assumptions for cost estimating. For the Government to sell protection supplementary to old-age and survivors insurance would have the advantage of providing a way for the supplementary protection to follow the worker from job to job. On the other hand, employers can now buy such protection for their employees from private insurance companies if they so desire. The cost is high but it would also be high if operated by the

Government. No clear need for Government operation in this area has yet been demonstrated.

Because of the interest in vesting provisions, it has sometimes been proposed that certain minimum vesting be required in a plan as a condition of approval for tax offset. There are other desirable features of private plans which might also be required. However, this type of regulation should be approached with great caution, if at all. By and large, the provisions of private plans should be left to individual decision and collective bargaining. Only by leaving individuals and groups free to experiment and to deviate from what is now considered desirable will the private plans be able to pioneer in new fields and solve some of the problems which have been raised. . . .

# 18. VIEWS OF THE LIFE INSURANCE COMPANIES ON OASDI ISSUES

*Sound Policy for Social Security: A Statement by the Life Insurance Business, 1958.*

THROUGH INDIVIDUAL POLICIES, group insurance, annuities, and pension plans, the life insurance business for many years has furnished people with facilities to build their own security on a voluntary basis. Well over 100 million individuals are providing a substantial measure of protection for themselves and their families through these means.

In view of the related purposes of social security, life insurance executives have been keenly interested in the subject ever since the original Federal legislation was under study. Because of their experience with security plans and programs, life insurance men have been called on for advice and assistance from time to time, particularly in connection with the Federal old-age, survivors, and disability insurance system (OASDI).

In general, the life insurance attitude toward social security has been one of support and of cooperation. At the inception of social security, there was no opposition by the life insurance business, nor did the life insurance business oppose the addition of survivor benefits to the system when they were added in 1939. Legislative proposals seeking to make the system more effective within a framework of sound principles have had active support.

On the other hand, the life insurance business has criticized some legislative proposals in the social security field as not being in the public interest. In the main, these have been proposals which would over-liberalize OASDI benefits as measured by the sound floor-of-protection concept, or which would dangerously extend the Federal legislation into the fields of compulsory health or disability insurance.

From time to time, changes in economic conditions, changes in public attitudes, and changes in the Federal social security legislation itself, make a restatement of the policy position of the life insurance business with respect to social security necessary or desirable. The eighteen numbered points which follow, along with a brief discussion of each, represent the latest presentation of the views of the American Life Convention and the Life Insurance Association of America on the subject. They are founded on the same basic concepts and philosophy as have long guided life insurance thinking about social security.

### 1

**It is of immense importance to Americans generally, and to life insurance policyholders in particular, that the nation's social security structure be sound and well-balanced. Because of their broad experience in matters related to social security, life insurance executives have an opportunity of contributing helpful counsel toward this end.**

It is hardly necessary to cite the tremendous sums collected in payroll taxes and paid out to beneficiaries each year by the Federal OASDI system—and the even greater magnitudes in prospect for the future—to prove the quantitative importance of social security. More significant, however, may be the subtle changes social security legislation can induce in the thinking and outlook of the American people and in the nation's economy. Such changes could readily have a great effect, for good or ill, on the national character—and, of course, on life insurance policyholders. It thus seems clear that Americans generally, and life insurance executives particularly, should take a continuing interest in social security and devote continuing attention to it. Life insurance executives, because of their broad experience with related matters, are in a position to offer helpful counsel to legislators and to the public.

### 2

**The repeated enactment of legislation expanding the nation's social security structure amounts to a trend that, if continued, would result in overliberalization, which could have grave economic consequences. Increased education of the public in the long-range cost implications is an important step toward counteracting the trend toward social security overexpansion.**

Probably the central issue in social security is how best to guard against the dangers of overexpansion. The existence of such dangers is hardly debatable. Apart from earlier expansions, the OASDI legislation was liberalized substantially in 1950, 1952, 1954, and 1956. A similar legislative trend exists in other countries. If continued, the trend in the United States will result in overexpansion, if it has not already done so, and it could be carried to the point of seriously damaging the American economy.

The trend toward social security overexpansion stems mainly from the fact that benefit liberalizations have an immediate impact on the public consciousness, while the impact of the required tax increases is deferred. Increased education of the public in the long-range implications of social security, particularly with regard to costs, represents an important step toward combating the dangers of overexpansion. Constant vigilance and determined effort are also necessary.

### 3

**The economic security of the American people rests basically upon the productiveness of the national economy and upon the steady jobs at good wages which it provides. Social security legislation—which does not add to the supply of goods and services, but which operates merely to redistribute income—should be so framed as to minimize any tendency to restrict the economy's productiveness.**

The OASDI system and other social security measures should be clearly seen as adjuncts to the productive employment and regular earnings on which the economic security of most Americans rests. The OASDI system is merely a mechanism for adding to the security of persons not supported by regular earnings through a redistribution of income from those who are gainfully occupied. As such, it can perform a useful function, but the system may have an inherent tendency to reduce the incentives for productive effort, particularly among those eligible for benefits on withdrawal from regular work. The legislation should be so framed as to restrict this tendency as much as feasible. Otherwise, the increased security OASDI provides for its beneficiaries might be outweighed by diminished security for others, stemming from reduced national production as well as from the diversion of a portion of their incomes to the system.

### 4

**Business concerns—including insurance companies—can contribute to a reduction in the demand for social security benefit expansion through increased provision of suitable employment opportunities for potential beneficiaries. Efforts to expand job opportunities for the aging and the handicapped can be particularly helpful.**

It is generally recognized that most aging and handicapped persons would rather work in suitable jobs, if their health permits, than be without gainful employment—even if supported by OASDI benefits. It is also recognized that the outlook and attitude of the individual is ordinarily improved if he is a useful, productive member of the community. Moreover, to the extent that the abilities and skills of the aging and handicapped are utilized, the nation's production is increased, and the burden of social security is reduced.

Business concerns and other employers, including insurance companies, can accordingly make a contribution toward sound social security by reviewing their employment practices to the end of expanding suitable job opportunities for the aging and handicapped as far as feasible. However, it is recognized that individual concerns often find many advantages in observing mandatory retirement ages. The challenge is to develop practices under which such advantages might be retained, while job opportunities for the aging and handicapped are expanded.

**5**

**The fundamental aim of the OASDI system is to provide a basic floor of protection against want. This purpose can best be effectuated in accordance with the sound principle of benefits varying within limits so as to bear some relationship to the individual's previous average earnings.**

From its inception the fundamental purpose or aim of the OASDI system has been properly conceived as being to furnish a basic floor of protection against want. This concept has been widely accepted. While the protective floor should be high enough to be of real value in preventing want or destitution, it should not be so high as to require taxes, actual or prospective, that would unnecessarily reduce the living standards of self-supporting people, or their capacities and incentives to save. The benefit level in effect, following the 1956 Social Security Amendments, is adequate at present to provide a suitable protective floor, and any increase in benefits would be undesirable at this time.

It is sometimes urged that the existing OASDI system be abandoned and replaced with a system under which uniform monthly benefits would go to all beneficiaries. Such a change-over from the present approach, which has been followed for some 20 years, would be quite impractical. Moreover, the present approach—under which benefit amounts are related to the individual's previous average earnings and vary within the limits of a floor-of-protection range—gives an appropriate recognition to varying costs of living, particularly in different geographic areas, and to the individual's past contributions to the economy.

## 6

Private pension plans, personal savings, insurance coverages, and other voluntary efforts should be relied upon to furnish such protection as groups and individuals may desire in addition to a basic floor of protection. The OASDI legislation should be so framed as to avoid discouraging such voluntary efforts.

Above the basic social security floor, groups and individuals should be free to decide whether they wish to build additional protection for themselves, and if so, they should be free to decide on the methods to be used. Private pension plans, personal savings, insurance coverages, and home ownership are among the means commonly employed. It is far preferable that these voluntary approaches be available and utilized than that the OASDI system, through repeated tax and benefit increases, be converted into a sort of uniform, compulsory, national pension plan. Apart from other considerations, such a transformation of the system would spell grave interference with personal freedom and would dampen the spirit of initiative and self-reliance among the American people. The OASDI legislation should be so framed, on the contrary, as to avoid any discouragement to the development of voluntary pension plans and other voluntary means of protection.

## 7

In the case of those with above-average earnings, private pension plans and other voluntary mechanisms should have full responsibility for providing such protection as groups and individuals may desire with respect to that portion of their earnings which is above average. Consequently, the annual limit on taxable earnings under the OASDI system should not exceed the average full-time earnings of gainfully occupied persons.

A particularly important issue as to the dividing line between the responsibility of OASDI to furnish basic protection and the responsibility of voluntary mechanisms for additional protection, concerns the annual limit on earnings (the "wage base") to be taken into account by OASDI for tax and benefit purposes. This limit is now $4,200, having been increased in two stages from an initial figure of $3,000. At no time should this figure exceed the average earnings of regularly employed people. For higher-than-average earnings to be taken into account by OASDI would simply mean that extra benefits—above a floor-of-protection level—would go to the minority of persons who have had such above-average earnings. These are the very people best able to build their own extra protection on a voluntary basis. Inasmuch as average earnings of regularly employed people are now no greater than $4,200, the OASDI limit on annual earnings should not be increased at the present time.

### 8

Continued adherence to the sound principle under which the OASDI system is maintained on a self-supporting basis through special taxes levied on those covered under the system, and their employers, is essential. Also, it is important that OASDI tax rates be maintained at levels to yield revenues approximately equal to benefit disbursements.

One of the principles which has become firmly established in the OASDI legislation over the years is that the system must be self-supporting through the special taxes levied on those covered under it and on their employers. It is also firmly established that the tax rates applying to employers and employees at any one time should be the same. It is essential that these sound principles be maintained, and in consequence, any need for future tax rates beyond the ability or willingness of people to pay must be avoided.

Closely related to these principles is the increasing recognition that no useful purpose would be accomplished by further substantial growth of the OASI and DI Trust Funds. Considered together, the two Funds are already more than adequate as a contingency or buffer reserve. On the other hand, it would not be desirable, or at all feasible, to build them up by the $250 or $300 billions necessary for them to be on a full reserve basis. The wisest course is for Congress to continue to set the OASDI tax rates at levels sufficient to yield revenues which, over a short period of years, will approximately equal prospective benefit disbursements, with due allowance for administrative expenses and interest income.

### 9

As a matter of principle, the OASDI system should cover all employed and self-employed persons. However, in applying this principle to the few groups remaining excluded, Congress should take some account of the wishes of the members of each group.

From the inception of OASDI it has been contemplated that the system will eventually cover everyone. The efficiency of the system is impaired if people are continually moving in and out of coverage as they change from job to job. As a matter of principle, the system's coverage should consequently be extended to the few remaining areas of employment and self-employment still excluded. However, in effectuating this principle, Congress might wisely take some account of the wishes of the groups involved, as has been done in past legislation extending OASDI coverage.

**10**

The maintenance of a retirement test, or "work clause" in the OASDI legislation is essential to avoid the payment of unneeded benefits to persons with regular, full-time earnings. The "work clause" should be so devised that the individual would always have some financial incentive to increase his production efforts and earnings.

Since its inception the OASDI system has contained provisions designed to prevent the payment of benefits to persons engaged in regular gainful activity. The valid purpose of these provisions has been to avoid the heavy costs and the unwise use of social security monies that paying unneeded benefits to persons with regular earnings would mean. The amount of earnings permitted under the so-called "work clause" without loss of benefits has been increased by successive amendments from $14.99 a month to $1,200 a year. Any further increase in this figure is undesirable at the present time, lest the "work clause" be rendered too weak to accomplish its purpose in full.

However, the schedule in effect following the 1956 Social Security Amendments, that sets forth the number of monthly benefits to be withheld for specified annual earnings in excess of $1,200, does need revision. It should be revised so that the individual will always have some incentive, in terms of augmented after-tax income, to increase his productive efforts and earnings. At present, in many instances, the work clause operates as a financial incentive to partial or complete retirement for persons who would otherwise choose to remain more fully employed or self-employed.

**11**

So-called "increment" provisions, under which an individual's OASDI benefit amount increases automatically on a basis of the length of time he has been covered by the system, are unsound. No such provisions, whether applying to coverage before or after age 65, should be reintroduced into the OASDI legislation.

At one time the OASDI legislation provided a one-percent automatic increase, or so-called "increment," in the basic amount of the wage-earner's benefit for each year he had engaged in covered employment. This provision was unsound, in relation to the basic-floor-of-protection concept, as the individual's needs do not vary with the length of time he was covered by the system; and Congress wisely removed the provision in 1950. Since then there have been recurrent proposals for new "increment" provisions, including proposals for an increment to apply only after the individual reaches age 65. However, since the average age of actual retirement under OASDI is now about 68, such a special increment would amount to little more than an unneeded benefit increase in most instances. Moreover, the presumable objective of the proposal—to encourage people to continue in gainful activity after reaching age 65—can be accomplished better by an appropriate "work clause" amendment, as mentioned in item 10 above.

## 12

**Increasingly, individuals qualify for monthly benefits under both the OASDI system and one or more other governmental benefit systems in a combined amount that is excessive and unjustifiable. Existing legislation should be strengthened so that the total of benefits will be reduced appropriately in such instances.**

In addition to the OASDI system, the Federal Government operates numerous other retirement systems and workmen's compensation and veterans' programs. State and municipal governments also operate many varied programs of this sort. Increasingly, people qualify for benefits under two or more of them. In some but not all of these instances the benefit total is excessive and the duplication is unjustifiable. While existing laws contain some provisions to reduce the total benefits payable in such cases, more adequate legislation is needed. Social security and other governmental funds should not be misused to provide windfall benefits for a relatively small minority of fortunate individuals.

## 13

**The lump-sum payments provided in the OASDI legislation are traceable to an unsound money-back concept in the original social security enactment, which has no proper place in the program. In no event should the dollar amounts of the lump-sum payments be increased.**

An anachronism in the OASDI legislation is the section under which lump-sum payments ranging up to $255 are made whenever a person "insured" by the system dies. The unsound money-back concept on which this section is founded has been abandoned in all other respects. It would be best if the entire section were repealed. As a minimum, it is important that there be no increase in the dollar amounts of the lump-sums.

## 14

**The OASDI provisions for cash disability benefits are surrounded by grave long-run dangers. In the absence of evidence that such dangers can be surmounted, the existing disability provisions should not be extended or expanded in any way.**

When amendments adding cash disability benefit provisions to the OASDI legislation were under consideration by Congress in 1956, life insurance witnesses called attention to the serious dangers involved. Among other points, the heavy costs, the negative effects on rehabilitation programs, and the administrative problems, particularly the pressures for lax adjudications, were mentioned as grave consequences that in all likelihood would become apparent in the course of time. There have been no intervening developments suggesting that these dangers have become less serious or were then overstated. In the absence of evidence indicating that the dangers inherent in the disability benefit provisions can be successfully surmounted, it seems clear that these provisions should not be extended or expanded in any way. It would be particularly hazardous to increase the amounts of the benefits, either directly or through the addition of dependents' benefits, because to do so would reduce the necessary margin of financial incentive to the individual to overcome his handicap and return to gainful activity.

## 15

**The best method of coping with the problem of disability is through effective programs of rehabilitation. Federal legislation aiding state programs of rehabilitation should be strengthened, if and as a need for such strengthening can be demonstrated to exist.**

It was emphasized by spokesmen for the life insurance business, when the 1956 Social Security Amendments were under consideration, that the best method of coping with the problem of disability is through effective rehabilitation efforts. Significant accomplishments in this regard have been registered by voluntary organizations. State rehabilitation programs, with generous Federal support, have also had considerable success. The State programs were somewhat strengthened, under the 1956 Social Security Amendments, by provisions calling for the referral of applicants for OASDI cash disability benefits to State rehabilitation agencies. Should it become clear that further strengthening of the Federal provisions would contribute effectively to rehabilitation efforts, legislation to that end should be enacted.

## 16

**While government has a responsibility of providing necessary hospital and medical care for the needy, a governmental system of compulsory health insurance would be thoroughly undesirable. Steps in that direction—such as a Federal program of hospital or medical benefits for the aged, whether inside or outside the OASDI system—should be avoided.**

•State and local governments have a traditional responsibility of providing adequate hospital and medical care for those who need it but are unable to pay for it. Recent Federal legislation aids the States in meeting this responsibility with respect to those on the public assistance rolls. For the Federal Government to go further and cover everyone, without regard to need, under a compulsory health insurance system would be most undesirable. Among many reasons, such action would operate to undermine the present high standards of medical care in the United States and to sweep away the rapidly increasing amount of protection provided through voluntary health insurance.

From time to time various limited steps toward a compulsory Federal health insurance system have been urged. In particular, it has been proposed that hospital and perhaps medical benefits be provided through OASDI for some or all of the system's beneficiaries. Any such legislation, whether or not utilizing OASDI as an administrative mechanism, would be undesirable for the same general reasons that an all-inclusive system of compulsory health insurance would be undesirable. Also, such a limited plan would necessarily tend to lead to a fully developed system.

## 17

**With improved health conditions and increased life expectancy among the aged, there is no justification for reduction in the OASDI retirement ages—a step which would increase costs substantially and reduce the nation's productivity. Even if accompanied by provisions for reduced benefits, reduction in the retirement ages would be definitely undesirable.**

For two decades after its inception the OASDI legislation provided a retirement age of 65 for both men and women. In 1956 the retirement age was reduced to 62 for women, with the provisions optional on a reduced-benefit basis for female wage earners and wives. Many current proposals would make further reductions in the retirement ages of the system. All such proposals are unsound. Among other points, health conditions among the elderly have been steadily improving; and students of the aging process, as indicated earlier, are agreed on the desirability of continued employment for aging persons, which most who are in good health desire. Also, unless the reduced-benefit principle is applied, the costs to the OASDI system would be heavy. More important, whether or not that principle is applied, there would be a heavy social cost in that many able-bodied persons would be induced to discontinue gainful activity.

## 18

**With the OASDI program gradually picking up its full beneficiary load, Federal participation in the financing of state programs of old-age assistance should be terminated. This may best be done by the incorporation in the Federal old-age assistance legislation of a sliding scale which would gradually eliminate Federal grants over a period of years.**

When the original Social Security Act was adopted, it was contemplated that, as the old-age benefit provisions gradually approached maturity, slowly picking up the full beneficiary load, the old-age assistance provisions would come to cause less and less drain on the Federal budget. Actually, on the contrary, Federal outlays for old-age assistance have been steadily increasing ever since. Legislation to effectuate the original plan, and reverse the present trend, is long overdue.

As a practical matter, the complete and sudden withdrawal of the Federal Government from old-age assistance financing would present most States with a difficult budgetary problem. The best approach would be to incorporate a sliding scale into the Federal old-age assistance provisions which would gradually reduce the Federal matching percentages over a period of years, and eventually terminate the Federal grants.

# 19. SOME ISSUES AND GOALS IN OASDI

WILBUR J. COHEN, *Industrial and Labor Relations Review,* July, 1959.

IT IS IMPORTANT to remind ourselves that just a few years ago old-age insurance was a relatively small program. Benefits just prior to the 1950 amendments averaged only about $26 a month for a single retired individual. Total disbursements under the program in early 1950 were running at about three quarters of a billion dollars annually, less than 10 percent of the over $8 billion paid out in 1958. And the number of persons receiving old-age assistance on a needs test basis exceeded the number of aged persons drawing old-age insurance up until 1951.

Congress made a vital decision in 1950 "to reaffirm the basic principle that a contributory system of social insurance . . . is the most satisfactory way of preventing dependency."[1] It decided that Old-Age and Survivors Insurance really would be the first line of defense in meeting the income-maintenance needs of retired aged persons. By 1951 the number of aged persons receiving old-age insurance had exceeded the number receiving old-age assistance. A new dimension had been added to our social institutions. The reiteration of this policy in 1954 by a new Administration, after careful study and review of all the controversies of the previous twenty years, enabled the system to accelerate the performance of the role set out for it by Congress in 1950.

Today, Old-Age, Survivors, and Disability Insurance (OASDI) is the

---

[1] For an elaboration of the factors influencing the Congress's decision, see House of Representatives Committee Report on the Social Security Act Amendments of 1949, Report No. 1300 (81st Cong., 1st sess.) (August 22, 1949), pp. 2–3.

largest social insurance program in the United States, dwarfing any other social insurance program and even the veterans' programs. In protection afforded to employees and their wives, it exceeds the coverage of all private pension plans in the United States and is equivalent to about one half of the face value of all the life insurance protection—public and private—in the nation.[2] And, moreover, it does this in a way which has not adversely affected initiative, thrift, or voluntary pension plans, has preserved emphasis on self-responsibility and wage differentials, and has operated at the phenomenally low administrative cost of only 2 percent of benefit payments,[3] while disbursing benefits totaling nearly $40 billion in the past twenty years on an efficient basis without any taint of political manipulation or scandal.

A group of business executives appointed in 1957 by the Secretary of Health, Education, and Welfare surveyed the operations of the Bureau of Old-Age and Survivors Insurance. They found that the Bureau is "carrying out its mission in a sound and vigorous manner" and commented favorably on their "impression of both efficiency and friendliness created by the typical OASI district office."[4]

It is this enviable record that makes it possible to discuss the issues involved in still further broadening, expanding, and improving the program.

The topic could be approached by dealing intensively with the key issues for 1960 or the longer-range issues. Each contains sufficient content for a full-scale paper. But it would be unwise to discuss one without the other, for both are linked together and it is only fair to see both in some perspective.

## THE MAJOR GENERAL ISSUES

The larger general issues seem to me to be these:

The most immediate short-range new policy issue is whether insurance protection to cover some or all of the health costs of beneficiaries should be included in the OASDI program and, if so, what protection to offer and to whom, how to administer the program, and in what way to finance the costs and relate the program to the longer-run issue of comprehensive health services.

The longer-range issue is the question of how to achieve social adequacy of the cash benefits during the coming decade in the light of developing and changing needs, growing private arrangements, the relationship of social security to private pension plans, and the increasing ability of our economy to pay for a more adequate program.

---

[2] T. N. E. Greville and J. A. Lazerson, *Estimated Amount of Life Insurance in Force as Survivor Benefits under OASI–1957*, Actuarial Study No. 47, Social Security Administration, 1958, p. 15. The approximate total face value of all survivors' insurance benefits under OASDI for 1960 probably will be in the neighborhood of $500 billion.

[3] Robert J. Myers, "Old-Age, Survivors, and Disability Insurance: Administrative Expenses," *Social Security Bulletin* (March, 1958), p. 15.

[4] *Social Security Bulletin* (August, 1958), p. 3.

A persistent question, both in the short- and long-run, is how to finance the costs of maintaining an acceptable program which takes into account social adequacy and equities and does not adversely affect a number of other complex principles believed essential to our economy.

## SOME DIFFICULT SPECIFIC ISSUES

Some of the more important and difficult specific questions which have to be weighed before coming to any conclusions as to recommendations for changes in the OASDI program are the following:[5]

1. What should be the retirement age for men and women? Should it be the same for women as for men?

2. Should a "retirement test" continue to be a condition for receipt of insurance benefits? If there is a "retirement test," what should it be?

3. Should greater flexibility be introduced in the system by allowing persons to retire before a normal retirement age at an actuarially reduced benefit and/or by increasing benefits to persons who delay retirement beyond the normal age?

4. Should there be a more liberal definition of disability for older persons age 55 or 60 who are disabled for work in their regular occupations? Should short-time disability be included in the OASDI system rather than under state plans?

5. Should those who are already retired, disabled, and widowed be blanketed into the insurance program for minimum benefits? How should this minimum be determined? Who should pay this cost? How would these provisions affect attitudes toward the contributory, wage-related insurance program?

6. Should there be a government contribution to the system; if so, when, how much, and on what rationale? How much of the cost should be borne through payroll taxes?

7. Should insurance benefits be automatically adjusted to changes in prices and wages? If so, how should this cost be financed?

8. Should any changes be built into the system so that it will be automatically adjusted to the business cycle to have a countercyclical effect? If so, should these relate only to the contributions or also to specific provisions in the benefit structure?

9. What would be the impact of any of the above possible changes in the federal system on private pension plans and industrial relations?

Keeping these specific questions in mind, I shall attempt to formulate a tentative set of short-range and longer-range goals. It will be clear that I do not attempt to answer all the questions just raised, but it is hoped that the answers to those questions which are discussed reflect an awareness that the unanswered questions also have important social, economic, and financial implications.

---

[5] Some of these questions relating to retirement age and the retirement test are discussed in my book on *Retirement Policies under Social Security*, 1957. Several of them are discussed in Robert M. Ball, *Pensions in the United States*, 1952; in John J. Corson and John W. McConnell, *Economic Needs of Older People*, 1956, and Eveline M. Burns, *Social Security and Public Policy*, 1956.

My own formulation of long-range goals for our OASDI program is based upon several assumptions. These may be briefly summarized as:

There is no need or justification in our economy for any aged retired or disabled person or family, where the breadwinner has died, being in want.

The need for recourse to assistance should be reduced to an absolute minimum.

Social insurance methods have proved their effectiveness and acceptability and should be strengthened.

In an expanding economy, we can allocate more of our resources toward the needs of our dependent population without adversely affecting the incentives of the productive population.

In addition to our social insurance needs, there are other important health, education, and welfare needs that have a valid claim on our expanding resources and which must be taken into account in determining social priorities in meeting human needs.

## SHORT-RANGE PROPOSALS FOR IMPROVING OASDI

There are nearly 15 million persons who are drawing social security benefits or who are insured and could draw them if they retired. This includes those eligible persons age 50 and over who are disabled and those who are eligible survivors (widows and dependent children).

### Hospital and Nursing Insurance[6]

The aged and disabled have relatively low incomes and a greater than average need for hospital and nursing services. Those who do have voluntary hospital coverage have utilization experience which will continue to make for increasing premium costs, while others have no protection. The voluntary plans, the hospitals, and the individual all can be benefited by extension of social security to cover part of the costs of hospital and nursing services.

Substantial protection in this area can be provided for a total of about one-half of one percent of taxable payrolls on a level-premium basis. This would mean about one-quarter of one percent on employees, an equal amount on employers, and three-eights of one percent on the self-employed. A somewhat more limited system could be financed for a total of about a quarter of one percent of payrolls and a much more comprehensive scope of medical care for about one percent of payrolls, on a level-premium basis.

To keep within a limited cost, two major types of protection could be provided initially: a limited duration of hospital care of perhaps 30, 50, or 60 days a year, and a limited amount of essential nursing service, including visiting nursing service in the home. The legislation might pro-

---

[6] For some of the controversial issues involved in, and some implications of this proposal, see Wilbur J. Cohen, "The Forand Bill: Hospital Insurance for the Aged," *American Journal of Nursing* (May, 1958).

vide that, as experience or funds warrant, the benefits might be increased up to 70 or 120 days. Other aspects which might be considered to help keep the plan within certain cost limits are: providing that, initially, benefits be payable only to persons age 70 or age 72 or over or, alternatively, to those who are "retired"; providing for collection of contributions for six to twelve months before benefits begin; and allocating the contributions to a separate trust account. Consideration could be given to providing certain outpatient services and skilled nursing home services when connected with a hospital.

Administratively, consideration might be given to placing the initial responsibility for putting this plan into operation by a board (similar in composition to the former Social Security Board), if certain novel discretionary decisions are necessary, such as the authority to enter into agreements with nonprofit plans on a national or state basis which, in effect, would enroll the social security beneficiaries under plans such as the Blue Cross. Also, such a board might be desirable to handle appeals on any matters specifically relating to health benefits.

### Average Benefits

Although prices rose about 8 percent and wages 12 percent during the four years from 1954 to 1958, Social Security benefits were increased only 7 percent in 1958 over the 1954 levels. The average benefit being awarded to persons first coming on the benefit rolls in 1959 is estimated to be about $85 but only $72 for all those drawing benefits.

To increase benefits to an average of about $100 a month would mean an increase of about 20 to 25 percent. Since other improvements are necessary in the program, it may not be possible to achieve such an increase all at once. Therefore, the increase might be achieved in steps: an immediate increase of 5 to 10 percent, and another 10 to 15 percent increase in two or four years. These steps might be included in any legislation providing for the suggested initial increase.

### Maximum Earnings Level

An increase in the maximum earnings level—now $4,800—would serve both to increase benefits as well as to bring additional income to the system and strengthen the financial base. This might be done in two steps, corresponding to the general benefit increase, by increasing the $4,800 to $6,000 within the next two years, and to $7,200 about two or three years later.

### Minimum and Maximum Benefits

The minimum monthly benefit could be increased to $50 for those who have contributed at least 5 years. The maximum family benefit for those with several children should be increased automatically from $254 (which is twice the present maximum primary benefit of $217) to about

$300 or $350 as the maximum earnings level and maximum benefit increases.

### Widows' Benefit

Widows have the very lowest incomes among all beneficiaries. Logically, they should receive 100 percent of the primary benefit amount (as does a single retired worker) instead of the 75 percent they receive at present. An increase to 100 percent, however, might cost slightly more than one-half of one percent of payroll. Hence, it might be also necessary to increase this amount in two or three steps. An initial increase could be to 80 or 85 percent.

### Maximum Eligibility Age for Children

Increasing from 18 to 21 the maximum eligibility age for children might enable some to stay in school and finish college. This would involve a very small cost and would accomplish a socially desirable objective.

### Disability Insurance

Since disability insurance benefits are paid from a separate trust account, it is necessary to consider their financing separately from the financing of OASI benefits. Two changes might be considered:

1. Repealing the limitation to pay benefits beginning only at age 50.
2. Paying the cost of rehabilitating disabled persons from the disability account.

Both changes would not only help disabled people but would aid the general taxpayer by reducing some welfare costs now paid out of general revenue. Many disabled persons now have to apply for public assistance or vocational rehabilitation or both. Both programs are financed from general revenues and the federal government is paying about 60 percent of the total cost of each program. Both programs are limited at the present time, in part, by lack of funds. Many additional disabled persons could be rehabilitated by providing that the disability account would pay for their rehabilitation; this would also save the system funds in the long run as these persons returned to work.

Appropriate adjustments would have to be made in the amount of contributions allocated to the disability account to finance these changes fully.

### LONGER-RANGE OBJECTIVES

Since 1939, opinions on proposed changes in the old-age insurance program have tended to diverge on particular issues, although it should not be overlooked that there is very wide agreement on such basic issues as the maintenance of a contributory, wage-related program and, even between management and labor, on such a question as the maintenance of a retirement test.[7]

The more general the statement of the objective, the wider is usually the extent of the agreement. Both management and labor might be able to join in a formulation of such objectives as comprehensive, adequate, and sound protection for everyone, with a minimum of compulsion and a maximum of voluntarism, with no red tape, without any employees needed for administration, at no cost to anyone, with prompt, courteous, and efficient administration, and with no adverse effects on initiative, thrift, employment, or self-reliance!

Such a general formulation, then, while it may be helpful under some circumstances, does not always aid in deciding specific complex issues. Any discussion of specific proposals concerning OASDI indicates that there are many issues and objectives in the program on which there is no general agreement among labor, management, the insurance industry, public welfare personnel, social workers, and social insurance students. Yet, in the American pragmatic way, we have made significant progress in improving OASDI. However, representatives of some of those groups who are most concerned about costs, incentives, and relationship to private plans repeatedly ask for a definition of the *ultimate* objective of the program. Is it 50, 100, or 110 percent of wages for anyone who wishes to retire at any age? If not, what is it?

The specifics of the program today are the results of the balancing of conflicting factors of yesterday. Is it possible to state long-run objectives in terms which will help guide developments in the future? Recapitulating some of the previous discussion, here are some long-run goals, stated in objective terms, which are very tentatively suggested for discussion, clarification, and revision:

*Contribution Coverage.* 100 percent of those regularly working for a living.
*Potential Beneficiaries.* 100 percent of those in the eligible age group who have "retired."
*The Minimum Primary Benefit.* Approximately equal to the average old-age assistance payment (excluding medical care).
*The Maximum Primary Benefit.* At least four to five times the minimum benefit.
*The Maximum Family Benefit.* Between two and three times the maximum primary benefit.
*The Average Benefit.* Equal to at least 50 percent of "average earnings," subject to the following: (a) at least 85 percent of all aged retired persons hav-

---

[7] See the five areas of agreement in *Pensions in the United States*, A Study Prepared for the Joint Committee on the Economic Report by the National Planning Association (82d Cong., 2d sess.), 1952, pp. 25–38. See also items 8 and 10 in *Sound Policy for Social Security*, A Statement by the Life Insurance Business, 1958. It should be noted, however, that there would not be general agreement between labor and management on many—if not most—of the other points in the Life Insurance document.

ing a total income from all sources of about two thirds of "average earnings," and (b) not more than 5 percent of the aged in receipt of old-age assistance.

*The Maximum Earnings Base.* About 90 to 95 percent of the full earnings of men age 25–45 working four quarters a year.

*Normal Retirement Age.* For men—at the age at which about 50 percent or more are not in the labor force.

*Eligibility for Disability Benefit.* Inability to engage in substantial gainful work irrespective of age.

*Widows' Benefit.* 100 percent of the primary benefit.

*Hospital Costs after Retirement.* 100 percent of semiprivate care with adequate arrangements for alternative services to minimize unnecessary hospitalization.

## EQUITY, ADEQUACY, AND RELATED FACTORS

. . . The problem of making a specific determination of benefit adequacy in relation to equities is perhaps the most difficult of all issues in social insurance. It involves some interrelated aspects of economics, finance, sociology, political science, and social psychology. In a country such as ours, with its vastness, its wage differentials, the mobility of its population, and the many different kinds of family spending units, benefit adequacy is a composite of many elements. Although it may be desirable, it would be presumptuous to attempt to solve this complex issue with any single phrase or any single formula.

From time to time, the complexity of this issue has been minimized by use of the facile phrase that the benefits in the OASDI program should provide a "basic floor of protection." Congressional committees, government agencies, business and insurance groups have become fascinated by this elusive concept. Some people think of the floor as a bare, rough-hewn cabin floor, others as a solid oak floor nicely polished and waxed. It is also possible to think of it as a floor with a kind of Bigelow carpet on it not only to keep one's feet warm but also to give some aesthetic pleasure. Undoubtedly, the great attractiveness and usefulness of the "basic floor of protection" formula has been that it can mean different things to different people. Its value is in what it conceals, rather than in what it reveals.

In sharp contrast to Great Britain's experience, no group in the United States has had the knowledge, courage, or wisdom to attempt to define a specific benefit standard. The research of Booth, Rowntree, and others in Great Britain led Beveridge, in 1942, to the acceptance of the physical efficiency standard for social insurance benefits.[8] Such a standard would be unacceptable in the United States as a basis for formulating social insurance policy.

While we have developed and used budgetary standards for determining relief payments and minimum wages for women, and as guides for

---

[8] Sir (now Lord) William Beveridge, *Social Insurance and Allied Services* (New York: The MacMillan Co., 1942), pars. 193–232, pp. 76–90.

other kinds of social legislation, we have not used them in OASDI or Workmen's Compensation, and only slightly and indirectly in unemployment insurance.

## OPINION SURVEYS

One approach seldom used in formulating social insurance policy is to ask people what they think should be paid under the program. There has been a noticeable unwillingness on the part of those persons studying or formulating social insurance policy to use the Gallup poll method[9] because of the fear that this democratic approach would be criticized as "unscientific" and would also result in a benefit level which would bankrupt the country and put the Townsend plan to shame. But what evidence we have on this matter indicates that such "conventional wisdom" is not rooted in fact. Survey experts report that the average American is more "reality conscious" than he is given credit for and that his level of economic aspirations is usually below the effective capacity of our expanding economy.

John W. McConnell and Robert Risley approached this problem by the subjective-survey method. In 1948 they found in Elmira, New York, that the minimum amount which the chief income producers thought necessary for retirement varied from less than $50 to over $300 a month.[10] Yet, despite this wide variation, there was a clustering between $76 and $175 with the median at $125. This was at a time when the average primary old-age benefit was $25 a month and the average benefit for a man and wife was about $39.

Although replies to a question of this sort are a subjective measure, affected by innumerable known and unknown factors, they serve as one important benchmark of adequacy. McConnell and Risley did not ask whether all or any portion of this minimum income should be supplied through social insurance. Hence, while a very vital part of the information needed for determining the level of social insurance benefits is missing, the replies indicate that the average individual's perception of the desirable level of governmental retirement payments is realistically grounded.

McConnell and Risley concluded from their study: "That the needs of

---

[9] For some results of opinion surveys on how much people in 1935, 1938, and 1939 thought should be paid under the social security program, see Hadley Cantril (ed.), *Public Opinion, 1935–1946* (Princeton: Princeton University Press), pp. 541–42. See also the results of a survey taken in California in 1952 by the Pomona College Social Science Research Center, Floyd Bond *et al.*, *Our Needy Aged: A California Study of a National Problem* (New York: Henry Holt & Co., 1954), p. 304.

[10] *Economic Security: A Study of Community Needs and Resources* (Ithaca, N.Y.: New York State School of Industrial and Labor Relations, Cornell University, July, 1951), Bulletin No. 18, pp. 2–4, 69–71.

people, in their own opinion, are modest rather than excessive, is clear. They are not reaching for the moon."[11]

The Gallup poll approach is in many ways just as necessary as—and in some ways superior to—the traditional budgetary standard approach. The presumed objectivity of a budgetary standard is, after all, only the cumulative total of a series of subjective determinations. Should cigarettes and beer be included, or not? Should you include a second-hand car, a TV set (and repairs!), money for church, union dues, and newspapers? If these items are put in, the dollar level of the budget naturally comes out higher than if they are left out.

These comments should not be interpreted to mean that budgetary standards are useless or unnecessary. They play a valuable role in helping to define the level of living we are talking about. But what people think they want their level of living to be should be given as much—or more— weight than a pseudoscientific standard prepared by budget experts which, after all, is determined by including those items which some people think form an acceptable standard at the time.

There is no single, simple objective standard for determining the long-run adequacy of all types of social security benefits. Concepts of adequacy can and do vary. Beveridge's concept of adequacy for social insurance benefits in Great Britain differs from ours in the United States. Beveridge stated that social insurance "should aim at guaranteeing the minimum income needed for subsistence," but he also noted that "determination of what is required for reasonable human subsistence is to some extent a matter of judgment; estimates on this point change with time, and generally, in a progressive community, change upwards."[12]

It is relatively much easier to indicate in what respect particular benefits are inadequate at a given moment of time than to define "adequacy" as a timeless standard. Yet we must make a greater effort to determine what we mean by adequacy in each program.

It is possible for benefits to be inadequate for some individuals while they may be "too adequate" for others. The latter situation may arise when more than one benefit is payable for the same risk or when allowance is made for the nontaxable status of benefits. It is not always possible to solve both inadequacy and overadequacy by the same device. As our private programs proliferate, these problems may become more acute and more difficult to solve.

Determining the appropriate level of social insurance benefits is not simply a matter, however, of asking people what they want, or bringing together some family-budget specialists who will determine what people need. Some of the other considerations which must be taken into account

---

[11] *Ibid.*, p. 3.
[12] Beveridge, *op. cit.*, par. 27, p. 14.

are the amount and distribution of costs, the effect on incentives, personal responsibility, and similar important elements which are not easily evaluated in objective terms, the relationship of the benefits to the prevailing distribution of wages and incomes, and the balancing of present consumption wants and needs with future wants and needs. Moreover, even if a desired level of living for beneficiaries is agreed upon, how much of this should be met through public, compulsory, tax-supported arrangements and how much through individual and private responsibility can not be determined by a fixed mathematical formula, and is certainly subject to change.

## DISCUSSION QUESTIONS

1. The economic and social problem of the aged has become increasingly important in the past quarter century. Explain the reasons for this.

2. Discuss the following policy issues in old-age insurance:
   *a*) The contributory principle.
   *b*) The benefit level.
   *c*) The retirement test.
   *d*) Relating benefits to length of contribution.
   *e*) The size and implications of reserve financing and pay-as-you-go financing.

3. Should old-age insurance be financed in part or in whole from general revenues? Discuss the implications.

4. How should the value of retirement benefits be protected against the effects of inflation?

5. Explain the reasons for the development of private pension plans. Indicate their magnitude and implications for the economy from the viewpoint of savings and mobility.

6. What changes in old-age insurance would be necessary in order to dispense with the need for old-age assistance?

7. Do you think the nation can afford an adequate program of security for the aged? Explain.

## SELECTED REFERENCES

Board of Trustees of the Federal OASI Trust Fund. *Annual Report.* Washington, D.C.: U.S. Government Printing Office.

British Parliament. *Report of the Committee on the Economic and Financial*

*Problems of the Provision for Old Age*. London: Her Majesty's Stationery Office, 1954.

BURGESS, ERNEST W. (ed.). *Aging and Retirement*. University of Chicago Press, 1954. This collection of papers also appears in *American Journal of Sociology* (January, 1954), entire issue.

CANADIAN PARLIAMENT. *Report of the Joint Committee on Old Age Security, June 28, 1950*. Ottawa, Canada: E. Cloutier, Printer to the King, 1950.

CLARK, ROBERT M. *Economic Security for the Aged in the United States and Canada*. Ottawa, Canada: Department of National Health and Welfare, 1959.

COHEN, WILBUR J. *Retirement Policies under Social Security*. Berkeley: University of California Institute of Industrial Relations, 1957.

CONFERENCE ON AGING. University of Michigan. *Annual Proceedings*.

CORSON, JOHN J., and McCONNELL, JOHN W. *Economic Needs of Older People*. New York: Twentieth Century Fund, 1956.

DRAKE, JOSEPH T. *The Aged in American Society*. New York: Ronald Press Co., 1958.

HOLTZMAN, ABRAHAM. "Analysis of Old Age Politics in the United States," *Journal of Gerontology*, Vol. IX (January, 1954), pp. 56–66.

HOUSE COMMITTEE ON WAYS AND MEANS. *Social Security Act Amendments of 1954. Hearings, on H. R. 7199* (83rd Cong., 2d sess.). Washington, D.C.: U.S. Government Printing Office, 1954.

INSTITUTE OF GERONTOLOGY. The Southern Conference on Gerontology, University of Florida. *Annual Proceedings*.

MASON, BRUCE. "The Townsend Movement," *Southwestern Political and Social Science Quarterly* (June, 1954), pp. 36–47.

MATHIASON, GENEVA (ed.). *Criteria for Retirement*. New York: G. P. Putnam, 1953.

MERIAM, LEWIS, and SCHLOTTERBECK, KARL. *The Cost and Financing of Social Security*. Washington, D.C.: The Brookings Institution, 1950.

MERRIAM, IDA C. *Social Security Financing*. Social Security Administration, Division of Research and Statistics, Bureau Report No. 17, 1952.

NATIONAL ASSOCIATION OF MANUFACTURERS, INDUSTRIAL RELATIONS DIVISION. *Retirement Security in a Free Society*. Economic Series No. 67. New York, 1954.

RAUSHENBUSH, STEPHEN. *Pensions in Our Economy*. Washington, D.C.: Public Affairs Institute, 1955.

SENATE COMMITTEE ON LABOR AND PUBLIC WELFARE. *Studies of the Aged and Aging* (85th Cong., 2d sess.). Washington, D.C.: U.S. Government Printing Office, 1957.

SHENFIELD, BARBARA E. *Social Policies for Old Age*. London: Routledge and K. Paul, 1957.

STARK, J. R. "Equities in the Financing of Federal Old Age and Survivors Insurance," *National Tax Journal*, Vol. VI (September, 1953), pp. 286–92.

UNITED NATIONS, DEPARTMENT OF ECONOMIC AND SOCIAL AFFAIRS. *The Aging of Populations and Its Economic and Social Implications*. New York, 1956.

# CHAPTER

## IV The Employment Security Program: Unemployment Insurance and the Employment Service

## INTRODUCTION

THE SOCIAL SECURITY ACT of 1935 provided the stimulus for the establishment of a federal-state system of unemployment insurance. Only Wisconsin had enacted such legislation before 1935. With the fear of interstate competition removed by the employment tax offset provision in the Social Security Act, all 51 "states" passed such legislation by July, 1937.

The federal legislation provides wide latitude for the state programs. As a result, one finds a rather complex system with great diversity in the substantive provisions for unemployment insurance in the 51 jurisdictions. In general, benefits are paid only to individuals previously depending for their livelihood on their earnings in covered employment but who are involuntarily unemployed and are able and willing to work and are seeking work. Since this is a social insurance program, no means test is required. Benefits are paid as a matter of right when unemployed claimants qualify as insured workers by reason of past employment in jobs under the law. There is great variation concerning benefit amount and duration among the states. In almost all states, only employer contributions based on payrolls finance the program.

The federal-state unemployment insurance system completed its twenty-fourth year of operation, and twenty-first year of benefit payments, on January 1, 1960. More than $23 billion in benefits had been paid to insured claimants. About 8 million workers drew some benefits during 1958, at an average weekly rate of $30.58. Over 45 million workers were in covered employment. By 1959, more than $28.2 billion of collections and interest had been paid into the unemployment trust fund, leaving a net balance of more than $6.9 billion—an amount equivalent to almost 4 years of payments at the average benefit levels over the previous 10 years.

For most of the program's history, unemployment insurance appeared to be on the defensive. Unions complained about low benefits, excessive

226

disqualifications, and inadequate coverage and duration. Management thought these provisions adequate and were concerned with benefit costs, contribution rates, and experience rating. Public concern was manifested in the problem of malingering, anomalies, and abuses. On the whole, there was little basic public understanding of the program, its strengths and weaknesses, and its role in our economy.

This can in part be explained by the fact that, except for three brief and mild recessions, the program operated under conditions of relatively high employment levels. The benefit paying system functioned efficiently, and with reasonable speed.

The shortcomings in weekly benefit amount and especially duration of payments were highlighted by the large layoffs which began in 1957. Concern was also expressed about the exclusion of many groups, including farm labor, domestic service, employees for nonprofit institutions, most state and public employees, and particularly employees of small establishments.

In 1958 Congress enacted for the first time a form of extended benefits, entitled Temporary Unemployment Compensation. Twenty-two states, embracing 70 per cent of the covered labor force, either acted under provisions of the federal legislation or enacted their own temporary extension of benefit duration.

There is considerable controversy concerning the direction which unemployment insurance should take in the future. This controversy revolves around several critical issues in unemployment insurance. Among these, the following stand out:

*First,* should the present federal-state system remain unchanged, leaving the substantive questions of benefit amount, benefit duration, conditions of eligibility, and methods of financing almost entirely within the control of the individual state?

*Second,* if that course is followed, how can interstate competition in benefit costs be avoided? Such competition has, it is alleged, compelled each state to be on the alert so as not to impose costs upon its employers which are more onerous than those costs on employers in competitive states.

*Third,* to what extent should there be federal provision for benefits and duration and with respect to other substantive matters in unemployment insurance? Such federal provision could be in the form of a single federal law replacing the present state-by-state system. Such legislation has been strongly favored by organized labor but has vigorous opposition from management. An alternative approach is to retain the present federal-state system but to require minimum federal standards as to benefits, financing, and similar matters. Such legislation has been proposed with the support of organized labor but has failed to receive congressional approval.

*Fourth,* within the realm of state action, a central issue revolves around the question of benefit levels. The states have made substantial progress in increasing weekly benefit amounts. As a proportion of average weekly wages, however, such benefits represent approximately 35 per cent for the nation as a whole. It is urged by many, particularly in the trade unions, that this ratio is too low and benefit amounts should be raised to approximately half of average weekly wages. There is strong opposition to such benefit levels based on the fact that such levels will undoubtedly increase the cost of financing unemployment insurance and also on the fear that higher benefits might adversely affect workers' enterprise in job holding and job seeking.

Unemployment insurance is a highly controversial area of social insurance. It is an important facet of industrial relations. In a dynamic economy it has many important implications. In addition to knowing how unemployment insurance and the employment service operate, it is essential to consider the proposals made for changing the program. To help answer some of these questions a broad knowledge of social insurance and the nature of the economy are both essential.

# 20. STRUCTURE AND MAJOR FEATURES OF UNEMPLOYMENT INSURANCE

*Social Security in the United States*, Social Security Administration, 1957.

THE FIRST UNEMPLOYMENT INSURANCE LAW in the United States was passed by Wisconsin in 1932, but it did not come into full operation until after the Social Security Act became law 3 years later. The Federal act made it to the advantage of the States to establish unemployment insurance. By July 1937, all States, Alaska, Hawaii, and the District of Columbia had passed laws for this purpose.

The Social Security Act gave the State two incentives. The act set up a Federal unemployment tax on employers in industry and commerce who had eight or more employees in 20 weeks of the year (four or more, beginning in January 1956). It made it possible, however, for employers to be relieved of paying most of this tax if they were contributors under a State unemployment insurance system. Therefore a State that taxed employers to pay for unemployment insurance did not put them at a disadvantage in competing with similar businesses in States that had no such tax. Congress also authorized grants to States to meet necessary and proper costs of administering State systems. A State program has to meet certain Federal requirements in law and administration if employers are to get their offset against the Federal tax and if the State is to receive Federal grants for administration.

Effective January 1, 1955, employees of the Federal Government were brought under the unemployment insurance system.

The Federal Unemployment Tax Act, which is now part of the Internal Revenue Code, lays a tax on employers at the rate of 3 percent of workers' pay in covered jobs, not counting anything over $3,000 paid to a worker in a year. The employer can offset against as much as 90 percent of this tax the amount he has paid under an approved State unemployment insurance law or from which he has been excused under the experience-rating provisions of the State law, in accordance with his experience with unemployment risk. All States reduce the contribution rates of employers whose workers have little unemployment; some excuse an employer from making any contribution at all in a particular year. In 1956 the average contribution rate of employers under State laws was 1.3 percent of their covered payroll.

The remaining tenth of the Federal tax—0.3 percent of covered payroll—is collected by the Treasury and goes into general Federal revenues.

In the Employment Security Administrative Financing Act of 1954, Congress provided for earmarking, for purposes of employment security, the excess of collections of the Federal unemployment tax over Federal and State administrative expenditures; added the first permanent provision for Federal assistance to States with low reserves; and provided for return to the States of the excess of collections after a $200 million reserve is built up to be used for payment of benefits and, under certain conditions, payment of State administrative expenses.

Congress appropriates money for grants to States for State administration of the program. In the fiscal year 1957 funds allocated to the States, including amounts for administration of public employment services, totaled $250 million. The Bureau of Employment Security in the United States Department of Labor is responsible for determining each year whether the State program still meets Federal requirements for these grants and the tax offset and for recommending the amounts of the grants. The Secretary of Labor certifies his determination of the facts to the Treasury.

## Administration

The Federal partner in the Federal-State program of unemployment insurance is the Bureau of Employment Security in the United States Department of Labor. Prior to 1949 this Bureau was a part of the Social Security Administration. Each State has an employment security agency. Seventeen of these are in the State Department of Labor and one is in the State workmen's compensation agency. The others are independent departments of the State government or independent boards or commissions. The overall agency which administers unemployment insurance ordinarily administers the employment service also. Claims for benefits are taken in the 1,700 local offices of the employment service in the various States.

### Federal Requirements

All contributions collected under the State laws must be deposited in the unemployment trust fund in the United States Treasury. The fund is invested as a whole, but each State has a separate account to which its deposits and its share of interest on investments are credited. The State may withdraw money from the account at any time but only to pay benefits.

Benefits must be paid through public employment offices or other federally approved agencies. The State must have methods of administration that will ensure full payment of benefits when due. Workers must have a right to appeal a decision of the State agency concerning their claims. Benefits cannot be denied to a claimant because he refuses to accept a job under certain conditions designed to protect the established standards as to prevailing wages, working conditions, and union affiliation.

These and some other requirements of Federal law are intended to assure that a State participating in the program has a sound and genuine unemployment insurance system, fairly administered. The State itself decides what workers it will cover, how workers will qualify for benefits, how much they receive a week and for how long if they continue to be unemployed. The State decides what the employers' contribution rates will be. The State unemployment insurance agency makes rules for payment of benefits and handles and decides claims of unemployed workers.

### State Unemployment Insurance Programs

Unemployment insurance differs from State to State and only the general pattern of the State programs can be outlined here.

*Qualifying for Benefits.* In general, an unemployed worker can receive benefits if he meets the following conditions:

1. He must register for work at a public employment office and file his claim.

2. He must have been employed in a job covered by the State law. Generally, this must be a job in private industry or commerce, such as jobs in factories, stores, mines, offices and so on. In most States, it must have been a job with a firm that had at least 4 employees in 20 weeks of the year. More than two-fifths of the States cover firms with fewer than 4 workers.

3. He must have earned a certain amount of "wages credits" in covered jobs. That is, he must have had a certain amount of pay or worked for a certain time, or both, in a period set by the law before he lost his job.

4. He must be able to work and available for work and ready to take a suitable job if one is offered him.

In general, a worker cannot get unemployment benefits if he is sick or unable to work for any other reason.

A few States pay unemployment benefits to a worker who becomes sick after he has filed a claim for unemployment insurance and registered for work; benefits continue so long as no work which is suitable, except for the disability, is offered or refused. Three States have separate provisions to pay disability benefits to workers insured under their unemployment insurance laws when the worker's unemployment is due to sickness or other disability; in a fourth State the temporary disability insurance program is administered by the State workmen's compensation agency but covers substantially the same workers as are covered by unemployment insurance.

**Benefit Payments.**     States also differ in the weekly amount of the benefits they pay to unemployed workers with similar wage credits and in the length of time a worker can continue to get payments if he cannot find a suitable new job.

In general, the weekly amount is intended to be about half the worker's previous weekly pay except that there are minimum and maximum amounts on the payment. Some States increase the amount for workers who have dependents. The maximum weekly benefit for a worker without dependents ranges among the States from $25 to $45 a week. The minimum weekly amount for any worker who qualifies ranges from $3 to $17. All States pay partial benefits for partial unemployment. All but four States require a waiting period, usually a week, after a worker becomes unemployed before his benefits can begin.

In most States, a worker's past earnings or employment under the law determine the length of time he can continue to receive benefits if he continues to be unemployed. In some, it may be as short as 6 weeks; in most, as long as 26 weeks. Fourteen States have a "uniform potential duration" of benefits for any qualified worker. Uniform duration ranges among these States from 16 weeks to 30 weeks.

**Disqualifications.**     A claimant may be disqualified from benefits even if he has the wage credits he needs to be insured. He is generally disqualified if:

1. He has quit his job voluntarily without good cause. (Some State laws say without good cause "attributable to the employer" or "connected with the work.")
2. He was discharged for misconduct in connection with his work.
3. He has refused or has failed, without good cause, to apply for or accept suitable work.
4. He is unemployed because of a stoppage of work as the result of a labor dispute.

In all States, disqualification means that a worker must serve a longer waiting period before he can get benefits. Some States not only postpone the benefits otherwise due him, but also reduce them. A few States may cancel all the benefit rights of a disqualified worker; then he cannot receive anything under the system until he has again had enough covered employment to build up the necessary wage credits.

# 21. MAJOR OBJECTIVES OF FEDERAL POLICY WITH RESPECT TO THE FEDERAL-STATE EMPLOYMENT SECURITY PROGRAM

*Employment
Security
Review,*
**August, 1955.**

IN APRIL, 1955, the Secretary of Labor issued a statement of the major objectives of Federal policy relating to the Federal-State employment security program. Quoted below are the overall objectives and the objectives that apply specifically to the unemployment insurance program.

### Overall Objectives

1. To aid, through an effective employment service system, in getting the best possible job for the worker and the best possible worker for the job.

2. To provide adequate income insurance for unemployed workers when suitable jobs are not available, and through this system to help maintain purchasing power.

3. To promote the establishment of income insurance programs for non-work-connected disability.

4. To assist in the improvement and optimum utilization of the Nation's manpower resources, including the promotion of employment opportunities.

5. To assist in maintaining and improving our manpower readiness for defense mobilization.

6. To develop and disseminate employment, unemployment, and labor market information in order to assist in achieving economic stabilization and growth, and to meet the informational needs of labor, management, and the public.

### Objectives of the Unemployment Insurance Program

Unemployment insurance is a program—established under Federal and State law—for income maintenance during periods of involuntary unemployment due to lack of work, which provides partial compensation of wage loss as a matter of right, with dignity and dispatch, to eligible individuals. It helps to maintain purchasing power and to stabilize the economy. It helps to prevent the dispersal of the employers' trained labor force, the sacrifice of skills, and the breakdown of labor standards during temporary unemployment. To accomplish these general objectives and to meet the national interest in an effective and reasonably adequate and uniform program of unemployment insurance throughout the country, the program should meet the following specific objectives within the framework of a Federal-State system:

1. To cover so far as feasible all workers subject to the risk of involuntary unemployment.

2. To admit to benefits those workers who have demonstrated a recent and substantial attachment to the covered labor force, without providing arbitrary qualifying and requalifying requirements. (For example, to use an individual base period and benefit year with as short a lag as possible between the base period and the benefit year; to use a qualifying requirement in terms of employment or wages which will be effective at all benefit levels, and which will be realistic in relation to the wages of covered workers and to the weekly benefit and duration of benefits recommended.)

3. To provide eligible claimants income sufficient in weekly amount to meet their nondeferrable expenditures, replacing enough of wage loss so that most workers need not turn to other forms of aid, but not so much in relation to recent earnings as to weaken incentives to return to work. (As an immediate goal, to provide weekly benefits for individual workers equal to not less than one-half their gross weekly wages in covered employment, up to a maximum that will provide such benefits to the great majority of covered workers; to include payments for partial unemployment as well as total unemployment with an earnings allowance sufficient to provide an incentive to work and to cover the normal additional expenses of working.)

4. To provide income sufficient in duration to insure protection through temporary periods of unemployment. (As an immediate goal, an amount equal to at least 26 weeks of benefits for total unemployment for all eligible workers at all benefit levels, if they remain unemployed that long.)

5. To limit the unemployment to be compensated to that due to lack of work, by requiring claimants to be able to work and by temporarily disqualifying claimants who leave work voluntarily without good cause, who are discharged for misconduct connected with their work, who refuse suitable work without good cause, or who are unemployed because of direct participation in a stoppage of work due to a labor dispute at the establishment at which they were last employed, but without rigid requirements and harsh penalties. (Specifically, not to require an active search for work irrespective of circumstances; not to limit good cause for voluntary quitting to good cause connected with the employer or the employment; and not to penalize disqualified claimants by disqualification for the duration of the employment or by canceling their benefit rights but, with respect to voluntary quitting, discharge for misconduct, and refusal of suitable work, to postpone benefits for a specified period immediately following the disqualifying act, during which it may be considered that the claimants' unemployment is due to their own actions, without good cause.)

6. To help maintain desirable labor mobility by providing benefits for unemployed individuals who have worked in more than one State or who have moved to another State in search for work, through interstate arrangements for combining wages, for payment of benefits, and for holding of benefit appeals.

7. To provide financing for benefits by payroll taxes on employers, or on employers and employees, which yield funds adequate to insure payment of benefits in bad years as well as good years and, as far as possible, operate to reduce taxes in bad years and increase them in good years; to establish a tax structure which will encourage employers to stabilize employment, without interfering with the overall objectives of the program.

8. To provide benefits promptly when due, through appropriate provisions (concerning notices to employers and time for appeals) and through appropriate administrative procedures.

9. To administer the program so that claimants and employers understand their rights and responsibilities, that misrepresentation by either claimants or employers is subject to suitable penalties, and that improper payments are eliminated.

10. To increase opportunities for re-employment of claimants through proper coordination with the Employment Service.

11. To provide public information useful to employers and workers, as well as to agencies and organizations concerned, on the number and characteristics of the unemployed and the contribution of the program to individuals and to the economy.

# 22. UNRESOLVED ISSUES IN UNEMPLOYMENT INSURANCE

MARGARET S. GORDON
and RALPH W. AMERSON,
*Unemployment Insurance,*
University of California,
1957.

UNEMPLOYMENT INSURANCE IS now an accepted part of our social security program. Only a small minority of Americans would seriously argue that it should be abandoned. In this sense the system is no longer controversial. But it is still the most controversial of the existing public programs in the sense that battles over proposals for substantial modification of statutory provisions are waged in an atmosphere of particularly heated disagreement. More than any of the other programs, unemployment insurance has an impact on prevailing wage levels and on the functioning of the labor market. For this reason, the controversies of the next decade or two over changes in federal and state unemployment insurance laws are likely to be no less contentious than those of the recent past. What are the major issues around which these battles will revolve?

## 1. Who Should Be Covered?

The trend toward expansion of coverage will undoubtedly continue, but the chances of being included in the system vary a good deal among the groups of workers now excluded.

Workers in firms with less than four employees are likely to be covered in the not too distant future. Originally it had been thought that the inclusion of very small firms would create administrative difficulties, but the experience of the states that cover all firms with one or more workers has been encouraging. Bills which would amend the federal Unemployment Insurance Act to apply to all firms with one or more employees have been supported by both the Truman and Eisenhower administrations. Enactment of such legislation at the federal level would undoubtedly bring all the states quickly into line.

In addition, coverage will probably be gradually extended to state and local government employees not presently protected. Now that federal government employees are covered, the pressure on the states to extend protection to their own government employees will be considerably stronger, although resistance in some states will be greater than in others. Another group of workers who are likely to be covered sooner or later are employees of nonprofit organizations.

Opposition to coverage of the other excluded groups is much more pronounced. Although most self-employed workers are now covered by Old-Age and Survivors Insurance, inclusion of the self-employed in the unemployment insurance system would present serious difficulties. The chief problem would be one of determining whether, in any given case, a self-employed worker was involuntarily unemployed.

Resistance to the inclusion of agricultural laborers is strongest of all. Because of wide seasonal variations in the employment of farm laborers, farm work tends to be unsteady and the cost of coverage would be high. The California Department of Employment for example, has estimated that benefit costs for California agricultural workers would be 11 to 15 per cent of taxable wages in agriculture. A number of experts argue, moreover, that casual workers (among whom they would include farm laborers) should not be covered by unemployment insurance, which is not well adapted to handle the special problems presented by such workers. Those who support the coverage of farm laborers argue that, with the low wages and unstable employment prevailing in agriculture, this group is particularly in need of protection.

The case of domestic servants in private households is somewhat similar, although the costs of insuring this group would by no means be as high as in agriculture.

## 2. The Problem of Eligibility Provisions

The tightening of eligibility and disqualification provisions, as we have indicated, has been a major trend in the development of the unemployment insurance program. It is a tendency which has been clearly associated with the reliance on experience rating, with its inducements to employers to minimize the number of cases of unemployment to be charged against their accounts.

There is little likelihood that the trend toward tightening of base-period earnings requirements will be reversed. As wage levels rise, there will undoubtedly be continued pressure toward upward adjustment of minimum earning provisions. Along with this there will almost certainly be increasing emphasis on provisions calling for distribution of base-period earnings over several quarters, notwithstanding the vigorous resistance of representatives of seasonal workers. It is entirely possible, also, that more of the states will swing over to requirements stated in terms of minimum weeks of employment, despite the more comprehensive record keeping necessitated by this type of provision.

The future of disqualification provisions is less clear. A good many experts argue that the trend toward increasing the severity of penalties for disqualification has gone too far. For example, there is good ground for questioning the justification of provisions which disqualify a claimant for the duration of the entire period of ensuing unemployment, except perhaps in the case of conviction for clear-cut and deliberate fraud. Some experts would argue that federal standards are needed to establish reasonable maximum periods of disqualification.

### 3. What Is an Adequate Benefit Level?

There is little doubt that some of the most intense battles of the next decade or two will be waged over benefit levels, and particularly over the provisions for maximum benefits which now determine the weekly amounts received by the majority of claimants.

The critical problem in the controversy over benefit levels is the absence of agreement over the criteria to be used in determining adequacy of benefits. There are few who would seriously argue that the principle of relating benefits to previous earnings should be abandoned. But what proportion of previous weekly earnings represents an adequate benefit level? The 50 per cent standard adopted in the early draft bills—and reiterated as a recommendation to the states in the President's Economic Report of 1954—is admittedly somewhat arbitrary.

It is impossible to consider the merits of arguments over what proportion of former weekly earnings constitutes an adequate benefit level without introducing the criterion of *need*. On the basis of today's living costs, what proportion of his former weekly earnings does the unemployed worker with a family of average size need in order to maintain nondeferrable expenditures? Should the proportion be somewhat higher —as many experts would argue and as benefit formulae in practice recognize—for a low-income worker than for a high-income worker? And what about the secondary wage-earner, for example, the working housewife, in a family—should his or her benefits represent a smaller proportion of former earnings than those of the principal wage-earner?

These questions cannot be satisfactorily answered, as most informed observers now recognize, in the absence of comprehensive statistical information bearing on the incomes and expenditures of unemployed workers. The federal government has recently initiated a special research program designed to obtain this kind of information. The results of a pilot study conducted in Pittsburgh—in cooperation with Duquesne University—represent a significant first step toward accumulating the needed data.

The Pittsburgh findings clearly indicated that the great majority of workers included in the study received very little income other than their unemployment benefits while unemployed. Typically the incomes of these workers during unemployment declined to considerably less than 50 per cent of their former weekly earnings—as would have been expected in the light of current benefit-wage relationships. Their expenditures during unemployment tended to exceed their incomes by considerable margins. Expenditures for food, shelter, and household operation were maintained at the expense of spending on apparel and other deferrable items. To a considerable extent, these unemployed workers borrowed, or drew on whatever savings they had, to meet the gap between income and expenditures during unemployment. The study also showed that, where the unemployed worker was a secondary wage-earner, the family fared much better than did single claimants or families in which the chief wage-earner was unemployed.

Another criterion which cannot be neglected in any discussion of benefit adequacy is the problem of incentives to work. What is the maximum proportion of weekly earnings that unemployed workers might receive as benefits without a serious increase in malingering? Some informed observers would argue that the answer to this question would suggest, at least in principle, a reasonable upper limit (well under 100 per cent of weekly wages) to the level of benefits. But whether, in practice, it would ever be possible to discover what this upper limit ought to be is highly doubtful.

It now seems not at all unlikely that these questions may be worked out to a considerable extent around the collective bargaining table. The 60–65 per cent of take-home pay adopted in the Ford-UAW supplemental unemployment benefit plan—and substantially followed in many other SUB agreements—is certain to have an impact on legislative deliberations over benefit levels, even though a relatively small proportion of all workers are covered by these plans. And, of course, there remains the possibility that the prevailing percentage in SUB plans may be modified from time to time. But, if this happens, unions and employers will need access to the results of studies similar to the Pittsburgh survey in connection with their negotiations.

An aspect of benefit adequacy that cannot be neglected is the problem of duration of benefits. But since this is intimately related to the question of how much protection the system should offer against severe unemployment, it will be discussed below.

### 4. Should Financing Provisions Be Changed?

Despite the widespread dissatisfaction with experience rating, there is little likelihood that the system will be abandoned. Although Alaska, with its high unemployment insurance costs and inadequate reserves, has recently given up experience rating, it is unlikely that many other states will follow suit, at least in the near future. It must be remembered, not only that experience rating is a well-established feature of our state laws, but that it could not easily be abandoned without revision of the Federal Unemployment Insurance Tax Act. A federal tax of 3 per cent would be completely out of line with present-day unemployment insurance costs in the absence of the experience-rating features of the federal law

Even though experience rating is not likely to be abandoned, substantial modifications will probably be proposed and seriously debated. Some experts argue that the federal law should be amended to give employers credit under the tax-offset plan for contributions they are excused from paying not only under experience-rating systems but also under other methods of tax rate reduction which states might adopt. This would give a state the option of continuing experience rating or adopting some other system of rate reduction. Other informed observers seriously question whether zero rates, or rates very close to zero, should be permitted under state tax schedules and whether the growing practice of non-charging should be encouraged. And many economists would press for an attempt to develop tax formulas, particularly provisions governing shifts from one tax schedule to another, which would prevent the raising of tax rates during periods of business recession.

Another important issue is whether workers (as well as employers) should be taxed to finance the program, as under Old-Age and Survivors Insurance. Certain labor spokesmen have recently advocated such a change, arguing that (1) unions would pay more attention to cost considerations in advocating legislative changes and (2) employers would be more receptive to proposals for raising benefit levels if the tax were levied on both employers and employees.

Finally, the need for raising the maximum annual earnings to which the payroll tax applies will become more pressing as time goes on. As incomes rise, the exemption of all wage payments over $3,000 to individual employees becomes increasingly obsolete.

## 5. The Problem of Severe Unemployment

The last of the major issues to be considered is whether our unemployment insurance system, as now designed, offers adequate protection against severe unemployment.

A good many critics of the present system would argue that benefit and duration provisions should be progressively liberalized to the point at which the system would offer much more effective protection against the severe and prolonged unemployment that might accompany a serious depression. Even in a mild recession, these critics would argue, the proportion of claimants who exhaust their benefit rights rises sharply, and in a severe depression there would be millions of unemployed who would be protected only for a relatively short period. Furthermore, although benefits average about a third of weekly earnings in covered employment, the actual proportion of total wage loss compensated is much less than this, because of incomplete coverage, waiting periods, disqualifications, exhaustion of benefits, and other factors. It has been estimated that in the 1949–1950 recession, unemployment benefits represented only about 20 to 25 per cent of the income lost through unemployment.

Others would sharply oppose this point of view on a number of grounds: (1) that protection of this type would be so costly as to impose a serious financial burden on industry, (2) that the payment of benefits to unemployed workers over long periods would encourage malingering, (3) that English experience in the 1920's clearly indicated that unemployment insurance tends to break down when benefits are paid for long periods, and (4) that other types of emergency government measures would have to be relied on to combat the mass unemployment that would accompany a severe depression.

It is the duration provisions that are chiefly at issue, of course, in this connection. Although these provisions may well be liberalized to a moderate extent over the next several decades, radical changes in the direction of greatly lengthened duration of benefits seem unlikely. What we *are* likely to see, however, is a variety of proposals designed to extend the duration of benefits for particular groups of workers under special circumstances. Michigan is reported to be utilizing a little-known provision of its law which permits benefits to be paid up to 44 weeks to workers enrolled in certain types of training courses. With the growing interest in the need for training programs to encourage the development of new skills in a period of rapid technological change, similar provisions may be proposed in other states. Another, and somewhat more debatable, type of modification was proposed in a bill that was introduced, but not passed, in California in 1955, under which weekly benefits could be paid for 52 weeks if unemployment in the claimant's area or industry exceeded 6 per cent.

It may well be that significant changes in the unemployment insurance system in the next several decades will grow out of proposals of this type. If a high level of employment continues to prevail, unemployment is likely to be a specialized rather than a general problem, chiefly affecting particular groups of workers who encounter discrimination because of race, sex, age, or physical handicaps, or who are displaced as a result of rapid technological change. As the unemployment insurance program evolves, it may be gradually modified in the direction of offering more effective protection against at least some of these specialized types of unemployment.

In the meantime, it is important not to minimize the significance of the contribution made by our unemployment insurance system as it has evolved over the last twenty years. Despite its defects, the system protects workers against complete loss of income during periods of joblessness and helps to protect the economy against the possibility of a cumulative deflationary spiral during business recessions.

# 23. THE PRESENT STATUS OF UNEMPLOYMENT INSURANCE IN THE UNITED STATES

WILLIAM HABER and
WILBUR J. COHEN,
1960.

## I

## ABSENCE OF AGREEMENT ON OBJECTIVES OF UNEMPLOYMENT INSURANCE

UNEMPLOYMENT INSURANCE in the United States has now been in existence for nearly a generation. This is not a long period in the history of a social insurance institution. It is perhaps long enough, however, to hazard an appraisal of its performance, to identify the areas in which progress has been made, and to indicate in what manner this important institution may be said to have succeeded or been inadequate in its mission.

Unfortunately, there has been some confusion concerning the objective of unemployment insurance. To many persons, indeed there are several objectives. For the fact is that no fully developed or consistent body of unemployment compensation theory preceded the enactment of the first hastily drafted laws. Nor have the amendments of recent years been based on consistent principles. More often they have responded to the demands of pressure groups or to the needs of administrative considerations.

While the various provisions in the state unemployment insurance laws reflect to greater or lesser degree the several points of view concerning the objectives of unemployment insurance, its principal function has gradually come to be recognized as that of providing a basic level of economic protection to individuals whose income has ceased or been reduced because of temporary unemployment. "Unemployment compensation is justified primarily as a method for providing benefits needed to maintain unemployed workers and their families."

Others, however, justify unemployment insurance, at least in part, as a device for stabilizing consumer purchasing power, as a method of reducing fluctuations in business and for stabilizing employment in the individual firm. Unemployment compensation is also conceived as a method for achieving better utilization of the labor force, with certain safeguards to prevent its being used to depress labor standards or to limit the mobility of labor.

In our view, unemployment insurance should be governed primarily by a single purpose—the provision of adequate protection, as a matter of right, against unemployment for all ordinarily employed workers who are involuntarily idle. Experience has demonstrated that multipurpose systems produce internal contradictions and may often limit the full realization of the primary objective. Speaking generally, unemployment insurance provides income to individuals who customarily depend on wages from covered employment and who, because of lack of work, are unemployed. Benefits which are a proportion of previous wages are paid as a matter of right. Workers must satisfy the qualifying requirements, register for work, file a claim for benefits, be able and available for work, not refuse suitable work, and not be otherwise disqualified under other specified provisions of the law. Qualifying requirements, weekly amounts, and the maximum number of weeks are fixed by law. The costs of benefit payments are borne from earmarked taxes or contributions paid generally by employers and measured by the wages earned.

## No Objective Criteria

Appraising the present status of our unemployment insurance system is beset with several difficulties. There are, in the first place, no widely accepted objective criteria for judging the performance of this legislation. Since the program has been in existence for nearly 25 years, this is quite startling in itself.[1]

Failure to reach a closer agreement is to be explained by at least two factors. The first is the dispersion of policy decision on these matters among the 51 states. (In the terminology of unemployment insurance, the District of Columbia is included as a "state," thus making a total of 51.) Differences in economic circumstances and political views explain in part the great diversity which exists among the states with respect to the substantive provisions in unemployment insurance. In sharp contrast to Old-Age, Survivors and Disability Insurance, where only agreement by the nation's Congress is essential, what may be considered a reasonable objective in unemployment insurance in one state may be quite objectionable in another. Such a situation is bound to prevail in the absence of federal minimum standards.

In addition, unlike Old-Age, Survivors and Disability Insurance, unemployment insurance has a more direct bearing on industrial relations, on labor turnover, and on employment practices. The benefit level may, under certain circumstances, affect the re-employment rate. It is intimately related to layoff and recall policy and affects other aspects of the collective bargaining contract as well. The areas of public disagreement in unem-

---

[1] *Issues in Social Security: A Report to the Committee on Ways and Means of the House of Representatives* by the Committee's Social Security Technical Staff (Washington, D.C.: U.S. Government Printing Office, 1946), pp. 368–70. "There are no criteria which will permit a precise measure of the adequacy of benefits or duration. Moreover, there is no agreed body of principles which can be used to evaluate amounts, duration or disqualification; what is considered to be appropriate . . . depends . . . on what is considered to be the basic objectives of unemployment compensation. There seems to be no general agreement as to these basic objectives . . ."

ployment insurance are far greater, tensions are more apparent, and there is stronger resistance to compromise. And the fact that the system has operated under conditions of relatively high employment levels may also explain the diversity of objectives. Not all states felt any serious impact during the several recessions since the end of the war. In many, benefit costs have been exceptionally low and the 3 per cent payroll tax overfinanced the system in many areas.

As a result, many states have accumulated large reserves. Benefit payments for the year 1940, for example, represented only 5 cents to each dollar of tax collections. And the postwar developments further contributed to low benefit outlays and consequent large reserves. In recent years experience rating has in effect operated to place the program on a current financing basis, with total annual contributions roughly equaling annual expenditures and leaving available reserves largely untouched. This was not the case, of course, during the recent recession when all states paid out more than they collected in tax contributions.

The recession of 1957–58 provided the first serious test for our federal-state unemployment insurance system. Unemployment in 1958 averaged more than 4.8 million persons, representing 6.8 per cent of the labor force. And actual benefit payments for the year represented 3.2 per cent of taxable payrolls. This is in sharp contrast to the period 1938–47 when benefit costs averaged only 0.9 per cent and the period 1949–58 when such costs averaged 1.6 per cent of taxable wages.

The recession compelled the general public, the Congress, and the legislators to give some thought to the soundness, the solvency, and the adequacy of our unemployment insurance plan. For the first time federal legislation providing for supplemental unemployment payments was adopted for a temporary period. The recession also provided the first test for the collective bargaining–negotiated Supplementary Unemployment Benefit plans which supplemented the state benefits to over 300,000 workers in 1958 alone.

## II

### UNEMPLOYMENT INSURANCE HAS MADE SIGNIFICANT PROGRESS

The evidence is quite clear that unemployment insurance has made a major contribution to the needs of the unemployed and to the economy. During its history, beginning in 1936 to December 1958, it has collected over $25.4 billion in payroll taxes and earned over $2.8 billion of interest on the fund. It has paid out over $21.4 billion in benefits to insured unemployed workers. It had accumulated a reserve in excess of $8.6 billion at the end of 1957, and was still more than $6.9 billion as of the end of 1958. And the 0.3 of 1 per cent of taxable payroll paid direct to the federal government by covered employers provided over $750 million in excess of the sums necessary for the operation of the state unemployment security programs.

The automatic operation of the system is one of its real advantages. As unemployment mounts, payments expand. Unemployment insurance thus serves as an efficient instrument to compensate for wage loss, to provide purchasing power, and to underwrite an important segment of the wage earner's living standards. Its automatic character is especially favorable to check a business decline by making available compensation in lieu of wages. The 1953 benefit payments of $962 million to 5.5 million beneficiaries jumped to over $2 billion to 6.6 million beneficiaries in 1954. And in the more recent recession, benefit payments increased from more than $1.7 billion to 5.6 million beneficiaries in 1957 to more than $3.5 billion to 7.9 million beneficiaries during 1958. There can be no question that benefit payments of such magnitude helped to sustain the demand for consumer goods, to prevent other unemployment, and thus to hasten the recovery from the recession.

In addition, there has been a record of progress and improvement under the present federal-state system. This progress has not been uniform in all the states nor in all aspects of the program. It has, nevertheless, been sufficiently impressive to give substantial support to those who espouse the present federal-state system, under which substantive improvements depend largely on state action.

Finally, unemployment insurance has come to be recognized as a program for the general welfare by the courts, by employers, by labor, and by the general public. It now undoubtedly represents a permanent part of public policy in dealing with unemployment. Many groups are evidencing a critical interest which is indispensible in the development of an improved system. Unemployment insurance is an established institution in American life.

### Coverage Expanded and Duration Increased

From the inception of the program, the average number of workers covered by unemployment insurance has more than doubled from approximately 20 million to 45 million by May, 1959. The original federal law applied to employers of eight or more; in 1956 the law became applicable to employers of four or more workers. And, while in 1938 only ten states covered firms with one or more employees, in 1958 eighteen states did so.

There has also been a general improvement in the legislative provisions for duration of benefits. The original legislation providing for a duration of about 16 weeks was soon found inadequate and produced a rather high "exhaustion ratio." Thirty states with almost 67 per cent of the covered workers now provide a maximum duration of payments for 26 weeks. As of 1958, thirteen states now have a uniform potential duration, in seven of these for 26 weeks or more. The smaller amount of progress in this area is, no doubt, a reflection of our experience with the average duration of unemployment since 1945.

### Weekly Benefits Increased

There has been improvement also in the weekly benefit amount. The early laws provided for a weekly benefit equal to about 50 per cent of full-time weekly earnings. The effective realization of this objective was severely restricted, however, by the imposition of a maximum weekly benefit amount. With the increase in wages during the war period, these maximums were soon raised and all states increased the maximum amounts. Average weekly benefits have advanced steadily from $10.56 in 1940, $20.76 in 1950, $24.93 in 1954, and during recessionary 1958, topped $30.58. When Temporary Unemployment Compensation benefits are included, the average weekly benefit in 1958 was $30.78. The Social Security Act incorporated no standards for benefits in the federal-state system of unemployment insurance. Hence, there is no central pattern of benefit provisions comparable to that in coverage and financing. The states have developed quite diverse and complex formulas for determining workers' benefit rights. Forty-six states have increased their maximum one or more times since 1954.

Finally, to these gains in the improvement of unemployment insurance coverage, duration, and benefit amount one must also add the improvement in administration, the steadily increasing proportion of the unemployed to whom it applies, the reduction in the waiting period to one week, including its entire abolition in five states, the payment of benefits when due, and the increased efficiency and improved experience of the federal-state employment services in the referral and placement of the jobless workers. Murray Latimer writes that "the improvement in these factors has not proceeded as rapidly as some would like; but measured by any standard except the standard of almost absolute perfection, the record is quite good."[2]

### III

### HAS PROGRESS BEEN ADEQUATE?

### Coverage Limitations

While substantial progress has been made, unemployment insurance still fails in several important respects. There are gaps in coverage. These deny the protection of unemployment insurance to about 13 million employees, a denial not easy to justify. An Administration proposal to extend coverage would add an additional 3.2 million workers to the covered group—2.0 million are still excluded in small firms and some 1.2 million

---

[2] Murray W. Latimer, *Interstate Conference on Unemployment Insurance* (Salt Lake City, 1955).

workers in nonprofit institutions. Further broadening of coverage would include all persons who have a substantial attachment to the labor force, including some hired farm laborers, workers for certain federal instrumentalities, those on American aircraft serving overseas, and other groups not now covered.

This form of protection against the risk of joblessness is no less important to the wage earner if he works for a small employer than if he works for an employer of thousands. Unemployment is no less painful if the layoff is from a job with a state or federal government or from a job in agriculture; nor is the threat of a layoff as nominal in these activities as many people believe. Social insurance cannot justify treating one group of wage earners in a different manner merely because by accident they work in a retail store or for a smaller employer, or because the worker is laid off from a public department. Such employees, excluded from insurance plans because of alleged administrative reasons, when in need have to go on relief, submit to a means test, and face the community as a public charge. Experience has conclusively demonstrated that difficulties which would be involved in the extension of coverage are neither significant nor insurmountable.

## The Lag in Weekly Benefits

As wages increased, the benefit percentage declined in view of the fixed weekly maximum amount. As a result, in 1958, the average weekly unemployment insurance benefit represented 36.3 per cent of the average weekly wage. This is an improvement over the preceding year. It is still, however, substantially below the original goal designed to compensate about 50 per cent of average wages. Weekly benefit amounts have obviously increased, and, in many instances, quite substantially. They have declined, however, as a proportion of average weekly wages.

In 1939, the maximum benefit exceeded 60 per cent of the average wage in thirty-five states; in all states but one, the maximum benefit exceeded 50 per cent of the average wage. In 1958, in only seven states did the maximum benefit exceed 50 per cent of the average wage; in not a single state was the maximum in excess of 60 per cent.

Most of the period in which the unemployment insurance program has operated has been characterized by steadily increasing wages. In most instances, increases in dollar maximums for unemployment benefits have lagged far behind wage increases. This explains the fall in the ratio and the fact that it has remained practically static since 1952. Two states—Utah and Wyoming—have written a new principle into their laws, under which benefit maximums automatically increase (or decrease) with increases (or decreases) in the state's prevailing wage levels.

These facts are not in dispute. Those who oppose further and more rapid liberalization point out that such comparisons overlook the fact that many of the unemployed receive considerably in excess of one half of their wages. Further, it is not fair to compare the average benefit of those who receive insurance payments with the average wage of covered workers.

Beneficiaries undoubtedly receive an average wage considerably lower than that of the covered group. Marginal employees possessing lower skills and receiving lower wages are laid off first. As a result, their weekly benefit probably represents a considerably higher proportion of their wages than the over-all figures suggest.

Layoffs under recent or current labor market conditions affect marginal groups more than others. Mass layoffs, even for short periods, would quickly correct the differences between the average wages of covered workers and the average wages of the recipients of unemployment insurance.

It is also argued that unemployment insurance benefits are tax-free and it is not fair to compare them with average weekly wages which are subject to the withholding tax. There is some merit in this observation. However, for a married wage earner with dependents, the withholding tax would be quite nominal except for those in the higher wage brackets.

## The Issue of Dependents' Allowances

Twelve states now provide additional allowance for dependents, which vary from $1.00 (in the District of Columbia) to $5.00, usually with a limitation on the number of dependents for whom additional benefits shall be paid. In each of the last three years, about two fifths of all beneficiaries in these twelve states had compensible dependents. A dependents' allowance increased the benefit of those who received it about 20 per cent on the average, while aggregate state expenditures for dependents' allowances amounted to only 6.4 percent of all payments.

The limited elasticity in family budgets might argue for dependents' allowances. On the other hand, varying weekly benefits with the number of dependents may not be appropriate to a wage-related program. At the same time, in view of the fears which employers have about higher benefit levels interfering with work incentives, a variable benefit program provides some protection. Higher benefits for a married person with one or more children does not represent as much of a hazard from the viewpoint of work-seeking incentives as such a benefit might provide for single people or married people without children. Further, wives and other secondary wage earners not being heads of families, would be ineligible to receive the higher benefits. As a result, the weekly maximum of $55 in Michigan and $82 in Massachusetts actually goes to an exceedingly small percentage of beneficiaries

## Failure of Benefits to Provide Basic Needs

For more than 15 years the controversy about the adequacy of benefits has been continued on the basis of broad assumptions as to presumptive needs. Several local studies, undertaken by state agencies, suggested that a majority of the families drawing unemployment insurance benefits were spending considerably more than their benefits and were thus using up savings or borrowing.[3]

One such study in a region of heavy unemployment in the Albany-Schenectady-Troy area of New York State in the spring and summer of 1957 showed that beneficiaries in family units with little or no income except for the $33 per week unemployment benefits spent on the average of $26 for food alone and $75 to $94 altogether, or more than twice the benefit amount during the survey weeks.[4]

An earlier study in the Pittsburgh area indicates that there, also, the weekly unemployment insurance checks do not adequately meet the needs of the unemployed family heads.[5] The findings in these studies tally with the general observations and experiences of those who are familiar with the impact of unemployment in many sections of the country.[6]

These findings hardly suggest that there is serious danger of the unemployed being pauperized by benefit levels which make possible the maintenance of high living standards and thus threaten incentives and mobility. The conclusions may not apply with equal force to single claimants nor to secondary earners.[7] Even here, the evidence hardly suggests that there is serious danger of pauperizing or malingering.

In negotiating a SUB plan for automobile workers, the companies undoubtedly made a careful study of what their employees actually require in order to carry on without a serious distortion in the living standard during short layoffs. Their agreement to provide 65 per cent of take-home pay, now part of the collective bargaining contract, comes closer to what is required to provide the sort of income security during short-term layoffs contemplated by the framers of our unemployment insurance legislation.

---

[3] See *Unemployment Compensation, A Survey of Benefit Adequacy 1956–1957*, conducted by the Pan-American Consulting Corporation, Inc., in cooperation with the Florida Industrial Commission and the U.S. Department of Labor; and, *Adequacy of Benefits under Unemployment Insurance*, a staff report prepared for the Steering Committee of the Federal Advisory Council, conducted by the U.S. Department of Labor, Bureau of Employment Security, Unemployment Insurance Service (Washington, D.C., October, 1958).

[4] *Expenditures of Unemployed Workers*, Bureau of Applied Social Research of Columbia University under contract with the Division of Employment of the New York State Department of Labor in cooperation with New York State's Interdepartmental Committee on Low Incomes (Spring, 1957).

[5] *Survey of Unemployment Compensation Beneficiaries in Pittsburgh, Pennsylvania*, study conducted by Duquesne University; U.S. Department of Labor, Bureau of Employment Security (Washington, D.C., October, 1955).

[6] A somewhat different interpretation of the Pittsburgh study is taken by the Unemployment Benefit Advisors, Inc., see "Pilot Study of Benefit Adequacy in Pittsburgh," *Research and Education* (Washington, D.C., January 31, 1956).

[7] *Summary of Findings, Survey of Unemployment Compensation in Michigan, 1955*, Hope College, Department of Economics and Business Administration (Holland, Michigan, February, 1957).

Further improvement in the weekly benefit amount, considerably above the gains made so far, must remain on the legislative agenda for unemployment insurance in the period immediately ahead. The Federal Advisory Council on Employment Security in a majority report recommended that "the great majority" of eligible claimants should receive at least one half of their normal full-time gross weekly earnings. The President made a similar recommendation. To achieve this objective it was the Committee's recommendation that the maximum benefit amount be fixed at two thirds of the state-wide covered average weekly wage.[8]

## INADEQUATE SUPPORT OF PURCHASING POWER

The President in his 1959 Economic Report stated that the "primary objective of our federal-state system of unemployment insurance is directly to aid those experiencing involuntary loss of employment . . . by sustaining the aggregate purchasing power of consumers at a level higher than would otherwise prevail," and in this manner these payments "contribute significantly to the stabilization of the whole economy."[9]

During the recession of 1957–58, the decline in the aggregate of personal incomes was extremely small. Between August, 1957 and April, 1959, the dollar volume of the nation's total output fell about 5 per cent and the physical volume fell about 6 per cent. In earlier times personal incomes would have responded decisively to so severe a drop in production over a short period, and a spiraling depression might have developed. This time personal incomes after taxes fell only about 1 per cent and the decline was well over before the recession ended. The explanation is to be found in the more or less automatic workings of certain of our institutions, such as the substantial sums pumped into the income stream through unemployment compensation benefits.[10]

While the average dollar in trade is estimated to turn over six times in a year, the unemployment insurance dollar may turn over even a dozen times in a year. Because of the way it is paid out, and the economic condition of the people it serves, and the manner in which it serves their immediate needs, it could be said to be twice as effective as any other kind of a dollar. A study in Grand Rapids, Michigan, indeed, showed that the "real value" to the economy of an unemployment insurance dollar was $12 because of this trend toward a rapid turnover.[11]

Nevertheless, while the general objective has been to provide about

---

[8] *Report of the Committee on Legislative Review* to the Federal Advisory Council (December 2–3, 1958), p. 7.

[9] *Economic Report of the President*, transmitted to the Congress, January 20, 1959 (Washington, D.C.: U.S. Government Printing Office, 1958).

[10] Arthur F. Burns, "Some Lessons of the Recession," *The Reporter* (December 11, 1958), p. 16.

[11] Max W. Horton, Michigan Employment Security Commission, February 11, 1958.

half of average wages in insurance payments, because of coverage limitations and benefit ceilings, such payments do not exceed 20 to 30 per cent of the lost wages. One should not minimize the outlay of nearly $2 billion in 1949, and somewhat more than that sum in 1954, nor the $4 billion of benefit checks in 1958. Its importance from the humanitarian point of view is obvious. However, this is not enough. What should be provided is a more substantial proportion of lost earnings.

## IMPORTANCE OF PRESERVING RELATIONSHIP OF BENEFITS TO EARNINGS

Improving benefit levels by raising the maximum amount payable is also necessary and desirable in order to relate the weekly benefits more closely to differences in earnings. We rejected the uniform weekly benefit for all wage earners, and sought to provide a formula which would vary such weekly benefits with the earnings of the insured worker, subject to the minimum and maximum amounts. This, we reasoned, was more consonant with our ideas of an enterprise economy and with the prevailing wage differentials in American industry.

The effect of the benefit ceiling, however, has been that a vast majority of the beneficiaries now receive a uniform weekly benefit—the maximum allowed under the state legislation. Maximum benefit amounts are at a level that in April–June, 1958 about half of the claimants in the country as a whole were at the maximum while in three states (Illinois, Louisiana, and Ohio) the proportion at the maximum was 80 per cent or more. The objective of providing a differential benefit based on earnings is thus largely defeated. Twenty-one states now have maximum weekly benefit amounts set at $35 or above. If the objective of providing 50 percent of wages is coupled with a $35 per week maximum amount, all wages over $70 are not taken into account. Since, however, the average weekly wage in the manufacturing industry was $83.58 in 1958, with the average weekly benefit being $30.58, the effect of the ceiling is to disregard a substantial portion of the normal wages in calculating the weekly benefit.

## EFFECT OF TIGHTER ELIGIBILITY REQUIREMENTS

The federal acts contain no requirements concerning eligibility and disqualification provisions excepting the labor standard provisions. All state laws require that a claimant, to receive benefits, must be able, available, and seeking work. He also must avoid being disqualified for leaving work voluntarily, and in some states the cause must be connected with the work. Further disqualifications are discharge for misconduct and refusal of suitable work.

As benefit levels and duration of payment have been improved, the states have tended to tighten the eligibility requirements, requiring longer periods of employment or higher wage earnings in the base period in order to receive benefits. This trend is likely to continue and the pressure for higher benefits and longer duration will adversely affect those with only a tenuous attachment to the labor force. That higher benefits require larger premiums cannot be disputed. Social insurance does not and should not lean solely or even primarily upon equity considerations, indispensable as these may be in private forms of insurance. To do so would defeat an important objective of social insurance, that of the widest practicable coverage.

## The Disqualification Problem

The evidence with regard to disqualification is less conclusive than one would assume, considering the intensity of the controversy which has revolved around that topic for some 20 years. In many states disqualifications have become considerably more stringent for certain types of cases in recent years. In all states, such provisions result in at least a postponement of benefits for one or more weeks in addition to any required waiting period; in some states it also involves a cancellation of benefit rights or a reduction of benefits otherwise payable. Major disqualifications may apply to voluntarily leaving work, to refusal to accept suitable work, to discharge for misconduct, and unemployment due to a labor dispute. Minor disqualifications apply to special circumstances such as pregnancy, wage earners with marital obligations, students, and fraudulent misrepresentation. Whether such a trend should be checked or reversed depends upon the social policy as to whether a covered employee, clearly in the labor force and clearly unemployed, gets *any* benefits for *any* weeks. Thus, many covered employees, otherwise eligible, cannot get any benefits because of such disqualification provisions.

One of the explanations for the tendency to tighten disqualification provisions grows out of the fact that only the employer contributes to the financing of this program. It is generally assumed that every employer should be responsible for such unemployment which is attributable to him. Perhaps an additional explanation is to be found in the high levels of employment since 1940 and to the prevailing notion, very much exaggerated, that there is much abuse and malingering in unemployment insurance. To the average person, unfamiliar with the operation of the labor market, the payment of cash benefits to anyone during a period of relative labor shortage appears paradoxical.

These factors have combined to make legislatures receptive to proposals designed to restrict and to deny benefits to those who leave their work voluntarily, even for good cause, and to increase the penalties against those who fail to accept suitable work. While there is no dispute as to the extent of this development, its significance has been somewhat exaggerated. A large proportion of those disqualified from benefits should probably be disqualified even under the most liberal interpretation as to eligibility under a program designed to pay only for involuntary unemployment. A small proportion are undoubtedly the victims of the tighter benefit provisions. Complete cancellation of benefit rights or the denial of benefits for the entire duration of unemployment would seem to be a gross inequity. Even a ten-week penalty appears needlessly harsh. It is the sense of injustice rather than the magnitude of the problem which explains the bitter reaction against the recent tightening in disqualifications. Employers are probably making a serious error in pushing this development.

All insurance programs, whether private or public, must maintain constant vigilance against those few persons who wish to "get something for nothing." Public concern that some individuals will seek benefits to which they are not entitled legally is realistic, and legislative provisions and administrative procedures must be devised to minimize possible abuse. The problem is one of determining what methods will best shield the program against abuse, while enabling it to achieve its objectives.[12]

### Trends in Unemployment Insurance Costs

The strong resistance to more liberal benefits cannot be explained alone by increasing costs. These, in fact, have been relatively stable over a long period. Since the beginning of the program, a period of over 20 years, benefit costs as a ratio to taxable wages were 1.5 per cent.[13] In the decade since 1949, a period which included three recessions, the ratio of benefits to taxable wages was only slightly higher, being 1.6 per cent. The average annual tax rate paid by employers over the past 10 years was but 1.3 per cent of this taxable payroll, and even during the rather severe recession of 1958 the tax rate was 1.4 per cent.

This appears to represent the average long-run costs of our unemployment insurance program under present benefit liabilities and the economic circumstances prevailing in postwar periods. More frequent or more serious recessions would, of course, increase both rates and costs materially. The accumulated reserves have absorbed the shock of increasing costs during recessions. Thus, during the 1958 recession, $2.39 was paid in benefits for every $1.00 of collections. Previous highs were $1.78 in 1954 and $1.76 in 1949, both moderate recession years. A total of more than $3.5 billion in benefit payments was recorded in 1958—more than $4 billion, in fact, when account is taken of benefits under Temporary Unemploy-

---

[12] Fred Slavick, *Voluntary Quit Disqualification in Unemployment Insurance—The Iowa Experience*, Bureau of Labor and Management, College of Commerce, State University of Iowa (Iowa City, Iowa, December, 1958), p. 65.

[13] Statistical calculation "since the beginning of the program" excludes the abnormal experience during the war years—1941 through 1944. Thus, an 18-year period is used.

ment Compensation. In the recession of 1958, *all* states paid out more than they collected. This evidence suggests that recessions may be as costly, if not more costly, for unemployment insurance than are depressions.

The estimates by W. S. Woytinsky, made in 1948, concluded that for 2 per cent of *taxable wages* we can improve our unemployment insurance system to provide a uniform duration of 26 weeks, benefits approximately 50 per cent of taxable wages, and dependents benefits as well.[14] Expressed as a per cent of *total wages* paid in covered employment, the nominal burden of unemployment insurance costs is even more striking. A recent study based on our experience for the last decade indicates that a combined state and federal tax rate equivalent to 3 per cent of *total wages* paid in covered employment would have sufficed to finance, on a national basis, the most far-reaching among several proposals to liberalize unemployment insurance benefits introduced in Congress, plus dependents' allowances conforming to the most generous provisions currently in effect under state law.[15]

These estimates suggest that a good system of unemployment insurance is not overly expensive. It is, in fact, cheap insurance.

## THE FINANCING OF UNEMPLOYMENT INSURANCE

Unemployment insurance is both a taxing and a benefit payment program. In fact, the federal law is primarily a taxing statute. The federal government imposes a uniform national payroll tax of 3 per cent on employers having four or more employees for 20 weeks in the taxable year, with certain types of employment being exempt. The tax applies to the first $3,000 of annual wage of each employee. Employers are permitted to offset up to 90 per cent of this tax if they pay unemployment insurance taxes to a state with an approved law. Thus, in actual practice, a federal tax of 0.3 per cent goes into the general funds of the Treasury to defray the administrative costs of the program. Congress appropriates funds which are allocated to the states quarterly by the Bureau of Employment Security for the payment of their administrative expenses.

### The Influence of Experience Rating

Employers may, of course, pay less than 2.7 per cent of taxable payrolls to the states and still gain the 90 per cent offset of the federal tax. Additional credits are allowed under the Internal Revenue Code for employers in states which determine the employer's contribution rate ac-

[14] W. S. Woytinsky, "The Cost of Unemployment Insurance," *Social Security Bulletin* (May, 1948), and "The Cost of Unemployment Insurance: Part II," *Social Security Bulletin* (June, 1948).

[15] George F. Rohrlich, *Public Policy Implications of Unemployment Insurance Financing*, Industrial Relations Association, Annual Meeting (Chicago, December, 1958), p. 5.

cording to the unemployment risk of the employer over a three-year period of experience.

The first experience rating provisions became effective in Wisconsin in January, 1938, with all the other states following in rapid order by 1948.

Many who have opposed unemployment insurance liberalization have done so in good faith and in the belief that benefit increases are unnecessary. However, others insist the explanation is to be found in the experience rating system of financing our unemployment insurance laws which prevails in nearly all the states. This system makes it possible for many employers to keep their unemployment insurance costs considerably below the state or national average. Further liberalization may endanger the favorable rates enjoyed by these employers.

Whatever factors are responsible for the rapid adoption of experience rating, and there is general agreement as to the reasons, it seems that the system is here and will remain; further, that it has certain desirable features which strengthen rather than weaken our unemployment insurance laws. At the same time, experience rating should not be permitted to operate in a manner which may interfere with the basic objectives of unemployment insurance. It seems to have done so. Experience rating explains in part the increasing toughness of disqualification and eligibility provisions. The unfavorable impact of higher benefit levels upon the insurance rate of the employers with the lowest contribution rates influences the strong resistance to more adequate levels.

**A "Deceptive" Reserve**

The Social Security Act provided that the taxes collected by the states are to be deposited in the Unemployment Trust Fund in the United States Treasury and interest credited to the state accounts. States can draw from this fund only for the purpose of paying benefits.

The accounts are not expected to balance on a year-to-year basis. Evaluation of the financial soundness of the system as a whole or of the program in individual states is rendered difficult by the absence of any clear formulation of the period of time, presumably one which includes both good and bad employment years, over which the funds are expected to balance. In short, precise actuarial calculation of unemployment is not entirely possible.

In terms of over-all national figures, the 23-year record is impressive. In only four calendar years—1945, 1950, and 1958—did outpayments exceed inpayments plus interest earned. Moreover, at the end of 1958 the trust fund balance stood at almost $7 billion. At the rate of 1958 withdrawals, the highest year in history, benefits could be paid for nearly two years without any additional inpayments.

The reserves have, except for the years 1945–46 and 1957–58, shown a steady growth. At the end of 1958 these reserves were equivalent to almost two years' collections at the standard rate of 2.7 per cent, or to four years of collections at the average rate of 1.4 per cent which actually prevailed during 1958.

The reserve, of course, is not a national pool. Here is where the problem lies. Such a pool may be of little help to "hard-hit" states. The employment experience among the states is, of course, not uniform. For example, Alaska, Michigan, and Pennsylvania were seriously hit by the 1958 recession and their reserves suffered substantial depletion.

In such a predicament not many alternatives are open to the affected states. It is politically difficult, if not impossible, to reduce benefits. Increasing tax rates puts a relatively heavier burden on employers in some states than is borne by their competitors elsewhere. Nevertheless, such steps have been taken by many states; experience rating provisions have been postponed and other devices used to increase income into the fund.

Another alternative is for a state to secure an interest-free loan from the Federal Unemployment Account under terms of the Reed Act, the Employment Security Administrative Financing Act of 1954. A state can secure such a loan by request if its reserves were smaller than the amount of benefits paid out during the year.

Five states with reserves less than benefit payments in the preceding year were eligible at the end of 1958 to borrow from the federal loan fund provided by the Reed Act. These were Alaska, Delaware, Michigan, Oregon, and Pennsylvania. In addition, twelve states had reserves which were less than twice the amount of benefits paid in the year 1958. The fund was entirely used up in 1959, and our brief experience with it clearly indicates the need for a more adequate loan fund or a national reinsurance system capable of meeting the problem likely to be created by more frequent or serious recessions than that of 1958.

### The Need for a National Reinsurance Fund

When the Social Security Act was adopted, the object was to eliminate interstate differences in cost of unemployment insurance. The way it has worked out, these differences have not been entirely eliminated; as a result, employers in certain states, such as Michigan, have been placed at a distinct disadvantage for this reason alone. In recent years there has been a growing recognition that large-scale unemployment, which may be centered in such highly industrialized states as Michigan, results from factors which are not controllable by individual employers and are not localized within a state.

There is no good reason why a state like Michigan or Pennsylvania or any other state should be penalized because of a recession which is national in origin and has a more serious impact on that state. Some experts in unemployment insurance have advocated a nation-wide system of reinsurance which under the Federal Unemployment Account would assume all or a substantial portion of the costs of excess benefits above specified percentages of taxable payrolls. Several proposals embodying this principle, including the Kennedy Bill, have received legislative consideration.

Such a fund could, for example, be financed by changing the 0.3 of 1 per cent unemployment insurance tax retained by the federal government to 0.4 of 1 per cent or more, if necessary. And the equalization or reinsurance fund could carry the unemployment insurance costs which exceed a fixed percentage of the payroll in any state. If such a fund were in existence, it would not be necessary for the unemployment insurance costs of employers in the recession-hit states to increase the tax rates in 1959 and 1960, as is definitely required if their funds are to remain solvent.

### The Problem of Duration of Benefits in Recessions

Unemployment insurance is admittedly inadequate to deal with persistent unemployment associated with serious economic depressions or with joblessness in "depressed areas" suffering from chronic unemployment. The program is designed to meet the costs of relatively short-time joblessness for wage earners whose regular and recent attachment to the labor market is clearly established. Area redevelopment programs may be of aid in "depressed" communities. Monetary and fiscal policies including public works may aid in raising the general level of business and unemployment. Unemployment insurance, however, is a limited program and should not be expected to carry the total burden of privation created by an economic cataclysm.

The recession of 1957–58, however, hardly falls within this category. Whether measured in terms of the decline in the volume of production, or in employment or unemployment, the magnitudes were rather small. Unemployment did not climb much above 5 million, or about 8 per cent of the labor force, in the worst month. Even so, the inadequacy of the duration provisions of unemployment insurance laws became apparent early in the recession when 2.6 million workers used up their benefit rights.

For the first time "extended benefits" were made possible by congressional enactment in 1958 of the Temporary Federal Unemployment Compensation Law. Public notice was taken of the fact that about only two out of every three unemployed were either covered, eligible, or in receipt of jobless benefits. And the role of unemployment insurance as an income maintenance program for the unemployed worker and his family, and as a built-in stabilizer for his family, received increasing recognition.

The Act provided for the temporary extension of benefits in states which entered into agreement with the Secretary of Labor to pay them. Temporary benefits were payable to claimants who had exhausted their benefit rights under state unemployment insurance laws (or the federal program for Korea veterans and federal employees). A state might participate fully, partially, or not at all.

Additional benefits were limited to one half of the total amount which were payable to the claimant pursuant to the law under which he last exhausted his benefit rights. The temporary benefit for a week of total unemployment was the same in amount as the regular weekly unemployment insurance benefit.

Seventeen states chose to participate fully under this Act, and paid temporary benefits under all programs: state, UCFE, and UCV. Five other states—Colorado, Connecticut, Illinois, Ohio, and Wisconsin—enacted their own temporary extension of duration independently of the federal law. The terms of additional benefit payments in these states were similar to those in the federal TUC program. Together, these 22 states contained about 70 per cent of the nation's covered labor force. Twelve states, Puerto Rico, and the Virgin Islands partially participated in the federal TUC program, paying temporary benefits under UCFE and UCV programs only. The remaining 16 states had no plan, but took interstate claims for temporary benefits as agent states only.

When the TUC Act of 1958 expired, it was extended three months for current claimants under the same terms and provisions of the former act.

The program provided substantial aid to the unemployed. Shortcomings of the Act were that it was temporary in character, failed to embrace all the states, and that it did not deal with the matter of coverage or the size of benefits.

The quick recovery from the 1958 recession sidetracked the problem of a permanent extension of benefit duration for normal times and particularly for recession periods. It would be unfortunate to leave this matter for emergency treatment in the next recession.

Arthur F. Burns, former Chairman of the President's Council of Economic Advisors, sums up this growing conviction: "Now that our economy is once more expanding, we are in a position to proceed deliberately and to carry out permanent improvements in unemployment insurance, not only with a view to mitigating individual hardships, but also with the objective of increasing the resistance of our economy to a future recession."[16]

## IV

### IS IMPROVEMENT IN BENEFIT LEVELS POSSIBLE? SHOULD WE RELY ON PRIVATE SUPPLEMENTATION OR FEDERAL STANDARDS?

Is it possible to improve our unemployment insurance system without dismantling the present federal-state system? Can it be done without a radical change in experience rating? Has the moment arrived for federal standards?

Three alternative methods of dealing with the problem suggest them-

---

[16] Arthur F. Burns, *op. cit.*, p. 18.

selves. The first is the system of supplementary unemployment benefits through collective bargaining. The development of private supplementation of unemployment insurance benefits has followed the fringe benefit pattern in American industrial relations. It has already been applied to old-age retirement benefits, to workmen's compensation, and to illness and disability. The general principle is that the public scheme at best provides only a floor of protection for the entire population. Such protection must, of necessity, impose only moderate costs upon the employer since these costs must be borne by all, whether there are profits or not. As a result, organized workers in a favorable bargaining position and in growing industries and profitable firms have won substantial fringe benefits supplementing public payments in several programs. The most extensive developments have been made in the retirement pension area.

The widespread dissatisfaction with the benefit levels in unemployment insurance, coupled with the slow progress made via legislation, made this matter a logical item on the union fringe benefit agenda. And in 1958, after two years of the most intensive agitation, under the pen name of the Guaranteed Annual Wage, the idea was translated into collective bargaining contracts with the major auto producers. It has since spread to nearly all producers of automobiles, and in addition, to other industries such as steel, rubber, aluminum, agricultural equipment, and can making. In all, well over two million workers are now covered by some form of SUB plan. The union was able to win through collective bargaining what it failed to secure through legislation. The limitation of unemployment insurance was thus, in part, corrected.

Private supplementation provides a certain degree of flexibility to the unemployment insurance structure. It permits the legislative benefits to remain at "reasonable" levels from the viewpoint of costs and at the same time makes possible considerable improvement in the benefits of wage earners whose employer is in a favorable profit position or whose employees are in a relatively strong bargaining position. The pressure to improve benefits would, under such a development, be transferred to the collective bargaining arena.

There are, however, many real limitations to this approach. Quite apart from the anomalies which supplementation has introduced, under the most optimistic forecasts it is unlikely that the private supplementation plans will affect more than three or four million employees. The vast majority of the wage earners covered by the unemployment insurance laws would not benefit directly from such supplementation. They may, in fact, be harmed since the union's efforts might be concentrated in winning supplementary benefits, and its pressure for improving the program through legislation may be reduced.

About 45 million employees are now provided the protection of unemployment insurance. The large majority of these are not directly affected by the provisions of collective bargaining contracts. Significant areas of employment are relatively unorganized. Substantial dependence upon the collective bargaining route to improve unemployment insurance will not aid these groups. Supplementary unemployment compensation results in uneven protection for unemployment.

Will state action alone be adequate? Are federal standards called for? These are important questions being posed right now. The recession of 1957–58 and the resulting substantial increase in public welfare rolls has put the focus on the jobless and the deficiencies in our unemployment insurance program.

The experience of the states during the recession has called attention to the need for some sort of federal standards. These standards would eliminate or reduce the gap between states which generally have maintained relatively high levels of benefit adequacy and duration and the states which have generally maintained relatively low standards. As a result, the majority report of the Committee on Legislative Review to the Federal Advisory Council concluded that minimum federal standards are necessary if benefits adequate in amount and duration to meet the needs of the unemployed are to be provided.[17]

### The Kennedy Bill

A bill, introduced in 1958 by Senator John F. Kennedy and supported by 31 senators, sought congressional approval of a program of federal benefit standards in unemployment insurance. Major provisions of the Kennedy Bill would:

Require states to establish a minimum benefit of not less than 50 per cent of a worker's weekly pay and not less than two thirds of the state's average weekly pay. The unemployed worker would receive the lesser of the two benefits set by the state equal to or above these minimums.
Require states to pay benefits for at least 39 weeks to all eligible employees.

Senator Kennedy said his bill, if passed, would "cushion any recession, alleviate individual hardship, and speed national recovery."

### Alternative Courses of Action

The federal interest in promoting and maintaining a healthy national economy is well established. Unemployment insurance has an important role to play in this endeavor, but it can do so only if such provisions as benefits and duration, among others, are reasonably adequate. Where they are not adequate, the federal government has an obligation to try to bring about the necessary improvement. To accomplish this it may: (1) continue, as now, to urge and encourage the states to act; or (2) establish federal minimum standards.

In the first of these two courses of action the states have acted to raise

---

[17] *Report of the Committee on Legislative Review,* to the Federal Advisory Council (December 2–3, 1958), p. 5.

benefits and duration on many occasions, as the volume of enacted legislation over the years will show. On the whole, however, the tendency has been to go slow in making necessary improvements. Such a tendency in our rapidly changing economy has provided inadequate results in the process of program improvement, especially with regard to such elements as the level of the maximum weekly benefit amount and the minimum earnings requirement.

There are a number of reasons why there is strong opposition to federal standards. Federal standards, it is held, would be an improper intrusion into the internal affairs of the states and restrict their freedom to adopt to local conditions. Since the unemployment insurance laws are state laws and benefits are paid from state funds, financed from contributions made by employers in the respective states, the states should have complete freedom to experiment and to adopt the provisions they want. Secondly, federal standards might force some states into insolvency. Thirdly, federal standards would be a departure from the system of unemployment insurance as originally enacted by Congress. Although the original legislation has been amended on several occasions since 1935, Congress has not enacted any federal minimum benefit standards in the twenty-odd years which have elapsed. Finally, enforcements of the requirements on various points would involve the federal government very deeply in state operations. Federal standards would increase problems of conformity and compliance, particularly with respect to eligibility and disqualification.

The case for federal standards centers around the claim that voluntary action by the states has not been sufficient. First, the federal government has a direct financial interest in an adequate system of unemployment insurance benefits. This became clearly evident during the past ten years and especially during the 1957–58 recession. The federal government has long accepted a responsibility for adequate protection of the unemployed. Heavy unemployment has its origin in the national economy rather than that of the individual states, and even localized pockets of unemployment are often attributable to technical market changes beyond the control of individual states. Federal standards are necessary, in the third place, to assure throughout the nation levels of protection that meet at least minimum objectives. With the unemployment insurance program as it now stands, claimants having identical earnings and employment experience are entitled to widely different treatment in different states. One major objective of the Federal Unemployment Tax was to eliminate interstate tax competition as a deterrent to the establishment of an unemployment insurance program. Federal standards are needed to help remove the competitive advantage now enjoyed by employers in states with inadequate provisions. And further, federal standards would not change the structure of the federal-state system. Some federal standards are obviously included in the federal legislation, including one standard directly relating to benefits. Sixth and last, federal standards being in terms of minimum requirements would not impose a dead level of uniformity on the entire country. Above the minimums of protection for the unemployed required by the standards, state legislators would be free to frame provisions adapted to their own industries, economic conditions, and social objectives.

Our unemployment insurance system should be strengthened now, under favorable economic conditions, so that it can meet the stress to which it will be exposed later. If federal standards in financing and benefits are essential to provide such improvements—and we think that they are—we should not shrink from such a course. In our judgment, such minimum standards are essential if our unemployment insurance is to make its maximum contribution to the wage earner and to the economy.

# 24. SUMMARY OF MAJOR PROPOSALS TO MODIFY THE FEDERAL-STATE UNEMPLOYMENT INSURANCE PROGRAM, 1934-1959

WILBUR J. COHEN,
1960.

I. Enlarge State Responsibility.
  A. Increase the tax offset from 90 per cent to 99 per cent.

> This was the majority recommendation of the Study Committee on Unemployment Compensation and Employment Service to the Commission on Intergovernmental Relations, 1955. See *A Study Committee Report on Unemployment Compensation and Employment Service* (Washington, D.C.: U.S. Government Printing Office, June, 1955). This committee recommendation was rejected by the Commission.

  B. Increase the tax offset from 90 per cent to 100 per cent.

> This proposal was recommended between 1946 and 1948 by various employer groups. It was embodied in a bill, H.R.5736, introduced by Representative Harkness on March 4, 1948. The proposal resulted in sharp differences of opinion among state agency representatives. Congress took no action on the proposal.

  C. Increase the Federal Loan Fund.

> A loan fund was first adopted in 1944 as the "George loan fund" which expired at the end of 1951. Subsequently, the loan fund was made permanent in the Employment Security Administrative Financing Act of 1954, known as the "Reed Bill." The Mills-Simpson Bill,

H.R.7177 and 7178, introduced on May 18, 1959 (86th Cong., 1st sess.) proposed increasing the maximum amount in the loan fund from the present $200 million to $550 million. An additional one tenth of 1 per cent would be levied on employers to finance the cost of increasing the loan fund.

D. Repeal the Federal Unemployment Tax Act.

See suggestion in paper by William Papier, Secretary of Ohio State Advisory Council on Unemployment Compensation, "The Role of Unemployment Compensation," to the Conference on Social Security, The University of Michigan, November 19, 1959.

II. Change to a Federal Grant-in-Aid Program for Benefits.
  A. 100 per cent federal grant to the states.

Report of the Advisory Council to the Committee on Economic Security, 1934. See House Hearings on H.R.4120 (74th Cong., 1st sess.), 1935, pp. 881–88. See also Report of the Committee on Social Legislation of April 10, 1935, to the Business Advisory Council, U.S. Department of Commerce, Washington, D.C., May 16, 1935.

  B. Federal sharing on a 50–50 grant basis.

Recommendation of the Social Security Board, 1946, *Annual Report*, 1946, pp. 485–86. This proposal involved decreasing the federal unemployment tax to 1 per cent and no credit for contributions under state laws. Out of the proceeds of the 1 per cent tax, the federal government would grant the state half the total costs of its program, including benefits as well as administration. The states could finance their half of the costs in any way they desired.

  C. Reduce the federal offset.

Various alternatives are possible by reducing the existing federal offset of 90 per cent to some lower figure. With the additional income to the federal government it would be possible to finance regular or special benefits, partially or wholly, as might be determined.

  D. Federal sharing of the cost of an auxiliary program.

This proposal by Father Joseph M. Becker involves the federal government offering to share one third of the cost of a separate auxiliary program during periods of abnormal unemployment. The remaining two thirds of the cost would be met by each state in any way it chose. Reserves would be kept separate to make it unmistakably clear that the regular and the auxiliary program have different functions and operate on different principles. See *Hearings on Unemployment Compensation before the House Committee on Ways and Means* (86th Cong., 1st sess.), April, 1959, pp. 537–58.

III. Federal Minimum Benefits Standards.
  A. Minimum federal benefit standards for states.

The original Wagner-Lewis bill of 1934, H.R.7659, provided for some minimum federal benefit standards. See *Hearings before a Subcommittee of the House Committee on Ways and Means* (73d Cong., 2d sess.), March 21–30, 1934, p. 3.

    B. Minimum federal benefit standards for states, with an average contribution rate below 2.7 per cent of taxable payrolls subject to a "solvency" test of the size of the state fund. Contribution rates reducible by experience rating or flat rates.

        There was no reinsurance provision in this proposal. H.R.6635, the Social Security Act Amendments of 1939, as passed by the House of Representatives, contained such a proposal. See *House Committee Report No. 728* (76th Cong., 1st sess.), June 2, 1939, pp. 24–25, 65–68, 102–3. The provisions were deleted by the Senate and dropped in the Conference Report on the bill.

    C. Minimum federal benefit standards and a reinsurance fund.

        The Kennedy-Karsten bill, S.791 and H.R.3547 (86th Cong., 1st sess.), 1959, provides for both federal minimum benefit standards and a reinsurance fund. For a summary of the provisions of the bill see *Congressional Record*, January 29, 1959.

IV. Federal Reinsurance of State Costs.

    A. The proposal for 50–50 grants to the states is in effect a reinsurance of state benefit structures. See II.B in this outline. The same general principle could be applied by utilizing different variations of this formula.

    B. The reinsurance provisions of the Kennedy-Karsten bill could be applied independently of the federal minimum benefit standards.

    C. Use of the "excess collections" from the federal tax as authorized by section 904($h$) of the Social Security Act to finance state benefits.

        See testimony of Wilbur J. Cohen in *Hearings before the Senate Committee on Finance on H.R.12065* (85th Cong., 2d sess.), May 1958, pp. 183–93.

V. Federal Solvency Standards.

        Various proposals have been advanced from time to time to require the states to meet a certain minimum size of reserve to be eligible for certain loans, grants, credits, or approval under the federal law. See, for instance, the requirement in the Kennedy-Karsten bill that when the state's reserve fund drops below 6 per cent of taxable wages, a minimum contribution rate of 1.2 per cent must be maintained in order to be eligible for a reinsurance grant.

VI. Supplementation Plans.

    1. Federal supplementation from general revenues of extended duration only.[1]

---

    [1] This summary does not include all the variations of supplementary emergency plans proposed in 1942, 1944, 1945, 1952, and 1958. These proposals dealt with both the amount and duration of benefits.

The Senate passed this provision in 1945 to extend the duration of benefits to 26 weeks. The bill was referred to the House Committee on Ways and Means which voted 14 to 10 to postpone action on the bill.

2. Federal supplementation from general revenues of benefit amount and duration during "high-level unemployment periods."

This bill was introduced by Mr. Prouty, H.R.11634, March 25, 1958 (85th Cong., 2d sess.). It provided for an increase of 30 per cent in benefits being received by insured unemployed individuals and an increase of up to 20 weeks of benefits at prevailing state rates to unemployed individuals who exhaust their benefits. See *Congressional Record*, March 25, 1958, p.A2771, daily issue, for summary of the proposal.

3. Cyclically graduated compensation—the Galbraith proposal.

Professor Galbraith's proposal is that unemployment insurance should be increased as unemployment increases and should be diminished as full employment is approached. As unemployment increased he would raise total payments to nearly approximate wages. When unemployment is high he would pay benefits for as long as unemployment lasted. See John Kenneth Galbraith, *The Affluent Society* (Boston: Houghton Mifflin Co., 1958), pp. 292–307.

4. Federal payment from general revenues for benefits to noncovered individuals.

This proposal was included as Title II of the Mills-McCormack bills, H.R.11326 and H.R.11327 (85th Cong., 2d sess.), 1958. It provided that individuals employed in noncovered employments who could meet the eligibility conditions in state laws would receive benefits according to the state law up to 16 weeks of benefits. A similar proposal was included in the McNamara amendment offered as a substitute for H.R.5640 (the extension of the 1958 TUC law), March 25, 1959 in the Senate but was defeated 38 to 49. See *Congressional Record*, March 25, 1959, pp. 4645–46, daily issue.

VII. A Contributory Plan: The Advisory Council Plan of 1948.

The Advisory Council plan, among other things, involved a minimum federal contribution rate on both employers and employees and a federal benefit standard on disqualifications. See *The Reports of the Advisory Council on Social Security to the Senate Committee on Finance*, Senate Document No. 208 (80th Cong., 2d sess.), 1949, pp. 137–236.

VIII. A Federal System.

For a statement of the advantages of a federal system see *The Reports of the Advisory Council on Social Security to the Senate Committee on Finance*, Senate Document No. 208 (80th Cong., 2d sess.), 1949, pp. 206–11.

# 25. ADEQUACY OF BENEFITS

*Adequacy of Benefits under Unemployment Insurance*, U.S. Department of Labor, 1958.

SOME OF THE objectives of the program are accomplished through the payment of benefits, some through the financial structure of the system, and some through the bringing together of claimants seeking work and employers seeking workers. *This report is concerned only with those objectives that can be achieved through the payment of benefits.*

There is substantial agreement on the *general* minimum objectives of benefit payments:

1. To replace enough of the current wage loss of unemployed workers who meet the program's requirements so that most such workers would not have to turn to other programs for aid, under normal or recession conditions. To this some would add that the program should forestall exhaustion of savings or resort to credit for basic needs; others suggest that the program cannot be so liberal as to make unnecessary a moderate use of savings during unemployment. Some would urge that benefit levels should enable workers substantially to maintain their customary level of living without diminishing their savings appreciably. As to the period during which these goals would operate, some would say "moderate recession" rather than "recession"; others, on the other hand, would expect the program to meet its objectives not only in a period of recession, but in a period of more serious economic dislocation as well, at least in its early stages.
2. To compensate for wage loss in such a way as to help provide a sense of security for the covered work force—the feeling of assurance based on the knowledge which individuals have that they will surely be compensated for periods of involuntary unemployment should they become unemployed.
3. To help maintain essential consumer purchasing power, thus helping to brake a downturn in business activity and sustain the confidence of the community, locally or nationwide as the case may be.

There is less agreement on *specifics.*

\* \* \* \* \*

## WEEKLY BENEFIT AMOUNT

### Purposes and Principles—Major Views

The weekly benefit is designed to replace *part* of the current weekly wage loss of eligible workers. On this there is little, if any, disagreement. But there is disagreement on how large that part should be for different claimants. Some of this disagreement arises from differences as to the function that the benefit check is to perform: what it is expected to do for an unemployed worker. Among those who agree on objectives, there are differences on ways to carry them out.

There is general agreement that the benefit should not be so large as to affect adversely the incentive to work. Without an adequate financial differential in favor of working, the payment of benefits would defeat one of the major objectives of the employment security program: to facilitate the speedy reabsorption of workers into suitable jobs. Payments made to claimants who would be working in a suitable job except for the benefit are needless payments and mean losses in productivity.

A variety of opinions have been expressed on the differential between benefits and wages necessary to help maintain the incentive to work. These opinions are related to varying concepts of what "take-home pay" is. Some would define it as gross wages less withholding taxes, social security deductions, and a variety of expenses connected with employment, such as transportation, clothing, and lunch. Others define take-home pay simply as gross wages less withholding taxes. Some of those who support the first definition would urge a differential of as much as 50 percent between benefits and gross wages as necessary to maintain the incentive to work. Without conceding the validity of the restrictive definition of take-home pay, others would maintain that a 15 to 35 percent differential between benefits and wages after taxes is sufficient to maintain work incentives. A recent operational manifestation of the opinion of this latter group can be found in some of the current union-management contracts providing for supplemental unemployment benefits.

What impels the beneficiaries of unemployment insurance to work or not to work is not merely a matter of the level of benefits. This is a subject that requires much research before easy answers can be given. The "incentive to work" must include, for example, the stimulus provided by seniority rights. Millions of workers have a regular attachment to a payroll, and their job and job rights depend on their reporting for work if the plant is operating.

Moreover, the objective of the employment security program is *not* to secure the speediest possible re-employment of workers at whatever wages and whatever skills they can find jobs. One of the functions of unemployment insurance is to give workers short-run carrying power so that they may be able to preserve, to the best of their ability, their skills and their earning power. This is to the advantage not only of the worker and his family, but of the nation's productivity as well.

There has been increasing acceptance of the thesis that the benefit must be sufficient to cover, for most beneficiaries, that proportion of past wages that goes for nondeferrable living expenses. Some express this somewhat differently, holding that the objective should be to provide a benefit amount sufficient to relieve hardships and to allow purchase of basic necessities. Agreement on either statement of the proposition has not meant agreement on specifics. "Most beneficiaries" in the first statement of the proposition means 50 percent of the beneficiaries to some, 75 percent to others, and 95 percent to still others. Moreover, there has been no universally accepted definition of nondeferrable expenses or basic necessities. The concept of nondeferrable expense is further complicated by the prevalence of durable goods buying on the installment plan, which enlarges the area of fixed payments within the family budget.

In this connection, some place great stress on what the benefit can do not only for the family that receives it but also for the community. The benefit, it is argued, helps maintain purchasing power, provides a brake on downturns in business activity, and helps sustain the confidence of the community and the general level of economic activity.

Many avoid answering these knotty questions by arguing, on principle, that the benefit must be the same proportion of wages for all eligible claimants if the wage-loss principle is to be maintained. Most of this group would accept as a legitimate goal maintenance of the concept that was generally acceptable as reasonable or feasible when the program started: that benefits should approximate 50 percent of wages. Here, again, arises the question of whether the wage-loss to be compensated in part should be calculated on the basis of gross or take-home pay. There is increasing acceptance of the desirability of 60 percent of wages as a goal, while some would urge a somewhat higher percentage, say from 65 to 75 percent of wages. Many States have increased their benefits—between minimum and maximum—to more than 50 percent of wages. The proportion of wage-loss compensation is 65 percent or more under most State workmen's compensation laws for temporary total disability and about 65 percent of wages net of taxes withheld under supplemental unemployment benefit agreements between unions and management.

Those who would urge a more factual basis for the setting of the proportion of wage loss would start with the proposition that the weekly benefit should be sufficient to cover that proportion of his past wages which a worker spends, when employed, for items he cannot do without when unemployed. They would then try to make some reasonably scientific definition of the content of the nondeferrable "bundle" and use the best statistical data available on the income and expenditures of claimants or of workers with characteristics similar to those of the claimant group.

What data there are on the income and expenditures of workers suggest that workers with low incomes have to spend a higher proportion of their earnings for food, shelter, and household operation than workers with higher wages, and that those with family responsibilities have to spend a higher proportion of their income for these living essentials than workers without dependents. Many therefore urge that lower-paid workers and workers with dependents receive a higher proportion of wages than other workers. Experience has shown that it is possible to define classes of "dependents" on the basis of simple presumptions and yet

cover those dependent in fact in such cases without detailed questioning of claimants. Some object that any administrable definition of dependent must leave out some classes of relatives who in individual cases are equally dependent on the claimant. Others maintain that only workers who have evidenced substantial ability to support their dependents during periods of employment should be eligible for dependents' allowances.

There are many, however, who maintain that to vary payments according to number of dependents is wrong in principle. They believe that dependents' allowances inject a determination or presumption of need into the program and are foreign to an insurance concept. They generally believe that payment of benefits at a uniform proportion of wages is more in conformity with insurance principles. Many of these would agree on the desirability of paying higher proportions of wages to workers with low earnings, but, within wage classes, would pay a uniform proportion, averaging out the different proportions spent on basic essentials by workers with different numbers of dependents.

Whichever principle is agreed upon, the degree to which the benefits received by eligible claimants reflect that principle depends on a number of elements other than the proportion of wage loss itself: the wage base used as a measure of wage loss, the minimum, and the maximum weekly benefit.

It seems agreed that the wage base, taken together with the fraction of wages payable, must minimize the effects of periods of no earnings or reduced earnings on a worker's benefit. It is contended that, in theory, the worker's usual weekly wages in a reasonably recent period would provide a desirable base, but there appears to be some disagreement as to whether "usual" should be taken to mean "full-time" or "average." The original laws generally specified "full-time."

It also seems agreed that the minimum weekly benefit should not be inconsequential but should make a significant contribution to the beneficiary's welfare and warrant the administrative expense of processing claims and payments. All who agree on this statement would not necessarily agree on what it should mean in dollars. However, if qualifying requirements have been properly established and the proportion of wage loss is sound, setting the minimum should not be a critical problem.

Of greater significance and difficulty is the setting of the maximum. Here, too, it is easier to agree on a statement of principle than on the ways to effectuate it. Few, if any, would deny that the maximum should be high enough to permit the wage-loss principle to operate satisfactorily. Some would conclude from this that there should be no maximum—so long as the proportion of wages has been set properly for each worker. Most would say that there must be a maximum so that individuals with unusually high wages will not draw a disproportionate share of available funds. Additional support for a maximum perhaps derives from the fact that a high-wage worker need devote a smaller proportion of his earnings to cover the basic necessities than does a lower-paid worker. In fact, a maximum operates to provide progressively lower proportions of wages to workers in the highest wage brackets. This is in accordance with sound principles—*if the maximum is high enough.*

### Analysis and Application of Possible Criteria of Adequacy

There are many measures with which the adequacy of the weekly benefit amount can be tested. Some of them involve simply a review of the benefit provisions of the law. Others concern the experience with the actual payment of benefits. Still others deal with the general experience of beneficiaries during unemployment as a context for viewing benefits. No one criterion by itself can provide a total conclusion regarding adequacy. A composite approach along these lines, however, can offer a broad basis for evaluation.

*Review of Benefit Provisions of State Laws.* An examination of the law itself will yield many significant judgments regarding benefit adequacy. For example, if a benefit of 50 percent of wage loss is accepted as a goal, the law itself reveals much.

Weekly benefits were expressed in the earliest laws as a percentage of a reported "full-time weekly wage," usually 50 percent. For administrative reasons, the reporting of full-time weekly wages for individual workers was replaced by the reporting of quarterly earnings. This necessitated the computation of weekly benefits as a fraction of quarterly or annual earnings. Most States originally computed benefits as $\frac{1}{26}$ of highest quarterly earnings in a base period—equivalent to 50 percent of weekly earnings if the claimant worked 13 weeks in the quarter. Because there are not always as many as 13 weeks of employment in the quarter of highest earnings, or simply in order to liberalize benefits, the fraction of quarterly earnings has been raised to more than $\frac{1}{26}$ in most States. This fraction now generally ranges from $\frac{1}{25}$ to $\frac{1}{20}$ or to higher fractions in a few States for certain workers. Nine States, however, base the weekly benefit on total annual earnings in the base period. In these States, it is not possible to say just how weekly benefits are related to weekly or quarterly earnings. In four States, the weekly benefit is based on average weekly wages.

The States have generally increased not only their rates of wage-loss compensation but their minimum and maximum benefits as well. The earliest laws included no fixed minimum weekly benefit amount; workers received a percent of full-time wages, if this was less than a specified amount. The most common minimum became $5. . . .

Most significant of the changes that have been made in the weekly benefit amount provisions of State laws have related to the maximum weekly payment. Fifteen dollars was the maximum in all but two States in 1938. . . .

Some States have legislated increases in the maximum frequently in order to keep pace with steadily rising wage levels. Under such condi-

tions, fixed dollar maximums soon become obsolete. There are now four States which have flexible maximums, related to the average weekly wage in the State. In these States, benefit provisions specify a constant relationship between the maximum weekly benefit and the average weekly wage in covered employment, this relationship to be maintained by administratively adjusting the maximum periodically to accord with changes in the average wage.

**Ratio of the Maximum to Average Weekly Wages.** It has become customary to compare the maximum weekly benefit amount with the average weekly wage of covered workers. This ratio, however, should be evaluated against some acceptable criterion which, if satisfied, would be expected to yield the proper benefit-wage-loss relationship for the great majority of individual workers.

There are those who would set and maintain maximum benefits at either three-fifths or two-thirds of the average weekly wage of covered workers. This particular criterion, in many respects, represents a minimum measure of benefit adequacy since it automatically means that only claimants whose wages range from the minimum qualifying amount up to an amount equal to approximately one-third more than the average weekly wage will receive 50 percent of their wage loss. Minimum criteria of this nature are useful, however, since if benefits appear inadequate under such a criterion, most people would agree it would be desirable generally to raise maximum benefits.

At the present time 4 percent of the covered workers are in the six States where the basic maximum benefit is at least 50 percent of the average weekly wage. Three percent of covered workers were in such States in 1952. Currently 33 percent of covered workers are in States where the basic maximum benefit is less than 40 percent of the average weekly wage. The comparable figure for 1952 was 37 percent.

Significant changes would have to be made in many State laws to have maximum benefits constitute either three-fifths or two-thirds of the average weekly wage. As of September 1958, only 5 States could attain these standards by increasing their maximum by $10 or less; 6 States would have to increase their maximum by $20 or more.

**Weekly Benefit Payments.** Meaningful as these simple tests are, of perhaps greater significance is what the law allows for eligible claimants and beneficiaries. Data are readily available on the average weekly payment for total unemployment and the distribution of weekly payments by amount.

There are differences, no doubt, between the average of weekly benefit amounts for which eligible claimants qualify and the average of payments to beneficiaries in a month, quarter or year. Similarly, there are most likely differences between the distributions of amounts to which insured claimants are eligible on the one hand, and the distributions of actual payments on the other. The second figure in both these comparisons is affected by differences in the number of payments made to workers with different benefit amounts. Moreover, fluctuations over time in economic conditions influence such data. During periods of heavy unemployment in high-wage industries, there is likely to be a greater concentration of benefit payments at or near the maximum than would be the case at other times, thereby causing a rise in the average payment. In practice, therefore, such figures on benefit payments must be used cautiously in drawing conclusions about the adequacy of benefit provisions of State laws.

It would be desirable to compare average payments with the average wage of beneficiaries, but the latter figure is rarely known. Most States do not know the average wages of their claimants; in most States estimates cannot be readily made for many workers because of the maximum limitation on wages reported per year. Because of these difficulties, average benefit payments to claimants are sometimes compared with the estimated average wage in covered jobs since this figure is readily available in all States. However, there is considerable uncertainty over the relationship between the average wage of claimants and the average wage in covered jobs. Again, largely because of variations in economic conditions, this relationship varies from State to State and over time thereby limiting the usefulness of the ratio of average benefits to average wage in covered jobs.

*Proportion of Insured Claimants Eligible for the Maximum Benefit.* Among the measures of adequacy related to actual experience under benefit provisions is a simple and yet quite telling criterion: the proportion of insured claimants eligible for, or the number of payments being made at, the maximum weekly benefit amount. If the wage base and the proportion of wage-loss compensation have been properly set, the proportion of either insured claimants or payments at the maximum should be nominal. Under this assumption a finding of a significant number of claimants or payments at the maximum would indicate that the program does not operate on a wage-related basis, as intended, but, instead, more nearly resembles a flat-rate system. If a judgment is made suggesting that 10 or 25 percent constitutes a desirable upper limit to the proportion of claimants or payments at the maximum, then the increase in the maximum benefit necessary to effectuate this judgment can be estimated. While it is likely that some would disagree with the suggested figure of 10 percent, it seems unlikely that many would desire to have a system under which one-fourth or more of all beneficiaries were receiving the maximum benefit since a condition of this nature strongly implies that the system is failing to maintain its announced wage-loss-benefit relationship. . . .

*Application of the 50 percent Replacement Concept.* The general concept of replacing 50 percent of wage loss can be applied in another way. This is by determining the number of claimants who are actually receiving 50 percent of their wage loss. In addition, the average wage

at which a claimant will receive 50 percent of his wage loss can be calculated and then compared with the average weekly wage in the State.

In most States, workers who regularly earned $60 or less per week
would be compensated for at least 50 percent of their wage loss if unemployed. At the present time some 5 States, with 2 percent of the covered
work force, replace 50 percent or more of the wage loss incurred by a
worker whose weekly wage was equal to the statewide average weekly
wage. In all but one State at the present time, a worker whose average
weekly wage is equal to two-thirds of the statewide average weekly
wage will receive a weekly benefit, excluding dependents' allowances,
amounting to about one-half or more of his wage loss. The actual range
for this latter worker is from 48 percent to 67 percent.

**Dependents' Allowances.** This discussion of possible criteria has thus
far been concerned with basic benefits. There are 11 States, however,
which augment basic benefits with dependents' allowances. In a benefit
adequacy analysis, a significant question regarding dependents' allowances is whether or not they should be added to the basic benefit when a
general judgment regarding benefit adequacy is being made. One possible criterion for making this judgment rests on how significant dependents' allowances are in terms of both number of beneficiaries affected and
amount of benefits paid. To get an answer to this question, the pertinent
entitlement provisions of State laws having dependents' allowances need
to be analyzed along with the actual results of the operation of these additional benefits.

Maximum dependents' allowances range from a low of $6 per week to
a high of $25 per week. During the first 9 months of 1958, the number of
beneficiaries in these States who had compensable dependents ranged
from 10 percent to 63 percent of all beneficiaries in the State. Dependents' allowances increased the benefit of those who received it by 20
percent on the average, but overall benefits in these States by only 8 percent. These figures varied from State to State because of the difference
in the definitions of "dependents" and in the amounts payable for those
dependents.

**Net Wages as a Basis for Measuring Adequacy.** There are those who
maintain that wages net of withheld taxes, rather than gross wages, should
be used as a measure of wage loss. One argument advanced for the use
of net rather than gross wages points out that taxes withheld at the earnings source today constitute a significant proportion of gross wages, and
that the worker lives on net, not gross, wages. Moreover, when comparing
ratios of benefits to wages for different periods of time, it seems reasonable to make some allowances for the fact that withholding taxes have
taken bites of varying size out of workers' wages since 1943. The various
criteria suggested above can be related to net wages as well as to gross
wages. The major difficulty confronted in using net wages is that taxes

fall unevenly on families of varying incomes and sizes. Data on average benefit payments to workers with different numbers of dependents related to gross and net wages, along with information about the impact of withheld taxes on workers' levels of living and expenditure habits, would give added effectiveness to the use of net wages in measures of adequacy.

The percentage of wage-loss replacement depends, of course, on whether one uses gross or net wages in the calculation. The comparisons discussed above were based on gross wages. Different comparisons result if net pay is chosen as a standard of measurement. Currently, a worker whose average weekly wage is equal to the state-wide average weekly wage can receive 50 percent or more of his gross weekly wage loss in only 5 States. The same worker, with no dependents, will receive 50 percent or more of his "net" wage loss in 29 States. If this worker has 3 dependents, he will receive a basic benefit of 50 percent or more of his "net" wage loss in 10 States.

Recent union-management agreements which call for supplementary unemployment benefits generally provide for a supplemental benefit which when added to the regular unemployment insurance benefit will replace 65 percent of the worker's wage loss calculated on the basis of the worker's wage net of Federal taxes.

At the present time, only one State's maximum benefit is high enough to meet this measure when it is applied to either a worker with no dependents or a worker with three dependents who earns the statewide average weekly wage. Nineteen States would have to raise maximum benefits by $10 or more in order to replace 65 percent of the net wage of such a worker with no dependents, and 24 additional States could do so by raising maximum benefits by between $1 and $9. For a worker with three dependents, 37 States would have to raise their maximum by $10 or more and 7 States by between $1 and $9 in order to match this standard.

***Cost of Living and Benefits.*** The preceding discussion has emphasized —and properly so in a wage-loss system—the importance of maintaining proper relationships between benefits and wages. It is important that changes in wages be recorded so that necessary changes can be made in the provisions for weekly benefits. It has been urged, also, that changes in benefits should accord not only with changes in wages but also with changes in the cost of living, or in the Consumer Price Index of the Bureau of Labor Statistics. This comparison does not seem valid in a short-term insurance system. If, by judicious amendment of maximum benefit provisions, a proper relationship between benefits and wages can be maintained, it appears too much to ask that benefits be changed in accordance with prices as well. Benefit rights are established in accordance with the worker's more recent wages—inflated or deflated as the case may be. For some beneficiaries, in fact, wages used as a basis for benefits may already have been changed—up or down—in response to changes in the Consumer Price Index. It may be of some interest to see what the benefit will buy in 1939 or 1945 dollars, but this need not be a controlling consideration in a short-term wage-loss system.

To rule out the need for variation of benefits with average changes in consumer prices does not rule out the usefulness of frequent examination of the proportion of workers' incomes that goes for "the nondeferrable bundle." There is an important difference between increasing benefits because living costs on the average went up, and increasing benefits because beneficiaries now spend *relatively more* of their income for food and rent and other fixed costs. Fortunately, the proportion of wages that goes for nondeferrable expenses does not seem to fluctuate as much as the Consumers Price Index itself.

The basic data in this area are those collected from time to time on consumer income and expenditures as well as "objectively derived" family budgets. The latter are usually constructed for specific family types and sizes, and used as guides for computing living costs or for administering public assistance. The relating of such benefits to such data as a measure of adequacy, however, must be qualified by the knowledge that the incomes of many families of the size and type for which the budgets were constructed may not be representative of the incomes of beneficiaries. Moreover, unemployment insurance cannot provide a worker with a "modest but adequate" standard of living, as described by one type of "objective" budget, if his wages do not. Information on the cost of the different items in a budget, and of various combinations of them, are useful in an analysis of the amount of protection that benefits provide. They will help measure the extent to which benefits provide a basic minimum layer of protection, or something more or less. Also pertinent in such analysis is information on the relative importance of different sources of income at various income levels, at different ages, and among different family types and sizes. Unfortunately, "objective" family budgets are not compiled or priced very often, or on a State basis.

*Experience of Beneficiaries during Unemployment.* More directly related to benefits are data yielded by studies of beneficiaries which describe their financial experiences, particularly those that reflect the impact of unemployment. While various "objective" standards may be devised as attempts to define nondeferrable expenditures, it is also valuable to know something of the kinds and amounts of spending which workers do or do not defer when unemployed. The influence of unemployment on income and the role played by benefits during such periods seen in relation to cash available and the expenses that are met furnish another index of adequacy. Such analyses must take into consideration all the circumstances of the beneficiaries studied with respect to their family needs and responsibilities. Thus the type and size of the family take on importance as does the significance of the beneficiary's earnings to the family and whether or not other family members contribute income. Other adjustments, both financial and nonfinancial, made by the beneficiary and his family provide additional indication of how well benefits are fulfilling their objectives.

To get information of this nature requires personal and, often, lengthy interviews with beneficiaries. This is not meddling but a needed inquiry into the disposition of insurance funds, what protection they provide, and how much real security they represent. In the final analysis, no definitive answer to the question of adequacy of benefits can be approached without information of this nature. The criteria that have been discussed above all represent partial measures of benefit adequacy but, without factual information gathered on beneficiary experience during periods of unemployment, the above criteria lack some necessary substance.

In recent years, several State employment security agencies have conducted this type of beneficiary study. These studies contain some revealing information about the role played by benefits during a worker's unemployment. One general conclusion that can be drawn from these studies is that there are significant differences among the unemployment experiences of the single claimant, the claimant who is the head of a family, and the claimant who is a secondary wage earner in a family. In comparing levels of cash income and spending before and during a period of unemployment, these studies show that total monthly cash outlays for all expenses usually declined by modest amounts after the onset of unemployment in contrast with more severe declines in cash incomes. As might be expected, the decline in the income of the single claimant or of the household where the head was unemployed was considerably greater than was the case of the household with an unemployed nonhead.

The surveys clearly indicate that, during their current spell of unemployment, beneficiaries did not receive benefits which compensated for as much as 50 percent of their actual wage loss. This was partly due to the fact that not all weeks of unemployment were compensated because of delayed filing, waiting weeks, disqualifications, and so on. For single claimants and families with the chief wage earner out of work, the relatively low level of total benefits received takes on added significance when one considers that the net wage earnings of the claimant had constituted, on the average, from 75 to 100 percent of the total cash income available to the household before his unemployment. Wages of the nonhead claimant made up a much smaller proportion of the family's income before unemployment.

Looking at how far benefits went in covering total expenses and nondeferrable expenses[1] during unemployment, the various surveys indicate that, on the average, the weekly benefit amount paid to single beneficiaries

---

[1] As used in this analysis, nondeferrable expenses included expenditures for the following items: food, shelter, utilities and medical care. These items do not represent a recommended nondeferrable bundle but rather appear to be the minimum group of expense items that most would agree should be included.

constituted between 57 and 73 percent of their total weekly expenses and was enough to cover, or more than cover, their nondeferrable expenses. Somewhat by contrast, the average weekly benefit amount paid to heads of households covered between 38 and 48 percent of their total weekly expenses and between 60 and 78 percent of their nondeferrable expenses. Thus, current benefit levels appear to be more nearly adequate in terms of the expenditures of single claimants than those of the families with unemployed heads of households. Similar comparisons for claimants who were nonheads of their households show a much smaller proportion of expenses covered by the weekly benefit amount. However, it must be remembered that the family unit of the nonheads have significant sources of cash income, other than benefit payments, during unemployment.

# 26. DISQUALIFICATION PROVISIONS IN STATE UNEMPLOYMENT INSURANCE LAWS

*Comparison of State Unemployment Insurance Laws as of January 1, 1958, Department of Labor, 1958.*

THE FEDERAL ACTS contain no requirements concerning eligibility and disqualification provisions excepting the labor standard provision. Each State establishes its requirements which an unemployed worker must meet to receive unemployment insurance. All State laws require that a claimant, to receive benefits, must be able to work and must be available for work, i.e., he must be in the labor force. He also must be free from disqualification for such acts as voluntary leaving without good cause, discharge for misconduct connected with the work, and refusal of suitable work. These eligibility and disqualification provisions delineate the risk which the laws cover; the able-and-available tests as positive conditions for the receipt of benefits week by week and the disqualifications as a negative expression of conditions under which benefits are denied. The purpose of these provisions is to limit payments to workers unemployed primarily as a result of economic causes. The eligibility and disqualification provisions apply only to claimants who meet the qualifying wage and employment requirements.

In all States, claimants who are held ineligible for benefits because of inability to work, unavailability for work, or disqualification are entitled to notice of determination and to an appeal from the determination.

**Ability to Work**

The variations from State to State in the language setting forth the requirements concerning ability to work are minor. The addition of the words "physically able" or "mentally and physically able" in a few State laws has had no significant influence on the benefit decisions under the State laws. One evidence of ability to work is the filing of claims and registration for work at a public employment office, required under all State laws.

**Availability for Work**

Availability for work as well as ability to work is evidenced by registration for work at a local employment office. Nonavailability may be evidenced by refusal of work, offered by the employment service or by a former employer, which the unemployment insurance officials consider suitable for the claimant. In addition, 27 State laws require that a claimant must be actively seeking work or making a reasonable effort to obtain work. . . .

**Disqualification from Benefits**

The major causes of disqualification from benefits are voluntary separation from work, discharge for misconduct, refusal of suitable work, and unemployment due to a labor dispute. In all States disqualification results in at least a postponement of benefits for one or more weeks in addition to any required waiting period; in some States it involves also a cancellation of benefit rights or a reduction of benefits otherwise payable. Unlike the status of unavailability for work or inability to work, which is terminated as soon as the condition changes, disqualification means that benefits are denied for a definite period, specified in the law, or set by the administrative agency within limits specified in the law, or for the duration of the period of unemployment; frequently the disqualification lasts for the duration of the benefit year, or longer.

The disqualification period is usually for the week of the disqualifying act and a specified number of consecutive calendar weeks following. . . . The theory of a specified period of disqualification is that, after a time, the reason for a worker's continued unemployment is more the general condition of the labor market than his disqualifying act. The time for which the disqualifying act is considered the reason for a worker's unemployment varies among the States and among the causes of disqualification. It varies from 3 weeks . . . in New Hampshire to 1–24 weeks . . . in Texas. In two States the maximum disqualification period for one or more causes may be as long as the maximum duration of benefits. A number of States have a different theory for the period of disqualification. They disqualify for the duration of the unemployment or longer, by requiring a specified amount of work or wages to requalify or by canceling a disqualified worker's wage credits. . . .

Twenty States follow the same pattern for disqualifications for voluntary leaving, discharge for misconduct, and refusal of suitable work. In States with provisions of different severity for the different causes, misconduct is most often the cause with the heaviest penalty; refusal of suitable work ranks second; and voluntary leaving, third.

The provisions for postponement of benefits and cancellation of benefits must be considered together to understand the full effect of disqualification. Disqualification for the duration of the unemployment may be a slight or a severe penalty for an individual claimant, depending on the duration of his unemployment; that, in turn, depends largely on the general condition of the labor market. . . .

## Disqualification for Voluntarily Leaving Work

In a system of benefits to compensate in part for wage loss due to lack of work, voluntarily leaving work without good cause is an obvious reason for disqualification from benefits. All States have such a disqualification provision.

*Period of Disqualification.* In 15 States the period of disqualification for voluntary leaving is a specified number of weeks; in 22 States, a variable number of weeks; in 16 States, for the duration of the unemployment or longer.

The disqualification imposed for voluntary leaving without good cause may be summarized as follows:

| Provision | | Number of States |
|---|---|---|
| All States | .... | 51 |
| No reduction of benefit rights | 33 | .... |
| Reduction of benefit rights | 18 | .... |
| Maximum period of 6 weeks or less | .... | 14 |
| No reduction of benefit rights | 10 | .... |
| Reduction of benefit rights | 4 | .... |
| Maximum period of more than 6 weeks | .... | 21 |
| No reduction of benefit rights | 11 | .... |
| Reduction of benefit rights | 10 | .... |
| Disqualification for the duration of unemployment or longer | .... | 16 |
| No reduction of benefit rights | 12 | .... |
| Reduction of benefit rights | 4 | .... |

## Discharge for Misconduct Connected with the Work

The provisions for disqualification for discharge for misconduct follow a pattern similar but not identical to that for voluntary leaving. There is more tendency to provide disqualification for a variable number of weeks "according to the seriousness of the misconduct." In addition, 17 States provide for heavier disqualification in the case of discharge for a dishonest or criminal act or other aggravated misconduct.

*Period of Disqualification.* Twenty-eight States have a variable disqualification for discharge for misconduct. . . .

The disqualifications imposed for discharge for misconduct and discharge for aggravated misconduct are summarized below:

|  | Number of States with specified provision for— | |
| --- | --- | --- |
| Provision | Misconduct | Aggravated misconduct |
| All States......................................... | .... 51 | .... 17 |
| With no reduction of benefit rights................. | 33 .... | 5 ..... |
| With reduction of benefit rights.................... | 18 .... | 12 ..... |
| Maximum period 6 weeks or less..................... | .... 11 | .... 0 |
| With no reduction of benefit rights................. | 8 .... | 0 ..... |
| With reduction of benefit rights.................... | 3 .... | 0 ..... |
| Maximum period limited but over 6 weeks............ | .... 30 | .... 2 |
| With no reduction of benefit rights................. | 17 .... | 1 ..... |
| With reduction of benefit rights.................... | 13 .... | 1 ..... |
| Disqualification for the duration of unemployment or longer........................................... | .... 10 | 15 |
| With no reduction of benefit rights................. | 8 .... | 4 ..... |
| With reduction of benefit rights.................... | 2 .... | 11 ..... |

## Disqualification for a Refusal of Suitable Work

Disqualification for a refusal of work is provided in all State laws with diverse provisions concerning the extent of the disqualification imposed, smaller differences in the factors to be considered in determining whether work is suitable or the worker has good cause for refusing it, and practically identical statements concerning the conditions under which "new work" may be refused without disqualification. To protect labor standards the Federal Unemployment Tax Act provides that no State law will be approved, so that employers may credit their State contributions against the Federal tax, unless the State law provides that:

Compensation shall not be denied in such State to any otherwise eligible individual for refusing to accept new work under any of the following conditions: (A) If the position offered is vacant due directly to a strike, lockout, or other labor dispute; (B) if the wages, hours, or other conditions of the work offered are substantially less favorable to the individual than those prevailing for similar work in the locality; (C) if as a condition of being employed the individual would be required to join a company union or to resign from or refrain from joining any bona fide labor organization.

*Criteria for Suitable Work.* In addition to these mandatory minimum standards, most State laws list certain criteria by which the suitability of a work offer is to be tested. The usual criteria are the degree of risk to a claimant's health, safety, and morals; his physical fitness and prior training, experience, and earnings; the length of his unemployment and his prospects for securing local work in his customary occupation; and the distance of the available work from his residence. . . .

The disqualifications imposed for refusal of suitable work are summarized below:

| Provision | Number of States | |
|---|---:|---:|
| All States........................................ | .... | 51 |
| No reduction of benefit rights............................. | 36 | ..... |
| Reduction of benefit rights................................ | 15 | ..... |
| Maximum period of 6 weeks or less......................... | .... | 15 |
| No reduction of benefit rights............................. | 12 | ..... |
| Reduction of benefit rights................................ | 3 | ..... |
| Maximum period of more than 6 weeks...................... | .... | 22 |
| No reduction of benefit rights............................. | 14 | ..... |
| Reduction of benefit rights................................ | 8 | ..... |
| Disqualification for the duration of unemployment or longer........... | .... | 14 |
| No reduction of benefit rights............................. | 10 | ..... |
| Reduction of benefit rights................................ | 4 | ..... |

## Labor Disputes

The disqualifications for unemployment due to labor disputes differ considerably from those for voluntary leaving, discharge for misconduct, and refusal of suitable work.

*Definition of Labor Dispute.* The laws differ in the use of terms— for example, labor dispute, trade dispute, strike, and strike and lockout. Nine States exclude lockouts, presumably to avoid penalizing workers for the employer's action; four States exclude disputes due to the employer's failure to conform to the provisions of a labor contract, and five States, those due to failure to conform to any law of the United States or the State on such matters as wages, hours, working conditions, or collective bargaining, or disputes where the employees are protesting substandard working conditions.

*Location of the Dispute.* Usually a worker is not disqualified unless the labor dispute is in the establishment in which he was last employed. . . .

*Period of Disqualification.* In 49 States, labor-dispute disqualifications last, in general, as long as the labor dispute. In 34 of these States the period of disqualification ends whenever the "stoppage of work because of a labor dispute" comes to an end or the stoppage ceases to be due to the labor dispute. In 12 States, disqualifications last while the labor dispute is in "active progress," and in Arizona and Connecticut, while the workers' unemployment is due to a labor dispute. A few State laws allow individuals to terminate a disqualification by showing that the labor dispute (or the stoppage of work) is no longer the cause of their unemployment. Thus the Missouri law specifies that bona fide employment of the claimant for at least the major part of each of 2 weeks will terminate the disqualification and the New Hampshire law, that the disqualification will terminate 2 weeks after the dispute is ended even though the stoppage of work continues. In contrast, the Ohio law extends the disqualification for a reasonable period of time necessary for the establishment to resume normal operations. Under the Massachusetts law a claimant may receive benefits if, during a stoppage of work due to a labor dispute, he obtains employment with another employer and earns wages of at least $500 (the amount required to qualify); however, base-period wages earned with the employer involved in the dispute cannot be used for benefit payments while the stoppage of work continues.

Only two States provide for a definite period of disqualification. In New York a worker who lost his employment because of a strike or lockout in the establishment where he was employed can accumulate "effective days" after the expiration of 7 weeks and the waiting period, or earlier if the controversy is terminated earlier. In Rhode Island a worker who became unemployed because of a strike in the establishment in which he was employed is entitled to benefits for unemployment which continues after a 6-week disqualification period and a 1-week waiting period.

*Exclusion of Individual Workers.* The California law applies the disqualification only to individuals who left work because of the dispute. In Texas the unemployment must be due to the claimant's stoppage of work. Kentucky, Minnesota, Ohio, Rhode Island, and Wisconsin limit the disqualification to workers whom the dispute caused to lose or leave their employment. Utah applies a disqualification only in case of a strike involving a claimant's grade, class, or group of workers if one of the workers in the grade, class, or group fomented or was a party to the strike; if the employer or his agent and any of his workers or their agents conspired to foment the strike, no disqualification is applied. Minnesota provides specifically that an individual is not disqualified if he is dismissed during negotiations prior to a strike. The other States provide that individual workers are excluded if they and others of the same grade or class are not participating in the dispute (42 States), financing it (31 States), or directly interested in it (41 States). A few States omit "others of the same grade or class." Only Alabama, Delaware, and New York have no "escape clause."

## Disqualification of Special Groups

Under all State laws, students who are not available for work while attending school, women who are unable to work because of pregnancy, and women who quit their jobs because of marital obligations which make them unavailable for work would not qualify for benefits under the regular provisions concerning ability to work and availability for work. However, 35 States make special mention of pregnant women or married women or both, and most of them restrict benefits more than under the usual disqualification provisions. Sixteen States have special provisions concerning the benefit rights of students. New York has a general provision that any claimant who leaves work voluntarily under circumstances which show a bona fide withdrawal (temporary or permanent) from the labor market is disqualified until he presents certification of a bona fide return to the labor market. . . .

### Disqualification for Fraudulent Misrepresentation to Obtain Benefits

Forty-seven States have special disqualifications covering fraudulent misrepresentation to obtain or increase benefits. These disqualifications from benefits are in addition to the provisions for the repayment of benefits paid as the result of fraudulent claims or their deduction from potential future benefits and the provisions of fines and/or imprisonment for willfully or intentionally misrepresenting or concealing facts concerning employment and earnings which are material to a determination concerning the individual's entitlement to benefits.

***Recovery Provisions.*** All State laws contain some provision for the recovery, by the State agency, of benefits paid as the result of fraud on the part of the recipient.

# 27. OBJECTIVES AND APPRAISAL OF EXPERIENCE RATING

CLINTON SPIVEY, *Experience Rating in Unemployment Compensation*, 1958.

EXPERIENCE RATING has four principal objectives and advantages which make the case for its use in the unemployment insurance program. If these four major objectives can be proved desirable, this would give satisfactory evidence that experience rating as a method of setting unemployment compensation tax rates is justifiable in our present system. At this time the objectives will be merely described to give the background necessary for the study.

### Proper Financing of the Program

A very important objective of experience rating is the provision of funds adequate for the operation of the program without tying up unnecessarily large sums in reserves. This concept of replenishment, as presently practiced, aims at securing an amount of contributions each year which will replenish the average annual amount of benefits paid out in the past three years. A three-year period is used because the Federal law states that an employer's rate must be assigned on the basis of not less than three years' experience with unemployment or with other factors directly related to the risk of unemployment. This three-year experience requirement tends to level the peaks and valleys of replenishment costs.

### Employer Incentive to Stabilize Employment

At the inception of the unemployment compensation system stabilization of employment was considered a primary objective. The experience of several large firms in regularizing employment helped to prepare the way. Elizabeth Brandeis, writing at this time, said:

A satisfactory program for enhancing security against unemployment must include both an attempt to reduce the hazard to its smallest possible proportions, and provision for compensating the unemployed that remain.

Experience rating is thus viewed as a preventive measure resting on the assumption that employers have a substantial degree of control over unemployment and that differential rates will serve as an effective incentive for employers to stabilize their operations. The proponents contend that the employer, responding to the incentive of the avoidance of a higher tax or the reward of a lower tax and being able, within limits, to control the volume and duration of his employment, will manage his business in such a manner as to minimize unemployment of his workmen. This objective is undeniably a desirable one. The soundness of this objective, however, rests on the extent to which the individual employer can regularize his employment.

As early as 1939, with unemployment compensation in effect only four years, it was thought that experience rating would offer very little stimulation to individual employers to counteract the effect of technological and cyclical forces. Employers have other and more powerful incentives, such as higher profits, to stabilize employment whenever possible. With the range in tax rates becoming increasingly narrow in recent years and with the added popularity of non-charging provisions, the strength of the experience rating incentive has been increasingly challenged.

Where individual firms have the ability to decrease the irregularity of employment, the gains achieved may be at the expense of the stability of other employers. For example, the action of an employer in diversifying his products to fill in slack seasons may cause some other employer to lay off workers because part of his market has disappeared.

### Equitable Distribution of Premium Costs

A basic principle of the American economic system is that the special costs inherent in the production of a given product should be included in the price of that product instead of being partially subsidized by other products which compete in the market place for the consumer's dollar. Advocates of existing law maintain that experience rating provides a system of cost accounting which allows the dollar value of the wage loss actually compensated to be charged to the responsible industries and employers through the devise of contribution rate differentials. That experience rating fulfills this principle of cost distribution is by no means universally accepted.

The economic desirability of allocating costs by experience rating has been questioned. Opponents contend that unemployment is a general social problem and the costs thereof should be shared on a joint basis rather than having some industries penalized and other inherently stable industries rewarded. According to this view, it is not wise social fiscal policy to put the burden of the unemployment taxes on industries characterized by unemployment not under their control.

### Achievement of a More Stable Economy

Both the financial aspect and the benefit aspects of unemployment compensation must be taken into consideration in evaluating the ability of experience rating to help stabilize the economy. Regarding the financial aspects, it has been asserted that most unemployment insurance plans tend to accentuate business cycles. The tax rates are reduced during periods of high employment when such taxes are most easily paid and are increased during periods of unemployment when they can be least afforded. Since this argument relates not to experience rating itself but rather to particular formulas used to vary rates, efforts will be made to determine which, if any, of the five experience rating formulas are cyclical and to what degree.

Looking at the benefit aspects, payment of unemployment insurance helps to maintain purchasing power in periods of business decline. This element of purchasing power is both important and timely, but has definite limits. It is timely because unemployment compensation payments are made early, soon after unemployment begins. By avoiding the forced liquidation of workers' assets, such as homes, automobiles, and furniture, benefit payments help prevent the aggravation of a business downturn. Various segments of retail business may, therefore, be maintained at a level substantially higher than would be possible without unemployment insurance.

## TYPES OF FORMULAS FOR EXPERIENCE RATING

Although experience rating has been vigorously opposed both on theoretical and practical grounds over the years, it has flourished and grown. All state laws, except that of Alaska, have in effect some system of experience rating by which individual employer's contribution rates are varied from the standard rate. State experience-rating provisions have developed on the basis of the additional-credit provisions of the Social Security Act. Under the Federal standards no reduction from the standard rate can be granted to any employer "except on the basis of his (or their) experience with respect to unemployment or other factors bearing a direct relation to unemployment risk. . . ."

While five different systems of experience ratings are in use by the states, each having its own peculiar effect on the actual rates established for various employers, the structural form of all systems follows a similar pattern. There are, however, marked differences. For example, risk may be measured by benefits paid to eligible workers, wages paid to workers in covered industries, payroll decline, or combinations of these or other factors.

## Reserve Ratio Formula

The reserve ratio was the earliest of the experience-rating formulas and is still by far the most popular. It is used in 32 pooled-fund states and one reserve-account state. Although the various ratio plans differ in detail, they all have one common feature—a separate account maintained for each employer. On each employer's record is entered the amount of his payroll, his contributions, and the benefits paid to his workers. The benefits are subtracted from the contributions and the resulting balance is divided by the payroll to determine the size of the balance in terms of the potential liability for benefits inherent in wage payments. Mathematically, the basic reserve ratio formula may be expressed as follows:

$$\text{Reserve percentage} = \frac{\text{Cumulative contributions} - \text{Cumulative benefits}}{\text{Annual taxable payroll}}$$

The balance carried forward each year under the reserve ratio formula is ordinarily the difference between the employer's total contributions and the total benefits received by his workers since the law became effective. In the District of Columbia, Idaho, and Louisiana calculations of contributions and benefits are limited to the last five years if that works to an employer's advantage. Michigan law excludes the year 1938 and a specific portion of benefits for the year ending September 30, 1946.

The employer must accumulate and maintain a specified reserve percentage before his rate is reduced. Rates are then assigned according to a schedule. The higher the ratio of the reserve to the employer's taxable payroll, the lower will be his rate. The formula is designed to make sure that no employer will be granted a rate reduction unless over the years he contributes more to the fund than his workers draw in benefits. As the total funds available for benefits have increased, the rates for a given reserve have been decreased. In 21 of the 33 states using the reserve ratio plan, provision has been made for higher rates should the state funds decrease.

## Benefit-Ratio Formula

Benefit-ratio systems also use benefit payments as the measure of experience, but contributions are eliminated from the formula. Benefits are related directly to payrolls. The ratio of payments to payrolls is the index for rate variation. The five states that have adopted the benefit-ratio formula all use a three-year period for the measurement of risk. The formula for the benefit ratio is:

$$\text{Benefit ratio} = \frac{\text{Benefits (last three years)}}{\text{Taxable payrolls (last three years)}}$$

The ratio in effect shows the per-dollar cost of benefit payments for each employer over the past three years. Under this plan the ratio varies directly with the degree of risk of unemployment; a high benefit ratio is the equivalent of a high degree of risk. The theory is that if each employer pays a rate which approximates his benefit ratio, the program will be adequately financed.

The contribution rates actually assigned employers are usually higher than the ratio of the benefits charged to the taxable payroll during the experience period. This difference occurs because the rates are further varied according to the level of the state fund in terms of dollar amounts or of a proportion of payrolls.

### Benefit-Wage-Ratio Formula

Six states use the benefit-wage-ratio as a measure of experience. It is radically different from all the other plans. It makes no attempt to measure all benefits paid to the workers of individual employers. The relative experience of employers is measured by the number of separations of workers which result in benefit payments. The duration of their benefits is not a factor. The number of separations is weighted by the wages earned by the workers during each base-period and is recorded on each employer's experience-rating record as "benefit wages." In some states a portion of these benefit wages is not charged if the employer rehires the claimant prior to the exhaustion of his benefits. The benefit-wage ratio is equal to the total of such charges divided by the employer's total taxable wages. Mathematically:

$$\text{Benefit-wage-ratio} = \frac{\text{Benefit wages (last three years)}}{\text{Total taxable wages (last three years)}}$$

The assignment of rates in the benefit-wage-ratio states is considerably more complicated than in either the reserve-ratio states or the benefit-ratio states. First, a "a state experience factor" is computed, which is equal to the ratio of total benefit payments in the state during the experience period to total benefit wages. In other words, the workers, who drew benefits, receive a certain amount of benefits for every dollar of benefit wages paid, and the same amount of taxes per dollar of benefit wages is needed to replenish the fund. The total amount to be raised is distributed among employers in accordance with their benefit-wage ratios; the higher the ratio, the higher the rate.

Computation of the employer's rate consists of multiplying his benefit-wage ratio by the state experience factor. (Usually, the actual computation does not need to be carried out. The laws contain tables giving rate schedules for each of a series of state experience factors.) The complete formula for the determination of an individual employer's ratio may thus be expressed as follows:

$$\text{Rate} = \frac{\text{State total benefits}}{\text{State benefit wages}} \times \frac{\text{Employer's benefit wages}}{\text{Employer's total taxable wages}}$$

Only one separation per beneficiary per benefit year is recorded for any one employer. There is considerable variation among states as to when the employer's account is charged. In Alabama and Oklahoma the charge is made at the time of the second week of benefit payments. In Illinois and Virginia no charge is made until the benefits paid equal three times the base period weekly wage. Texas charges the employer's account when benefits equal one week's wages.

### Compensable Separations Formula

In essence, the compensable separations formula used by only one state, Connecticut, is very much the same as the benefit-wage-ratio formula. The maximum charge for any employee in any one period of unemployment is incurred as soon as he has collected any benefits at all, although additional charges are made for later spells of unemployment. The major difference between the Connecticut formula and the benefit-wage-ratio formula is that the measure of the charge to the employer is the worker's weekly benefit rate instead of his base period wages.

The schedule of unemployment insurance tax rates in Connecticut for 1955 ranged from 0.5 percent for employers with the best employment experience to 2.7 percent for employers with the poorest experience and for employers not yet eligible for reduced rates.

The merit-rating provisions of the unemployment compensation law outline in detail the method by which rates are determined. A merit-rating index is computed for each employer who has been liable for contributions for the three fiscal years immediately preceding the computation of rates and who is not delinquent in contributions. This index is computed by dividing each employer's total payroll during the experience period by all compensable separations charged against his account less credits. It may be expressed by the following formula:

$$\text{Merit-rating index} = \frac{\text{Taxable payroll during experience period}}{\text{Compensable separations charged} - \text{Merit-rating credits}}$$

Generally speaking, an employer's taxable payroll is the sum of wages paid his employees up to $3,000 a year each for work subject to the law. If an individual leaves his job and receives unemployment compensation benefits within four weeks, a compensable separation is charged to his employer's account. Only the first week for which benefits have been paid in a period of unemployment is chargeable. The charge is the amount of the total weekly benefit rate of the individual, whether the claimant receives total or partial benefits for the week. If the employer rehires an individual within seven weeks after benefit payments commence, he is entitled to a credit against the charge in accordance with a predetermined table.

Each employer can verify the amount of his payroll used in the computation by totaling the taxable payroll as reported on his quarterly contribution returns covering this period. A summary of charges is mailed to each employer just prior to the computation of the indexes.

## Payroll Variation Plan

Seven states, including New York, which is classified under the reserve ratio, employ some form of payroll decline system. These plans are different from all others in that they accept as the measure of unemployment risk a factor entirely removed from benefit payments. Under these plans an employer's experience with unemployment is determined by measuring the declines in his total payroll, either quarterly or annually, on the assumption that total payrolls reflect the employer's ability or inability to provide employment. Where annual declines are used, the effect of seasonal and other types of intermittent unemployment is ignored. The declines are expressed as a percentage of payrolls so that the experience of employers with large and small payrolls may be compared. If an employer's payroll shows no decrease or only a small percentage decrease over a given period, he will be eligible for the largest proportional tax reductions.

Mississippi and Washington measure the stability of the last three years' annual payrolls on the theory that over a period of time the greatest drains on the fund result from declines in general business activity. Rhode Island measures the stability of payrolls each quarter over a three- to five-year period. These changes reflect not only changes in general business activity but also seasonal or irregular declines in employment.

\* \* \* \* \*

## STABILIZATION OF EMPLOYMENT

A definition of stabilized employment is needed before one can evaluate the effects of experience rating on unemployment. Depending on the particular formula used there are many devices for obtaining stability in terms of a small amount of benefits chargeable to a particular employer without the employer having created a single new job or having reduced the total volume of unemployment one iota.

Does stabilization mean the employment of the same work force throughout the year or simply the employment of the same sized work force? Can stabilization be measured by employment statistics alone or should it be considered in terms of man-hours or labor turnover?

A tentative definition of stabilization would be "the maintenance of a labor force of approximately the same size for approximately the same number of hours per week over a particular period." Such a definition would rule out all extreme work spreading, but would allow some flexibility of hours in order to avoid minor fluctuations in employment. Dovetailing of employment between two or more firms would have to be excluded, illustrating the difficulties of a rigid definition.

In many ways "stabilization" devices increase the hazards of unemployment for some workers. Many employers are encouraged to spread work too thin and are discouraged from adding workers for temporary jobs lest they injure their experience rating. Many of the "stabilization" devices are practicable only for large companies which can produce for stock or can shift workers to various jobs. There is no social gain if when some employers avoid benefit payments to their employees they increase the insecurity of employment for workers outside their plant.

The four major causes of unemployment have been described as (1) frictional, (2) seasonal, (3) cyclical, and (4) technological. It is becoming more and more evident that cyclical and technological changes are the chief causes of mass unemployment. Up to the present time the United States has not contemplated fully insuring workers against either of these hazards. Benefits can, of course, be drawn for such causes, but since such unemployment extends over a long period of time and benefit payments are of relatively short duration the worker is not fully covered. Unemployment compensation has been designed to operate primarily in the fields of frictional unemployment and seasonal variation.

## STABILITY OF THE ECONOMY

The ability of experience rating to achieve a more stable economy has been studied from its *benefit* and *financial aspects*. The benefits of the unemployment insurance program have become an important factor in offsetting the unfavorable cumulative effects of unemployment on consumer spending. Although experience rating has no connection with benefit payment per se, it does have an indirect relationship. Unemployment compensation funds would be larger were it not for experience rating. If the funds were larger there is every reason to believe that benefits would be increased. For the period 1938 to 1955 inclusive, benefit disbursement under state unemployment insurance laws was $14.5 billion. Hundreds of thousands of wage earners throughout the United States have participated as a matter of right in the distribution of this vast sum of money.

The hundreds of thousands of workers who have participated in the program have not been the sole beneficiaries. The distribution of over $14 billion in benefits has, without a doubt, had far-reaching effects in individual states and in local communities. Money has been put into circulation and the purchasing power of communities has been stabilized to the benefit of industry and trade. It has been said that the distribution of this vast sum has not had any apparent effect upon the relief rolls. Yet, had there been no unemployment compensation, the administrators of the program agree, each state would have had to provide through taxation much larger sums for relief.

Although benefits are inadequate in light of the present take-home pay, the value of unemployment compensation in helping achieve a more stable economy should not be underestimated. More significant than benefit payments in judging the influence of experience rating on the stability of the economy are the financing aspects of unemployment compensation. The evidence gathered in this study indicates that under each existing system the employer may find himself burdened with a high tax rate during periods when he is least able to afford it. When profits are high and deflationary measures are called for, he may contribute at the minimum rate allowed by law. Furthermore, the $3,000 limitation on taxable payrolls accentuates this cyclical affect since taxable payrolls are a much lower percentage of total payrolls during good periods than during depressions. There appears little evidence that the existing experience-rating systems are capable of producing countercyclical tax effects.

## PROPER FINANCING OF THE PROGRAM

Proper financing of the unemployment compensation program is considered to be one of the important objectives of experience rating. The advocates of experience rating claim that without it the various state funds would today contain two or three times the amount presently held. They feel reserves of this size would be too large.

There is found to be a substantial variation in the degree of adequacy of state funds. Some reserves are relatively so small that they could be quickly used up in the event of a sharp and continuing upturn in the volume of unemployment. Although only two states have encountered major difficulty in raising funds sufficient to pay their benefit liability, the success of the program, such as it is, can undoubtedly be attributed more to the low levels of unemployment over the past twenty years than to any inherent adequacy in the financing structure of the state systems.

## EQUITABLE ALLOCATION OF COSTS

The proponents of experience rating also justify the system as a means of allocating equitably the costs of unemployment. Their argument is that the cost of unemployment, properly considered, is a part of the cost of producing goods and services.

This allocation of the costs of unemployment benefits among the consumers of goods and services produced by the taxed enterprises represents an incomplete analysis of the shifting process. The burden of a payroll tax may be borne by the employer who originally pays it; it may be shifted forward to the consumers of the goods and services of the taxed industries; or it may be shifted backward to the workers of the taxed industries. To trace the incidence is an extremely complicated task. As an illustration of this complexity take just a few of the issues involved in backward shifting. The proportion of wages to total costs, as well as the demand and supply conditions for labor, vary from one industry to another, from employer to employer, and from one geographic area to another.

There is a basic inconsistency between two of the arguments advanced for experience rating. If experience rating is to allocate costs it must do so through increased prices to consumers. A perfect allocation would result in the complete unloading of the tax by employers. On the other hand, if the payroll tax serves as an incentive for stabilization then the employer is assumed to bear the tax. If the employer bears the burden he cannot shift it: if he shifts it he cannot bear it. Similarly, if the payroll tax is shifted to the workers then there is no basis for maintaining that the tax would provide an incentive to stabilize employment. The incentive for employment stabilization may be through profits rather than by way of the tax burden. Assuming the tax is shifted those paying less than the maximum rate get larger profits.

The wisdom of placing the burden of the unemployment taxes on industries characterized by unemployment not within their control has been questioned. A majority of the Committee on Experience Rating of the Interstate Conference of Employment Security Agencies in 1940 stated:

> We must conclude there exists in our present economic pattern wide variation in the stability or regularity of employment due to forces beyond the control of the individual employer or even of groups of employers. The highest degree of instability exists in the construction industry, in mining, and in the capital goods or durable goods industries. These are what might be termed the corner stones of the business and employment structure. It follows that a penalty imposed on the basic industries—principally because of uncontrollable factors—will have adverse effects on the whole national economy. Such a tax is clearly against national policy.

Those opposed to experience rating see no element of fairness in the system's cost allocation. They view the differential tax as a highly discriminatory tax.

## EMPLOYER INTEREST IN PROPER ADMINISTRATION

Experience rating adds markedly to the administrative expense of unemployment compensation. Even in its simplest form there is a considerable volume of record keeping that serves no function other than the useless and even harmful one of tax differentials.

The proponents of experience rating feel that despite complications, the promotion of an active employer interest in the program justifies the system. With the employer's desire to reduce costs by protesting the payment of improper claims, a more effective policing of the system by the state administrative officials is achieved. Without experience rating, the advocates say, the claimant may freely make allegations as to the reasons for his separation without much fear of the discovery of wrongful testimony. Effective employer interest aids in preserving benefit funds for those entitled to them and helps to insure that those not entitled do not receive them.

The National Association of Manufacturers has collected data on contested claims which they feel clearly reveal that employers have not tried to delay or prevent the payment of proper claims. They offer much evidence, on the other hand, that employer interest in the system has resulted in the denial of many unjustified claims which might otherwise have been paid.

That experience rating promotes an active employer interest is certainly not denied by its opponents. They feel that there is an over-zealous interest which shifts the emphasis of the employer from trying to prevent unemployment to trying to avoid payment of benefits by one or another of the following means:

1. Work-spreading.
2. Hiring ineligible workers such as students or workers with little or no prior wage credits.
3. Laying-off the workers with the lowest accumulation of wage credits.
4. Hiring or laying-off of workers at such times as will prevent the paying of partial benefits.

Each state law contains a set of disqualification provisions which differ in their content and phraseology. Experience rating has had an influence in this area since an employer's tax rate is increased or decreased according to his experience with unemployment. Regardless of whether the payroll tax is shifted each employer acts as though he were paying the tax and were responsible for the unemployment being compensated. Consequently, some employers believe that unemployment should not be compensated if it involves no fault of the employer.

In April, 1955 the Secretary of Labor issued a statement of the major objectives of Federal policy relating to the Federal-state employment security program. He said it was Federal policy

. . . to limit the unemployment to be compensated to that due to lack of work, by requiring claimants to be able to work and available for suitable work and by temporarily disqualifying claimants who leave work voluntarily without good cause, who are discharged for misconduct connected with their work, who refuse suitable work without good cause, or who are unemployed because of direct participation in a stoppage of work due to a labor dispute at the establishment at which they were last employed, but without rigid requirements and harsh penalties.

Such a policy does not require an active search for work irrespective of circumstances; nor does it limit unemployment due to good cause connected with the employer or the employment. When there is a question of disqualification, benefits are postponed for a specified period during which the cause of the claimant's unemployment is considered.

## SUMMARY

Public interest in state unemployment compensation laws is clearly increasing. Such laws vitally affect the lives of millions of American citizens, the operation of American industry, and the well-being of every community. There is bound to be increasing public concern with the provisions and administration of each state unemployment compensation law, whether or not it provides for employer experience rating.

There has already been some evidence of public interest. The question of whether major league baseball players should receive unemployment benefits has made front-page headlines and provoked editorial comment. Fraudulent claims, the payment of benefits during labor disputes, and the effect of benefits on the relief load have been the subject of extended public discussion during the past few years. There are other factors besides experience rating to stimulate the interest which many contend is needed for a more efficient administration of the state program.

If unemployment compensation is to remain on a state basis it is essential that some provision be made to permit states to limit tax collections to the amount necessary to support their benefit liabilities. At the present time the only method by which states can limit their collections is by experience rating. This study indicates experience rating is in many instances unsound in principle and almost impossible of equitable administration. The net effect of experience rating is inequitable and erratic tax reductions. It is suggested that states be permitted to limit their collections by flat rate (or horizontal) reductions, which would apply to all employers alike. A flat rate imposed on payrolls automatically results in a high income to the unemployment fund during high employment levels and in a reduced income when payrolls are at a low level. When both payrolls and individual employer rates vary from year to year, automatic adjustment is more difficult of attainment.

Although this study indicates existing laws have fallen short of their goal in many respects, if for no other reason than political acceptability, experience rating will be continued. Within this framework of political realism consideration might well be given to the appropriateness of revising the requirements in the Federal law so that states may be given greater freedom in selecting the type of experience system. A simple requirement might be adopted which would provide that after a state's reserve had reached a certain size in relation to payrolls, say one or one and one-half percent of the total payroll for the last three years, the state could reduce rates by whatever system of experience rating it might choose or by flat reductions. Conversely, if the reserve dropped below the specified requirement the state would increase its rates, or if it so chose, obtain a loan from a Federal pool.

# 28. THE PROBLEM OF ABUSE IN UNEMPLOYMENT BENEFITS

Joseph M. Becker, *The Problem of Abuse in Unemployment Benefits—A Study of Limits,* Columbia University Press, 1955.

At the end of an investigation like this, one would like to be able to say: (1) The extent of abuse was precisely so and so. (2) Therefore the provisions of the law should be (liberalized or tightened) precisely thus and so. The reader . . . knows that such precise conclusions are still out of reach.

The first must always be somewhat out of reach because the problem of abuse is in part qualitative, as explained before. It is more out of reach than it need be, because where the problem is quantitative the data which would permit exact measurement are often lacking. . . .

The second is out of reach for an additional reason. The conclusion that any given provision of the law is desirable or undesirable must rest logically on a consideration of all the advantages and disadvantages of that provision. The present investigation was concerned only with possible disadvantages, and not with all of those. Even if data on improper payments were complete, one could not immediately draw conclusions concerning the desirability or undesirability of the law under which the payments were made. Arriving at the first conclusion is a necessary, but not a sufficient, condition for arriving at the second. So obvious a point would not need to be made if it were not so often overlooked in practice.

Hence . . . we can reach only general and tentative conclusions as regards both the amount of abuse and the desirability of changing the law. . . .

\* \* \* \* \*

## FAVORABLE EVIDENCE AND CONCLUSIONS

Favorable evidence is evidence for proper payments, and hence is an indirect measure of improper payments. The latter cannot be greater than what remains after the subtraction of proper from total payments. Such indirect measurement is needed to supplement the attempts at direct measurement. The data produced by the latter are so fragmentary that they leave much room for judgment. The favorable evidence exercises a control on that judgment. . . .

The favorable evidence produced . . . will impress different readers differently. It will probably suffice for most of them to conclude that even in the reconversion period the system as such was not discredited. In this worst of periods abuse was not great enough to constitute a serious indictment of the whole system. The most fervent friends of the system may consider that the favorable evidence suffices to prove that a program on the lines of the Kilgore bill would have worked satisfactorily. Less fervent friends may consider that it at least proves there was no necessity for suspending all benefits temporarily, as the extreme opponents of the bill suggested. Some readers will not find the evidence sufficient even for the latter conclusion.

Whether one finds the favorable evidence sufficient for coming to some conclusion depends very much on what advantages one sees in a system of unemployment benefits. In deciding the kind of program most suitable for a reconversion period (past or future) one should keep in mind at least the following advantages conferred by unemployment benefits in the recent conversion.

The chief advantage was the lessening of hardship to the unemployed individual. Both those who actually experienced and those who feared it were shielded by the system.

The number of the unemployed as a proportion of the labor force was small, but it was a large number absolutely. On the average, there were more than two million persons unemployed throughout the whole of the reconversion period, or about five million man-years of unemployment. That represents a significant amount of human suffering, and its alleviation must be put down as a great advantage of having a system of unemployment benefits. The number of different persons who were unemployed during the reconversion period was far greater, of course, than two million. Contributing to that average figure were some who were unemployed for only a few days and others who were unemployed for months. Although the incidence of unemployment was low in general, it was high for particular areas, industries, and classes of persons.

Unemployment benefits conferred the greatest help on the long unemployed; but the others profited also. The short-term unemployed do not know that they are short-term while they are unemployed. The employed do not know how long they will be employed.[1] For all wage earners unemployment benefits provided psychological security. That was another

---

[1] "A second conclusion which workers draw from their experience is that good jobs are scarce and hard to find. It seems curious that this view should have been widespread even in a year of peak employment such as 1947." This was one of the findings of Lloyd Reynolds and Joseph Shister in their study of a New England manufacturing center in 1947: *Job Horizons* (New York: Harper and Brothers, 1949), p. 85.

large advantage of having the system in operation during the reconversion period, an advantage that attaches to all insurance. Even when the total number of unemployed is relatively small, the individual wants to have protection against the chance that he personally will form part of that small number.

And, of course, it was not certain that the total number of unemployed would be small. The guesses of some economists were better than those of others; but they were still guesses. In economics the large swings of aggregate demand are still not subject to accurate prediction; the economists who were right this time in their predictions may be wrong the next time. Looking back on the reconversion period we can see that aggregate unemployment was never a serious threat. But we ought not transfer our present certainty back into the planning period. Before the event some of our soundest economists were unable to do more than warn that both inflation and deflation were possibilities.[2] A strong demand for labor during the reconversion period was probable, not certain. In that uncertainty it was an advantage to have the safety net of unemployment benefits stretched beneath the working population while the transition from war to peace was being accomplished. If large-scale unemployment developed for a while, the system was there to be used. If unemployment was small, so also would be the costs of the unused system.

There was still another advantage from providing unemployment benefits in the reconversion period—that of national unity. Citizens providing their fellow-citizens with generous defenses against possible disaster cannot help but bind the citizens more closely together. We should have lost some of that advantage if we had been less magnanimous either in the benefits provided or in the terms on which they would be granted—if we had adopted a "subsistence" rather than a "status" norm. We should have lost all that advantage if, as was suggested, we had suspended operation of the system altogether. Russia decided to suspend unemployment benefits for its sector of Germany. When a commission representing the Big Four met in Germany during the reconversion period to re-establish the German social security system, Russia objected to the inclusion of unemployment benefits. "There will be no unemployment in our part of Germany for the next twenty years," the Russian delegate argued.[3] The other three countries, with a different viewpoint, evidently, of the dignity of the individuals from unusual hardship, went ahead without Russian cooperation and set up a unified system of unemployment benefits for the other

---

[2] For example, J. M. Clark: "In reconversion there will be both shortages and surpluses, and it is impossible to predict with certainty whether the prevailing trend will be toward inflation or deflation; hence it is necessary to be prepared for both"; "Economic Controls in Postwar Transition," in *Economic Reconstruction*, S. E. Harris, ed. (New York: McGraw-Hill Book Co., 1946), p. 183.

[3] Interview with George E. Bigge upon his return from Germany as American social security representative.

three zones. We could hardly do less for our own citizens. Such solicitude for the individual cannot but strengthen the sense of community, of national solidarity. Unless the cost is very great in terms of violations and lessened work, it is worth the investment. It is very likely that the program of unemployment benefits, along with other similar programs, shares the credit for a reconversion period which was comparatively free from the violence and bitterness that marked the period after the First World War.

It is true that less desirable jobs "went begging," while claimants shopped around for better jobs, especially during the fall of 1945. But that is in the nature of our unemployment benefits system, as it is presently constituted, and one of its advantages. It is not merely a subsistence but also a status program. It is meant to save the unemployed person from loss not only of the bare means of subsistence but also of the status he had acquired before he lost his job. A part of its goal is to enable the unemployed person to do with less hardship what he would have done in any case. It is not merely a disaster program but also one designed to soften some of the day-by-day hardships that are part of the modern insecure way of earning a living. If it is an "artificial" way of guarding the worker's status, the blame can be put at the door of the "artificial" structure of industrial society, which makes the wage earner's status unbearably insecure. Substantial improvement in the situation must come, not from abolishing social security programs, but in changing the underlying structure of society which makes such programs necessary.

. . . Undecided at the start of the investigation—even as between the extreme positions of Kilgore and Williams—at its end I feel no difficulty in approving a system at least as liberal as the one that resulted from the 1945 amendments, the one in existence during the reconversion period. Particular provisions in particular State laws were, perhaps, unwise, but the system as a whole seems not to have been unduly liberal.

The investigation leaves me with an especially strong impression that unemployment benefits exerted no significant effect on the level of employment and the progress of reconversion. Certainly, the more extreme fears and charges under this head find little support in the history of the period. . . . If significant abuse existed in the reconversion period, it probably was not abuse as defined by the norm of employment. The charge which received the most attention seems to have had the least foundation. If true, the conclusion has considerable significance; for the community can afford to expand its social security programs as long as they strengthen, but not long after the point where they begin to weaken, the productive system.

There are two other favorable aspects of the program which might be conveniently mentioned here. Both are the fruits of the specific line of investigation.

The first emerges from a consideration of the *characteristics* of violators. Violators are not spread uniformly through the claimant population. The situation is "spotty." The concentration of violators varies by sex, by cultural group, by industry, by State.

Everything indicates that females predominate among the nonworking violators. The labor-force pattern of females differs so much from that of the males that they almost require a program of their own. There is no doubt that they constitute a special problem. . . .

Violators tend to be more numerous among the lower-income, less-educated workers, who have more to gain financially and less to lose socially by violations. They are also the ones who most easily violate the law through ignorance. Violators are more numerous among the employees of the seasonal industries, in the industries which use piece work, among the longshoremen, and in localities where many workers habitually shift between industry and agriculture. They are more numerous, probably, in the more liberal States. They are certainly more numerous in States which have given less attention to policing their claims.

This "spottiness" is a favorable aspect of the situation for two reasons: it dispels the suspicion that the whole system is bad, and it points to the feasibility of administrative control once we have discovered where violations are concentrated.

The other favorable feature of the evidence turned up by the specific line of investigation is that the materials convey an impression of considerable "flexibility" in the system. The system is responsive to changes of public opinion. If at particular times particular groups of claimants take undue advantage of the freedom granted, the disqualification policy can be tightened temporarily to take care of the situation. It is not necessary to wait for legislative action. The community seems to have at hand an instrument flexible enough to control any situation, even such a superlatively difficult one as the reconversion period. . . .

## UNFAVORABLE EVIDENCE AND CONCLUSIONS

. . . [Previously] evidence was presented showing payments made contrary to the law. These illegal payments went to working violators and nonworking violators.

### Working Violators

Fairly objective measurement is possible in the case of payments to the employed, but it has remained largely a possibility. Most States are still (in 1951) not able to make an estimate, supported by data, of the number of working violators among their beneficiaries and of the amount of benefits paid to them. In the reconversion period the States knew even less about the situation.

Delaware and Massachusetts had the two best sets of data. The former's is statistically more complete (for the UC program); the latter's has the longest history and includes the RA program.

Delaware found that more than 10 percent of all its beneficiaries became working violators during 1946; more than 12 percent during 1947. The percentage of benefits going to these violators (and the weekly average of violators) was much less, of course: 1.28 percent in 1946, and 1.93 percent in 1947. About a quarter of the violations were serious enough to be subjected to the fraud penalty. There were a number of factors, especially the factor of uncovered employment, which made these figures an undercount. The extent of the undercount is probably not significant.

Thus, in Delaware in 1946 and 1947 about 11 percent of all beneficiaries were working violators; in New York for the same period the corresponding rate was about 1 percent. The difference may represent the greater diligence of New York in preventing violators or the greater diligence of Delaware in detecting violators. The findings of the New York "experimental office" would lead one to accept the second as the major explanation. The contrast between New York and Delaware has significance for the general situation because most States in the reconversion period resembled New York rather than Delaware in their attempts to discover working violators.

The rates of Massachusetts are lower than those of Delaware. In the UC program during the reconversion period somewhere between 2 percent and 4 percent of the beneficiaries seem to have been violators in the course of a year, and about 0.5 percent of all benefits were paid to them (the violators).

The RA program showed higher ratios. The proportion of benefits going to working violators was about twice as high as in UC during the reconversion period. That was exclusive of benefits drawn illegally by veterans who were receiving subsistence allowances at the same time. The results of the RA and UC audits are not strictly comparable for beneficiaries, but there, too, the RA rates were evidently higher.

The Massachusetts postaudit has been in operation longer than has that of Delaware, and it does not screen as closely. Both facts would tend to make the Massachusetts rates lower. But the lower rates might also be due in part to differences in industrial structure or to different amounts of agency errors.

It is not possible to construct a "national average" figure from the experience of Delaware and Massachusetts. One of the important facts to grasp about this violation is that the situation is "spotty." The difference in results between particular and general audits makes that abundantly clear. Violations are concentrated more heavily among the workers of some industries and among certain social classes. Moreover, this sort of violation seems to spread quickly once it takes root, and can infect a whole firm or even a whole industry in one State while being almost absent from the same firm or the same industry in another State. Hence, it is unsafe to generalize from the sparse data available at present. Whether the national rate during the reconversion period—or now—is higher than that found in Delaware or lower than that found in Massachusetts cannot be determined with solid probability on the basis of existing data.

If I were forced to make an estimate, because some practical decision turned on it, I should put it somewhere between the Delaware and the Massachusetts results, estimating that on the average about 1 percent of benefits (and of beneficiaries each week) were improper, and about 6 or 7 percent of beneficiaries over the year. But I should be very conscious of the uncertainty of the estimate.

On the subject of willful violations—that is, the proportion of working violators who are cheaters—the most intelligent statement which can be made is that no one knows. On the one hand is the fact that the majority of the violations are small—some for only a part of a week, some for one or two weeks—which might indicate ignorance rather than willfulness. On the other hand is the fact that those who have to interview these violators believe that most of them are willful.

### Nonworking Violators

The figures are even less certain for nonworking violators than for working violators. For one thing, the data usually cannot be cleared completely of working violators so as to leave only nonworking violators. This qualification must be kept in mind or the total number of violators will be overestimated. In cases which seemed to refer chiefly to nonworking violators, the available evidence showed that the incidence of violation could be high, especially among long-duration claimants. Violators could apparently comprise 10 to 20 percent of 20-week RA beneficiaries in 1946 Among 10-week UC and RA beneficiaries combined, California found that apparent violators made up 15 percent in 1947. In Illinois in 1948 the corresponding rate was about 20 percent. These were beneficiary rates. The corresponding benefit rates would not have been lower, however, because the beneficiary rates referred to a point in time.

The incidence of violation for the whole claimant population must have been much lower than for these special groups; but there is no way of calculating it for the reconversion period. The way in which the census and the claims measures of unemployment reversed their usual relationship probably indicates a significant proportion of violators in the total claimant population; but there is no way of reducing that general impression to a quantitative estimate. Some light is thrown on the situation by the Buffalo-Rochester contrast. Most of the difference between the disqualification rates of Buffalo and Rochester in 1946 probably represents nonworking violators. Since the *weekly* difference averaged about 2 percent, it means that about 2 percent of the benefits paid in Buffalo in 1946 may have been paid to nonworking violators. The percentage that such violators made of all beneficiaries over the year would, of course, have been much higher. The situation in Buffalo was probably representative of the other war-production centers during the reconversion, and the war-production centers accounted for a large part of total claims.

## All Violators

Working and nonworking violators together—what proportion of all benefits did they receive during the reconversion period? . . . The only source of data free of that limitation pertains to a later period: the New York Test Office as it was operated in 1950. It cannot answer the above question directly, therefore. But it can provide a rough control on what is a reasonable answer.

Although it confirmed the principle that "investigation makes a difference" (doubling the staff doubled the number of disqualifications), the investigation produced results which were on the whole reassuring. They seemed to indicate that in normal times, for New York at least, not more than 1 or 2 percent of all benefits went to violators, working and nonworking combined. That was the difference in disqualification rates between the test office and the control office in the early months.

That rate is not directly applicable to the reconversion period. Neither is it directly applicable to the country as a whole. In Delaware, for example, improper payments to working violators alone equal that rate. And there are a number of reasons for thinking that even for New York itself the rate represents an underestimate. Nevertheless, so low a rate coming from so careful an investigation exercises considerable control on what is a plausible estimate for the amount of improper payments. The California "20 percent" estimate becomes more unlikely than ever in the light of these New York results. However, an estimate of 3 or 4 percent does not seem impossibly high for the reconversion period, with its abnormal conditions among veteran and female claimants.

Even the New York experiment yielded no direct data on the percentage of improper claimants; but of course it would have been much higher than the percentage of improper claims. It was estimated at about 10 percent over the year. That is, about 10 percent of all the different claimants in the year may have been violators. The estimate would have to be raised somewhat for the reconversion period.

Of the two rates the claim rate is the more important. But the claimant rate is not without its significance. For one thing, it is an index of the violation potential. For another, it represents the greater danger to the program from the viewpoint of public relations. Ten persons drawing benefits improperly for one week are more of a threat to the good name of the program, especially if they talk about it, then is one person drawing benefits improperly for ten weeks.

## Conclusions from the Unfavorable Evidence

The evidence for the existence of working and nonworking violators may be enough to decide some persons against the reconversion program represented by the Kilgore bill. Previously undecided, I reached a decision, unfavorable to the bill. . . . I was not much impressed by the possibility that the Kilgore program, if enacted, would have diminished the supply of labor and thus have perceptibly retarded the process of reconversion. Senator George's declaration that it would increase unemployment by 25 percent finds no strong support in the available evidence. But I was impressed by the possibility that the Kilgore proposals would have increased the proportion of benefits going to violators, especially to the nonworking variety.

The extension of coverage to the whole working population would have increased greatly the administrative problems of the period. If the additional groups—domestics, farm laborers, teachers, casual workers, anybody who earned as little as $150 a year in wages—had presented no more than the normal problems of administration, just their added bulk would have swamped the agencies. But as a matter of fact they would have been more difficult to handle. They were excluded originally precisely for that reason. Available trained personnel would have had to be assigned in disproportionate numbers to solve the technical problems of the proposed new groups. But trained personnel were spread too thin in the reconversion period to handle even the smaller task adequately.

The higher benefit scale would have narrowed still more the gap between war-based benefits and peacetime wages. That could have been a step in the wrong direction. If the adoption of the Kilgore scale for UC had led to raising the RA scale correspondingly—as it almost certainly would have done—it could have been two steps in the wrong direction. It would have made more difficult the transfer of displaced warworkers, including veterans, back to their prewar work. But the effect need not have been great. Only workers with dependents would have been eligible for the high benefits against which Senator Vandenberg directed his argument, and such workers are less likely than others to prefer benefits to a job.[4]

The super-duration provision, of two consecutive years (for practically everybody who was or had been in the labor force), would have been the source of more serious difficulties. With such a provision it would have been much more difficult to weed out the nonworking violators among the warworkers, especially the women. The States depended to a considerable degree on the operation of exhaustions to accomplish that task.[5] There was no greater single help to administrators than the fact that most of the war-born nonworking violators were automatically eliminated by the middle of 1946. Even the fifty-two consecutive weeks of the veterans program were probably too many. Officials of the Veterans Administra-

---

[4] One employer representative with much experience (he spent his full time covering the unemployment compensation cases of one of the largest companies in the country) told me that he had found that this group caused the least trouble of all.

[5] Note the resignation in New Jersey's "there is no way presently of testing their availability for peacetime work."

tion have expressed the opinion that a better arrangement would have been—and would be if there is another "reconversion period"[6]—two separate benefit years of twenty-six weeks each. It should be recalled, also, that the original draft bill prepared by the Social Security Board provided only twenty-six weeks of benefits altogether.

\* \* \* \* \*

The unfavorable evidence also enables one to understand and in part to evaluate the action of some States in tightening their programs since the reconversion period. The action has taken forms such as the following.

*Adding Special Disqualifications for Female Claimants.*[7]

*Changing from a Uniform to an Individual Benefit Year, with Consequent Changes in the Base Period.* Under a uniform benefit year a claimant's benefit rights are not tied as closely to his recent employment history. In New York, for example, in some circumstances a claim could be based on employment that was more than two years in the past. Of the fifteen States with a uniform benefit year in 1945, seven[8] had changed to an individual benefit year by the end of 1951.

*Tying Experience Rates to Individual Benefit Payments.*[9] This is an effective and apparently the only really effective way of keeping the employer in the program as an active policing agent. Up to the present he has been needed in that function. The increased policing activity of the agencies after the reconversion period is in part due to employer pressure. If the agencies continue their activities, the importance of this function of employers will diminish; but it will still be important.

*Adding a Requirement That a Claimant "Actively Seek Work."* This calls for a more extended comment. Its rapid spread as a statutory requirement was the most marked single effect of the alleged abuses of the reconversion period. In 1945, after ten years of experience, only six States had the requirement in their laws. By 1949 twenty-two State laws contained it.

---

[6] On May 14, 1952, the House Committee on Veterans Affairs approved unanimously and sent to the House floor a bill providing educational and other benefits for the veterans of the Korean War. It was patterned on the "G.I. Bill of Rights" of the Second World War, with one conspicuous exception: it did not include readjustment allowances. John D. Morris, of the Washington Bureau of the New York *Times,* reported in his article of May 14, 1952: "The bill contains no provisions for special unemployment benefits. This was omitted because of many veterans' abuse of the World War II system . . ." If this is true (in a personal letter Mr. Morris said that he had been given this reason by members of the committee) it must be added to the list of "reconversion reverberations."

[7] Canada, also, added special conditions of eligibility for female claimants in the 1950 amendments to its unemployment insurance law.

[8] Namely, Arkansas, Colorado, Connecticut, Massachusetts, New York, Rhode Island, and Utah.

[9] Michigan went farthest in this direction, in 1947, modeling its law on that of Wisconsin; but even New York took a long step in the same direction in 1951.

The Bureau of Employment Security looks askance at the spread of the requirement as a separate legal provision, pointing out that it is not really needed because it can be interpreted as a part of the requirement, already in the law, that a claimant be available for work: "A separate statutory provision lends itself more readily to rigidity in its application than would a similar requirement imposed as an interpretation of the usual availability provision."[10]

There is no doubt that the provision lends itself to misuse. Because it is an easy mechanical way of deciding that a claimant is not available, local office office personnel are tempted to overwork it. Where the availability questionnaire is used, this requirement is usually a part of it and takes the form here of asking the claimant to list the names of employers from whom he sought work in the past week. In that form it is by no means the most important part of the questionnaire. If it is made the most important part, as I have seen happen in some local offices, the questionnaire is ruined. The other information elicited by a good questionnaire is far more valuable than are the names of a few companies to which the claimant says he went in search of work.

However, there is something to be said in favor of the provision. A legislature has no way of directly influencing policy except by introducing legal provisions. This provision was the shortest and most effective way of reversing, in some States, a previous policy of accepting registration with ES as sufficient activity on the part of the claimant. If it is understood as a way of emphasizing the fact that more may be required of a claimant than such registration, there is no objection to it.

The data on improper payments produced by the combined general and specific lines of investigation are fragmentary. They suffice only as the basis for an intelligent impression. Incomplete as they are, however, any judgment on the general situation which ignored them would be unbalanced. They supply the only kind of evidence we have at present for gauging the degree of pressure on the defenses of the system and for coming to some kind of estimate as to what is likely to happen if we increase/decrease the incentives to file improper claims or lower/raise the defenses of the system against such claims.

The final word must be, however, that an impression based on such incomplete data must be uncertain. There is real need for better data.

---

[10] U.S. Dept. of Labor, Bureau of Employment Security, Unemployment Insurance program Letter No. 213 (June 28, 1950), p. 6.

# 29. THE SCANDAL OF UNEMPLOYMENT COMPENSATION

Kenneth O. Gilmore,
*Reader's Digest,*
April, 1960.

In July 1957 a 65-year-old man bade a last farewell to colleagues at an industrial plant in Pittsburgh. His long career completed, he looked forward to a leisurely retirement, well-fixed with a monthly $188 pension from his company, an $1,800-a-year slice of a deferred profit-sharing plan, plus his regular social security pension checks. Yet immediately he registered as a job seeker at the local U.S. Unemployment Office, knowing full well that nothing would be available to him as long as younger men were seeking work in his specialty.

During the next 7 months this man picked up $35 every week without doing a lick of work. Then, after a wait, he automatically qualified for another effortless $33 a week for 30 more weeks. It added up to over $2,000, all tax free, and all in addition to his regular retirement income.

This is not an isolated case. Despite crude attempts of Federal authorities to cover up and conceal, the fact cannot be hidden that today our unemployment-compensation apparatus is in horrible disrepair. The solid planks on which it was built years ago have been so warped by the pressures of our growing welfare bureaucracy that hundreds of millions of dollars are being wasted on loafers, quitters, honeymooners, schemers, parasites and a host of others for whom it was never intended.

When Congress enacted social security legislation 25 years ago, requiring every State to set up basic unemployment compensation laws, the objectives were straightforward and simple. To qualify, unemployed workers had to be "ready, willing, and able to work." Benefits were to go to legitimate wage earners who had clearly lost jobs through no fault of their own, to tide them over until they could find employment.

The collapse of these standards is shocking. All types of freeloaders have joined the unemployment-aid roster:

In Wisconsin, a mine-hoist operator demanded sick leave for arthritis, only to go touring country fairs as a sulky-driver in harness races. Eight weeks later, when he showed up for work, he was fired for misconduct. At that point he applied for benefits, and it was finally ruled that his behavior should not prevent him from receiving compensation.

There's the girl who worked in a musical comedy in New York for about a year, then took a vacation in Miami. She stayed on as a nightclub dancer at $100 a week for 6 weeks. When the show headed for Las Vegas, she quit and went back to New York. Her homecoming was sweetened with jobless aid.

After classes let out for the summer vacation, a Georgia schoolteacher who was paid by the year collected unemployment in North Carolina. He claimed that his monthly school checks were for work he had done in the school term.

In Hollywood, a 12-year-old child actor spurned parts as an extra paying up to $28 a day, yet was declared eligible for unemployment benefits. Why? The youngster was accustomed to speaking roles at $100 to $150 a day, so lesser parts were beneath him.

These are recent, documented cases, summarized in bulletin form at the U.S. Department of Labor and distributed by the hundreds to keep State unemployment officials abreast of legal precedents. In every one of them, benefits were granted even though all the facts cited here were brought to the attention of authorities. They epitomize an untold number of instances in which unemployment protection has been stretched beyond belief.

The result is a multibillion-dollar colossus that continues to expand in all directions. Of the $23 billion in jobless pay handed out during the past two decades, nearly half has been eaten up in just the last 5 years. In 1959 1 out of every 12 members of our civilian labor force collected an unemployment check.

Set up as a Federal-State insurance system, unemployment compensation has long been dominated by Federal officials bent on building up a Washington-run welfare apparatus. Along with their continual efforts to cut down the authority of the States, they have waged a relentless campaign—with bulletins, speeches, memorandums, letters, and a flood of statistics and literature—for larger, longer, and laxer benefit payments.

Under this pressure, benefit protection for four of every five workers has been boosted over 200 percent since the system began. In Connecticut, claimants can collect as much as $1,742 over a half year; in California, $1,430. People have been able to draw compensation for 40 or more weeks in 21 States, beyond 50 weeks in 7 States.

The money for all this comes directly from the 2 million employers who are taxed by each State according to the size of their payrolls. However, they must send in additional millions of dollars to the Federal Government, where it is appropriated to the U.S. Bureau of Employment Security (BES), a Federal supervisory agency within the Department of Labor. The BES then channels cash back to the States for their administrative expenses, retaining an average $6 million a year for its own expenses. That's not the half of it, however. Every cent collected from employers may be impounded in Washington if States do not bow before BES and Federal rule, and employers may be penalized with a Federal tax that is 10 times greater.

Says Dr. Edison L. Bowers, professor of economics at Ohio State University and chairman of Ohio's Advisory Council on Unemployment Compensation, "We have been gradually approaching a complete Federal system by the back door—a system in which the State legislatures and the State administrators relinquish their rights and responsibilities in return for administrative funds."

In Pennsylvania, where many of the favorite BES concepts have been faithfully followed, legal problems have created an appalling mess. The official record there shows that workers who had retired on pensions were showered with $20 million in unemployment payments during a 3-year period; and further, that in 4 years more than $45 million had been squandered on persons who voluntarily quit work or were fired for misconduct. On top of that, a recent investigation by the State chamber of commerce revealed that in one 3-month period some $2 million was given to students, pregnant women, retired and seasonal workers, and numerous borderline wage-earners.

In one city, for instance, 85 women, mostly housewives, work 8 months of the year at a factory that makes chocolate bunnies, chicks and eggs for the Easter season. In the spring the plant closes down for the summer. Since no other factories in the area have openings, these women can collect as much as 30 weeks' compensation. Many of them have accumulated enough wages to draw the maximum benefits. Result: a 4-month paid vacation.

One of the worst abuses in Pennsylvania is a scheme of benefit distribution whereby certain claimants can collect for two 30-week periods without lifting a finger in between. They draw the double bonus because of a loophole they have discovered in an extremely technical provision of the State law. Significantly, the chamber of commerce study disclosed that one-half of all benefits paid to these "double-dippers" goes to retired workers. Yet efforts to halt this practice have failed, and little headway has been made toward a cleanup.

Employers can contest benefit claims which they consider unjustified, but they have fared badly before administrative tribunals in Pennsylvania. In a recent 12-month period more than two-thirds of their appeals to referees and the board of review were turned down. Consider the case of an inspector in a plant handling defense work. Because he failed to check the measurements on an important machine, $2,000 worth of material had to be scrapped. He was fired. Nevertheless, benefits were granted by a board of review even though the record showed that the inspector had been issued previous warnings by the company because of his carelessness.

Pennsylvania's unemployment finances are in a shambles. Last April it had to borrow $96 million from Washington to keep from nose-diving into the red. In addition to that, it lapped up over $80 million from a gigantic recession fund created by Congress in 1958. For 6 months every person on the rolls who had run through all his compensation hauled in an additional 15 weeks of benefits.

Contrast this situation with that in Ohio, a large industrial state like

Pennsylvania. Last fall Ohio's unemployment fund stood at a solid $407 million, without any loans from Washington. Nevertheless, Ohio's Bureau of Unemployment Compensation has been sharply criticized by the BES. Why? One complaint: Ohio should purge from its law a section which barred benefits to persons sent to jail or discharged from jobs for misconduct or dishonesty. Let 35 days roll by, said the BES, and then permit the dishonest person to collect aid. It reasoned that the average unemployed man in Ohio located a job in 5 weeks; therefore, why not grant compensation to the jobless crook after that much time had elapsed? Somehow, by then his dishonesty would have no relation to his unemployment.

Such is the incredible logic of the BES giveaway experts whose welfare philosophy has been thrust on other States besides Ohio. The Bureau has urged every State to limit to a mere 6 weeks' disqualifications for all cases of voluntary leaving, discharge for misconduct, and refusal of suitable work. So, in New York a secretary quit her job for no reason, waited out 42 days of disqualification, and then climbed on the unemployment bandwagon.

In just this way millions of dollars are slipping out to persons who sit out short penalty periods, then rake in benefits. Indeed, BES-promoted laxity has become so flagrant that only 18 States now bother to impose heavier disqualifications for aggravated misconduct such as forgery, larceny, embezzlement, arson, intoxication, sabotage, or dishonesty.

Alfred L. Green, executive director of New York's division of employment, has pointed out that this situation is "typified by the case of the man who received unemployment benefits after he was fired for stealing $25,000 from his employer. Under penal law that's larceny. Under the unemployment insurance law it is misconduct in connection with his employment, and benefits are paid after a suspension period. When the employer was notified that the benefits had been charged to his account, he was, to put it mildly, irritated."

The BES hacks away at restrictions set up by States to prevent compensation from becoming an outright grab bag. It has notified all States that it is "unnecessary as well as undesirable" to have legislative provisions which exclude women from jobless aid because of pregnancy or marriage obligations. The result? In Rhode Island a woman clerk married a man from Mississippi and quit her job to live in the South. When she claimed unemployment compensation, her employer objected—but an administrative ruling declared that it is a woman's duty "to live where her husband designates." For that reason she got unemployment benefits.

In New York Mrs. Sheila Shaw drew 9 weeks of unemployment compensation after she quit her $45-a-week clerk-typist job to become a bride. Her employer appealed. When the case finally reached the State supreme court appellate division, the employer was turned down. The court put marriage in the same class "as an illness or other event of important personal consequence to the worker."

Snapped Albany's Knickerbocker News: "If employers are going to pay for honeymoons, they should do it outright—not with under-the-counter payoffs through the unemployment-insurance fund."

BES has also notified States to write their laws "in broad terms with no specific requirement that claimants be actively seeking work." As a result, workers all too often just register at the local employment office and relax while paid specialists do their job hunting for them.

In scores of labor disputes strikers collect benefits completely contrary to the original intent of the law. In New York last fall, 25,000 striking steelworkers pocketed $9 million in benefits because compensation is allowed in that State after a strike lasts 7 weeks. "It's outrageous for an employer to have to finance a strike against himself," says John A. Williams, chairman of the New York State Conference on Unemployment Insurance. "It makes a mockery of the fundamental principle that States should not take sides in disputes between employers and employees."

In defense of this practice, New York's chief compensation administrator counters that after 7 weeks a striker's reserves are likely to be exhausted and "since today we don't let people starve, the government is going to provide funds" in either "unemployment insurance or relief."

Is it reasonable to believe that New York steel strikers would have starved after 7 weeks without compensation? Did they starve in other States? The United Steelworkers of America has (or did have before the strike) a huge unemployment fund. Other national unions chipped in to help the steelworkers take care of its own. The millions in unemployment compensation money handed out to the New York steel strikers was in addition to funds received from their own unions.

While all the rackets mentioned thus far have beaten the system within the law, unemployment assistance is also plagued by illegal abuses. In the last three recorded years 170,000 cases of fraud were officially reported. Yet BES statistics show only 32,000 prosecutions and 25,000 convictions. The officially admitted take by gypsters: more than $12 million.

States have a variety of methods for cross-checking the validity of claims, some better than others. But in thousands of cases benefits are granted solely on the word of the applicant. How much fraud thus slips by is not known, despite the millions of dollars BES has spent financing 30,000 detailed investigations of claimants in 41 States. BES simply refuses to disclose the total amount of fraud found in any one of these States.

Now the situation threatens to grow worse. Legislation before Congress would put the States completely under the thumb of BES by imposing mandatory Federal benefit rates in all States to run 9 months for anyone who qualifies for jobless aid. Big unions are already beating the drum for this Federal takeover of jobless assistance.

Even more disturbing, a majority of the Federal Advisory Council on Employment Security, a group of citizen consultants handpicked by BES and the Labor Department, has called for Federal benefit requirements. Not only must this not happen, but Federal invasion of State unemployment compensation must cease. "It seems inevitable that, if present trends continue, the States will be reduced to the status of rubber stamps or the system will break down of its own complexity," warns William Papier, director of research and statistics at Ohio's Bureau of Unemployment Compensation.

No one questions that jobless assistance is a necessary and important program for the protection of legitimate workers made idle by conditions beyond their control. But it's time for unemployment compensation abuses to be cleaned up.

What can you as a citizen do about this? Here are suggestions:

If you know of any cheaters, report the facts to employment officials or to your local newspaper.

Find out if your State law needs to be tightened to prevent what you consider unjustified payments. If you decide that something should be done, communicate with your legislator. Write your governor. Get your neighbors interested.

Find out if your Congressman intends to support national legislation that would turn over unemployment compensation entirely to the Federal Government.

Most important, take a personal stand against the insidious "get it if you can" philosophy that keeps abuses alive. Just because it's technically legal to dip into the public till, don't let yourself be persuaded that it's the right thing to do.

This last is the real test. For America's moral fiber will be fatally weakened unless we as responsible citizens take action ourselves. We cannot afford to become a nation of loafers, system beaters, and dole grabbers.

# 30. ANALYSIS OF "READER'S DIGEST" ARTICLE, "THE SCANDAL OF UNEMPLOYMENT COMPENSATION"*

U. S. Department
of Labor,
1960.

1. The article cites the case of a retiree from a Pittsburgh industrial plant who looked forward to leisurely retirement, but filed a claim for unemployment compensation and "during the next 7 months this man picked up $35 every week . . . without doing a lick of work. Then . . . he automatically qualified for another $33 for 30 more weeks. It added up to

---

* For Mr. Gilmore's reply to this article, see the *Congressional Record* (86th Cong., 2d sess.) (Washington, D.C.: U.S. Government Printing Office, 1960), p. A-5814 (daily issue).

over $2,000, all tax free, and all in addition to his regular retirement income."

The facts:

This claimant cannot be identified in our records. If the author of the article will provide the Pennsylvania agency with the name of the claimant, and if as stated in the article the claimant did not want work, the claimant will be liable for prosecution for fraud. Action could be taken for the recovery of the fraudulent benefits and a fine imposed. The benefits would be fraudulent because for each of the 60 weeks he is said to have received benefits, he had to sign a statement that: "I was able to work and available for suitable work." In addition, every fifth week for which he claimed benefits, he received a special interview at which he was asked what he had been doing during the prior 5 weeks. These interviews are for the purpose of identifying claimants who are not entitled to benefits.

Pennsylvania's law and those of 30 other States do not prohibit individuals in the labor market from receiving unemployment insurance while drawing a pension. Administratively, however, the States investigate more carefully the availability for work of retirees than of those not receiving retirement pay. (See point 10.)

2. "The planks on which it (unemployment insurance) was built years ago have been so warped by the pressures of our growing welfare bureaucracy that hundreds of millions of dollars are being wasted on loafers."

The facts:

All laws in the beginning and today require any individual receiving benefits to be available for work. This is frequently paraphrased as meaning "ready and willing to work." From the beginning and still today an available individual has been regarded as one who does what a reasonable person in his circumstances would do to get work. Loafers, etc., have never been legally entitled to benefits. Any claimant may be offered any job known to the employment service which the agency regards as suitable for him in terms of his past employment and training. A claimant who refuses such an offer, without cause acceptable to the agency, is subject to a disqualification for work refusal.

The statutory causes of disqualification and the period of disqualifications have been generally made more severe. Thirty-five States have elaborated on the four original causes of disqualification. The maximum period of disqualification has increased in many States. For example, in 1938 the maximum disqualification for voluntary leaving in any State was 9 weeks. The most common was five or less. Now 22 States disqualify for more than 6 weeks, and 16 States disqualify for the duration of the unemployment.

Throughout the article are innuendoes that there are many payments which were not intended by the original law but which have been made possible by existing law. Benefit payments are made only by State employment security agencies under the terms of State laws. At almost every session the provisions of the State laws are reviewed by the legislators, and if they deem it necessary amendments are enacted. The State laws and procedures have been tightened over the years to give greater assurance that only workers genuinely in the labor market receive benefits. The qualifications, for example, in terms of earnings and length of employment, which a worker must meet to be eligible for benefits have steadily risen. Originally not one State held special extended interviews to explore the worker's continued availability for work. All States have now adopted this procedure.

3. *"In Wisconsin, a mine-hoist operator demanded sick leave for 'arthritis,' only to go touring country fairs as a sulky driver in harness races. Eight weeks later, when he showed up for work, he was fired for misconduct. At that point he applied for benefits, and it was finally ruled that his behavior should not prevent him from receiving compensation."*

The facts:

*Mulford Callam* v. *Montreal Mining Co. and Industrial Commission* (Circuit Court, Dane County, Sept. 9, 1957) (BSSUI,[1] MC-15.05–17).

The initial determination in this case denied benefits on the ground of misconduct discharge. On appeal, the examiner reversed this determination and allowed benefits. The commission, in turn, reversed the examiner and denied benefits. Finally, the circuit court allowed benefits, without disqualification.

Callam, the claimant, worked in a mine for about 8 years as a hoistman. He suffered from chronic rheumatoid arthritis which had grown progressively worse. In the latter part of June 1955, on his doctor's orders, he asked for a sick leave from his superintendent. The superintendent told him that the company did not grant sick leaves but that, if his doctor recommended he take off, Callam should do so and return when he was able. Callam absented himself from work for 8 weeks after June 30, 1955. He stayed at home the first 3 weeks recuperating. He then left the city with his family for a tour of area and county fairs at which he entered and sometimes drove a harness-racing horse in races. Callam came home on August 24, 1955, and reported for work. He was told that his employment had been terminated. On August 4 and 5 the employer had tried unsuccessfully to reach Callam by telephone and in person. On August 5 the employer had sent him a registered letter asking that he report for work or obtain a leave of absence within 15 days or his employment would be ended. Callam never received this letter, although he had left a forwarding address. The court pointed out that considerable latitude needed to be left to an employee's discretion as to whether or not he is able to continue at work.

Callam did not think he was able to return to work until August 24 and he had medical evidence to back up his contention. There is no contrary evidence

---

[1] Benefit Series Service, Unemployment Insurance.

other than the commission's conclusion that driving a harness race in two 3-minute heats was just as strenuous as operating a mine hoist. . . .

The commission in effect has substituted its discretion for that of the workman. Perhaps Callam was mistaken in his judgment as to when he could return to work but does that constitute misconduct under the statute?

The Supreme Court of Wisconsin in the Boynton Cab case "flatly holds that the term 'misconduct' does not include 'mere mistakes, errors in judgment, or in the exercise of discretion' on the part of a discharged worker, and we think at best that nothing more than a mistake or an error in judgment on the part of Callam is here involved."

Comment:

This is a court decision and not an administrative determination.

The court based its decision on a definition of "misconduct connected with the work" that was laid down by the Wisconsin Supreme Court in 1941 in what has become the leading American case on the subject.

The mine superintendent told Callam to follow his doctor's orders and absent himself from work until he was able to return. Nothing in the facts indicated that what he did was contrary to his doctor's orders. Medical evidence did indicate that he was unable to return to work until August 24, 1955. In other words, he did just what his superintendent had told him to do.

4. *"There's the girl who worked in a musical comedy in New York for about a year, then took a vacation in Miami. She stayed on as a nightclub dancer at $100 a week for 6 weeks. When the show headed for Las Vegas, she quit and went back to New York. Her homecoming was sweetened with jobless aid."*

The facts:

New York: Unemployment insurance appeal board, decision No. 60, 435–57 (August 16, 1957; BSSUI, VL-315–5).

The initial determination and the referee both disqualified the claimant for voluntarily leaving her employment without good cause. The appeal board reversed them and allowed benefits.

The claimant, a dancer, was 18 years old at the time she filed her claim. Her first job after leaving school was with a musical comedy in which she worked for about a year. When this job ended she went to Miami for a vacation, but obtained a job there in a night club and worked for 6 weeks until April 13. This employment was terminated when the night club closed at the end of the season. She had been hired for the run of the show in Miami, Fla. Her contract of hire did not obligate her to perform in the same production with an employer elsewhere. She declined to go with the show to Las Vegas for these reasons: She did not want to travel to Nevada. The salary would have been about $102 or $105 a week, out of which she would have had to pay her own living expenses in Las Vegas. She was one of the last employees to be hired and would be one of the first to be terminated in the event of a layoff. Her mother disapproved of her traveling to a distant part of the country because of her age. The appeal board concluded that she should not be disqualified because her contract of hire did not require her to accept the Las Vegas offer and because her youth and limited traveling experience were a good ground for her refusal to travel and to be employed in a distant part of the United States.

Comment:

When this claimant's musical comedy employment ended and she decided to vacation in Miami, she did not claim any unemployment benefits. However, when a chance came to work while in Miami she took advantage of it.

The testimony in the case showed that this 18-year old was living with friends in Miami. This kept her living costs down and provided chaperonage. In Las Vegas she would have had to live at a hotel where her costs would be higher and the guardianship of family and close friends would not be available.

5. *"After classes let out for the summer vacation, a Georgia schoolteacher who was paid by the year collected unemployment in North Carolina. He claimed that his monthly school checks were for work he had done in the school term."*

The facts:

North Carolina: Appeals deputy decision, docket No. 548-UCV-57 (July 12, 1957, BSSUI, TPU-105–43).

The claims deputy denied benefits to the claimant on the theory that he was not unemployed; the appeals deputy reversed him and allowed benefits. This claimant was a Korean veteran and filed his claim for benefits under the program provided by the Congress in the Veterans Readjustment Assistance Act of 1952.

The claimant had been teaching school in Georgia. After he lost this job, he moved to North Carolina in search of employment. Under the claimant's teaching contract with the Warrenton Elementary School, Warrenton, Ga., he had been required to and did perform services from September 1, 1956, to June 1, 1957. The school, however, paid its teachers, including the claimant, monthly on a 12-month a year basis. Claimant was released from his teaching job on May 29, 1957. After that he no longer had any obligation to the Warrenton school and was free to take other work and was willing to do so. His checks, after May 1957, were considered wages that he earned and accrued during the September 1–June 1 period.

Comment:

The North Carolina law (sec. 96–8 (10) (a)) says that "an individual shall be deemed totally unemployed in any week with respect to which no wages are payable to him and during which he performs no services." The pay checks which this claimant received during the summer of 1957 were for work performed during the 9-month school period. They made him no less unemployed than if the school had paid him the same total salary but divided it into 9 equal monthly checks.

6. *"In Hollywood, a 12-year-old child actor spurned parts as an extra paying up to $28 a day, yet was declared eligible for unemployment benefits. Why? The youngster was accustomed to speaking roles at $100 to $150 a day, so lesser parts were beneath him."*

The facts:

California: Unemployment insurance appeals board, benefit decision No. 6574 (January 30, 1959, BSSUI, AA-195-23).

The initial determination and the referee's decision denied benefits to the claimant from August 18, 1957, on the ground that he was not available for work. This was reversed by the appeal board.

The claimant, a 12-year-old actor, had 7 years' experience in movies and TV production. During 1951–53 his maximum annual earnings had been under $700. He earned $1,858 in 1954, over $5,000 in 1955, and again in 1956. As of October 7, 1957, he had earned over $4,900 in calendar year 1957. His normal rate of pay as an actor was from $100 to $150 a day or from $350 to $400 a week. The number of days which he had worked as an actor during the past several years had exceeded, to a considerable degree, those worked by the average child who received work in the entertainment field. In 1957, when he filed his claim, minimum rates for extras were $21.51 per day and $97.15 per week.

During the past few years, there had been a surplus of children seeking extra work and Central Casting Corp., the agency through which the major studios usually employed extras, had generally not been accepting their requests for registration for extra work.

Actors and their agents generally considered that for an established actor who had attained normal rates of pay above the Screen Actors Guild minimum (as was the case with this claimant) seeking work as an extra would lower his professional prestige, harm his acting career, and destroy his established rates of compensation.

In the present case, the claimant has firmly established himself in the acting profession and has consistently, over a period of several years, secured a substantial amount of work and income in the entertainment field. In addition, he has attained a stature in his profession which allows him to consistently command rates of pay in excess of those set forth in the collective bargaining agreements negotiated by the Screen Actors Guild. Under these facts, . . . we find that there existed for the claimant a reasonable labor market and one which offered the claimant reasonable prospects for continued regular employment therein. Also, in view of the claimant's established position in the entertainment industry, his currently established rates of compensation and, based upon his recent employment experience, his apparent prospects for continued regular employment at such rates, it is our further opinion that the claimant's exclusion of work as an extra player, which paid wages of $21.50 or $28.33 per day, was not an unreasonable restriction.

Comment:

The basic criterion used by the Board to determine the availability of child actors for work has been whether or not they have firmly established themselves in the entertainment field.

The California board decided three other child actor cases on the same day as in this case—Nos. 6575, 6576, and 6577. In 6575 and 6576 benefits were allowed. In 6577 benefits were denied even though the claimant who had done free-lance work in motion picture, radio, and TV production for about 4 years, was willing to accept all types of work which he could perform in the entertainment and modeling fields, including extra work at the minimum scale. This claimant had earned about $575 in 1955, about $3,500 in 1956, and about $2,500 in the first 8 months of 1957. The appeal board said that these earnings indicated that he had not sufficiently established himself in the entertainment and modeling fields so that he could expect to secure employment on a reasonably regular or full-time basis.

7. *"Of the $23 billion in jobless pay handed out during the past two decades, nearly half has been eaten up in just the last 5 years."*

The facts:

The article omits the reasons why the amount of benefits paid out in recent years has been considerably greater than in earlier years. There are two major reasons for the rise: (a) a larger number of workers are now covered; and (b) the benefit amount, which is based on the going wage structure, has steadily increased to reflect the constant rise in the level of wages. The article omits the further fact that the rise in benefit amounts has not kept level with the rise in wages. The article also omits the fact that the 5-year period referred to included the 1958–59 recession.

8. . . . The article . . . states that the program "has long been dominated by Federal officials who are engaged" in a continued effort to cut down the authority of the States.

The facts:

Any examination of the tremendous variation in State unemployment compensation programs reveals the falsity of any charge of Federal domination. It is obviously ridiculous to say that 50 State legislatures and the Congress of the United States are dominated by the Bureau of Employment Security in Washington.

9. *"The BES then channels cash back to the States for their administrative expenses, retaining an average of $6 million a year for its own expenses."*

The facts:

The funds are collected by the Internal Revenue Service, and appropriations out of these funds are made by the Congress for the States' administrative expenses. Congress also appropriates the money for Bureau expenses. This is the same process by which other Government agencies obtain their funds.

10. *"In Pennsylvania . . . workers who had retired on pensions were*

*showered with $20 million in unemployment payments during a 3-year period."*

The facts:

Because of the strong implications of withdrawal from the labor market, the States investigate more carefully the continued eligibility and availability for work of retirees than they do with regard to claims by younger workers. In addition, a number of States have special disqualifications for workers receiving pensions. But not all retirees are in the same situation. Some are forcibly retired from one job—and continue working for many years afterward in other jobs. Others are not interested in working. The personal circumstances of each must be carefully investigated and weighed. The worker who retires voluntarily from his last employment may be disqualified for voluntarily quitting his job without good cause. Mere eligibility for retirement has never been accepted in any State as good cause for quitting a job. Unless the worker has other and substantially better reasons for quitting, the voluntary retiree will be disqualified. By contrast, the worker who is forced to retire is in no different situation from any other worker who is laid off. He has lost his job for a reason for which he is not responsible even though he may be receiving a pension or old-age insurance payments. A typical example of the State approach to the determination of the rights of retirees under usual availability provisions is this statement by the New York Division of Employment:

> Cases of workers who have been retired for age by an employer are closely examined. The amount of pension paid by the employer or the union and of old-age insurance benefits under the Social Security Act and ascertained and weighed in determining such worker's availability, that is, his desire to work. Particular emphasis is given to cases where acceptance of work would entail forfeit of such payments. Restrictions by claimants regarding the type of work and wages sought are evaluated against the prospects of finding employment. An active search for work is required in these cases.

If a worker retires voluntarily, especially strong evidence is required to demonstrate a later return to the labor market and possible eligibility for benefits.

Facts examined in making determinations on the availability for work of pensioners include these:

The circumstances of separation from previous employment, that is, voluntary or mandatory separation.

The willingness of the claimant to accept such suitable employment as is obtainable in the current labor market in the light of conditions surrounding the employability of older workers.

Physical capacity of the claimant to do the kind of work for which he is otherwise qualified.

The reasonableness of the restrictions imposed by the claimant as to wages, type of work, location (travel, transportation), hours, etc.

The kind and extent of efforts made by the claimant to obtain employment.

The amount of pension and old age benefits received and their effect on a genuine desire to work, the conditions of continued receipt of such payments, and the willingness of the claimant to forfeit the entire amount, or any part of it, if necessary, to accept employment.

11. *"In one city 85 women, mostly housewives, work 8 months of the year. . . . In the spring the plant closes down for the summer. Since no other factories in the area have openings, these women can collect as much as 30 weeks' compensation."*

The facts:

Information from Pennsylvania is to the effect that these women are actively in the labor market during the off season and that a number, in fact, do get some work. The workers are regularly tested for their willingness and ability to work. Since they regularly work 8 months of the year, they could not possibly draw 30 weeks of benefits (over 7 months). They would be disqualified immediately if they refused to return to work at the beginning of the season.

12. *"One of the worst abuses in Pennsylvania is a scheme of benefit distribution whereby certain claimants can collect for two 30-week periods without lifting a finger in between. They draw the double bonus because of a loophole they have discovered."*

The facts:

This is not a loophole in the Pennsylvania law. There are only 13 State laws which have specific statutory provisions to prevent payment of benefits in a second benefit year without intervening employment.

The article assails the provisions which permit workers to draw benefits continuously from the end of one year through the beginning of the next benefit year. The article does not explain that benefits are payable in any year only on the basis of earnings and employment in a recent base period. The worker, therefore, cannot receive benefits in 2 consecutive years unless he has had sufficient earnings in two consecutive base periods. It is only the accident of when the long-unemployed worker was laid off that determines whether he will have a period of idleness between his periods of benefit entitlement or whether the first period of benefit payments will run into the next. The article also overlooks the fact that the longer a worker remains unemployed the more stringent becomes the State investigation of his availability.

13. *"In a recent 12-month period more than two-thirds of their (employer) appeals to referees and the board of review were turned down."*

The facts:

The article omits the fact that three out of four workers lose their appeals when they appeal to referees and the board of review.

14. *"Consider the case of an inspector in a plant handling defense work. Because he failed to check the measurements on an important machine, $2,000 worth of material had to be scrapped. He was fired. Nevertheless, benefits were granted by a board of review even though the record*

*showed that the inspector had been issued previous warnings by the company because of his carelessness."*

The facts:

Pennsylvania Unemployment Compensation Board of Review, decision No. B-47651, May 21, 1958 (reaffirmed October 10, 1958).

The claimant had worked as a floor inspector in a plant manufacturing parts for jet engines for about 6 years. His basic functions were to approve machines, check the piece which the machine was producing against a blueprint, and master the gage on the job. On January 16, 1958, he failed properly to gage the pieces on the job. As a result, the pieces produced were scrapped. Checking the operation of the machine periodically was the duty of the machine operator as well as the claimant. The machine operator was suspended for 3 days. The claimant was discharged for his failure properly to set the gages and failure to make proper inspection of the machine. The board, through its referee, held three separate hearings at which the employer was represented by its accounting firm and several members of its managerial staff. Fifty-three pages of testimony were taken. After considering the testimony, it was the board's conclusion that there had been a failure to prove any deliberate and willful action on the part of the claimant. "We feel that the claimant's actions were actions of misjudgment and as such do not constitute misconduct within the meaning of the act."

Comment:

The three hearings held in this case indicate the detailed care with which the facts were explored by the referee and the board of review. The testimony taken showed conflict as to the extent and nature of previous warnings and commendations that had been given to the claimant. Dispute existed also as to the workload given to the claimant and the ability of one person to do an adequate job of inspection on the number of machines assigned in an area so large as the one which the claimant had to cover. The board's decision was a factual conclusion in the face of the parties' disagreement on the details of the claimant's duties, conduct, and precise cause of separation.

15. *"For 6 months (in Pennsylvania) every person who had run through all his compensation hauled in an additional 15 weeks."*

The facts:

This false statement implies that no matter what the duration of benefits is, the unemployed workers will continue to draw benefits to the very end of the period. The "additional 15 weeks" of benefits referred to by the article were paid out under a Federal law passed by the Congress during the 1958 recession to help workers who were not able to find jobs during the recession within the number of weeks during which the State paid benefits. Seventeen States including Pennsylvania participated in this Federal program. As a matter of fact, of the 251,000 Pennsylvania claimants who began to draw TUC benefits, as many as 115,000—or 46 percent —dropped out before the end of the 15-week period. Clearly, workers continue to draw benefits only while they cannot find work.

16. The article is critical of 5- and 6-week disqualification periods and attributes them to "BES-promoted laxity." The cases selected for discussion are misconduct cases involving dishonesty. *"In Pennsylvania . . . in 4 years more than $45 million had been squandered on persons who voluntarily quit work or were fired for misconduct."*

The facts:

The unemployment insurance program was not set up to punish workers for dishonesty or for any other reason. That is a function of the criminal courts. The unemployment insurance program should only deny benefits to a worker for as long as his unemployment is the result of his own unreasonable actions. Obviously, a good deal of guessing must necessarily take place in trying to predict how long a particular individual's unemployment will be attributable to his own actions. Instead, the Bureau looks to the experience of the average worker. The Bureau's recommendation— and that of many States and students of the program—is that the disqualification in each State should be as long as, or slightly longer than, the period it normally takes workers in that State to find work.

The reference "that only 18 States now bother to impose heavier disqualifications for aggravated misconduct" carries a misleading implication. Originally, no State had such a provision.

17. *"In Rhode Island a woman clerk married a man from Mississippi and quit her job to live in the South. When she claimed unemployment compensation, her employer objected—but an administrative ruling declared that it is a woman's duty 'to live where her husband designated.' For that reason she got unemployment benefits."*

The facts:

Rhode Island: Board of review, appeal No. 5029 (March 14, 1958; BSSUI, VL-155.2–39).

The initial determination denied benefits for voluntary leaving without good cause. The claimant's appeal was decided by the board, without any intermediate referee stage.

The *Reader's Digest* version is correct in the facts. The board said:

We have held in previous cases that where a claimant is required to leave her job to join her husband who moves to or is a resident of another State she is acting under a duty imposed upon her by law to live where her husband designates. Accordingly, in doing so, claimant is fulfilling an obligation to the law. Claimant is acting from a compelling reason which in our opinion justifies a voluntary leaving. There is no basis for the imposition of a penalty for voluntary leaving without good cause under the facts in this case.

Comment:

The initial determination, made by the State employment security agency's staff, disqualified the claimant when the employer objected. The claimant appealed from this to the board. The board, composed of a public representative, a labor representative, and an industry representative, unanimously reversed this disqualification.

The board's decision was in accord with an earlier court decision.

In 1953 the Rhode Island Superior Court had approved a decision that a clerk who left Rhode Island to be near her marine husband at a California camp for 2 or 3 months before he left for overseas duty, had left her work with good cause (*Champagne* v. *Department*, P.A. No. 2846).

18. "*In New York Mrs. Sheila Shaw drew 9 weeks of unemployment compensation after she quit her $45-a-week clerk-typist job to become a bride. Her employer appealed. When the case finally reached the supreme court appellate division, the employer was turned down. The court put marriage in the same class 'as an illness or other event of important personal consequence to the worker.'*"

The facts:

New York: *Matter of Shaw* (Appellate division, supreme court, July 31, 1958; 6 A.D. 2d 354; 177 N.Y.S. (2d) 1, affirmed by the court of appeals without opinion, 158 N.S. (2d) 128 (1959)).

Benefits were allowed this claimant without disqualification, at all levels, from the initial determination to the court of appeals.

Sheila Shaw had been employed as a clerk-typist for 2 years by the General Mutual Insurance Company in Albany. She left her job to be married and to live with her husband in North Tonawanda, New York, some 280 miles from Albany. She was married on July 23, and did not look for work until August 23, when she filed her claim. Ultimately (on October 29), she found a job as a typist.

The court pointed out that the statute did not define the meaning of "good cause." "Usually it would be expected to be some cause connected with the employment itself; unsatisfactory hours or wages, strain of the work, transportation or other related difficulties." However, said the court, when the statute is read in context, it is clear that leaving employment "for good cause" may exist because of conditions which have no direct bearing on the work itself. The court pointed to such things as personal illness, illness in the family which may require the individual's help, his desire to continue his education, or an inheritance of enough money so that the individual would not be required to work for a while, as examples of reasons that might constitute a temporary withdrawal from the labor market in good faith.

Thus, leaving employment for good cause may be integrated with a temporary withdrawal from the labor market; and while they may not be fully coextensive, not every bona fide temporary withdrawal from the labor market would be "good cause" for leaving employment (having enough money not to need to work, for example), it would seem that "good cause" ought to be read as a cause having some reasonable foundation.

We think marriage ought to be treated as such a cause as well as illness or other events of important personal consequences to the workers. This is especially so where it is manifest that the woman who is married intends to return to the labor market.

The bride of the Victorian era would no doubt regard her marriage as a permanent withdrawal from the labor market, if, indeed, she had ever been in it; but the economics of modern marriage require that many married women work and they intend to remain and do remain in the labor market after marriage.

Comment:

This claimant filed her claim only after she was settled in her new home and ready to go to work. She was married on July 23 and filed her claim 3 weeks later. The court emphasized the claimant's actual return to the labor market and the fact that she did find a job.

19. In the midst of a discussion of laxity in disqualifications for which the article blames the Bureau occurs this sentence: *"In scores of labor disputes strikers collect benefits completely contrary to the original intent of the law."* The next sentence refers to 25,000 strikers in New York who received benefits. The implication is twofold: (a) The Bureau recommends the New York type of disqualification, and (b) this type of disqualification is to be found in many States.

The facts:

The disqualification of workers for unemployment due to a labor dispute, or for any other reason, is determined by State legislators who regularly review the State unemployment insurance laws.

Actually, only two States now have such a limited disqualification for unemployment during labor disputes. Moreover, the Bureau does not recommend this type of disqualification. The Bureau believes the disqualification should continue as long as there is a causal relationship between the stoppage of work and the unemployment.

20. The article points out that in the last 3 years, *"170,000 cases of fraud were officially reported. Yet BES statistics show only 32,000 prosecutions and 25,000 convictions. The officially admitted take by gypsters: More than 12 million dollars."*

The facts:

The amount of fraud is small and many cases are detected before benefits are paid. This statement gives a false impression as to amount of fraud and as to the effectiveness of State activity. For the years 1956, 1957, and 1958 overpayments as the result of fraud amounted to about one-fifth of 1 percent of all benefits paid. The article is particularly remiss in not mentioning that regardless of prosecutions two-thirds of the benefits paid out as the result of fraud was recovered. Also the article fails to mention that penalties are imposed by the State agencies even if they decide not to prosecute. Although the figures the article cites refer to claims which were not detected until after benefit payments had been made, these penalties are levied on all fraudulent claims including those that are detected before benefits are paid. During these 3 years almost 200,000 administrative penalties were imposed.

21. The article refers to the more than 30,000 benefit random studies as *"detailed investigations in 41 States"* and adds that *"BES simply refuses to disclose the total amount of fraud in any one of these States."*

The facts:

The cases to be investigated were selected with the objective of testing the basic claims methods in the State and not to measure the extent of fraud throughout a given State. The results have value in improving local office functions but have no relationship to the amount of fraud in a State since the sampling method is not done on a statistically sound basis for that purpose. For this reason, and to avoid misuse of the data, the Bureau informed all the States in September 1954 when it sought this information from them that "Information obtained from survey reports to the Bureau which identifies an individual State will be released only with the agency's specific consent." The writer of the article was told this and was invited to write to the individual States for the material if he so desired.

22. *"The Federal Advisory Council on Employment Security, a group of citizen consultants hand-picked by BES and the Labor Department."*

The facts:

The Federal Advisory Council is a statutory body consisting of equal representation from management, labor, and the public. The management members are selected by the Secretary of Labor taking into consideration lists submitted by the National Association of Manufacturers and the U.S. Chamber of Commerce; the labor representatives are selected from a similar list prepared by the AFL-CIO. The public members are selected by the Secretary of Labor.

# 31. SUPPLEMENTAL UNEMPLOYMENT BENEFITS

MARGARET S. GORDON
and RALPH W. AMERSON,
*Unemployment Insurance,*
University of California, 1957.

As A RESULT of recent developments, no discussion of unemployment insurance would be complete without a consideration of supplemental unemployment benefits.

Essentially, supplemental unemployment benefits are additional benefits paid to unemployed workers from private funds accumulated for the purpose. Under existing plans, these supplemental benefits are paid by employers under the terms of collective bargaining agreements. In many respects, they are similar to other types of "fringe benefits" included in union contracts, such as pensions and health and welfare plans.

The first agreement providing for supplemental unemployment benefits was signed by the Ford Motor Company and the United Automobile Workers in June, 1955. Similar agreements were negotiated soon after between the UAW and the other major automobile producers. SUB plans, as they came to be called, have also been adopted in a number of other industries. It was estimated late in 1956 that approximately 2 million workers were covered by such plans, chiefly in the steel, shoe, glass, electrical, maritime, and farm implement fields, as well as in the auto industry.

The Ford agreement provided for contributions by the employer into a trust fund, amounting to 5 cents an hour for each worker covered by the plan. Only employees with at least a year of seniority would qualify for these benefits, which were to equal, when added to state unemployment insurance benefits, 60–65 per cent of the worker's weekly take-home pay. The laid-off worker would get 65 per cent of his take-home pay for four weeks and 60 per cent for the remaining weeks of eligibility for supplemental benefits. Thus the company would be paying the difference between regular unemployment benefits and 60–65 per cent of take-home pay, but in no case would supplemental benefits amount to more than $25 or less than $2 a week. Although the maximum duration of benefits was to be 26 weeks, the actual duration in any given case might be considerably less, depending on (1) the worker's seniority, (2) his previous employment experience, and (3) the position of the trust fund.

The negotiation of supplemental unemployment benefits grew out of the drive for guaranteed annual wage plans, similar to those that had existed in a few firms for many years. But SUB plans represent a substantial modification of the guaranteed wage proposals. By accepting the obligation to pay supplemental benefits for a limited period to laid-off workers, employers incurred a much more limited type of liability than would have been involved in the typical guaranteed wage plan. But at the same time unions gained a concession which they considered a substantial advance toward greater job security for the worker. The unions argued that, not only would benefits be more adequate under these plans, but employers with SUB plans would be less likely to lay off workers, while employers facing union demands for new or liberalized SUB plans would be more likely to support liberalization of public unemployment benefit levels.

The Ford agreement provided that benefits would not be payable under the plan unless administrative rulings or statutory amendments in the states in which at least two-thirds of its workers were employed had established the legality of supplementation. It was not long before this condition was met. By late 1956, 26 states (including most of the leading automobile producing states) had taken action to permit supplementation, chiefly through administrative rulings but in a few states through legislative enactment. Indiana, North Carolina, and Ohio, however, had rejected supplementation. Ohio voters, in November 1955, rejected a referendum which provided that the receipt of a supplemental unemployment benefit would not disqualify a claimant for unemployment insurance.

Agreements in other industries differ from the Ford plan in some respects, but all SUB plans are linked with public unemployment insurance systems in a similar manner, except "individual account" plans such as those in the glass industry. Under the glass industry plans, each covered worker has an individual account from which withdrawals, in specified amounts, may be made in the event of illness or unemployment.

Although SUB plans may be expected to spread to additional industries, most informed observers expect their expansion to be somewhat limited, at least for some time to come. One estimate suggests that they are unlikely to include more than a total of 5 or 6 million workers in the coming few years. There is a good deal of opposition to the plans, not only on the part of employers, but also on the part of union members in some industries. Workers with relatively high seniority ratings in industries with comparatively stable employment are reported to be unenthusiastic about giving up wage gains or other fringe gains that might be achieved in return for a type of protection which would be likely in practice to benefit only low-seniority workers who happened to get laid off.

SUB plans are not equally well adapted to all industries. They appear to be best adapted to industries in which workers are ordinarily employed on a full-time, continuous basis but in which temporary layoffs affecting substantial numbers of employees occur from time to time. In industries with unusually stable employment conditions, on the other hand, there is less need for this type of arrangement, while in industries characterized by short-term, casual, or sharply seasonal employment, SUB plans of the usual type would not be workable.

Even though SUB plans may not spread rapidly, they are likely to exert upward pressure on state benefit levels. Worker dissatisfaction with current state benefit levels is bound to be enhanced, while employer groups may offer less resistance to liberalization of regular unemployment benefits as a means of forestalling the spread of SUB plans. At the same time, employer groups are likely to support legislation designed to limit the expansion and liberalization of SUB plans by imposing restrictions on the terms and conditions under which state unemployment benefits can be paid to jobless workers covered by SUB plans.

# 32. SIGNIFICANT FINDINGS ON THE IMPACT OF THE 1957-58 RECESSION

WILLIAM HABER, FEDELE F. FAURI, and WILBUR J. COHEN, The University of Michigan, 1959.

—Both unemployment insurance and public assistance programs made an important contribution to meeting some of the hardships and economic losses caused by unemployment during the recession.

—Unemployment insurance benefits and *all* public assistance payments (for all five categories) totalled $7 billion for the 12-month period. About $4 billion was for unemployment insurance and $3 billion for public assistance. The increase in total disbursements above the level of a year before was, however, only about $2.1 billion.

—Unemployment insurance benefits in October, 1958 were about $2 billion above the annual rate of August, 1957, while general assistance payments were at an annual rate of about $100 million above the August level.

—Unemployment insurance benefits, nevertheless, fell substantially below the 50 per cent of average wages recommended by President Eisenhower. The amount and duration of benefits was too limited and coverage too restricted.

—While over two million persons exhausted their unemployment insurance benefits in the ten months January-October, 1958, the total amount of state reserves for unemployment insurance at the end of October, 1958 was $7 billion—or about twice the $3.5 billion in benefits paid out in the previous 12 months.

—*If unemployment insurance benefits had been paid at a rate of 50 per cent of average wages instead of the approximately 37 per cent actually paid, and if coverage had been broadened, and the maximum duration of benefits had been 39 weeks in all states for the entire period of the recession, about $1.5 to $2 billion additional would have been disbursed to unemployed individuals.*

—General relief was not available in all localities to meet the needs of able-bodied unemployed persons. In some localities no relief was available to "employable" persons. In some communities, residence and settlement requirements made it impossible to give aid to some needy unemployed persons or their families.

—In 16 states, the localities had to supply all needed funds and thus the potential expansion of the program to meet the emergency was severely limited by the fiscal resources of the particular locality.

—Although federal funds were available to the states to help persons who became needy through unemployment when the individual was aged, disabled, blind, or where there was only one parent in the home, no federal aid was available for direct relief to other groups.

## RECOMMENDATIONS

The experience of the recession indicates that the existing built-in stabilizers in our income maintenance programs were not—and still are not—satisfactory to meet another similar reoccurrence. A free-enterprise economy must make more effective provision than we now have for meeting the unemployment hazards which occur from the free play of economic forces in the market place.

The full potential of our unemployment insurance system was not utilized during the recession for the alleviation of hardship and the support of our economy.

The tragic part of the situation was that there was $7 billion in unemployment insurance reserve funds which were not touched during the recession. If state and federal unemployment laws had been more adequate and had permitted $1.5 to $2 billion of these reserves to be used to pay benefits to the unemployed, many personal hardships could have been avoided. There would still have been about $5 billion of reserves left if unemployment insurance benefits had been more adequate.

Among the most urgent improvements in federal and state legislation which are vitally needed while the lessons of the recession are still fresh in our memory are:

1. Coverage should be broadened to cover all persons who have a substantial attachment to the labor force including the 1.8 million persons in small firms who are not covered in 33 States and some of the hired farm laborers and other groups not now covered.

2. The maximum duration of benefits should be increased to at least 30 weeks in a benefit year in all states. Provision should be made for longer duration whenever the average unemployment in a state reaches recession levels of say 6 to 9 per cent.

3. Steps should be taken to establish an equalization fund in order to reduce the excessive costs of unemployment insurance in states suffering from a high incidence of unemployment caused by national economic conditions.

4. The great majority of eligible claimants should receive at least one half of their normal full-time gross weekly earnings. States and employers should be given a period of six years to accomplish this objective. The great majority of eligible claimants in a state should receive at least 40 per cent of their normal full-time gross weekly earnings for the first two years following the effective date of the standards; for the next two years, not less than 45 per cent, and after that not less than 50 per cent. In order to provide benefits at these levels, states would have to make

changes in their benefit structure including increasing the maximum weekly benefit amount.

5. The Federal Temporary Unemployment Compensation Law which expires March 31, 1959 should be extended until permanent federal standards and supporting state legislation are enacted to improve the benefit duration and financing arrangements of state laws.

6. Since a major impact of the recession was on younger workers with families, it was especially unfortunate that most state unemployment insurance laws did not provide for benefits in relation to the number of dependents. Only eleven states had such provisions. Dependents' benefits should be included as an integral part of each state unemployment insurance program.

7. Because a social insurance system does not protect all individuals from want during extended periods of unemployment, federal and state funds for direct relief should be made available to assure all *needy* persons a floor of protection against want in all localities. Such a program should be designed to assist needy individuals to become self-supporting.

# 33. THE UNITED STATES EMPLOYMENT SERVICE IN A CHANGING ECONOMY

WILLIAM HABER,
1960.

I

## SOME QUESTIONS CONCERNING THE PERFORMANCE OF THE PUBLIC EMPLOYMENT SERVICE

THE PUBLIC EMPLOYMENT SERVICE in the United States occupies an important position in the organization of the American labor market. In periods of national emergency, when labor shortages are widespread, we look to the local employment office and its network of state and national employment services to assist in meeting the manpower requirements of a strained economy. Without an effective national network of local employment services, labor surpluses in one area or region would not be expeditiously available to areas of substantial labor shortage. In two world wars and in the Korean action in the early 1950's we relied heavily upon our public employment services for the "allocation" of manpower in accordance with our over-all national objectives.

And in "normal" times, our network of local and state employment services can and do play a vital role in uniting the jobless man and the manless job. In its simplest form it serves as an "employment exchange." When effective, it helps to reduce waste of manpower by shortening the period of job seeking; it can be an important repository of comprehensive information about all aspects of manpower requirements. Its facilities are available to all and are of particular service to groups in our working population who are in special need of assistance in finding employment. These include new workers entering the labor market for the first time; juvenile workers with limited employment experience; older and handicapped workers, who meet special obstacles in their quest for jobs and need guidance and assistance in their search; members of minority groups whose employment prospects are dimmed by discriminatory hiring practices; special groups, such as veterans, whose employment problems receive a particular priority because of public policy, and migratory workers who meet our seasonal agricultural needs. In a special category, perhaps, should also be included workers in depressed areas where employment prospects are relatively meager and who may need special assistance, including the possibility of relocation to another area. All these categories, in addition to wage earners who have no special employment problems, have access to the job information, counseling, testing, and guidance services which a "good" employment service can provide.

These aids-to-employment functions contribute to the fuller utilization of our manpower resources and play a part in effectuating the nation's objective of maximum levels of employment as outlined in the Employment Act of 1946. They also aid employers and improve personnel practices generally since they provide special services in selection and placement, screen applicants by means of tests, provide job descriptions, and thus enable the employers' personnel officers to do a more careful job of selection.

Unemployment in our society is not exclusively the result of massive general economic forces. A substantial volume of temporary joblessness grows out of employer policies and individual choices. Much of it is related to the continuous changes which take place in the labor market: the influx of young people; changes in the educational, training, and skill requirements of our industries; seasonal fluctuations in demand for goods and labor; displacement which accompanies technological progress; the decline of old industries and areas; and the persistence of excessive levels of unemployment in depressed areas. These problems are perennial; they are accentuated by depressions and recessions, but are not created by these economic dislocations. And they may well be of greater significance in magnitude in the 1960's than in the past. Such developments, including "structural unemployment," when coupled with what is usually referred to as "frictional" joblessness that arises because many workers are always between jobs, may well represent a substantial proportion of the total manpower waste chargeable to unemployment.

It has long been assumed that an efficiently "organized" local labor market, properly coordinated on a regional and national basis, can eliminate or avoid a substantial portion of such unemployment; that idle jobs can be filled more quickly; that jobless men can be directed to work; that youthful workers can be given the necessary vocational guidance; that the technologically displaced can be counseled as to their occupational outlook; that labor surpluses in one area can be advised of areas where there are labor shortages; in brief, that "normal" unemployment, associated with "structural" and "frictional" aspects of our labor market, can be kept at a minimum.

The Wagner-Peyser Act, which established the basic structure of our present federal-state employment service, was enacted in 1933. The Social Security Act, whose unemployment insurance provisions led to the creation of a state-wide employment service in all states, was adopted in 1935. It can thus be said that we have had about a quarter-century experience with our present federal-state system of employment services.

How well has it performed? To what extent have employers come to rely upon the employment service as an important source of their labor supply? The statistical record suggests that most employers do not depend upon the public employment service to recruit their labor requirements. This is especially true for the larger firms. Is the reason for this situation to be found in the fact that such firms have their own personnel departments, are more often unionized, are bound by seniority rules regarding layoffs and recall and thus have fewer hiring transactions?

The labor force has been increasing in the postwar period; why has the volume of job placements by the U.S. Employment Service failed to expand at least at the rate represented by the increase in total employment? Or is the size of the labor force and the level of employment an improper index of employment service performance?

The record also suggests that an overwhelming proportion of the nonagricultural job placements made by the employment services in most areas consists of unskilled and semiskilled workers and employees in trade and service industries. Employment in these activities has been expanding most rapidly. Do employers make sufficient use of the employment service to obtain skilled workers, technically trained employees, white-collar workers, and professional employees, or do such workers tend to shun the employment service? If not, why do they represent such a small proportion of the total placements?

To what extent is it proper to judge the employment service's performance by the volume of placements? Is this appropriate in a free labor market with a wide variety of hiring channels? Should that be the primary criterion for appraising the performance of a public employment service? If that is so, then have we not overloaded it with specialized tasks for youth, for farm labor, for the handicapped, for minority groups, for the older worker? Can a public service avoid these responsibilities? Since we have assigned them to the employment service, are we unfair in also expecting it to achieve high placements in general employment, in the "main stream operation," and have we not involved it so deeply in the administration of unemployment compensation that the major preoccupation of the upper staff officials is with the payment of benefits, rather than with the job placement of unemployed workers?

To what extent is the problem one of adequate appropriations? Would more adequate funds make the service more attractive to large employers? —to skilled and professional workers? Would it attract more trained and generally more competent personnel? Has adequate provision been made for additional facilities and staff resources in keeping with labor force growth, industrial change, and labor market developments?

How is one to explain the survival and the phenomenal growth of private fee-charging employment agencies in the face of increasing appropriations and expenditures for the operation of public employment offices whose services are free? What have they got to offer the employer or the job seeker which the public agency lacks? Can it be that private agencies are sometimes preferred by employers because freedom in selection, referral, and hiring is greater, since there is no obligation concerning employment discrimination. And should the public employment service seek to compete with the private agency? What about the suggestion of the private fee-charging agency that the public service should confine itself to aid only the unemployed, and allow the commercial employment service to cater to the needs of the employed who seek to change jobs? We obviously cannot expect a commercial agency to provide a wide variety of market services which are in the public interest but for which no fee can be charged.

What about the suggestions made by a prominent labor leader that all employers should be required to list their job openings with a public employment service? He urged that failure to do so should disqualify such an employer from the experience rating provision in our state unemployment insurance laws. Would this be a desirable development? Is compulsory use of the employment service by employers desirable or should one trust to its utilization on the basis of the service rendered?

Should the employment service be given greater responsibility in labor market administration? Should it, for example, be given authority to facilitate area transfers of unemployed and be authorized to advance travel costs resulting from such transfers? There are also vital national security interests and manpower mobilization obligations; can we permit the public employment service to become less effective?

It is clear that in the public image the role of the employment service is highly limited and needs to be modified. In that image the public employment service is seen too often as an agency which has a vital role in the administration of the state unemployment compensation laws, or as the public agency which provides job aids to specialized groups in need of such assistance, and, except in situations of national emergency, the public employment service is seen as performing only an incidental role in the placement of the mainstream of the American labor force.

There are no simple answers to each of these questions. The facts are not readily available. An extended inquiry involving consultation with those who utilize the employment service, or fail to do so, both workers and management, would be necessary if these questions are to be answered adequately. Apart from the facts, however, some of the issues raised involve matters of public policy. They have an important bearing on the utilization of our business resources, economic well-being, and national security. Whether our public employment service in normal times should seek a higher placement penetration rate, for example, is such a question. Similar policy issues grow out of the suggestions that, except for the unemployed and the groups requiring special assistance, the placement task should be left to the employer and the fee-charging commercial agency.

## Improving the Employment Service

A substantially higher proportion of the American work force now looks to the public employment service for placement assistance than was true 10, 15, or 20 years ago. The service has unquestionably made much progress and plays a more important role in the "management" of the local labor market than at any time in its history. Nevertheless, most students would agree with the following catalogue of the employment services' limitations and shortcomings:

1. From the viewpoint of job placement, "the heart and core of all local employment office services," the record of the employment service has failed to keep pace with the growing labor force and expanding employment levels. Secretary of Labor James P. Mitchell, in his 1958 address in Chicago to the Interstate Conference of Employment Security Agencies, said, "The employment service stands or falls upon its main purpose, placement, and all subsidiary activities fail when placement fails." And he called attention to the fact that "nonagricultural employment has increased by over nine million workers in the last ten years, and yet, in that same period . . . nonagricultural placements made by the employment service have declined."

The failure of job placements to increase in selected activities can be explained. And some of the reasons are impressive. The index of placement potential is not in the level or volume of employment but rather in the stability of the employment transactions; further, the large increases in employment, for example, have been in activities where the employment service has relatively little influence as a factor in job placement. This is true of government employment, which increased 39 per cent since 1947. It is also true of construction employment, which expanded by 42 per cent. Insurance, finance, and real estate jobs went up 40 per cent in this period. And nonproductive workers increased rapidly and often while production workers have been declining. These are job areas where the employment service, for one reason or another, has little or no influence. In construction there are traditional hiring arrangements; in government the civil service does the hiring; and the other expanding areas are concerned with the types of jobs less important in the public employment service "portfolio."

It is also suggested that there is a substantial decline in labor turnover. "The vast preponderance of hiring transactions result from labor turnover—the need to obtain replacements rather than employment growth." In developing a more stable work force, in the reduction of the separation rate and a declining accession rate—developments growing out of union seniority plans, homeownership, and pension plans—to cite a few of the reasons—the combined effect is a smaller placement potential for the employment service.

While these explanations introduce "mitigating factors," the hard facts nevertheless indicate that, when measured in terms of placement, the inevitable crucial yardstick, the relative importance of the employment service, especially in activities where "new hires" are increasing, has been declining.

While placement must remain the major objective of a public employment service, it is not possible to agree that the system is a success or a failure in relation to a specified volume of placement, representing a certain proportion—a fluctuation rate—of all placements in an area or an industry. The British employment service, for example, older, more established, and under unified national administration, is also concerned with the same problem. After a half-century of operation, its "penetration rate" is said to be low.

Short of requiring that all vacancies should be listed with a public employment service, a requirement which would be strongly resisted except in times of war, employers and employees will pursue their accustomed ways in filling vacancies and in job seeking. The requirement that all vacancies should be listed would, of course, improve our knowledge of the local labor market, reduce waste and frustrations which now accompany job seeking, and immediately increase the volume of placements made by the public employment service. Such a step is not to be recommended in normal times. The employment service should win acceptance by the quality with which it performs rather than by compulsory job listing.

2. It is emphasized that too large a proportion of the placements made by the employment service is concerned with trade service occupations and lower skilled labor jobs; that skilled people generally shun the employment service, and the highly skilled, professional, and white-collar fields generally look upon the employment service as a "last resort." The job finding patterns of these workers and the prevailing hiring patterns

of employers disclose limited confidence and limited use of these facilities. As a result, only a mere dent has been made in placement of professional, technical, and higher skilled trades. Since all the forecasts are that the number of unskilled jobs will be declining and nonproduction workers with technical skills will be expanding, the importance of a vigorous program to expand activities in these occupations becomes clear. Considerable progress has been made and there is evidence of a widespread awareness nationally and in many states of the importance of enlarging the employment services' role in these occupations. Even so, the services' preoccupation in most states and areas has been with other problems and pressures, and its prestige and reputation has suffered.

3. A third limitation is that the employment service is too deeply involved in the administration of unemployment insurance. This is, of course, unavoidable. No one could seriously suggest that unemployment compensation should be administered by an independent agency. Whether the unemployed applicant for insurance is in fact available for work requires the participation of employment service personnel. In many states, however, it is required that even claimants who expect to be out of work for a very short time must be processed as job applicants. This is unproductive use of employment staff time and is inevitably at the expense of other efforts which might be made in behalf of other applicants facing a less optimistic job outlook.

Much more can be done to emphasize the employment service functions in local offices and through extending further the separation of these activities from unemployment compensation activities. In some states, separate local managers are provided. There is urgent need for further experimentation and study of local experience to determine the value of a further separation of responsibilities.

4. The employment service is overloaded with special programs for the hard-to-place workers. The placement record suffers from the adverse selection of those who utilize its facilities. Such a criticism is widespread. It is not merited. A public agency cannot avoid meeting the employment needs of those who are most disadvantaged in seeking work. The handicapped, the older worker, new and inexperienced workers, minority groups—these must depend upon the public service for aid in job finding. As a result, we have, in fact, several employment services operating in each office. There can be no question that, as a consequence, the mainstream activity, the placement service for workers without special problems, suffers.

It is easier to state the problem than to suggest a remedy. It should be clear, however, that the loading of specialized tasks upon the employment service requires adequate staff and financing, if the mainstream placement activity is not to be neglected.

5. The public employment service is faced by a substantial expansion

of the commercial placement agencies. Private fee-charging employment agencies have grown in size and number since the end of World War II to an extent which deserves deeper analysis than this report can attempt. That their number has increased is clear; we do not have data on the volume of their transactions. The obvious question is: Do these agencies provide a level of service enough higher or substantially different than that of the public agency that applicants (and in some cases, employers) are willing to pay a fee for their use?

The private agencies, in capturing a greater segment of the employment market than in the prewar period, appear to have demonstrated at least two things: (1) a promotional capacity which is apparently effective, and (2) the ability to "deliver" on all business secured. The public agency might well study the promotional methods used by these agencies in an effort to discover which points are most persuasive.

The private agency, surviving as it must by giving the employer full satisfaction, has not diverted its energies into fields which have no direct placement value. The public agency, to be sure, cannot avoid doing that; it must implement public policies directed to special purposes (placing the handicapped, providing special services to veterans, overcoming racial discrimination, providing counseling service to graduating students, etc.). The public system must continue to perform these special tasks; at the same time, however, it must employ a more aggressive and imaginative program to capture a larger share of the job market.

6. The importance of an expanded research program has already been emphasized. Many states fail to recognize the importance of a continuous appraisal of programs and policies. Research staffs and funds are inadequate. The major responsibility in this area must be with the Bureau of Employment Security in Washington. It must take the leadership in developing and stimulating occupational and labor market research if we are to prepare for employment problems of tomorrow.

# 34. THE GROWING ROLE OF EMPLOYMENT SECURITY

Edwin E. Witte,
*Employment Security Review,*
June, 1958.

In a time of widespread unemployment, such as prevails at present, there is some recognition of the functions of public employment offices by nearly everybody. Public employment offices were first established during depressions in the 1870's and 1880's as local and temporary services. They became permanent services in quite a number of States during the depression of the 1890's or soon thereafter. The U.S. Employment Service was started in World War I to facilitate the transfer of workers to war industries.

In this early period, placement of workers in jobs, or more accurately referral to jobs, was almost the sole function of public employment offices. To this was added, in some of the temporary employment offices established in periods of depression, the function of assignment of unemployed workers to relief jobs provided from municipal or charitable funds—a function which has recurred in more recent times whenever relief work has been started.

By the time of World War I, there was considerable enthusiasm for a nationwide employment service which would serve as a central labor market. This would be a common market to which all employers needing help would come, as well as all unemployed workers. In line with this concept, an order was actually issued before the close of the war, requiring all employers engaged in war work to report all their hirings to the U.S. Employment Service which then, at least in some offices, recorded them as placements of the Service.

The flimsy nature of this sort of central labor market, plus the almost complete withdrawal of congressional appropriations immediately after the Armistice, pretty effectively put an end to the idea of an employment service which would be the central market for all hiring of workers throughout the country. But the U.S. Employment Service has had a continuous, although at times somewhat uncertain, existence since 1918.

Early in the Roosevelt Administration, the Wagner-Peyser Act was passed and the U.S. Employment Service was given pretty much the cast it has had ever since. It is a Service with public employment offices throughout the country. These offices are conducted and staffed by the States, but since 1942 the national government has paid their entire costs. There is interstate clearance and some coordination, but with the control resting essentially with the States.

The idea of a central labor market, in the old sense, has pretty much disappeared. It is no longer thought that all hirings should be made or cleared through the public employment offices. Everywhere, far more workers are hired at the gate than are referred by the public employment offices. Incidentally, this seems also to be true in every other free country of the world. The percentage of persons hired after referral by a public employment office is higher in England and other western European countries than in the United States, but in none of them do these offices constitute an exclusive, central labor market, as once was envisioned to be desirable and possible.

Instead, the objective of the placement services of the public employment offices has become one of assistance to employers in finding needed help and to workers in finding jobs. This is a service to which employers often resort when they cannot readily find the workers they need through other methods. Similarly, workers come to the employment offices in the largest numbers when they have difficulty in finding jobs. This places upon the public employment offices the burden of finding for employers the hard-to-get workers and also the burden of finding jobs for workers who cannot find them otherwise. This is a most difficult task and one in which no employment office can have a "thousand" batting average. But it is in meeting this hard task that there lies the real value of the placement services of the public employment offices, rather than in mere numbers of placements.

In a time of recession, the number of placements relative to applications for work is necessarily small. This is, undoubtedly, very discouraging but should not be so regarded. The people who are helped to get jobs when jobs are hard to find receive a service of great value both to them and to the community. And there are still employers who have trouble finding all the men they need, particularly workers with unusual skills. At a time like the present, when there are so many more workers looking for work than there are jobs, it is most wasteful if the unfilled job and the unemployed workers who can fill that job are not brought together.

At this time, the functions of the public employment offices in connection with unemployment insurance overshadow the placement services, at least in volume. This is a function which the public employment offices did not have until the State unemployment insurance laws came into operation in the second half of the 1930's. But it is a function which the employment offices have wherever there is unemployment insurance.

The basic idea in giving the public employment offices responsibilities in connection with unemployment insurance is not so much that there must be a registering and paying office in unemployment insurance. It goes back to the concept that unemployment insurance offers partial compensation only for wage loss due to *involuntary* unemployment. It is not all unemployment which is compensated but only unemployment which is involuntary, at least in its continuance. From the time when unemployment insurance was first instituted, it has been a part of the concept that the unemployed workers must be willing and able to work. "Willing and able to work" is a subjective test which must be translated into objective standards which can be applied in the workaday world.

The tests which are applied, whether unemployment is or is not involuntary, are much the same in unemployment insurance laws the world over. These are that the claimant for unemployment insurance must be registered for work at a public employment office, must report regularly or otherwise keep in touch with the employment office, and must accept suitable work when offered. The latter is not an easy test to apply but is an essential if unemployment insurance is to be other than a handout to just about everybody who applies. Thus, the public employment offices have a function in connection with unemployment insurance which goes to the central purpose of the latter institution, without which it cannot operate properly and beneficially.

## A Time of Challenge

In a time like the present, the registration of unemployed workers at the public employment offices seems to many to be pretty futile. There are so few calls for workers that registration of the unemployed for work seems almost a waste of time. With so many unemployed and so few jobs, I fear attempts to find jobs are merely made perfunctorily. But it is in connection with the hard placements that the employment offices render their most valuable services. In what may be called "normal times," when many of the unemployed are on short layoffs and expect to go back to their old jobs, there is but limited value in trying to find them other work during their layoff periods. In a time of recession, when many layoffs are for an indefinite period and just about everybody expects they may be prolonged, finding another job is for many workers their greatest need. It is in such a time that the public employment offices are put on their mettle and in which they are called upon to demonstrate their true value.

As I see it, there are possibilities for service to the unfortunate unemployed even if efforts to find them other jobs prove unsuccessful. In the New Haven studies of the unemployed conducted in the late 1930's by Prof. E. Wight Bakke, the current President of the Industrial Relations Research Association, it was developed that one of the major characteristics of the unemployed is withdrawal from their prior friends and associates. They usually cease to go to church or to the lodge, and often sever relationships with their neighbors and even their relatives, unless they too are unemployed. Their associations are with others in the same situation as they are; and nothing produces loss of self-respect and status as the loss of employment coupled with inability to get other work. Even the children suffer, not only from a sense of insecurity, but often from the cruel jibes of their fellows.

Unemployment breeds more Communists and other radicals than any other phenomenon of the present day. To a very considerable degree, how the unemployed are treated will determine how serious are the psychological and social consequences of widespread unemployment. The employment office is one place the unemployed must visit. How they are treated by the people who take their registrations and who, at least, should try to help them get a job, may determine not only how much lasting harm unemployment produces but the future of our system of free enterprise—in fact, the entire way of life in future years.

In addition to placement and unemployment insurance services, the public employment offices in the last decades have developed what might be called "community services." Among these, the oldest are statistical and research services. Long since, it has occurred to people that one way to count the unemployed is to record those who use the employment offices—not only to record their numbers but to note their sex, age, occupation, length of unemployment, what jobs they get, and other characteristics and information about them. It is now recognized that data of this kind obtainable through the employment offices will not give us all that we need to know about the prevalence of unemployment and the unemployed—not even the total number of unemployed. But the data we get through the employment offices are a valuable part of the total obtainable information—which is now much better than that which we had about the unemployed at an earlier date.

The employment service is also the source of data as to future prospects regarding employment. This is obtained, principally, through field visits of employment office personnel with the personnel people and other representatives of employers. Contacts of this kind are desirable to enable the employment offices to most satisfactorily perform their placement and unemployment insurance services. Through these contacts, local offices obtain accurate information on the immediate expectations of employers with regard to layoffs, recalls, and additional hirings.

### What Can They Do Best?

More recently—in fact no further back than 10 or 15 years—the testing programs of the employment offices have been developed. Applicants for work, particularly youths or those who have been long unemployed, are given aptitude and other tests to discover what occupations and positions they are suited for and how well they can perform the skills they claim. Tests of this kind are desirable, not only to get good men for employers, but to help workers find the niche for which they are best suited. They are most valuable for young and new workers, but are also very important for those who have been long unemployed. Employers who can do so will make their own and additional tests, but testing is also a necessary function of the present-day employment service and a valuable one to both employers and workers.

In the British and continental employment offices, besides testing there is very extensive vocational guidance, particularly for young workers. Some people in the employment offices know a great deal about industrial prospects in the years ahead. To become the principal source of vocational guidance information, however, involves hazards—principally the one that the future is almost impossible to forecast in a rapidly changing world.

I do not want requirements imposed, such as prevail in totalitarian countries, that children must get their jobs or their first regular jobs through the employment offices. But I see value in establishing close contacts with the school people, especially those concerned with giving information and advice to prospective entrants into employment. And I deem it a function of the U.S. Employment Service to continuously study job opportunities and other aspects of the employment problem; and to publicize the results of such studies. The *Dictionary of Occupational*

*Titles,* with standardized descriptions of all job classifications, is a good example of a well-performed service of this kind.

Placement, unemployment insurance, and community services are the main functions of the public employment offices today. Combined, they do not amount to the sort of central labor market which was the ideal envisioned by the early-day champions of the U.S. Employment Service. But the functions actually performed are of greater value to employers and workers and to the entire public than a central labor market would be. They are even more important in times of recession and depression than in more prosperous times. The present is a difficult period for the public employment offices, but also one of great responsibility and opportunity.

# DISCUSSION QUESTIONS

1. There are strong differences of opinion concerning the objectives of unemployment insurance. Explain why this is so.

2. What are some of the major criticisms leveled against the present federal-state unemployment insurance system by labor and management?

3. Discuss the pros and cons of experience rating in unemployment insurance.

4. What can be said for the proposal to require employees to contribute toward the financing of unemployment insurance?

5. Does the addition of dependents' weekly benefits make unemployment insurance a welfare program? Discuss.

6. The opposition to the adoption of federal benefit standards in unemployment insurance is based on a fear that it represents a first step toward the federalization of the program. Is this an adequate reason for opposing federal standards?

7. In view of the substantial variations in the costs of unemployment insurance benefits among the states, a reinsurance plan on a federal basis has been suggested. Explain the case for and against such a plan.

8. Discuss the advantages and disadvantages of supplementary unemployment benefits (SUB) as against a general liberalization of the public program.

9. Unemployment insurance is now designed to be a first line of defense against unemployment. Should the program be modified and, if so, how, to meet problems created by a serious recession or by persistent unemployment?

10. Should the role of the employment service be confined to providing a "work test" to applicants for unemployment insurance or to providing a more efficiently organized labor market? Which of these objectives should predominate? Discuss.

11. "A public employment service represents unfair competition to private fee-charging employment agencies." Discuss.

# SELECTED REFERENCES

ALTMAN, RALPH. *Availability for Work, A Study in Unemployment Compensation.* Cambridge, Mass.: Harvard University Press, 1950.

ATKINSON, RAYMOND C. *The Federal Role in Unemployment Compensation Administration.* Washington, D.C.: Social Science Research Council, 1941.

BECKER, JOSEPH M. *The Problem of Abuse in Unemployment Benefits: A Study in Limits.* New York: Columbia University Press, 1953.

——— *Shared Government in Employment Security: A Study of Advisory Councils.* New York: Columbia University Press, 1959.

BENNETT, SAMUEL V. *Unemployment and Relief from the Local Government Point of View.* Chicago: Public Administration Service, 1955.

BUREAU OF EMPLOYMENT SECURITY. *Comparison of State Unemployment Insurance Laws.* Washington, D.C.: U.S. Government Printing Office, 1959.

BURNS, EVELINE. *British Unemployment Programs.* Washington, D.C.: Social Science Research Council, 1949.

FELDMAN, HERMAN, and SMITH, DONALD M. *The Case for Experience Rating in Unemployment Compensation and a Proposed Method.* Feldman & Smith, Industrial Relations Counselors, 1939.

GRAY, HERMAN. *Should Unemployment Insurance Be Federalized?* New York: American Enterprise Association, Inc., 1946.

HIBBARD, RUSSEL L. "Minimizing State Unemployment Compensation Taxes," *American Economic Security,* Vol. XI (January-February, 1954), pp. 28–36.

INTERNATIONAL LABOUR OFFICE. *Unemployment Insurance Schemes.* Studies and Reports, New Series No. 42. Geneva, Switzerland, 1955.

INTERSTATE CONFERENCE OF EMPLOYMENT SECURITY AGENCIES. *Annual Proceedings.*

LESTER, R. A. *Providing for Unemployed Workers in the Transition.* Committee for Economic Development. New York: McGraw-Hill Book Co., 1945.

LESTER, R. A., and KIDD, C. V. *The Case against Experience Rating in Unemployment Compensation.* Lester & Kidd, Industrial Relations Counselors, 1939.

SMIGEL, E. O. "Public Attitudes toward Chiseling with Reference to Unemployment Compensation," *American Sociology Review,* Vol. XVIII (February, 1953), pp. 59–67.

SOCIAL SECURITY TECHNICAL STAFF. *Issues in Social Security: A Report to the Committee on Ways and Means of the House of Representatives* (79th Cong., 1st sess.). Washington, D.C.: U.S. Government Printing Office, 1946.

TAX FOUNDATION, INC. *Financing Unemployment Compensation.* Project Note No. 23. New York, 1953.

TILLYARD, SIR FRANK. *Unemployment Insurance in Great Britain, 1911–1948.* Leigh-on-Sea, Esses: Thames Bank Publishing Co., 1949.

"Unemployment Compensation," *Yale Law Journal* (December, 1945).

"Unemployment Compensation in Other Countries," *Employment Security Review* (January, 1957).

*Vanderbilt Law Review.* "A Symposium on Unemployment Insurance," Vol. VIII (February, 1955), entire issue.

WATSON, ANDREW D. *The Principles That Should Govern the Structure and Provisions of a Scheme of Unemployment Insurance.* Rev. ed. Ottawa, Canada: Unemployment Insurance Commission, 1954.

WERMEL, MICHAEL T. *The Benefit Formula in Unemployment Insurance.* Pasadena: Benefits and Insurance Research Center, California Institute of Technology, 1957.

WOYTINSKY, W. S. *Principles of Cost Estimates in Unemployment Insurance.* Washington, D.C.: Social Security Administration, 1948.

# CHAPTER
# V

# Medical Care and
# Health Insurance

## INTRODUCTION

INSURANCE AGAINST medical costs was one of the earliest forms of social insurance established in foreign countries; today, it is undoubtedly the most prevalent form of social insurance in operation in the world. Yet, at the beginning of 1960, of the major industrial countries of the world, only the United States does not have a public system of health insurance or nationwide comprehensive public medical care covering all or a major proportion of the population.

Governmental responsibility for medical care has a long history in the United States. The health functions of local and state governments go back to the very beginning of the country. The federal government provides hospitalization and other types of medical care for seamen, veterans, Indians, members of the armed forces and their dependents, and certain other groups. The federal government also makes arrangements for financing health insurance for its employees and their dependents. The various state and federal workmen's accident compensation laws, in effect, are compulsory health insurance laws limited to injuries and diseases arising out of industrial employment. Medical care for patients with tuberculosis and mental illness has long been the responsibility of state and local governmental agencies.

In earlier times sickness was considered the primary, if not the exclusive, responsibility of the individual and his family and, in a very limited degree, of local and state governments. With new scientific discoveries, industrialization of the economy, the concentration of populations in urban areas, and knowledge of the benefits of modern medicine, a growing concern with health matters arose among workers and their families as well as among numerous professional groups, such as doctors, social workers, and economists. Fear of dependence upon charity or relatives during periods of prolonged illness has been a major factor in drawing public attention to problems of meeting the costs of medical care. Public opinion polls taken in recent years have shown an overwhelming majority interested in medical care and in the prepayment of costs for such care.

Although there is great interest in financing and organizing medical care in the United States, the methods to be adopted for dealing with these questions are still highly controversial. In view of this fact, some common understanding of the terms and ideas is essential to proper understanding of the subject.

Health insurance in other countries usually covers both medical services and cash payments for wage loss due to sickness or disability. In the United States, however, these two aspects of a health program have been considered separately. Consequently, "health insurance" customarily applies only to medical services or medical costs, whereas the term "disability insurance" applies to the cash payments for wage loss. Undoubtedly, the reason for this separate consideration has been organized medicine's vigorous opposition to compulsory insurance with respect to medical services or costs in contrast with its lesser (and unsuccessful) opposition to compulsory insurance with respect to cash payments for wage loss due to disability.

In public discussion, health insurance is frequently confused with socialized medicine. Socialized or state medicine, however, is usually distinguished from health insurance in that it is financed from general tax revenues, doctors are employed directly or indirectly by the government on a full-time or part-time salaried basis, and the facilities are often owned and operated by the government. Medical care for veterans, the tuberculous, or the mentally ill are examples of socialized medicine in the United States. In reality, medical care always has a social or socialized aspect because of public assumption of responsibility for certain groups, such as the indigent or the physically handicapped, and public concern over standards of care, such as medical licensure provisions.

Several countries already have in operation a system of socialized or state medicine. A more proper term would be "public medical care," a parallel to the use of the term "public education," since there is much similarity in the basic principles of both such services. Although Great Britain and the U.S.S.R. are usually considered as the outstanding examples of such public medical care, Australia, Chile, Czechoslovakia, New Zealand, Norway, and Sweden have inaugurated programs, in whole or in part, of public medical care.

Total annual expenditures for health and medical care in the United States were approximately $4 billion for 1939–40. The figure was nearly six times as much by 1960. About 10 per cent of the 1940 expenditures were from public funds, compared with 21 per cent in 1958. Health insurance benefits, almost nonexistent before World War II, covered 18 per cent of personal health care by 1958. It is significant that both trends have been occurring simultaneously.

The amounts spent each year by individuals and families for medical care represents, on the average, 4 to 5 per cent of consumer incomes. Families in the lowest-income groups spend a somewhat greater proportion of their incomes but less in actual dollar amounts. But such average figures can be misleading since, individually, there is uncertainty as to the magnitude of the cost that will fall upon the individual or a family. In any year the actual costs of medical care fall unevenly, with a small group having to bear a disproportionate share of the total.

The basic problems of general public concern in the field of health arise from the various barriers to adequate medical care which now exist. Although there are differences of opinion as to the extent of unmet medical needs and the reasons for failure to meet these needs, there is general acceptance of the fact that unmet medical needs constitute an important social problem. Numerous statistical studies have shown that, among the poor, sickness comes oftener and lasts longer. Death comes earlier than in the homes of the well-to-do. Many families have to borrow from small loan companies, credit unions or other lending agencies, or friends or relatives to pay for medical care; but not all families are able or wish to borrow. As a consequence, many medical bills remain unpaid. In addition, many people put off going to a doctor or making use of other medical care because of the cost. According to several public opinion polls, from 30 to 60 per cent of the American people sometimes have put off going to a doctor or dentist because of the cost.

The shortage and maldistribution of medical personnel and facilities, particularly in low-income rural areas, have a tremendous effect upon the adequate provision of medical care. The combination of low-income families and inadequate facilities make it difficult for many persons to receive any medical care at all. Even some with incomes large enough to pay for all or part of their medical care needs are handicapped by shortages of personnel or lack of adequate facilities in their localities.

For the most part, physicians, other health personnel, and hospitals are concentrated in the urban, higher-income areas. Good medical care depends upon the availability of many kinds of medical personnel and of hospitals and related facilities. There are still some communities, especially in rural sections, where such personnel and facilities are wholly inadequate or entirely lacking.

Although the American Medical Association was critical and skeptical of any type of health insurance for many years, it is now enthusiastically in favor of voluntary health insurance. Voluntary health insurance plans have had a much shorter history in the United States than tax-supported programs of medical care. The health insurance movement has won widespread acceptance from the American people and now over 70 per cent have some form of health insurance protection.

The best known of the voluntary health insurance plans are the Blue Cross plans which were developed in the 1930's to help the hospitals keep going and which insure against hospitalization costs.

Blue Shield plans are controlled by state and local medical societies and are characterized by free choice, individual private practice, fee for service payment. They are limited primarily to physician's care for hospitalized patients.

To a growing extent insurance against the costs and losses of sickness is being handled through commercial insurance companies on an "indemnity" basis. Contracts under this type of insurance usually provide for specified and limited payments when the insured requires medical and surgical care. The volume of such commercial insurance increased considerably during recent years.

Voluntary prepayment plans have made valuable contributions to those whom they serve in providing security against the high costs of medical care and, to the country, in the useful experience they have accumulated in organizing the financing of medical care. However, few provide comprehensive medical services and important segments of the population, such as some of the aged, lower-income workers, and rural groups, are not covered.

One of the important policy issues in this area is whether voluntary plans will be under the control of the hospitals, medical profession, or commercial insurance carriers, or whether the interest of the consumers of medical care will be represented in the over-all policy-making control of the voluntary plans. Another major current issue is whether medical care should be guaranteed to all or to some persons in the community as a matter of right either through compulsory insurance or otherwise. Another issue is whether remuneration of physicians and other medical personnel will be so modified that the change may become basic in medical practice. The question of whether voluntary health plans can and should be meshed in with any national health plan emphasizing comprehensiveness of care is also an important question. Other issues of current interest are included in the discussion questions at the end of the chapter.

# 35. CONSUMER SPENDING FOR MEDICAL CARE

Health Information
Foundation,
New York, 1958.

As PART OF their rising standard of living, American consumers today are spending more money on medical care[1] than ever before in their history. Part of the increase reflects merely population growth and the

---

[1] Medical care as used in this article is defined as the entire gamut of personal health services purchased by private individuals: hospital services, drugs and medicines, appliances, services of physicians and dentists, etc. Spending by government at all levels, business, and philanthropy is excluded.

rise in prices for medical care; but even on a per capita basis, and with prices held more constant, medical spending has increased. For his larger outlay, the American consumer today receives a greater quantity and variety of medical services, while the quality of these services has improved.

Along with the rise in medical spending has come a substantial shift in the relative proportions spent for the various services which comprise medical care. Today proportionately more than formerly is being spent for hospitals, for the costs of health insurance, and for ophthalmic and orthopedic appliances. On the other hand, a smaller share of the medical care dollar now goes for physicians, dentists, and other professional services, while that for drug preparations and sundries has been relatively constant.

Underlying the increases in medical spending has been the income rise in recent years. Nevertheless, spending for medical care has increased proportionately more than income. Medical spending is now a more important part of the family budget than ever—that is, it represents a larger share of the nation's personal expenditures on consumption for all goods and services.

In 1929 Americans disbursed almost $3 billion as aggregate personal consumption expenditures for medical care.[2] Over the next four years, as economic activity in general contracted, annual expenditure dropped by about one-third, reaching a low just under $2 billion in 1933. In the following year it picked up, and it has increased each year since then, a record unequalled by 10 of the 12 major groups of personal consumer expenditures. By 1957 the total had reached $15 billion,[3] about five times as high as in 1929. From 1929 through 1957 the aggregate volume of medical care spending increased annually at an average rate of 6 per cent.[4]

Part of the increase in the total volume of medical care spending stems from the steady growth of the U.S. population. But even on a per capita basis medical expenditures increased substantially, from about $24 to $89 between 1929 and 1957,[5] or 4.8 per cent per year.

The increase in spending for medical care also represents the influence of rising prices. However, with medical care prices held constant

---

[2] For 1929–47, data are those published in U.S. Dept. of Commerce, *Survey of Current Business, National Income Supplement*, 1954 edition. All later data on medical expenditures are from the recently revised, unpublished estimates by the same agency.

[3] If spending by government, business, and philanthropic agencies is included, the total is estimated at $20.5 billion. I. C. Merriam, "Social Welfare Expenditures in the United States, 1956–57," *Social Security Bulletin*, No. 21, Vol. 10 (October, 1958), p. 22.

[4] All average annual rates of increase cited in this article are computed by the compound interest formula applied to terminal points.

[5] Adjusted to civilian (including institutional) population.

on the basis of changes in the medical care component of the Consumer Price Index, the increase in medical spending per capita was still substantial and represented a "real" increase in quantity of services purchased. The figure rose from $32.86 in 1929 to $64.78 in 1957 (both in 1947–49 prices), or just less than double. The rate of increase averaged 2.5 per cent annually, while the comparable rate for real gross national product[6] per capita was 1.7 per cent.

### The Components of Medical Spending

Growth in medical spending since 1929 reflects a rise in spending, not only for the total, but also for each major component of the medical care aggregate, both in gross and per capita terms. This growth also reflects marked shifts in the relative amounts spent on some components, and sometimes in their rank order.

Thus, for the services of physicians, largest of the components from 1929 through 1954, spending rose from $959 million in 1929 to $3,693 million in 1957, and on a per capita basis from $7.89 to $21.93. But although impressive, this increase was far overshadowed by those of the other components. The share of spending for physicians in the medical care dollar dropped from 32.6 to 24.5 cents, and its rank from first to second.

In contrast, spending for hospitals[7] ranked fourth in 1929 (after physicians, drugs, and dentists) but gained steadily and since 1955 has been in first place. Its volume grew from $403 million in 1929 to $3,884 million in 1958, on a per capita basis from $3.31 to $23.07. In 1929 spending for hospitals accounted for only 13.7 cents of the medical care dollar, but by 1957 its share was nearly double at 25.8.

In like manner, expenditures to cover the costs of providing hospitalization and medical care insurance[8] rose from $108 million in 1929 to $1,064 million in 1957, from 89 cents per capita to $6.32. This component rose at a slightly higher rate than hospitals, although in dollar volume the amount of the increase was far less, since it began at a much lower figure. It moved from seventh to fifth place and its share of the medical care dollar also almost doubled, from 3.7 to 7.1 cents. Another component which rose relatively was spending for ophthalmic products and orthopedic appliances.

For drug preparations and sundries, volume of expenditures increased from $604 million to $3,098 million, a rise at the same rate as for all components combined. This category claimed 20.6 cents of the dollar in

---

[6] Total output of the economy in constant dollars.

[7] Comprises the current expenditures of nonprofit hospitals and payments by patients to proprietary hospitals and sanitariums.

[8] Premiums less claims: accident and health insurance, mutual accident and sick benefit associations, and group hospitalization associations. Also covers administrative and medical expenses of group health associations and student fees for medical care. Includes costs of insurance against loss of income due to illness.

both 1929 and 1957, although there was some fluctuation in the interim. Its rank dropped from second to third.

For dentists' services, in contrast, even though the rise in volume from $482 to $1,705 million was also substantial, the share of the medical dollar dropped from 16.4 to 11.3 cents, and its rank from third to fourth. Other professional services[9] also rose in absolute volume, but declined with relation to the others.

Not only in current dollars but in constant dollars[10] as well, per capita spending for each major component rose from 1935 to 1957.[11] But the relative rates of increase were considerably different than in current dollars. For example, expenditures for hospitals, physicians, and dentists rose relatively least in constant dollars between 1935 and 1957, averaging 2.8, 3.5, and 3.8 per cent annually, respectively. The comparable increases in spending were higher for ophthalmic services and orthopedic appliances, and drugs (each 5.9 per cent).

These increases in "real" expenditures for the major components of medical care correspond generally to increases in the quantity and variety of services and commodities received by the public, as indicated by data from other sources on the actual utilization of these services. As one example, in 1928–31 an annual average of 2.6 out-of-hospital doctor visits number for the entire population had risen to 4.8.[12] Similarly, the proportion who reported seeing a doctor at all in the course of a year climbed from 48 to 63 per cent.

Also, the average annual number of patient-days in general and special hospitals in the United States rose from 0.88 in 1935 to 1.25 in 1956. Births in hospitals increased from just under 800,000 to about 3.8 million. And the expansion in variety and quality of all types of medical commodities and services (new and better medications, appliances, etc.) has been widespread.

### Fluctuations in the Rate of Growth

Although the volume of medical care spending increased between 1929 and 1957, the pace of increase has been very uneven, responding in

---

[9] Osteopathic physicians, chiropractors, chiropodists and podiatrists, private-duty nurses, and miscellaneous curative and healing professions.

[10] The medical care component of the Bureau of Labor Statistics' Consumer Price Index is used here to "deflate" the current dollar amounts of expenditures. However, for most items it is available only since 1935; some of the expenditure items are not included; and it represents the price changes of a specific "market basket" of medical care items purchased by urban wage earners and clerical worker families. Nevertheless, it is widely used to represent the price trends for medical care. See E. A. Langford, "Medical Care in the Consumer Price Index, 1936–56," *Monthly Labor Review*, No. 80, Vol. 9 (September, 1957), pp. 1053–58.

[11] Comparable figures are not available at all for "other professional services" and only since 1951 for insurance.

[12] Health Information Foundation, *Progress in Health Services*, Vol. VII, Nos. 5 and 8, 1958.

substantial measure to social and economic change. For example, World War II and its aftermath provided considerable impetus to medical spending, while the periods of general economic contraction provided some check.

During World War II, despite the withdrawal of a large segment of the population and medical personnel from civilian life, the average annual rate of increase in medical spending reached about 11 per cent, far exceeding the prewar rate. Even this was exceeded by the 15.4 per cent of the postwar years, reflecting both sharp price increases in medical care and the return of servicemen to civilian life. Even since then the increase has been very rapid, averaging 7.7 per cent annually.

However, when considered on a per capita and constant dollar basis, the magnitude of increase in these various periods, and their relative rank order, are vastly changed. In constant prices, increase in spending per capita was most rapid during the war years, 1941–45 (averaging 8.5 per cent annually). The next most rapid increase took place in the prewar years, 1933–41 (5.5 per cent). The per capita increases in constant prices during the postwar years, 1945–48, and subsequently, 1948–57, have been at much lower rates (3.6 and 2.3, respectively).

As with the aggregate, expenditures on most major components of medical care have generally responded to changes in social conditions and in the level of economic activity. For example, the highest rate of increase for most components occurred during the war and the immediate postwar years. But on a per capita and constant dollar basis, the picture is considerably more complicated, with great variation in relative rates of spending.

In the earlier years, contractions in the general level of economic activity resulted in reductions in the volume of medical expenditures. But today even the impact of recession is almost negligible. For example, consumer spending for medical care in the depression of 1929–33 declined over 9 per cent annually. But in each subsequent period of economic recession, 1937–38, 1948–49, and 1953–54, there was actually an increase in volume, and in each at a progressively higher annual rate— 0.6, 3.9, and 7.7 per cent, respectively. On a per capita basis, there were increases during the last two of the three recession periods. And even for each component of medical spending, contractions in the general economy have been exerting consistently less influence in holding down increases in recent years in rates of consumer spending for them.

## Medical Care Spending and Income

Part of the increase in spending for medical care follows from the increased income of American consumers. Thus, disposable personal income, i.e., income after taxes, rose from $638 per capita in 1929 to $1,812 in 1957, nearly tripling. Medical care spending increased less rapidly than disposable personal income in the prewar period (0.7 per cent for each 1 per cent change in income), but more rapidly since World War II (1.4 per cent for each 1 per cent), and somewhat more rapidly for the period 1929–57 as a whole.

Medical expenditures constituted 3.5 per cent of disposable personal income in 1929, then rose to 4.4 in 1932. During the war years, the proportion fell to a low of 3.1 in 1943, and subsequently rose again. By 1957 spending for medical care accounted for 4.9 per cent of disposable personal income, the highest figure as yet in this series of data.

Medical care has also become a more important part of the average individual's budget and of his level of living—i.e., it has increased substantially as a proportion of all personal expenditures by consumers. In 1929 medical care constituted 3.7 per cent of each dollar spent for all consumer items, but rose to 4.3 by 1933. Between that time and 1948 the proportion fluctuated irregularly between 4.0 and 4.3, but thereafter the rise was sharp. By 1957 the corresponding figure was 5.3 per cent, an increase of over 40 per cent since 1929.

For the consumer, individually and as a member of a family group, medical spending usually runs steadily higher when income is higher. Thus urban families with low incomes in 1950 spent very little on medical care—$91 was the average for families with incomes under $1,000 and $96 for those in the $1,000–$2,000 class. The average was higher for medium-income families ($226 for $4,000–$5,000) and highest at the upper incomes—$373 for $7,500–$10,000 and $446 for $10,000 and over.

But the increasing absolute amount of medical spending with rising income actually constituted a consistently decreasing proportion relatively. Medical spending accounted for 14.5 per cent of the average income of families in the under-$1,000 class and 6.1 per cent for $1,000–$2,000, while for the $10,000-and-over families the figure was only 2.4 per cent of average income.

In summary, American consumers have been shifting their buying habits in the direction of a greater emphasis on medical care. Underpinning this rise has been the rise in income and standard of living generally. Medical care is now becoming a more important part of the American standard of living, while as an "industry" it is becoming a more important part of the American economy.

# 36. PRIVATE HEALTH INSURANCE:
# Changing Patterns of Medical
# Care and Supply in Relation
# to Health Insurance

HERMAN M. and
ANNE R. SOMERS,
*California Law Review,*
August, 1958.

THE GROWTH OF private health insurance in the United States has been phenomenal. As recently as 1940 less than 10 per cent of Americans had any hospital insurance, only 4 per cent had some surgical coverage and slightly over 2 per cent any form of non-surgical medical insurance. By the end of 1957, the percentages were roughly 71, 64, and 42 respectively. Between 1948 and 1956 annual premium payments increased four-fold, from less than $0.9 billion to over $3.6 billion.

This development had its origin in the Depression but the greatest impetus came during the period when Americans were politically embroiled in debate over proposals for national compulsory health insurance and Californians were disputing the Olson and Warren proposals for a similar state program. Private health insurance plans were rapidly advanced as alternatives to governmental programs. Equally important was the simultaneous growth of organized labor and collective bargaining. The wartime wage stabilization program and its encouragement of "fringe benefits," the effect of National Labor Relations Board and U.S. Supreme Court decisions in making such benefits a routine matter for collective bargaining, management's increasing concern for "human relations" in industry, and the continuing post-war emphasis on "health and welfare plans" all helped to accelerate the growth of voluntary health insurance.

This marriage of medical care and industrial relations has had a decisive influence upon the growth and character of health insurance and other medical institutions. The vast majority of insured persons and perhaps three-fifths of all Americans owe their health insurance to an employee benefit plan, paid for in full or in part by their employers, who are now contributing about $1 billion a year.

Health insurance, once a controversial issue, is now a fully accepted instrument for dealing with medical costs. Its achievements are impressive. Yet, there remains considerable controversy as to whether the voluntary mechanism will prove adequate to the need. A deep sense of uncertainty pervades the atmosphere and frequently erupts into conflict even among those who appear to have prospered most from recent developments. Professional and trade journals bristle with accusations and suspicion. Doctors and insurance executives attack each other, but unite in blaming consumers for alleged abuse of health insurance. Medical societies and hospitals are in combat over the issue of "corporate medicine," the loaded term used to describe salaried practice in hospitals. And some now see in organized labor and its growing influence in medical institutions a threatening ogre comparable to that represented in former years by the federal government. Some of these conflicts are discussed later in this paper.

More thoughtful participants in these developments, however, see beneath the surface tensions and conflicts "certain social, political or economic trends that are almost inexorable." The main purpose of this paper is to identify the most important of these powerful trends and the issues and prospects they pose for the future of voluntary health insurance. To do this, it is essential to examine not only health insurance institutions themselves but also the two underlying factors which condition the character of health insurance: consumer demand for medical care and the technology and organization of its provision or supply.

Health insurance is primarily a financial mechanism for bringing supply and demand into a satisfactory and mutually sustaining relationship. But so large and dynamic an institution cannot be neutral in its own influence upon the nature of demand or the organization of supply, even when its administrators so intend. Health insurance has altered the nature and extent of both the demand and the supply just as surely as the latter have influenced the nature and course of health insurance. The three sets of phenomena, each of which is in a process of rapid transition, are partly mutually interactive in their effect on one another and partly independent. . . .

While this paper is primarily concerned with voluntary programs, it must be kept in mind that these programs are not the only important mechanism for supplementing direct consumers' expenditures for medical care in the U.S. today. Despite its sensational growth and its near monopoly of the health insurance field, a far larger proportion of the nation's total medical care bill is still financed through public programs than through private health insurance. In 1956, about 30 per cent of total U.S. medical expenditures was financed by government—local, state and national. If the area of comparison is narrowed to personal health services, disregarding public expenditures for military and community health services, the public sector accounts for 21.4 per cent as compared to 18.9 per cent for voluntary health insurance.

Ideally, therefore, a thorough analysis of the private programs should include an examination of public programs, as the two areas are interrelated. Space does not permit. In any event, it is an axiom of American political life that government is generally permitted to do only what private institutions cannot or will not do. It may be reasonably predicted that government participation in the health insurance field will increase only to the extent that the private institutions fail to fulfill the expectations they have helped to create. The nature of these expectations, the extent to which they are being fulfilled under existing health insurance arrangements, and the potentiality for future fulfillment are the main themes to be pursued.

## THE NEW DIMENSIONS OF DEMAND

During the past 20 years, profound changes have taken place with respect to the extent and nature of demand for health services. At the root of these changes is the scientific revolution in medicine.

### A. The Scientific Revolution in Medicine

Scientific, technological, and economic advances have combined to increase the effectiveness of medical care to a point where it is now a decisive factor in personal and national welfare. This is less a truism than might appear at first glance. The essentiality of medical care is a relatively recent phenomenon. A distinguished medical authority put the matter sharply: "I think it was about the year 1910 or 1912 when it became possible to say of the United States that a random patient with a random disease consulting a doctor chosen at random stood better than a fifty-fifty chance of benefiting from the encounter." Today, 50 years later, medicine has penetrated mysteries of the human body and mind and mastered techniques of surgery, chemotherapy and psychiatry which were not dreamed of at the beginning of the century. At a rapidly accelerating pace, the complex of knowledge and skills now embraced under the composite term "medical care" has increasingly gained the power to give or to withhold life, to give or to withhold the functional capacity which may determine the value of life not only for the seriously disabled but for the great majority of all people who suffer some degree of chronic disability.

This is, of course, not an achievement of the superior wisdom of our century. As Bernard of Chartres put it, the men of any generation are like dwarfs seated on the shoulders of giants. If we are "to see more things than the ancients and things more distant" it is "due neither to the sharpness of our sight, nor the greatness of our stature." But "simply because they have lent us their own." The indispensable foundation for the capacities of contemporary physicians and surgeons traces back to the pioneering inquiries and insights of the early Egyptians and Greeks and the European Renaissance. The discovery of asepsis was no less important and remarkable in its time than the antibiotics and sulfas in ours— and the latter could only follow, not precede, the former. However, as knowledge and skill are cumulative, their expansive force tends to grow geometrically and thus it is that the recent advances in science and technology have made the earlier days of our own century seem like ancient times indeed.

Similarly, it is not possible for medicine to progress or even be meaningful in isolation from the total environment of which it is a part. The achievements of modern medicine stem directly from progress in general scientific research. Engineering advances have been vital to the practical application of scientific medicine. Industrialization, economic progress, social organization, and the spread of humanism and democracy have all contributed to the advance of health and physical well being and the present state of the medical arts. The causal factors explaining the health progress of the nation are multifold, complex, and interdependent. No one knows how much to attribute to medicine as such. But it is clear that medical science is an indispensable ingredient in the amalgam and, even more, that the utility and effectiveness of the other contributing factors such as basic research and improved nutrition find their expression in large part through applied medical arts.

The overall picture of health advance is well known. In the first half of our century the mortality rate declined by almost half. Between 1915 and 1955 alone infant mortality was cut 75 per cent. The ravages of typhoid, diarrhea, dysentery and other infectious diseases have been drastically curtailed. Between 1900 and 1956 the mortality rate from tuberculosis, pneumonia and influenza dropped more than 90 per cent. A baby born in 1957 could be expected to live 23 years longer than one born in 1900.

An even more dramatic comparison, in that it minimizes the non-medical factors, can be made from the records of military death rates: "Where 650 men on the Union side died of disease in the Civil War, there were 250 in the Spanish-American War, 160 in the First World War, and 6 in the Second World War. An improvement of one hundredfold in 90 years."

The evidence as to the increasing effectiveness of modern medicine is vast and incontrovertible. Dr. René Sand, the great Belgian epidemiologist, has said: "We can buy human life. Each country within certain limits decides its own death rate." While the phrase has a probably deliberate melodramatic touch, the essential point is patent: the degree of accessibility or nonaccessibility of modern medical care is now a demonstrably crucial factor in personal and national welfare and is subject to conscious policy influence.

## B. Medical Care as a Civic Right

There is today a broad consensus in this country that people should receive the medical care they need. In 1952 The President's Commission on the Health Needs of the Nation, sixteen eminent citizens representing educational, industrial, labor, agricultural, and consumer interests, as well as the various health professions, after a year of study and voluminous testimony, agreed upon a set of guiding principles for approaching the nation's health problem. The first of these was: "Access to the means for the attainment and preservation of health is a basic human right." The Commission also said, "We set as a goal for this Nation a situation in which adequate health personnel, facilities, and organization make comprehensive health services available for all, with a method of financing to make this care universally accessible."

This concept of medical care as a "right" has now become part of our political vocabulary. A 1957 study of tax-supported medical programs in Pennsylvania begins as follows, "Democratic societies are by definition committed to a series of ethical assumptions emphasizing the value of human life and well-being. We interpret these humanitarian principles to mean that each individual has the right to command certain fundamental necessities, among them, medical care."

This new public attitude toward medical care stems partly from the growing health consciousness of the American people, partly from their increasing familiarity with the new medical potential. During World War II and the Korean War, for example, the whole vast armory of American medical resources and skills was put at the disposal of the humblest Army private from Mississippi and a whole gamut of free medical services was provided to his dependents. Millions of civilian war workers obtained, for the first time in their lives, access to first-class medical care on a non-charity basis. The trend has, in lesser degree, continued since the war, thanks primarily to the new methods of financing medical care, both public and private. Today, more people are directly experiencing the benefits of the scientific revolution in medicine than ever before.

The new attitude also stems from the changing socio-economic climate of post-war America. It comes from more education, higher incomes and greater mass purchasing power. Knowledge, accompanied by general rising standards of living, brings expectation and demand. People may not take literally Dr. Sand's dictum—"We can buy human life"—but an increasing number of Americans appear to have adopted the view that "adequate medical care" is as much implicit in the right to "life, liberty and the pursuit of happiness" as, for example, public education.

This revolution in individual attitudes is intertwined with new community attitudes. We are continuously reminded that industry and the economy, our productivity, resources, and security suffer conspicuously and often unnecessarily from the losses caused by illness, absenteeism, and disability. In recent years, it has been progressively emphasized that health and medical care are essential sources of military and national strength. And we are equally often reminded that this does not simply rest in the laps of the gods. Little wonder then that medical care is changing from the status of a "private luxury" or a "blessed benevolence" to that of a "civic right."

Equally important, however, is the fact that when Americans speak of "adequate medical care" they do not have in mind any finite or definable quantity or quality. The incoherence and potential enormity of this new demand, if present economic barriers were removed or reduced, has led some to fear that health insurance could, like the Sorcerer's Apprentice, be almost drowned in the flood which it might unloose without being able to control. For example, Professor Ginzberg has cautioned, "There is a marked difference between society's commitment to provide free education . . . and a commitment to provide adequate medical care for all in need. Education can be quantitatively delimited. Moreover, it requires that the individual exert himself. The limits of medical care are much more elastic. . . ."

There is, however, accumulating evidence that both the extent and nature of the potential demand for medical care are more subject to definition and measurement than was thought possible only a few years ago. Several kinds of studies have greatly increased our knowledge of present and future demand patterns: the public health survey with its emphasis on basic demographic, morbidity, and disability data; studies of medical care expenditures; and of medical care utilization. Together they shed a good deal of light on the possibility of meeting this new demand through voluntary health insurance.

## C. The Changing Pattern of Basic Needs

Increasing life expectancy has altered our population picture and this in turn has resulted in marked changes in the incidence and pattern of illness. Four times as many persons in the United States today are 65 or over as in 1900. As a proportion of the total population they have more than doubled: 4.1 per cent in 1900 to 8.6 per cent in 1955. The number of aged and aging will continue to increase rapidly. Based on 1955 death rates, there will be at least 21 million 65 or over by 1975, as compared to 14 million in 1955. How much they will continue to increase relative to the whole population is uncertain and depends mainly on the future birth rate. If this continues at its recent very high level, the increase in the proportion of the aged may be relatively small. On the other hand, a decline in fertility, which appears more likely, would mean a rapid increase in the proportion of the aged. The 1958 estimates of the Social Security Administration indicate a range from 9.4 per cent to 10.7 per cent for 1975 and from 9.7 per cent to 12.9 per cent in 1990. In any case, it appears that by 1975 persons 45 and over will constitute about one third of the population.

Such demographic changes have been accompanied by marked changes in morbidity patterns but overall illness rates have not declined. Increased longevity means primarily a shift in incidence from disease of the young to diseases of the aging and the reduction in mortality means more illness among the aged. At the beginning of the century, the three leading causes of death were influenza and pneumonia, tuberculosis, and diarrhea and enteritis—all acute infectious diseases which affect primarily the young. By 1950, the three leading causes of death were diseases of the heart, cancer, and vascular lesions of the brain—chronic degenerative diseases associated primarily with older age groups and characterized by insidious inception, long duration and a high proportion of residual disability.

Whereas the incidence of acute illness, including respiratory and other communicable diseases, gastrointestinal disorders, and accidents, is greatest among the young and declines with age, the pattern is reversed for chronic illness. Compared to the population as a whole, those 65 and over experience two to three times as much chronic illness. Persons 45–64 also have a strikingly higher degree of chronic illnesses than young people. The result is that total days of disability increase sharply with advancing ages as does the average rate of hospital utilization. The aged average about three times as many days of disability a year and over twice as many days in the hospital as the general population.

About half of the hospital beds in the country are now occupied by the mentally ill, and more than half of all Veterans Administration hospital patients are psychotics. It is not difficult to understand why mental illness is often called the nation's foremost health problem. On an average day in 1956, 722,000 persons—almost equal to the combined population of Nevada and New Hampshire—were patients in psychiatric hospitals. For a quarter-century there has been a steady and alarming increase in mental illness. In part, this is due to a better understanding and ability to recognize the nature of mental disease and society's relatively new willingness to accept it as such. In part, however, the influence of longevity is evident. The incidence of mental illness is far more pronounced among the aged than in the general population.

It appears clear that a progressively larger proportion of the nation's total demand for medical services will relate to the growing problem areas—chronic and mental illness. The corollary of this shift is an increasing need for long-term preventive, rehabilitative, semi-custodial, and medical social services in contrast to the great current emphasis on treatment of acute illness. Most chronic diseases are months or years in developing and require early diagnosis if they are to be handled effectively. The period of treatment is, by definition, extensive. If "cure" is achieved there is often required a long "post-cure" rehabilitation. People rarely die now of the once deadly disease of diabetes, but they do require continuous medical supervision. Thus the expanding influence of chronic illness has been an important factor in enlarging the concept of "adequate medical care" to include a broad spectrum of services running from earliest positive promotion of health to ultimate rehabilitation.

These new tendencies are by no means confined to long-term disability. The progress in science and technology has had significant effects on the need for other types of medical care as well. Consider the case of pneumonia. Thirty years ago, old people frequently died of it in three days. "Now," as the director of the Massachusetts General Hospital says, "they may be cured, but after 30 days of illness, with doctors and nurses in attendance. The death rate is lower, and the patients live, but they have had ten times as many days of disability and medical attendance." The effect of such medical advances on the average medical costs of the aged is well documented and a source of major difficulty with respect to current health insurance.

The maternal death rate has been cut about 85 per cent since 1900, but now expectant mothers see doctors regularly during their pregnancy and commonly use hospital facilities for delivery, which was not the case 50 years ago. The dramatic decline in infant and child mortality has gone hand in hand with development of, and a growing demand for, the new specialization of pediatrics. Obstetrics and pediatrics have become two of the most important aspects of modern medicine. Both are committed to continuous health maintenance rather than episodic treatment.

The continued high incidence of automobile and other accidents, now the fourth most common cause of death, and the exploration of new fields of surgery, especially of the brain and heart, call for the same "life or death" virtuosity which has distinguished the great surgical pioneers of the past. But success in these endeavors adds evidence to the point. Those who are saved from death by the miracles of modern surgery will frequently require long periods of indispensable care and supervision.

With such progress and change, the once-supposed clear-cut dichotomy between health and illness becomes increasingly blurred and the concept of medical need becomes very difficult to pinpoint in space or time. There is rather a continuous spectrum with varying degrees of emphasis. It begins before we are actually ill; it does not cease when we are discharged from the hospital. Continuity and comprehensiveness are becoming essential aspects of effective medical care.

### D. Changing Health Mores

The greatly enlarged potential demand for medical care implicit in the new patterns of medical need has already been partially translated into utilization and expenditure figures, both of which have been going up steadily since the early Thirties. The U.S. Bureau of Labor Statistics, after eliminating the factor of price rise, found that expenditures per family for medical care in 1950 were nearly 2½ times as much as in 1934–36, although family size is now smaller. Moreover, the figures do not include the additional value of employer contributions to health insurance nor the expansion in public medical care programs.

Between 1948 and 1956, private expenditures for medical care rose from $7.3 billion to $12.1 billion. Adjusted for price changes, the real increase was 27 per cent. Note the extent to which this increase has been associated with the expansion of health insurance. During this nine-year period, direct payments by consumers fell from 88 per cent of the total to 70 per cent, while insurance benefits rose from 8 per cent to 25 per cent. While health insurance—benefits plus overhead—represented only 12 per cent of all private expenditures in 1948, it accounted for 57 per cent of the $4.8 billion increase between 1948 and 1957.

The evidence supports the view that health insurance has probably stimulated greater utilization of all medical services—the uninsured as well as the insured. But it does not support the fear that potential demand is indefinitely expansible, subject to no predictable limits, and thus that general care is not insurable.

In the first place, the stimulus has not been as great as may appear. The overall increase of 27 per cent, in constant dollars, took place in a period of prosperity when almost all consumer expenditures were increasing as well. The proportion of per capita disposable personal income going for medical expenditures increased only 8.5 per cent between 1948 and 1956. Even in 1957, only about 5 per cent of family expenditures, an average of $280, was devoted to medical care, hardly a sum or a proportion to suggest that Americans are being profligate with health services.

But there is more direct evidence on this core question. Studies, both here and abroad, indicate that in the early years of any new health care program which reduces previous economic barriers, demand is rapidly increased, reflecting a backlog of unsatisfied need. But after this transitional and often difficult period of adjustment, a stable and adequate means of financing usually results in a stabilized demand. This is emphasized in a recent study of the Windsor, Ontario, Medical Services plan, which provides comprehensive physicians' services on a prepaid basis—hospital services are provided by Blue Cross—to 191,000 subscribers, 85 per cent of the population. After about 20 years of operation, the demand for physicians' services seems to have become stabilized at a point about ⅓ above the average for the uninsured. In 1954, 68 per cent of Windsor Medical Service subscribers visited a doctor compared to 58 per cent of members of non-comprehensive plans and 51 per cent of the uninsured.

Strikingly similar findings are reported for enrollees of the Health Insurance Plan of Greater New York (HIP), the largest comprehensive prepayment plan in the United States, which has been in existence about 10 years. HIP officials report that about 75 per cent of its enrollees see a doctor at least once a year compared with 57 per cent for the general New York City population. With respect to number of visits to doctors, the Kaiser Foundation Health Plan in the San Francisco Bay Area reports an average of 4.5 visits to doctors' offices per patient per year, also after a decade of operation, while the California Health Survey found an average of 5, including home calls, for the general population. These comparisons suggest that removal or substantial minimization of the economic barrier results in a significant, but neither inordinate nor totally unpredictable, rise in the demand for health services. As the Windsor study concluded, "The distribution of services in the population appeared to be stable over time; many people received only a few services and a few received many. As a result, the use of comprehensive services can be predicted statistically, so that insurance principles are applicable."

*The Trend to Hospital.* Changes in health mores are also revealed by relative changes in the utilization of the different types of services. The most dramatic change has been the increase in the proportion of private medical expenditures going for hospital services: a rise from 25 per cent in 1948 to 34 per cent in 1956. The corollary has been a relative decline in the role of the other major components of medical care: the proportion going to physicians dropped from 32 to 30 per cent; for medicines and appliances, from 25 to 21 per cent; for dentists from 11 to 9 per cent.

If the category "physicians' services" were broken down and payments for surgical and obstetrical fees, almost always associated with hospitalized care, were added to the hospital category, the proportion of all costs going for hospital-associated illness would rise to over 40 per cent of the total. These figures are partially discounted by the far greater price rise in hospital costs than for medical costs generally, but even after adjustment is made for this factor we find that hospital expenditures increased by 30 per cent in constant dollars while all other medical expenditures increased 20 per cent between 1948 and 1956.

A major transformation has taken place in the role of the hospital in the medical care pattern of the American people. Almost three times as many Americans are admitted to hospitals today as 20 years ago. Six out of every 100 were hospitalized during the year 1935 but by 1955 the proportion was 13 out of every 100. Hospital insurance is by far the most prevalent form of health insurance with in-hospital surgical insurance second.

There appears to be a disparity between the character of medical need revealed by the morbidity and disability studies and the actual patterns of expenditure and health insurance coverage. Whereas the emphasis in the former is on long-term chronic illness and continuous preventive and maintenance care, the emphasis in the latter is on short-term illness and acute emergencies. As a result of this dichotomy, major policy debates have taken place for years as to whether there is a conflict between the type of insurance consumers need and the kind available. Public health experts and others who emphasize demographic and morbidity data have stressed the need for comprehensive care. The American Medical Association and others who formerly opposed comprehensive insurance could point persuasively to actual patterns of utilization.

The reasons for the "trend to hospital" are too many and too complex for adequate treatment here. However, some understanding of the major causes is essential to any effort to predict the future course of this trend and hence the appropriateness of the present dominant pattern of health insurance. There appear to be three broad sets of factors:

1. There has been a widespread appreciation of the new central role of the modern hospital both as symbol and physical embodiment of the scientific revolution in medicine. The hospital stands for the oxygen tent, the blood bank, the operating room, and the other miraculous instruments through which modern medicine has demonstrated its ability to save or to deny life. The American people have insisted on taking advantage of this life-saving institution in greater and greater numbers.

At the same time, hospital care, rightly or wrongly, is generally associated with high, even catastrophic, costs. It is not surprising that, in spite of the admonitions of the public health experts, the average American appears to have felt that his first insurance requirement was against these costs. The attitude of insurance carriers, doctors, and other interested parties reinforced this conviction.

2. There is a mutually interactive relation between demand and supply. Once hospital insurance became the dominant health insurance pattern, it is understandable that in the almost total absence of other types of health insurance people would try to stretch the available protection to cover parts of their uninsured costs. A disproportionate supply of one type of medical service can lead, at least temporarily, to a distorted demand for that service. In any case, health insurance has now replaced income-level as the major socio-economic influence on the hospitalization of Americans. Recent studies are consistent in pointing to the decisive influence of health insurance in raising utilization rates: the insured enter hospitals more often and use more days on the average than the uninsured. The Health Information Foundation (H.I.F.) 1953 survey found that hospital admission rates were 14 per 100 for the insured, 9 per 100 for the uninsured. The insured averaged 100 hospital days per 100 persons a year; the uninsured 70.

This has resulted in widespread charges of "abuse" of hospital insurance by patients and/or doctors. There is wide difference of opinion among the experts as to the extent of such "abuse," if any, and its significance, but there is an increasing consensus as to the built-in tendency toward overutilization of hospital services in the dominant health insurance pattern. This conclusion is reinforced by evidence that, under comprehensive health insurance, hospital utilization rates are significantly lower than where only hospital and surgical costs are covered.

According to Dr. Frederick Mott, "Blue Cross subscribers nationally utilized an average of 995 days of hospital care per 1000 persons in 1956. In Michigan the figure was 1100 days per thousand. On the other hand, the utilization figure for Kaiser Plan subscribers in Northern California was 624 days, for Group Health in Seattle it was 562 and for Group Health in the District of Columbia it was 546." A recent study of comparative hospitalization experience of HIP and Blue Shield subscribers in New

York City, with similar Blue Cross coverage, found that approximately 8 out of 100 HIP enrollees were hospitalized in a year as compared to 10 out of 100 Blue Shield enrollees.

The contention is that the availability of physicians' services on a pre-paid basis for out-patient diagnosis and early treatment tends to reduce the incidence of hospitalized illness. This theory is receiving increasing recognition. For example, Dr. George Wheatley, vice-president, Metropolitan Life Insurance Company, quotes with approval this statement by another doctor, "I think an insurance policy sold without office or outpatient coverage is a greater cause of abuse and increased cost than any other single factor."

3. In addition to health insurance, many other socio-economic factors are known to influence hospital utilization. The effect of age in increasing utilization rates has already been noted. Contrary to popular belief, despite higher female admission rates during child-bearing years, male utilization of hospitals is higher than female due primarily to longer stays.

Among the insured, the lower the income the higher the admission rates and the greater the number of hospital days used. The effect of increased education is closely related. A 1951 New York study indicated that persons with less than 9 years schooling averaged significantly longer hospital stays than those with more education, regardless of age or insurance status. With respect to hospital admissions, however, the situation is at least partially reversed. An important British study found that marriage appears to be a safeguard against hospitalization. The same phenomenon appears to prevail in this country. This and the high male utilization rate suggest the important role of home nursing facilities. Home environment and even sheer loneliness may be swelling hospital lists, especially of the aged. During the past few decades, the hospitals have been increasingly called on to provide services which other facilities might have provided more economically.

From these three factors it would appear that the increasing utilization of the hospital is, in large part, well warranted by its increased technological importance in modern medical care and by the backlog of need on the part of many people to whom it was previously denied. In part, however, demand has been artifically skewed by the general limitation of insurance to this particular type of service, by the lack of other community facilities and services, and by inadequate consumer appreciation of the importance of preventive care.

But this situation appears in a stage of transition. Health insurance itself has helped to stimulate health education as well as health consciousness. The people are becoming more critical. As early as 1953, the Health Information Foundation-National Opinion Research Center study of Blue Cross-Blue Shield and Aetna subscribers found that ¼–⅓ were dissatisfied with their present insurance coverage, primarily on the basis of too narrow protection. Organized labor is pressing, with increasing success, for "supplementary benefits"—out-patient diagnostic services, home and office doctor visits, dental care, drugs, eye care, etc. These are already beginning to spread. The continued growth of HIP, the Kaiser Plans, and a number of other comprehensive prepayment organizations, in spite of the frequent opposition of state medical societies, is testimony to the persistent strength of the demand for comprehensive coverage. So is the rapid growth of the new "major medical" and "comprehensive" policies sold by the commercial carriers and the somewhat belated but now strenuous efforts on the part of a few Blue Cross and Blue Shield organizations to extend out-patient and non-hospitalized medical coverage.

Leading authorities in medical economics agree on this point. For example, Dr. Odin Anderson has said, "The drive toward greater comprehensiveness of benefits has been so relentless that the principle itself is not an issue any more and current discussion and worry are now directed to 'how comprehensive' and how can it be administered." Dr. Mott has said, "In this evolutionary situation [with respect to health insurance] the most powerful force shaping events is the increasing demand of the public for more comprehensive services and more complete financial protection."

The new demand is in part a tribute to the success of hospital and surgical insurance in their limited fields in pointing the way towards further advances. In part it is a simple recognition of the fact that the largest and most stubborn part of medical costs still involves non-hospital, *i.e.*, noninsured costs. The growing demand for "comprehensive" health insurance —which, of course, does not mean coverage of all costs, but does mean a much greater coverage than is now available—appears to signify a reconciliation of basic need with expressed demand. The capacity of voluntary health insurance to cope successfully with this demand will be a major determinant of its future.

# 37. HEALTH ISN'T FREE

*Business Review*, Federal Reserve Bank of Philadelphia, December, 1958.

WHEN YOU FIRST become vaguely conscious of a feeling of discomfort somewhere in the equatorial region you are inclined to ignore it. If the discomfort degenerates into a nuisance or a pain that aspirin tablets no longer dispel, you reluctantly consult a doctor. After a professional pummeling and poking, the doctor finds the cause of your trouble. It has a Latin name, and requires immediate surgery says the doctor with profound gravity. Your face betrays even greater gravity as you exclaim, "An operation!" And so, for the first time in your life, you enter a hospital carrying a valise instead of a bouquet.

### On Going to a Hospital

On checking in at the hospital, there is a long questionnaire to be filled out. Cavalierly, you answer all the questions—just a matter of routine—except the one about who is your next of kin.

You are not expected to tip the nurse who conducts you to your room. She tells you to get undressed, go to bed, and promptly disappears. Apprehensively, you await the surgeon with his kit of tools, but nothing happens. Just about the time you conclude that you have been forgotten, a succession of nurses appears—one to lead you to the scale for a weighing, another to take your temperature and pulse, another to take your blood pressure, and the needle nurse to get samples of your blood.

After another long period of apparent neglect, comes a squad of nurses with a rig that looks like a portable filling station after it is assembled. Your hunch was right. The juice flowing by little drops into your blood stream is glucose and saline—an energy reinforcement and a shock absorber. About the time you are fueled up, the surgeon makes his appearance. He engages you in cheerful conversation and avoids all shop talk except to say that you will have your operation at 8 o'clock tomorrow morning and that you will not be given any breakfast. After a loudspeaker announcement asking all the visitors to leave the hospital, a nurse hands you a paper cup and a small capsule, designed to help you to fall asleep.

The capsule made short work of the night. A pair of nurses in spotless uniforms gives you full attention. Another capsule and another needle and you get dressed up for the party with the queerest toggery you ever saw. The queerest toggery you ever . . . the queerest toggery you . . . the queerest tog . . . the queerest . . . the queer . . . the . . .

It is most uncomfortable to be lying on a steeply slanted roof on top of a tall building with a tin sheet for a cover and no pillow. But there you lie at a dizzy height—way, way up. Way up, "Wake up!" says the nurse standing beside your bed, and you ask why all the delay, why didn't they perform the operation, and she tells you that it's all over. Then why can't you be let alone? Why the brushing of teeth and the bathing fetish? You will surely come apart if the nurse insists on going through with the bathing ceremony! With persistence on the part of the nurse and no cooperation on your own, bathing is completed and, miraculously, you have not come apart.

The days of convalescence get longer and longer, especially after you graduate from the horizontal to the vertical. The body has long since recovered from the shock of surgery, and finally comes the day when the surgeon says you may go home. When you check out, there is another shock—the bill. At $18 a day for so many days, the largest item is likely to be room service. Then there are numerous extras, such as laboratory fees, drugs, operating room, anesthesia, X-ray, and perhaps blood service, physiotherapy, oxygen, and surgical dressings. The total bill may be $500 or more. Nor is that the end.

Some time later, during convalescence at home, you receive in the mail another shock—the surgeon's bill. That may be $300, more or less, depending upon the nature of the surgery. Not counting loss of income through absence from the job, the operation may cost $800—a serious blow to the family budget.

Everyone is a potential hospital patient. In the course of a year, at least one out of ten persons becomes a bed case for medical attention. Prior to the first time you land in a hospital, you probably had regarded yourself as a superman—perpetual strength in perpetual motion. Hospitalization teaches you that the body you live in is a fragile retort of flushing chemicals and fleeting emotions. With the help of enforced rest the human body usually recovers very nicely from the physical shock of surgery.

Recovery from the psychic shock to the pocketbook-nerve is achieved by some people through the purchase of health insurance. About 70 million people are insured against the hazard of hospital expenses. Under these policies the insurance companies indemnify the beneficiaries for hospital expenses incurred. Another form of protection, perhaps less well known, is Blue Cross.

## BLUE CROSS

Blue Cross is a prepayment program between a number of hospitals which offer their services and a large number of people who want protection on a regular basis against the hazard of hospital bills. It is a nonprofit corporation which removes most of the money worries of hospitalization. The basic principle of Blue Cross is a service contract—that is, one providing benefits, not dollars, coupled with a Blue Cross member hospital contract, under which payment is made to the hospital for the service benefits guaranteed by them. It is a prepayment plan whereby the subscribers buy their hospital service when they are well so as to reduce the shocks of money worries when they are ill.

### How It Works

Blue Cross is no Santa Claus, but another form of protection utilizing the insurance principle. The subscriber pays for what he gets, and the payments are made in advance in manageable monthly installments, and the payoff comes on the day of adversity.

The subscriber may buy the hospital service by entering into an individual contract with Blue Cross or he may subscribe as a member of a group—usually the firm or company he works for. Under the group subscription plan, a single remittance is customarily made by the firm for all of its employee-subscribers, and some firms absorb part or all of the cost on behalf of their employee-subscribers.

Monthly payments under the group plans range from slightly over $2 for individual protection to approximately $7 for family protection, where all members of the family are covered. Rates vary with the type of contract and in Pennsylvania are subject to review and adjudication of the State Commissioner of Insurance.

The benefits to subscribers, depending on the contract, cover most of the hospital costs such as semi-private room, meals, nursing service, operating room charges, drugs, anesthetics, electro-cardiograms, laboratory fees, etc. Subscribers under a group plan need not terminate their hospitalization service upon retirement. Upon payment of the going rates, subscribers may continue their Blue Cross protection through the period of retirement. This is a particularly attractive feature because the need for hospitalization usually increases with age.

**A Prodigious Growth**

Blue Cross has had a phenomenal growth in the comparatively short period since its inception. No one knows when he will need hospital care nor what it will cost him. The hospital bill for one patient with heart disease may be $250 and for another with the same disease it may be $2,500. The amount depends upon the procedures required for proper treatment, the drugs administered, the length of stay, and many other factors—all beyond the patient's control.

In 1932, a National Committee on the Costs of Medical Care discovered that 50 per cent of the cost of all medical care in the United States was incident to hospitalized illness or disabilities. Furthermore, it was found that the 10 per cent of the people who are hospitalized each year had to bear 50 per cent of the medical care costs for that year. These are the reasons for the widespread acceptance of the Blue Cross plan for providing hospitalization under which payment is made to the hospital for the service benefits guaranteed by them.

The Associated Hospital Service of Philadelphia was started in 1938, with an office force of five people, a typewriter, borrowed furniture, a box of pencils, and a $30,000 loan. Today, Blue Cross of Philadelphia occupies eight floors of a 12-story building it owns in central city; has 550 employees, a telephone switchboard with 73 trunk lines, a teletype system, electronic data processing machines, and a forest of files. All this is required to accommodate its 2¼ million subscribers and the 85 member hospitals in the Philadelphia metropolitan area. Payments to hospitals on behalf of subscribers rose steadily from less than $5 million in 1945 to approximately $45 million in 1957. Payments in 1957 averaged $122,000 every day of the year. In the twenty years of operation, Blue Cross has paid out over $300 million of hospital bills for approximately 3 million subscriber cases who have benefited by receiving hospital care. In 1938, the Mayor of Philadelphia took out the first membership card. Now, 68 per cent of the population of Greater Philadelphia is covered by Blue Cross.

The Lehigh Valley Blue Cross has had a similarly rapid rate of growth during its comparatively short period of existence. Its membership grew from 26,000 in 1940 to almost 350,000 in 1957, and hospital claims paid since 1940 rose from less than $100,000 to approximately $6½ million. Wherever Blue Cross hospital protection is available, people are quick to take advantage of its facilities.

It is significant that there are more than 80 non-profit Blue Cross Plans throughout the United States, serving over 55 million subscribers. All Blue Cross Plans must meet the requirements of the American Hospital Association. All of them render service benefits, as distinguished from cash indemnities. Their boards of directors include representatives of hospitals, the medical profession, and the public, and directors serve without pay. Within a period of 25 years, payments of hospital bills for subscribers of Blue Cross Plans rose from $15,000 a year to more than a billion dollars in 1957. This is a rate of growth few industries can match.

## SOME HOSPITAL ECONOMICS

Maintenance of the country's 7,000 hospitals costs the American people $5½ billion annually, and they have more than $12 billion invested in them. Blue Cross does not own or run any of these institutions, but it has a direct interest in the voluntary hospitals which serve its subscribers whose bills it pays.

Hospitals are indispensible but peculiar institutions with a strange history. Originally, our hospitals were charitable institutions for the down and out. Now they are health-restoring centers for the down and in.

A hospital is like a hotel that merged with a restaurant, a laboratory, and sometimes a nurses' training school, medical college, pharmacy, library, and nursery to boot. It takes quite a variety of skills to manage a hospital—bookkeepers, engineers, dieticians, doctors, dishwashers, maids, nurses, laboratory technicians, surgeons, physiotherapists, internes, elevator operators, etc. The doctors are not under the control of the hospital but they decide who is to be admitted, how long each patient is to stay, and the nature of the treatment. Thus, medical practitioners exert considerable influence over the expenses incurred by these institutions, as they must. It is a rare hospital indeed that does not have a shortage of beds, nurses, rooms, ice water, and money, and an abundance of patients, visitors, flowers, hypodermics, and complaints. Running a hospital requires a depth and breadth of understanding that is out of this world. The manager ought to be a doctor of medicine, law, psychology, economics, bacteriology, engineering, dietetics, sociology, and backing-up drain pipes. The wonder is that hospitals run as well as they do.

### The Cost of Medical Care

Medical care costs money, and in recent years it has been costing more and more. The costs of services, as distinguished from goods, are usually slow in responding to economic developments, but when they rise, they soar. The cost of medical care more or less paralleled the rising cost of living in the early postwar years. After 1951, however, cost of medical care rose much faster than the over-all cost of living and now the cost of medical care is 44 per cent above the 1947–1949 base, in contrast with the consumer price index, which is 23 per cent above the base. Moreover, it is somewhat disturbing that the rising cost of medical care shows no signs whatsoever of letting up despite the fact that it costs $1.44 to buy the medical care that cost only a dollar a mere decade ago.

Since 1947, the cost of medical care has gone up faster than any of the other major items in the consumer price index except transportation. . . .

### Doctor Bills and Hospital Bills

When illness strikes, people are prone to growl and grumble about doctor bills, but those whose illness lands them in the hospital have a much better conversation piece for griping. Look at the accompanying table and

PERCENTAGE INCREASES IN COST OF MEDICAL AND
OTHER SERVICES, 1947–1957

| B.L.S. Item | Index (1947–1949 = 100) | | |
| --- | --- | --- | --- |
| | 1947 | 1957 | Percent Increase |
| Hospital room rates | 87.4 | 187.3 | 114 |
| Public transportation | 88.6 | 178.8 | 102 |
| Men's haircuts | 94.3 | 159.3 | 69 |
| Laundry service | 94.2 | 137.4 | 46 |
| Automobile repairs | 95.5 | 139.7 | 46 |
| General practitioners' fees | 96.9 | 134.5 | 39 |
| Dentists' fees | 95.2 | 127.4 | 34 |
| Movie admissions | 98.4 | 130.5 | 33 |
| Shoe repairs | 97.1 | 125.6 | 29 |
| Surgeons' fees | 96.2 | 120.9 | 26 |

see how hospital room rates have gone up in contrast with doctor bills and costs of other services. During the past decade, hospital room rates more than doubled, which is in striking contrast with the 26 per cent increase in surgeons' fees, the 34 per cent increase in dentists' fees, and the 39 per cent rise in fees of general practitioners. The cost of haircuts, laundry service, automobile repairs, and public transportation all rose more than doctors' bills and less than hospital room rates.

### YOU CAN'T PAY BILLS WITH INDEX NUMBERS

"The medical care index, like the whole of the Consumer Price Index, is designed to measure only the change in price for items of *the same quality and quantity customarily bought* by urban wage-earner and clerical-worker families." So says the Bureau of Labor Statistics, which created and maintains the index. The italics are our own, for thereby hangs a tale of considerable moment to hospitals, doctors, Blue Cross, and all people served by them.

Someone has said that hospital care today is as different from such care fifteen years ago as today's aircraft differs from that fifteen years ago. Medical science has not been standing still. Although hospitals do not practice medicine, they supply the housing, machinery, tools, and all the other supplies and facilities required by the doctors who practice medicine within their walls with ever-advancing technology. A complicated piece of machinery like an artificial heart or an artificial kidney, which keeps a patient alive while the surgeon is operating on the organ, may cost $300 just to set up the machine and run it while the surgery is being performed.

Hospitals are constantly being called upon to perform a variety of services. Surgery is not the only function. Hospitals are offering increased diagnostic and treatment services. They are called upon for more private and semi-private accommodations; they are performing more outpatient service; they have expanded programs of medical and nursing education, and also have expanded programs of public education. These are all necessary functions but it costs money to perform them.

Hospital costs go up or down with fluctuations in occupancy. In a hospital, the unit of production is the bed occupied by a patient; an empty bed produces no revenue and it entails overhead costs that must be borne by the patients receiving care. The ideal situation would be to have all beds occupied all of the time, but a hospital just cannot schedule production like a cheese factory.

Improvements in diagnostic and treatment procedures have shortened the average length of stay of patients, and that likewise contributes to higher per diem costs. Higher bed turnover, to borrow a term from industry, increases nursing costs and housekeeping expenses.

Rising salary and wage levels are major causes of increasing hospital costs. Hospitals must compete with industrial and commercial concerns in the general labor market to get their complement of employees with diversified skills and talents, and as a result of rising wage-salary scales generally, hospitals are under constant pressure of rising costs to get and keep adequate staffs.

Still another cause of rising hospital costs is the readier disposition of a rapidly growing population to utilize hospital services when needed. Scarcely a generation ago, people were scared of hospitals and shied away from them like the plague. Indeed, there was a time when, in the opinion of some people, hospitals delayed rather than hastened the restoration of the health of its patients. In this generation, however, it is the rare person who does not accept hospitalization on recommendation of his doctor; the annual in-patient admission rate has increased from 8 to 12 per cent of the total population.

## Curbing the Costs

As might be expected, no two hospitals are alike nor are their cost curves alike. Identical treatment of identical cases may cost 30 to 40 per cent more in one hospital than in another. Variations in cost arise from differences in age of buildings and equipment and differences in managerial policies and performance.

Efforts to reduce hospital costs are exerted in four major areas: more effective utilization of facilities, improved personnel practices, better procurement procedures, and improved accounting practices. C. Rufus Rorem, Executive Director, Hospital Council of Philadelphia, points out (in the March 1957 *Journal* of the American Hospital Association) four major areas that have been effective in controlling the cost incurred by hospitals in serving patients.

More effective utilization of beds and diagnostic and treatment facilities. (Reduction of number of beds per room to permit alternative use by various types of patients; increased special services to vertical patients referred for study and treatment by physicians; better scheduling of admissions, discharges and professional procedures to avoid the necessity of expanded facilities for beds and scientific equipment.)

More effective use of professional and institutional personnel. (The employment of practical nurses, aides and technicians to perform certain functions under the direction of professional nurses.)

More scientific procurement and use of supplies and materials. (The adoption of uniform standards to permit large-scale buying for departments; simplification of sizes and types to reduce manufacturers' cost; joint buying of commodities where specifications can be applied to generally used items; systematic storage and issuance procedures; group conferences and action among hospital purchasing agents concerning purchasing methods; standards of quality, delivery schedules, etc.)

Uniform accounting and statistics. More effective use of uniform accounting and statistics would enable hospitals to appraise the results of varying methods and practices, and to compare the experiences with those of other institutions. The information obtained through adequate and uniform records and reports, if properly applied would, in my opinion, increase services in most hospitals without additional expense.

Blue Cross has a very real interest in keeping hospital costs at a minimum because all of its income collected from subscribers is used to pay hospital bills except for costs of administration. In Philadelphia, 93 cents of every dollar collected from subscribers is available to pay hospital bills.

Some people say that Blue Cross Plans, by their very nature, promote unnecessary hospitalization, that some doctors either on their own or under pressure of their patients are too quick to send patients to hospitals and too slow to discharge them. The problem, whatever its magnitude, is a medical problem and should be solved by the medical staff. Doctors themselves should and must decide what is best for their patients. Concerted efforts are being made to eliminate the abuses of Blue Cross privileges. Blue Cross has tightened its contract provisions with subscribers. The Pennsylvania Insurance Commissioner has authorized Blue Cross Plans to make expenditures for instituting reforms to eliminate abuses in the use of hospital care.

Blue Cross of Philadelphia has given widespread publicity to an effective plan devised by the Sacred Heart Hospital of Allentown for the elimination of unnecessary use of hospital facilities. In order to eliminate Blue Cross "boarders," that hospital set up a plan for admitting patients based upon the degree of urgency, and systematic procedures were established to shorten the stay of each patient. The plan includes features such as quicker transfer of patients to specialists, scheduling of X-ray and laboratory tests before admission, speeding up requests for consultation, moving up the check-out time before 11 a.m. to save a day's room charge, no shifting of patients from private rooms to semi-private or wards where shortages usually prevail, and penalizing doctors for nonconformance with the rules.

Blue Cross rates have gone up from time to time as a consequence of rising hospital costs, increased use of hospitals, and improved hospital care provided. The statement has been made that Blue Cross is in danger of pricing itself out of the market. Blue Cross rates, however, have gone up only because hospital costs have gone up; so what the statement really means is that hospitals may price themselves out of the market. The probability of that happening is just about as great as the chance that people will stop eating because the cost of food is too high.

Suppose that all of our hospitals were modern and up to date, that all were adequately staffed, that all inefficiencies were eliminated, and that all costs had been cut to the irreducible minimum. As a result of all this, it might be possible to reduce your hospital bill materially. Whatever the reduction in the size of the bill, it would still be a shock to the individual. This is not to say that unnecessary costs should be tolerated, but there is no escape from the simple and obvious truth that it costs money to run a hospital and, as someone has said, "It isn't so much the cost of the thing as the uncertainty of it that causes most people to complain about hospital bills." The insurance feature of Blue Cross eliminates that big uncertainty and substitutes for it a small constant cost. For family protection, that amounts to the price of a daily pack of cigarettes.

# 38. SOME FUNDAMENTALS OF HEALTH INSURANCE

THE HEALTH
INSURANCE
COUNCIL, 1956.

PEOPLE TODAY ENJOY better health and better health care than ever before in history. An almost constant stream of news reports about startling advances in medicine has served to intensify the public's interest in matters relating to health. Yet, meeting the costs of medical care, as well as regular living expenses, is a serious problem for many families when sickness or accident strikes.

Voluntary health insurance, during the past two decades, has been of increasing service to the nation's families in solving this problem. Of such insurance, that issued by insurance companies is a major and growing segment, and *now protects more people than all other types of health insurance put together*. Many doctors are consequently recognizing a need to have the latest information on insurance-company health insurance. . . . Doctors are often asked for advice by patients and others who are considering the purchase of health insurance. They may wish to buy it for themselves. They are often called upon by patients for certifications on which benefit payments will be based. Also, a growing proportion of most physicians' incomes is derived from the insurance-company benefit payments. And, from a broader viewpoint, the continuing growth of voluntary health insurance serves as a safeguard against unwise compulsory legislation.

## SOME FUNDAMENTALS OF HEALTH INSURANCE

Physicians, like many other people, sometimes find it difficult to keep up-to-date on health insurance. Any difficulty is entirely natural, however, because the voluntary health insurance movement has been developing with great rapidity in recent years, and it has moved in diverse directions.

A brief review of a few basic facts about health insurance may consequently be a helpful beginning to consideration of health insurance fundamentals. And a grasp of such fundamentals is essential for insight into what the insuring organizations are trying to do, and into why they use certain methods, while avoiding others.

### The Scope of Health Insurance

At present, well over 100,000,000 people have at least some health insurance. Collectively, they are covered through policies and subscription contracts issued by hundreds of insurance companies, dozens of Blue Cross and Blue Shield plans, and numerous independent plans.

Despite the wide variety of health insurance contracts available, the protection they provide can be classified into five main types: loss-of-income protection, hospital expense protection, surgical expense protection, and major medical expense protection.[1] Most people with voluntary health insurance have two or more of these types of protection, often through the same policy.

Outside the scope of "health insurance," as the term is commonly used, are several insurance forms which nevertheless, in the aggregate, provide many millions of dollars in benefits each year to sick and injured people.

In particular, the insurance forms not usually regarded as a part of health insurance include (*a*) policies protecting against accident only; (*b*) the provisions for permanent and total disability benefits in many life insurance policies; (*c*) the medical benefit features of automobile, business, and residence liability insurance policies; and (*d*) the medical benefits of workmen's compensation insurance.

Exclusive of these forms of protection, the term "health insurance" may be said to mean voluntary policies or other contracts which provide benefits on account of loss of productive time, or on account of medical, hospital, or related bills, if occasioned by accident, sickness, or maternity.

### The Functions of a Health-Insuring Organization

Physicians no doubt realize that insuring against health hazards involves many perplexing problems. Yet despite the special problems encountered in the health field, insurance experts recognize that the general function of a health-insuring organization is much the same as the function of an organization issuing any other type of insurance.

In health insurance, as in other insurance branches, the insuring organization seeks to develop contracts or arrangements under which—

*a*) It will receive money in the form of relatively small, regular premiums paid by a relatively large number of persons subject to a common hazard or group of hazards; and

*b*) It will use the money thus assembled to pay relatively large benefits to a relatively small number of persons actually stricken by a hazard insured against.

Thus, any health-insuring organization is essentially a means by which people are enabled to join with one another to ease the economic burdens of illness and injury.

In the short run, benefit payments may exceed premium receipts, or

---

[1] Regular medical expense protection ordinarily provides benefits only with respect to the cost of doctor's visits for nonsurgical care. Major medical expense protection, in contrast, ordinarily provides benefits toward meeting almost all types of expense for the treatment of unusually costly illness and injuries.

receipts may exceed payments. The insurer's resources will consequently decrease or increase—with the net result also reflecting various additional items of outgo and income such as operating expenses on the one hand and interest income on the other.

In the long run, however, benefit payments are closely related to premium receipts. Over a period of time, aggregate premiums must be adequate to support the benefits offered, while competition among insurers serves to keep premiums at a minimum consistent with sound practices. In long-run terms, then, lower benefit payments mean lower premiums, while higher benefit payments mean higher premiums.

### Stock and Mutual Insuring Organizations

Like business corporations generally, many insurance companies have stockholders who provide the capital and assume the risks and responsibilities of ownership and management. Also, of course, the stockholders expect to receive dividends out of such profits as may be earned.

The many mutual insurance companies, on the other hand, are owned by their policyholders. They have no stockholders, and any surplus funds developing inure to the benefit of the policyholders. Blue Cross and Blue Shield plans, as well as most independent plans, are organized in a substantially similar way.

While these distinctions may be worth noting, they should not be overemphasized. From the customer's standpoint, the important thing about an insurance company or any other business enterprise is the way the business is conducted, not the way it was chartered.

Moreover, as suggested, all organizations offering health insurance are in keen competition with one another. Their subscription charges or premium rates must be substantially competitive. In insurance, as in any other field of business, a concern that charged appreciably more than its competitors for the same goods or service, would soon see its patronage dwindle to the gain of other concerns that were offering more for the money.

### Group and Individual-Policy Health Insurance

A major proportion of voluntary health insurance protection is furnished through group insurance. In general, group insurance is a low-cost, wholesale method of furnishing protection to the employed population. The group method is used not only by insurance companies but also by Blue Cross, Blue Shield, and the other health-insuring organizations. In fact, Blue Cross, Blue Shield, and the others rely mainly on group underwriting techniques.

In the individual contracts of insuring organizations, the approach is a retail one. Many families do not have group insurance, and the health insurance requirements of many other families are not fully met through the group approach. For such families, it is well worthwhile to pay the "retail" premiums required for individual policies in order to have needed protection not otherwise available.

## Cancellable and Noncancellable Health Insurance

A majority of health insurance policies and subscriptions are cancellable. In general, a cancellable contract is one that remains in force from year to year only if both the insured and the insurer wish to continue it. Of course, in the event of the contract's termination, the insured person is entitled to full payment on any claim originating while the contract was still in force.

Noncancellable health insurance is available only from insurance companies, with more and more of them coming to offer it. While the policyholder need not renew a noncancellable contract, the company guarantees to renew it, year after year, upon payment of the premium. Because noncancellable policies assure lasting protection, they ordinarily require higher premium rates than do cancellable contracts.

Also to be noted, noncancellable policies usually are carefully underwritten from a standpoint of the applicant's health. Less strict underwriting is necessary in the case of cancellable policies, with the result that some persons can obtain them who would not qualify for noncancellable protection.

## Subjective Aspects of Illness

Most of the difficulties encountered in developing successful health insurance policies and plans stem from the human or subjective side of illness. As physicians well know, human health is a very complicated matter. There are those who clearly are well, and those who unquestionably are sick, but there remain many who are not definitely either the one or the other.

In fact, many physicians consider the rendering of medical treatment to be more of an art or skill than a rigid science. They recognize that agreement cannot always be expected on answers to such questions as: Does the patient need to go to a hospital? Is a private nurse needed? May the patient leave the hospital? When can he return to work?

The patient's appraisal of his own condition is subject, of course, to much wider variation than is medical opinion. Insurance company physicians have learned that among several persons having the same condition, so far as can be determined by objective tests, one may shrug it off and go to work as usual. Another may take to his bed. Still another may make an emergency call to his family physician, while a fourth may demand to go to a hospital.

## Subjective Effects of Insurance Benefits

The difficulties inherent in health insurance arising from the subjective aspects of illness are magnified as soon as sickness benefits are introduced.

Some who would go to work, in the absence of benefits, will remain at home if benefits are payable. Likewise, some who would not call the doctor, without the help of insurance toward meeting the bill, will do so if insurance benefits can be had.

In general, the tendency of health insurance to increase the public's demand for health care is desirable. With earlier and more adequate attention, the illness may be less serious, and complications may be avoided.

But certainly, the reduction of monetary restraints by health insurance tends in some measure to increase needless work absences, fruitless doctors' visits, and hospital stays of no real value. Even in such cases, outright fraud is seldom involved. More often, the insured individual rather unconsciously tends to develop a greater-than-normal concern about his health.

## Problem of Control

Insurance companies are of course aware of these subjective considerations. In fact, a central problem in devising workable health insurance plans is to develop ways and means of dealing with them.

On the other hand, the companies are willing and able to pay policy benefits whenever they serve a necessary and useful purpose. In fact, by paying for helpful medical attention that would not otherwise be provided, health insurance makes a definite contribution toward improving the nation's health.

On the other hand, insuring organizations do not wish to pay unnecessary benefits, and they should not do so to any substantial extent. For them to pay very many needless benefits would mean that premium charges would have to go up without any increase in the true value of the benefits offered. As a result, many policyholders would let their insurance lapse, and the entire plan of insurance might have to be discontinued. And in any case, the company would be remiss in its duty toward the great bulk of its policyholders. They should not be asked to pay inflated premiums in order that unneeded benefits may go to a few less prudent or less conscientious policyholders.

Consequently, the central problem mentioned above is one of control—of how health insurance may best provide benefits when needed without providing benefits when not needed. It may be added that this problem, obviously, is faced not only by insurance companies but also by Blue Cross, Blue Shield, and all other health-insuring organizations.

## Defining Risks and Specifying Benefits

The development of a careful statement of the risks which the policy insures against, and of the benefits payable under it, is the first step toward solving the problem of control. Carefully outlining the scope and benefits of the policy, of course, does not make certain all benefits paid will be of real value, but it does serve to define the area within which the control problem exists.

Some policies, of course, have much broader scope and provide much more liberal benefits than do others. The less liberal policies naturally have lower premiums, and they are provided for those not able or not choosing to purchase more adequate protection. While health insurance sales representatives ordinarily advise prospective purchasers to buy fully adequate policies, final decision is obviously up to the purchaser.

**What About the "Fine Print"?**

With reference to policy terms, a word is in order about the "fine print." While many users of this expression may merely be referring to policy restrictions and limitations generally, there may be others who have the notion that such provisions are, literally, printed in small type. Actually, health insurance policies are printed in large type, and it is illegal for any policy to give more prominence to its positive benefit provisions than to the restrictions and limitations it may contain.

Of course, insurance policies and service-plan contracts do contain some restricting or limiting provisions, at least to the extent necessary to spell out the risk insured against. Other limiting provisions are not ordinarily found in group insurance, which even provides benefits with respect to injury occurring or sickness commencing before the effective date of the policy.

In the case of individual and family policies, however, the safeguards inherent in the group method are lacking. Consequently, a few limitations are essential in such policies, while a few others are considered desirable by many companies.

For instance, an individual policy may restrict the benefits payable in case of an aviation accident which occurs in other than scheduled passenger flying. While restrictions of this sort are sometimes considered detrimental to the policyholder's interest, they actually serve to protect the average or typical policyholder against unnecessarily high premiums. It would be unfair to the typical policyholder, who does not engage in amateur aviation, to increase his premiums in order to provide benefits for those who do.

From a broad viewpoint, insurance men recognize that the amateur flyer, to continue the example, may well need insurance protection against his special risks. However, they also recognize that such protection should not be provided through regular policies at regular premiums. The indicated solution is the development of special policies with high enough premiums to support the benefits offered. Insurance companies have made encouraging progress toward developing such policies.

**Overinsurance**

In any field of insurance, overinsurance is present if the policy benefits are more than sufficient to compensate for the losses suffered or the costs incurred. For example, if a hospital expense policy provides a $15 daily benefit, the policyholder would be overinsured if in his locality he could obtain satisfactory hospital accommodations for less.

The point at which overinsurance begins is often difficult to determine. For example, if a man's take-home pay is $70 a week, overinsurance would clearly be present if his loss-of-income provides weekly benefits of a larger amount. But suppose his policy provides $65 a week. Suppose also that, as he recuperates from an illness, he feels he would rather continue to rest at home, drawing his benefits, than return to work for the sake of the small difference in income.

In such a case, the temptation to protract the convalescence period more than is desirable from a health standpoint is essentially the same as if the weekly benefit had been over $70. Something closely akin to over-insurance is present—something that goes to the heart of the basic control problem. Insurance companies rely largely on the coinsurance principle in dealing with this "something."

### Coinsurance

In the health field, "coinsurance" signifies a sharing of the risk by the insured person and the insuring organization. In the broad new type of health insurance—major medical expense protection—a specific coinsurance percentage is stated in the policy.

The coinsurance principle is also employed in the customary types of health insurance, although not in terms of an explicit percentage. For example, a surgical expense schedule may provide a benefit of $150 for an appendectomy, although it is known that the customary surgeon's fee in the area for that operation is about $200.

The point is that when the coinsurance principle is applied—either explicitly or implicitly—*the policy benefits are not meant to recompense the individual completely* for the income loss he has suffered or for the medical expense he has incurred. As a coinsurer, he is expected to carry a portion of the risk himself.

In general, the insurance company endeavors to set the benefits available under a policy at as high a level as possible, while still leaving an adequate financial incentive to the insured person to avoid unnecessary work absences and needless health expenditures. But in any case, the fact that for the insured person to incur needless bills would be against his direct, financial self-interest as a coinsurer serves as a key means of solving the control problem. Coinsurance enables the companies to be largely successful in providing benefits when they are needed, while preventing the payment of needless benefits.

### Coinsurance and "Service-Benefit" Plans

Generally speaking, health-insuring organizations other than insurance companies provide so-called "service benefits" instead of cash benefits. While "service benefits"—in the full meaning of the term—are provided by most independent plans, the expression is not strictly accurate when applied to Blue Cross and Blue Shield subscriptions. Inaccuracy exists because these plans do not guarantee that the subscriber will be able to obtain service. Blue Cross, for example, does not guarantee to obtain needed hospital accomodations for its subscribers, but merely to pay the hospital in full, under the terms of the contract, for such accommodations as the subscriber or his physician succeed in obtaining.

While millions of purchasers have shown their preference for cash-benefit policies, such policies are sometimes criticized because the co-insurance principle is invoked. An unfavorable contrast is made with "service-benefit" arrangements, which ordinarily do not leave an uninsured margin within the scope of the coverage.

However, as has been seen, the primary purpose of coinsurance is to enlist the financial self-interest of the insured persons themselves in preventing the payment of needless benefits. But the providing of needless benefits is equally harmful to the interests of the participants, whether the benefits are in the form of cash or not. So, "service-benefit" plans have need for some equivalent of coinsurance in order to cope with the control problem.

In Blue Cross and Blue Shield, the participating hospitals and physicians agree that, if the aggregate subscription fees paid by or for the insured persons prove inadequate to compensate them at the stipulated rates, they will accept *pro rata* reductions in their remunerations.[2] By such agreements, the hospitals and physicians become the ultimate underwriters or reinsurers of the plans they are affiliated with, and hence have a direct incentive to prevent overutilization of their services.

In practice, this theoretical possibility of control in Blue Cross and Blue Shield is not always adequate to check excessive demands for hospital and medical care. If x-ray and other ancillary services, for example, are available to the patient at no out-of-pocket cost, there is little incentive for him to exercise restraint. The eventual effect of any lack of success in solving the control problem is, of course, to increase subscription charges for participants generally.

### The Individual's Capacity to Coinsure

Apart from the question of whether those considering the purchase of health insurance are willing to assume a portion of the risk as coinsurers, there is a question of whether they are able to do so. While it is sometimes contended that most people are not able to bear any portion of their health expenses directly, this contention is hardly realistic.

---

[2] While physicians affiliated with Blue Shield may—as ultimate underwriters—be called on to accept downward adjustment in their remuneration, cash benefit contracts operate to enhance the likelihood that the physician will receive 100 cents on the dollar for his services. The policy benefits are guaranteed and are payable in full regardless of possible epidemics or other forces that might cause the premiums charged to prove inadequate.

For one thing, no type of health insurance can be really meaningful for persons who are not normally self-supporting, and who consequently are unable to pay premiums. The self-supporting people for whom health insurance does have real meaning normally have both regular income and some savings, a portion of which can ordinarily be used to meet health expenses. To the extent this is done, coinsurance is entirely practicable.

In some cases, a portion of the medical or hospital bill may remain unmet. In such cases, it is usually feasible for the insured persons to make use of some postpayment arrangement. Installment purchasing and other types of postpayment are common features of the general economy, and are not without value in the health field.

### Insurance and Budgeting

The risk-sharing function of insurance is of greatest value to the participants in an insurance plan when the risk insured against in an insurance plan is a very serious one and when its occurrence is unpredictable. When insurance methods are applied to risks that are not very serious and which materialize fairly regularly, then the value of the insurance to the participants in the plan diminishes. Companies offering health insurance consequently encourage families to budget against minor items as far as they can.

Common colds, digestive disturbances, and minor injuries, for example, occur fairly frequently in the average family, and ordinary prudence requires some allowance in the family budget for the relatively small costs of their treatment. If such allowance is made, no real financial difficulties are likely to develop, and certainly none that could be significantly alleviated by the use of insurance. Indeed, there is but little more reason to seek to insure against minor, recurring health outlays than to seek to insure against one's grocery bills or against any other regular expense.

To the extent the family does budget against its minor health expenditures, it saves its share of the unavoidable operating expenses of an insurance plan covering such expenditures. Moreover, insurance operating costs become relatively great when the benefits offered are small, and hence the family's opportunity to save is greatest on those minor health expenditures most easily budgeted against.

### The Use of Deductibles

One of the chief methods of separating budgetable items from more serious financial blows is through the use of "deductibles." A deductible can take various forms, such as a specified amount of money, a specified number of doctor's visits, or a specified number of days of sickness. Deductibles in the form of specific amounts are a particular feature of the broad new type of health protection, major medical expense insurance.

For example, a policy may exclude any payment for bills aggregating less than $50 or $100 and may reduce larger claims by such an amount.

Many families can meet expenses of $50 or $100 out of regular income or savings, and in such cases the deductible should not place an inordinate strain on the family's finances.

Moreover, deductibles generally enable the same premium to purchase much larger benefits, payable in cases of more serious illnesses. Also, the use of deductibles helps to restrain unnecessary demands for service.

### Determining Premiums

In health insurance, as in other fields of insurance, premiums comprise two elements:

The *pure premium,* an amount calculated on an average to just cover the cost of the benefits offered; and
An *expense and safety allowance,* which is intended to cover an equitable share of the necessary operating costs of the insurance, together with a small margin for safety and profit.

Pure premiums are directly proportionate to the chances of the hazard's occurrence and to the benefits that would then be payable. This proportionate relationship is not greatly affected by the expense and safety element. In consequence, bargains in health insurance are not easy to find, at least so far as the policies of any one company are concerned. The best bargain is a policy that fits the family's needs particularly well, while the poor buy is a policy that does not meet its needs.

### Should Premium Rates Be the Same for All?

Because of differences in the risks involved, premium rates for health insurance may vary with age, sex, occupation, and similar factors. It is sometimes suggested that such variations be eliminated, and premium rates made uniform for all. Sometimes the suggestion goes further, and it is proposed that premiums be set at a low level for people with low incomes and at a higher level for people with higher incomes.

These suggestions are really proposals to transfer purchasing power from one group to another. The proposed transfers are extraneous to the insurance operations on which they would be grafted. Moreover, they could not be put into effect so long as free competition exists in the health insurance field.

Under competitive conditions premium rates are bound to vary in direct proportion to the cost of providing the benefits. If an insuring organization attempted to charge one group of persons extra premiums in order to provide benefits at less than cost for another group, a competing insurer could be expected to enter the picture and offer the first group of persons the same protection at a lower price. The original insuring organization could not then continue to offer protection to the second group of persons on a less-than-cost basis, but would necessarily have to increase the premiums to a self-supporting rate.

## Conclusion

. . . [This article], in presenting some health insurance fundamentals, has focused on those which bear directly on the policies issued by insurance companies. To round out the discussion, however, contrasts have frequently been drawn between the cash-benefit approach of the insurance companies and the approach employed by Blue Cross and Blue Shield.

In conclusion, it may be emphasized that each of the two approaches has its advantages, as does the approach used by the independent plans. American consumers are consequently fortunate in having a choice among the different types of protection resulting from the different approaches.

Moreover, there is much reason to hope that out of the competition of the various insuring organizations of different types may come better policies and plans than any now available. Certainly, the development of health insurance so far, and its increased public acceptance, have stemmed largely from competitive forces.

# 39. PRIVATE HEALTH INSURANCE: Problems, Pressures, and Prospects

Herman M. and
Anne R. Somers,
*California Law Review,*
October, 1957.

WHILE MOST HEALTH INSUREES are compensated for only a moderate proportion of their medical expenditures, about one-quarter on average, the importance of this protection has been very great in supplying to the insured population a sense of basic security in regard to the most dreaded of unpredictable family costs. In recent years Americans have become more intelligently health conscious than ever before and a greater proportion have become acquainted with good medical care. Whatever the present shortcomings of voluntary health insurance, there should be no depreciation of the substantial achievements to date.

But these very achievements, together with changing demographic and morbidity patterns, are rapidly altering the need and demand for medical care. Arrangements which represented progress only a few years back are no longer adequate nor appropriate. The currently dominant pattern of health insurance—hospital plus surgical coverage on an indemnity basis—is becoming obsolete. This is one reason that health insurance is becoming inordinately expensive.

The rising demand for more "comprehensive" benefits is consonant with the needs of a population with an increasing number of aged, increasing incidence of chronic illness, and a growing recognition of the need for continuous health maintenance as opposed to concentration on episodic costs. In the nature of our society, it can be predicted that in one way or another this demand will eventually be met. If voluntary health insurance is to survive as a major instrument for financing medical care it must solve the problem of providing more extended services and means must be found, either through private insurance or otherwise, to furnish protection to the aged, the chronically ill and other "poor risks," as well as the short-term unemployed.

The principal barriers to such goals now appear to be primarily cultural and political rather than technological or economic. From the actual operational experience of private health insurance a number of facts, which were unknown or in question only a few years back, have clearly emerged:

1. The hospital utilization rate, which has a crucial effect on the cost of hospital insurance and which has been accelerating at a disturbing pace, can be kept within insurable bounds without artificial restrictions or damage to medical care, by avoiding the present built-in incentives for nonessential utilization. Health insurance enrollees with comprehensive coverage utilize only 60–80 per cent as many hospital days as those with hospital-surgical coverage only. The comprehensive plans have demonstrated that the present distorted 2 to 1 ratio of hospital to medical insurance expenditures can be substantially reversed. If the minority pattern could be generalized, the problem of hospital insurance costs might be solved on a voluntary basis, while simultaneously serving other desirable objectives, e.g., more prevention and rehabilitation.

2. Recognition of the desirability of moving toward the goal of comprehensive medical care insurance implies no neglect of hospital-surgical coverage. On the contrary, the great progress achieved in this area in the past two decades must be preserved, not frittered away, through abuse, inflation or public misunderstanding. Institutions like B.C., which have demonstrated their social utility, will be strengthened by a closer attention to overutilization, costs and the promotion of outpatient insurance. Of primary importance is the recognition of B.C.'s "public utility" role and the needed increase in public and consumer representation on its policy-making bodies. This should help to restore B.C.'s control over costs and its ability to preserve its service-benefit structure and to expand its benefit coverage.

3. The next step toward the goal of comprehensive medical care insurance—coverage of outpatient physicians' services—is clearly feasible. Such insurance can be provided at a price which the average consumer can and is willing to pay. Consumers are willing to accept coinsurance, extra charges, and other reasonable cost controls if the suppliers of services demonstrate equal willingness to accept some controls and economy measures.

At the heart of the matter lies the development of service as opposed to indemnity plans. The former provide the better means for quality as well as cost controls. Group practice, either in private clinics or hospital outpatient departments, today offers the best promise of combined efficiency and quality in medical care. In some parts of the western and north central states, it is already the dominant form of medical organization and it lends itself well to prepayment service programs. However, solo fee-for-service practice, which will continue to attract many doctors and patients, although probably as a declining minority pattern, can also be satisfactorily organized on a prepayment basis, provided the profession is willing to accept and abide by fixed-fee schedules and effective professional supervision. Essential to the successful coverage of physicians' services on a voluntary basis is professional self-discipline by doctors and other suppliers of services through formal or structural means.

4. The fast-changing technology and environment of medical care will continue to require continuous adjustments in organization and financing. No particular forms will prove universally and perpetually correct. It is therefore indispensable for success that freedom for experimentation in the application of technological and administrative advances be assured. The present legislative and other restrictions on such freedom are creating an impasse which threatens the capacity of voluntary health insurance to cope successfully with its present challenges. In fact, positive incentives and aids to advance the development of new types of outpatient institutions and services may now be necessary to help overcome the effects of the long-hostile environment. Financial aid, in the form of governmental or foundation grants or loans, is needed for the construction of such new facilities, including group-practice clinics.

5. There is still an opportunity for private health insurance to cover a substantial proportion of those now excluded from protection if the over-all benefit emphasis is shifted from hospitalized to nonhospitalized illness, as suggested, if group insurance techniques can be further extended to these groups, e.g., through group conversion policies for the retired and longer coverage for the temporarily unemployed, and if costs are better spread through wider risk-sharing. Essential to success in this respect is the curtailment of experience rating and a deliberate return to the principle of community rates.

If this cannot be done and if the coverage of the aged and other "poor risks" is indeed unfeasible under voluntary insurance methods, then the sooner acknowledgement of that limitation is made and other desirable means of filling the gap are found, the better private health insurance will be able to do the remainder of the job.

If the aged and other excluded groups continue to be squeezed between the mounting costs of health care and the nonavailability of voluntary health insurance, it seems probable we will move towards some form of public social insurance for this segment of the population. The most likely immediate approach appears to be extension of the OASDI program to provide hospital and surgical care for the aged and dependent survivors, and perhaps eventually to the disabled. Self-interest may induce the private carriers to endorse such a public program as a way "off the hook." If a limited program is denied and the vacuums remain, the pressures for a more extensive government program may multiply.

In the crucial stage of evolution immediately ahead voluntary health insurance may determine its own role and, indirectly, the role of government for many years to follow. If the voluntary programs can succeed in taking the bold steps which offer some promise for coping with current and increasingly apparent inadequacies, the government role may continue in more or less the same pattern as at present. Otherwise the growing volume of consumer demand coupled with the financial crises of hospitals, medical schools, and other branches of medicine will lead to greater government intervention. At the moment the power of decision still rests to a major extent with the providers of service and the insurance carriers. If they default or fail, the major influence in public policy determination may move into other hands.

# 40. HEALTH AND MATERNITY INSURANCE AND RELATED PROGRAMS IN OTHER COUNTRIES

*Social Security Programs Throughout the World,* U.S. Department of Health, Education, and Welfare, 1958.

A TOTAL OF 59 countries have some kind of a health and maternity insurance or related program. Most countries that have a pension program also have a system of health and maternity benefits, but a few have only one or the other of these types of measures.

All of the Western and Eastern European countries possess some kind of health and maternity insurance program. Only two countries in North and South America lack any provision of this sort, although in a few cases only maternity benefits are provided. Programs are also found in four Middle Eastern countries, although in one maternity benefits only are involved and in another only cash payments are made from a provident fund. Six Asian countries have health and maternity insurance measures, several of them having been introduced within the last few years. There is only one program among the independent nations of Africa.

Although a few of the European systems were established in the 19th century, the majority of the health systems are of a somewhat more recent date than the pension programs. In fact, a considerable number of the systems have only been set up since the ending of World War II.

## Types of Systems

The great majority of health programs are social insurance programs, under which both cash benefits and medical services are provided in respect of ordinary sickness as well as maternity. These programs are financed in considerable measure from special insurance contributions paid by employees, employers, or both, and eligibility for benefits and services is normally linked to payment of contributions or coverage in insured employment during a specified minimum period. Eligibility for medical services as well as cash benefits under most of these programs is contingent upon coverage under social insurance.

A somewhat different arrangement prevails in about a sixth of the countries. In these, only cash benefits for sickness and maternity are provided through social insurance. Medical services in contrast are furnished by the government under a separate program to all residents, rather than only to social insurance contributors. These programs, under which a variety of medical services are furnished in effect as a public service by the government, are in some countries referred to as a national health service. Among countries where such a method of providing medical care is used in whole or part may be mentioned Australia, Czechoslovakia, Ireland, New Zealand, Sweden, the U.S.S.R., and the United Kingdom.

A few of the remaining countries provide certain cash benefits for wage loss, but no medical-care services are provided under the insurance program or for the population as a whole under public programs. These include the four State temporary disability insurance programs in the United States (although California provides hospitalization benefits), Iraq, Israel (cash maternity benefits only), and the Philippines. In Canada, various hospitalization and related services are to be provided under its new program, but, on the other hand, no cash sickness benefits are payable. It may also be noted, finally, that cash benefits in a few countries, as in Australia and New Zealand, are provided on a social assistance rather than a social insurance basis.

## Coverage

The risks of income loss from sickness and maternity, with which these programs deal, exist mainly for persons working for the account of another. They are present to a much lesser degree for self-employed persons working for their own account, and they do not really exist at all for persons who are not gainfully employed. Only a few countries cover self-employed persons for cash sickness benefits, in view of the difficulty of establishing that they have undergone a genuine wage loss when they are sick. Accordingly, the coverage of nearly all of the cash benefit programs is limited largely to employees in general, or to particular classes of employees. Some of the newer systems apply only to employees of larger firms in industry, commerce, and related branches. A few countries in Europe also exclude higher-paid salaried employees.

In the large number of countries where medical as well as cash benefits are provided on a social insurance basis, the coverage of the medical-care provisions is generally the same as that for cash benefits (with the exception of benefits for dependents, mentioned below). It should be noted that many of these countries include persons receiving pensions under their pension program as potential beneficiaries of medical care under their health insurance program. This is sometimes done without cost to pensioners, while in other cases they are charged a specified percentage of their pension for coverage for medical care. A number of countries also maintain special systems for certain classes of employees such as railroad employees, seamen and public employees. In addition, some countries have provisions authorizing voluntary coverage under health and maternity insurance for workers who leave covered employment, self-employed persons, or others.

The coverage of medical-care provisions in countries where such care is not provided under social insurance but as a public service, in contrast, usually extends to virtually all residents. There are usually, however, certain special provisions concerning aliens in this case.

The provision of health and maternity benefits in some countries is organized around membership in various types of mutual sickness clubs, societies, or funds. Membership in such societies is usually made compulsory for specified categories of employees. Members' contributions are paid to the societies, which also receive government subsidies and sometimes employer contributions as well. The societies in turn provide benefits at levels which may not be below certain statutory minimum standards. This type of coverage is found, for example, in Belgium, Denmark, Iceland, Japan and Switzerland.

Nearly a fifth of the countries are introducing their health and maternity insurance systems gradually in different parts of the country. Typically, benefits are first provided in the capital city and perhaps certain other centers, and are then gradually extended to other urban or rural areas. The pace of the extension is usually controlled by the rapidity with which new clinics and hospitals can be financed and erected in different regions, for the furnishing of medical benefits.

### Source of Funds

In the large number of countries relying on social insurance, the usual methods of financing social insurance are used in the financing of their health and maternity insurance programs. That is, a fixed percentage of earnings is generally payable as a contribution by employers and employees. These contributions go into a central fund from which all benefits, including both cash and medical benefits, are financed.

A majority of these countries also provide for some type of government contribution or subsidy to the social insurance system, so that tripartite financing is numerically the most common arrangement. There are, however, various other combinations of revenue sources. Some countries use only employee and employer contributions. In others, particularly where benefits are provided through mutual sickness societies, only employees and the government participate in the financing. In contrast, certain countries including most of those in Eastern Europe rely on employer contributions exclusively.

A number of countries place a ceiling on the maximum amount of earnings of an individual worker during a given period on which contributions are payable. It should also be recalled that a sizable group of countries integrate the financing of health and maternity benefits with that of other types of social security benefits and allowances, and require only a single contribution for the entire group of benefits.

In most countries where medical care is provided to all residents, by means of some type of national health service, the government usually pays all or the greater part of the cost of this service.

### Cash Sickness Benefits

A cash payment is made under nearly all of the programs when a worker is prevented from working due to a nonoccupational sickness or injury. To qualify for such a payment, the worker must actually sustain a wage loss, that is, must be incapacitated and not receiving sick leave; and he must also normally provide medical certification of his inability to work.

The rates at which these benefits are paid are nearly always something less than full wages. A basic reason for this is to provide an incentive to workers to return to work rather than to continue drawing sickness benefits. In the majority of countries the benefit rate is generally somewhere between 50 and 75 percent of average earnings during the last preceding year. There frequently are also supplements provided in the case of recipients who are supporting a wife or children. A maximum benefit is usually fixed, or else is in effect operative by reason of the general ceiling on earnings that may be considered for contribution and benefit purposes. A number of countries reduce the usual benefit rates somewhat while beneficiaries are hospitalized, the reduction usually being greater for single persons than for those with dependents.

Cash sickness benefits are not ordinarily payable if sickness lasts for only a few days. This waiting period under most of the systems is from two to seven days in length. A primary purpose of the waiting period is to keep down benefit and administrative costs, by ruling out claims for the large number of quite brief illnesses during which the loss of income is small.

Sickness benefits are usually payable weekly, although they may be computed on a daily or other basis. A maximum limit on the aggregate number of weeks during which such benefits may be drawn is usually fixed. The most common limit is 26 weeks, although some countries provide for a considerably longer period or even for unlimited duration. Some countries also make provision for special extension of their ordinary 26-week maximum duration to perhaps 52 or 78 weeks in individual cases, such as when recovery seems probable within the period of extension, for special types of diseases, etc. In most countries, the cash sickness benefit is converted to an invalidity pension at the end of the maximum duration of the former, if it is then evident that the pensioner is going to continue to be incapacitated permanently or for a long period.

Most social insurance systems provide for some kind of funeral benefit, which is commonly payable under sickness insurance rather than the pension insurance program. Funeral benefits take the form of a lump-sum grant which is generally equivalent either to several weeks earnings of the deceased, or else to fixed amounts in all cases. It is often provided, however, that if the recipient is not the spouse or an orphan of the deceased worker, the grant is limited to the actual costs of the funeral, subject to a specified maximum.

### Medical Benefits for Sickness

As noted above, most foreign social security programs that provide cash benefits in respect of sickness provide medical benefits as well. The general rationale of this two-fold set of benefits would seem to be that the cost of his medical care is a severe financial burden to a sick worker in much the same way as is his loss of wages, and that therefore this is a risk to be insured against in the same way. There is also the important consideration that the earlier that effective curative care makes it possible for workers to return to work, the lower will be the cost of the cash sickness benefits payable to them.

A wide variety of methods are currently being used under the social insurance systems of different countries in providing medical benefits. It is possible in general to distiguish three main patterns, although numerous countries use some combination of these different methods or of variants thereof. Under one general type of method used, insured patients pay the bills of doctors, hospitals, druggists, etc., in the first instance themselves, and then later receive reimbursement from the social insurance system in respect of such bills. Under a second method, the social insurance system pays the doctors and hospitals directly for services they have rendered to social insurance recipients. The third general method used in some countries is for the social insurance system to acquire its own dispensaries, clinics and hospitals, as well as its own medical staff, and to provide services directly to the insured population it covers.

The particular kinds of services provided as medical benefits under social insurance also differ somewhat from country to country, but they usually include at least general practitioner care, some hospitalization, and essential medicines. They also often include specialist care, dental care, a wider range of medicines, and perhaps certain appliances (artificial limbs, spectacles, dentures, etc.). They sometimes also include home-nursing services, or transportation expenses of patients.

Where medical benefits are provided in the form of reimbursement for bills paid or of direct payments to doctors and hospitals, the payment by the social insurance system may cover the whole cost in some countries, but only a part of the cost, e. g., 75 percent, in others. In the latter case, the insured patient himself bears the remaining part of the cost of the treatment. Where medical services are provided directly by the social insurance system or as a public service, patients are also sometimes required to pay a fixed fee per visit, prescription, etc. The general purpose of requiring recipients to share a part of the charge for medical services in these various ways is presumably to hold down their cost, both by obtaining a part of the revenue directly from individual patients themselves, and also by providing an incentive to patients not to make unnecessary use of the services.

Some countries place no time limit on the duration of medical benefits, while others prescribe a maximum duration such as 26 weeks for any one illness. A limit is also sometimes placed on the duration of hospitalization paid for by the system, even though there may be no limit on other services. Some countries with a fixed limit permit its extension in special cases, as when a cure is foreseeable during the period of extension or in case of diseases of importance to the community or of special types of diseases.

### Cash Maternity Benefits

The great majority of countries provide cash benefits to working women covered by the insurance system for a specified period of time before and after they are confined. It is a prerequisite of such maternity benefits that a woman abstain from paid work during the period that benefit is received, that she suffer an actual loss of wages, and usually that she take advantage of the prenatal and postnatal care provided by the system. There is a wide range in the percentage of regular earnings payable as a maternity benefit, with most countries paying somewhere between 50 and 100 percent of wages. The benefit usually can start around 6 weeks before the expected date of confinement, and is commonly payable up to 6 weeks after the confinement.

In addition to the basic maternity benefit, a number of countries also provide a special nursing allowance to mothers who nurse their own children. This is commonly paid at a rate of 20 or 25 percent of the maternity benefit, and may continue for up to 6 months or longer. Some systems also provide a small grant for the purchase of a layette, or else provide the equipment itself in kind. Finally, some health and maternity insurance systems pay a lump-sum maternity grant in the event of each birth, for use in meeting such special additional expenses as may be involved. This lump-sum payment is sometimes made to wives of insured men as well as to women workers. It should be noted that in certain other countries similar birth grants are furnished under the family allowance program.

## Medical Benefits for Maternity

Nearly all of the programs which provide medical benefits for sickness also provide prenatal care to working women covered by the insurance system as well as obstetrical and postnatal care. The obstetrical care may in some cases be limited to that furnished by a midwife, although care by a doctor is usually available if required. In addition, care in a maternity home or hospital is usually furnished where necessary, as well as essential medicines.

The particular method used in different countries for providing these maternity services, that is, whether by reimbursement, direct payment, or direct provision of services, is the same as that used for medical benefits generally.

## Benefits for Dependents

The majority of systems that provide medical benefits to insured workers on a social insurance basis, also furnish much the same medical services to dependents of insured persons. Such dependents always include the spouse and children; and sometimes also other adult or minor relatives living with the insured and dependent upon him. Under certain systems, however, the benefits provided to dependents are somewhat more restricted than those available for insured persons. For example, the maximum duration of hospitalization may be somewhat briefer for dependents, or possibly a larger percentage of the cost of medicines may be required if the patient is a dependent. Where dependents are covered, medical care in respect of maternity is generally provided to the wife of an insured man just as are other types of medical care.

Since the total number of dependents ordinarily exceeds the total number of covered workers, it is obvious that extension of eligibility for medical care to dependents greatly increases the volume of medical services to be provided under a social insurance system and, thus, the cost of such services. This has led some of the newer health and maternity insurance programs, such as those of India and Burma for example, to omit medical benefits for dependents at the outset. It is intended to bring in the dependents, however, as rapidly as facilities and finances of these systems permit.

It should be noted that, in those countries where medical care is provided in the form of a public service, dependents are of course eligible for medical services on the same basis as other persons. Some countries in fact provide certain services for children, e. g., dental care or special foods, that are not available to the rest of the population.

Some health and maternity insurance systems also pay a funeral benefit in case of the death of a dependent of an insured person. The amount is usually somewhat smaller than that paid for the death of an insured person, and also is generally smaller for children than for adults.

### Qualifying Conditions

Nearly all health and maternity insurance programs require claimants for cash benefits, in addition to being incapacitated, to have completed some kind of a minimum qualifying period of contribution or insured employment. The general purposes of imposing this condition are to ensure that benefits are limited only to persons who regularly derive their livelihood from employment, and consequently to those who suffer a genuine wage loss when ill; and to secure a reasonable balance between expenditure and revenues.

The length of the qualifying period required for cash benefits differs considerably from country to country. For cash sickness benefits, the period ranges from as little as one month, unless no period at all is required, up to as much as 6 months or longer. It usually must have been served within a fairly recent time span, such as during the last 6 or 12 months immediately preceding the claim. For cash maternity benefits, the qualifying period is generally somewhat longer. It is often fixed, for example, at 10 months of contribution or employment during the last year or two preceding the claim.

As regards medical benefits, some of the social insurance systems require the same qualifying period as for cash benefits. In this case, a worker becomes and continues to be eligible for both types of benefit at the same time. Other systems prescribe a somewhat briefer qualifying period for medical than for cash benefits. In fact, a certain number of social insurance systems require no qualifying period for medical benefits and thus, in effect, provide such benefits to any worker who is currently and actually in insured employment. There is also, of course, no qualifying period required under those programs which furnish medical care as a public service.

There are normally no separate qualifying conditions pertaining to the provision of medical benefits to dependents. Under a relatively few systems, however, special longer periods of employment are necessary than for insured workers themselves before medical services will be provided to dependents.

### Administration

Much the same general patterns of administrative organization exist for health and maternity insurance programs as for old-age, invalidity and survivors insurance programs. The largest number of countries provide for such programs to be administered by some type of self-governing semi-autonomous institution, under government supervision. Some of these institutions own and operate their own medical facilities, through which at least a part of the medical benefits provided under the program concerned are furnished.

In a certain number of other countries, responsibility for most of the detailed administration of the program is placed in the hands of a large number of local or occupational sickness funds or societies, which workers are required to join. These bodies collect contributions from their members, pay cash benefits, and also arrange for the furnishing of medical care to their members, often through contracts with doctors and perhaps hospitals in the region. These smaller funds in a number of countries are affiliated in turn with larger federations, which may carry on various coordinating activities at the national level.

Health and maternity insurance programs in most of the remaining countries are administered by government departments. Such administration is often linked with that of other types of social security benefits, the entire range of benefits being administered as a single integrated program.

# 41. PRESIDENT TRUMAN'S NATIONAL HEALTH PROGRAM

PRESIDENT HARRY S. TRUMAN,
Message to the Congress,
November 19, 1945.

In my message to the Congress of September 5, 1945, there were enumerated in a proposed economic bill of rights certain rights which ought to be assured to every American citizen.

One of them was "the right to adequate medical care and the opportunity to achieve and enjoy good health." Another was the "right to adequate protection from the economic fears of . . . sickness. . . ."

Millions of our citizens do not now have a full measure of opportunity to achieve and enjoy good health. Millions do not now have protection or security against the economic effects of sickness. The time has arrived for action to help them attain that opportunity and that protection.

\* \* \* \* \*

To meet these problems, I recommend that the Congress adopt a comprehensive and modern health program for the Nation, consisting of five major parts, each of which contributes to all the others.

FIRST—CONSTRUCTION OF HOSPITALS AND RELATED FACILITIES

\* \* \* \* \*

SECOND—EXPANSION OF PUBLIC HEALTH, MATERNAL AND CHILD HEALTH SERVICES

\* \* \* \* \*

THIRD—MEDICAL EDUCATION AND RESEARCH

\*   \*   \*   \*   \*

FOURTH—PREPAYMENT OF MEDICAL COSTS

Everyone should have ready access to all necessary medical, hospital, and related services.

I recommend solving the basic problem by distributing the costs through expansion of our existing compulsory social insurance system. This is not socialized medicine.

Everyone who carries fire insurance knows how the law of averages is made to work so as to spread the risk and to benefit the insured who actually suffers the loss. If, instead of the costs of sickness being paid only by those who get sick, all the people, sick and well, were required to pay premiums into an insurance fund, the pool of funds thus created would enable all who do fall sick to be adequately served without over-burdening anyone. That is the principle upon which all forms of insurance are based.

During the past 15 years, hospital insurance plans have taught many Americans this magic of averages. Voluntary health insurance plans have been expanding during recent years; but their rate of growth does not justify the belief that they will meet more than a fraction of our people's needs. Only about 3 or 4 percent of our population now have insurance providing comprehensive medical care.

A system of required prepayment would not only spread the costs of medical care, it would also prevent much serious disease. Since medical bills would be paid by the insurance fund, doctors would more often be consulted when the first signs of disease occur instead of when the disease has become serious. Modern hospital, specialist, and laboratory services, as needed, would also become available to all and would improve the quality and adequacy of care. Prepayment of medical care would go a long way toward furnishing insurance against disease itself, as well as against medical bills.

Such a system of prepayment should cover medical, hospital, nursing, and laboratory services. It should also cover dental care—as fully and for as many of the population as the available professional personnel and the financial resources of the system permit.

The ability of our people to pay for adequate medical care will be increased if, while they are well, they pay regularly into a common health fund instead of paying sporadically and unevenly when they are sick. This health fund should be built up nationally in order to establish the broadest and most stable basis for spreading the costs of illness and to assure adequate financial support for doctors and hospitals everywhere. If we were to rely on State-by-State action only, many years would elapse before we had only general coverage. Meanwhile health service would continue to be grossly uneven, and disease would continue to cross State boundary lines.

Medical services are personal. Therefore, the Nation-wide system must be highly decentralized in administration. The local administrative unit must be the keystone of the system so as to provide for local services and adaptation to local needs and conditions. Locally as well as nationally, policy and administration should be guided by advisory committees in which the public and the medical professions are represented.

Subject to national standards, methods and rates of paying doctors and hospitals should be adjusted locally. All such rates for doctors should be adequate and should be appropriately adjusted upward for those who are qualified specialists.

People should remain free to choose their own physicians and hospitals. The removal of financial barriers between patient and doctor would enlarge the present freedom of choice. The legal requirement on the population to contribute involves no compulsion over the doctor's freedom to decide what services his patient needs. People will remain free to obtain and pay for medical service outside of the health-insurance system if they desire, even though they are members of the system; just as they are free to send their children to private instead of to public schools, although they must pay taxes for public schools.

Likewise physicians should remain free to accept or reject patients. They must be allowed to decide for themselves whether they wish to participate in the health-insurance system full time, part time, or not at all. A physician may have some patients who are in the system and some who are not. Physicians must be permitted to be represented through organizations of their own choosing, and to decide whether to carry on in individual practice or to join with other doctors in group practice in hospitals or in clinics.

Our voluntary hospitals and our city, county, and State general hospitals, in the same way, must be free to participate in the system to whatever extent they wish. In any case they must continue to retain their administrative independence.

Voluntary organizations which provide health services that meet reasonable standards of quality should be entitled to furnish services under the insurance system and to be reimbursed for them. Voluntary cooperative organizations concerned with paying doctors, hospitals, or others for health services but not providing services directly, should be entitled to participate if they can contribute to the efficiency and economy of the system.

None of this is really new. The American people are the most insurance-minded people in the world. They will not be frightened off from health insurance because some people have misnamed it "socialized medicine."

I repeat—what I am recommending is not socialized medicine.

Socialized medicine means that all doctors work as employees of government. The American people want no such system. No such system is here proposed.

Under the plan I suggest, our people would continue to get medical and hospital services just as they do now—on the basis of their own voluntary decisions and choices. Our doctors and hospitals would continue to deal with disease with the same professional freedom as now. There would, however, be this all-important difference: whether or not patients get the services they need would not depend on how much they can afford to pay at the time.

I am in favor of the broadest possible coverage for this insurance system. I believe that all persons who work for a living and their dependents should be covered under such an insurance plan. This would include wage and salary earners, those in business for themselves, professional persons, farmers, agricultural labor, domestic employees, Government employees, and employees of nonprofit institutions and their families.

In addition, needy persons and other groups should be covered through appropriate premiums paid for them by public agencies. Increased Federal funds should also be made available by the Congress under the public-assistance programs to reimburse the States for part of such premiums, as well as for direct expenditures made by the States in paying for medical services provided by doctors, hospitals, and other agencies to needy persons.

Premiums for present social-insurance benefits are calculated on the first $3,000 of earnings in a year. It might be well to have all such premiums, including those for health, calculated on a somewhat higher amount such as $3,600.

A broad program of prepayment for medical care would need total amounts approximately equal to 4 percent of such earnings. The people of the United States have been spending, on the average, nearly this percentage of their incomes for sickness care. How much of the total fund should come from the insurance premiums and how much from general revenues is a matter for the Congress to decide.

The plan which I have suggested would be sufficient to pay most doctors more than the best they have received in peacetime years. The payments of the doctors' bills would be guaranteed, and the doctors would be spared the annoyance and uncertainty of collecting fees from individual patients. The same assurance would apply to hospitals, dentists, and nurses for the services they render.

Federal aid in the construction of hospitals will be futile unless there is current purchasing power so that people can use these hospitals. Doctors cannot be drawn to sections which need them without some assurance that they can make a living. Only a Nation-wide spreading of sickness costs can supply such sections with sure and sufficient purchasing power to maintain enough physicians and hospitals.

We are a rich Nation and can afford many things. But ill health which can be prevented or cured is one thing we cannot afford.

FIFTH—PROTECTION AGAINST LOSS OF WAGES FROM SICKNESS AND DISABILITY

* * * * *

## Conclusions

I strongly urge that the Congress give careful consideration to this program of health legislation now.

Many millions of our veterans, accustomed in the armed forces to the best of medical and hospital care, will no longer be eligible for such care as a matter of right except for their service-connected disabilities. They deserve continued adequate and comprehensive health service. And their dependents deserve it, too.

By preventing illness, by assuring access to needed community and personal health services, by promoting medical research, and by protecting our people against the loss caused by sickness, we shall strengthen our national health, our national defense, and our economic productivity. We shall increase the professional and economic opportunities of our physicians, dentists, and nurses. We shall increase the effectiveness or our hospitals and public health agencies. We shall bring new security to our people.

We need to do this especially at this time because of the return to civilian life of many doctors, dentists, and nurses, particularly young men and women.

Appreciation of modern achievements in medicine and public health has created widespread demand that they be fully applied and universally available. By meeting that demand we shall strengthen the Nation to meet future economic and social problems; and we shall make a most important contribution toward freedom from want in our land.

# 42. AMA ATTITUDES TOWARD COMPULSORY HEALTH INSURANCE

DAVID R. HYDE
and PAYSON WOLFF,
*Yale Law Journal,*
May, 1954.

FEDERAL HEALTH INSURANCE proposals were a culmination of two lines of development: the recognition of the insurance principle as adaptable to meeting medical costs, and the increasing scope of governmental interest and participation in the provision of medical care. The public and many individual doctors have accepted both patterns, often from direct contact with voluntary prepayment schemes on the one hand, and with state and federal health services for fractional segments of the population on the other. Organized medicine has generally resisted each of these developments. However, these encounters with innovation seem but skirmishes in comparison to the bitter struggle which followed the merging of the two lines into compulsory health insurance.

### Development of a National Health Program

While prepaid governmental medical care has become a major issue in this country only recently, European experiences stimulated some mild interest here nearly forty years ago. The AMA at this time received reports from abroad with equanimity and began to consider the possibility of adopting such programs in the United States. But by 1920 its position was clearly one of opposition to government controlled or regulated medical service. In 1932, the majority report of the Committee on the Costs of Medical Care indicated tentative approval of tax-supported health insurance, and received wide attention in medical circles. It was in 1935 that the New Deal became interested in the passage of a health insurance law as part of the social security program. By 1938 the issue of compulsory health insurance had assumed more threatening proportions for the AMA. The President's Technical Committee on Medical Care, appointed to study the 1935 Social Security Act, recommended a program of medical care and sickness insurance. In an Address to the Congress, President Roosevelt asserted that medical care for the people was a matter of public concern.

At this point the AMA abandoned its resistance to the insurance principle for meeting the costs of medical care. The issue became whether medical society or governmental auspices for health insurance provided the best solution. Organized medicine opposed anything which might divest it of any part of its control over medical services.

The first serious legislative proposal for a national health program was introduced by Senator Robert Wagner of New York in 1939. It followed closely the program of the President's Technical Committee and provided for grants-in-aid to the states to enable them to develop plans of their own choosing—subject to basic standards set by the Federal Government. Despite a favorable interim report from the subcommittee which studied the bill, the AMA's own study committee submitted twenty-two distinct arguments against it and no further action was taken. The next significant health measure was the first Wagner-Murray-Dingell Bill, of 1943. This provided for a federal system of medical and hospital benefits, with medical care payments from a fund composed of equal payroll contributions from employer and employee. Senator Wagner denied that the bill would socialize the medical profession, pointing to provisions maintaining the doctor's freedom to remain outside the program, to choose his own patients, and to determine by what method he should be paid. However, the bill provided that each patient could select the doctor of his choice only from participating physicians. Moreover, the Surgeon General was given extensive powers to set fee schedules and limit the size of the doctor's panel of patients. These proposals brought forth violent reaction from organized medicine and the bill died in committee. A similar Wagner-Murray-Dingell proposal followed President Truman's special message to Congress in November, 1945, but even with outspoken administration support the bill was no more successful than its predecessor.

In 1946 and 1947, however, Senator Robert A. Taft sponsored an alternative measure to the administration's program. The Taft Bill, instead of health insurance, proposed locally-administered federal subsidies to the states to assist "those families and individuals in the state having insufficient income to pay the whole cost of" health services. The AMA did not react unfavorably, but fearing the possibility of lay administration at the local level, it was unenthusiastic. Also in 1947 the newly-elected Republican Congress considered a significantly modified Wagner-Murray-Dingell Bill. Conforming to criticism of the earlier bills, the sponsors assigned the duties formerly designated for the Surgeon General to a five-man board in the Federal Security Agency, and control of the proposed program was further decentralized; but more services were offered, and more groups were covered.

The last major administration health insurance bill was inspired by the Ewing Report of 1948. This Report endorsed a national health program and was instrumental in the identification of its author with compulsory health insurance. Ewing's proposals received the full backing of President Truman in the 1948 presidential campaign. AMA anxiety was heightened by the election returns and the prompt introduction in January, 1949, of a bill similar to the 1947 Wagner-Murray-Dingell proposal.

## AMA Tactics of Opposition

Organized medicine's earlier attempts to block the passage of compulsory health insurance displayed an essentially *ad hoc* approach. The earliest proposals for national health insurance required little more than vocal opposition by medical spokesmen. With the introduction of Senator Wagner's 1939 Bill, however, the AMA and many state societies intensified their campaign against government medicine. The AMA's cause was almost entirely taken up by the newly formed National Physicians Committee for the Extension of Medical Service, which served as the propaganda arm of organized medicine. Although the AMA denied any official connection with this organization the NPC was headed by AMA members and supported by its fund-raising machinery. For nearly ten years, the AMA itself confined its official opposition to state insurance to public addresses, to editorials in the *Journal*, resolutions in the House of Delegates, and testimony before legislative committees.

The NPC undertook organized medicine's first concerted effort to influence public opinion. Working largely through doctors, the Committee is reported to have distributed 25 million pamphlets. But the occasional crudeness of its methods reduced its effectiveness. In 1948, the press protested the NPC's "attempt to buy editorial opinion" through a $3000 prize offered for the best published anti-national health insurance cartoon. And when the NPC distributed copies of a letter signed by "Reverend" Dan

Gilbert, Editor of the notorious *Defender* and former associate of Silver Shirt Gerald Winrod, severe criticism from AMA members followed. By the end of 1948 the NPC's utility as a rallying point for organized medicine was negligible.

Similarly, Dr. Morris Fishbein, Editor of the *Journal* and the recognized spokesman for organized medicine, had become the "symbol of old reactionary leadership" in the profession, at a time when favorable public opinion was becoming increasingly important. The AMA's decision in 1946 to hire a special public relations counsel was an important step officially taken to curtail Fishbein's activities. Finally, in 1949, the Board of Trustees announced the "retirement" of Dr. Fishbein after thirty-seven years of "devoted service."

By the end of 1948 it was apparent to AMA leadership that a more positive and drastic program was needed to forestall the enactment of compulsory health insurance. The Ewing Report, followed by the Democratic victories in the fall, increased the likelihood that Congress would pass a national health program. Moreover, the new British experiment in socialized medicine had fostered public interest and discussion concerning the adoption of a similar program in the United States. The discrediting of The National Physicians Committee and the retirement of Dr. Fishbein cleared the road for new, more effective opposition techniques.

The interim session of the House of Delegates convened in St. Louis the month following the November elections "in a spirit of great urgency." The delegates voted to assess each AMA member $25 to build a $3,500,000 "political war chest to fight socialized medicine." Despite considerable adverse criticism from members the AMA went ahead with plans for an enlarged Washington office and an advertising campaign to "educate" the American people. And it soon announced that its "National Education Campaign" would be conducted by the public relations firm of Whitaker & Baxter.

The experts whom the AMA chose to lead its campaign were already well known for their successes in California politics. Chief among these was their victory, on behalf of the California Medical Association, over Governor Warren's proposal for state-wide compulsory health insurance. Whitaker & Baxter were called in immediately after Governor Warren announced his legislative program in January, 1945. In accordance with the procedure they had evolved for short, urgent campaigns they "started at the top and worked down." They obtained public endorsement from the leaders of more than one hundred state organizations, enlisted the support of more than two hundred newspapers, made speeches to some nine thousand physicians, and induced doctors, druggists, insurance executives, and dentists to speak to hundreds of "thought leaders." A state-wide "Voluntary Health Insurance Week" promoted membership in the society sponsored California Physicians Service. Medical groups bought forty thousand inches of paid advertisements, and sympathetic merchants, another thirty thousand. At the end of three months, Warren's bill was defeated by one vote. In 1947 a similar bill failed by a wider margin, and today, state health insurance is given little or no chance of passage in California.

The Chicago office of the AMA's National Education Campaign, with a staff of thirty-seven, was established in January, 1949. To overcome opposition from within the profession to the Campaign and its $25 assessment, public speaking tours and circulars were successfully employed and intense doctor support was stimulated. During the first year of the Campaign all but a few members displayed posters and nearly 20 million pamphlets were distributed to patients; Congressmen were contacted by their personal physicians and urged to support AMA views. A Campaign "Blueprint" published in February indicated that the first year's strategy would be to mobilize lay group leaders who, in turn, would urge the membership of their groups to back the AMA in communications to legislators. .

By December, 1949, the National Education Campaign Headquarters reported that it had the public endorsement of 1829 separate organizations ranging in size from a few to more than five million members. In addition nearly 55 million pieces of literature had been distributed to an estimated 100 million people at a cost of more than $1,000,000. Traveling press representatives and selected spokesmen operating through "Speakers Bureaus," and 250,000 physicians, druggists, and insurance men under less formal organization, had spoken, written, and distributed AMA material. Half of the first year's budget was allocated to "defense and attack," the other half to "extending and improving the services of the voluntary health insurance system." The latter was to be organized medicine's affirmative answer to the Ewing program. Insurance companies and doctors were urged to promote the sale of voluntary health insurance policies under the slogan "The Voluntary Way is the American Way." The rate of enrollment in 1949 was nearly one million each month.

The National Education Campaign soon produced a marked effect. Former congressional supporters of the President's plan in Congress began to withdraw their backing, and by November many sponsors conceded that there was no hope of enacting any health insurance law in the first session of the Eighty-First Congress.

Realizing that its 1949 success provided only temporary respite, organized medicine planned its 1950 Campaign to end conclusively the threat of national health insurance. The House of Delegates, in December, 1949, voted to impose permanent yearly dues of $25 for all AMA members. There were "fringe bills" to defeat and, most important, there was a decisive congressional election to be won.

Much of the strategy of the 1950 Campaign was a continuation of the previous year's Blueprint. Furthermore, an intensive two-week advertising campaign was timed to influence the congressional elections. $1,100,000 was set aside—one-half for newspaper advertisements and the remainder equally divided for radio time and magazine space—to arouse public opposition to compulsory health insurance.

Since the AMA could not openly endorse any candidates, it urged individual members to engage in political action supplementary to the National Education Campaign. Member doctors formed Healing Arts or Medical-Dental Committees to help defeat supporters of national health insurance. Previous experience in special elections had demonstrated the effectiveness of such committees. During the 1949 election in the 26th Pennsylvania Congressional District, the Healing Arts Committees mailed more than 190,000 letters, made more than 120,000 personal telephone calls, placed a series of twelve advertisements in every newspaper in the District, and purchased radio time to urge the election of John P. Saylor and the defeat of his Democratic opponent, who had endorsed the President's program. The total vote approached the District's turnout for the 1948 presidential election and more than 20,000 Democrats switched their votes to elect Saylor.

During the 1950 campaign, doctors in many congressional districts formed their own political committees. In Wisconsin, the Physicians for Freedom helped to defeat Representative Andrew Biemiller through posters, advertisements, and campaign literature included with monthly bills to patients. In Florida, similar tactics were used against Senator Claude Pepper in his unsuccessful bid for renomination. Tallahassee hospital patients received breakfast trays upon which were placed cards reading, "This is the season for canning Pepper." And in Ohio the Physicians Committee for Taft was politically active in enlisting support.

The National Education Campaign and the Healing Arts Committees were rewarded by the election returns. Some of national health insurance's most active supporters were defeated. The president of the AMA called the results "very reassuring" and announced to the House of Delegates that in the light of the recent campaign "any compulsory health insurance bill in Congress today would go down to defeat by at least a 2 to 1 vote."

Despite the fact that national health insurance seems a dead issue, organized medicine has maintained a continuing interest in political affairs. The Democratic platform in 1952 made no mention of national health insurance. Governor Stevenson stated his opposition to such a plan but commented on the need for assistance in financing the costs of illness. The Republican platform unequivocally stated opposition to federal health insurance and General Eisenhower left no doubt that he was opposed to "socialized medicine." A non-partisan organization, the AMA took no official sides. But by October a "National Professional Committee for Eisenhower and Nixon" was mailing letters from the National Education Campaign's former address, urging that medical and related groups support the Republican ticket. The letterhead featured the names of former

AMA Presidents Henderson as chairman, and Cline and Irons as vice-chairmen, as well as Whitaker & Baxter.

Since the defeat of the Truman-Ewing plan, controversy concerning the role of the Federal Government in the health insurance field has centered around proposals to aid voluntary projects. The Magnuson Report, prepared by President Truman's Commission on the Health Needs of the Nation, recommended federal grants to subsidize either these plans or potential subscribers having low incomes. In a 1954 Message to Congress, President Eisenhower advocated a different measure: federal "re-insurance" of voluntary plans. At present, most voluntary schemes place a limit upon the protection given their subscribers. This leaves the cost of catastrophic illness to be borne largely by the individual. Under re-insurance the Federal Government, in return for premiums received from the plans, would insure against claims over a certain figure so that coverage could be extended to include high-cost services. The AMA opposed the Magnuson recommendations because they called for Government subsidies. They have similarly condemned re-insurance, fearing that it might lead to subsidization and constitute an "opening wedge to socialized medicine."

Throughout its recent campaign to halt governmental inroads into medical affairs the AMA has adopted an essentially emotional approach. The basic issues are obscured by the AMA's use of catch-phrases, like "socialized medicine," and such devices as mass distribution of the famous Sir Luke Fildes painting, "The Doctor," captioned "Keep politics out of this picture." Organized medicine's counterproposals, advocating local controls or private, voluntary remedies, often provide inadequate or partial solutions. By presenting the profession's views realistically, the AMA's campaign against Government health programs could lead to enlightened discussion of the merits rather than exchange of invective.

# 43. HOSPITALIZATION INSURANCE FOR OLD-AGE, SURVIVORS, AND DISABILITY INSURANCE BENEFICIARIES

Report to the House
Committee on Ways and Means
by the Secretary of Health,
Education, and Welfare,
April 3, 1959.

IN RESPONSE to a request from the Ways and Means Committee of the House of Representatives, this report has been prepared to present the results of a study of alternative ways of providing insurance to finance hospital and nursing home care for old-age, survivors, and disability insurance beneficiaries, and of the practicability and costs of the several methods considered.

The primary purpose of this introduction is to identify the arguments that are advanced both for and against Federal action in this area.

There is general agreement that a problem does exist. The rising cost of medical care, and particularly of hospital care, over the past decade has been felt by persons of all ages. Older persons have larger than average medical care needs. As a group they use about two and a half times as much general hospital care as the average for persons under age 65, and they have special need for long-term institutional care. Their incomes are generally considerably lower than those of the rest of the population, and in many cases are either fixed or declining in amount. They have less opportunity than employed persons to spread the cost burden through health insurance. A larger proportion of the aged than of other persons must turn to public assistance for payment of their medical bills or rely on "free" care from hospitals and physicians. Because both the number and proportion of older persons in the population are increasing, a satisfactory solution to the problem of paying for adequate medical care for the aged will become more rather than less important.

In our society the existence of a problem does not necessarily indicate that action by the Federal Government is desirable. The basic question is: Should the Federal Government at this time undertake a new program to help pay the costs of hospital or medical care for the aged, or should it wait and see how effectively private health insurance can be expanded to provide the needed protection for older persons?

### Reasons Advanced as to Why the Federal Government Should Not Take Action

Here are some of the reasons that are advanced by those who support the adoption of a "wait and see" position:

1. As recently as early 1952, only about 25 percent of the 12.7 million persons aged 65 and over had any form of health insurance. Today about 40 percent of the 15.3 million persons in this age group have some type of health insurance. Whereas a decade ago, few insurance plans were open to older persons, many prepayment plans and insurance companies now provide such coverage and others are experimenting with special arrangements to cover the aged.

It is reasonable to expect that the proportion of the aged population covered by voluntary insurance will increase, and perhaps for a time at a faster rate than over the past 6 years. However, as the proportion rises, further increases become relatively more difficult to achieve. If the same average yearly increase in the proportion covered as that during the past few years is maintained, private hospital insurance will reach about 56 percent of the aged population in 1965 and 68 percent in 1970. If the same increase in coverage of OASDI beneficiaries that was recorded between 1951 and 1957 continues, about 70 percent of the aged beneficiary group will have some form of health insurance by 1965.

If recognition is given to the fact that voluntary insurance may never be able to reach certain groups—for example, persons already in long-stay institutions, those with the very lowest incomes and others for whom the premium cost of individually purchased insurance is more than they are able to pay—the present achievement of voluntary insurance in relation to its potential is even greater than the 40-percent coverage of persons 65 and over would suggest. It is recognized, of course, that a part of the problem will remain even after private insurance has reached its maximum development.

2. A compulsory program to provide insurance against the cost of hospital care for OASDI beneficiaries or other aged persons would in large part undercut voluntary efforts to meet this particular need. Some older persons would purchase insurance to cover the cost of types of services not covered by the Government program, such as private room accommodations in the hospital or surgery or physicians' home and office visits. But there would be little opportunity left for private insurance against the cost of those hospital services that were paid for by the Government program. A decision to initiate a compulsory insurance program would be virtually irreversible.

3. Pressures would develop for extending a hospital benefits program to include other components of the medical care bill. The costs of short-term hospitalization on the average represent between 25 and 30 percent of the present medical care bill for the aged. Furthermore, voluntary insurance coverage of medical expenditures other than hospital bills is much less adequate than that for hospital benefits. Thus it would be difficult to limit a Government program to hospital or hospital and nursing home benefits. The eventual cost burden that might result if an initial program of hospital benefits were expanded to include other types of service could be at least two or three times as large as the cost for hospital benefits alone.

4. It is difficult to estimate with any accuracy the future cost of medical care. Many persons are concerned with increases in medical costs beyond those originally anticipated that have occurred in other programs. They believe that the eventual costs of hospital benefits alone may be much more than the estimated cost based on current practices and experience.

5. Pressures would also develop for extending insurance against the cost of hospital and other medical care to the working population and their dependents. Workers who were paying social security taxes to cover the cost of health benefits in old age might object to waiting until they reached retirement age to get such protection and be willing to pay additional contributions in order to have such insurance for themselves and their dependents immediately. A decision to provide hospital insurance

for the aged might thus lead to much more far-reaching Government action.

6. Federal action would result in a diminution of responsiveness to varying individual and local situations, and the attenuation of personal relationships and personal concern which almost inevitably accompanies a displacement of local and private arrangements by centralized governmental programs.

### Reasons Advanced as to Why the Federal Government Should Act

Here are some of the reasons advanced by those who believe this problem can only be solved through action by the Federal Government:

1. A decision against Government action at this time would merely postpone an effective solution of the problem of medical costs for many of the aged. The basic difficulty that private insurance faces in its efforts to extend hospital insurance protection to the aged is that they are a high-risk, high-cost group. A premium charge based on the experience and covering the entire cost of a reasonable level of protection for an aged group will be higher than many aged persons can afford to pay. Existing insurance has attempted to meet this situation by scaling down the benefits and protection provided, by spreading part of the cost over younger age groups, or by a combination of these methods. Limited protection leaves a large part of the original problem unsolved. If the higher than average cost of adequate medical care for the aged is accepted as a social cost that should be shared by the entire community, Government is in a better position than private industry to distribute the cost burden broadly and equitably.

2. It is possible that a public program of hospital benefits for the aged—by taking over this special problem—would help assure the continued acceptance of private insurance and prepayment arrangements as the method of handling the costs of medical care for the great majority of the population. A broad spreading of the risk and costs can be much more readily achieved by private insurance for the employed members of the population under 65 and their dependents than for the entire population. Employee benefit plans would also be relieved of the special charge which some of them are now carrying through various methods of continuing health insurance coverage for retired persons, thus removing these costs as a possible deterrent to employment of older workers and lessening the pressures against changes of jobs.

3. A publicly supported program of hospital benefits for the aged could provide more extensive and more adequate protection than has characterized much of the private insurance available to aged persons. There would be no lifetime limits on the total costs that would be covered, no cancellation of the insurance, no exclusion of preexisting conditions, and there could well be a higher maximum than is usual in insurance company policies on the number of days of hospital care that would be paid for during a year, as well as coverage of the cost of all hospital extras.

4. A little over 70 percent of all persons aged 65 and over are now eligible for benefits under the OASDI program. Eventually more than 9 in 10 aged persons will be eligible. The OASDI mechanism provides a ready and equitable method of spreading the cost of hospital care for the aged over the entire working population. A small increase in the present social security taxes would provide immediate protection for those now eligible for benefits. Persons now at work would in turn become entitled to the same protection when they reached retirement age. The individual's contribution toward the cost of medical care in old age would be spread over his working lifetime without breaks in coverage due to change of residence or employment.

5. For any specified level of protection, the cost of hospital insurance under OASDI would be relatively low because of the size of the group, the compulsory coverage resulting in lack of adverse selection and the fact that the collection of contributions and identification of eligible persons would utilize existing tax reports and wage records.

Fears as to rising costs under a public program are often greatly exaggerated. Costs may rise in absolute terms without an increase in costs in relation to the gross national product or in costs as a percent of taxable payrolls. Changes in medical knowledge and practice that no one can forsee may, of course, substantially increase or decrease future medical costs. Such changes would affect the total resources used for medical services no matter what method of paying for care was involved.

# 44. MEDICAL CARE IN GREAT BRITAIN

ANNE TAYLOR MOORE,
*The New Republic,*
April 6, 1959.

THE BRITISH National Health Service is now a decade old. And yet to many of us, even to many medical men who should know better, the British health plan calls up a series of confused images—or no image at all. A British MP, the Rev. Llewellyn Williams, returned flabbergasted from a recent American tour and described to the House of Commons "a consultant, attached to a large city hospital and a medical school in a university, who believed that all doctors in this country are directed by Whitehall, exactly like soldiers in the Army."

Perhaps the best evidence of the acceptance of state medicine in England is the fact that neither the Conservative nor the Labour Party today would risk its political future by attempting to abolish the Service. In the Parliamentary debate last July, commemorating the tenth anniversary of the plan, Labour and Conservative MPs emphasized their respective and important roles in its growth and development. Aneurin Bevan, the fiery first Minister of Health under the new system, termed the Service "a marked success—indeed so successful that there is now competition in claiming its paternity."

During three separate trips to England in the past three years, I have talked with a large number of patients, interviewed some 50 doctors both in and out of the Health Service, visited eight hospitals and interviewed two front bench Labour MPs, one a Parliamentary Secretary, the other a Minister of Health in the 1945–51 Labour Cabinet. On two occasions, I experienced state medicine as a patient, both in an NHS doctor's "surgery" and in a hospital clinic. I have thus had some opportunities to observe how doctors and patients regard British medical care.

To understand the British reaction one should first understand that what is commonly though not quite accurately called "socialized medicine" did not spring full-blown on July 5, 1958, from the brow of Labour's Bevan. Its most illustrious ancestor was the National Health Insurance Act of 1911, the triumph of a Liberal, Lloyd George. The 1911 Act provided about one-third of the British population (the lower-income working class) with medical services in the doctor's office and in home visits. However, its benefits were available to only the contributing working member. Specialist and hospital services were not part of the plan.

The major and dramatic difference between the 1911 and 1948 health measures was the method of financing. While the 1911 Act was an insurance program, subsidized by the state (*i.e.,* a group spreading the risk of illness through contributions which make each member eligible for specific benefits), the 1948 Act assumed responsibility for the health of the *total* population. It offers services based on medical need and is financed mainly from taxes which are collected by the National Exchequer.

At first, there were at least three major misconceptions about how the Service would work. Both doctors and patients feared there would be no free choice of doctors, that private medicine would be all but obliterated, that the doctor-patient relationship (sacred to both) would somehow be destroyed when the doctor became a "state servant."

Yet, today, only two percent of the people care to remain outside of the Health Service to receive private medical care. The other 98 percent are registered with NHS general practitioners who are reimbursed on a per-capita basis. A small segment prefer to go to a private physician for some complaints and their NHS doctor for "run-of-the-mill" disorders. Some NHS doctors have a small number of private patients, and many doctors in private practice report that they are losing some of their patients to Health Service physicians. In some instances, where the patient's financial circumstances appear marginal, doctors suggest that patients have a needed operation under the NHS.

The main criticism of the Service I heard from patients is the long wait endured before being admitted to a hospital. Doctors admit there is still a shortage of hospital beds, and they are asking for more hospital space, yet they insist that a bed is always found for emergency cases. On the other hand, patients feel that the initial fears about the doctor-patient relationship have proved unfounded. They see no evidence of a lack of individual attention. In the few instances where patients are dissatisfied, they are at liberty under the NHS to change to another doctor. In cases where the patient feels there is evidence of medical negligence the matter is brought before a special committee under the local NHS Council. Both doctor and patient present their side of the issue—this in contrast to countries where purely private medicine exists and such matters are usually handled through costly and complicated legal procedures.

Doctors have varied and various complaints about the Health Service, though at the same time they say they are in favor of the idea of the Service and hope for improvements as time goes on. The minority view is represented by a group of doctors called Fellowship for Freedom of Medicine (Ltd.), who have banded together to protest the socialization of medicine. They charge that a "deterioration in the standard of Medicine" has taken place since "the Appointed Day," and they believe in "putting more responsibility for his health on the patient." Critics of the Fellowship suggest that it is more concerned with maintaining the "prestige" of the medical profession than in the health needs of the total community.

On the whole, salary scales do not satisfy the doctors. In 1953, they were given their first raise, and a Royal Commission is now looking into the entire subject of remuneration. Since the inquiry is a searching and time-consuming one, two interim raises have been given NHS doctors—one in May, 1957, the other this January, of roughly five and four percent respectively. There also persists a sharp controversy over the present method of payment—a fee for general practitioners based on the number of patients they handle. Some doctors feel this method is just, in that it rewards a doctor for good doctoring—more leisure for keeping patients well; others insist that doctors under the present system fear losing patients if they don't give them what they ask for—their bottle of medicine or favorite green pills—whether the prescription will help or not. There is no way at present for giving a higher fee to the older practitioner who is often more experienced in his profession. Also, the economic motive forces doctors to attain, if they can, a maximum list of patients (3,500), which gives rise to a dispute over whether any doctor can adequately serve that number without undue strain on the doctor. It may well be that the Royal Commission will recommend another basis of remuneration when its report, promised for this summer, is published.

The prevailing opinion in America, I find, is that Britain's medical experiment must be a luxury which few countries could support. The American press does little to contradict this notion.

A news story in the *New York Herald-Tribune*, reporting on the tenth anniversary of the Health Service, called it "a success, an expensive success to be sure." Yet Professor Richard Titmuss of the London School of Economics, one of the fiscal architects of the Service, is convinced that the cost—approximately three percent of the national budget—is reasonable. In 1956 his opinion was reenforced when a special committee (referred to by the name of its chairman, C. W. Guillebaud) after inquiring into the cost of the Health Service, reported that there was little room for further economy. Those who hoped that the Guillebaud Report would expose alleged scandals and extravagances inherent in state medicine were sorely disappointed.

The total cost of the Health Service has grown from £435 million in 1949–50 to an estimated £735 million for the present year. If these figures look alarming, it must be remembered that the *percentage* of the national income spent on the Service has remained the same, indeed, has slightly decreased.

Who benefits most from 10 years of the NHS? Naturally the poorer classes to whom this kind of medical care was never before easily available, as well as the middle classes who frequently found it financially burdensome to be ill under private medicine. The present Minister of Health, Derek Walker-Smith, stresses the striking change in the pattern of disease over the past decade. These happy figures cannot be wholly ascribed to the Health Service—higher standards of nutrition, better housing, new drugs and surgical techniques are also contributing factors. Still, within a decade, the infant mortality rate in England has dropped from 33.9 to 23 per thousand, the maternal mortality rate has fallen from 1.02 to .47, the number of tuberculosis patients went from 552 to 107 per million of the population. Statistics like these seem to show that when medical care is available to all segments of the population, in a preventive as well as curative way, the whole community is the beneficiary.

Finally, one of the major benefits to be derived from any national health program is that it places on government responsibility for taking the long view; planning for the future is not lost sight of in the concerns of the moment. Government officials active in health affairs are well aware of both immediate and future problems. The Ministry of Health, cognizant of the present shortage of dentists is, through preventive approaches like the fluoridation of water, hoping to effect important benefits to the nation. Surplus TB beds are being devoted to other purposes—non-tubercular chest conditions, geriatrics and mental health. The long wait for assignment to hospital beds has been reduced by 11.5 percent while attendance at out-patient clinics has risen by 12 percent. The Health Ministry, through local medical councils, is bringing about a more even distribution of doctors by controlling areas in which new practices are allowed and encouraging doctors, through financial inducements, to go into under-doctored areas. Government planning to reduce the liabilities of the Health Service have already proved partially effective.

One can fairly conclude that Britain's gigantic medical enterprise has come through its first decade, not without problems, but with the whole-hearted sanction of most of its patients and practitioners.

# DISCUSSION QUESTIONS

1. The American people are said to have the best medical care. Why then all the excitement and controversy about health insurance and medical economics? Is this an artificially stimulated controversy?

2. Blue Cross, Blue Shield, and other privately sponsored health insurance plans provide protection against the costs of illness for over 100 million Americans. Yet the AFL-CIO favors a compulsory governmentally sponsored health insurance program. Why?

3. Health insurance and socialized medicine are not the same. Explain the difference and illustrate from American programs the extent to which socialized medicine already exists.

4. Explain the dramatic development of private health insurance in recent years. Indicate the role of collective bargaining in this development.

5. The American Medical Association's attitude toward health insurance has undergone significant changes in the past quarter century. Explain the reasons why its views on private health insurance have changed.

6. The American Medical Association in recent years has opposed compulsory governmentally sponsored health insurance. Explain the reasons for this.

7. President Truman said his compulsory health insurance plan is not socialized medicine. Do you agree? Why?

8. Health insurance may include either indemnification to the insured person for medical costs or payment of the costs to the provider of the medical service. Explain the difference in philosophy and effect on the economics of medical care.

9. What are the major features of the British National Health Service? Explain why such a program developed in England, while in the United States an entirely different development occurred.

10. The British National Health Service appears to have strong support in Great Britain and vigorous opponents in the United States. Explain the reason for this.

# SELECTED REFERENCES

American Hospital Association, Blue Cross Commission. *Blue Cross Guide.* Chicago, annually.

American Medical Association. *Voluntary Prepayment Medical Care Plans.* Chicago, annually.

AMERICAN MEDICAL ASSOCIATION. "Report of the Commission on Medical Care Plans: Findings, Conclusions, and Recommendations," *The Journal of the American Medical Association* (January 17, 1959) (special edition).

ANDERSON, ODIN W., and FELDMAN, JACOB J. *Family Medical Costs and Voluntary Health Insurance: A Nationwide Survey.* New York: McGraw-Hill Book Co., 1956.

BACHMAN, GEORGE W., and MERIAM, LEWIS. *The Issue of Compulsory Health Education.* Washington, D.C.: The Brookings Institution, 1948.

CHAMBER OF COMMERCE OF THE UNITED STATES. *A Look at Modern Health Insurance.* Washington, D.C., 1954.

COMMISSION ON FINANCING OF HOSPITAL CARE. *Financing Hospital Care in the United States.* New York: McGraw-Hill Book Co., Blakiston Division, 1954–55.
Volume I: *Factors Affecting the Costs of Hospital Care* (John H. Hayes, ed.).
Volume II: *Prepayment and the Community* (Harry Becker, ed.).
Volume III: *Financing Hospital Care for the Non-Wage and Low Income Groups* (Harry Becker, ed.).

COMMITTEE ON MEDICAL CARE TEACHING, ASSOCIATION OF TEACHERS OF PREVENTIVE MEDICINE. *Readings in Medical Care.* Chapel Hill: University of North Carolina Press, 1958.

DICKINSON, FRANK G., and RAYMOND, JAMES. *The Economic Position of Medical Care, 1929–1953.* Bulletin 99. Chicago: American Medical Association, 1955.

GOLDMAN, FRANZ. "Comprehensive Medical Care: Basic Issues," *Social Service Review,* Vol. XXIX (September, 1955), pp. 267–84.

HOUSE COMMITTEE ON INTERSTATE AND FOREIGN COMMERCE. *Health Reinsurance Legislation. Hearings . . . on H. R. 8356* (83d Cong., 2d sess.). Washington, D.C.: U.S. Government Printing Office, 1954.

—— *National Health Plan. Hearings . . . on H. R. 4312 and H. R. 4313* (81st Cong., 1st sess.). Washington, D.C.: U.S. Government Printing Office, 1949.

"Medical Care for Americans," *Annals of the American Academy of Political and Social Science,* Vol. CCLXXIII (January, 1951), entire issue.

NATIONAL HEALTH ASSEMBLY. *America's Health—A Report to the Nation.* New York: Harper & Brothers, 1949.

*The Nation's Health: A Ten Year Program.* A Report to the President by Oscar R. Ewing, Federal Security Administrator. Washington, D.C.: U.S. Government Printing Office, 1948.

NEW YORK ACADEMY OF MEDICINE, COMMITTEE ON MEDICINE AND THE CHANGING ORDER. *Medicine in the Changing Order.* New York: The Commonwealth Fund, 1947.

THE PRESIDENT'S COMMISSION ON THE HEALTH NEEDS OF THE NATION. *Building America's Health: A Report to the President.* Washington, D.C.: U.S. Government Printing Office, 1952–53.
Volume 1: *Findings and Recommendations.*
Volume 2: *America's Health Status, Needs and Resources.*
Volume 3: *America's Health Status, Needs and Resources—A Statistical Appendix.*
Volume 4: *Financing a Health Program for America.*
Volume 5: *The People Speak—Excerpts from Regional Hearings on Health.*

Ross, James S. *The National Health Service in Great Britain: An Historical and Descriptive Study.* New York: Oxford University Press, 1952.

Senate Committee on Education and Labor. *National Health Program. Hearings . . . on S. 1606* (79th Cong., 2d sess.). Washington, D.C.: U.S. Government Printing Office, 1946.

—— *National Health Act of 1945.* Reports Relating to the Bill (S. 1606) to Provide for a National Health Program, Senate Committee Prints Nos. 1–5. Washington, D.C.: U.S. Government Printing Office, 1945–46.

Senate Committee on Labor and Public Welfare. *National Health Program. Hearings . . . on S. 545 and S. 1320* (79th Cong., 2d sess.). Washington, D.C.: U.S. Government Printing Office, 1948.

—— *National Health Program, 1949. Hearings . . . on S. 1106, and S. 1679* (81st Cong., 1st sess.). Washington, D.C.: U.S. Government Printing Office, 1949.

—— *President's Health Recommendations and Related Measures. Hearings . . .* (83d Cong., 2d sess.). Washington, D.C.: U.S. Government Printing Office, 1954.

Serbein, Oscar N., Jr. *Paying for Medical Care in the United States.* New York: Columbia University Press, 1953.

# CHAPTER
# VI

# Related Social
# Security Programs

## INTRODUCTION

JUST AS THERE WERE social security programs in operation prior to the enactment of the Social Security Act in 1935, so, too, today, there are a number of social security programs outside the Act. Still other programs are being proposed as additions to, or modifications of, existing programs.

This chapter contains readings relating primarily to programs of a government character either existing or proposed. Because of the large number of public plans covering special groups, especially in the retirement and health fields, five programs are discussed in the limited space available in this chapter. These five programs are: temporary disability insurance, workmen's compensation, the railroad social security programs, public assistance, and children's allowances.

Although a nationwide program covering the risks of nonoccupational temporary disability does not exist, four states and the railroad employees have coverage of temporary disability and many plans of employers, public and private, contain provisions for payment.

Cash benefits for sickness or disability must be distinguished from health insurance, which deals with medical services. For this reason disability insurance has not been included in Chapter VI, dealing with medical care and health insurance. Although there are many interrelationships between disability insurance and health insurance, many problems are inherent in each program separately.

Many of the public provisions for social security have a very close relationship to private provisions. In California, for instance, the state temporary disability insurance law permits "contracting out" by firms when the sickness benefits in the private plan exceed those provided in the state plan. Several thousand private pension plans now supplement the old-age insurance program. Union and employer health and welfare plans also supplement social security or provide protection with respect to risks not yet covered by legislation. In various proposals for health insurance it has been suggested that local voluntary medical service arrangements provided by unions, consumers, employers, medical societies, or similar groups could supply the medical services outlined under the national or state plan.

The railroad social security program now consists of a retirement and disability insurance program first enacted in 1934; an unemployment insurance program enacted in 1938; and temporary disability insurance and survivors' insurance programs enacted in 1946. These programs are administered entirely on a federal basis. The original law of 1934 (which was held unconstitutional) and the subsequent laws of 1935 and 1937 were enacted with the joint support of railroad employers and railroad labor. The 1946 amendments, however, were supported by railroad labor and opposed by railroad employers, whereas the 1948 amendments were enacted with the joint support of both groups.

The railroad programs raise a number of fundamental questions on the one hand and practical problems on the other. Should governmental social security plans be established on an industry-wide basis? How can a separate and different schedule of contributions and benefits for railroad employees be coordinated with the general social security programs for industrial employees? In what respects should provisions in social security legislation for railroad employees be the same as, or different from, social security legislation for other groups generally?

There are many laws providing income maintenance to veterans and their families and for health and welfare purposes. These laws are, in effect, social security programs for veterans and their families. Veterans have both "health insurance" and "socialized medicine"; as well as pensions, disability and old-age benefits, life insurance, and other programs.

The pension and disability programs for veterans also raise certain basic questions. Should veterans and their families be guaranteed a minimum income from social security, through veterans' programs, or from both programs simultaneously? Should veterans or their families always receive higher benefits than nonveterans? If families receive both benefits, the question then arises, when military service is credited under social security plans, what adjustment, if any, should be made when a veteran or his family receive veterans' benefits based upon the same period of military service?

Similar problems of interrelationships arise with respect to social insurance benefits and workmen's compensation. All states now have some form of workmen's compensation. In order to assure that there will be no gaps or overlaps in various benefits it is necessary to make specific provisions in social insurance laws or proposals to achieve such objectives. For instance, proposals for payment of social insurance benefits to persons permanently or temporarily disabled must be coordinated with permanent or temporary disability benefits under workmen's compensation. This is not an easy task because of the different levels of benefits, the different sources of the revenues for the benefits, the different administrative organizations, and the different philosophies in the programs.

One of the problems requiring further study arises from the fact that, for workmen's compensation, cash benefits for temporary unemployment due to sickness or disability differ from the cash benefits for temporary unemployment due to loss of a job or to nonindustrial sickness or disability. Although all these various benefits have been enacted by the states, very little consideration has been given to the interrelationship of the benefit levels. In some states the benefits are higher in one program, whereas in other states the opposite is true. Different methods of computing wages and benefits as well as different minimum and maximum benefits are used in the various programs in the same states.

With the passage of the Social Security Act in 1935 the federal government undertook responsibility for sharing in the cost of assistance to special groups requiring long-time and expensive care—the needy, the aged, dependent children, and the blind. In 1950, provision was made for sharing in the cost of assistance to the permanently and totally disabled and for sharing in the costs of medical care paid to the providers of such care. Through grants-in-aid to the states, the federal government matches (within certain limits) the amount paid by the state to these individuals. The programs are administered through state agencies in accordance with state plans submitted to and approved by the Social Security Administration. Each state is free to decide the level of living which it will use in determining whether an applicant is needy.

Marked differences in the resources of the states have resulted in wide variations among states in public assistance payments. Unlike social insurance, fulfillment of all the various eligibility requirements for public assistance does not assure automatic receipt of aid. Poorer states, which are generally those with predominantly rural population, have often had insufficient funds to meet, on the basis of their own established standards, their share of the need of all who are eligible for public assistance.

The social security system in the United States is unique in a number of different ways. The United States has developed the most comprehensive system of any country in the world of private social security protection by means of private insurance, supplementary company pension plans, union health and welfare plans, and similar programs. It also has one of the most extensive programs of veterans' pensions, unemployment insurance, and related social security programs for veterans and their families. Cash assistance payments to needy individuals based upon an individual determination of need are very extensive in the United States as compared with other countries. Finally, the United States is the only important English-speaking country in the world which does *not* provide for some sort of cash allowances for children. In order to appraise the total social security protection available to individuals and their families in this country it is therefore necessary to look at all of the arrangements that exist for the purpose of providing such security whether they are public or private, comprehensive or piecemeal, or voluntary or compulsory.

# 45. OTHER PROGRAMS RELATING TO SOCIAL SECURITY

*Social Security in the United States,* Social Security Administration, 1957.

MUCH OF ALL the work that government does is important to social security or social welfare in a broad sense. That is, it is designed to help people to lead useful, self-supporting lives. Public education, for example, helps prepare children to carry the responsibilities they will have as members of families, workers, and citizens. Public health services prevent much unnecessary sickness and death that would cause poverty and dependency among families and heavy public costs. The Social Security Act of 1935 contained provisions for grants to States for public health services and for vocational rehabilitation services to help handicapped people regain their ability to earn.

It is not possible here to consider or even mention all the public programs—Federal, State, or local—that are important to social security. The following pages list some that are closely related to programs under the Social Security Act because they help assure families and individuals that they will have some income in old age, unemployment, disability, and other adversities.

## WORKMEN'S COMPENSATION

Workmen's compensation laws are designed to make sure that a worker receives prompt medical care and cash benefits when he is injured in connection with his job or benefits are paid to his dependents if he is killed. This was the first form of social insurance to develop widely in the United States. All States, Alaska, Hawaii, and Puerto Rico now have such laws. Federal laws cover Federal employees, longshoremen and harbor workers, and private employees in the District of Columbia.

### Types of Laws

There are many different kinds of workmen's compensation laws. Some States require all employers covered by the law to take out insurance. In other States, an employer may choose not to come into the insurance system, but the workmen's compensation law takes away the defenses against workers' claims that the employer would have had under the common law. Most laws permit the employer to insure with private insurance companies. In seven of the 18 States that have State insurance funds, however, employers are required to use the State fund in insuring their risks; these are known as the "exclusive" funds. In the other 11 State insurance systems the fund is "competitive," and employers choose between insuring with the State fund or a private carrier. Under all but a few acts an employer may qualify as a "self-insurer" by giving proof of ability to carry his own risk.

No State's law covers all jobs. Some cover only kinds of work that are considered dangerous, some only employers who have more than a given number of employees. Workmen's compensation laws usually exclude farm and domestic workers, casual labor, and employees of charitable or religious organizations.

Laws also limit the kinds of injuries that can be compensated. The usual definition of a compensable injury or death is one "arising out of and in the course of employment." Most of the early laws covered only injuries due to accidents, but the majority now include some or all diseases attributable to the worker's occupation. Some States exclude injuries due to the employee's intoxication, willful misconduct, or gross negligence.

### Benefits

Workmen's compensation laws provide for cash benefits to an injured worker and benefits to the family of a worker who is killed. The payments are usually based on the worker's wages at the time of the injury. Practically all laws place top and bottom limits on the weekly amounts payable to a disabled worker or to survivors. Most also limit the number of weeks for which benefits must be paid and/or the total amount paid in a given case. Some, however, provide for death benefits to a widow throughout her life unless she remarries and for benefits to surviving children until they reach a given age. Some place no time limit on the benefits payable to a worker so long as he continues to be totally disabled.

All the workmen's compensation laws require that medical care be furnished to injured employees, though about one-third limit the length of time during which it is supplied or the total cost or both. Practically all laws provide benefits to help meet the burial expenses of workers who are killed.

### SOCIAL INSURANCE FOR RAILROAD WORKERS

Persons who work for railroads and certain affiliated companies have greater protection under social insurance than any other large group of workers in the United States. This protection is provided under two Federal laws, the Railroad Retirement Act and the Railroad Unemployment Insurance Act. In addition, railroad workers and their dependents are protected under the old-age, survivors, and disability insurance part of the Social Security Act until the worker has 10 years of coverage under the Railroad Retirement Act. From an over-all financial standpoint, benefits under the Railroad Retirement Act are, in effect, reinsured by the Federal

Old-Age and Survivors Insurance Trust Fund and the Federal Disability Insurance Trust Fund.

### The Railroad Retirement Act

This law provides benefits for insured workers who have retired because of old age or disability and for the aged wives or dependent husbands of beneficiaries. It also provides annuities and lump-sum payments to survivors of insured workers.

Old-age annuities are payable to retired workers at age 65 or over after 10 years' railroad service or at ages 60–64 after 30 years' service; annuities which begin before age 65 are reduced for men but not for women employees. Reduced annuities remain at the reduced rate after the retired worker reaches age 65. Disability annuities are payable to workers permanently disabled for any regular gainful employment if they have had 10 years' service. A worker who is currently connected with the railroad industry and is permanently disabled for his regular occupation (but not necessarily for other work) may receive an annuity if he has reached age 60 and has had 10 years' service, or if he is under age 60 but has had 20 years of employment covered by the act.

The survivor benefits under this law include lump-sum payments, and monthly payments that are made under certain conditions to the worker's widow or dependent widower at age 60 and his or her children and to a widow, regardless of age, who has an entitled child in her care. If the worker leaves no widow, dependent widower, or eligible children, a monthly benefit may be paid to his or her dependent parents at age 60.

The amounts of monthly payments depend on the worker's past earnings and length of railroad service.

The system is financed by contributions under the Railroad Retirement Tax Act. The total tax rate, divided equally between employers and employees, is 12.5 percent of the worker's earnings under the system, not including earnings above $350 a month.

Railroad employment was excluded from coverage under old-age and survivors insurance when the Railroad Retirement Act of 1935 amended the 1935 Social Security Act. Now Congress has set up ways to correlate the two systems. At the death or retirement of a worker who has railroad service but not the 120 months needed to qualify under that program, his wage records are transferred to the Social Security Administration. Earnings under both programs are combined to determine whether he is insured under old-age and survivors insurance and, if so, the amount of the benefits. At the death of a worker who has more than 120 months' creditable railroad service, wage records are similarly combined. If he had a current connection with the railroad industry at the time of his death, benefits to his survivors will generally be paid by the Railroad Retirement Board; if not, generally by the Social Security Administration. A retiring worker can qualify for retirement benefits under both programs if he has worked long enough under each to be insured, but at his death the survivors can qualify under only one program based on the combined earnings record.

### The Railroad Unemployment Insurance Act

This law provides payments to qualified railroad workers who have been out of a job for more than a certain number of days within a 14-day "registration period" either because they are unemployed or because they are sick. Days lost from both causes cannot be combined in the same registration period. In the first registration period in a year, a worker receives a benefit for each day after the first 7 days lost because of unemployment or sickness; in later periods the benefit is paid for each day after the first 4. Disability benefits and unemployment insurance may each be paid for a maximum of 130 days in a benefit year.

To qualify, a worker must have had at least $400 in a year in pay from an employer subject to the act. Special maternity benefits may be paid to women workers.

## VETERANS PROGRAMS

The United States provides a great variety of payments and services to persons who have served in the Armed Forces in wartime or to their survivors and, in some circumstances, to members of the families of living veterans. These are given, of course, in recognition of special wartime sacrifices. The benefits have a relation to past military service. In any case, veterans' programs may be considered to have a relation to social security. . . .

The Veterans' Readjustment Assistance Act of 1952 provides unemployment compensation for veterans with service on or after June 27, 1950. Benefits are paid by the State employment security agencies at the rate of $26 for each week of involuntary unemployment, up to a maximum of $676. If a veteran qualifies for unemployment compensation under any other law, either State or Federal, he may receive under the Unemployment Compensation for Veterans law only the difference between $26 and the amount of unemployment benefits to which he is entitled under the other unemployment insurance law. Where the weekly amount of benefits under any other law is $26 or more, no payments can be made from UCV funds until other benefits are exhausted. Veterans must meet the eligibility and disqualification provisions of the State laws. No benefits are paid while veterans are receiving mustering-out pay or education or subsistence allowances.

By the end of April 1955, 3.8 million veterans eligible for these benefits had been released from service; 831,000 had filed claims for UCV benefits; 615,000 had received one or more benefit payments; and 106,000 had exhausted their benefits. The total payments had aggregated $193 million.

## RETIREMENT SYSTEMS FOR PUBLIC EMPLOYEES

The Federal Government, States, and many localities have retirement systems that cover some or all of their employees. Most of these systems make payments to a qualified employee who retires either in old age or because he is disabled. Some also provide annuities for survivors.

### Federal Employees

Most civilians who work for the Federal Government are covered by the Civil Service Retirement Act. Other Federal laws cover some special groups, such as Foreign Service officers. Federal employment not covered under any other system is generally included under the Social Security Act.

The Civil Service Retirement Act provides annuities to qualified employees who retire because of age or disability, to the widows and minor children of employees who die, and, in certain circumstances, to the survivors of annuitants. Old-age annuities are also payable to persons who have been in Government service but have left it before retirement age, if they have not withdrawn their contributions. The amount of payments depends on the employee's earnings and length of service. Persons covered by the system contribute $6\frac{1}{2}$ percent of their base pay. The law requires matching payments from the employing agency and further implies that the Government will furnish such additional amounts as are required to finance the system.

### Employees of States and Localities

General or special retirement systems administered by States or localities are in effect for almost three-fourths of the persons employed by these governments. Under practically all these systems, the employee contributes to the cost. Most of the systems provide for retirement because of disability as well as in old age. Conditions for receiving benefits and amounts of benefits vary widely. Usually an employee must have had a considerable period of service to qualify or to receive a substantial annuity. Usually also a person who leaves his government job before retirement age has his contributions returned but does not qualify for an annuity.

Except for special systems for policemen and firemen, most of these programs make only limited provision for the survivors of an employee who dies. Generally it consists of a refund of contributions or continuing payments to the survivors of an annuitant who has chosen to take a reduced payment for himself so long as he lives.

When the Federal system of old-age and survivors insurance was extended in 1950, about 1.5 million State and local public employees who were not covered by retirement programs were made eligible for coverage under agreements between States and the Federal Government. Beginning with 1955, coverage was made possible for 3½ million more State and local government employees (except most policemen and firemen) who are covered by a retirement system. The 1956 amendments to the law provide for the coverage of certain State and local government employees, including policemen and firemen, under special provisions which apply only to certain States.

The Social Security Act permits a State to enter into a voluntary agreement with the Federal Government to accept Federal old-age and survivors insurance for any one or more "coverage groups" of employees of the State or its political subdivisions. Where a State or local retirement plans exists, a majority of its members eligible to vote must favor Social Security coverage in a secret referendum before coverage of a particular "coverage group" under the Federal program can be effected. When the State does make such an agreement, all employees in the groups affected come under the Federal system except those doing certain kinds of work not covered by the Federal law. The State may, if it wishes, include or exclude certain kinds of work from the agreement. In January 1957, almost 2 million State and local government employees had been covered under the Federal system through voluntary agreements; half of them were also members of State or local systems.

## STATE PROGRAMS FOR TEMPORARY DISABILITY

Four States—Rhode Island, California, New Jersey, and New York—pay temporary disability benefits to partially compensate wage earners for loss of wages caused by nonoccupational illness or injury. In general, coverage is similar to that of unemployment insurance. The first three operate their systems in connection with their unemployment insurance programs; in New York, disability insurance is administered by the Workmen's Compensation Board.

Rhode Island provides benefits through an exclusive State insurance fund in which all contributions are deposited and from which all benefits are paid. California and New Jersey provide a State fund, but employers may contract out to private insurance carriers or as self-insurers, if their plans meet the requirements of the law. In New York the employer must make his own arrangements for insuring his workers, either by purchasing a group accident and health policy from a private insurance company or from the State insurance fund or by adopting an approved plan of self-insurance.

An employee payroll tax of 1 percent of wages—up to $3,600 in Rhode Island and $3,000 in California—is used exclusively to finance benefits under the State-operated systems in these two States. In New Jersey, the State-operated system is financed by an employee contribution of 0.5 percent of the first $3,000 and an employer contribution of 0.25 percent which may be modified by experience rating. In New York, workers pay

0.5 percent of their wages up to a maximum of 30 cents per week, and the employer bears any additional costs of the program.

Weekly benefit rates are designed to replace one-half or more of the wage loss. The maximum weekly benefit is $30 in Rhode Island, $35 in New Jersey, $40 in California and $45 in New York. The minimum weekly benefit is $10 in California, New Jersey, and Rhode Island and $20 in New York. After a waiting period of 7 consecutive days, disability benefits are payable for a maximum duration of 26 weeks in Rhode Island, California, and New Jersey and 20 weeks in New York. California provides, in addition to weekly cash benefits, hospital benefits of $10 a day for 12 days in a period of disability. None of the laws provides for benefits to dependents of a disabled wage earner.

## PUBLIC ASSISTANCE

In 1935 the Social Security Act authorized Federal grants to States to pay part of the costs of aiding people who are old or blind and children whose need is due to certain causes. In 1950 Congress added Federal grants to States for aid to permanently and totally disabled persons.

These four assistance programs have one condition in common. People aided under any of them must be needy, according to the definition of need used in the State. In this, public assistance is different from social insurance. A person qualifies for an insurance benefit on the basis of his past work under the insurance system. When he meets the conditions for benefits, he receives his benefit regardless of any savings or resources other than earnings he may have.

In public assistance, as in unemployment insurance, the Social Security Act left the States free to decide whether or not they wished to take part in a program under the act. If, however, a State wishes to receive a Federal grant-in-aid for one of these programs, it must have a plan approved by the Federal authorities as meeting general requirements laid down in the Federal law.

The Bureau of Public Assistance of the Social Security Administration, acting under the supervision of the Commissioner of Social Security, is responsible for considering such conformity of State laws and plans and for recommending the amounts of Federal grants. The Secretary of Health, Education, and Welfare certifies to the Treasury that Federal requirements have been met. The Bureau also provides services and conducts studies to aid States in carrying out their programs.

### Federal Grants to States

The Federal grant to a State meets half the cost of administering the State's program. It also covers part of the amount the State gives, because of need, to persons aged 65 or over, blind persons, totally and permanently disabled persons over age 18, and families with children who have lost support or care because of a parent's death, incapacity, or absence from the home. In the year 1956 the Federal share of all assistance payments under the Social Security Act amounted to 54 percent.

Federal law leaves it to the States to define blindness and total and permanent disability. In general, the States aid people who are totally blind or have so little sight they cannot earn a living. Permanent and total disability does not necessarily mean that a person is completely helpless. It can be interpreted to mean a physical or mental defect or condition that keeps him from performing useful work he otherwise could do.

Most States providing this type of assistance take this broader view. The assistance agency decides whether the person is disabled in the meaning of the program on the basis of the findings of doctors, social workers, vocational advisers, and other experts. It considers his physical and mental condition, education, age, experience, and so on. When his condition can be improved, he can be helped to get the necessary services.

Federal money may be used for aid to children until the child reaches age 18 (prior to July 1957, it was required that a child between 16 and 18 be regularly attending school). The child must be living in a family home with one or more relatives. Federal money may be used to help meet the needs of the parent or other relative who is caring for the child, as well as the needs of the child himself.

To be approved for the Federal grant, the State plan for aid to any one of these groups of needy persons must be in operation throughout the State. The State must share in the cost, and a single State agency must administer the plan or supervise administration. The aid must be given directly to the needy person, in money, except that the agency may pay other persons for medical care they have given the recipient. The State agency must provide if requested a fair hearing for any person whose application for aid is denied or whose payment is decreased or stopped. These and a few other requirements of the Federal law are intended to ensure that Federal money is used fairly and for the purposes for which Congress appropriates it.

The amount of the Federal grant to a State depends on what the State itself spends. The Federal Government shares in payments to recipients up to only a certain amount. Except in Puerto Rico and the Virgin Islands, these limits are $60 a month for an aged, blind, or disabled person; $32 a month for a parent or other relative caring for a child and $32 for the first child and $23 for each additional child aided in the same home.

The Federal grant reimburses the State for a given part of the average amount of payments under these maximums. It meets four-fifths of the cost of the first $30 of the average payment to recipients of old-age assistance and aid to the blind or the disabled, and half the rest of that average. In aid to dependent children, the Federal share is fourteen-seventeenths of the first $17 of the average monthly payment per recipient and half the remainder.

In Puerto Rico and the Virgin Islands the Federal Government pays 50 percent of the assistance payments within a maximum of $30 for old-age assistance, aid to the blind, and aid to the permanently and totally disabled, and $18 and $12 for aid to dependent children. In addition there is a limitation on the total amount granted annually from Federal funds.

Beginning July 1, 1957, the Federal Government will also share on an equal basis State expenditures for payments to suppliers of medical care (including expenditures for insurance premiums for medical care) up to a maximum amount determined by multiplying $6 per month times the number of adults on the rolls and $3 per month times the number of children. . . .

### The Federal-State Partnership

In January 1957, old-age assistance, aid to the blind and aid to dependent children were being given under the Social Security Act in all 48 States, Alaska, the District of Columbia, Hawaii, Puerto Rico, and the Virgin Islands. Federal-State programs for aid to the totally and permanently disabled, for which Federal grants were not made before October 1950, were in operation in 42 States, the District of Columbia, Hawaii, Puerto Rico, and the Virgin Islands.

The Federal-State partnership under the Social Security Act has greatly extended and improved aid to needy old or disabled persons and children who have met with misfortune. It has also been important in helping to develop a new attitude toward people in need.

Once "relief" was commonly given in the form of food or other necessities handed out to people who asked for help. It was often assumed that such people could not manage their own lives. Most of the people on the public assistance rolls are too old or too young or too disabled to support themselves. Some, including relatives caring for dependent children, must stay home to care for others. Like other people, however, they want to and should manage their own lives as fully as possible. Under these programs, therefore, their assistance is chiefly money. (Some agencies pay a doctor or hospital directly for necessary medical care for recipients.) This money payment, which they are free to spend as they think best, just as they would any other money, helps them maintain their self-respect and their desire and efforts to be independent.

In addition to financial aid and medical care, States are increasingly providing social services to help needy persons become self-sufficient to the full extent of their capabilities. To help achieve this goal, special Federal grants to States for training are authorized to increase the number of professionally qualified personnel available for employment in public assistance programs.

### GENERAL ASSISTANCE

Many people who must have money to meet their basic needs cannot get public assistance under the Social Security Act. They may not be among the special groups aided by those programs. That is, they may not yet have reached 65 and they may not be blind or permanently and totally disabled or children in need for one of the reasons named in the Federal act. Or they may be in one of these groups and still not eligible for the Federal-State program because they fail to meet some requirement of the State, such as citizenship or residence within the State for a certain time.

General assistance is a form of aid that States or localities furnish for needs they recognize among persons not included in the federally aided special assistance programs or not getting enough help from such programs to meet their needs. This aid is given usually in cash but sometimes in the form of orders for groceries, rent, or other items.

In hard times, many of the people on the general assistance rolls are in need because the earners in the family cannot get jobs. When employment conditions are good, many or most of those on the rolls are in need because they are sick or disabled or because of the illness or death of others on whom they normally depend. The provisions of the Social Security Act for aid to the permanently and totally disabled did not become effective until October 1950. Since that time this program has been assuming responsibility for many seriously disabled persons who previously received general assistance, but it is not yet in full operation throughout the country. Even when it is, it will help meet only part of the need directly attributable to sickness and disability.

States and localities provide general assistance under their own laws and regulations and meet the whole cost out of State or local funds or both. The conditions under which aid is granted and the amounts of assistance differ widely from place to place, reflecting the resources and attitudes of the State or locality.

## SERVICES FOR MATERNAL AND CHILD HEALTH AND CHILD WELFARE

The health and welfare service programs for mothers and children are service rather than cash income programs. No money is paid to any mother or child under these provisions. Everything that Congress appropriates for grants to States goes to State health and welfare agencies to support services. The largest part goes to pay the salaries of doctors, dentists, nurses, medical social workers, child welfare workers, and other professional people who help give children a better start in life. Some goes to pay for hospital and convalescent care of crippled children, some to pay the cost of foster care of children who cannot be cared for at home.

The Social Security Act authorizes Congress to appropriate $16.5 million for maternal and child health services, $15 million for services for crippled children, and $10 million for child welfare services (authorization for grants for child welfare services has been increased to $12 million beginning with the fiscal year ending June 30, 1958). From the amounts

Congress actually appropriates, grants to States are made according to general rules in the act. These grants are administered by the Children's Bureau of the Social Security Administration, acting under authority delegated to it by the Secretary of Health, Education, and Welfare and the Commissioner of Social Security.

The Bureau's staff includes specialists in child health and welfare, who help States to develop and improve their programs. The Bureau also encourages and carries on studies concerning the well-being of children and helps parents and others to learn about ways to promote child health and welfare.

## The Basis of Federal Grants

The Federal law emphasizes services for children living in rural areas and in areas of special need. Each State receives a flat amount for each of the programs. The rest of the money is apportioned according to different factors.

In grants for maternal and child health services, each State's share depends in part on the number of births in the State in relation to the total number in the Nation, the proportion of births in rural areas of the State, and the State's need for help in providing these services.

Each State's share in grants for services to crippled children depends in part on the relative number of rural children and the financial need of the State. The State share, however, is governed largely by the number of children under 21 years of age.

In grants for child welfare, the State share is affected by the proportion of the State's rural population under age 18 in relation to the total rural child population.

In order to take full advantage of the Federal provisions, the State itself must supply part of the money spent for these programs.

Before the beginning of each year, the State health or welfare department or the other official agency concerned makes a plan for its work during the following year. The plan tells what work it proposes to do, how many people will be needed to do it and what training or experience they must have had, how much State and local money will be used, and how much Federal money is requested. The plans for each program must be approved by the Children's Bureau before the State can receive its share of the Federal money to help carry it out.

## State Programs

All 48 States and Alaska, the District of Columbia, Hawaii, Puerto Rico, and the Virgin Islands receive Federal grants for these programs. The following examples illustrate some of the services, among many others, that these programs are providing.

*Maternal and Child Health.* Under State plans, local health departments provide health supervision by doctors in prenatal clinics, child-health conferences, and schools, and by public health nurses in clinics, schools, and homes. The grants also provide money for postgraduate education in the care of mothers and children to train needed doctors, dentists, nurses, and other health workers.

*Services for Crippled Children.* State agencies locate crippled children and give them a diagnosis, without charge. In line with what the doctor finds necessary, the agency helps the parents plan for whatever medical, surgical, hospital, or other care the child may need. In some cases, the State agency itself pays for such care.

*Child Welfare Services.* State welfare agencies use Federal funds for service to children who are dependent, neglected, or delinquent. The child welfare worker in a State or local public welfare agency helps children whose problems have been brought to the agency's attention by the schools, the police, the juvenile court, neighbors, or the child's parents. The agency then arranges with the family or others in the community to have the child receive the services he needs.

# 46. MYTH AND REALITY IN WORKMEN'S COMPENSATION

Herman M. Somers,
International Association of
Industrial Accident Boards
and Commissions, 1956.

This is the first time I have attended your convention in the flesh. But I have been attending in spirit and mind for many years. I have read with care and admiration your proceedings, committee reports, and resolutions. In such publications, I find not only the spirit of dedicated administrators but frequently of scholars and reformers. Over the years, you have exhibited the courage and wisdom to bring together at your meetings, spokesmen for every viewpoint, technical skill, and special interest—doctors, claimant and defense lawyers, university scholars, insurance officials, representatives of management and of labor, along with government administrators. You have not hesitated to welcome opinions antagonistic to your own. This has not only contributed greatly to the quality and usefulness of your deliberations but it has been a forceful expression of your faith in the democratic way to progress, an expression made all the more valuable because it is, unfortunately, not always practiced by other professional associations.

Your informed discussions of the highly technical aspects of compensation administration—such as disability rating, second-injury funds, industrial radiation and occupational disease, the techniques of rehabilitation, and many complex medicolegal issues—with the conspicuous exception of finance and insurance, have become a treasure house of invaluable data and guidance for technicians not only in your own work but in the growing variety of related areas. From my own recent experience I can tell you that when the President's Commission on Veterans' Pensions was established last year, one of the first sources it turned to was the disability compensation experience under your programs.

The records of your proceedings are enough to disarm any critic. Whatever shortcomings the outsider may point to in workmen's compensation, you can show, on the record, that you said it first. Nowhere will one find such candid—though loyal—criticism of most aspects of compensation. When I was first informed of the type of model bill the Department of Labor was undertaking, about two years ago—I understand the term has now been changed to "comprehensive check list"—I observed that the Department could find all the recommendations it needed in the proceedings, the self-appraisals, of this organization.

In inviting me here, your president asked me to avoid detailed treatment of any such practical particulars which properly dominate your own discussions, but rather to look, as an outsider, at the whole of workmen's compensation and its present role in the United States. While it would be easier to talk about some narrower subject, I have accepted his suggestion because I agree that a bird's-eye perspective is now sorely needed and deserves the attention of all of us, even though much of its aspect is painful.

If one does stand off and tries to get a view of the problem as a whole, one soon sees why dealing with the particulars alone is inadequate and in some degree unreal. As is often the case with long-established and accepted social institutions, which have won their initial victories, we become as much attached to the forms as to the purpose. There is a natural tendency to look at the comforting myths, derived from past triumphs, instead of the uncomfortable realities which imply new and more difficult obstacles ahead.

For example, partly through sheer habituation, the myth develops that the particular structure in effect is the only possible or reasonable design for achieving the objectives of the program, and that friends of the program must not question it. A challenge to the current organization of the program is looked upon as concealed opposition to the program itself and its purposes, and is thus disregarded.

At your meeting two years ago in Quebec, as some of you may recall, a young man on the program made some rather severe criticism of how the program was running. He was sharply called to task by one of your senior colleagues—whose honorable service goes back to the first decade of workmen's compensation—who chided him for his youthful inability to remember the harsh injustices suffered by injured workers before workmen's compensation. Similarly, my academic colleague, the late Domenico Gagliardo, in his widely used book, *American Social In-*

*surance,* concludes his chapter on workmen's compensation by evaluating its success in relation to the inhumane conditions which prevailed at the turn of the century.

It is important to remember history, and workmen's compensation is rightly celebrated as a great pioneering landmark in American social legislation. But it is fruitless, and probably dangerous, to fall into the temptation of evaluating a program whose job must be done in 1957, and thereafter, in terms of 1910. The whole social, ethical, and economic environment of workmen's compensation has been radically altered. It is in terms of the new environment and new conditions that the job must now be done and in which our effectiveness will be tested. The current challenge to workmen's compensation does not derive from failure to recall conditions of 50 years ago; it comes primarily from the failure to adopt our institutions to the present.

Permit me to list, and describe briefly, a few of the current conditions . . . which basically influence workmen's compensation in a way which was not true when the structure was originally designed—six sets of current realities which must be faced up to when we consider what needs doing in workmen's compensation.

1. As a result of collective bargaining or unilateral employer action, a host of industrial disability and death benefit programs now overlap with workmen's compensation. Millions of workers are eligible for short-term nonoccupational disability benefits. Often these benefits are so much higher than workmen's compensation that some union leaders report a "black market" usage of nonoccupational benefits in occupational injury cases.

Less common, but spreading, is the practice of granting occupational disability benefits to supplement workmen's compensation up to the level of nonoccupational disability benefits or some other agreed standard.

Increasingly, industry is making available early or disability retirement programs for permanently disabled workers who must retire prematurely. Group life insurance is even more widespread. Benefits are usually set at one year's pay, longer periods are becoming more common, and are available to survivors regardless of whether death is caused occupationally or otherwise. Frequently such insurance also covers dismemberment from whatever cause.

Parenthetically, it may be added that where the issue of causation arises, for all practical effects a nonoccupational disability gets to be defined simply as one which does not qualify for workmen's compensation. Any contraction in workmen's compensation eligibility tends to expand the other programs—just as any decline in workmen's compensation benefits relative to wages may simply increase the role of the supplementary benefits. Workers have some reason to believe that if workmen's compensation were to narrow down or even disappear, they would have little difficulty obtaining similar protection through employee benefit plans.

2. In addition to cash benefits, industry is increasingly offering the protection of direct health services or medical care insurance. Hospitalization and medical care benefits are soaring. At the end of 1954, according to reports of the Social Security Administration, private employee benefit plans gave hospitalization coverage to more than 31 million employees (and more than 44 million dependents); and medical care coverage to over 17 million employees (and over 21 million dependents). The figures are probably higher now. While all these benefits are limited in extent it is the trend which is significant. Hardly a bargaining negotiation goes on today in which health insurance benefits are not introduced or improved.

Needless to say, also, many workers not covered by employee benefit plans are covered by other forms of health insurance. According to the Health Insurance Council, by 1955, 66.3 per cent of the population was insured in some degree for hospital expense; 56.6 per cent for surgical expense; 34.2 per cent for medical expense; and 3.2 per cent for major medical expense.

Although not so impressive numerically, great potential significance lies in the spread of industrial health services, on an in-plant basis, in union or union-management health centers, or in community centers such as Permanente and New York's H.I.P. Services are generally provided without regard to cause of disability and, under such arrangements, it becomes continuously less practical to attempt to segregate occupational from non-occupational causation.

Jerome Pollack . . . noted this trend in the whole field of health insurance and declared: "Splitting care into occupational and nonoccupational compartments reduces its quality, as either segment alone is incomplete and general medical care often misses the occupational origin of disease. Where general medical care is organized in such fashion as to assure high quality care, of adequate comprehensiveness, it may offer the needed setting which combines impartiality, competence, and a primary focus on the welfare of the individual."[1] Consider carefully the implications of this view for workmen's compensation.

3. The Social Security Act Amendments of 1956 provide the most recent, and perhaps the most significant, example of the extension of public social security programs into the field of disability, at one time almost the exclusive province of workmen's compensation.

The new legislation provides for payments to permanently and totally disabled workers at age 50, starting in July, 1957. No medical care is included, although a financial incentive for undertaking rehabilitation is

---

[1] Jerome Pollack, "Medical Care and Rehabilitation under Workmen's Compensation," *American Journal of Public Health* (May, 1955), p. 648.

provided. Because no benefits are allowed for dependents, the present maximum is $108.50 per month, currently less than the amount potentially available under most workmen's compensation laws. But, as you all know, OASI benefits have in recent years shown a tendency to increase more rapidly than workmen's compensation. As the disability program is attached to the old-age retirement program, the disabled will now be the beneficiaries of the great political support in this country for generous old-age pensions.

Unless present trends are reversed, we may look forward to the day when a permanently and totally disabled person will be better off, at least from a cash point of view, as a client of the Social Security disability program than as a workmen's compensation recipient. Already, the Social Security program offers more attractive duration features than many workmen's compensation laws. Under Social Security there is no maximum total amount provision, and the duration runs until the beneficiary automatically qualifies for retirement benefits at 65, a potential of 15 years at the basic level, after which additional benefits are allowable for dependents as well.

The Social Security Act provides that a disabled beneficiary who is also receiving workmen's compensation benefits shall have his federal benefit reduced by the amount of his workmen's compensation. Thus, if an occupationally, permanently and totally disabled worker is eligible for $105 a month in federal benefits, but is receiving $100 from workmen's compensation, he will receive only $5 from OASI. But, such a man, if and when his workmen's compensation benefit rights are exhausted, will suffer no disadvantage; he will then be paid by the federal government the whole $105. True, requirements for qualifying for the federal benefits are now quite stringent, and many a workmen's compensation recipient will find himself ineligible. But the law is new. We can be certain that eligibility will become less and less difficult with passage of time.

I am wondering whether any employer associations or insurance carriers have yet thought of the obvious proposal they might bring before state legislatures in the near future. They may point out that permanently and totally disabled workmen's compensation beneficiaries who are receiving less than $108.50 a month, and who could qualify for the federal benefits, would suffer no loss if they were cut off from workmen's compensation cash benefits entirely. No harm to the worker and it would save money for home industry! Legislators could be impressed.

I also wonder what reaction you are likely to encounter among workers entitled to workmen's compensation who suddenly discover they are not much better off than if they had never been covered by workmen's compensation.

4. Other public programs also impinge upon workmen's compensation. The Federal Old-Age and Survivors Insurance program now offers generous protection to the widows and children of workers who die from

whatever cause, including occupational injury. Maximum benefits for a widow with one child come to $162.80 and for a widow and 2 dependent children run to $200 a month, which exceeds the maximum available under most workmen's compensation laws. The potential duration of OASI benefits is also much greater. According to the Social Security Administration some 50 million of the nation's 56 million children are now assured of monthly benefits under OASI and 90 per cent of the married women with children under 18 are protected against loss of support because of the husband's death.

Since 1950, the Social Security Act has provided for grants-in-aid to the states for public assistance to the totally and permanently disabled. The program is now in effect in 45 jurisdictions and over a quarter of a million cases a month receive assistance. Disabled workers who do not qualify for this category of assistance may qualify for another of the assistances. Additional federal funds have recently been made available to increase medical care benefits in all these programs. A means test program is not something to which any worker will feel attracted, but it does offer some minimal guarantee which did not exist before.

Four industrial states and the railroad industry now pay cash benefits for temporary nonoccupational disability. Together with the private plans already mentioned, about 42 million workers, almost 70 per cent of the labor force, have some form of money income protection against such disability, according to the Social Security Administration.

The Veterans Administration provides medical care to veterans regardless of cause of disability. Under some circumstances, cash benefits are available for nonservice-connected injuries, as well as survivorship benefits for nonservice-connected death. There are now 23 million veterans. Together with their dependents they constitute about half of the population. As the veteran population ages, benefits from nonservice-connected disability will replace service-connected benefits as a major factor of cost and an important element of all social security benefits potentially available to American workers.

5. Present conditions have led to an increasingly articulated feeling that, on balance, workers may now be sacrificing more than they are gaining in workmen's compensation.

It is often reiterated that workmen's compensation was designed as a balanced *quid pro quo* between management and labor. In return for *limited* liability, the employer accepted liability irrespective of fault. The worker gave up the right to damage suit and potential unlimited compensation in return for an exclusive remedy of limited but steady and assured benefits without legal action. This "social bargain" is often referred to as if it were a contract binding for all time instead of legislation continuously subject to re-examination in the light of new conditions. It is implied also that if the considerations granted by the two parties were approximately in balance in 1910, they are still in approximate balance in 1956.

When workers, as their part of the bargain, gave up the right to sue, it was felt that they were not giving up a very valuable asset, because the courts were then known to be highly conservative, and inclined to ungenerous and rigid interpretation of labor's claims. During the past 20 years, the courts have radically revised their outlook. The probability of recovery in most cases has been greatly increased due to statutory as well as judicial changes. The public attitude has altered. Labor is now not only backed by strong unions but has available skilled, experienced, and effective lawyers who specialize for the plaintiff's side in such cases. Awards exceeding $100,000 are becoming more common.

When workers, as their part of the bargain, acquired the principle of "liability without fault" it was rightly considered an important and unique gain. But, in intervening years, other injured persons in tort cases have gradually been acquiring through judicial interpretation a similar principle, which might be called "liability through insurability," which in practice minimizes the issue of fault, without any sacrifice of the right of unlimited damage award.

When, as part of the bargain, workers were given "assured" benefits—without necessity for litigation—it was anticipated that compensation would be geared to approximately two-thirds of wages in weekly payments. As it has turned out, and as your discussions have so often pointed out, benefits average not much more than half the expected levels, litigation has in fact been flourishing, and lump-sum payments are still prevalent in many states.

Among the occupationally injured workers, it is the temporary, short-term disabled, who fare relatively best from workmen's compensation. The long-term, seriously disabled, and the survivors of death cases do most poorly. But it is precisely in the area of short-term disability that the worker now has the most adequate alternative resources for care and benefits through private plans and, in some cases, public programs. Moreover, it is in long-term serious disability cases that a damage suit is likely to be most effective and profitable, as the experience under the Federal Employers Liability Act and the Jones Act so clearly demonstrates.

Furthermore, with the availability of Social Security total disability benefits at age 50—and the age is very likely to be lowered in future years—as well as survivorship benefits for widows and children, the consequences of a loss in a tort case will now appear less disastrous to a potential claimant. With basic protection of minimum income assured through other channels, the risks inherent in damage suits have been lowered. The possible profit has increased.

Some workers have become dubious as to whether the original bargain still represents a reasonably balanced exchange under present conditions, and, as you well know, there is increasing discussion as to whether they ought not to "renegotiate the bargain." Their leaders are looking more attentively to the experience of railroad workers and seamen who are not under workmen's compensation, and to western Europe. In England, workers have had, since 1948, an *additional* remedy. In addition to guaranteed compensation, a British worker may sue where negligence can be proved. This does not jeopardize his basic cash compensation even if the case is lost. It is reduced only 50 per cent if he wins. In West Germany, injured workers may sue the employer in the labor courts for damages *in excess* of social insurance benefits if the employer has violated safety regulations or has been grossly negligent.

Let me quote from a recent address . . . :

". . . the State compensation system you wish to preserve will come under attack from more than one quarter if it continues to fall behind the times; and one very real possibility is the eventual development of a movement to go back to damage suits, or, as in England, to add damage suits to compensation recoveries. If this sort of thing happens, employers will really have some costs to worry about, and the present cost of workmen's compensation, which now averages only about one percent of payroll for the country as a whole, will look small indeed. Does anyone really suppose that working people are going to go on indefinitely putting up with acts under which they are limited to twelve or fifteen thousand dollars for the very same injury which in a damage suit gives the railroad worker a quarter of a million dollars."[2]

Recent decisions of the highest courts of Illinois, New York and Massachusetts suggest that the movement to damage suits may already be past the stage of "just talk." No matter how ill-advised or unpleasant we may find this development, it will do little good just to call the advocates unpleasant names. Rather, we must look into, understand and take corrective action upon the factors which have caused such proposals to multiply. They cannot be wished away.

6. There is a world-wide trend towards coordination of all disability programs. In some countries, the administrative distinctions between occupational and nonoccupational temporary disability have been virtually eliminated. In this country, more and more, occupational disability is being considered and discussed not as a distinct social problem, as was the case during the early development of workmen's compensation, but as part of the general problem of disability.

Nonoccupational disability is estimated to be anywhere from 10 to 20 times more numerous than occupational disability. Not more than 5 per cent of total and permanent disabilities are covered by workmen's compensation. According to recent studies of the Chamber of Commerce of the United States, employers in major industries already spend about 10 per cent of payroll for health, welfare, and pension programs, of which workmen's compensation constitutes an average of less than 1 per cent,

---

[2] Arthur Larson, "Model-T Compensation Acts in the Atomic Age," address to the 10th Annual Convention of the National Association of Claimants' Compensation Attorneys, Los Angeles, California, July 29, 1956.

one of the very few items which has not been moving up in cost proportionately.

One of our great universities, with the financial support of a famous philanthropic foundation, is about to launch an inquiry into workmen's compensation in relation to other forms of public and private provision for disability, occupational and nonoccupational. Everywhere, the question is raised regarding the need for rationalizing workmen's compensation with other types of social insurance. Clearly, the need for a separate and independent system of workmen's compensation is no longer taken for granted.

These six points, and others which could be added, are all interrelated. They add up to a glaring reality that workmen's compensation is living in a different environment than was envisaged by its founding fathers. To remain viable, social legislation must adjust continuously to the shifting realities of a dynamic society. We must run fast in order to stand still. The very survival of workmen's compensation may be threatened by the perpetuation of a myth that legislation whose basic pattern and structure is now more than a half century old, and based heavily upon a 19th century British law which has since been abandoned by the British themselves, can continue to meet the new needs of new generations. To live we must boldly face new challenges with new devices—yes, even completely untried approaches.

Herein seems to me to lie a basic inadequacy of the recent model bill —or comprehensive check list—approach of the federal government. To frame a bill based on a combination of the "best" features in existing legislation obviously has its value. Whether or not you happen to be one of those who objected to the method of its preparation, surely it is true that if every state were to adopt the best aspects of legislation in all the states, workmen's compensation would be stronger than it is today. Certainly, the sharp raising of existing standards, which the list calls for, would allow workmen's compensation to come much closer to performing the job for which it was intended. The effort deserved a better reception than it received from influential groups who may yet learn at a heavy price that they have misunderstood their own long-range interests while being excessively preoccupied with short-range appearances. The check list called attention to—and was itself a reflection of—the mounting crisis in workmen's compensation. At the very least it showed awareness that workmen's compensation is in danger, not so much from outside attack but from internal neglect.

But the check list approach assumed that all the necessary answers could be found in existing laws and that the present framework within which our difficulties have arisen would prove adequate for the future. I happen to agree with the large majority of the specific proposals in the list which are, after all, largely endorsements of IAIABC resolutions. But the central issue is whether the workmen's compensation program needed for the future can be devised by a process of picking and choosing shiny nuggets among the existing laws and even enlarging upon a few.

To cope with the realities of this new age requires the courage and the innovation of the men who fought for and founded workmen's compensation. They were not committed to the past; their job was to create the new. That job now rests with you—if it is to be done. It is a most difficult task, but it is in your power to achieve it.

What, specifically, can be done? You, in the light of your vast collective experience, will know that better than I. But I can suggest three general directions which may be worth consideration.

*First*, make yourself *indispensable* once again to a larger number of workers. You must meet the invasion of multiple new programs in areas which were once your exclusive domain by enlarging the scope of benefits available primarily or exclusively through you. One obvious path is greater emphasis upon the persons and injuries which are least protected by other programs. For example, it is the workers in small firms, unorganized industries, agriculture, and domestic service who tend to be left out of the growing number of competing benefits. But, by and large, workmen's compensation has neglected them too. These groups, discriminated against by private and public programs alike, are coming to be referred to as a category of second-class citizens. Here is an opportunity to make workmen's compensation the indispensable support of that large group of American workers who need protection most and receive it least.

To be able to finance effective coverage for such groups may require some adjustment in present financing arrangements. There is nothing sacrosanct about that either. We are perhaps the only major nation which attempts to allocate costs precisely in accord with the charges attributable to particular employers.

Similarly, it is the long-term, seriously injured worker who is relatively neglected under most programs, including workmen's compensation. Here is an opportunity for you to fill an essential gap by a change in emphasis.

On the other hand, at a time when the role of workmen's compensation is relatively shrinking, nothing could be so foolhardy as voluntarily and unnecessarily to shrink your area of responsibility even further. For example, I am told that in at least two States there is a campaign to remove from workmen's compensation coverage persons with cardiac conditions —for their own good of course, as we are told. Mind you, we are living in an age of full acceptance of growing social insurance. If your program fails to provide protection, another will. This applies not only to cardiacs but to the entire field of diseases which in so many States remain substantially uncovered. Either you move towards expansion or you will contract. There is no standing still.

*Second*, you can place yourselves in a position of excelling in certain essential services which other programs do not or cannot offer as fully. Most conspicuous are total medical care and rehabilitation. Your meetings have often rung out with the conviction that rehabilitation may now be the primary job, the culmination, of workmen's compensation, that properly understood it should be the heart of the entire program, and that the future of workmen's compensation may rest on what it achieves in this area. Certainly I need not describe to this audience the economies, the constructiveness, and the public popularity of rehabilitation. Rehabilitation as an organized program started out as a branch of workmen's compensation. Workmen's compensation is still in a most favorable position to be the agency which can best assure to its beneficiaries the maximum amount of physical and occupational rehabilitation providing for all services and maintenance until the job is done, and continuing compensation for anatomical loss thereafter. But such opportunities do not remain forever. The longer workmen's compensation delays in assuming this responsibility in full dimension, the more rapidly other agencies will move into the vacuum. Society, like nature, abhors a vacuum.

Another possibility lies in the highly controversial area of disability evaluation and the basis of compensation. Virtually all competing programs base their benefits upon capacity to work or to earn. Only in the veterans' program and in workmen's compensation is physiological loss or damage, as such, an important factor in establishing the right to award. If this trend in workmen's compensation were expanded, you would accomplish at least two objectives. You would enlarge the area of service and benefits which your program can offer as distinct from other disability programs. Moreover, it would help disarm the advocates of damage suits who have been arguing that only through such action can the occupationally injured man receive deserved compensation for sheer anatomical loss and disfigurement in addition to loss of earning capacity.

May I add parenthetically that if I thought such a move had only tactical political advantages for you I would not advocate it. Anne Somers and I investigated this question at length last year for the President's Commission on Veterans' Pensions. We concluded that, on grounds of ethics and justice, and as an inducement to rehabilitation, as well as for administrative efficiency, physiological loss should be compensated.[3]

*Third*, the time seems to have arrived when it would be to the advantage of workmen's compensation to find a way of coordination with other social insurance programs, without losing its individual identity. All around us the social insurances are expanding and increasing. So long as workmen's compensation is "odd man out," new developments may take place in disregard of workmen's compensation. For example, it seems

---

[3] A large portion of this study has been published. See "Disability Rating: Veterans Administration Contrasted with Workmen's Compensation Experience," in *Compensation for Service-Connected Disabilities* (84th Cong., 2d sess.), House of Representatives Committee Print No. 281, pp. 209–45.

clear that the issue of the adequacy and distribution of present remedies can best be measured and dealt with in the total context of social insurance. Solutions to the problem of coordination are likely to prove most difficult and elusive, but potentially they may prove the most rewarding.

These are merely samples of the direction that new planning might explore in addition to the much-needed general raising of standards as suggested in the comprehensive check list.

But even bold new thinking must be based on adequate information. Here may lie your most immediate and most readily solvable problem: We simply do not have enough concrete information about what, in fact, has been happening to workmen's compensation in recent years—neither enough information for program planning nor enough to answer critics convincingly. Your Statistics Committee has been doing a splendid job of encouraging and giving technical leadership in the improvement of basic administrative and operational data. It is, however, necessary to have basic research to answer questions going beyond these boundaries.

For example: How many states can now tell us what happens to workmen's compensation beneficiaries? How many manage to live on the cash benefits? What are their other resources? Is it true that many of the long-term disabled require outside assistance, public or private? What happens to recipients who exhaust their rights, either cash or medical? Are many of them on relief, as is often alleged?

How many states know the degree and extent of overlap between workmen's compensation and other benefits? To what extent is it true that some families receive benefits from several public programs for the same contingency? In such cases what is the relative importance of workmen's compensation?

What happens to claimants who are denied benefits because the particular injury does not technically qualify? To what extent are such people thrown upon other public programs for support? What are the characteristics of such people? What really created the condition of need?

How do workmen's compensation benefits compare with benefits for nonoccupational disability under private employee benefit plans? Is there really a tendency to make claims for the latter rather than the former, simply because they appear more attractive? What are the consequences?

We need better information on these and many other basic questions if we are to proceed effectively—or even to know where it is necessary not to proceed. Although obtaining such information will require large cooperation from other public and private sources, including insurance carriers, the obstacles to cooperation can be overcome. It is safe to say they had better be overcome. It is well to recall that, according to Lord Beveridge's own testimony, the events leading to his recommendation that the whole workmen's compensation program in England be eliminated started with the failure of British employers to furnish adequate information. The leadership of IAIABC in this area could be crucial. Workmen's

Compensation agencies can not only launch out upon inquiries of their own, but ought to encourage inquiry by outside groups, universities and foundations.

From all these remarks you might get the impression that I am here to play Cassandra. That is not my intention. While I regard the situation of workmen's compensation as serious, I am hopeful about the final outcome. In theory, workmen's compensation remains a sound approach for dealing with occupational disability. Within its framework it is possible to bring to bear on the problem of work injuries an integrated program of high-quality medical care, rehabilitation, equitable cash compensation, and injury prevention and so bring to workers the full benefits which have long ago become justified by the changed society in which they find themselves.

The problems are not insuperable or beyond your capacities to resolve. Your generation of workmen's compensation officials follows immediately upon the heels of pioneers. You are still part of the pioneering tradition which was required to create workmen's compensation. Today the same bold vision of the future is required to recreate and revitalize. That job is part of your proud heritage.

# 47. EXPERIENCE UNDER STATE DISABILITY BENEFIT LAWS

ROBERT TILOVE, *Proceedings* of the New York University Eleventh Annual Conference on Labor, 1958.

FOUR STATES have had compulsory disability benefit laws for almost a decade now. In 1957, they covered a little over 10,000,000 workers and paid about a quarter-of-a-billion dollars in benefits.

What does experience tell us about the merits of these programs?

That question is very much alive. Repeated proposals have been made to the legislatures of the industrial states for similar enactments, in connection with which there have been a number of studies by state agencies or commissions.

The first of these laws—Rhode Island—goes back to 1942. New York —the youngest of the four—will mark its tenth anniversary next April 13. The New York enactment might well have served as a powerful precedent since it was the first state to establish disability benefits through a new tax, instead of simple diversion of an unnecessary portion of the unemployment compensation tax. And yet there have been no additional laws of this kind in almost ten years.

That this development has not spread further is partially attributable to a stalemate over the form which such a law should take, a conflict between those who advocate private coverage only—along the lines of New York —and those who advocate a state fund only—along the lines of Rhode Island. This question of basic structure has been argued sporadically over the years, although objective analysis has been far less noticeable than a simple clash of pressures in the state legislatures.

Despite the contrary opinion of those who believe that data are merely the tactical instruments of economic or political warfare, this paper is written in the belief that facts can sometimes be convincing. On that supposition, it would seem useful to examine experience under the state disability benefits laws to see whether the facts have a bearing on the further enactment of compulsory coverage, and on the form which it ought to take.

Each of the four state laws is significantly different. Rhode Island provides benefits exclusively through a state fund, administered by the unemployment compensation agency. California has a state plan administered with unemployment insurance, but it permits groups of employees to contract-out, if they are able to provide superior benefits. New Jersey has the same system, except that it does not require that anything more than the statutory benefits be provided as a condition for contracting-out, and it involves a partial contribution from the employer, which California does not. The New York law is different from all the rest: it compels coverage, but leaves it to be provided entirely by private arrangements, whether by contract with an insurance company, a contract with the State Insurance Fund, or by self-insurance.

These four laws have changed over the years. What are they like today?

## The Rhode Island Law

The Rhode Island Temporary Disability Insurance Law provides for weekly benefits equal to 1/20th of high-quarter base-year earnings, with a minimum of $10 and a maximum of $30. The waiting period is a calendar week in which the worker was disabled on the last regular working day. Benefit duration runs from a little over 7, up to 26, weeks, according to base-year earnings.

Coverage of the Rhode Island law is co-extensive with unemployment insurance, applying to firms with one or more workers. Eligibility depends on base-year earnings of at least 30 times the weekly benefit amount. The base year used for eligibility, benefit amount, and duration consists of the last four calendar quarters preceding the benefit year, which begins for each worker with his first valid claim for disability insurance.

Rhode Island pays benefits for disability attributable to pregnancy, but they are now limited to the six weeks prior to expected childbirth and six weeks after childbirth, except if there are unusual complications. Payment of wages does not disqualify for disability benefits. Disability benefits are also payable simultaneously with workmen's compensation, provided the two combined do not equal more than 85 per cent of the average wage, nor more than $58 a week.

The program is financed strictly by an employee contribution equal to 1 per cent of the first $3,600 of earnings. This contribution was originally part of the financing of unemployment compensation, but was found unnecessary for that purpose. For a brief period in its history, the Rhode Island law called for an employee contribution of 1½ per cent of taxable wages, but the extra ½ per cent was discontinued after one year (on June 30, 1957) when federal legislation (the Knowland Amendment) made available reserves of $29,000,000 accumulated out of the 1 per cent employee contribution when it was part of the unemployment compensation law.

Rhode Island benefits are provided exclusively through the state fund, administered by the Department of Employment Security, which also administers unemployment compensation.

### The California Law

The California Unemployment Compensation Disability Benefits Law was enacted in 1946, and again, as in Rhode Island, by diversion of a 1 per cent employee contribution which was found unnecessary for the financing of unemployment compensation. Benefits began December 1, 1946.

Coverage is identical with unemployment insurance, involving employment of one or more workers and $100 of quarterly payroll. The employee contribution is based on the first $3,600 of earnings.

Eligibility depends on base-year earnings of at least $300. The base year is a period of four consecutive calendar quarters preceding the period of disability by a gap of several months. There is a one-week waiting period, except that it is waived in the event of hospitalization. Maximum duration is 26 weeks.

The weekly benefit rate is based on high-quarter base-year earnings, with a minimum of $10 and a maximum of $50. The California law originally provided maximum benefits of $20, increased to $25 in 1948, to $30 in 1952, to $35 in 1954, and to $50 in 1958. Benefits are not paid for pregnancy. California recently added disability benefits on top of workmen's compensation for *permanent* disability, but it otherwise limits the duplication so that the combined payment will not exceed the basic weekly disability benefit amount. Benefits are payable in addition to wages, but only if the combination would not exceed prior wages.

A unique feature of the California law was the addition, in 1949, of cash benefits for each day of hospitalization. This began at the rate of $8 a day for up to 12 days of hospitalization, and was increased to $10 a day in 1953. Effective January 1, 1958, this was increased to $12 a day for up to a maximum of 20 days of hospitalization.

The California law provides for a state fund which automatically assumes coverage, but with the right of contracting-out. The state plan is administered by the Department of Employment, which also administers unemployment compensation. A unit of employees may, by majority decision and consent of the employer, elect to provide the required benefits by a voluntary plan, provided it secures state approval by matching the statutory benefits in every feature and exceeding them in at least one respect.

### The New Jersey Law

The New Jersey Temporary Disability Benefits Law was enacted in 1948; benefits became effective January 1, 1949. Coverage is the same as for unemployment insurance: four or more workers in 20 or more weeks. Eligibility is conditioned on earnings of at least $15 in at least 17 weeks within the year preceding the claim.

After a seven-day waiting period, benefits range from $10 to $35 a week (originally $22 a week), based on ⅔ of the first $45 of earnings, plus ⅖ of the remainder of the average weekly wage. The average weekly wage is determined on the most recent eight-week period. Maximum duration ranges from 13 to 26 weeks, depending on the number of "base weeks" within the 52 weeks preceding the claim. The duration limit applies to any period of 12 consecutive months.

New Jersey does not cover pregnancy and does not pay disability benefits if workmen's compensation is payable—but it allows duplication with wages if the two do not exceed prior wages.

The New Jersey benefits are financed jointly by employers and employees, in amounts which represent diversion of contributions originally made for unemployment compensation. Employees contribute ½ per cent of taxable wages (up to $3,000 a year). Employers contribute ¼ of 1 per cent of wages. If they are covered by the state plan, this may vary with experience from 0.10 per cent to 0.75 per cent of taxable wages. If the employer has a private plan, its obligation is simply to pay the remainder of the cost.

The New Jersey law starts by providing the benefits through a state plan which is administered by the Division of Employment Security in coordination with unemployment insurance. Employers have the right, with agency approval, to contract-out, provided the employees approve (assuming they contribute).

Payment is not made for pregnancy disability. Payment of wages during a period of illness is disregarded under the New Jersey law, provided the combination of wages and benefits does not exceed 100 per cent of the wages. However, disability benefits are not payable at the same time as workmen's compensation.

## The New York Law

The New York Disability Benefits Law was enacted April 13, 1949—effective for benefit payment, July 1, 1950. It covers establishments employing four or more workers on 30 or more days in the year. This differs from unemployment insurance, which now covers smaller establishments. The categories of excluded employment are very much like those in unemployment insurance, but not identical.

The benefit is equal to 50 per cent of average wages in the most recent eight-week period, payable after a one-week waiting period for each period of disability.

Eligibility begins after four consecutive weeks of employment, and continues as long as the employee is eligible for unemployment insurance. The minimum benefit is $20 and the maximum $45 (originally $26). Originally, the maximum duration was 13 weeks, but this was increased to 20 weeks effective July 1, 1956, and 26 weeks effective June 1, 1958.

Benefits are not payable if wages are paid during illness in an amount equal to at least the disability benefit rate, nor are they payable if workmen's compensation is paid. Disabilities attributable to pregnancy are not covered, unless they follow termination of pregnancy and return to covered employment for at least two consecutive weeks.

The New York benefits are financed jointly by employers and employees. Employees are obligated to contribute ½ of 1 per cent of taxable wages (up to $.30 a week). The employer pays the remainder of the cost. The employer is free to assume the employee cost as well.

New York does not provide any state plan or state fund with automatic coverage, except for workers who become disabled after they have been unemployed for at least four weeks. Coverage matching the requirements of the law is mandated. Each employer makes his choice as to means of provision. He may secure a contract with an insurance company, or he may self-insure. One of the insurance companies he may choose is the State Insurance Fund, a state-operated carrier originally established for purposes of providing workmen's compensation coverage. But New York's State Insurance Fund bears no resemblance to the state plans which assume automatic tax-rate coverage in New Jersey and California.

An employer can satisfy the requirements of the New York law by providing strictly statutory coverage, or he may provide more. An unusual feature of the New York law is the right of employers to discharge their obligation by providing medical benefits—hospital, surgical, or medical benefits—in lieu of a portion of the cash weekly indemnity. An employer may substitute for up to 40 per cent of the weekly cash indemnity otherwise required under the law. Tables of actuarial values established by the chairman of the Workmen's Compensation Board govern this system of substitution.

The operation of the program is supervised by the Workmen's Compensation Board, which makes direct payment of benefits only to two limited categories of claimants: covered workers who become disabled after they have been unemployed for at least four weeks, and those few workers whose employers have entirely defaulted in disability benefit payments.

\* \* \* \* \*

Does experience with these statues have a bearing on the question whether a state should enact a compulsory disability benefit law?

### Extent of Voluntary Coverage

One basic consideration has been whether compulsory coverage is necessary. The argument has been made in the past that voluntary plans have been increasing, and may, therefore, be depended on to do the job. A number of states have therefore made surveys of the extent of voluntary disability benefits. These surveys all show essentially the same thing. There is a large degree of voluntary coverage, and it has been growing over the past years. But it is equally true that there is a substantial percentage of the labor force which is not covered, to be found in the industries characterized by small units or by comparatively low levels in wages and other standards of employment.

Voluntary development is always slow in these industries: the employers can hardly be relied on to assert individual leadership toward improvement of conditions since these industries are generally highly competitive, and with slim margins. Growth of voluntary plans for employees in large-unit industry is no indication at all that these improvements will also be extended, in any reasonable period of time, to the great majority of employees in the unorganized, small-unit, and marginal sectors of the economy.

That being the case, there is a legitimate question whether it is worthwhile to engage in an expensive and protracted study to determine whether voluntary coverage covers 51 per cent, or even 70 per cent, of the working population or will soon do so. The argument runs easily in either direction, no matter what the facts may be. One way it has been argued is that *if* coverage is *not* very extensive, then compulsion is necessary. The other way of looking at it is that *if* coverage *is* extensive, then the state ought to compel the lagging minority to live up to the standards already established by the majority. It would seem desirable for research in this general subject to be more definitely concentrated toward the discovery of facts which might make a difference.

### The Welfare State

In arguing compulsory coverage there has always been, of course, the broad question of governmental philosophy: whether the state should intervene to compel the payment of sick benefits. What can we say within the purview of this paper, except that it is part of the entire argument about the welfare state? It involves the fear that government may become too important, business too hemmed-in with regulations and requirements, and individual initiative and self-reliance undermined by constant provision of economic security by the government. Naturally, it is impossible to isolate the effect of the disability benefit laws themselves to discover whether they have, in fact, tended to encourage dependence on the state or to undermine the economic self-reliance of the individual.

Besides, even if it were not simply a question of weekly cash sickness benefits, but of a whole raft of welfare provisions, how would we know whether attitudes of self-reliance were, or were not, being affected? How is that to be measured?

This is perhaps as apt an occasion as any for an excursionary suggestion that a sociological project might well be devised to attempt the application of more or less objective tests by which changes in the climate of attitude and opinions might be determined over long intervals of time. This would be something in the nature of a device to take a picture of the forest without being obscured by the trees. To use another analogy, you may be in the middle of a great current of history, but if the current is big enough and broad enough, it might be difficult to know what was happening to you: a set of instruments would be necessary to find out where you are drifting. This is particularly true, of course, in matters of shifting *mores*. It is perhaps not beyond the ingenuity of man to devise objective measurements, to secure more timely descriptions of our social movements, particularly in matters of attitude and opinion, than the historian can provide by his hazardous retrospection.

Of course, coming back to disability benefits, the general objection that an individual's self-reliance may tend to be undermined by welfare plans of one kind or another loses much of its force when you recognize that so far as the individual is concerned, there is little difference between a voluntary group plan and (on the other hand) state legislation. In either event, he is provided for without individual budgeting. Consequently, the argument about individual self-reliance, putting aside its force or validity, is really limited to those individuals who are employed in substandard industries, and it is hard to make out a glamorous case for keeping rugged individualism alive *only* among shipping clerks and the sales help of non-chain variety stores.

### Competitive Costs

Another argument that always comes into play is that enactment of compulsory coverage in one state will subject its business to a competitive cost disadvantage vis-a-vis the next state. Here again there is not much you can say solely on the basis of disability benefit laws.

### Fear of Malingering

A perennial argument centers around the theory that widespread compulsory coverage will result in malingering. The term "malingering" carries a suggestion of fraud, but actually the wider problem is whether benefit payments impede early return to work. Fears of this kind have apparently not materialized under the existing programs; so far, there has been no evidence that a problem of this kind has been widespread. People would rather work at full wages than receive 50 per cent or less in disability benefits, and if they are unemployed, they can generally receive unemployment insurance in the same amount as disability benefits. It is only in special circumstances when the benefit (which is tax-exempt) becomes a high percentage of the wage that some indifference about return to work may enter.

A decade back, a question of widespread malingering was created out of Rhode Island experience. Statistics showed much heavier claims in the late spring and summer months than at other times, and the obvious inference was that summer was a good time to stop working anyhow. The explanation of the Rhode Island agency that it had a fixed benefit year which began with the first Sunday in April, so that workers who had exhausted benefits from the previous benefit year could reapply for a fresh run of benefit payments was a little difficult for the half-interested layman to follow. However, in 1950, Rhode Island amended its law so as to provide for an individual benefit year and the seasonality of claims disappeared.

Rhode Island had a problem for a long while with the fact that its disability benefits were payable on top of workmen's compensation. About 25 per cent of the claimants who collected both received thereby more than their full-time wages. Obviously this has to raise a question of reluctance to return to work. That problem has since been curbed to some extent by a limitation that the combination may not exceed 85 per cent of the wage. However, this is a problem which arises from a special type of statutory provision, and certainly does not go to the heart of compulsory coverage *per se*.

The basic safeguard against malingering is the difference between the benefit rate and the full-time wage. The question tends to become a matter of serious concern only in those limited areas where the differential is absent: the claimant is unemployed anyhow, or the law permits disability benefits to be paid on top of workmen's compensation or on top of wages. And it may also tend to be a potential problem with workers who are secondary breadwinners with household duties.

Duration of claims is longer among those disability claimants who are already unemployed than among employed workers who are out sick. Lack of available employment may have something to do with this longer duration, because the wage incentive for pronouncing recovery is absent, but the situation is certainly not a simple one. Unemployment may, in fact, have helped to induce the illness, and, on the other hand, poor health may help to account for the unemployment in the first place.

The payment of disability benefits on top of workmen's compensation is a curious development. They are both intended for precisely the same purpose: to idemnify the single wage loss. The duplication takes place—

in Rhode Island and in California—only because workmen's compensation and disability insurance are different laws with different financing, and we tend to think of them, even today, in different compartments of our minds.

It is worth noting, too, that in both states, disability benefits are financed entirely by employee contributions. Apparently, where employees pay the whole cost, there is an almost irresistible logic that the employee builds up an individual equity which cannot be denied. That approach was also evident in the trouble which Rhode Island had in curbing the amount of benefits to be paid for pregnancy disabilities.

A related question concerns whether disability benefits should be payable to an employee who receives wages while out ill. Disqualification because of wage payments discourages supplementation; on the other hand, full payment of both raises the problem of reluctance to resume work. Solutions proposed include (*a*) benefit payment, with adjustment of wage continuance at the employer's discretion, or (*b*) allowing a combination of the two payments up to a fixed percentage of the wage.

In summary, then, the argument over whether a state ought to mandate disability benefit coverage remains largely one of governmental philosophy. The question of how far voluntary coverage has gone appears more and more to be rather immaterial to the issue. As to the fear of significant malingering, while certain types of provisions have given rise to real problems, no credible evidence has yet been produced from the experience of the existing programs to suggest that this is a real source of concern unavoidably connected with compulsory coverage.

\* \* \* \* \*

This paper has obviously not attempted to deal with all of the problems on which there has been illuminating experience under the disability insurance laws; rather, it has limited its analysis to the major questions which must be considered in adoption of a state disability benefit law.

On the merits of compelling temporary disability insurance, experience with the four state disability benefit laws by itself tells us nothing conclusive. To be sure, it has demonstrated that these programs can work smoothly and efficiently and without imposing any onerous costs. And a good deal of the force has been taken out of the expressed fear of widespread malingering by the fact that it has not developed into a large and unmanageable problem in any of the states, but has been a potential source of concern only in relation to limited types of provisions, such as relation to wage continuance or workmen's compensation. Nevertheless, the fundamental and continuing clash over whether the state should mandate this form of benefit coverage remains largely a question of governmental philosophy as to the appropriate welfare role of the state, the employing unit, and the individual.

The deadlock over the enactment of any more of these state laws which has persisted over the past nine years is partly attributable to a stalemate

over the basic structure of such a law between those who advocate an exclusive state fund and those who advocate exclusively private coverage. In the balance between economy of operation, on the one hand, and, on the other hand, flexibility for individual employing units to improve benefits beyond the statutory minimum or to accommodate to the needs of particular groups, there is much to be said for the system of contracting-out with which California and New Jersey have had experience. Neither the fears of the insurance companies that such a system would inevitably eliminate private plans nor the contradictory fear of the advocates of an exclusive state fund that such a system would be ruinous for a state plan has materialized, and while this development is still in flux, there are strong indications that a system of contracting-out can in fact achieve an equilibrium between voluntary plan and state plan coverage.

It is possible that more fruitful answers would result if there were greater use of the pragmatic spirit which we consider a national characteristic, utilizing either voluntary private arrangements or the facilities of the state, or both, as experience indicates, without being constrained by the dogmatic labels which have so often been attached to each.

# 48. IMPROVING STATE WELFARE PROGRAMS

Aime J. Forand,
*Congressional Record,*
April 15, 1959.

Mr. Speaker, although great improvement has been made in the welfare programs in this country during the past quarter century, experience has shown that much more needs to be done, especially in the State programs.

I am today introducing a bill providing for such improvements.

This bill, H.R. 6422, is designed to alleviate the plight of those many families throughout the country who find themselves in need as a result of unemployment and other factors beyond their control and for whom no provision is now made under Federal law. This bill, which would authorize the Federal Government to assist the States in meeting the full range of needs now confronting their public welfare agencies, is similar to bills I have introduced in previous Congresses, but is given a new urgency by the persistence of unemployment currently affecting some 5 million American workers and their families.

This bill, entitled the "Public Welfare Act," incorporates the recommendations of leading national welfare organizations representing both public and voluntary agencies. Taken together with the bill, H.R. 4700, previously introduced by me to extend health benefits to beneficiaries of the old-age, survivors, and disability insurance program and the bill establishing minimum benefit standards in the unemployment insurance program which I am likewise supporting, this bill rounds out the program of immediate improvements in our total social security program urgently necessary to meet the most pressing needs today confronting large segments of our population. As such, the basic provisions in the bill have the support of the American Federation of Labor and Congress of Industrial Organizations; the American Public Welfare Association; the National Association of Social Workers, and other groups representing those affected by our social security measures.

We are rightfully proud of the steady growth in coverage and benefits under the social insurance aspects of the social security program and the extent to which this has reduced dependence on public assistance among the able-bodied aged, surviving widows, and the older disabled group. Last year improvements were also made in the financing of public assistance and in the child welfare program. But pride in progress cannot be allowed to blind us to the areas of insecurity and hardship that still remain. Extensive and persistent unemployment over the past year has served to remind us of the vulnerability of our working people to the hazards of the modern economy. We must move toward a national policy which, first, reduces the chances of any individual or family in the United States becoming needy but, second, provides its own built-in assurance that if this contingency befalls, provision will be made to meet those needs. This is the purpose of my bill.

### Role of Public Welfare

Public welfare provides the ultimate protection to individuals under our total system of social security. When all other resources fail, it is to the State and local public welfare agencies that an individual must turn for help. If a worker cannot find a job, when his unemployment insurance rights and savings are exhausted he becomes dependent upon public assistance. If a worker or farmer or small businessman becomes ill, he may find his savings quickly exhausted in heavy medical and living expenses. Then he has no choice but to turn to his State or local public welfare office. But under the present assistance provisions of the Social Security Act, the Federal Government takes no responsibility for assisting the public welfare agencies in meeting the needs of people who do not qualify under the four existing categorical programs of old-age assistance, aid to dependent children, aid to the blind, and aid to the permanently and totally disabled. As a result, in most States provision for the needy unemployed is miserably inadequate and even, in some localities, virtually nonexistent. In other States with a heavy incidence of unemployment, funds for the purpose have been repeatedly exhausted despite every effort to make adequate provision. It is self-evident that the States with heavy and persistent unemployment not only have a disproportionate need but are in the worst fiscal position to meet that need from State and local resources.

## Unemployment a National Responsibility

Unemployment is an attribute of the national economy, and the development of policies to assure individual security is a national responsibility. The Federal Government should not only take steps to prevent unemployment and to assist depressed areas in making needed economic readjustments, but it should also assume its fair share of responsibility in protecting all its people, wherever they may live, against its hazards. The first line of defense is through a strengthened unemployment insurance program; the second is through a strengthened program of public welfare which is the purpose of this bill.

## Adapting Public Welfare to Change

Public welfare, under our Federal system of government, is the primary responsibility of the States and their political subdivision. The grant-in-aid system, which has developed extensively as an instrument of public policy since 1933, is designed to combine the advantages of decentralized administration with the broader financial base of the Federal Government and the need for basic national programs in areas of national concern. My bill, following this extremely successful principle, is designed to give the States the maximum latitude in adapting their own public welfare programs to changing needs. It does not affect the existing provisions of titles I, IV, V, and XIV of the Social Security Act, but rather offers the States the option of combining all or part of these specialized public welfare programs for particular groups into a comprehensive program of aid for all needy persons and of needed social services. The administrative and policy advantages of such a simplified plan are obvious, especially to the individual in need of public welfare aid, who today often finds himself bewildered by a variety of agencies, eligibility standards, and requirements. Many State welfare policymakers and administrators would welcome the opportunity to move in this direction but are today prevented by the limitations of Federal law. On the other hand, there is no compulsion upon the States under my proposal to abandon any specialized welfare program which is felt to be serving the best interests of a particular group.

## Flexibility to Meet Actual Need

The rapid growth in our social insurance programs has created a substantial change in the character of the public welfare function which has not yet been reflected in changes in Federal and State law. Increasingly, public welfare is being called upon to meet the unusual or unpredictable situation or to provide for needs which have not yet been provided for through social insurance or other preventive measures. Thus, the nature of the public welfare task tends to change in emphasis. Today, for example, many retired OASDI beneficiaries are obliged to turn to public welfare for help when they become ill. But soon it is hoped we can provide hospital and related benefits for these people as a part of the insurance program. No one wants a large public welfare program, but we do want one which is sufficiently flexible and comprehensive to meet actual need as it occurs. The only way to do this is through legislation which provides the machinery, the policies, and the built-in financing provisions to meet such needs whenever they arise. We do not want to be confronted again with the need for emergency legislation as we were in 1933—or even last year, or again this year, with our unemployment insurance program. We want a strong institutional structure that can be quickly adapted to actual needs whether they arise from economic factors, social change, or disaster situations.

The State public welfare agencies have been handicapped in adapting their own programs and in making the best use of their own resources and personnel by the rigid compartmentalization and restrictive scope of Federal aid. This bill proposes to remedy this situation by providing the optional alternative of a single public welfare plan with more adaptable provisions relating to eligibility, financing, and scope of service. In return for this greater flexibility, States are required to provide assistance for all persons who qualify within their own standards of need without arbitrary exclusions such as those based on residence. The bill also recognizes the importance of individual determinations and service as an intrinsic element in all public welfare functions thus making it possible to bring about a closer coordination of all welfare programs in a single public welfare agency. The advantage of such a simplified approach to the person who needs help, to the administrator, and to the public constitutes a major argument for giving early consideration to this proposal.

### Specific Provisions

In the statement which follows a more detailed explanation of the provisions of this bill is given.

*First: General.* The bill provides a new title XVI for the Social Security Act under which a State could submit a comprehensive public welfare plan for assistance to needy persons and welfare services as defined in the bill. States that wish to do so could continue to operate programs of assistance under the existing provisions to titles I, IV, X, and XIV but the new matching provisions described below are applicable only to title XVI and the usual provision is made to preclude assistance payments to any individual under more than one title of the act. For most States the scope, flexibility, and financial provisions of title XVI would probably prove an inducement to change, but the optional feature would ease the transitional process and make it possible for a State, which wished to retain certain programs—as, for example, aid to the blind—on the present basis, to do so.

*Second: Coverage for Assistance.* This bill makes it possible for a

State to receive Federal aid for assistance to any needy person, including those who are in need because of unemployment, and not exclusively for those over 65, blind, permanently and totally disabled, or those meeting the restrictive definition for aid to dependent children—as at present. Administration by categorical groups would, however, be optional with the States, provided the basis for establishing the categories was reasonable. Assistance could not, however, be paid to persons residing in public institutions other than medical institutions nor to patients in an institution for tuberculosis or mental disease.

*Third.* Financial ceilings or the maximum average payments subject to Federal aid would be increased to $75 a month for all adults and $50 for all children. Present maxima in old age assistance, aid to the blind, and aid to the permanently and totally disabled are based on an average of $65 a month; in aid to dependent children the present ceiling is an average of $30 for each individual.

*Fourth.* A new and simplified system of matching would replace the present formulas. Under the proposed formula the total of all assistance payments—within the average ceilings as shown in 3 above—would receive a 62 percent Federal reimbursement in any State whose average per capita income was the same as that of the United States as a whole. For States above this average the percentage of Federal reimbursement would be proportionately decreased but would in no case fall below 50 percent. For States with a lower than average per capita income the percentage of Federal reimbursement would be proportionately increased but the maximum level of reimbursement would be 80 percent. Under this formula the needy in both the high and low income States would benefit: The former by the higher reimbursable ceilings and the latter by the higher rate of reimbursement.

*Fifth.* Welfare services provided by the public welfare agency would be subject to the same rate of reimbursement as assistance payments. Increasingly those persons turning to public welfare agencies for aid are those with special needs requiring knowledgeable service for their solution. Such service can often help speed the return of the individual to self-support, secure for him the care he needs from other sources, prevent serious or long-term future difficulties, and reduce the cost to the public of extended dependency. For example: Many people needing medical care or rehabilitative service do not know what provisions are available or how to go about applying for them. Many people are lingering in general or mental hospitals simply because they have no other place to go—and no one to help them find such a place; many people living in areas where their former source of livelihood has ceased to exist need help in moving to areas of new opportunity; many children might be saved from juvenile delinquency or other forms of costly social maladjustment if their parents received helpful guidance at the crucial time or—in cases where substitute family care was necessary—the child welfare services of the public welfare agency could make prompt and adequate provision for their adoptive or foster-care placement. An advantage of this bill to the child welfare program is the fact that it permits child welfare workers to apply assistance funds to the placement of needy children requiring foster care. The grave injustice done to this neediest group of children under the present act, which denies assistance to children not living with a close relative, was pointed out by the welfare report of the Commission on Inter-Governmental Relations.

**Sixth.** Simplified administration, with consequent benefits to those requiring public welfare aid as well as to those who do its work and pay its cost, is provided in this bill in several ways. Matching on the average of all payments, the optional elimination of categorical administration, and the provision of the same reimbursement formula for all types of aid would permit reduction in paperwork with subsequent reduction in the cost of overhead administration. The bill also requires that the program be administered by a single agency at each level of government. From the point of view of the individual or family requiring help the advantage of a single agency is obvious.

**Seventh: Availability of Benefits.** The bill makes it a condition of the broadened base of Federal financial assistance provided by this new title that its benefits should be available to all qualified persons without residence or citizenship requirements. No public welfare program can be considered to be fulfilling its function as the ultimate guarantee against individual need if it arbitrarily excludes needy persons solely because of their length of residence. The very factors that make it essential for the Federal Government to share the broad public welfare responsibilities of the States make it equally essential that such aid be available to all.

**Eighth: The Virgin Islands and Puerto Rico.** This bill rights a long-standing injustice toward our fellow American citizens in the Virgin Islands and the Commonwealth of Puerto Rico by extending to these jurisdictions the same program provisions as apply in the States and Territories.

**Ninth: Confidential Assistance Records.** This bill restores to all persons receiving assistance under this title the protection formerly required by all titles that the facts concerning their receipt of assistance be treated as confidential information.

**Tenth: Personnel Training.** The bill recognizes the serious shortages in qualified public welfare personnel by providing special financial aid on a continuing basis for training such personnel.

# 49. FAMILY ALLOWANCES

James C. Vadakin, *Family Allowances: An Analysis of Their Development and Implications*, University of Miami Press, 1958.

## A FAVORABLE VIEW

Family allowances may be considered desirable from several points of view. In the first place, such allowances improve the well-being of children, particularly those in large low-income families. In so doing, they will not only contribute to child welfare and to the making of a more educated and intelligent future citizenry, but from a strictly economic standpoint, they can lead to an improvement in the nation's human resources and its future work force. Therefore, allowance payments are not simply "spent" but rather are "invested" in such a manner as to increase long-run productivity.

Family allowances can assist materially in the providing of a national minimum level of living. This is true both during periods when the family breadwinner is employed and when his earnings are interrupted by sickness, disability, unemployment and the suffering of other risks. In the absence of any sort of allowances for dependents, the fixing of minimum wages and other social insurance benefits with no regard to varying family size and need is a very unsatisfactory and most unrealistic practice, as was learned in Australia and New Zealand three decades ago. When correlated with various social insurance measures, family allowances make these programs more effective in the fulfillment of their intended purposes.

Of most important significance, however, is the role which can be played by family allowances in the general area of monetary and fiscal policy and the maintenance of full employment. In a basically unplanned capitalistic society, there is no guarantee that the free operation of market forces will ensure complete utilization of resources. Experience has shown that, under such a system, economic activity may fluctuate all the way from full employment to widespread unemployment. In this day and age, there is widespread acceptance of the concept that the government has the positive function of pursuing such monetary and fiscal policies as will ensure the maintenance of a full employment economy. (In the United States, this view is embodied in the Full Employment Act of 1946.)

Essentially, full employment hinges upon the maintenance of a sufficiency in aggregate effective demand. This, in turn, depends upon the level of consumption and the level of investment. Inflation results when the levels of consumption and investment exceed that amount needed to provide full employment. Deflation and unemployment occur when the level of these expenditures becomes deficient. There is very little question but that family allowance payments increase consumption expenditures. Our previous analysis showed that a program such as that in Canada produces a vertical redistribution of income in the direction of lower-income groups. Persons in these groups have a very high marginal propensity to consume, and quite likely will spend the allowances promptly and wholly. As this purchasing power is spent, it increases the level of consumption not only by the amount of the initial expenditures but, through the action of the multiplier principle, to an even larger extent (varying with the magnitude of the leakages). Furthermore, by means of the acceleration principle, these added consumption expenditures will also tend to create a necessity for increased investment. The actual amount of acceleration leverage will, of course, depend upon the nature of the increased consumption expenditures involved (i.e., whether they are spent for goods requiring a large or small amount of capital equipment for their production).

Whether or not the foregoing results will be beneficial depends, of course, upon the level of economic activity existing at a particular time. It may be argued very cogently that the imposition or operation of a family allowances program in a full employment situation characterized by excessive inflationary tendencies would only serve to aggravate these conditions further, particularly by means of the increased consumption expenditures flowing forth into a market already short in its supply of goods and services. While it is true that the progressive taxation measures used in financing the program might tend to have an offsetting deflationary effect by reducing funds available for investment, the net effect of allowances payments during such a period would clearly be of an inflationary type.

On the other hand, during a period characterized by deflation and unemployment, the effects of a family allowances program would be highly salutary. By means of their favorable influence on the level of consumption and investment, such payments would work in the direction of stabilizing both income and employment at a time when this was sorely needed. If it became necessary, in order to prevent a dampening influence on investment because of the taxes needed to support the program, allowances payments could be met through deficit financing. (In this connection, it might be pointed out that family allowance payments made during a depression have an advantage over public works expenditures insofar as they would not intrude into the realm of private enterprise.) That family allowance programs would be beneficial in depressed times cannot be gainsaid.

While it is essential to guard against the twin evils of inflation and depression, the potential dangers of a family allowance program during prosperity would seem to be far outweighed by their beneficial results during a cyclical downswing. Furthermore, regardless of the cyclical phases involved, it is important to recognize that family allowances pay-

ments produce an over-all stabilizing effect upon the economy. Benefits are continuous and non-seasonal, and are spent very largely for stable consumer goods. This, in itself, injects into an economy a considerable degree of much desired stability. At the same time, insofar as the transfer payments involved bring about an increase in income, these payments are, in the end analysis, paid for, at least in part, out of such an increase in income.

From the standpoint of Keynesian teachings, family allowances would clearly be regarded as being economically beneficial. Not only did Keynes himself advocate such allowances as part of the British Government's wartime program, but his writings contain numerous indications of the desirability of just such a measure, as witness the following statement:

> Whilst aiming at a socially controlled rate of investment with a view to a progressive decline in the marginal efficiency of capital, I should support at the same time all sorts of policies for increasing the propensity to consume. For it is unlikely that full employment can be maintained, whatever we may do about investment, with the existing propensity to consume.[1]

Whether viewed from their effects on the standard of living, the improvement of human resources, or the maintenance of full employment and prosperity, it may be argued that family allowances programs produce beneficial economic results.

## AN UNFAVORABLE VIEW

In accordance with the tenets of more orthodox (classical) economic teachings, family allowances could be regarded as being undesirable and dangerous, not only economically, but politically and socially as well. Such a position does not condone or disregard the facts concerning income distribution in relation to family size and the consequent problems of child welfare. Indeed, orthodox economists are as much interested in improving the well-being of children and the general welfare of the community at large as are those economists who hold contrary points of view. The question is not one of ends sought, but one of the means and policies which should be adopted in order to achieve desired goals.

The foregoing position is based on the assumption that the market economy, which implies private ownership of the means of production, freedom of enterprise and competition, is the type of economic system which, in the end analysis, is best suited to raising the standard of living and achieving other desirable improvements in the condition of mankind. If allowed to operate freely in accordance with the laws of supply and demand, as expressed through the pricing system, the forces of the market will guide individuals in such a manner as to result in the fullest and most economical utilization of resources. If at any time there is not full employ-

---

[1] J. M. Keynes, *The General Theory of Employment, Interest and Money* (New York: Harcourt, Brace and Co., 1936), p. 325.

ment, there is a tendency towards it; and the free operations of the forces of the market will bring about equilibrium at a full employment level. Lapses of full employment and from maximum utilization of resources are not attributable to inherent faults in the system of capitalism but rather to the imposition of inflexibilities into the system which prevent its effective operation. These inflexibilities are brought into being by the actions of business monopolies, trade unions, and government "planners." State intervention in economic affairs should be kept to a minimum, and should be directed not at "tinkering" with the mechanism of market forces, but in ensuring their unimpeded operation. Contrary to the charges of their opponents, modern orthodox economists are not "economic royalists" and are not opposed to all government intervention *per se*. An outstanding spokesman of the classical school, Professor A. C. Pigou, stated the position taken towards governmental action in the economic sphere very clearly when he declared:

> That the state must act in very important ways is universally agreed. The real question is not whether the state should act or not, but on what principles, in what degree and over what departments of economic life its action should be carried on. The issue is not one of yes or no, but of more or less; of delimiting an uncertain frontier, or weighing, in different departments, conflicting advantages, the balance of which sometimes tips to one side, sometimes to the other.[2]

Thus, while the necessity and even the desirability of certain governmental action are recognized, such action should be carefully undertaken, and should not be aimed at or result in the destruction of the free enterprise system.

Family allowances are objectionable for a number of reasons. First of all, they involve rewarding of individuals, at least to some degree, on the basis of their needs. It is granted that family allowances in a nation such as Canada are not intended as a reward for having children, that children in large low-income families are unfairly deprived of essential needs, and that family allowances if provided would in large measure be spent by parents in such a way as to improve child welfare. However, such allowances do involve a radical departure from the principle of rewarding individuals on the basis of their economic contribution, and may hence entail the creation of questionable values. There are other methods by which child welfare could be promoted. For one thing, educational facilities and other measures aimed at creating equality of opportunity could be provided. In cases of need, services in kind could be given, and on a much wider scale than that now in existence. The payment of universal cash allowances, not just in cases of need but as a continuing proposition, may result in a dangerous undermining of the foundation and principles of the capitalistic system.

---

[2] A. C. Pigou, *Economics in Practice* (London: MacMillan and Co., Ltd., 1935), p. 110.

on producers' goods industries would be indirect, and would depend essentially on the effects of such allowances on the general level of economic activity;

3. the payment of allowances of a reasonable size, such as in Canada, will not depress wage rates. While this seems clear during prosperous periods, no basis for judging the effects during a recession exists, since governmentally financed programs have been in operation only during the more prosperous period since the early 1940's. However, French experience indicates that this might become a problem in a recession, particularly if the level of payments is unusually high;

4. family allowances will exert no influence on mobility since the coverage of this type of program would be universal; and

5. family allowance payments of a "reasonable" size, such as those in Canada or probably even somewhat higher, will not adversely affect incentives. However, there is an indefinable point beyond which benefits should not be raised, as indicated by the unfavorable French experience.

A program based on the French model, using the compensation fund device, has a tendency to redistribute income horizontally rather than vertically, thus defeating in some measure the purpose of the program. There is also a greater likelihood that family allowances may depress wage rates. Our study would seem clearly to warrant the conclusion that if a nation is not bound by the dictates of historical development and wishes to adopt a family allowances system, a program patterned after the Canadian model would be more efficacious from an economic viewpoint.

As regards the broader aspect of family allowances in terms of economic philosophy, theory and policy, it is difficult to render any "right" answers or decisions. In this respect, much greater limitations are involved than was the case when the purely child welfare or demographic aspects of such programs were discussed. The economic implications should provide the strongest cause for halt, and for careful analysis in our thinking. Quite aside from the question of desirability or undesirability, which in the end analysis resolve themselves into matters of making careful yet subjective judgments in the light of one's own economic philosophy, the presentation of the opposing views towards family allowances clearly indicates that many of the influences which such a program would exert cannot even be measured from a long-run point of view. Consequently, the only appropriate conclusion that one can scientifically draw, and even needs to draw at the present time in the United States, is that those broad economic aspects of family allowances which were outlined above are deserving of our most careful consideration. It would be most unwise to decide either for or against the adoption of a family allowances program in this country without such an analysis by the best economic minds that the nation has to offer.

# 50. A PROGRAM FOR THE LOW-INCOME POPULATION AT SUBSTANDARD LEVELS OF LIVING

*Recommendations of the Joint Committee on the Economic Report, Report No. 1311, 1956.*

## I. INCOME SECURITY, PUBLIC WELFARE, AND HEALTH CARE

1. The Congress consider legislation to establish social-insurance programs covering the risks of temporary and permanent total disability.

2. The appropriate congressional committees study the desirability and feasibility of dovetailing such programs, if established, with the workmen's compensation acts of the various States; such study will necessarily entail a review and evaluation of the adequacy of the existing workmen's compensation programs.

3. That the Federal Government, in cooperation with the States and private groups, develop a comprehensive health program covering the following:

*a*) Stimulation of means whereby families in rural areas may secure adequate health care;

*b*) Provision of additional funds to provide for adequate recruiting and training of professional workers in the field of health care;

*c*) Reduction in the cost to the individual of comprehensive health protection. This may necessitate contributing part or all of the cost of approved insurance programs for low-income families. The Congress may wish to consider whether it may be necessary, in order that voluntary health plans reach all of the population, to provide Federal financial aid to those in the low-income groups who are unable to purchase such protection; additional funds alone, however, would be useless to millions of our people in rural areas where there is a lack of doctors, nurses, and hospital beds;

*d*) Extension of the school-lunch and milk programs, and the distribution of surplus commodities to needy families; and

*e*) Expansion of Federal participation in public-assistance payments for medical care.

4. That the following changes be considered in the Federal grant-in-aid program of public assistance:

*a*) Establishing a single, unified system of Federal grants for general public assistance in place of the current and separate programs which, according to evidence presented to the subcommittee, tend to restrict unnecessarily the types of need for which Federal funds are available;

*b*) Basing Federal grants-in-aid for general public assistance on an equalization formula which takes into account the relative financial needs of the various States and State differences in per capita income;

*c*) Lowering the maximum residence requirements which the States can impose on public-assistance applicants; and

*d*) Making the Federal grants for child-welfare services available to all areas rather than limited as they now are to specially designated areas.

5. Including in the Federally aided public-assistance programs provision for services designed to encourage individuals to attain self-support and self-care and to preserve and strengthen family life.

6. That the Federal Government consider providing additional grants-in-aid to the States for the purpose of increasing the supply of trained professional workers needed to carry out the recommendations we present in this report.

## II. INCREASING EDUCATIONAL AND TRAINING OPPORTUNITIES FOR THE LOW-INCOME POPULATION

7. Direct Federal grants-in-aid to the States, initially for construction of school plant and equipment, based on an equalization formula which takes account of the relative economic need among the States.

8. That the Federal Government, through grant-in-aid programs, assist the States to expand guidance services and vocational counseling provided within the school systems.

9. The establishment of a national scholarship fund to aid those who could profit from additional education but who lack the necessary financial resources.

10. Expansion of adult education programs through Federal financial assistance extended to such institutions as the recognized and accredited colleges and universities; and, encouragement of vocational training and retraining programs sponsored by nongovernmental groups in our economy.

## III. AID TO ECONOMICALLY DEPRESSED RURAL AND INDUSTRIAL AREAS

### A. Depressed Agricultural Areas

11. Expansion of the credit programs now available to farmers, with increased emphasis on loans extended to low-income farmers.

12. In combination with expansion of credit programs for low-income farmers, a corresponding increase in the provision of technical assistance to the individual farm families receiving loans, such assistance to include development of an appropriate farm plan for the individual family and extending the technical guidance and leadership required to help the family carry out the plan proposed.

13. Consideration be given to the development of farm extension services to meet the needs of low-income farm families in particular, and to greater utilization of trained workers to assist the family improve all aspects of its family life. As a first step toward a better life, it should be possible to help the family get improved subsistence from the land on which they are now living.

14. Consideration of the following program designed to meet these particular needs:

a) By means of technical assistance and Federal loan guaranties, aid recognized and approved local groups engaged in attracting new industry into the area, and develop other ways of providing off-farm employment. These programs (which also are recommended for extension to depressed industrial areas) should provide maximum stimulus to private investment in areas now depressed but which possess advantages of location or resources that, in combination with such investment, make economic growth practical and feasible;

b) Assist in the development of a program for financing approved cases of out-migration of individual families;

c) Expand vocational counseling and job placement services in depressed agricultural areas; and

d) Expand in rural areas the federally aided nonfarm vocational training programs.

## B. Depressed Industrial Areas

15. Substantial expansion of existing programs of technical assistance to depressed industrial areas and to small producers within the area.

16. Credit aids be extended, when such assistance is economically desirable, to existing local industries, and to approved local groups engaged in planning and constructing "ever-available" plants for the purpose of attracting diversified and expanding industries. Credit aid may possibly take the form of loan guaranties designed to promote maximum stimulus to private investment.

17. That the Federal Government share in planning and conducting appropriate economic surveys to determine the scope of current and potential local resources.

18. Expansion of the small-business program, with particular emphasis on aid to depressed areas, and coordinated with a strengthened program of decentralization of defense contracts.

19. Extension of vocational counseling, job information, and placement services of the Federal-State employment services so that workers in depressed areas will be aware of job opportunities in other communities. In addition, these agencies should expand their function of alerting employers outside of depressed areas, as well as within, to the types of skills currently available in depressed areas.

20. That financial assistance should be provided to unemployed workers willing to undertake the approved retraining programs, and to those willing to migrate to areas of labor shortage.

## IV. ADMINISTRATIVE AND RESEARCH NEEDS

### A. Depressed Rural and Industrial Areas

21. That there be established in the executive branch of the Federal Government a central group charged with the responsibility of preparing a coordinated, comprehensive program aiding currently depressed industrial and rural areas and so designed as not to affect adversely other areas. Such a program must assist in maintaining the economic climate necessary to promote maximum economic growth of the economy as a whole.

22. Increased research along the following lines:

*a*) A continuing program of study is needed to analyze regional and technological shifts so that trouble spots can be detected early enough to make for practical preventive action, such as encouragement of new enterprises in an expanding industry in areas where a major enterprise in a declining industry is expected to close down.

*b*) An inventory of labor skills and economic assets should be compiled for each area now marked by concentrations of low incomes and chronic unemployment, to make it possible for public and private groups to match the available local resources with the needs of expanding industries so that new enterprises could be attracted to these depressed areas.

*c*) For each distressed area, improved and more detailed reports on unemployment, labor force, percent unemployed, and number of new jobs to be created;

*d*) Regular reporting of work stoppages by areas with some suitable measure of its relative importance in each area; and

*e*) More information on differences in cost of living and in wage rates between areas and communities.

### B. Low Income Resulting from Causes Associated with the Individual

23. Intensive studies to identify the population at substandard levels of living and the causes of their low economic status.

24. That the Federal-State employment services place greater emphasis on job-placement services for the older worker.

25. That, in all ways possible, government—Federal, State, and local—encourage industry to employ older workers willing and able to work and to make more jobs available to this group by redesigning work to fit their capacities.

26. That the appropriate departments and agencies of the executive branch prepare a report on the current status and size of the *low-income population* and the progress made in the alleviation of poverty and elimination of its causes, such report to be submitted to the Joint Economic Committee *during the 85th* Congress, and periodically thereafter.

# DISCUSSION QUESTIONS

1. Workmen's compensation was the first social insurance program in the United States. It has also been characterized by some as the worst social insurance program. Is this true? Explain.

2. Explain why only four states have adopted cash sickness benefits? In view of the widespread adoption of private plans, is there need for a public program?

3. What are the interrelationships between veterans' benefits and social insurance benefits? Is there a need for closer coordination between these programs?

4. What explains the reasons why the United States has not adopted a family allowance program?

5. Explain the reasons why railroad employees are protected by a separate social insurance system. Is this desirable?

6. Why should there be federal financial aid to the states for public assistance?

7. Should federal funds be made available for direct relief to needy persons without regard to residence?

8. Explain the persistence of low incomes in a high-level economy. Do you think poverty can be abolished? How would you go about it?

# SELECTED REFERENCES

### Disability

DAHM, MARGARET. *Experience and Problems under Temporary Disability Laws.* U.S. Department of Labor, Bureau of Employment Security, Unemployment Insurance Service, 1955.

### Workmen's Compensation

"The Current Status of Workmen's Compensation," *Industrial and Labor Relations Review* (October, 1953).

"Workmen's Compensation—Unfulfilled Promise," Herman M. Somers and Anne R. Somers, pp. 32–42.

"The Anomalies of Workmen's Compensation," S. Bruce Black, pp. 43–50.

"A Policy Decision for Workmen's Compensation," Jerome Pollack, pp. 51–62.

"Workmen's Compensation and Private Benefit Programs," Duncan M. Macintyre, pp. 63–72.

INTERNATIONAL ASSOCIATION OF INDUSTRIAL ACCIDENT BOARDS AND COMMISSIONS. *Workmen's Compensation Problems: Proceedings of the Annual Conventions.* Washington, D.C.: U.S. Government Printing Office.

REEDE, ARTHUR H. *Adequacy of Workmen's Compensation.* Cambridge, Mass.: Harvard University Press, 1947.

SOMERS, HERMAN M., and SOMERS, ANNE R. *Workmen's Compensation: Prevention, Insurance and Rehabilitation of Occupational Disability*, John Urley and Sons, Inc., 1954.

YOUNT, HERBERT W. "Workmen's Compensation—An Appraisal," *American Economic Security* (March–April, 1956), pp. 10–21.

## Related Social Security Programs

BELKNAP, LOREN C. "An Analysis and Criticism of the Program of Aid to Dependent Children," *Journal of Public Law* (Spring, 1957), pp. 25–54.

BLACKWELL, GORDON W., and GOULD, RAYMOND F. *Future Citizens All.* Chicago: American Public Welfare Association. 1952.

BOND, FLOYD A.; BABER, RAY E.; VIEG, JOHN A.; PERRY, LOUIS B.; SCAFF, ALVIN H.; and LEE, LUTHER J. *Our Needy Aged: A California Study of a National Problem.* New York: Henry Holt & Co., Inc., 1954.

BROOKINGS INSTITUTION. *Functions and Activities of the National Government in the Field of Welfare: A Report with Recommendations.* Washington, D.C.: U.S. Government Printing Office, 1949.

LEYENDECKER, HILARY M. *Problems and Policy in Public Assistance.* New York: Harper & Brothers, 1955.

TENBROEK, JACOBUS. "The 1956 Amendments to the Social Security Act After the New Look—A First Thought," *Journal of Public Law* (Spring, 1957), pp. 123–62.

DEPARTMENT OF HEALTH, EDUCATION AND WELFARE, OFFICE OF PROGRAM ANALYSIS. *Grants in Aid Administered by the U.S. Department of Health, Education, and Welfare.* Washington, D.C.: U.S. Government Printing Office, 1957.

## Children's Allowances

CORLEY, F. J. "Why Federal Family Allowances," *Social Order* (June, 1954), p. 249.

WILLARD, JOSEPH W. "Family Allowances in Canada," *International Labour Review* (March, 1957), pp. 207–29.

RATHBONE, ELEANOR F. *The Case for Family Allowances.* Baltimore: Penguin Books, 1940.

# CHAPTER

## VII

# The Economic and Social Implications of Social Security

## INTRODUCTION

TOTAL DISBURSEMENTS, federal, state, and local, in all public social security programs in the broad sense, including pensions to veterans and their dependents and governmental retirement and similar plans, amounted in 1959 to nearly $25 billion. Including estimated payments under private retirement and insurance policies and plans, union health and welfare plans, voluntary health insurance plans, and public expenditures for medical care, the grand total was in the neighborhood of $45 billion and is continuing to increase.

Disbursements for future years will be much higher. Under the present federal old-age, survivors' and disability insurance law, disbursements will greatly increase in future years.

A comprehensive social insurance program is estimated to average eventually between 15 and 20 per cent of payrolls, although not all of these costs may be borne on payrolls, depending upon the sources of revenues used and the extent of reserves.

Old-age, survivors', and permanent disability insurance may cost eventually between 9 and 12 per cent of payrolls, depending upon the level of the benefits provided, retirement and mortality rates, employment and wage levels, and similar factors.

Unemployment insurance is estimated to average about 2 per cent of payrolls over the course of an eight- or ten-year business cycle, although in years of full employment disbursements may amount to only 1 per cent of payrolls, and in periods of heavy unemployment they might average 4, 5, or 6 per cent of a lower level of payrolls.

Cash benefits for temporary disability are estimated to average 1 to 1½ per cent of payrolls.

Health insurance—that is, medical services to insured persons and their families—is estimated to average about 3½ per cent of payrolls in the early years of the program, and as personnel and facilities expand, to average 4 to 5 per cent of payrolls in later years.

These are average costs for a "normal year." In a year of high employment they could be somewhat less; in a year of heavy unemployment they would be somewhat more. The above estimates, whether in dollars or percentages of payroll, are subject to a considerable margin of error, depending upon changes in and the growth of the economy.

In evaluating the economic and social implications of private and public measures of economic security, consideration should be given to the following comment of the Advisory Council on Social Security in 1948:

> In the last analysis the security of the individual depends upon the success of industry and agriculture in producing an increasing flow of goods and services. The very success of the economy in making progress, while creating opportunities, also increases risks. Hence, the more progressive the economy, the greater is the need for protection against economic hazards. This protection should be made available on terms which reinforce the interest of the individual in helping himself. A properly designed social security system will reinforce the drive of the individual toward greater production and greater efficiency and will make for an environment conducive to the maximum of economic progress.

One of the most pervasive economic problems affecting social security arises as a result of inflation. Inflation acts to decrease the value of social security benefits. Individuals who are on fixed incomes feel the effect of inflation adversely. In order to adjust the benefit structure to rising prices and earnings, social security programs have had to adjust their basic benefit levels. Inflation causes serious problems for all types of social security systems whether they are insurance, pensions, assistance, or some combination, and whether they are related to wages or need. An important factor, of course, is that inflation introduces new financial considerations into the social security program at a time when the government is having other financial difficulties. Any change in benefits or contributions necessitates considering long-run financial implications.

The social and economic implications of these vast programs are far reaching. They have an effect on savings and investment, on incentives and production, on the relation of government to business and to individual plans and aspirations.

A large proportion of the present reserve is being "set aside" for future distribution and expenditures. The economic consequences of these developments call for study and analysis. Some of the significant issues of public concern are included in the discussion questions at the end of this chapter.

# 51. SOCIAL INSURANCE: A PROBLEM IN INSTITUTIONAL ECONOMICS

J. Douglas Brown,
*American Economic Review*,
May, 1957.

Few areas of inquiry in the field of economics demonstrate more clearly the importance of an institutional approach to the discipline than the area of social insurance. At a time when one wing of economics is finding more and more uses of mathematics in the development of the theoretical analysis of the behavior of markets and prices, another wing, more concerned in the role of the human factor in the economic equation, is seeking the aid of the full spectrum of social science to discover the interrelations of economic policy and the enhancement of our way of life. It is good that this is so.

The traditions of the discipline of economics are broad enough and deep enough to encompass a widely varied attack upon the essential problem of how man organizes his productive efforts to assure the best possible livelihood for himself and his fellows. It is a matter of personal taste and predilection whether one prefers to analyze by the most precise methods the operation of any or all measurable phenomena, or to range more widely in the exercise of both analysis and judgment in developing new structures and devices for the improvement of the economic machinery of our society.

The economist with a mathematical bent warms to the deductive process of a tightly reasoned demonstration from assumed economic premises. If the premises are approximations of reality and the deductive process is sound, results of much value to understanding are achieved. Like in all scientific proof, however, the essential consideration in the evaluation of results is in large measure *esthetic*. Is the solution neat and tidy? Is it beautifully symmetrical and simple? Does it "click" into place and fit situations other than those used in the demonstration? On the assumption —the basic faith of all scientists—that this is an orderly world, such an esthetically satisfying solution may reveal truths of far-reaching application. They may eventually change the premises of all future policy.

The economist who by predilection moves outward into the world finds the very complexity of social, economic and political forces exciting. He enjoys the inductive process of absorbing, weighing, blending and building a multitude of items of evidence into a more or less definite picture of truth. If he is passively inclined, he stops with such a picture. He may be content to be an economic historian, even of the current scene. Others are led by the zeal for action to convert judgment into policy—

new policy to improve our way of life. They become what might be properly called political economists.

The test for continuing membership of the political economist, thus described, in our honored profession is not the precise tools he uses to arrive at propositions of economic importance, but rather that he studies *all* available evidence, freely, thoroughly and effectively, by those tools most appropriate to the evidence. This opens up for him the vast range of disciplined analysis which has been developed by historians, political scientists, economists, sociologists and social psychologists. He may even find helpful approaches, not in mathematics alone, but in the whole range of science. Perhaps most telling of all will be those highly suggestive insights which he may gain from great literature and philosophy. The mathematical economist may profit most by intensive concentration in the depth of his subject—a thrilling experience for many able men. The political economist must ever broaden his area of interest, and continue a kind of adult liberal self-education reaching out from his central interest and objective.

With acknowledged bias, the writer would like to demonstrate the nature of the work of the political economist by marshalling certain unsolved problems in an important area of public policy, social insurance. It is believed that such a demonstration will not only indicate the variety of evidence and approaches necessary in the attack upon such problems—and thereby support the conclusions made above—but may also encourage some younger economists to leave the ivory towers of deductive analysis and venture forth into the rough and ready life of an economic frontiersman where the rifle and the ax may be more appropriate tools than the slide rule.

The unsolved problems in social insurance policy which follow are purposely chosen to be typical and varied, rather than necessarily the most pressing in importance in every case. To make each problem more meaningful, some considerations, often contradictory, will be outlined. In some cases, the writer will offer a judgment as to the better solution of the problem. But it must be noted immediately that such a judgment is ever subject to change in the light of newly acquired evidence.

I. *Does social insurance protection enhance or reduce worker motivation?*

It is vital to continued progress in a free, competitive economic system that government enhance rather than attenuate the normal drives of the individual to improve his livelihood, so long as these drives are legitimately exercised. It has been proved time out of mind in history that response is more effective than command in raising the level of production in a society. No institutional factor should be superimposed by government which, on net balance, reduces rather than enhances motivation. This is a core problem.

Social insurance in the United States has evolved as an extension of the differential wage system. To the extent that benefits are related to wages, the motivation to increase the rate and regularity of earnings is carried over into the social insurance system. This is in sharp distinction to relief payments which are related to need, not past earnings. It is also to be distinguished from flat benefit systems used abroad. If benefits under the system vary in any reasonable degree with earnings, the motivation inherent in the wage system should, at least, not be attenuated by the social insurance system.

But it may be argued that a reduction in the degree of risk faced by the wage earner on the introduction of a system of benefits (particularly unemployment benefits) reduces his motivation to retain employment or seek new employment when laid off. The problem of the planner of social insurance is to so relate benefits to normal earnings to afford reasonable protection without reducing motivation in any serious degree. This becomes a problem in which psychology, economics and public administration must be joined in seeking a solution. The solution will not stay put as conditions change and any solution will be a compromise. But the significant point is that there is an increasing body of evidence which on thorough analysis suggests sound policy. We no longer need to guess.

At a more philosophical level, a good deal of thinking has been done on what constitutes the object of worker motivation. We are learning that security is a goal as well as a support. There is in most normal individuals a striving to attain a higher and higher level of security. As the level of education and foresight increases, the three-dimensional quality of rewards for sustained effort become increasingly important. Witness the rapid extension of fringe benefits in both progressive companies and in union contracts. Many such benefits provide elements of security. They make the reward for effort a more attractive package than if current wages alone were afforded.

The nub of the problem is whether the reward of a higher level of security is realistically related to the greater quantity or quality of effort contributed. This is a psychological problem and not a mathematical one. In private benefit programs, differential benefits can be carried to high ceilings. Unfortunately in social insurance in the United States, a sound policy of differential benefits has been limited in application at the upper ranges by ever-present political considerations.

II. *What should be the proportionate cost and the proportionate benefit under social insurance programs compared to normal earnings?*

Under private benefit programs, the answer to this question might be readily developed. An appropriate level of benefits might be one-half of normal earnings. The cost of such a level of benefits can be computed in actuarial terms and the resulting figure applied in the individual case. This is an example of clean-cut equity. But even in the most orderly of private firms, such equity in its pure or raw state is seldom applied. An employed group is a social entity in which old and young, higher-paid and lower-paid work in close association. Some who are older cannot afford to pay the costs of the level of benefits established and yet will soon need benefits of at least that level. Others have a long span of contribution ahead or are less likely to become eligible for benefits for some time. In the light of this complex situation, the employer, recognizing the need to favor group morale rather than individual equity, serves to attenuate the extremes of differentiation. In private retirement annuity programs, minimums and maximums are established, accrued liability is absorbed, and guarantees given. This is but the recognition that economics must adjust itself to social psychology and to certain well-tested attributes of social groups.

In social insurance programs, this balancing of equity and adequacy must be carried further than in private company programs. It is easy to see that the goal of differential benefits as a reflection of differential effort is compromised to some extent by the need to recognize a group interest in adequacy. Fortunately in the United States, the proportion of normal earnings required to assure adequate minimum benefits is sufficiently modest to permit a large part of total contributions (employee and employer combined) to be used to sustain differential benefits above the minimum. We have, however, departed markedly from any premise of paying benefits equal to approximately one-half of lost earnings, even within the bracket of earnings covered by contributions. The problem remains for continuing study and political debate whether the existing proportionate contributions as opposed to graduated levels of benefit are in sound balance. The politician may be content with a pragmatic solution. The political economist cannot get off so easily.

III. *What is the appropriate area of operation of social insurance as contrasted to needs-test relief or self-support?*

The simplest definition of the area of operation of social insurance can be based upon the premise that it is an extension of the wage system. It can be argued that social insurance has the function of making the wage system workable in an economic system with inherent qualities of fluctuation and mobility and in which individuals become old, disabled and unemployed. The individuals who are dependent upon the wage system to support themselves and their families are assumed to be in the labor market. But when is a person in the labor market? This is a tough problem which no single discipline can solve.

In the area of social insurances related to life risks such as death, dependent old age, or permanent and total disability, an historical test of past participation in the labor market is available. Employment at minimum earnings for minimum periods within a zone of time can be used to establish a workable test. But in the area of current risks covered by social insurance, such as unemployment and temporary disability, the historical test falls short. It can be used to establish elibility at the onset of the contingency but it may provide no effective check on continuance in or re-entry into the labor market on the part of the beneficiary. There is also the problem of whether the individual has ceased to be "marketable" or whether a market exists.

There are many type illustrations of this problem of the relation of the beneficiary of term social insurance and the labor market. The following may be suggested:

*a*) A married woman establishing eligibility for unemployment insurance benefits in seasonal employment does not seek regular employment.

*b*) A skilled worker laid off on the closing of a plant refuses to seek employment except in an occupation no longer in demand in the community.

*c*) A worker disabled by temporary illness loses his incentive to secure regular employment.

*d*) A community undergoes the loss of its principal industry with little likelihood of replacement.

These illustrations are sufficient to indicate the tenuous line between the economic and the psychological factors which arise in applying the test of continuance in the labor market in social insurance. The practical answer has come to be to apply whatever tests of attitude may be readily at hand, such as the offer of reasonably suitable jobs when available, and to permit the exhaustion of benefit rights to do the major task of clearing the rolls of those leaving the labor market.

IV. *What is the proper role of employee contributions in a social insurance system?*

The obvious answer that employee contributions are intended to spread the cost of social insurance benefits is far from sufficient. If the objective to spread cost were the exclusive goal, the use of a general income tax would be more effective. Also, there are many problems for the economist concerning the effective incidence of payroll taxes. There is little certainty even in a relatively static situation in respect to the degree of shifting of the tax. The considerations involved in a policy of employee contributions include more than those narrowly economic in nature. They include basic attributes of individual and group psychology.

It is a normal expectation in human experience that benefits involve sacrifice and that rights involve obligations. This is true in both the economic and the political spheres of life. A benefit gained without contribution is almost sure to be undervalued. Differential contribution for differential benefit pervades the whole market structure in both goods and services. Why should it be expected that individual attitudes toward social insurance benefits be different? Even highways are now divided between toll and free.

Not only does contribution on the part of the individual tend to enhance value, but by a subtle psychological interconnection it tends to enhance responsibility. A person feels an interest in something in which he has invested and from which he expects to benefit, whether it be a home, a car, a church or an operating system. He will be disposed to object to waste, inefficiency or abuse which affects the object of his interest. The accumulation of individual interests becomes reinforced when they merge into a group interest with articulate expression by the natural leaders of the group. By this process, a psychological reaction of the individual leads to political responsibility in the general citizenry when individuals contribute directly and specifically to their own protection.

This justification of employee contributions in social insurance in psychological and political terms may be questioned by the economist who wants to keep things simple and logical in economic terms. But an institution as complex as social insurance won't stay simple. It perversely wanders through the whole maze of social science and the ramifications of public administration. An interesting question for future debate is whether unemployment insurance in this country would be better administered today if the principle of employee contributions had been universally accepted and sustained. Another question is why can't income tax legislation be designed to avoid discouragement to the survival of the contributory principle in all forms of benefit programs.

V. *How much does a social insurance system contribute to reducing the amplitude of economic fluctuations?*

In the early discussion of unemployment benefits in this country, there was much talk about stimulating the employer to stabilize employment in his firm. The concept of prevention of lay-offs was developed from that of preventing accidents under workmen's compensation insurance. From this transposition of concepts, the justification of merit rating under unemployment insurance arose. Even the devasting effects of a serious depression failed to diminish the faith shown in the efficacy of the concept. It is true, however, that many converts in industry had their faith supported by a strong direct interest in a low rate of contribution determined more by the nature of their business than by any added incentive to stabilize.

Whatever slight effect merit rating under unemployment insurance may have had on the prevention of lay-offs, the far greater impact of this and other social insurances on the fluctuations of business must be sought on the side of benefit payments. It is significant that, in this respect, unemployment insurance has a close parallel in old-age insurance. So long as eligibility for full old-age insurance benefits is related to withdrawal from the labor market, there will be a very considerable fluctuation in the volume of benefits paid according to the extent to which withdrawal is encouraged or discouraged by the state of the labor market. In times of good business, retirements are delayed or re-employment sought; in times of bad business, employers may lay off older workers eligible for benefits and favor younger workers in filling their needs.

A question for study might be: how much does the varying volume of benefit payments tend to compensate the variations in the volume of wages paid? To be of most interest, such a study should be made in an industrial area in which eligibility for social insurance benefits is high when lay-offs or retirements occur. The statistical series which would result from such a study might be suggestive, but they would be far from indicating the whole effect of social insurance benefits upon business conditions.

More subtle than the effect of an increased volume of benefit payments in time of business recession upon the total purchasing power available is the effect of the assurance of benefits, if needed, upon the individual consumer. There has been much discussion of the role of confidence in the decisions of the business enterpriser. Does the availability of social insurance benefits have a real effect upon the confidence of the wage earner-consumer as he makes his decisions to embark upon commitments to pay for the host of items now offered for installment purchase? To answer this question would require techniques in the area of social psychology.

Apart from the fluctuations of social insurance benefit payments and their availability to the individual when most needed, is the mounting volume of long-continued payments to retired workers and survivors. When permanent and total disability benefits are paid, they will add to this continuing flow. Unlike the return on investments, such regular payments will almost entirely find their way into immediate use in the purchase of consumers' goods and services. In the olden days, the rich old lady in Boston was a steadying influence on the economy of that city. Perhaps we have created a few million counterparts, much lower in income per individual, but accumulatively far more effective.

The foregoing examples of problems for study in the field of social insurance are sufficient to indicate the need for the more inclusive approach of institutional economics to make progress in this field. It may be argued that, like the famous Powder River of the West, such an approach becomes "a mile wide, an inch deep, and runs up-hill." Granted, there are grave dangers of superficiality in institutional economics just as there are the dangers of artificiality in mathematical economics. But the problems of the world await analysis and, for some, the satisfaction of aesthetic proof do not compare with those of participating in the development of effective public policy.

It must be added that, in the case of social insurance, the political economist in his institutional approach is dealing with an area of economics which is only now coming into its own. This is the study of the enhancement of human resources as the most precious ingredient in any economic system, not land, capital or labor (in the old sense of purchasable services), nor markets, prices or credit. Because the individual is the end of human activity, the economist has tended to leave him to the humanist, on one hand, or the psychologist on the other. But the individual and any aggregate of individuals is the most subtle and the most critical element in the economy of a firm, a community, or a nation today. They make prosperity possible, and national security sure. If badly used, they make poverty and war inevitable.

The study of human resources, whether in the U.S.S.R. or the U.S.A., may help determine which of these two great institutions will survive. Such study is challenging enough to make one willing to work with less exact tools, if there is promise of progress toward new knowledge.

# 52. THE ECONOMICS OF PENSIONS

Robert M. Ball,
*Pensions in the United States,*
National Planning Association, 1952.

The economic security of the retired aged, like the security of us all, depends on the success of industry in producing an increasing flow of goods and services. But, a high level of production alone will not prevent insecurity for the individual. It is necessary, as well, to have institutional arrangements such as pensions to make sure that all have the continuing right to share in consumption after retirement. There are thus two basic factors in the provision of economic security—production and the institutional arrangements for income maintenance.

These two factors are to a considerable extent interacting. Not only does the production potential of a country establish the outside limits of what is possible in the provision of goods and services to the various groups of consumers but the nature of the arrangements for income maintenance may themselves have something to do with the level of production.

Pensions are a device for making sure that the retired aged will have income when they need it. The justification for pensions lies in the security which they give the individual. Nevertheless, in considering the design of pension arrangements it is important to consider their probable effect on total production. They may be justified as security measures even if they were to have a depressing effect on the volume of production, but it is certainly desirable to keep any factors which inhibit production to a minimum and to promote factors which are favorable to a large volume of goods and services.

This section of the report will consider some of the economic effects of pension arrangements and will raise those economic questions which seem most deserving of further study.

## IS OUR STANDARD OF LIVING THREATENED BY THE INCREASE IN THE NUMBER OF THE AGED?

Probably the most fundamental economic question connected with the growth of the aged population is whether the flow of goods and services going to the retired aged will be so great in the future that the gainfully employed will find it difficult to produce enough for the aged and at the same time have enough for themselves, their children, and their wives. As indicated earlier, it is extremely unlikely that the percentage of persons working past the age of 65 can be very much increased. There seems to be little doubt that the growing proportion of aged in the population will mean an increasing number of retired aged in relation to the number of gainfully employed. Alarmist stories of what this situation is supposed to do to the community standard of living are familiar to all.

It does not appear, however, that there is any real basis for alarm. The relative sizes of the groups of those gainfully employed and those not gainfully employed *is* one of the basic determinants of the volume of goods and services available per person. The larger the number of persons not gainfully employed in comparison with those who are, the greater the number who must share in consumption in relation to the number there are to produce what is to be consumed. But those over 65 who are not working at present make up only a little over 10 percent of all persons not

TABLE I

*Nonproducers in Relation to the Gainfully Employed*

| Year | Persons not gainful workers per 100 gainful workers | Aged persons not workers or wives of workers as percent of all persons not gainful workers | Year | Persons not gainful workers per 100 gainful workers | Aged persons not workers or wives of workers as percent of all persons not gainful workers |
|---|---|---|---|---|---|
| 1870......... | 209 | 1.9 | 1920......... | 149 | 4.2 |
| 1880......... | 189 | 2.3 | 1930......... | 152 | 5.0 |
| 1890......... | 170 | 2.8 | 1940......... | 140 | 7.9 |
| 1900......... | 161 | 3.2 | 1950......... | 137 | 9.4 |
| 1910......... | 147 | 3.7 | 1952......... | 135 | 10.0 |

gainfully employed. Children under 18 make up over half of those not in the labor force, and housewives nearly one-third.

The percentage of retired older people among those not gainfully employed will almost certainly grow over the next 25 years, but the ratio of all persons not gainfully employed to those gainfully employed at the end of that time will be about the same or even improve. The trend over a considerable period of time, as shown in Table I, has been in the direction of fewer and fewer nonproducers in relation to the gainfully employed.

What the population picture will be 25 years from now is, of course, uncertain. It is possible, however, to predict with some confidence the approximate number of persons who will be 65 and over and the approximate number who will be of working age and under 65, since most persons who will be in these groups have already been born. Migration is not likely to be an important factor. What uncertainty there is arises primarily from the possibility of significant changes in mortality rates.

There is considerably greater uncertainty about the size of the dependent child population, because the birth rate over the next 25 years is more difficult to predict than mortality rates. There is also uncertainty about the size of the gainfully employed group, because no one knows whether the average age at retirement will be higher or lower than at present. Moreover, it is uncertain to what extent women will participate in gainful employment during the next 25 years and at what age young people will begin work. Reasonable assumptions on these doubtful points, however, still lead to the conclusion that the total number of nonworkers per active worker will probably not increase over the long range, or if so by only a slight amount, but it is more likely that there will be a further moderate long term decline. Over the next few years, however, there may be some increase in the ratio because of the very large number of births since 1945. The effect of these births on the labor force will not be felt until about 1960–65 but in the meantime they tend to raise the ratio by increasing the number of nonproducers. Any increase over the long range that might occur would arise only if birth rates are very high continuously or if employment conditions become very unfavorable so that many persons drop out of the labor force. In 1975 the ratio of nonworkers to workers will probably be very much as it is today or even somewhat more favorable, perhaps 120 to 130 nonproducers to 100 workers (and certainly no more than 140 to 100) as against 135 to 100 today. By then, however, assuming the same rate of retirement as today, the nonworking aged will probably represent not 10 percent of the nonproducers as they do now, but 13 percent.

Since older persons who can work by and large seem to prefer to, it is highly desirable (assuming full employment for younger workers) to increase production by giving as many of the aged an opportunity to work as possible. The population picture, however, is not such as to cause alarm if we are successful in continuing to employ as large a proportion of the aged as at present. It would, of course, be a significant loss to the economy if in the future an even smaller proportion of the aged were to work. If, for example, retirement at age 65 became general, the group requiring pensions in 1975 would be perhaps 20 million (including 1.5 million more wives) instead of 14 million and the national product would be reduced during periods of full employment by the extent of the contribution of about 4.5 million workers.

Not only may there be somewhat fewer nonproducers per worker in

1975 but almost certainly each worker will be able to produce more. This has been the trend over the last 100 years and there is every reason to believe that it will continue.

The increase in the productivity of workers comes about largely because of an increase in the amount of capital equipment which the worker can command and improvements in management and the methods of using that equipment. The best available estimates indicate that over the past several decades, the average increase in output per man-hour has been more than 2 percent per year.

In the fiscal year 1952, the national income was about $285 billion. On the assumption of a 2 percent per year increase in productivity and a 1⅓ percent per year increase in the labor force, the national income in 1975 would be about $600 billion in terms of 1951 prices. This would mean a per capita income of $3,000 (1951 prices) as compared with the present per capita income of $1,830.

It is quite clear that if we are at all successful in continuing economic progress, our standard of living is not threatened by the growing number of retired aged.

## WHAT IS THE SIZE OF THE PENSION COMMITMENTS WE ARE MAKING?

Although our standard of living is not threatened in absolute terms by pensions, it is still possible that "too much" of the future national income is being committed to retired persons in comparison with the rest of the population. Are the pension commitments which we are making for 1975 to the 14 million or so aged nonworking persons reasonable when measured against a $600 billion national income?

In one sense this question cannot be realistically considered in terms of present dollar commitments. If we achieve a $600 billion national income in 1975 (1951 prices), pensions will undoubtedly be more liberal in order to reflect the higher standard of living.

Although there have been occasional sharp ups and downs, the general trend of wages and the level of living has been upward throughout the history of the United States. This long-range trend of money wages and the standard of living will undoubtedly continue to be in this direction during the next quarter century. The future price trend is less certain but it is likely to be upward.

The dynamic character of these fundamental economic factors creates serious problems for pension planning. A worker and his employer start contributing toward a retirement benefit when the worker is a young man, but when he reaches age 65 he will find that the money amount which seemed adequate at the time the system was established is now completely insufficient.

There are two different factors present here. If the price level has risen it means that the same money amount at a later date will not buy as much as it would when the system was planned. Even if prices did not rise, however, the amounts would still be considered inadequate because the general standard of living of the community will have risen. What were once considered luxuries become necessities and a content of living which seemed adequate in 1900 was below the poverty line in 1950. It is not enough, therefore, for pensions to maintain a constant purchasing power. They must keep pace in the long run with the rising standard of living.

It is extremely unlikely that the dollar benefits which would result from present commitments will keep pace with a rising level of living. This would happen only if there were a sufficient drop in the price level to reflect the increases in productivity. It is much more likely that the dollar benefits now promised will have to be increased.

It seems best, therefore, to measure pension commitments for 1975 on two different bases, (1) assuming as a minimum the maintenance of the purchasing power of benefits, and (2) assuming liberalizations sufficient to keep up with a rise in real wages. Legal commitments of course may well be lower than is shown by any of these estimates. If one were to assume a rising price level over the next 25 years and pension payments were not increased enough to maintain their purchasing power, then pension payments as a percentage of national income would be lower than indicated in any of these estimates.

The validity of the dollar estimates which follow are dependent on the achievement of a $600 billion national income. This is not true of the percentage figures which are, perhaps, the more significant. If productivity increases less than has been assumed, then pensions will not be liberalized as much as they otherwise would. The national income will also be smaller, however, and, in that event, pensions might represent about the same percentage of the lower national income as liberalized benefits might represent of a much higher national income.

On the basis of maintaining the 1951 purchasing power promised in the present law, the old-age and survivors insurance program will in 1975 be paying about 10 million persons past 65 approximately $8 billion (1951 prices) or 1.2 percent of a $600 billion national income. Assuming that the program is constantly liberalized to keep up with a rising level of living and that its coverage is extended to include all employments not now covered under any Government plan, it will be paying in 1975 about $14 billion, or 2.3 percent of the estimated national income.

All other Government retirement plans will be making to those 65 and over payments of about $2.5 billion (0.4 percent of the national income) on the assumption of guaranteeing the purchasing power of present provisions, and about $5 billion (0.8 percent of the national income) under the assumption of adjustments taking into account a rising level of living.

It is much more difficult to get an idea of the commitments being made through private plans, but they may be of this general magnitude: under the assumption of a guarantee of purchasing power—$600 million, or 0.1 percent of the national income in 1975; under the assumption that benefits will be constantly liberalized to reflect a rising standard of living, that eligibility conditions will be greatly liberalized, and that coverage will be gradually increased from the present 15 percent of the labor force to over half of the labor force by 1975, $3 billion, or 0.5 percent of the national income, would be the figures.

Taking all the retirement plans together, a guaranty of purchasing power might result by 1975 in retirement pay representing 1.6 percent of the national income. With benefits constantly liberalized to keep up with productivity increases and with greatly expanded coverage, retirement pay in 1975 might represent 3.7 percent of the national income.

There would seem to be little point in hazarding a guess concerning the level of retirement pay in periods even more remote than 1975. It is possible that sometime after 1975 the American economy will be adversely affected by a depletion of major natural resources and a failure of invention and imports to provide adequate substitutes. We are, for example, using up our easily available oil resources at an extremely rapid rate and conceivably even coal and iron might be scarce in the next century. The rise in the level of living, which short of atomic war seems reasonably certain over the next 25 years, could be reversed in the long run. On the other hand, the development of new sources of power such as atomic energy might mean a rapid acceleration in the rate of productivity increases. We may be sure, in any event, that radical changes in the productivity of the economy in the remote future will call for adjustments in retirement pay.

## WHAT IS THE EFFECT OF PENSION ARRANGEMENTS ON THE TOTAL VOLUME OF PRODUCTION

First of all, are there factors in some retirement plans which may have an adverse effect on the total volume of production? Although no quantitative measurement is possible, the answer to this question is in the affirmative. Certain plans may adversely affect the employment of older workers and the mobility of labor.

### Effects of Present Pension Arrangements on the Employment of Older Workers

If pension arrangements are such as to decrease the employment of older workers and if, as a result, the total number of persons at work is reduced, there is a decrease in production which can be attributed to pensions. It is easy, however, to exaggerate the loss of production associated with the failure to employ all older workers who seek jobs. Older workers are, of course, only one group among several whose capacities are frequently under-utilized. Industry may also fail to employ fully the handicapped, women who seek work, racial minorities or other groups. In the recession phase of the business cycle, older workers may be employed in place of other workers and under such circumstances production is not lost by laying off the older person. Nevertheless, attention should be given to the effect of pension arrangements on the employment of older workers. Pensions may affect the employment of older workers either through being a barrier to their employment or through encouraging retirement at an earlier age than is necessary.

The extent to which private pension plans discourage the hiring of older workers is largely a question of whether or not the older person seeking work brings with him to a new job substantial retirement rights. In hiring an older worker who does not already have rights to a deferred annuity, the employer is faced either with the expense of providing a pension greater than his responsibility to the worker on the basis of length of service would justify, or with the onus of later retiring him on an inadequate pension. The employer's solution of this dilemma may be not to hire the older worker at all. However, since all industrial workers now bring with them to the new job substantial retirement rights under old-age and survivors insurance, lack of early vesting probably has less effect in many private plans on the hiring of the older worker than before the 1950 amendments to the Social Security Act. It is now possible for employers to grant to older workers pension rights commensurate with remaining years of service, or for that matter no private plan rights at all, without running as grave a risk of community censure. Private pensions, then, are no longer necessarily a barrier to the employment of older workers, although in practice some employers may refuse to hire those who are beyond the age of eligibility for retirement plan participation. It would be highly desirable to study the detailed operations of private plans with a view to determining how best to eliminate those factors which may still have an undesirable effect on the employment of the older worker.

It would also be desirable to know to what extent, if at all, the granting of private pensions results in encouraging employers to retire those who are able to work and in encouraging workers to retire even though employers are willing to keep them on. Moreover, how many of those who retire from their regular jobs take up some other kind of gainful employment? In other words, to what extent does the pension actually result in fewer older people making an economic contribution and to what extent does it merely provide income for those who would not be in employment anyway?

In the past, private pension plans have been associated with a policy of compulsory retirement at a fixed age. In a study of pension plans in Minneapolis conducted by the University of Minnesota Industrial Relations Center in the spring of 1950, it was found that "of the nonpension firms 93 percent keep on 'most or all' hourly employees, and 87 percent keep on 'most or all' salaried employees after 65; but of the pension firms only 33 percent keep on 'most or all' hourly paid and only 26 percent keep on 'most or all' salaried employees after 65." To what extent can a flexible retirement age be introduced into these plans?

As indicated in part I of this report, experience under the public program so far indicates that workers past 65 generally prefer to continue in employment if they are able to do so in spite of the availability of retirement benefits in the amount now payable. Preference for work rather than retirement is perhaps less categorical where part-time employment is involved. It is true that some individuals may, under the present old-age and survivors insurance retirement provision, refrain from taking or increasing the amount of their part-time employment because the earnings would exceed $75. A part-time job, if it nets earnings barely more than retirement pay, may not be worth taking from the beneficiary's point of view if it means losing the retirement benefit. For this reason, the amount which an individual can earn before his benefit is suspended should be high enough to permit part-time employment without penalty. It should not be so high, however, as to create a preference among any large number of people for part-time jobs over full-time employment.

There is no evidence to indicate that the retirement test in old-age and survivors insurance has caused any significant number of people to forego employment in order to secure benefits. The elimination of the retirement test on these grounds would, therefore, be inadvisable and would greatly increase costs. If old-age and survivors insurance paid an annuity at age 65 without regard to employment, it would be paying benefits in 1975 not to 10.5 million persons 65 and over, but to 12.5 million. The additional benefits would go, by and large, to persons who were still earning as they had at younger ages.

### Possible Effect of Pension Plans on the Mobility of the Labor Force

Pension arrangements would also have adverse effects on production if they were to inhibit a desirable degree of mobility in the labor force. It is important that many workers be willing to change jobs. New industries can be developed only with the help of workers from older industries. Without geographical and industrial mobility among American workers the development of the automobile industry, for example, would have been impossible. From the standpoint of the public interest and to promote the welfare of the individual, we should in general encourage workers to try out at better jobs in which they may be more productive. We should not put grave penalties in the way of enterprise and initiative.

Some private plans, particularly those without vesting privileges, set a very high price on a worker changing his job. This is particularly true of older workers who have been with a company for a long period of time. Under many plans the worker gets nothing if he leaves before retirement age and, in leaving, may forfeit pension rights worth $10,000 to $15,000. Some plans are purposely designed this way as a method of holding experienced workers. Other plans omit all provision for vesting, not in order to hold workers but in order to keep down the cost of the plan. If the plan pays only those who stay on and gives nothing to those who leave, it may cost only a third as much as a fully vested plan would cost. The collective bargaining plans, for example, generally do not have vesting because the unions were interested in securing as high benefits as possible with the funds available for those about to retire at the time the plans were inaugurated.

The provision of early vesting is desirable from the standpoint of the worker and the economy. Many companies, too, now believe that they gain more in high morale by a generous policy of vesting than they would gain by holding workers through the design of the pension plan. The worker who stays on because of the promise of a pension is not always the one the company wants most to keep. In addition to high costs, perhaps the biggest barrier to the widespread adoption of early vesting is the frequent lack of interest on the part of young workers in deferred annuities—if there is something coming to them many want the cash when they leave the employer—and the feeling on the part of a group within management that the company has little obligation to the worker who leaves of his own free will.

The degree to which those private plans without substantial vesting inhibit a desirable degree of mobility among the working force, depends to a considerable extent on the adequacy of the public plan which does follow the worker from job to job and the amount of additional protection furnished by the supplementary private program. If nonvesting private plans supplied most of the retirement income or if there were no public plan at all, the effects of private plans on mobility might well be considerable. Under present arrangements, however, where in mass production industry the public pension will supply from one-half to three-fourths of the retirement income for hourly workers, the effect is considerably weakened. Under these circumstances, other factors such as the security of employment and other special privileges of seniority are probably, in most instances, more important than pension rights in determining whether or not a worker is willing to leave a given employer.

Nevertheless, pensions when added to other factors may have an inhibiting effect on the willingness of a significant number of older workers to change jobs. To determine the extent to which this is true would require considerable research and study. Any such study should include the various Government programs. Nonvesting State and local government plans may act as a barrier to mobility to an even greater extent than private plans since, under these Government systems, the workers do not have the basic protection of old-age and survivors insurance. For Government workers, a change to another kind of job may have even more serious effects on pension rights than in the case of industrial workers.

The fact that certain jobs are not covered under old-age and survivors insurance may also prevent some workers from taking those jobs. The lack of coverage might result in a significant loss of production.

### To What Extent Do Retirement Systems Contribute to a Greater National Product?

To the extent that contributions to pension plans result in a reduction of expenditures that would otherwise be made they increase saving in the aggregate. It is recognized that at certain periods in the business cycle an increase in saving may create difficulties and require countermeasures. In the long run, however, it is likely that a higher rate of saving will facilitate the financing of an expansion in productive capacity. An increase in productive capacity will in turn permit a greater increase in production and the future standard of living. The effect of an increase in pension funds on investment is most clearly recognizable when the funds of private pension plans are invested directly in additions to productive enterprise. The same effect may also occur indirectly when the funds are invested in existing stocks or obligations of corporations or in Government bonds. In these cases funds will be released for new private investments if and when a demand for additional funds exists.

It is very difficult, however, to determine the extent to which pensions in the future will be financed from savings which would not have been made in any event for some other purpose. This is an important matter for further investigation. It is significant that in pension systems we are dealing largely with forced savings and savings dedicated to a specific purpose, a purpose, incidentally, for which people have not saved on a large scale in the past. Moreover, there are indications that a widespread public insurance program actually increases the interest of people in saving on their own and in buying private insurance. Coverage by a social insurance system brings adequate provision for old age within reach and gives people an incentive to add private savings and insurance. Without social insurance many would see little hope of avoiding dependence on relatives and old-age assistance. All in all, it is not unlikely that in spite of retirement systems people will want to accumulate nearly as much in individual savings as they would have otherwise.

Less tangible, but nonetheless real, are the contributions to production which pensions can make in other ways. Retirement plans can help to keep industrial leadership aggressive by making it easier to retire the unfit among the aged and thus promote young men of promise. In the same way, to the extent that pensions make for a healthier, happier labor force by relieving current workers of a source of worry, they undoubtedly make an indirect contribution to production. (Some plans, however, may have the opposite effect. In requiring long years of service they may make the employee too dependent on a particular employer and a particular job.)

Contrary to popular impression, certain kinds of retirement plans—

those which do not tie a worker to a particular job—promote risk-taking. With basic protection assured, workers and self-employed persons are more, rather than less, likely to take chances, to try out new jobs, to start new enterprises. It is one of the functions of insurance of any kind to spread a risk and so make it bearable for the individual; he can then afford to take a chance. It is a mistake to assume that insurance and social security arrangements promote caution. They are much more likely to promote enterprise and risk-taking—factors greatly needed in our economy. As stated by the Advisory Council on Social Security to the United States Senate Committee on Finance, "A properly designed social-security system will reinforce the drive of the individual toward greater production and greater efficiency, and will make for an environment conducive to the maximum of economic progress." Moreover, as the Council pointed out, . . . the very success of the economy, while creating opportunities, also increases risks. Hence, the more progressive the economy, the greater is the need for protection against economic hazards."

An increasing volume of goods and services is dependent not only on the availability of raw materials, capital equipment, improvements in the organization of industry, and skilled and willing manpower, but also on the ability to employ fully the productive resources available. In the past we have periodically failed to achieve reasonably full use of our economic resources.

One factor in the prevention of depression periods or in mitigating their severity is the effectiveness of institutional devices for maintaining consumer demand. Recessions deepen into depressions partly because some unemployment causes additional unemployment as more and more persons are unable to buy what the economy can produce. Insofar as pensions give a large segment of the consuming public an assured regular income which is independent of the business cycle, they have a steadying effect on demand. Moreover, the availability of pensions for older workers who become unemployed and later drop out of the active labor force altogether compensates in part for the loss of earned income. Pensions then will, at certain phases of the business cycle, add to the total volume of production through maintaining purchasing power and thus employing otherwise idle manpower and capital.

All things considered, it is unlikely that existing pension arrangements have an adverse effect on the total volume of production. It is more likely that the effect is favorable.

## IS THE BURDEN ON THE COMMUNITY OF CARING FOR THE AGED GREATER OR SMALLER THAN IT WOULD BE IN THE ABSENCE OF PENSIONS?

Pension commitments do not, of course, measure the increase in the flow of goods and services going to the aged as a result of pensions. In the absence of organized plans, those who retire in the future would, in most cases, obtain at least the goods and services necessary for a minimum level of living. To a considerable extent they would be supported by children and other relatives and by the community through public assistance.

It is likely that retirement systems will result in the future in a larger proportion of retired persons obtaining a level of living above a bare minimum than would be true without such systems. (With or without retirement systems, some retired persons, of course, will secure a higher than minimum level of living as a result of individual saving.) The absence of a means test in old-age and survivors insurance and the relatively high level of benefits paid by some private systems makes this probable. How much of an increase in the flow of goods and services going to the aged can be attributed to pension arrangements cannot be accurately determined.

Retirement systems are not necessarily a burden to the community, however, even to the extent that they increase the flow of goods and services to the retired group over what it would be in the absence of pensions. They constitute a burden to the community only insofar as others must limit their consumption because the pensioners are getting more than they would in the absence of pensions. To the extent that the increased flow of goods and services going to pensioners is the result of increased production brought about by the pension arrangements themselves, there is no additional burden to the community. Moreover, to the extent pensions are paid for by the earlier contributions of pensioners, either direct or indirect, the pension arrangements would not require a reduction in consumption on the part of others.

Employee contributions to retirement funds, whether public or private, are in the nature of savings and the incidence of the contribution probably remains where the contribution is first imposed. The final incidence of the employers' contribution—whether on the worker in the form of lower wages, on the consumer in terms of higher prices, or on the owner because of lower profits—depends on the interaction of a variety of factors. The nature of the market for the product will determine the extent to which demand falls off if the price is raised and thus controls the ability of the employer to pass his contribution on in the price. Is there a strong labor union which makes it difficult to pass on the contribution as a lower wage? Will establishment of a pension fund and the employers' contribution be a substitute for a larger increase in wage rates which would have had to be granted in the absence of a pension plan? What is the degree of competition in the industry? What are the Government's wage and price policies? Perhaps all that may be safely said about the final incidence of the employer's contribution is that, in general, it does rest in part on the future pensioner in his role as wage earner and consumer. Taking into account both the employer and employee contribution, it may be said that to a considerable extent future pensioners are paying for their pensions by current reduction in expenditures.

Considering the extent to which pensions are financed by the earlier savings of pensioners and considering the contribution which pension arrangements make to production, it is not unlikely that retirement systems result in less of a burden on others in the community than would exist in the absence of these systems.

## PROBLEMS OF FUND ACCUMULATION

At present, the most significant economic characteristic of private pension plans is that they are primarily a method of collecting money now in order to pay benefits later. Most plans are relatively new so that there are few pensioners, probably only about 350,000 age 65 and over in the whole country (500,000 when the wives 65 and over are counted as recipients), but money is being set aside for the future retirement pay of many millions of current workers. Ultimately, the money going to retired workers in pensions may exceed that being set aside for current workers (the difference being made up by earnings on the accumulated funds). For the next few decades, however, pension payments will represent a relatively small proportion of what private industry sets aside to cover future payments. In 1951, as indicated in part I, perhaps $300 million was paid out in private pensions, including amounts paid to retired workers under 65, but about $1.8 to $2.0 billion was added to pension funds. What will be the probable size of this fund accumulation in the future, what will be its effect on the capital markets, and how effective will these funds be in providing future old-age security?

It is very difficult to make a reasonable estimate of what the rate of private fund accumulation will be, for many of the factors which enter into the estimates are highly uncertain. Some factors tend to decrease the rate of fund accumulation and other factors tend to increase the rate. Factors tending to decrease the rate include an increase in the number of pensioners as plans mature, an increase in benefit amounts to keep up with current wage and cost-of-living levels (which is more than offset, however, by higher contributions required if fully funded), and a decrease in funding for past service as these costs are gradually amortized. For example, a plan which cost 12 percent of pay roll during the first 12 years when past service credits were being funded might cost only 7 percent of payroll thereafter. Moreover, at present with taxes high there are advantages in funding generously and for funding past service credits within the shortest period in which the amount may be taken as a tax deduction (approximately 12 years). Under less favorable business conditions or with lower taxes the rate of funding could be considerably reduced.

Factors tending in the opposite direction include the need for additional funding as benefit amounts are increased (including additional funding for past service credits), the establishment of new plans, the meeting by more workers of minimum eligibility requirements for participation which are included in some plans, increased earnings as the funds build up, and, in those plans geared to wages, increased funding required by a rising wage level. It is perhaps not unreasonable to assume that over the next decade these various factors may offset each other. On the basis of 1951 prices, the average yearly increase in private pension funds during the next 10 years may well be around $2 billion or somewhat more. Together with interest, this would result in aggregate reserves of $33 to $39 billion a decade in the future as compared with present reserves of about $12 billion.

Under the present tax schedule, the excess of income over outgo in old-age and survivors insurance will average an additional $2 billion per year during the next 10 years, varying from about $1.5 billion in 1953 to $2.5 billion in 1960–62. Other Government programs will average about $1 billion additional per year, making the average yearly total of excess of income over outgo for all plans, public and private, about $5 billion. During inflation the accumulation of these funds has been convenient but, of course, the opposite will be true during a period of deflation. The impact of these funds in a deflationary situation is, therefore, an important area for study.

The effect on the capital markets of $5 billion a year of new funds is an additional major area for exploration. At present much of the basic information needed for analysis is lacking. Quantitative information on private pension funds and their investment is to a considerable extent not available. Analytical studies of current investment practices and comparative earnings are also needed.

Among the questions which should be studied are the following:

*1. Will pension funds continue to be invested in Government and industrial bonds to the same extent as at present, or will a larger proportion be invested in equities?*

At present about two-fifths of the private pension funds seeking investment in a given year are insured funds. Almost none of these funds is invested in equities. A growing emphasis on maximizing income and a desire to protect the fund against the effects of inflation have led to increased equity financing among trusteed plans. A recognition that pensions will need to be liberalized in the future as the standard-of-living rises reinforces this trend. Perhaps about a fifth of new money going into trusteed funds is invested in equities.

Although a few trusteed plans have bought business enterprises (for example, the General Tire & Rubber Co. fund bought the Dan Lee Mutual Broadcasting System in California), it is not likely that pension funds will become an important direct source of risk capital; the equity financing by trusteed plans has been very conservative. Yet to a considerable degree the money market is a single market and more funds for any purpose increase the supply available for all purposes.

## 2. What will be the effect of fund accumulation on the interest rate?

An answer to this question must await some determination of the extent to which these pension funds represent an increase in the volume of savings and the extent to which they merely represent a shift in the form of savings. If the volume of savings is increased will the increase be sufficient to affect the interest rate? A related question is whether the investment practices of these funds will have a concentrated effect on certain types of securities, lowering the rate of return for the safer investments, or whether the money market is fluid enough for the impact to be absorbed more or less evenly. The effect of fund accumulation on the interest rate is an important area for investigation.

## 3. Will the investment policies of the trusteed plans have a stabilizing effect on the stock market?

It is possible that the growing tendency for trustees of pension funds to invest in common stocks and to emphasize average yields over a long period of time rather than market value might have a stabilizing effect on the stock market. The funds are earning funds and there is usually no need to sell. The popular method of stock purchasing called dollar averaging, moreover, calls for regular purchases of the leading stocks regardless of the condition of the market. This theory, based on the idea that averaging is safer than trying to outguess the market, if applied on a large scale, results in a steady demand for the better-grade stocks and would help prevent sudden drops in price. On the other hand, since the pension trusts are exempt from income tax they can, if they wish, profitably take capital gains by shifting from stocks which they feel are overvalued to those which are undervalued, or they can shift part of their holdings from stocks to bonds if yield disparities are sufficiently narrowed. These practices could serve valuable market functions.

## 4. What will be the effect of a rising level of living, and possibly rising prices as well, on the contribution which the present type of funding can make to the financing of future benefits?

Funding under private plans is considered to be necessary because any given concern may go out of business and the pay-as-you-go method would result in inability to meet accrued obligations. Moreover, since costs rise steeply, funding is advocated as a way of reducing, through earnings on the fund, the payments to meet benefit costs which would be necessary in the future. Yet these funds may be less useful than is now generally expected. Unless the funds are invested in equities, a rising price level greatly reduces their usefulness, for as suggested earlier, benefits will need to be liberalized sufficiently to maintain at least purchasing power. For example, if we were to have a price rise averaging as much as 2 percent a year, in 35 years it would mean a price level twice as high as at present (35 years because of compounding). Under such conditions, pensions would have to be twice as high and funds invested at a fixed rate of interest 35 years earlier would be performing only half the job they had been designed to perform. On the other hand, if prices remain stable, benefits will nevertheless need to be liberalized to reflect productivity increases and a rising level of living. Under these circumstances as well, if the funds are loaned at fixed interest rates rather than invested in such a way as to share in the gains arising from productivity increases, yields on the funds will meet a continually declining proportion of benefit costs. The dilemma is a very real one. Is it desirable to risk the major part of a pension fund in stocks?

The Teachers Insurance and Annuity Association of America is now experimenting with one way of partly meeting this problem. This association, which covers some 70,000 college teachers with completely vested annuities, is now offering through an affiliate, the College Retirement Equities Fund, a plan which would base the part of retirement pay coming from this fund entirely on equities. The benefit payments will vary from year to year according to the market value and yields of the equities held by the Fund.

In the public pension programs, any attempt to finance a substantial part of benefit costs through an earnings fund runs up against the same difficulties. And, in addition, an attempt to meet part of the problem through buying equities in productive enterprises would put the Government in business and raise serious questions concerning the proper relationship of Government to private enterprise. Fortunately, in the Government programs the continued existence of the systems may be assumed and the security of the benefit can be made to rest on the taxing power of the Government so that funding is not as necessary as in private plans. Since the general Government program, at the very least, must maintain the purchasing power of the benefit, and should also allow for some increases as productivity improves, it may not be wise to rely heavily on funding as a way of meeting long-range benefit costs. The present assumption, inherent in the tax schedule for old-age and survivors insurance, that ultimately roughly a fifth of benefit outlays in a given year will be met by interest earnings may well prove to be too optimistic.

This is not to say that a public fund is worthless. The old-age and survivors insurance trust fund and those of other Government systems do not differ materially from those operated by insurance companies or private trusts. Yet there has been considerable confusion about the effect of the investment of the old-age and survivors insurance reserve in Government securities. It is alleged, for example, to result in double taxation for OASI benefits: first when the taxes are paid on covered earnings and again when redeeming the bonds held by the trust fund or when paying interest on the bonds. It is perhaps worth commenting on this point.

It is true, of course, that the Government will have to levy taxes to pay interest on the obligations issued to the trust fund or to redeem the bonds. However, these taxes are not for the purpose of paying OASI benefits. Rather they are to pay the general expenses of Government for which the money was borrowed from the fund—the cost of defense, for example. These taxes would have to be levied regardless of whether the bonds were held by the trust fund or by a private bank or insurance company. If the trust fund reserve could be held in cash as an idle balance, earning no interest, it would be necessary to levy not only the usual taxes to service the national debt, but additional OASI taxes to make up for the loss of interest to the trust fund. The fallacy in the notion that there is double taxation for OASI purposes lies in the assumption that payment of interest on part of the national debt is a cost of social insurance. Actually, the Federal debt exists quite independently of the social insurance program. Purchase of Government bonds by the trust fund does not mean that the national debt is increased, but merely that the bond purchaser is a public agency rather than a private investor.

# 53. WHY FINANCIAL NEED IN AN EXPANDING ECONOMY?

WILLIAM HABER,
*Public Welfare,*
January, 1957.

IT IS QUITE appropriate to be asked to discuss the reasons why there is such a considerable amount of financial need in an expanding economy. During a period of economic depression or a serious recession the existence of such need is understood and accepted. When there is a slump or business is declining, millions of wage earners are unemployed. For many who continue to hold on to a job, the hours of work may be drastically reduced and their take-home pay drop considerably below the normal level. Under such circumstances we readily understand the needs of people in want. We respond with the natural humanitarianism of our people and respond generously to needs, whether created by lay-off, old age dependency, illness or the death of the breadwinner; for most people associate such need with "poor times."

Since these are "good times" many people cannot quite understand why the social security and public assistance expenditures are so large and involve so many millions of people. Has something happened to the American character? Are our people losing, or have they lost their self-reliance? Are they being pauperized by the very measures which were passed to assist them when in want? For more than 15 years we have had unprecedented prosperity in the United States. Except for a brief readjustment associated with reconversion from war production to peacetime industries in 1945 and short recessions in 1949 and 1954, we have had full employment or nearly full employment for the American labor force. Many cannot understand why, under these conditions of high employment levels and the highest wages in our history, over 17 million individuals are in receipt of some kind of public payment—either social security, public assistance, or welfare service—in 1956.

I am asked to explain if I can why this takes place in an expanding and prosperous economy. It might be well if we began by examining several of the more important characteristics of an expanding economy. These aspects of our society, prosperous as it is, may help to explain the pressure and in fact the reasons why financial need is actually increasing although our economy is growing.

### The Population Explosion

The first of these characteristics is population growth. We have had and are continuing to have an unusually large increase in our population. Many Americans are not aware of the size and significance of the birth rate in the U.S. since 1940. Our present population of over 165 million will reach 190 million in 1965, less than 10 years. And by 1975, only 19 years from now, it is estimated that we will have a population of over 220 million people. We have not had such a rapid rate of growth in this century. By 1975 we shall have in the U.S. as many people as now live here plus a number equal to the population of Great Britain. This growth is part of our expanding economy. We have added 25 million to our population since 1940; we shall add another 25 million in the next nine years, and over 30 million more in the following 10 years. This population explosion will influence every aspect of our society—education, public health, social security and the volume of activity of every unit of government.

### A Larger Labor Force

The immediate result of our population expansion is the rapid growth in the size of our labor force. We now have 68 million people in our working group—men, women and youth. But nine years from now our work force will expand to 77 million. By 1975 we shall have 90 million people producing goods and services—nearly 50 percent more than we now have. This means that we shall have to build an economy that will create nearly a million new jobs every year. If we fail to do so we shall be increasing our unemployment. A large labor force, of the size we shall have in 10 and 20 years, makes possible a great increase in the volume of goods and services which will be available to all Americans. It suggests also a host of problems concerned with training and labor mobility, counselling and employment services.

## Steady Rise in National Income

Our expanding economy, as we would expect, has been accompanied by a large increase in our national product. The rise has been steady and now is well over $400 billion per year. Even when allowances are made for changes in the value of the dollar, we have made fantastic progress in increasing the volume of goods and services. We have never been as productive nor as prosperous as a people. And while there is no guarantee against recession or depression, most economists are agreed that there is a very good chance that the trend of the past 15 years will not be reversed or seriously retarded. If we can continue to increase our national product at a rate of three or four percent per year, we can double our real standard of living in about 25 years. It is not a wild dream at all to suggest that by 1980 the living standard of the average American family will be double what it is today.

## Automation and Change

Another characteristic of our growing economy is the rapid pace of technological change. Automation is on everyone's mind. It represents new ideas of substituting mechanical means for human hands and the human brain. We are investing billions of dollars in searching for new, better and cheaper means of making things. In time we shall depend even more than now upon industrial technology rather than manpower to do our work. This development and its greater speed in an expanding economy will have significant influences in many areas of our life. It may in time make possible a substantial reduction in the length of the work day and the work week. More leisure will bring with it other problems, including that of the intelligent use of leisure time. A shorter work day will create increasing opportunities for work away from home for women, especially married women—which will create child welfare problems.

Two other observations about our growing economy merit attention. One is the rather persistent inflation. The other is the uneven growth of expansion. The inflationary trend is a serious business. While we can probably avoid the runaway sort of price inflation—the kind that wipes out values in a few years—many economists are of the opinion we shall probably have price inflation of one to two percent per year. This may not appear very much. In 10 years, however, it can substantially decrease the purchasing power of a pension or a fixed income and drastically reduce the living standard of those dependent on such incomes.

Finally, while it is proper to refer to our economy as expanding, it is well to remember that it is not expanding evenly nor in a straight line. Full employment does not mean no unemployment. And "stranded areas," sick industries, pockets of unemployment, exist in the very midst of prosperity and growth. We have millions of employers. While most of them are prosperous, many are failing or just hanging on. Bankruptcies exist in the very midst of high average profits. And from two to three million jobless are always present. Our expanding economy is a free economy. And in a free economy growth and decline go on all the time, side by side. All this has obvious implications for the problem of financial need.

### Government Interest in Human Need

Before we examine these implications it is necessary to refer to the rather drastic change in our philosophy as a people and of our government towards human need. As a result of our experience during the depression of the 1930's, we began to focus more attention upon income maintenance programs than we ever had in the history of our country. We assumed public responsibility, again to a degree never undertaken before, to provide funds and services for the neediest part of our population. For the first time, in the early 1930's the states began to appropriate funds for public welfare. Again for the first time, the Federal Government did the same. And finally, in 1935, we adopted the Social Security Act. In the past 20 years we have time and time again confirmed what we did in 1935 and we now recognize that we have undertaken a firm obligation to underwrite income loss resulting from these dislocations.

Indeed, the deep scar which the depression left upon the American memory has not quite been healed. We are more sensitive to human need, to joblessness and to old age dependency as a result. Thus we are committed to provide an underpinning for the minimum standard of living, to provide a floor below which incomes will not be permitted to fall. In brief, we said that poverty will be dealt with by the community. We do this because, in the final analysis, the community will have to pay the price of neglect if it does not deal with the problem. This is our public policy. It has been affirmed almost annually since 1935 and confirmed in the significant amendments adopted to the Social Security Act in August, 1956.

Our expanding economy and growing population, coupled with the assumption of public obligations to underwrite minimum need, is bound to increase public expenditures. Let us explore the effect of the age distribution of our population upon the increase of need in an expanding economy.

### More Old People—Greater Need

The problem of the aged presents a most startling challenge. We have today some 14 million people over age 65 in the United States. By 1965 we shall have 17 million people over 65. And by 1975, the frame of reference I'm using for this discussion, we shall have 21 million in that age group. Let's stop a moment and reflect on the significance of this one figure—21 million people. When it comes to men, 50 percent of the people over 65 are not self-supporting. When it comes to women, 90 percent of people over 65 do not earn their own way. Here we have over 20 million people, of which some three out of four will be dependent upon some source of income other than that from their own labor. For how long? If you have reached the age of 65, or when you do, according to the statisticians you have a life expectancy of 14 years. We have undertaken therefore a public responsibility of old age assistance or old age insurance for roughly 15 million people by 1975.

It is no exaggeration to say that this is probably one of the most significant economic problems in the entire American economy. Old age assistance and old age insurance have significance for every citizen, every legislator, every taxpayer and every social worker. Unless we can do something about this problem, these costs are bound to go up whether we have prosperity or depression.

What can we do? There is no easy answer to this question. But one of the things we ought to try to do is to change the thinking of most people in America about retirement and change the thinking of employers about the employment of older people. For, unless in the next 20 years we can revise the employment pattern for our aging populations, these costs of old age security—whether in the form of assistance which in some states is still miserably low, or whether in insurance not directly based on needs tests—are bound to increase; and we cannot escape this obligation.

Why financial need in an expanding economy? At least one reason is that people are getting older, being squeezed out of employment, leaving the farms and living in urban communities where self-employment is not possible. Some have suggested that we should offer employers a substantial incentive in order to encourage the employment of older people. Perhaps a revision of the tax laws granting to each employer a $500 tax saving for every employee over 65 kept on would contribute to dealing with the problem. Were such an idea to be adopted it would probably be less expensive than might appear. Older people are also productive—as we found out during the war. We are a rich country, but not quite rich enough to disregard the production potential of millions of our senior citizens.

### Dislocations Affect Group 45–64

The problem of the next age category—those between 45 and 64—presents a different sort of challenge. We shall witness a very large increase in the number of people over 45 years of age. As was pointed out earlier, an expanding economy does not grow evenly and its very dynamic character creates serious dislocations. For many people, especially the young, these dislocations are usually of short duration and a layoff is soon followed by a better job. Occupational mobility, even when it involves moving to another locality, is not too difficult if one is young. But for those over 45 or 50, especially those with greying hair, a layoff may be more than a temporary readjustment. With the coming of automation, we may be in for a large amount of technological change. This will intensify

the problem of the older wage earner who is not quite old enough to retire. We are therefore likely to develop a far larger demand for vocational
retraining and counselling, for employment services and unemployment
insurance. Thus even an expanding economy calls for larger services and
financial need for many groups in our society.

### Effects of the Baby Boom

This can also be seen by looking at the problems to be created by the
startling increase in the number of very young. The baby famine of the
1930 to 1940 decade has been converted into the biggest baby boom in
our modern history. The shortage of babies 15 and 20 years ago explains
the difficulties we now experience in finding enough stenographers, clerks
and office workers. Ten years from now we shall have 11 million more
people in the age category from which we recruit our stenographers and
clerks. And the very young group—those born in the past 10 years—has
been growing most rapidly.

This means that we face unprecedented outlays for education. In the
next five years, for example, we shall have to build 470,000 classrooms
merely to catch up with our growing school population. It is estimated
that the minimum cost of meeting our education building needs alone
will exceed $12 billion. That also means more teachers, more child welfare
problems, and sadly, perhaps more juvenile delinquency. In brief, millions
of more kids spell for us a host of demands for education, schools, teachers, guidance and welfare, problems which revolve around that age category. We cannot escape these problems; they are characteristic of our
expanding economy. Expansion of our economy carries with it an obligation to meet the problems which accompany growth.

### Expansion and Expenditures Move Together

What I am trying to suggest is that prosperity and growth of the kind
we have been having, with all of its increasing wealth and higher living
standards, does not necessarily eliminate the need for public outlays for
the sort of services we now provide for the aged, the unemployed and
youth, for public health, counselling, and a host of others.

If, for example, we are to deal with the problem of delinquency, we
must do much more than has been done so far. We have barely scratched
the surface of this and other pressing problems. To go beyond will require
greater, not lesser, expenditures. It is vital for public welfare workers,
commissioners of welfare boards, legislators, editors, and citizens generally, to understand that these large outlays of public funds and their certain increase are the result of basic problems of our society. We have these
huge expenditures, and they are large not because our people have less
backbone in them, nor because they have been pauperized by the welfare
state, nor demoralized. Nor have we destroyed the old habit of thrift.
Rather they are due to the fact that we live in a highly urbanized and in-

dustrialized community growing rapidly and unevenly, and in its growth creating problems which a free and relatively well-to-do society will not and cannot permit to remain unattended.

It is, therefore, no indictment to say that these costs are high or getting higher. Many of these problems cannot, and some should not, be prevented. We can prevent illness, but to do so we may have to spend more on public health and preventive medicine and research. We cannot stop getting older no matter how hard we try and some may try very hard indeed. We can reduce the number of handicapped in time by more safety and rehabilitation. To do so is also costly. In fact, we should spend several times more on rehabilitation than we do now. Such spending will pay huge dividends in more productive and better adjusted citizens. We can reduce juvenile delinquency—not by spending less but by spending more.

Indeed, what I am suggesting is that these large outlays are not pathological; they do not suggest that something is radically wrong with our society. Quite the contrary, they represent the social cost of problems created by a growing, healthy, and in most respects, thriving community.

A natural question which suggests itself to most people who reffect upon these problems has to do with individual thrift. Why don't people save for the rainy day? Why must retirement costs be met by public assistance or old age insurance? Why survivors' benefits? Why not private savings? People do save!—But the persuasiveness of our advertising profession and its magnetic slogans induces them to put their savings into durable goods for the modern kitchen or into a television set or a car and for many, into a home. It is not easy to resist the allurements of the advertiser. As a result, liquid assets of the average wage earner are surprisingly low. In Flint, Michigan, for example, a city of relatively highly paid automobile workers with wages exceeding $90 per week, a recent study showed that the liquid assets of the average family are less than $400—hardly a month's wages.

### How Much Can We Afford?

The final question has to do with whether we can afford these large welfare costs. Granted that we accept the idea that financial need exists and will expand even in good times; that such expenditures represent our way of dealing with income loss and insecurity, with widowhood and child dependency, with old age dependency, with sickness and physical handicap; we still cannot escape the question as to whether we can afford all of this. Will such large outlays put us on the road to national financial bankruptcy? It is obvious that if such expenditures compel us to boost taxes to levels which discourage industry and endanger economic development and growth, then we face serious problems, indeed. Every congressman and legislator as well as every taxpayer is concerned with this problem. Are we taxing ourselves out of business?

A definite "yes" or "no" answer to this question is not possible. To begin with, we may have no choice but to support these 16 million or 17 million "unproductive" people. Whether we can afford it or not, we do not have a free choice. We are obligated to provide for need and our commitment is firmly established.

Whether we can afford to do so depends, in the final analysis, upon the size of our national product. We know that has been growing, fortunately, at a rather steady rate. With a 400 billion dollar annual national product we can afford to do many things we could not have afforded in the 1930's nor in 1945. It is much less painful to provide the large sums for these welfare, social security, and education expenditures now than it would have been at the national income levels of two decades ago. Our national pie is getting larger, and as a result a larger slice will be available to those segments of our population who are unproductive.

In 1956 dollars, we are producing goods and services valued at considerably over 400 billion dollars. If past experience is to be a criterion, and it is safe to count upon it, our national product and national income should grow at an average annual rate of three percent to four percent. On that basis, by 1965 we should have a national product not of 400 billion dollars but over 500 billion dollars. And barring catastrophes, by 1975 we should be able to double our national product and our standard of living. If that can happen, and I think it can, we need not wear long faces and be discouraged concerning the capacity of our economy to bear these costs. We are a growing country, and as long as we continue to increase our efficiency and productivity we simultaneously enlarge our ability to make these expenditures.

### How Willing Are We?

The question which is constantly disturbing is concerned with how much of this total national product the community is willing to set aside for the millions who are unproductive. I use the term, "unproductive," purely in a descriptive sense, and not in any derogatory manner. How much we are willing to set aside to support the aged, the dependent children, the unemployed and similar groups, depends on how important we consider their needs to be in relation to other needs in our society. In recent years, national defense costs have had a very high priority. At other times I suspect hospital construction or provision for mentally sick will have a higher priority than it has now. At the moment, the needs of education and school construction are rapidly developing into a higher priority than we have heretofore given these matters. Indeed, public welfare workers and members of boards and commissions have a responsibility, if they believe in the importance of this work, to win public understanding of it, in order to give these needs and the expenditures to meet them the priority they deserve.

For those who are inclined to be discouraged, it is pertinent to emphasize that this is probably the first time in the history of the world, and surely in the history of our country, when the abolition of poverty becomes a practical possibility. It has never been possible to talk about abolishing poverty in terms other than those of a dreamer. We have made fabulous strides in that direction in the past 20 years. We have learned how to make more and more things with less effort and to release more and more people to provide services. Our productivity and capacity for services has increased so remarkably that now for the first time, we are really in a position to assume our responsibility for meeting financial need. Perhaps this cannot be done uniformly on a national basis. Some regions and sections are less "well-off" than others. In time, however, the growing wealth of our country should make it possible for higher standards everywhere. The time to start is now when times are good and national income is growing.

# 54. TRENDS AND ISSUES IN SOCIAL WELFARE EXPENDITURES AND PROGRAMS

WILBUR J. COHEN,
*American Journal of Public Health,*
October, 1959.

DURING THE PAST ten years, the productive capacity of our nation has grown remarkably. Although the average rate of growth of the gross national product has been 3 per cent a year since 1900, during the past ten years it has been 4 per cent a year. Despite temporary setbacks, real family incomes have increased about 20 per cent over the last decade. If our economy continues to grow during the next ten years by at least the same rate it has grown during the past ten years—and there is every reason to believe it could grow at a somewhat larger rate—we have some very important choices before us in determining the course of our social welfare programs and expenditures.

The former secretary of health, education, and welfare, Marion B. Folsom, stated the challenge facing us very clearly:

In the new age we are entering, our society will have the resources and the power, the opportunity, to banish many more of the burdens that have beset mankind through the centuries. For the first time in human history a great nation will have the material resources, the wealth in being, to eliminate hunger and scarcity and poverty, to provide a decent level of living, for a whole people. Life may no longer have to be, for anyone, a grim struggle for bare existence.

Our society also will have, or can have, the knowledge and power to abolish—to a far greater extent than ever before—age-old burdens of disease and disability and pain. We will have far greater resources and opportunities than ever before to erase ignorance and to encourage more effectively the intellectual development of many more of our young people.

I say our society will have the resources and the power to do these things. But will we use this power—and use it wisely? Will we have the vision to assign the proper priorities for the investment of the resources available? Will we take a sufficiently long view in setting our goals? These are crucial questions.[1]

### Establishing Social Priorities

As we attempt to build upon and expand our existing social welfare programs, an ever-present factor comes into play with increased importance —the growing recognition of the need for more deliberately determining our short-run objectives in relation to our long-run goals.

Our expanding labor force and national product, the growth of our population—especially the number of children, the aged, and the disabled —the growth of suburban areas, the mobility of our population, the exodus of Negroes from the South to northern metropolitan areas, the influx of Puerto Ricans to the mainland, and the continued flow of persons from rural areas to urban centers, have created all sorts of social needs which press for immediate solution.[2] We need more schools, more roads, more hospital beds, and more housing. We want more teachers, more doctors, nurses, social workers—and we will have to pay them more to get them in competition with the demands of science, business, and other professions.

We not only want to expand our educational system, our social insurance programs, our health services, and to improve our public assistance programs, but we wish to improve the quality of the services given. We wish to have more extensive child welfare services and services for mentally retarded children, better programs to deal with juvenile delinquency and the mental health needs of both adults and children. We need more neighborhood centers, counseling and rehabilitation services, and recreational programs. This list could be expanded at great length. But more and more we are coming to recognize that while there remains much to do, and there is much more that we can do than we are doing, we cannot do all we want to do at once. Moreover, money alone is not the sole limiting factor. Increasingly, it may become of less importance. The lack of trained personnel may be an even more important bottleneck. Consequently, certain social priorities must be established in determining what we want to and can do first, how the costs are to be distributed, how we obtain the necessary trained personnel, and through what institutional means we will try to achieve our objectives.

---

[1] Marion B. Folsom, "Some Suggested Adjustments in the Use of Our Resources," address before the American Philosophical Society, April 24, 1958.

[2] For the reasons why our social welfare expenditures have increased see Wilbur J. Cohen, "The Impact of Social and Economic Forces on Health and Welfare Programs," in the *Objectives of Public Welfare Administration and the Leadership Role of the Public Welfare Administrator* (Chicago: American Public Welfare Association, 1958).

At both the professional and legislative levels we will have to give more weight in determining priorities for the training of personnel, as well as to the most appropriate institutions for dealing with our needs, whether through private or public auspices or combination of them. When we evaluate private arrangements we must give attention to the many kinds of efforts by individuals and families and to the activities of voluntary associations, employers, unions, collective bargaining, the nonprofit associations in health and welfare, and commercial insurance enterprises. When we consider the use of public arrangements we must define the roles of the federal, state, and local governments—not always an easy task. And when we come to consider the relationships between governmental and nongovernmental organizations we shall have to steer a difficult course between abstract principles and pragmatic experience which may test all our wisdom and skills.

We face a very different task today in charting a course for social welfare than we did in 1929 or 1935. Then we had the advantage of a relatively clean slate and the availability of talented and highly motivated personnel, but with the great disadvantage that many administrative problems had to be solved. We have gained "know-how" in administration. We have gained a reasonable degree of competence in financial, actuarial, and economic planning of programs. But today we have a pluralistic, piecemeal system with many vested interests—a jigsaw puzzle of many parts—with more diverse arrangements than we had in 1935. Furthermore, with each passing year it becomes more difficult to make basic changes in the structure as institutionalization and rigidities take hold. Recalling what Sir William Beveridge has said, we must be most careful that as we attempt to adjust our social welfare institutions to our changing needs that we do not permit the good to become the enemy of the better.

## The Magnitude of Social Welfare Expenditures

In discussing trends in social welfare programs the first important factor to note is the magnitude of existing expenditures for these purposes—because while they are substantially below our needs they are much more than most persons usually assume.

Total expenditures—public and private—for all social welfare activities in the fields of health, education, and welfare in the United States reached about $60 billion for 1957, according to the best estimate I can make.[3] This is equivalent to about 14 per cent of all the goods and services produced in the nation (the gross national product).

---

[3] For definitions and classifications of these expenditures see J. Frederic Dewhurst, and Associates, *America's Needs and Resources: A New Survey* (New York: Twentieth Century Fund, 1955), chaps. 10, 12, and 14. See also Ida C. Merriam, "Social Welfare in the United States, 1934–1954," *Social Security Bulletin*, No. 18, Vol. 10 (October, 1955), p. 3; "Social Welfare Expenditures in the United States, 1954–1955," *ibid.*, No. 19, Vol. 10 (October, 1956), p. 3; and annual articles in the October, 1957, and 1958 issues of the *Social Security Bulletin*.

This is an impressive and significant measure of the importance which the United States places on human values. Too frequently the objectives of our economic and political institutions have been advertised or evaluated solely in terms of materialistic accomplishments to our disadvantage both at home and abroad.

A review of existing social welfare programs and expenditures shows that, as a nation, we believe in developing the capacities and creativeness of the individual to the maximum, in strengthening family life, and in using a wide variety of public and private social welfare institutions to promote the general welfare.

Despite the gaps and shortcomings in our programs, it is clear that the American people have accepted the principle that government, business, and voluntary agencies should have as their goal the attainment of a "state of welfare" for all people.

In many instances, government and business are reluctant to admit or explicitly declare their acceptance of these goals for fear they may be charged with belief in the "welfare state" (whatever that might mean). But in the good pragmatic pattern of our heritage, legislators, businessmen, and others act increasingly in a socially conscious manner even when they vigorously deny the similarity in objectives with social workers.

### Ends and Means

As we scan the growth of social welfare institutions since the turn of the century and the proposals being considered for further improvement, the so-called "controversial" issues today revolve less around the fundamental "principle" of assuming social responsibility and more around such complex issues as alternative methods of administration and allocation of costs. These elements become important because of the concern about incentives, the relationship between governmental and nongovernmental agencies, and the proper timing of particular proposals in relation to other needs. These are all complicated questions involving technical decisions in which persons sharing the same broad goals and philosophy may have strong differences of "principle" on what to others may seem "details" or "methods."

Perhaps I can illustrate my point in another way. With the acceptance of the basic objectives of public responsibility in some of the fields of health, education, and welfare by the Eisenhower administration, the controversies turn now to such complex issues as the formulas for federal grants-in-aid to the states; the role of the states, localities, and the federal government in urban renewal and juvenile delinquency; who shall pay for extended unemployment insurance benefits; and similar financial and administrative questions. Increasingly, social policy formulation may involve knowledge and decisions on specific issues of great complexity and less on those which can be easily shown to involve exclusively great matters of ethical principles which will arouse emotional and moral crusades.

This may change the whole character of social action in social welfare issues.

### Increased Public Expenditures

Social welfare expenditures from public funds have grown significantly in the past decades. In 1890 all public expenditures for health, education, and welfare amounted to about 2.4 per cent of the gross national product. In 1929, just before the advent of the Great Depression, this figure had grown to 4.1 per cent. During the fiscal year 1957 (the latest for which information is available) the figure was 8.8 per cent. It is clear from a number of studies[4] that public expenditures for social welfare activities will continue to increase both in dollars and in relation to our total economy.

The Rockefeller Report issued in April, 1958, made a number of recommendations for changes in some of our health, education, and welfare programs.[5] The report includes projections of the public expenditures involved in their recommendations. For all three types of programs it is estimated that public expenditures of about $33 billion in 1957 should increase to somewhere between $62.5 and $75 billion by 1967.[6] Omitting education, for the other two types of programs it is estimated that public expenditures of $20 billion in 1957 should increase to between $38.5 billion and $45 billion in 1967. This will involve a doubling of dollar expenditures. Can we attain this goal in the next decade without unduly burdening our economy? I think we can, if we maintain a healthy, growing, expanding economy.

These expenditures for health and welfare amounted to 4.6 per cent of the gross national product in 1957. Depending upon the future gross national product, the projected expenditures for 1967, in the Rockefeller Report, range from 6 to 6.6 per cent of the gross national product. Thus, while public expenditures are estimated to double in terms of dollars, the increase is about 40 per cent in relation to the gross national product.

### Total Social Welfare Expenditures

Let us now look at the situation from the standpoint of all social welfare expenditures, public and private. A true measure of the impact of social welfare programs upon individuals and the economy involves the combination of both public and private expenditures. Unfortunately, a periodic total of both kinds of expenditures is not available. The Twen-

---

[4] "Veterans' Benefits in the United States," *Findings and Recommendations of the President's Commission on Veterans' Pensions* (the Bradley Commission), April, 1956, pp. 117–26. The Bradley Report contains projections of public income maintenance expenditures to 1985. Under one set of assumptions, expenditures for 1985, measured as a per cent of national income, are nearly twice those of 1955.

[5] *The Challenge to America: Its Economic and Social Aspects* (New York: Doubleday, 1958), p. 78.

[6] *Ibid.*, p. 68.

tieth Century Fund made an estimate for the year 1950,[7] and a projection for 1960, and with some modification and broadening in this approach I have prepared the estimate of $60 billion for 1957.

My estimates differ somewhat from Dewhurst's classification for 1950, the most important being that I have included payments for private life insurance and annuities. The 1957 estimates are preliminary and subject to revision. Mrs. Merriam's estimates deal only with the public civilian programs and differ somewhat from the Dewhurst's definitions and mine.

Private expenditures (or more specifically, all nonpublic expenditures) for health, education, and welfare are equal to about half the public expenditures or about one-third of the combined total. The private share is highest for health (about 66.6–70 per cent) and the lowest for education and welfare (about 20–25 per cent).

Private expenditures may be identified as direct consumer expenditures, such as individual and family expenditures for medical care and education; employer and employee contributions for retirement, disability, and life insurance; and philanthropic contributions to private agencies. Somewhat different forces are at work in these three areas. While we cannot explore here the vast impact of these forces, we can illustrate some of the likely differential effects upon different programs.

Contributions to health, welfare, and pension plans will undoubtedly increase in absolute amounts and probably relative to the gross national product, although this will depend upon the extent of changes in our social insurance programs. Payments by individuals for life insurance, while increasing in absolute amounts, may remain relatively stable in relation to the increased gross national product while payments for health insurance increase. There are conflicting forces at work which may change these trends as income increases and people make different decisions as to how they wish to spend their incomes.

### Health Expenditures

Several long-term trends are most evident in the field of medical care. These may be summarized as follows:

1. There has been an increase in the share of the national income allocated to medical care.
2. An increasing proportion of medical care costs is being met through insurance and through public funds.

Both trends appear likely to continue in the future. Total medical care expenditures have quadrupled during the past 25 years; the per capita expenditures have trebled; the proportion of the total spent from public funds has more than doubled; and a larger percentage—closer to 5 per cent at the present time, instead of 4 per cent as in the past—of our national income goes for medical purposes.

---

[7] The Dewhurst estimates for the calendar year 1950 were $12.3 billion for health, $10.5 billion for education, and $16.9 billion for welfare—a total of $39.7 billion.

Total medical expenditures average over $100 per year for every man, woman, and child in the nation. The total medical bill in the broadest sense of the term is thus about $20 billion for the country as a whole.[8] The consumer's share in these costs—while increasing in absolute amounts—has been decreasing relatively as the share from public sources increases. Philanthropy and business provide a small but slowly increasing share of the total.

With a growing and aging population, and the demand for more and better medical services, these expenditures will continue to increase. Medical expenditures are increasing approximately a half billion dollars annually. It will not be many years, at the present rate, until medical expenditures exceed $25 billion annually.

Insuring the costs of medical care has tended to increase expenditures for two reasons: (1) by eliminating the financial barrier to medical care and (2) by adding the overhead costs of providing the voluntary insurance protection. As voluntary insurance coverage continues to increase, these two factors will continue to operate unless there are economic or social changes in the provision of medical care which are not now visible.

Twenty-five years ago the use of the insurance method was a controversial issue in medical care. This is no longer true. Today, the public wholeheartedly accepts the insurance principle, as do the hospitals and, to some extent, the physicians. Every effort is being made to extend it on a voluntary basis and to expand it to cover a larger proportion of people and a larger proportion of medical costs. Nevertheless, a substantial proportion of low-income persons and high-cost services are still excluded from insurance coverage. It is doubtful whether existing voluntary arrangements can or should cover these areas completely. While the exact character and extent of financing from public funds is a controversial issue when approached from the standpoint of "principle," the most likely new approach to the problem may develop pragmatically as a result of the special health needs and costs of the aged.

## Philanthropic Contributions

Now let us look more intensively at the area of philanthropic contributions. Total religious and philanthropic contributions were $5.9 billion in 1955, or 1.5 per cent of the gross national product. In 1929 they were 1.2 per cent, while in 1930 and 1947 they reached 1.6 per cent.[9] If we assume a gross national product of $707 billion for 1967 (based on a 5 per cent growth rate) and assume that 1.6 per cent will be contributed from all philanthropic sources, then a total of $11.3 billion would be available—or nearly twice that of 1955.

---

[8] Ida C. Merriam, "Social Welfare in the United States, 1956–1957," *Social Security Bulletin*, Vol. 10, No. 21 (October, 1958), p. 28.

[9] Thomas Karter, "Voluntary Agency Expenditures for Health and Welfare from Philanthropic Contributions, 1930–1955," *Social Security Bulletin*, Vol. 2, No. 21 (February, 1958), p. 14.

There is no question that this amount could be used. There are many social welfare needs which are not being fulfilled for which voluntary agencies are suitable. Is it possible to raise this much money through existing arrangements?

The Rockefeller Report points out:

> Charitable contributions by individuals have risen to unprecedented levels. In addition, a fairly recent development in private philanthropy is the increase in corporate giving for educational and general welfare purposes. . . . We should give every impetus to accelerating the upward trend of corporate giving in the next decade.[10]

What effect a significant shift from individual to corporate giving will have on our voluntary institutions and agencies merits very careful reflection and review.

Philanthropic contributions for health and welfare purposes (omitting educational and strictly religious purposes) represent about $2 billion of around $20 billion of all private health and welfare expenditures, or approximately 10 per cent of the total. While the amount expended for philanthropic contributions has increased fivefold from about $400 million in 1930 to $2 billion in 1955, the proportion of the gross national product has increased from about four-tenths to about five-tenths of 1 per cent—about 25 per cent. If about five-tenths of 1 per cent of a gross national product of $707 billion were raised from philanthropic contributions for health and welfare purposes, the total would be about $3.5 billion annually—a 50 per cent increase over 1955.

It thus appears that philanthropic contributions are likely to be even a smaller share of total social welfare expenditures in the future unless there are some changes in our tax laws or sources of contributions, or an increase in philanthropy, as incomes rise.

### Total Social Welfare Expenditures for 1967

To present over-all projects for all social welfare expenditures,[11] public and private, for a decade ahead is a perilous attempt and most likely to be wrong in retrospect. But it will give us a provocative target to shoot at.

---

[10] *Ibid.,* p. 51.

[11] There are a number of points at which it is difficult to determine what should be included in "social welfare expenditures." Recreational expenditures and programs, for instance, are not included in the total. But, from the point of view of competing pressures on public, private, and consumer funds, and the relationship to mental health and prevention of delinquency, recreation might appropriately have been included. Consumer expenditures, as defined by the Department of Commerce in its national income studies, were $13 billion in 1955. Public expenditures were $715 million. Thomas Karter, "The Development of Organized Recreation in the United States," *Social Security Bulletin*, Vol. 5, No. 20 (May, 1957), p. 8. A total annual figure of $40 billion can be supported if a broad definition is used. (Dewhurst, *op. cit.,* p. 348.)

Increasingly, attention will have to be given as to the relationship between policies and expenditures for recreation and those for health, education, and welfare. The

In order to fill existing gaps and to meet the needs created by the explosive population growth ahead a substantial dollar increase in expenditures for health, education and welfare will be required. Some of the additional funds will come directly from the consumer (for medical care), some from private sources (private pension, health and welfare funds, and philanthropy), and a major proportion from public sources (for education, health services, and Social Security). If our gross national product grows at 3 per cent per year, it will be about $583 billion in 1967, in which case expenditures of $90 billion—about $30 billion more than at present—would come to about 15 per cent of the gross national product. With a gross national product growing at 4 per cent annually, we could reach a total product of $642 billion, which would make the total expenditure of $90 billion about 14 per cent—the same as today. The Rockefeller Report indicates a needed increase of $30–$42 billion in public expenditures alone. If our gross national product increases at a 5 per cent annual rate to $707 billion in 1967, we could increase present social welfare expenditures from $60 billion to $100 billion without increasing the proportion of the gross national product allocated for this purpose.

Assuming that this goal is an attainable objective from an economic point of view, the major policy question is how can we proceed to develop more effectively and more promptly the necessary social and fiscal policies and modifications of existing arrangements which will make it possible to reach this objective in an evolutionary manner consistent with other national goals and values, taking into account such policies as maximum individual choices, community responsibility for social needs, the role of voluntary agencies, and changes in tax policy?

Several devices come to mind: expansion of the social insurance principle; broadening of services; extension of research, demonstration projects, and training of personnel; and more effective use of the grant-in-aid system.

### Strengthening the Federal-State Cooperative Programs Relating to Social Welfare

There are many aspects of public policy raised by the projections and speculations I have but briefly and incompletely outlined in this article. I have outlined my recommendations in the social welfare field in detail elsewhere.[12] But I cannot refrain from including one specific here, namely, the use and improvement of the federal grant-in-aid system.

---

need for recreational facilities in educational settings, the question of recreational programs in relation to juvenile delinquency, and the role of public and voluntary agency responsibilities in recreation all indicate the many social policy questions involved.

[12] Health, Education and Welfare Policies and Expenditures for Economic Growth and the General Welfare," in *Federal Expenditure Policy for Economic Growth and Stability*, Joint Economic Committee (85th Cong.), November 5, 1957, pp. 919–55.

Federal grants-in-aid for all purposes (including highways, airports, public health, urban renewal, and many other functions) totaled about $3.5 billion in 1956 or 1.1 per cent of personal income.[13] From the standpoint of the national economy, or the federal budget, they are not large but are very important. The federal-state cooperative grant-in-aid mechanism is a great social invention which has demonstrated its usefulness but which has not yet been used to its maximum potentialities.

The federal-state cooperative grant-in-aid system of health, education, and welfare, which we have developed over many years in this country, enables us to achieve essential national objectives with decentralized administrative responsibility and with wide latitude for adjustment of many details to special circumstances. We should strengthen and broaden this system—rather than weaken or dismantle it as has been suggested in some quarters.

Federal grants to the states have not weakened the states but have strengthened them and preserved the federal-state system in this country. We will not be able to meet the rapidly changing and expanding social and economic needs of our nation without building upon the federal-state system. It is not difficult for a high school sophomore to catalogue in great detail various minor criticisms and defects of the federal-state system, just as it is possible to do so with the institutions of marriage, the family, democracy, or the Congress. But it is much more important to keep the large picture in mind and to recognize that the federal-state system enables us to seek and find ways to accomplish broad and important national objectives for the conservation of our human and natural resources with decentralized administrative responsibility and wide latitude for adjustment of specific policies to varying needs and changing circumstances.

# 55. ARE WE SPENDING ENOUGH FOR SOCIAL WELFARE?

Ida C. Merriam,
National Conference
of Social Welfare,
May 25, 1959.

Over the past 100 years, this country has doubled its output of goods and services roughly once every 24 years. We have taken the fruits of expanding productivity partly in the form of fewer hours of work, partly in greatly increased real levels of family income, partly in a substantial growth of social services.

---

[13] Sophie R. Dales, "Federal Grants to State and Local Governments, 1955–1956," *Social Security Bulletin*, Vol. 6, No. 20 (June, 1957), pp. 11–15.

For the first time in history we have the technical means of wiping out poverty. Even in a society of very great abundance, however, that possibility cannot be achieved automatically or easily.

One of the questions I want to touch upon is the role of social welfare spending in an economy of abundance. The general level of spending for welfare—or any other purpose—in a democratic society depends in part on the total resources available, in part on the general values of the society and the way in which particular needs are perceived, in part on the existence of institutional mechanisms through which choice can be effectively exercised. Social inventiveness may be as important as technological invention in determining the rapidity and direction of social progress.

In discussing the developing role of social welfare programs in this country, I shall try to identify some of the changes in goals and in institutional arrangements which have resulted in major changes in the level of social welfare spending, as well as some of the needs which are still unmet.

There was a brief time not too long ago when hopes for a world at peace led many economists and political leaders to look to social welfare spending as the major outlet for our productive capacity and energies. While we must all hope and work for the kind of world situation in which military spending in all countries will be cut to a tiny fraction of what it is today, it is probable that for some time to come social welfare spending must justify itself in competition with a heavy burden of military expenditures. What is the nature of the claim which social welfare can at this time legitimately and effectively make for its share of the national output?

One part of the claim is timeless in character. Underlying all modern welfare programs is the age-old demand for social justice. Another part of the claim is specifically related to the nature of the world in which we live —its complex technology, its interdependence, its dynamic character. Part of the reason for spending for social welfare is that in a modern, complex urban economy we must do so if the society as a whole is to prosper.

### Investing in Education and Health

It is accepted without question by those who have worked most closely with the problems of underdeveloped countries that an essential step toward economic development may be improved health and more widespread education for the people of the country. The economists call expenditures for such purposes investments in social overhead capital.

A developed economy requires an even higher level of investment in human resources. Continuing economic growth depends to a major extent on continuing innovation which comes increasingly from highly trained scientists and organized research. The number of jobs for unskilled workers has been decreasing in one field of work after another, and the new era of automation, atomic power, and space exploration on which we are entering can be expected to continue this process. Increasingly higher levels of professional training are called for in such fields as medicine and social work, as well as more persons with such training.

Broadly speaking, there have been three major stages or levels of support of education in this country. The first began early in the last century with the then highly controversial decision in state after state that every child should have an opportunity to get an elementary education in publicly supported schools. At the end of the century we were spending a little over 1 per cent of our gross national product on education. The extension of the normal span of schooling to include high school and some vocational training brought our total public and private expenditures for education by 1929 up to almost 3 per cent of the much larger national product.

The third period, when college and postgraduate training became accepted goals for large numbers of young persons, was signalized if not in a sense ushered in by the GI educational benefits program. In 1950, expenditures under this program alone amounted to 1 per cent of the gross national product if subsistence payments are included—and certainly many veterans could not have taken advantage of the scholarship funds without some income support. Today we are spending about 4 per cent of our national product for education. Somewhat over four-fifths of these expenditures are from public funds.

Clearly within the next decade, the construction of new school and college buildings, the further upgrading of teachers' salaries, the increasing emphasis on postgraduate education, the probable expansion of scholarship aid, these and other trends mean that more dollars and more resources will be devoted to education. How much larger a proportion of our total national output this will require depends on the future rate of growth of the economy. This is a point to which I shall come back later.

The advances of science and technology have also been primary factors in the increase in the proportion of our total resources invested in health and the dramatic improvements in the general level of health that have occurred in the last 50 and even more in the last 25 years.

Environmental sanitation began to assume significance in this country in the 1860's and 1870's and is taking on renewed importance today as water and air pollution and radiation hazards mount. The beginning of effective control of communicable disease early in this century marked another stage in health care, and one that in this era of jet travel also requires continuing attention on a world-wide scale.

Since 1940 we have greatly increased our total expenditures for medical research, particularly from federal funds, and this is an area in which it appears increases will continue to be made. Whatever new medical discoveries lie ahead, however, it is probable that for some time to come, personal medical care will be the most important factor in the further improvement of health. Two areas of particular concern are the problem of mental health and that of medical care for older persons.

The level of our total national expenditures for health services is likely to be significantly influenced over the next decade by the way we resolve the problem of methods of payment for care. Some method of spreading the risk and cost of heavy medical expenditures, for all groups in the population, becomes increasingly important. How this is accomplished will, in turn, affect the balance between the different kinds of preventive and treatment services that are provided.

In 1929, the first year for which we have such estimates, about 3.5 per cent of the gross national product was going into hospital and other medical services, hospital construction, and medical research. About one-seventh of the total was spent from public funds, primarily for care in state and local and in veterans' hospitals, and for general public health activities. Today we are using almost 5 per cent of our total output for health and medical services, and about one-fourth of the total comes from public funds. The increase in the public share has resulted from a number of separate developments—greatly increased expenditures for public hospital care, newer programs such as vendor payments for medical care under public assistance, and increased use of public funds for construction of private as well as public hospitals and other medical facilities, are among the more important.

Today, however, we still have only 75 per cent of the general hospital beds, and only 53 per cent of the mental hospital beds that the state hospital planning authorities estimate are needed. To make up these and related deficiencies and to assure that adequate medical services actually reach the entire population, we may well have to increase the proportion of our total resources used for health services. The investment, if we decide to make it, would yield important returns.

### Income Maintenance and Income Support

If education and good health are necessary conditions of economic development, social security programs are a necessary outgrowth of industrialization. Increasingly as technology becomes more complex and work more specialized, the individual is separated from the production of the essentials he and his family need for every day life. At the same time, the goods and services that a dynamic economy produces in ever greater abundance and diversity must be widely distributed and consumed if the process of production is to go on. With the organization of our entire economy dependent on a continuing flow of money incomes, some institutional mechanism for assuring a regular source of money income for the nonearning groups is essential.

There are certain periods of nonearning for which the need to plan is evident. These are what we usually refer to as the common risks—sickness and disability, unemployment, death of the breadwinner in the family, and old age or retirement after a specified age. For persons in such circumstances social insurance has proved a successful income distribution mechanism and one particularly appropriate to a dynamic economy. Benefits related—though not in strict proportion—to the individual's past earnings, can reflect individual differences in living standards without direct inquiry into personal circumstances and thus reinforce incentives to individual effort and encourage individual savings. The contributory basis of financing not only provides a stable source of funds but supports the concept of benefits paid without regard to other income. A broadly based social insurance program encourages the mobility of labor and the flexible adjustment to technological change that our kind of economy requires. And payments which to the individual family mean an assured source of income to buy food and shelter and other necessities, are for the economy as a whole an important supporting and stabilizing factor.

Historically, the first type of social insurance to be adopted in almost every country has been workmen's compensation—in other words, insurance against the risk most clearly associated with an industrial economy. In this country workmen's compensation laws were adopted in a number of states before World War I. We also had, prior to 1935, a long-established veterans' pension program, and retirement plans for some government employees as well as private pension plans for a few favored groups of workers.

The Social Security Act laid the foundation for a major new development which has not yet reached its full potential. Social insurance benefit payments now represent more than 3 per cent of our gross national product, compared with less than one-half per cent in 1929. They will continue to grow for some time to come, even without further changes in the existing programs, as a still larger proportion of the aged population is able to qualify for OASDI.

In addition to the clearly defined circumstances in which a continuation of money income is necessary in a developed economy, there must be some way of meeting individual need whatever its cause. As the general level of well-being rises, a society which stresses human values will find it increasingly intolerable that anyone should fall below some minimum level. Nor can a society as interdependent as ours afford sizable islands of poverty, or the continuing problems of poor health, limited education, and maladjustment which they create.

The Social Security Act also marked a turning point in this country in attitudes and programs designed to meet individual need. The substitution of cash payments for relief in kind moved dependent families into the money economy and the general consumer market. The use of federal grants-in-aid to help finance assistance—thus drawing on the superior financial resources of the national government while retaining state and local administration—was another innovation of far-reaching importance.

In 1929, we were using a little over one-half of 1 per cent of our national output for public aid and for institutional care for dependent groups—the expenditures for cash assistance and other aid cannot be separated. At the depth of the depression of the 1930's we were spending more than 4 per cent of a shrunken national output for public aid. Since 1950, the proportion of our rising total output going for public assistance has remained steady at eight-tenths of 1 per cent, reflecting the net effect of the growth of social insurance on the one hand, and on the other increased standards of public assistance in many states, additional federal matching funds, and population and other changes.

As a society we have accepted the idea of a socially provided continuing source of money income more completely with respect to aged persons than with respect to any other nonearning group. For persons aged 65 and over OASDI is now by far the most frequent source of income. At the end of 1958 three-fifths of all aged persons were drawing such benefits and another tenth were eligible to draw them when they or their husbands retired. (Most of the persons receiving private pensions are also getting social insurance.) Public assistance provided the major support for another 12 per cent of the aged population. Only 10 per cent had no income either from employment or from one of the public income-maintenance programs. Ten years earlier, at least 30 per cent of the aged had no income from these identifiable sources. It is clear that we have come a long way in terms of the number of aged persons who can rely on a regular payment to provide them some income security.

Opinions would differ as to how much satisfaction we should take in the size of the payments. The average monthly benefit paid to a retired worker under OASDI in March of this year was $72. For an aged couple the average was about $120 a month, but for an aged widow only $56. Many beneficiaries have other income. A recent survey showed, however, that in 1957 one-fourth of the beneficiaries had practically no money income other than their social security benefits. Home ownership was the most important asset and form of saving for most of the beneficiaries. Medical care costs appear to loom as one of their major problems.

By contrast, of the slightly more than 3 million persons under age 65 with long-term total disabilities, no more than 40 or possibly 45 per cent are getting some income from one of the public income-maintenance programs—including OASDI, the retirement programs for railroad and government employees, the veterans' program, workmen's compensation, and public assistance.

There is a natural reluctance on the part of the general public to provide an alternative to earnings for persons who are not visibly severely disabled. Moreover, some professional groups fear that too generous support may discourage the efforts and exertion that might lead to rehabilitation. New knowledge with regard to human behavior and human motivation is bringing into question the traditional view that a disposition to malinger and avoid work is normal to most men. We may find that many, if not most, individuals are better able to concentrate on learning to overcome their disabilities when there is an assured source of income for the family during the period of rehabilitation and readjustment. In any event we must recognize that only limited rehabilitation at best is possible for some considerable proportion of the disabled.

Somewhat similar ambiguities of attitude have affected unemployment insurance—and reinforced other factors that have led to the now generally recognized inadequacies of this program. In most states, unemployment insurance benefit amounts are in theory intended to replace about 50 per cent of the worker's normal earnings. Because maximum dollar amounts fixed in the statutes have not been increased as much as wages have increased in recent years, however, most workers now get substantially less than this. During the 12 months ending last September, three out of ten of the persons who had been drawing unemployment benefits exhausted their benefit rights before they were re-employed. Unemployment compensation has replaced only about 20 to 25 per cent of the wage loss resulting from increased unemployment in each of the three postwar recessions. The President has urged the states to increase the duration of benefit rights, as well as to raise benefit levels. The general feeling in this country, however, is that benefits should not continue over too long a period. We have not faced up to the question of what provision should be made for workers who cannot find employment at the end of 26 or 39 weeks. This question may become more pressing in the next few years if, as many economists suspect, we are entering on a period when the primary cause of unemployment will be not so much cyclical ups and downs of business activity as very rapidly changing technology and the consequent displacement particularly of older workers.

With nine out of ten children now protected under OASDI, and with vastly improved health and mortality, orphanhood has become a diminishing social problem to an extent that would have been almost inconceivable to a Conference of Social Welfare meeting in 1910.

For children in families where the father is employable but unable to find work, and for children in families separated by divorce or desertion we have provided a much less dependable basis of support. There are still 23 states in which no public assistance is available to employable persons in some or all communities. Even if we are willing to let the adults shift, we need to remind ourselves that the children in such families make up a large part of the human resources whose health and education and general outlook will greatly affect our future.

In evaluating the public assistance programs, one is torn between emphasis on the advances we have made since the 1930's in recognizing a responsibility to provide needy persons with at least minimum income and medical care, and emphasis on the need that is still unmet. One does not have to have new family budget studies—useful and desirable as they would be—to recognize unmet need in aid to dependent children payments that nationally average $29 a month per recipient, or maximums on such assistance that in 29 states reduce payments below what the state public assistance agency has determined to be the amount necessary for basic needs. In recent months more than one-third of all PA recipients throughout the nation and 20 per cent of the total population in one state have had to rely for an unknown portion of their diet on the few commodities now distributed as surplus food.

There has been considerable emphasis recently on personal inadequacies as a major cause of the remaining poverty, and no doubt many of the families with the most difficult problems can be so identified. Lack of income itself may, however, be one of the most devastating causes of family stress and of inadequate functioning on the part of the individual. Increasingly, the need for assistance will probably be concentrated among families who have, or could have, some earnings but not enough for an acceptable minimum level of living. To provide needed support while encouraging the maximum independence possible for such families may call on all our skill and social inventiveness.

There is today a heavy concentration of poverty among minority groups. Here it is not welfare spending as such that is needed, but a lessening of discrimination in employment, in housing, in education, and in other areas of social life. Other pockets of poverty are found among groups—such as migratory agricultural workers, or families in chronically depressed areas—who have remained outside of the institutional changes that have raised the levels of living of the majority of the population. The long-run solution for them may be a combination of further technological change, special training and retraining programs, and special efforts to bring health and educational services particularly to the children in such families. Until the long-run measures can take hold, however, there remains an obligation to meet existing needs more adequately than they are being met in many parts of the country today.

## Social Services

I come at last to the area in which I know many of you have a special interest—family and social work services. The rapidity of social change and the pressures of urban living are intensifying a variety of social problems which have existed for a long time. The rise of juvenile delinquency in all countries of the world is a phenomenon the more disturbing because neither the causes nor solutions to the problem are fully understood. The increase in the number of illegitimate births, to cite another example, and particularly the increasing proportion of such births among teenagers, has intensified the need for services of several kinds.

At the same time the growing professional skills of the social worker are making possible new types of specialized services as well as more effective development of older types. Casework services to children in their own families, help with family conflicts, encouragement and help in finding and using community resources—these may be needed by only a small proportion of the population, but they can be of strategic value in

preventing breakdown and fostering independence. The field of rehabilitation also has taken on new dimensions with the development of medical and restorative techniques, increased understanding of mental illness,
and greater casework skills.

There is a growing demand, also, for community services of another
kind. Almost one-third of all mothers with children under age 18 in this
country are now working in paid employment. A recent nation-wide
survey conducted by the Bureau of the Census for the Children's Bureau
found nearly 400,000 children under 12 who had to care for themselves
while their mothers worked; over a million children were looked after by
nonrelatives. Like many other community services, organized and supervised day-care arrangements for children are needed by families of all income groups. They would be of greatest benefit to those women who
must work to support their children, many of whom have limited earning
capacity.

When families were large and neighbors closer to one another's problems, someone could usually be found to take over temporarily when a
mother was ill or to provide the special help needed to keep an older person out of an institution as long as possible. Much informal help of this
kind permeates our society today. But in the big city, and even in the big
suburb, homemaker services of this kind must be organized if they are to
be available to those families who need them most. There are only 143
agencies, most of them voluntary agencies, in the entire United States that
now provide such services. At the recently held National Conference on
Homemaker Services there was general agreement on the need for some
assumption of public responsibility in this field.

The public assistance program is providing an increasing volume of
casework and rehabilitative services for needy persons. We don't have a
measure of how much is so spent. Public expenditures for social services
other than those provided in connection with public assistance, and for
institutional care, and vocational rehabilitation are now taking perhaps
one-tenth of 1 per cent of our national output, about the same proportion
as in 1935. Our statistics here are somewhat weak, but the general picture
is clear. Institutional care has become relatively less important, provision
of services to persons in their own homes a larger part of the total. For
perspective let me point out that one-tenth of 1 per cent of our gross
national product is not a small sum of money. It is now approaching $500
million. In 1955 private agency expenditures for family and other welfare
services were a little more than three times as large as the corresponding
public expenditures excluding those under public assistance.

As all social workers are acutely aware, further expansion of many of
these services is being held back by the shortage of trained personnel.
Even with scholarship and other training aids, these shortages will take
time to overcome. An even more difficult problem may be that of finding

an organizational base that makes possible a rational relation of specialized services to one another and to the families served.

## Keeping Up with Change

If they are to fulfill their functions adequately, the institutions of social welfare must have a dynamism at least as great as that of the economy and society in which they operate.

I have referred to some of the social changes of the past which have molded our existing welfare services and programs. Changes that one can already see ahead—and others that we cannot foresee—will have a similar impact.

Our population is growing, and growing fastest in the younger and older age groups. By 1970, we shall probably have at least 37 million more persons in the total population. There will be 16 million more children under 18, an increase of 25 per cent, and over 4 million more persons aged 65 and over, an increase of 27 per cent. Those in the working ages will increase about 17 per cent. Even with automation and increasing productivity, we will probably see a still larger proportion of women working outside the home.

Thus we shall clearly need to spend more on all types of social welfare programs simply to maintain the same per capita level of spending as today. But with an increasing proportion of children and old persons, and with continuing geographical shifts in population and the need for new facilities and organization of services which such shifts involve, a higher per capita level of spending will very likely be necessary to maintain the same level of service.

There is another reason why we shall need to spend more dollars for the same level of service. Barring all-out nuclear war, we can safely assume that the growth in productivity which has characterized our economy in the past will continue and probably at an accelerated rate. The additional output per capita may be distributed in part through lower prices for some goods and services. It will probably be distributed in large part through higher earnings levels—with or without price inflation. Higher earnings levels would be reflected in the salaries of teachers, doctors, social workers, and all the other professional and nonprofessional groups engaged in the provision of social services.

A considerable part of the increase in total social insurance benefits and in assistance payments since 1940 has resulted from changes made to bring benefit levels and standards of need in line with rising prices. The adjustments have not always been made promptly; nevertheless we have recognized a general obligation to maintain the real value—in terms of purchasing power—of the long-term insurance benefits. Presumably we will continue to do so.

But if our national output continues to grow, the incomes of the working population will go up even though the price level remains stable. One of the important questions of social policy for the future is the extent to which the groups whose income is largely from social insurance or public assistance should share in rising levels of prosperity. To the extent we wish them to do so we must expect to make continuing changes in the level of insurance benefits and in the minimum level of need that is met through public assistance.

### Paying for Social Welfare

Obviously, if we are to spend more for social welfare, we will have to devise ways of financing those expenditures.

A part, but in all probability a very limited part, of the increased expenditures for community services such as day-care or homemaker services, or even certain case-work services, may come from direct payments by the consumer or client. Those most in need of such services will not be able to pay in full, however, and the question therefore becomes one of how much can be done through voluntary contributions and to what extent it will be necessary to draw on public funds if such services are to be developed.

One of the strengths of social insurance has proved to be the contributory basis of the system. Workers have been willing to put aside part of their earnings to purchase income security on the installment plan, if you will. Indeed, if a referendum were taken, the majority might prove more than willing to pay higher contributions to buy more protection.

If as a people we want more public services of other kinds, we must be willing to buy them through increased taxes at some level of government. Increased tax revenues need not necessarily mean increased tax rates, quite aside from any reforms that might be made in the tax structure. Tax yields from the personal income tax increase considerably faster than aggregate personal incomes when income is rising and decrease faster when it is falling. The yield of sales and corporate profit taxes changes at about the same rate as aggregate income.

Several years ago the Twentieth Century Fund published a detailed and elaborate study of *America's Needs and Resources*. The study not only traced the long-term growth in the national output, it also attempted to estimate unmet needs and the additional expansion in output necessary to meet them. There is not time to describe the assumptions used in estimating need—the study is 1,100 pages in length. In general the method was to establish for each category of consumption a minimum standard—the Department of Agriculture low-cost diet, for instance—and to estimate the expenditures necessary to bring everyone below that standard up to it, while leaving those above it with unchanged income and consumption.

In 1950, the study indicated, total personal consumption expenditures would have had to be about $12 billion or 6 per cent higher than they actually were to assure a minimum standard of living for everyone. An increase of only 1 per cent in total expenditures for food would have sufficed, but a 50 per cent increase in personal expenditures for medical care was called for. To meet specified criteria as to minimum expenditures per school child, number of hospital beds per capita, etc., it was estimated that government expenditures for all purposes other than national defense should have been $20 billion or 36 per cent higher than they actually were. Projecting to 1960, the Twentieth Century Fund survey saw needed expenditures as still exceeding probable expenditures by 4 per cent for personal consumption and by 20 per cent for nondefense government programs. A total output of goods and services only 7 per cent larger than the estimated national output for 1960 could cover these unmet needs. In 1950, a 17 per cent expansion in gross national product would have been necessary to bridge the gap.

The dollar figures—even the population figures—in this study are already out of date. A new study of needs and resources would present many differences in detail. It would almost surely, however, reinforce two major conclusions of this survey—one, the progressive closing of the gap between our actual production and the amount needed to provide a decent minimum living for everyone and much more than that for the great majority of the population; and second, the concentration of unmet needs in those services and programs that are provided from public funds and through the activities of government.

There have been several recent studies of the possible trend of events during the 1960's that suggest some of the alternatives for social welfare in the next decade. Such economic projections are one of the important new tools that economists have forged in recent years. By carrying forward past trends in relation to probable or desirable developments, they can give us some idea of the boundaries within which we can move.

Just a few weeks ago, the Committee for Economic Development—which, as you know, is a group of leading businessmen and scholars concerned with economic policy—released a study on *Trends in Public Expenditures in the Next Decade* prepared for the Committee by Professor Eckstein of Harvard. This study assumes that our total national output will continue to increase at the long-term average rate of 3 per cent a year. The medium estimate of probable government spending assumes no major change in present attitudes or generally accepted goals. Within this frame, however, it allows for a fairly substantial increase in expenditures for education and moderate increases for certain other functions.

On these assumptions total government expenditures would take about the same proportion of the gross national product in 1968 as they did in 1958. With no change in present tax rates, or in the present division of responsibilities between the federal and state and local governments, federal revenues would rise faster than expenditures, resulting in a balanced federal budget by 1961 and a federal surplus of over $11 billion by 1968. State and local revenues, on the other hand, would rise less rapidly than state and local expenditures both because of the increased spending for education that is assumed and because of the fact that state and local revenues are less responsive than federal revenues to changes in aggregate national income. As a result, all state and local governments combined would be running a deficit of about $3.4 billion by the mid-sixties, with the seriousness of the fiscal problem varying considerably—as it does today—from one area and region to another. The study points out that given these long-run pressures, several alternative developments could occur—state and local tax rates could be raised or new taxes imposed, functions could be transferred to the federal level, new grant-in-aid or tax-sharing devices might be developed, or state and local services could be allowed to deteriorate.

The Rockefeller Fund Report of last year on the *Economic and Social Aspects of the United States Economy* approached the problem from a somewhat different point of view. Its first concern was with what we should be spending to meet the needs of a dynamic society. It saw those needs as including at least moderate and for its "desirable" projections, considerable increases in public expenditures for social welfare programs. The report also projects a very substantial increase in defense expenditures, based on another Rockefeller Fund study. An attempt was then made to estimate how large an increase in national output would be necessary to support such expenditures.

The report concludes that if total output increased by 3 per cent a year, government (at all levels) would need to take a slightly larger proportion of the total than at present to cover even the projected low level increases in public programs. A 5 per cent annual rate of growth would be necessary to provide for the desirable level of government expenditures and allow for a slightly increased rate of growth in per capita consumption of food, clothing, and other consumer goods.

A 5 per cent rate of growth is well within the bounds of possibility. Projections to 1970 which have just been released by the National Planning Association use as the most probable figure an average rate of 4.2 per cent. Economists differ as to how high a rate of growth we can sustain without some price inflation—which every economist agrees is an evil, though many would say a lesser evil than stagnation and large-scale unemployment.

Whatever the future growth of our productive capacity, we shall not escape the problem of choice as to its use. The choices are of many kinds and will be made through many different channels. There are the overriding decisions which determine our relations with the rest of the world. There are the local decisions which determine the character of the communities in which we live. Many of the choices will be made around separate programs.

The development of social insurance has brought into the realm of public policy and political decision the question of the share of the current product which should go directly to the aged, the disabled, the unemployed or survivor families. The answers we give to this question will affect the amounts we spend for assistance and for other welfare services. Rising levels of living for most families give greater urgency to the problem of a minimum level of income support for everyone. The new degree of public interest in education which has developed in the last few years is already reflecting itself in a variety of actions in local communities, and at the state and federal level. The rising demand for medical care is also working in a number of different directions. In some respects the most difficult choices to implement are those which require new types of community organization and community planning. Some of the potential choices we might make will remain hidden until research and new knowledge bring them to light.

One of the most important tasks for those of us who are concerned with social welfare may be that of clarifying, for ourselves and for others, the values and the processes involved in the choice of social welfare goals.

# 56. MANAGEMENT'S STAKE IN THE SURVIVAL OF CONTRIBUTORY SOCIAL INSURANCE

J. Douglas Brown,
American Management
Association, 1949.

Accumulating experience indicates that the survival of democratic capitalism as a political and economic system will depend in the main upon the genius of man in combining the three ingredients vital to the success of the system. These ingredients are *individual incentive, mutual responsibility*, and an *effective framework of protection against the corroding fear of insecurity*. As democratic capitalism has moved from the stage of a predominantly agricultural economy, through small industry, to a vast industrialized complex, the relative weighting among these three needed ingredients has shifted. The farmer and the shopkeeper of Colonial days thrived because of individual incentive, and the simple economy thrived with them. The factory system introduced new and intricate relationships of mutual responsibility. And now vast aggregations of interdependent economic activities, by their very size and impact upon the individuals who serve them, necessitate greatly enhanced safeguards against impersonal and overwhelming contingencies.

The people of the United States have been slow to recognize the importance of this third ingredient vital to the survival of democratic capitalism. They have been blessed so richly with bountiful natural resources and with high talent in harnessing these resources that they have been but little concerned in safeguards against potential epidemics of want. The depression of the thirties brought a degree of awakening, and stimulated the establishment of the partial system of safeguards under the Social Security Act of 1935. But, since that time, war and industrial conflict have diverted attention from a fundamental cause of *both* of these interruptions to peaceful progress—economic insecurity.

Wars often arise out of the insecurity of the masses of the people—focussed through the machinations of ambitious leaders. Our drive for peace on the international front is an attack on insecurity abroad by arousing the incentive and responsibility of less fortunate people to improve their lot—and providing them with the tools of improving their way of life.

Industrial conflict in an industrial nation may be pitched at either of two levels. That which arises—

1. Out of the failure of peaceful collective bargaining to satisfy one of the parties that they are getting their precise fair or their possible share from the proceeds of production. Such strikes are disturbing, inconvenient, and costly but not dangerous to our way of life.

2. Out of the development of great emotional pressures where a group feels that it is forced into want—where it feels that it is being deprived of the opportunity for a decent living—that the system works against them and grinds them down. Such conflicts are bitter, rebellious, hate-forming, and dangerous to our way of life.

It is this second kind of industrial conflict that we must remove if democratic capitalism is to work.

It is the second kind that breeds communism on the one hand and its reaction—fascism—on the other. It develops when men think with their bellies instead of their heads.

It makes persistent enemies of people and classes of people, not vigorous competitors under sportsmanlike rules of the game. It is not American or British; it is the unfortunate lot of older, crowded peoples, suppressed for years by wars and dictators.

It is this second type of industrial conflict that a framework of basic security will prevent and, from an industrial relations point of view, is its chief job to prevent. Social security does many things, but for management—and labor—it keeps economic differences in the sphere of economics and the bargaining table—and away from the area of violence and mass hatred.

Is not social security worth the price of sustained interest and support by the managements of this country? Is it not a justifiable kind of fire insurance against the conflagration of bitterness of industrial conflict which would follow any period of widespread distress?

It seems high time for renewed and effective action in the core area of our problem in industrial relations today—How can we establish an effective framework against the fear of insecurity in order to sustain individual incentive and to assure mutual responsibility under democratic capitalism?

The most effective governmental mechanism yet invented to meet this challenge is *contributory social insurance*. Contributory social insurance prevents insecurity while preserving incentive. Protection is based on a man's contribution to the nation's productive effort. Mutual responsibility is encouraged by joint participation of government, employer, and worker in administering and financing the program.

Contributory social insurance avoids the sweet dangers of paternalism. It encourages self-reliance. It prevents dependency before it occurs rather than alleviating it *after* the fact. Relief and assistance are necessary last resorts, but like all paternalistic measures, they breed dependency by making it comfortable. Even more serious in a democracy, they encourage subservience to the group or agency that gives the most generous "handouts." Relief and assistance may seem in the short run more popular and easier to administer, but, unless controlled and replaced by contributory social insurance *as rapidly as possible,* they will lead us down the primrose path to state paternalism.

An effective system of social security must enhance incentive, wherever possible, rather than impair it. Even America cannot waste that drive which has raised its standard of living over the years. The individual citizen must be aided in preserving his effectiveness and self-reliance. This can be done through social insurance under which eligibility and benefits are related to past earnings and productivity, and to probable future wages as well.

There has been much talk of "security" *vs.* "incentive" among those who question further extension of our social security program. In social insurance this supposed conflict is resolved. Incentive for most people arises out of the quest for security and more security, once its satisfactions are tasted. Security may mean a single room or a six-room house. Men will work hard to get either. They are willing to contribute to a social insurance program to make sure that they do not lose either, should illness or unemployment occur. It is because of this recognition of incentive and self-reliance that social insurance appeals to a wide range of American people left cold by talk of relief. Despite all the talk, few wage-earners like to go on relief, far less rely upon it in advance.

The great question in modern America today is not whether there will be some form of social security to prevent widespread distress but what form it will take.

Management has a deep interest in the answer to this second question—

Will the social security system reinforce or dull the normal incentives to higher skills, higher earnings and productivity?

Will the social security system encourage men once laid off to seek new employment and to move if necessary to find it?

Will the social security system be a workable base upon which to build private old-age retirement programs, permanent and total disability benefits, sick benefits, and guarantees of employment?

Finally, what will the social security system do to the essential quality of the industrial manpower of this country?

After twenty-three years of study of employer programs for worker security in this country, I am convinced of one thing—that they work best when the employer and employee *both* contribute.

The American employer has no interest in relief schemes. They are the symbol of an old day of industrial paternalism. We know that the American employee does not want to depend upon the passing of the hat, nor a casual check from a benevolent fund.

The contributory social insurances in the United States grew out of employer experience. They extend to all the principles found effective by leading employers. They put a floor on competition by shortsighted employers who had avoided the true costs of an effective labor force.

It is the managements of this country that have the greatest stake in the survival of the contributory social insurances in the competition against a growing demand for paternalistic relief. What would a $200 or even a $100 Townsend type pension plan do to the incentives of the American wage earner? What would a new and greater siege of WPA do?

If contributory social insurance is to be the American way of assuring security and avoiding paternalism, it is time we made that determination clear. The assistance method is fast winning the race, both in the number of persons receiving payments, and in the level of protection afforded. Contributory social insurance has been revised neither in *scale* nor *scope* to meet the great economic changes of the past decade. Unless it is strengthened and enlarged *now*, it may become a Cinderella displaced by its more demanding stepsisters, assistance and relief. It is high time that contributory social insurance was made a truly effective protection to the American people, by making the level of benefits adequate, the scope of protection reasonable, and the area of participation every one who works for a living.

In specific terms, what is management's interest in social insurance to-day?

The first job is to help revamp the social insurance system affecting old-age, survivors, and unemployment insurance. Nothing constructive has been done for ten years. We are now driving a prewar model, despite dynamic changes in prices and employment.

The Social Security Agency has made recommendations. If you don't like their recommendations, study those proposed by the Advisory Council on Social Security to the Senate Finance Committee. The Council was appointed by a Republican chairman when the Republicans were in control—and expected to remain so. Its membership was heavily weighted by businessmen. Most of its recommendations were unanimous. A committee of the American Management Association after similar study would come out with similar findings.

The report of this Council is lost in the political bickerings in Washington. Neither management nor labor has put on pressure—real pressure—for action. Meanwhile, the slow and steady political drift is toward state paternalism, a hundred million here, a billion there. In a few more years contributory social insurance will be a "has been"—a lost ideal.

Management as a profession is deeply interested in the human resources of this country. Decade by decade it has gained a clearer notion of what sustains and enhances those resources. Better, perhaps, than any other group, it knows how to balance those three great factors in human motivation—*incentive, responsibility,* and *security.* Its advice and support is sorely needed today in assuring that the social security system of this country will prevent bitter industrial conflict, maintain incentive and responsibility, and enhance the human resources of our country.

# DISCUSSION QUESTIONS

1. "The incentives, enterprise and thrift of the American people are said to be in danger by the continued expansion of social insurance and welfare programs." Discuss the pros and cons.

2. "The mobility of the American wage earner has been an important factor in the efficient allocation of manpower resources." Social insurance coupled with private pension plans may affect this mobility adversely. Discuss the factors involved.

3. How much social security can we afford? What criteria should be employed in answering this question?

4. "Social security expenditures are not productive. They are said to represent a diversion of wealth from productive resources." Discuss.

5. Advocates of social security expect these programs to reduce economic fluctuations. Explain on the basis of past experience to what extent this is so.

6. "Is social security a road to serfdom?" Discuss.

7. Some see in social security a conservative force underpinning the private enterprise system; others see it as a process leading to socialism. Discuss.

# SELECTED REFERENCES

BURNS, EVALINE M. *The American Social Security System.* New York: Houghton Mifflin Co., 1949.

——— *Social Security and Public Policy.* New York: McGraw-Hill Book Co., 1956.

COHEN, WILBUR J. *Retirement Policies Under Social Security.* Berkeley: University of California Institute of Industrial Relations, 1957.

CORSON, JOHN J., and McCONNELL, JOHN W. *Economic Needs of Older People*. New York: The Twentieth Century Fund, 1956.

HARRIS, SEYMOUR E. *Economics of Social Security: The Relation of the American Program to Consumption, Savings, Output, and Finance*. New York: McGraw-Hill Book Co., 1941.

KEAN, ROBERT W. "Inflation and Retirement," in *Congressional Record* (July 21, 1959).

MERIAM, LEWIS, and SCHLOTTERBECK, KARL. *The Cost and Financing of Social Security*. Washington, D.C.: The Brookings Institution, 1950.

MERRIAM, IDA C. *Social Security Financing*. Social Security Administration, Division of Research and Statistics, Bureau Report No. 17, 1952.

———— "Social Security Programs and Economic Stability," in National Bureau of Economic Research, *Policies to Combat Depression*, pp. 205–35. Princeton, N.J.: Princeton University Press, 1956.

RUSSELL, J. E. (ed.). *National Policies for Education, Health and Social Services*. Garden City, N.Y.: Doubleday & Co., Inc., 1955.

# CHAPTER
# VIII

# Appraisal and
# Criticism

## INTRODUCTION

ALMOST ALL of the previous seven chapters have contained some selections appraising and criticizing the present social security program and suggesting revisions in existing programs or the establishment of new programs. Insofar as possible these selections were designed primarily to deal with particular programs. The selections in this final chapter are designed to deal with more general issues covering more than one program or suggesting some basic changes in present programs.

The selections in this chapter for appraisal and criticism of existing and proposed social security programs are obviously incomplete, since a presentation of a full selection of readings that would take up all points of criticism would involve an entire volume in itself. In addition, the readings selected tend toward those that are critical rather than those which stress the accomplishments and progress made under the existing laws and plans. By the very nature of social legislation there is always a need for improvement and adjustment to changing needs and circumstances.

In appraising existing and proposed private and public programs the following comment is worthy of attention:

It is sometimes alleged that a complete system of social security would ultimately have the effect of discouraging self-reliance and even fostering unemployment by destroying the incentives to industry, by removing the rough but salutary influence of discipline. . . . We must and do assume that the bulk of mankind who are able to work are willing to work, and that they will strive for something more than a doghouse subsistence on a dole. . . . it is not fear but hope that moves men to greater expenditures of effort, to ingenuity and emulation, to sharp struggle for the values they seek in life—hope set in a framework of justice, liberty, fair play, and a fair share of the gains of civilization.—Report to the National Resources Planning Board, 1943.

In the kind of society in which we live it can be expected that there will be strong diversity of opinion on specific program changes in social security. The complexity and magnitude of the issues involved, whether they are the coverage of migrant farm workers, the liberalization of disability insurance benefits, the lowering of the retirement age, the increase in the level of old-age, unemploymnt or workmen's compensation benefits, the increase in contribution rates, or provision for hospitalization or medical care protection, raise fundamental questions such as those relating to incentives, costs, standards of adequacy, the role of public and private agencies, and the relationship between federal and state governments.

It appears that Congress and the state legislatures may have an increasingly difficult task in attempting to reconcile the far-reaching economic, fiscal, social, and related issues involved in these questions. The conflicts seem likely to be intensified rather than minimized and, unfortunately, the general public seems less likely to understand the implications of the issues as they become more complex. For, as Senator Paul H. Douglas, a recognized authority on social security, has said, when there no longer is an attempt at the outright repeal of welfare measures, then those interested in improving the programs find themselves forced to engage in defensive actions on minor issues which do not stir people, as did the controversies over establishment of the basic program.

Another factor is the disappearance of the depression as an element in the formulation of policy regarding our social welfare programs. For a long period of time, the bitter memory of the 1929–33 depression in the minds of millions of people, and the fear of another depression in the minds of countless others, was an important factor affecting attitudes and pressures with respect to different social security proposals. But, today, many of the voters and many young people have no personal knowledge of the Great Depression of 1929–33. It is a part of what they have heard and read in their history books along with the Civil War and the laying of the first cable across the Atlantic Ocean. For many other families, the fear of unemployment during the postwar period has given way to sustained prosperity.

Rather than being justified by changes or improvement in social programs on the basis of a crusade against the threat of unemployment or depression, changes in the program are justified by a continued increase in productivity and wages and the ability of the country to finance improvements in social welfare out of a growing national income. With the increase in the level of employment and earnings and the growth of private health, welfare, pension, and supplementary unemployment plans—as well as private insurance, savings, and home ownership—proposals for expanding the scope of public programs have become more controversial and more complex.

# 57. THE ROLE OF INDIVIDUAL THRIFT, PRIVATE ENTERPRISE AND GOVERNMENT IN ECONOMIC SECURITY

THE AMERICAN ASSEMBLY,
*Economic Security for
Americans: An Appraisal of
the Progress during the
Last 50 Years,* Columbia
University, 1954.

AT THE START of our discussions we agreed that a striving for security is part of the temper of our time. As our discussions proceeded, there was a meeting of minds on the point of view from which the whole problem of security should be approached.

First, the problems of security are not exclusively economic. We must give serious consideration to social, political, psychological, moral, and spiritual values and their bearing on our economic security. Of all these values, those that are spiritual are of major importance in terms of our security today, just as they were in 1620 and 1776.

Second, the stability of our economy and our ability to move forward rest on an increasing awareness of our dependence as human beings upon each other. This focuses attention upon the importance of the individual in our economy. What he does as he attempts to make the most of himself affects the way of life of fellow citizens he will never see. Thus, the individual should do everything within his power, through careful planning and thrift, to provide for the future and protect himself and his family against the accidents of life.

Third, the circumstances of misfortune can develop beyond the power of the individual to prevent them or cope with them. Many such can be anticipated and dealt with satisfactorily by private enterprise. There is a kind of misfortune, however, with which the individual cannot cope and which cannot properly be met by any single private enterprise effort. In this area widespread misfortune becomes a social problem—a problem which can be met only when all of our citizens join in contributive effort to provide remedies which use government as our instrument.

## General Findings

1. We Americans are far more conscious of economic security needs than we were 50, or even 25, years ago. This keener awareness of security problems is the result both of changed economic conditions and of changed social and political attitudes. Major factors contributing to the dimensions of our security problem are the great movement of American population from the land to employment in the cities, the remarkable increase in the American life span with its attendant underlining of the

problem of retirement security, and the increasing complexity of our industrial and economic system. We are, in a real sense, more interdependent than at any time in our history, and our present awareness of economic security needs is, essentially, a recognition of that interdependence.

2. The problems of economic security must be approached broadly, and not in any narrowly technical spirit. Our American security pattern must be appraised in terms that take full account of the human values involved and of the broad economic, social, and political implications of decisions in the security field. It is not enough to judge an economic security development according to its effects on the efficiency of the social security system itself. The criteria which must be brought to bear in examining any specific economic security proposal include for example: What will be the effect of this change on the productivity of our economy? On government spending and taxation? On individual opportunity, incentive, and freedom? On the integrity of the American family? On human personality, viewed not as an economic unit but as a whole being?

3. We believe that there is no inescapable conflict between security, on the one hand, and individual initiative and freedom, on the other. Our free economy is strong enough, even in a time when heavy defense expenditures are necessary for national survival, to carry the weight of a reasonable and soundly developed economic security system. We believe that we are a stronger people—not a "softer" people—because of the economic security developments of the past half century. We see no reason for fear that the attainment of a reasonable standard of protection against the security exigencies will threaten any of the traditional American virtues—the will to work, the will to save, the disposition to deal generously with a needy neighbor. A security program, wisely conceived and fairly administered, can, indeed, provide the necessary economic foundation for high national morale and for the development of the best of moral and spiritual values.

4. Our discussions have convinced us that the economic security problem must be approached with three big questions in mind: (1) What is the role of individual thrift in economic security? (2) What is the role of private enterprise? and (3) What is the role of government? All three of these elements—individual, private enterprise, and governmental—are present in our unique American economic security pattern, and we would preserve them all. We believe that an economic security system is best for the individual, and best for the nation, when it is built on the three supports of individual thrift, private security plans, and government action. In our Assembly discussions, and in this report, we have taken account of all three of these supports.

### The Role of Individual Thrift in Economic Security

1. Individual thrift is and should continue to be a major element in the American pattern of economic security. Private savings are an essential,

integral part of the solution to the individual's economic and social security, and the individual should be encouraged to provide all that he can for his family and himself. The achievement of a high standard of personal savings is essential to the dynamic operation of our economic system and can provide a significant safeguard against economic dislocations. The encouragement of individual savings should be kept in mind at every phase of legislative policy making, including tax policy.

2. We are satisfied, from the evidence before us, that the existence of government social security programs has not weakened the will to save in most American families. A majority of the participants believe that the social security system has, in fact, made the typical American more aware of security exigencies and thus more desirous of putting something by for his own security.

3. While, at present levels of employment and income, many American families have the ability to make appreciable savings towards their own economic security, most families cannot save enough, by their own devices alone, to provide adequate protection against the several security exigencies and, in addition, maintain a good standard of living. We are further aware that a disturbingly large number of families have incomes so low as to deprive them of economic security. These families are seriously disadvantaged. Continued effort must be exerted to increase the productive skills of these families, to provide more opportunities for the full utilization of those skills and, in the meantime, to aid them in meeting needs that they cannot meet themselves.

4. In speaking of individual "savings" we mean all the forms in which the American people put their accumulated savings: bank deposits, government bonds, life insurance, home ownership, corporate securities, and other net savings forms.

## The Role of Private Enterprise in Economic Security

1. The vigorous functioning of our incentive system is the most valuable form of security for most Americans. Strides have been made toward stability of employment in many segments of our economy. Further progress toward stability of employment is one of the greatest contributions that private enterprise can make to economic security.

2. Private pension plans have become a very important element in retirement security. Existing plans cover more than twelve million employees. With an institution of this magnitude, it is essential that private pension planning be sound and far-seeing and wisely integrated with government social security. It is the majority view of the participants that we are better off with a pension pattern partly private and partly governmental than we would be if all retirement resources were public in origin and administration.

3. Private enterprise is now providing, for many employed persons, medical care (through plant and industrial clinics and hospitals, and

through plans for medical, surgical, and hospital benefits and cash sickness benefits) as well as supplementation of social insurance programs. Private pension plans provide a great body of experience which should be drawn on in considering these other possible undertakings of private industry in the economic security field.

4. We believe that it is sound policy to continue tax incentives encouraging employers to establish, or agree to, private pension plans. Within reasonable limits, this tax exemption should be extended to the employee's contribution to a pension plan. In addition, many participants feel that close study should be given to the possibility of extending this tax exemption principle, within reasonable limits, to individual retirement programs.

5. In our discussions we have given considerable attention to the problem of vesting of employee benefits under a private pension plan. As a general matter, union leadership tends to think of private pensions as a form of deferred compensation, while management tends to consider a private pension plan as a means of retiring over-aged employees and providing an incentive to younger employees to stay with the company. We are confident that a sound and reasonable adjustment of these views is possible and that these differences can be reconciled in a manner that will not unduly hinder the free mobility of labor or lose to the company the advantage it seeks to achieve by a plan.

6. We believe that in private pension planning the maximum practicable flexibility should be exercised in determining the age at which a worker must retire. A majority of the participants believe that the elimination of all workers from productive employment merely because they have reached a certain age, without regard to their physical and mental condition and their own wishes, is economically wasteful and socially harmful.

## The Role of Government in Economic Security

1. There is an essential governmental role in any program to achieve economic security. We subscribe to Lincoln's statement that government should "do for the people what needs to be done, but which they cannot, by individual effort, do at all or do so well."

2. It is an important concern of government to provide, in every way possible, a favorable climate for economic security. Government should protect the purchasing power of the dollar to prevent erosion of savings and should pursue policies to stimulate economic activity at a stable level and to maintain economic growth.

3. In addition to income-maintenance systems like OASI and unemployment insurance, many government activities have impact on economic security. There are many programs in which government initiates action, or offers incentives, to improve economic security—to cite two of many that might be chosen, the income tax deduction for medical expenses and federal deposit insurance.

4. Unless the essential principles of our social insurance system

are widely understood by the American people, the system will be vulnerable to political pressures for unsound changes in the social security structure. To safeguard against this, every effort should be made to carry on an effective and continuing program of public education in this field.

5. A system, such as public assistance, based on a test of need, is the least desirable of governmental security systems. While we recognize the place of public assistance as a final source of economic protection, we believe that efforts should be directed to minimizing the necessity for recourse to a needs test.

6. It is agreed, with respect to government income-security programs, that a contributory program, in which benefits bear some defined relation to aggregate contributions, best meets the major problems of economic security with minimum violence to the essential criteria of a sound system as listed earlier in this report. In principle, we believe that such programs are better handled by wage-related financing than by drawing on general tax revenues.

7. The unemployment compensation system should be reviewed and modernized in the light of changed conditions since its inception.

8. At our sessions, there was considerable discussion of the need to review workmen's compensation programs and to correct such inadequacies of benefits or coverage as may be found.

9. Many of the participants believe that there is need for some form of temporary nonoccupational disability insurance. Limitations of discussion time prevented any agreement as to the best method of accomplishing this objective.

10. In the formulation of economic security programs attention should be paid to the fact that the assignment of responsibility for social insurances to different governmental units often leads to unwarranted losses of benefits, or to unwarranted gains in benefits; and there should be an attempt at coordination.

11. A number of participants believe that the OASI program should provide benefits for those who, before they reach retirement age, are forced out of the labor market by permanent and total disability from nonoccupational causes, and that OASI credits of the permanently and totally disabled should be maintained to retirement age. Other participants express doubts as to this proposal, particularly with respect to costs and administrative difficulties.

12. Time and time again, the importance of constructive rehabilitation efforts was emphasized in round-table discussions. It is not enough to provide money benefits for the disabled; whenever possible, the disabled person should be given necessary training and an opportunity to resume his place in productive employment. The problem of rehabilitation deserves the best thought of government and private enterprise.

13. This report makes no specific findings or recommendations with respect to medical care. In our discussions we frequently came up against

this problem, particularly in relation to medical care for the chronically ill and for our constantly increasing number of aged persons. Because of the complexity of the subject, an adequate analysis of its ramifications would require far more time than was available to us. We are keenly aware of the gravity of the medical care problem and of the need for realistic study and timely action in this security area.

14. We have considered at length the retirement test of the present OASI system. We approve of a retirement test in principle, but we believe that it should be adjusted, as far as practicable, so as to reduce any possible deterrent effect it may have on those seeking employment after retirement age. Several participants have suggested the substitution, for the present all-or-nothing provision, of a sliding scale whereby a worker's benefits would be reduced only by a fraction of the amount by which his earnings exceed a specified sum. Other participants make the point that, in any future adjustment of the retirement test, care should be taken to make sure that the employment of persons past retirement age does not operate to depress general wage levels.

15. It is the opinion of a majority of the participants that early universal coverage of all employed and self-employed persons, including the professional groups, is in the public interest. Among the advantages of universal coverage will be the prevention of any further increase in the transitional group of elderly persons not now within OASI coverage.

16. The problem of aged persons not now covered by OASI is a serious one. The presence of a number of aged persons who are now provided for only by the admittedly unsatisfactory needs-test system constitutes a continuing threat to the stability and integrity of OASI. This problem is, we believe, a transitional problem and should be recognized as such. No satisfactory plan to solve it has yet been proposed. We must redouble our efforts to see if a sound solution cannot be found.

# 58. PROBLEMS FOR THE FUTURE

First National City Bank,
*Monthly Letter,*
New York: May, 1958.

The rapid expansion that has taken place in Social Security benefit payments and tax costs poses a number of problems for the future.

Consider the area of retirement provisions—a vital matter for a country faced with an aging population and, at the same time, with the prospect of manpower shortages in the years ahead.

Today there are some 15,000,000 people aged 65 or over, about 8½ per cent of the population. By 1975, population experts expect the number of "senior citizens" will have grown to more than 21,000,000, nearly 10 per cent of the total.

It would seem only reasonable that national programs and policies should encourage the productive efforts of this growing segment of our population. Instead, Social Security retirement rules tend to discourage such efforts.

An example of this is the action taken in 1956, as mentioned earlier, to permit women to retire three years earlier than men at age 62.

Another example can be found in the so-called earnings test for retirement under the program. Under this test, Social Security payments are reduced roughly dollar for dollar for amounts earned above $1,200 a year by beneficiaries under age 72. After 72 there is no reduction. By boosting the amount that can be earned each year without a reduction in benefits, older workers would be encouraged to continue using valuable skills learned over a lifetime.

### Taxes and Inflation

There is also the matter of the direct role the Social Security program would play in generating inflationary forces if it is repeatedly liberalized and financed by constantly rising taxes.

When the program first started, the employer paid a tax of 1 per cent on the first $3,000 of wages and salaries of each of his workers. Now that tax —as much a cost of doing business as anything else—has gone up to 2¼ per cent on earnings up to $4,200 for each of his employes. By 1975, even assuming the present tax rate schedule is not increased, the business man will face a payroll tax of 4¼ per cent.

As this tax burden rises, pushing up operating costs, the natural inclination of the business man is to protect profit margins by raising prices. Moreover, the heavier tax bite reduces take-home pay and workers want larger pay raises. As we stand already, it costs an employer $90 a week or more in wages and employment taxes to get $70 a week into the take-home pay envelope of an employe.

As prices go up, Social Security checks don't go as far, and pressure is put on the Congress to boost monthly benefits to keep up with the cost of living. Taxes are then raised to pay for increased benefits and the spiral takes another upward whirl.

### Security and Self-Reliance

Finally, there is the basic question: How much further can we liberalize the Social Security program without endangering our productive system?

The humanitarian goals we set for ourselves cannot be achieved without a strong, productive economy. This, in turn, requires the initiative and inventive genius, risk-taking investment, and hard work of a self-reliant people.

If payments are pushed ever higher, and if coverage is expanded to take in all kinds of financial and physical misfortune, there is a danger that the sense of individual responsibility and self-reliance will atrophy.

It needs to be remembered that OASI and other government pensions account for only part of government social welfare outlays. In addition, there are such major programs as unemployment compensation and public assistance. Payments under the latter, which were supposed to "wither away" with the advent of the Social Security program, amounted to $2.9 billion last year—nearly double the amount paid out in 1947.

Last year total social welfare outlays, so-called transfer payments, topped $21 billion, up more than 70 per cent since 1949 and equal to nearly 9 per cent of the pay people earn—before deductions—in wages and salaries for working.

### A Foundation Not a Substitute

The Social Security program, as originally conceived, was supposed to provide protection against economic insecurity for the worker and his family when retirement or death cut off his earnings.

Thus, a "floor of protection" against want was placed under those who because of age could no longer support themselves. The program has unquestionably played an important role in helping to "prevent destitution in our national life," as President Eisenhower has put it.

No one begrudges a retired couple their tax-contributed income security. Indeed, this protection against want should be as broadly based as possible.

But it is quite another matter to expand the system so that it becomes a substitute for private savings, pension plans, and insurance rather than a foundation on which these other forms of protection can be soundly built. To do so would be to discourage individual work effort, planning, and thrift to the detriment of personal freedom and national economic progress.

# 59. DOES OUR SOCIAL SECURITY SYSTEM MAKE SENSE?

DILLARD STOKES,
*Commentary,*
June, 1954.

### INSURANCE, RELIEF, OR WHAT?

THE TRUE NATURE of Social Security in our country is almost unknown to the taxpayers who maintain and rely on it. After twenty years, "Social Security" is in the language, but these words connote its purpose and assumed benefits rather than the vast politico-economic complex depended upon to realize them. The aims of Social Security are admirable. Most of the results evident *to date* are good. So, by association, these virtues are imputed to the system itself.

Both Democrats and Republicans extol this sacred cow for the milk it gives, but they do not audit its feed bill or mention the possibility of its going dry. Politicians in both parties trade on colossal outlays for today and munificent promises for tomorrow. Can the promises possibly be honored? What will they really cost? And who, really, is going to pay for them in the long run? These very relevant political considerations languish for want of attention. But they do not die; they only bide their time.

The sole changes seriously being proposed today in Social Security are for the extension of its "coverage" to more people—usually in blocks of several millions—and for the raising of payments to all beneficiaries, either forthrightly or by easing the curbs now in force. That is the substance of the Eisenhower program now before Congress. It was the substance of the program recommended by Presidents Truman and Roosevelt. These programs open the tap a little more—but the situation actually requires a thorough examination of the design and efficiency of the whole system of waterworks.

What faces us here is a lapse of the political process. Since the founding of the Republic, policy on great matters has been *hammered out through conflicts of interest.* Hard-money pressure opposed soft-credit pressure. High-tariff pressure opposed cheap-goods pressure. Each faction was a check on every other; its own interest acted as a test of the policy that prevailed, or of the compromise that was reached by balancing the pressures (the latter being the most frequent solution). This process does not function when only one side of an issue finds partisans and attracts general support, as is the case with Social Security today. The only issues taken to the people are which party, and which candidate, can promise most to most people most plausibly.

This is not because politicians are rascals but because they are politicians. It is their normal and proper response to much pressure on one side, and little or none on the other. Here on one side is the interest of six million beneficiaries, and of sixty-six million others who hope to join them. This interest is taken up by the liberal wings of both political parties, prodded by powerful lobbies like those of the AFL, the CIO, the ADA, social workers, fraternal groups, and others. These greatly outnumber and outlobby the normally conservative professional, industrial, and financial interests, many of whom are restrained in their opposition by their hope of finding in Social Security a solution of employer-pension and disability problems.

Hence there was no steam behind the recent proposal of the Chamber of Commerce of the United States to change over to a pay-as-you-go, universal coverage pension plan. It was lost amid the attacks upon and defenses of the Social Security idea on an ideological level. There was little discussion of the merits and faults, as such, of the proposed change.

It is the burden of this article that the unanimity is very superficial and that Social Security presents real issues on which neither present nor prospective beneficiaries would be all of one mind did they know the facts. Until these are clear the political process cannot function.

A realistic survey of OASI—the Federal Old Age and Survivors' Insurance plan, the programs called Social Security—must reckon with three propositions. First: the sheer size of OASI, which is the biggest permanent enterprise this government ever has undertaken, or is ever likely to undertake. Second: the public illusions about Social Security, which are clustered in such a semblance of order as to form a complete yet largely mythical system. Third: the bankruptcy of design and policy, both social and financial, that handicaps the actual system, whose function, method, and economic nature have not been clarified. The myth about Social Security veils shortcomings, but they are there, and they must be remedied before Social Security can do its job and merit its reputation.

The factor of size might be taken for granted, but it would be better to put it into perspective first. Since its establishment in 1935, Social Security has collected taxes from 106,800,000 persons. What other enterprise, public or private, ever attracted or compelled the participation of so many Americans? Not the armed forces: there are only about 20 million veterans. Not the income tax: fewer than 60 million returns are made a year. Not even making a living: the 1954 labor force amounts to somewhere around 62½ millions.

Out of a population of 161 million, about 6 million people get OASI benefits, one for each 10½ workers. Here are the OASI high- and low-cost forecasts for the year 2000, just 46 years away:

|  | Low Cost | High Cost |
| --- | --- | --- |
| U.S. population* | 248 | 216 |
| Working force* | 96 | 84 |
| OASI beneficiaries* | 21 | 25.8 |
| As per cent of population | 8½% | 12% |
| OASI reserve fund* | $128,000 | Exhausted |
| Annual OASI cost* | $16,421 | $16,437 |
| Per productive worker | $171 | $195 |
| Productive workers per each OASI beneficiary | 4.54 | 3.25 |

\* (In millions)

Besides old-age pensions to be paid in the future, OASI promises workers in covered jobs protection in the nature of life insurance. After only 15 years of operation, this insurance amounts to nearly $300 billion. All life insurance of all kinds written by all the private insurance companies in the United States adds up to only $276 billion.

Private insurance is backed up by assets—mostly reserves required by law—of about $76 billion. Social Security insurance is backed by a "reserve fund" now hovering around $20 billion. After 46 years this fund will *either* have grown to $128 billion, *or* to a lesser total—*or* else it will have all been spent by 1997. The 1953 report of the Social Security trustees envisioned all three possibilities, there being no way to tell which will come to pass. As far as the expert can see, any one of the three is likely as any other.

One does not have to be an expert to see that colossal sums of money are involved. Next to these items of $300 billion and $128 billion, let us place others drawn from the American economy. The national debt is less than $275 billion. The total assets of all American corporations are $181 billion. The total of all bank deposits is $189 billion.

An enterprise as big as Social Security, which is going to get still bigger, is sure to be a dominant factor henceforth in the American economy, as dominant as steel output, foreign trade, consumer credit, and the value of the whole wheat crop all put together.

Most American families are insured by Social Security against the death or retirement in old age of their breadwinners. Workers pay premiums on this insurance through taxes withheld from their wages, and the employers pay equal taxes for their workers' benefit. Workers in covered employment thereby acquire the right to a monthly income for themselves and their families when they retire at sixty-five, or a monthly income for their wives, children, aged parents, etc., in case of death before retirement. The payments vary with the worker's earnings, and thus with the premiums paid. These OASI benefits do not depend on a "means test," as relief does, for they are not charity or relief. The workers pay substantially for what they will get, and they, or their survivors, will get substantially what they pay for. The benefits are paid out of a reserve fund built up for the purpose from premiums paid by prospective beneficiaries. Premiums now being paid by tens of millions of workers are building up the reserve fund to pay their benefits when they become entitled to them.

A familiar picture, is it not? Consider it well: it corresponds to the notion of Social Security held by a hundred million Americans. They take it for granted, they take it for fact—and they are dead wrong. *For every statement in the foregoing paragraph is demonstrably false.*

As a matter of fact, Social Security does not provide "insurance." The "contributions" are not "premiums," they are just taxes. The workers acquire no "rights," nor do their survivors. Payments to retired workers, or to surviving families—if and when paid—have little relation to the worker's earnings or to what he paid in to OASI. There is a "means test" for many, and there is an "earnings" test for everyone. Most of the money now being paid out by Social Security is relief: the people getting it did not pay for it, and millions do not get what they did pay for. The benefits do *not* come out of any "reserve fund." The trust account maintained under that name is neither a fund nor a reserve.

*Insurance* is a word known to nearly everybody. And so is the substance of Webster's definition, that it is "a contract whereby, for a stipulated consideration, called a premium, one party undertakes to indemnify or guarantee another against loss by a certain specified contingency or peril, called a risk, the contract being set forth in a document called a policy" (*New International Dictionary*, second edition).

The Social Security program is referred to in the law as "Old Age and Survivors' Insurance." Its revenue comes from taxes imposed by the "Federal Insurance Contributions Act." The government has published over 60 million booklets, leaflets, press releases, and other "educational material," all chock-full of words like *insurance, premium, policy*, etc.[1] This nomenclature has been taken up by the newspapers, magazines, and public speakers.

For this reason, the American people cannot be blamed for supposing they are buying insurance with the taxes they pay OASI, and that the other party—the government—"undertakes to indemnify or guarantee" them against loss of income due to old age and death, according to the published tables and formulas. Hardly can it be called quibbling over words to point out here that the taxes are not *buying* them insurance or anything else. For under Social Security the company—that is, the government—is bound to no obligations whatever. It can raise the premiums or the benefits, or reduce them, or cut them out, or change the conditions upon which benefits are paid, or do anything else it likes, and the policy-holder—that is, the taxpayer, the worker—has no remedy. The courts say that what he pays in is an income tax, and if he gets anything back it is a gratuity.

There are sinister stories about the fine print in insurance policies, but surely no private company was ever able to *change* the fine print at will, or to default on the policy and keep the premiums.

Many will say that such a default would violate the moral if not the legal rights of the victims, and surely Congress never would do anything so shocking. Ah, but Congress has done so!

The Social Security Act of 1935 provided that a worker would get back not less than what he put into the system. The act provided lump-sum refunds to those who reached sixty-five without qualifying for pensions, to the estates of those who died before reaching sixty-five, and to the estates of those who began drawing pensions but died before receiving an amount equal to the value of their contributions. Under this law, refunds were made to 178,583 workers and 318,665 estates. The same "right" to get back their money belonged to the other 33 million people who paid Social Security taxes during this period but did not die or retire. Whether their "rights" were moral, legal, or both, Congress wiped them out by the act of 1939. As a result, up to the end of 1952, a total of 6,400,000 persons

---

[1] Here is a sample statement, from a booklet put out in 1952 (2 million copies printed): "Your account number on your social security card identifies your old age and survivors' *insurance account*. Your card is the symbol of your *insurance policy* under the Federal Social Security law" (italics mine).

died without receiving pensions, lump-sum payments, refunds, or anything else. Yet they, and their employers, had paid in $725 million.

The act of 1935 assured the original 33 million OASI taxpayers "permanent" coverage by 1941. Most of these taxpayers had but two years to go when Congress passed the 1939 amendments and moved the date forward to the end of 1946.

During the 1940's the courts declared Social Security "rights" to belong to upwards of a million persons over whom there was dispute by reason of the nature of their employment. Regulations to cover them were drafted, but never took effect because in 1948 Congress took the "rights" away.

Having bought, paid for, and qualified for their Social Security incomes —as they were led to think—many persons retired to live on them and on what they could earn through non-covered work. These persons opened little shops, set up as repair men, part-time bookkeepers, dressmakers, or the like. In fine, these old people made plans for their old age on the basis of Social Security and its assurances. What they did was perfectly legal—until 1950, when Congress extended OASI coverage to the self-employed, and put a limit on their earnings. As a result, many were stripped of their OASI incomes—23,208 individuals suffered these cuts by the end of 1951. In some cases they were called on to pay back substantial sums. And to rub salt in the wound, these people were required by law to pay OASI taxes on their earnings so they would have Social Security in their "old age."

These are instances of "rights" taken away by specific act. However, OASI "rights" can vanish simply by the passage of time. There are 25 million persons who paid some taxes to OASI between 1937 and 1951, but at the end of the latter year were "uninsured." Some never paid over a period long enough to acquire protection. Many others were insured at some time but lost that status, as well as what they paid in. Another 41 million persons are "currently" insured, but may lose that status and find themselves, like the first 25 million, deprived of their right to benefits if they are out of a job too long, or work too long at jobs not under Social Security. There are 25 million who now have "permanent" insurance. They keep their "rights" regardless of where or whether they work (unless Congress takes them away). These "permanently" insured persons, however, are liable to a diminution of their benefits if they stop paying OASI taxes: the longer they have no covered earnings the less the average monthly wage credited to them.

On this average is based the retired worker's primary benefit. His monthly payment is 55 per cent of the first $100 of the average, plus 15 per cent of the next $200. Secondary benefits are fractions of the primary. The spouse and children of a retired worker each may get a monthly payment of half the primary. The surviving spouse and parents of a deceased worker may each get a monthly payment of three-fourths of the primary.

Each surviving child may get between a half and three-fourths. The maximum payable on any worker's account is 80 per cent of his average monthly wage, but not more than $168.75.

What is the relationship of these benefits to what was paid in? This year a $100-a-month worker pays $4 a month—$2 himself, $2 through his employer—for a monthly primary benefit of $55. A $300-a-month worker pays $12 a month for a benefit of $85. That is 200 per cent more "premium" for only 55 per cent more "insurance." A self-employed person, for the same "insurance," pays 25 per cent less premium than one who works for somebody else. This isn't all: about 10 per cent of the 6 million persons newly covered by the 1950 amendments were able to "buy," by paying "premiums" for six quarters, the same coverage others had paid premiums on for 14 years.[2]

Whether Social Security is administering a relief program is a matter of fact, not of words.[3] As distinguished from bought and paid-for benefits widely supposed to come from Social Security, *relief* is aid given by a public agency to needy persons who have not paid for it. Payments based on a substantial consideration are not relief just because somebody calls them that. A gratuity is no less relief because it is called something else, or because of a token consideration that, in fact, does not pay for it.

A Social Security report shows $15 billion in annuities will be paid present old-age beneficiaries, their spouses and children. The actual cost of these annuities is not less than $9 or $10 billion, yet these beneficiaries paid only $711,480,000 for them. (We disregard the "insurance" protection enjoyed by the primary beneficiaries for periods up to 13 years, the value of which was several times the $711 million they paid in; here we treat the sum of $711 million as though it were paid for the annuities alone.) These people, then, are going to draw over $14 billion more than they paid in. These $14 billion were clearly *not* paid for: what does this sum go for then, if not old-age relief? The point is not made to blame the old people's getting the aid. Many of them need it, and a wise economy will give it to them. But these considerations do not justify pretending the $14 billion came out of a "reserve fund" built up by the beneficiaries. Nor do they justify camouflaging the fact that the money really comes out of "premiums" currently being paid in by workers who are led to believe that *their* money is being saved up for *their* benefit.

Granted that this $14 billion ought to be paid out and that, like all wise

---

[2] An OASI booklet in 1951 gave the example of a $20-a-week housekeeper who can get $41 a month for life when she has paid OASI taxes for three years. (For $93.60, she gets an annuity worth about $4000.)

[3] The reference, of course, is to OASI alone, not to Old Age Assistance, Aid to Dependent Children, Aid to the Needy Blind, or Aid to the Permanently and Totally Disabled. These federal programs, though handled by Social Security, are set up by Congress as relief, and paid for as such out of separate funds appropriated out of the general funds of the Treasury. In the year ending June 30, 1954, they cost the federal treasury $1,340,000,000, or about $2 per month per taxpayer.

relief, it promotes the general welfare. Under our theory of government, funds for this purpose ought to come—and otherwise do come—out of the general funds raised by taxes levied according to ability to pay. The fiction that these OASI payments are something other than relief conceals what is going on. *That is, this charge for the general welfare is being exacted from one class of taxpayers, the wage earners.* And the whole burden falls on the poorest of these, for OASI taxes only the first $3600 of annual earnings.

Public relief and private charity have long been denied to those having other means of subsistence, but Social Security is generally believed to eliminate this supposedly humiliating condition. As an OASI booklet puts it: "This is an *insurance* program. [Participants] may qualify for benefits without regard to their financial resources, such as savings, property, or other insurance" (italics theirs). Quite so. A millionaire can draw the same OASI income for himself and his family that a janitor can. Neither must pass a "means test." But if the janitor's "means" include $76 a month paid him for mowing lawns, he will lose his Social Security payments for that month. So will his wife and children. The payments to 340,508 persons were cut off, under this regulation, at the end of 1952.

Also, widowers, surviving parents, and, in some cases, children, must prove "actual dependency" on the primary beneficiary. In view of all this, the assertion that Social Security does not now use a "means test" rests on some pretty refined hairsplitting.

There is on the books of the Treasury an OASI trust account of nearly $20 billion which will increase by more than $2 billion this year. The account is part of the public debt, and draws interest at about 2¼ per cent. How then can one say there is no Social Security "reserve fund"?

Suppose there were no account, and from year to year OASI paid its costs out of appropriations voted for the purpose. If a year came when outgo was more than the appropriation, what could be done? There are four answers: (1) a portion of the Social Security benefits for that year would not be paid; (2) the government would borrow the necessary funds and make them available to Social Security; (3) Congress would raise taxes to get the money; or (4) the funds would be diverted from some other use by cutting the budget of some other agency.

The same four courses—and no others—would be open to meet an OASI deficit under the "reserve fund" as it is now constituted.

There is no money in this "reserve fund" either as cash, or as a credit like a bank deposit on which checks could be drawn. There are vast evidences of federal debt, but these are not "bonds" in a familiar or negotiable form. This is not to say that the "reserve" is worthless—it is as good as the credit of the United States—but it does not exist as a "fund" ready and available when needed. When OASI calls on it the Treasury must find the money, if it is able and Congress is willing. To make good on the "reserve fund" would require the same operations as to meet a deficit. As an economic fact there is no "reserve fund" (as the term has been used and understood up to now).

Private insurance companies have put many billions of their reserves (but seldom over 20 per cent of the total) into government bonds. But they are not on the same footing as OASI, which invests in nothing else. First, the reason for drawing on the reserves. Private companies get most of their revenue from premiums. A sharp drop in these would reduce their liabilities. But a drop in OASI revenue would mean no such relief from liability. On the contrary, the same factors that caused the loss probably would bring more claims for benefits. When OASI runs into a deficit it probably will not be due to revenue loss at all, but to increased demands. Second, if the private companies meet their needs wholly out of their government bonds, whether these were sold, pledged, or cashed in, there would be no resultant rise in government paper held by the public, or in taxes, and no reduction of federal spending. One or more of these would be sure to follow an OASI deficit, with considerable impact on the nation's whole economy.

The foregoing passages have touched on some but by no means all of the popular illusions about Social Security. Most of these probably grew out of confused policy and lack of basic principles. Both these confusions and lacks are in the Social Security Act itself. The blame belongs to Congress, not the administrators. They err in emphasizing insurance, premiums, "rights," and so forth, but even here they can plead that the terms came from Congress and they just make the most of them.

The conditions of eligibility common to all Social Security benefits are (1) filing application; (2) adequate covered employment of the "primary" worker; (3) absence of other OASI benefits of equal or greater value; and (4) that the beneficiary not earn over $75 a month in covered employment. The first requirement calls for no comment, except that it is hard to see why it was written into the very law. The second is certainly natural and reasonable: it goes to the foundation of eligibility. The third belongs in a relief or charity program: what is it doing, therefore, in an "insurance" system? (If one is able to claim two or more benefits it can only be because he, or somebody else, bought and paid for them. So why should he not have them? The answer is that OASI simply is not an "insurance" system except in name.) The fourth condition is the daily instrument of many discriminations.

Besides these there are a host of conditions which vary from one class of beneficiaries to another and out of which it is impossible to make any logical pattern. Some are so whimsical and arbitrary that whether a person gets, or keeps, "current payment status" might as well depend on drawing numbers out of a hat. The inevitable result is more discriminations; some favor the rich over the poor, others the poor over the rich. Each touches only a handful of people, but those affected are wholly affected. And handfuls add up.

Consider the covered-earnings requirement: a wage earner (as well as his wife and children) loses his OASI payment for any month in which he makes over $75. But the limit for a self-employed person is not $75 a month but $900 a year. He can make over $75 in 11 months out of 12 without losing a dime of OASI benefit.[4] Those who find employment outside OASI coverage, as in public agencies, tax-exempt institutions, and the like, are freed from this condition altogether. So are 25,000 beneficiaries in foreign countries. Raising the limit will not erase this flaw; the discriminations will still be there.

To survey all the ifs and maybes that harass any one category of secondary beneficiaries would take another article as long as this one. But let us look at one or two of them in practice.

*Age.* A retired worker must be sixty-five to be paid. What about his wife? She, too, must be sixty-five years old, no matter how long they have been married, no matter whether she ever has worked, or is able to work now. The fact is that most husbands are older than their wives; the average is nearly four years. And that tells why in 1952, 1,440,000 persons over sixty-five had a "right" to OASI benefits but were not drawing them. It goes far, too, to explain why the average retirement is not sixty-five, but over sixty-eight.

The OASI rule, however, is different if the wife under sixty-five has a child under eighteen. In that case she and the child can each draw a benefit equal to half that of the retired husband. No widow, however needy, can draw a benefit until she is sixty-five, unless she has a child. If she has, she collects, no matter how well off she is. Yet all these husbands paid taxes to OASI at the same rate for—as they thought—the same security for their wives.

*Dependency.* This is not a condition for payment of benefits to a child, or to a wife or widow over sixty-five, or to the mother of a child under eighteen, whatever her age. But the husband or widower of a woman worker must establish his actual dependency. What is more, in his case it is not enough that the wife be "permanently insured" under OASI. She must, in addition, have worked during half of the three years just before her death or retirement. Moreover, the husband's dependency must exist at the time of the retirement or death. If a husband suffers a breakdown or loses his job the week after the wife retires or dies, there is no OASI protection for him, no matter how much his wife paid in "premiums." In such a case, a retired woman *might* be able to qualify her husband by going back to work. But if she died, Social Security would simply keep what she had paid in and leave the widower to shift for himself.

The point advanced here is not that any of these rules are wrong in and

---

[4] The self-employed beneficiary can earn $81 a month for 11 months in a row, and still be within the $900 annual maximum.

of themselves, but that they are a hodgepodge, and follow no rationale. The earnings of some are limited, of others not; some must be sixty-five, others not; some must be actual dependents of the primary, others not. The "rights" of the beneficiaries depend on time, chance, and statutory caprice to a degree that would provoke just criticism of a charity program and is intolerable in a system of "insurance" the worker buys and pays for.

The chaos just indicated came about with the shift, in 1939, from paid-for pensions to gratuities, without acknowledgement of the fact either by Congress or by the advocates and apologists of Social Security. The same act of 1939 not only modified the social policy being carried out, but altered the economic nature of the system without the necessary corresponding alteration of its governing principles. From this arises the public illusion that Social Security is guided by concepts that in fact were long ago abandoned. No others having been adopted in their stead, the system today has no basic controlling economic principle.

Because the picture in the public mind is that of the original system set set up in 1935, otherwise sensible people are heard debating *whether* OASI shall be put on a pay-as-you-go basis—which is about the same as arguing whether we shall have rain yesterday. OASI already *is* on that basis.

The 1935 act did contemplate a reserve adequate to meet the probable liability. Within four years the political process broke down. Under overwhelming pressures to "give more," Congress in 1939 greatly increased the benefits without doing anything to amass reserves to pay them. On the contrary, Congress kept down the accumulation originally provided for, by holding OASI taxes at 2 per cent (half from the worker, half from the employer) until 1950. New increases in benefits, both in number and amount, were voted in 1950 and 1952 without corresponding provision for reserves. More are scheduled to be voted this year.

The result is that today the dollar amount of the OASI "reserve fund" is not quite enough to pay benefits due to those already on the rolls. There is nothing—not a dime—to pay the benefits that will become due to the 25 million "permanently" insured persons whose taxes built up the greater part of the present fund. Nor is there any money on hand to pay the benefits that will become due to most of the 41 million persons "currently" insured, or the 10 million to whom the Eisenhower administration proposes to extend coverage. From this, it does *not* follow that any of these benefits will go unpaid if and when they are due. But it implacably *does* follow that, if they are paid, the money will come from taxes yet to be collected, on wages yet to be earned, the wages of children still in school, of children yet unborn. What more does it take to make Social Security today a pay-as-you-go system?

Social Security began with economic and social foundations that inspired reasonable faith in its commitments. Those foundations having been abandoned, tremendous commitments have been and continue to be added pursuant to social policies not declared, or even formulated, and pursuant to no economic theory. There is danger of these uncontrolled commitments mounting to a total of billions beyond the capacity of even this country to honor.

This calls for a survey of Social Security from the ground up. First the facts, to cull the untruths and make the half-truths whole. Then the social philosophy, to resolve whether current practice actually is carrying out the generally accepted purpose. And finally the economic basis, to assure accomplishment of what is undertaken.

The plight of the needy aged did not grow out of the last depression, but arose during the course of a century and a half at about the same rate as the United States grew away from the land. The new urban and industrial economy produced every year an increasing number of old people upon whom no realist could impose the pioneer tradition of providing for one's own wants, one's own family, and one's own old age. The depression did bring an era of climax. To those who had made no provision for their own old age were added millions who had, but had now lost their means, or their employment, or both. Beyond immediate relief for all, there was great pressure for a permanent program. Much of this opinion was based on the assumption that under modern conditions most people *cannot* provide for their own future, a premise manifestly too broad, since millions no better off than the others could and did, can and do. The most that is sure is that some cannot and many do not, and they make up the problem of the needy aged.

Congress in 1935 did not go along with this unsound assumption; it did, however, undertake to enforce old-age saving by all, the thrifty as well as the unthrifty. (For the needy who remained, a relief program, Old Age Assistance, was set up, which was supposed to diminish and disappear as Social Security matures.[5]) The essential social policy of the original plan called for the beneficiaries' getting, not charity, but only what they paid for. In fact, there was a guarantee that every worker, or his heirs, would get his money back. With a relatively modest reserve maximum of $46 billion, the plan was very near to being soundly self-maintaining. Except for those who were on relief, and who thus were outside the Social Security system, nobody was going to support anybody else.

We have seen that since 1939 this no longer is so, and a basic question arises: does the United States wish to continue a system under which every 3¼ (or perhaps 4½) productive workers will be required by law to maintain one OASI beneficiary—a stranger to them—in addition to their own families? A system that makes from 21 to 26 million persons pensioners of the federal government? Leaving Social Security as it is now

---

[5] OAA, however, is still here. The federal cost rose from $244 million in 1937 to $917 million in 1954.

would amount to an affirmative answer. If the answer is no, some of the present promises of OASI benefits will have to be withdrawn, and a statement of social purpose drafted on realistic lines. Indeed, this must be done in any case. For the *ideal* cannot be made *fact* until it is clear what the ideal is, and this requires more than a passion for giving more to more people.

Does the nation wish to support all old people? All old people who retire? All old people without other means? And in each of these cases, their dependents? Actual or nominal? With, or without, regard to *their* means? Does the nation desire to support all widows and orphans? Or only needy ones? Or none at all?

Shall the support be at a flat rate? By some equally arbitrary formula? Or based on previous earnings? Even continuing the present Social Security plan requires answers to these questions if the present mare's nest of whimsical conditions is to be cleaned up.

Shall the needy be given relief, and others brought into a system in which they pay for what they get, and get what they pay for? In that case, shall the plan be voluntary, or compulsory and universal?

These questions are not raised frivolously. The answers established by Congress in 1935 are no longer valid, for they were abandoned in 1939. The answers that took their place are not valid, for they express no policy and form only a permanent program of whimsical give-aways. They were not the product of the normal American governmental process but the response of Congress to the pressures of one bloc of interests. Because of the fiction that Social Security could give a great deal to everybody, at little or no cost to anybody, no adverse interest was evident. So none was spoken for either by the Democrats or the Republicans. Social Security has drifted too long without a course; it is time to chart one and see that it is followed.

Once the purpose and policy of Social Security are established, they require an economic structure. Here there is room only to notice the courses available if Social Security is kept more or less in its present form: (1) The reserve structure could be restored. (2) As many participants as possible could be brought into a reserve system, with those who could not (that is, all the present and many potential beneficiaries) shifted to another, where the government frankly paid the cost. (3) The present system could be placed on a pay-as-you-go basis, with the reserve theory altogether abandoned.

The first course would require the government to add to the reserves a new bond, and OASI taxes would have to be raised to a rate that would maintain the reserve at an adequate level. The bond would have to be about $125 billion, which would establish the public debt at $400 billion. This amount ought not to horrify anybody who is not horrified right now. It would not be a new debt, but merely posting the books to show a debt Congress already has assumed. At least $125 billion, plus its interest, must be collected in taxes to honor the commitments already made under the Social Security program. The only way to cut the total is to cut OASI payments, or to pay them to fewer people than is promised at present. In short, to withdraw some of these commitments.

Under the second course, if future beneficiaries paid their own way, the government might get off for not much more than the $22 billion committed to those now on the rolls. The saving would be a mirage as far as the whole economy is concerned, for Social Security must withdraw from it, in taxes of some kind, whatever is going to be paid out. But the people who paid the taxes would get the benefits, and vice versa.

Both the foregoing solutions share one serious weakness: the reserves would be built up in dollars, to pay benefits at fixed dollar rates. But let prices go on up, and the benefits would have to go up with them, and against that event the new "adequate" reserve will no more be adequate than the present one.

The third course accepts the cost of Social Security as a year-to-year charge on the economy and proposes to meet it from year to year. It is free of the vice of collecting more in any one year than is needed, as a reserve plan does, including the fictitious one now in effect, which takes an excess of more than $2 billion a year, yet otherwise is a true pay-as-you-go operation. It is open to the criticism that—if benefits continue on the present basis—payments will be much larger a few years from now, with a consequent steep rise in cost. That is true. But the same is true, and perhaps more so, of all reserve plans. In the years to come, if the reserve is not drawn on, it will be because OASI taxes are high enough to carry the cost. If the reserves *are* drawn upon, the money will have to be raised, as has been noted, just as though there were no reserve. In fine, no matter which scheme is adopted, the present Social Security program is being handed down to our posterity with the memo: "We promise. You pay."

There are too many of these memos on file for children now growing up and for their children who come after them. Unless the processes of government are used by this generation to bring OASI into line with reality, they are sure to be used by the next generation to repudiate its burdens. There is no necessity to ordain such an outcome. The Americans of this day, of this decade, once having faced the facts, can resolve their purposes, and build a Social Security that is equitable, adequate, and economically viable.

# 60. WHAT PRICE WELFARE?
## It's Time to Stop
## Expanding Social Security

*Barron's,*
**January 4,**
**1960.**

OF ALL THE bureaucrats entrenched in Washington today, few have demonstrated such remarkable staying power as Arthur S. Flemming, Secretary of Health, Education and Welfare. Since the days of F.D.R., under Democratic and Republican regimes alike, he has manned lofty posts in the Offices of Production Management and Defense Mobilization, the War Manpower Commission, the National Security Council and the Cabinet. Over the years, this perpetual public servant also has shown a conspicuous ability to capture headlines. Only a few weeks ago, he touched off what has come to be known as the Great Cranberry Rhubarb. No sooner had that nationwide uproar subsided than he encored with the Case of the Cancer-Causing Caponettes. Last week, the ever-busy Mr. Flemming again was back in the news. This time, he was musing in public about a broad expansion of that already massive program, Social Security.

The subject, of course, is of keen interest on Capitol Hill as well. Indeed, in every election year since 1950, eager Congressmen have stepped up Social Security benefits, added new groups of eligibles, or both. In 1960, besides considering further expansion along those familiar lines, the lawmakers will debate a far-reaching proposal to bundle in something entirely new—free medical, hospital and nursing-home care. Humanitarian by tradition and instinct, the U.S. surely does not intend to neglect its senior citizens. Yet sooner or later it must decide how much more of a financial burden can be imposed upon an already heavy-laden working population. With the New Year, payroll taxes moved up another notch; three further increases are scheduled in the next decade, and proposals that would exact still more are being bandied about. Moreover, the rising outlays for welfare even now are proving a drag on U.S. economic growth. Security for the aged is undeniably a worthwhile objective. It must not be pursued, however, at the expense of the nation as a whole.

*    *    *    *    *

That expense is becoming a factor to reckon with. Since Social Security was launched in 1935, benefit payments have increased sharply. Group after group has been added to the rolls, age limits have been lowered, and eligibility broadened. In 1956, Congress extended coverage to a whole new class of recipients, the disabled. Today, 13.4 million Americans are receiving monthly checks, which for the year just ended, totaled $10 billion. Nor will the process stop here, since the number of beneficiaries is mounting steadily. What's more, Congress is toying with dozens of ways to broaden the program. Some legislatures would reduce the age of eligibility from 65 for men and 62 for women to 60 (or less) for everyone. Others would lower or eliminate the minimum age of 50 for payments for disability. Still others would boost all benefits by 10%. Finally, Rep. Aime Forand (D., R.I.) proposes to add "free" medical, hospital and nursing-home care. This modest proposal, by Government estimate, would cost over a billion dollars in the first year, and far more thereafter.

\* \* \* \* \*

Beneficence, of course, is fine for those who receive it. Unfortunately, however, there is another side of the coin—the mounting burden on every breadwinner. Since 1937, the earnings base on which taxes are levied has been lifted from $3,000 to $4,800, and some now would raise it to $6,000. The tax rate, meanwhile, has climbed from 1% (on employee and employer alike) to 3%, an out-of-pocket expense of $288 a year for every worker earning $4,800 or more. Even with no further increase in benefits, the bite is scheduled to grow in 1963, 1966 and 1969, to a total of 9%. Moreover, adoption of the Forand proposals in 1960 would force an additional unscheduled increase in taxes next January.

The costs, then, are not inconsequential. Yet for more and more people, the benefits are increasingly dubious. For one thing, many of today's taxpayers are likely to be short-changed when they reach retirement age. In the early years of Social Security, an open-handed Congress deliberately held payroll taxes below the rates originally scheduled. Consequently, just to lift the system out of the red, levies in the past few years have had to be raised faster and oftener than anyone had contemplated. Today's taxpayers, as a result, are carrying more than their rightful share of the load. Under present law, their eventual pensions will not be proportionate to their contributions.

For that matter, the nation, too, is failing to get full measure in return for its vast outlays. A mounting share of current benefits goes to men and women who are far from poverty-stricken. According to a 1957 survey by the Social Security Administration, to illustrate, one beneficiary in every three owned real or personal property worth $10,000 or more. Today, about one in six collects a private pension as well. Then, too, the program discriminates against the man who continues to work after 65, despite impressive evidence that most individuals are better off, physically and emotionally, if they stay on the job just as long as they are able. Most significantly of all, it penalizes productive members of society in favor of the non-productive. As everyone knows, there is a hue and cry these days about the rate of U.S. economic growth, and a widespread desire to speed it by spurring investment and production. Yet Social Security instead diverts more and more of the potential savings of the average citizen into immediate consumption. In the process, the nation clearly is the loser.

* * * * *

None of the foregoing, of course, argues for repeal of the program. Virtually all Americans now accept Social Security as a floor upon which to build their own retirement plans. What should be challenged, however, is its constant and reckless expansion. Instead of vying to see who can promise the old folks most, Congress and the Administration ought to be joining forces in a worthier crusade: safeguarding the dollar. The real enemy of the disabled, the needy and the aged is inflation. Instead of robbing Peter in order to dole out ever-growing benefits to Paul, Washington would benefit both by fighting relentlessly for honest money. Unless it faces up to that primary task, its increasing handouts will accomplish no worthwhile purpose, public or private.

# 61. RESOLUTION AGAINST CONTINUED USE OF INSURANCE TERMINOLOGY IN SOCIAL SECURITY ACT

NATIONAL ASSOCIATION
OF LIFE UNDERWRITERS,
1959.

WHEREAS The National Association of Life Underwriters (hereinafter referred to as "NALU" is a trade association having a membership of over 77,000 life insurance agents; and

WHEREAS NALU and its members have long had a deep and abiding interest in the Federal program of old age, survivors and disability benefits (hereinafter called "Social Security"); and

WHEREAS the Congress of the United States is constantly being subjected to a multitude of demands to liberalize Social Security benefit levels and other important phases of the program further and further; and

WHEREAS in NALU's opinion such liberalizations and the necessary resulting increased social taxes (1) would seriously impair, and perhaps even destroy, both the incentives and the financial ability of this Nation's citizens to practice self-reliance and private thrift, (2) would thereby cause a severe adverse impact on the American system of private enterprise and the entire national economy by drying up the vast pool of investment capital created by private savings which is so vital to industrial expansion, the creation of jobs and the production of substantial tax revenues, and (3) would threaten the existence of the Social Security program itself by increasing the already heavy social tax burden to such an extent that the Nation's taxpayers—and especially the taxpayers of tomorrow—might be unwilling or unable to bear it; and

WHEREAS NALU believes that many of the demands for such liberalizations (such as, for example, those calling for further liberalization or elimination of the program's so-called "retirement test," or "work clause") spring from the erroneous conception generally held by the public that the Social Security program is an insurance program like those underwritten by private life insurance companies; and

WHEREAS NALU also believes that the foregoing misconception held by the public regarding the nature of the Social Security program has been largely fostered by the fact (1) that the provisions of the Social Security Act contain numerous specific references to "insurance" and (2) that over the years the Government officials and employees charged with administering the Social Security program, as well as writers on the subject, have frequently equated the program to *true* insurance programs by such devices as mistakenly likening Social Security taxes to "premiums" and the Social Security card to an "*insurance contract*"; and

WHEREAS the Social Security program is not a true insurance program in that, among other things, it confers no contractual rights upon the participants and may be altered, amended or repealed by the Congress at will, and the compulsory contributions thereto are not "premiums" at all but are factually and legally merely additional excise taxes in the case of employers and additional income taxes in the case of employees and self-employed individuals;

NOW, THEREFORE, BE IT RESOLVED by the Board of Trustees of The National Association of Life Underwriters, acting upon the recommendation of the Association's Committee on Social Security and its National Council, that in consideration of the recitals contained in the foregoing preambles, the Congress of the United States be and it hereby is urgently requested (1) to delete from the Social Security Act all insurance terminology used therein; (2) to change the name of the Social Security program itself to one which will accurately describe its true nature and purposes; and (3) to incorporate in the Act a declaration of policy that the program is not and is not intended to be an insurance program and that it shall henceforth not be represented as such in any way by any official or employee of the Federal Government.

BE IT FURTHER RESOLVED that copies of this resolution be sent to all members of the Congress, the President of the United States, the Secretary of the Department of Health, Education and Welfare and the Commissioner of Social Security.

## 62. NEEDED CHANGES
## IN SOCIAL WELFARE:
## PROGRAMS AND OBJECTIVES

Wilbur J. Cohen,
*Social Service Review,*
March, 1959.

WE ARE LIVING in a dynamic, ever changing social and economic order, in a revolutionary period of such fast-moving developments that we find major problems arising out of continuous adaptation to new circumstances. The use of new sources of energy, new technologies, new methods, and new products brings new relationships and new ideas.

In various areas, such as health and life expectancy, in the use of energy and the production of food, we have telescoped into the last five decades progress comparable to changes that took two thousand or even five thousand years. It is no wonder that with these changes there are many unsolved social developments which create a challenge to social welfare.

### SIGNIFICANT PROGRESS

Before considering some of these challenges, the reader must keep in mind that despite the enormity of some of our problems significant progress has been made in recent years in improving the social welfare of people in the United States. The history of the last twenty-five years indicates that our country has come to recognize and to implement the principle that the development and conservation of human resources is a primary obligation of responsible government. Working in harmony with private and voluntary groups, social workers and public welfare officials during this period have pointed out that public programs and policies should afford each person the opportunity to discover and develop his maximum capacities and to choose those pursuits in which his abilities can be creatively employed.

Illustrative of the progress made are the following:

In 1950—just a little over eight years ago—there were more aged persons receiving assistance than were receiving insurance payments. Today there are nine million aged persons receiving insurance benefits, compared to about two and one-half million aged persons receiving assistance. This is remarkable progress in such a short time.

Mortality rates today are substantially lower than they were in the past. This trend has been very significant in the last three decades. If the mortality rates of 1910–20 were still prevalent today, there would be five million *additional* children without one or both parents. This is a tremendous saving in broken families.

Today more people are protected by health insurance than ever before. In 1957, 72 per cent of the population of the nation had some hospital insurance, 65 per cent had surgical insurance, and 43 per cent had some insurance coverage for in-hospital medical care and medical care in a doctor's office or at home.

Some progress has been made in unemployment insurance. In April–June, 1958, the average weekly payment for total unemployment insurance for the nation as a whole was about 37 per cent of average weekly wages compared to 34 per cent in 1954. Unemployment insurance made a more significant contribution to meeting wage-loss in the 1957–58 recession than in any previous recession.

In 1940, 5.5 per cent of the population were receiving public assistance. This figure dropped to 2.7 per cent during 1945–46. The figure rose steadily after the war, as the readjustments and dislocations took place, to 3.1 per cent in 1947, 3.3 per cent in 1948, 3.8 per cent in 1949, to a post-war height of 4.1 per cent in 1950. Then, under the impact of changed economic forces and the 1950 amendments to the Social Security Act, the figure began to drop to 3.7 per cent in 1951, to 3.6 per cent in 1952, and to approximately 3.5 per cent during the years 1953–57. It now appears that it has not exceeded 4 per cent during the 1957–58 recession.

## IMPROVING ASSISTANCE PROGRAMS

This over-all decline in the relative number of persons receiving public assistance is frequently overlooked by persons who view with alarm increasing public welfare expenditures. The amazing point is that the number of public assistance recipients is not somewhat greater than it is and that payments and expenditures are not larger than they are.

Despite the progress made, there are many persons on public assistance rolls whose payments are inadequate. This situation is very uneven. Grants are more adequate in some states than in others, but, speaking generally, some inadequacies exist even in the better programs and better states. Assistance payments in every state are still too low and should be increased. The most urgent need is for state-wide standards for direct relief in every state, more adequate state financial participation to the counties, and federal financial aid to the states for this purpose, with federal standards assuring assistance without regard to residence, citizenship, race, religion, or national origin.

Moreover, all assistance in an area should be administered by a single state or county agency in the interest of equitable and effective service. Is this too much to ask of a great and growing nation?

While most—if not all—of the people of our country would say that it is the responsibility of government to aid any person in actual need, this principle is not carried out in practice on a nationwide basis. Some of our energy and leadership must be directed to improving existing programs, including the amount of monthly payments for the needy aged, blind, disabled, and dependent children. There must also be a sustained effort to reduce the need for individuals to receive assistance but, on the other hand, every person in need should receive assistance regardless of residence, citizenship, or any other arbitrary restriction. Neither of these two conditions is being met throughout the United States at the present time. In sixteen states all general assistance in 1957 was financed solely from local funds. These states are California, Colorado, Florida, Georgia, Idaho, Indiana, Iowa, Kentucky, Mississippi, Nebraska, Nevada, New Hampshire, North Carolina, South Dakota, Tennessee, and Texas. The wide disparity is evident from the fact that in twelve states the amount spent per inhabitant for general assistance was less than fifty cents for the year 1957, while in three states (Washington, Illinois, and Michigan) it was over $4.00.

Medical-care programs for needy persons require broadening and strengthening. There is also need for improved standards in nursing-home care, for increased preventive and diagnostic services, for the expansion of visiting nurse services, and for provision of dental care for dependent children.

Federal participation in aid to dependent children should be brought to a level that will assure equitable treatment of children and the preservation and strengthening of family life. The desirability of exempting some income of families receiving ADC should be explored, especially for those with children who are of working age. Families in which the child works or wishes to work should not be penalized. Consideration should be given to how the ADC program can assist in promoting good work habits, family solidarity, and financial responsibility.

The federal public assistance law should be broadened to cover all needy children, especially to give protection when the parent is unemployed. At the present time, the eligibility condition relating to absence from the home places a premium on desertion. Moreover, federal matching funds should be available for two parents, not merely for one as at present.

## RAISING BENEFIT STANDARDS

There is still a long way to go before there can be a real safety-net of public assistance ready to help anyone and everyone in need in the United States. Standards should be raised in public assistance and the other social security programs beyond the minimum subsistence concepts that evolved during the depression. Our world is vastly different from that of 1930–35, yet many of our social welfare standards come from the depression period. Standards have been adjusted in many cases to take account of changing prices, but they have not been modified to take account of our rising standard of living and our belief in prevention and rehabilitation and in the importance of protecting and strengthening family life.

Our nation is approaching a $500 billion gross national product in 1960. Is assistance being provided in relation to the economy of today and the kind of economy we are likely to have tomorrow or in relation to the economy and attitudes of a past period?

There is an urgent need to re-examine standards, benefits, and objectives in both public assistance and social insurance. The Bureau of Public Assistance of the Social Security Administration, in a study of basic living requirements budgeted by the states in 1953 for single persons receiving old age assistance, found that the median amount budgeted ranged from $37.66 to $90.00.[1] The distribution was as follows:

| | |
|---|---|
| $40.00 or less | 2 states |
| 40.00–49.99 | 8 states |
| 50.00–59.99 | 13 states |
| 60.00–69.99 | 15 states |
| 70.00–79.99 | 5 states |
| 80.00–89.99 | 4 states |
| 90.00 and over | 1 state |

The national median was $64.36 a month. When special items were added *to basic* requirements, the national median was increased to $68.66. These figures do not include any direct payments for medical care.

The fact that twenty-three states had a budgetary standard of less than $60 a month in 1953 indicates a need for review of these standards. It is reasonable to assume that in a large number of states there has been no real improvement in standards above the $30-a-month basis contemplated in the 1935 law, and some states today are still below the dollar-a-day standard which was the goal of social workers during 1930–35.

Similar studies indicate a need for a review of ADC standards. Although the amounts received by assistance recipients have increased since 1953, so has the cost of living. It is reasonable to assume that no substantial basic change has occurred to alter the significance of the 1953 figures cited.

A study made in Boston in 1946 showed that from 39 to 50 per cent of various beneficiary groups in old age and survivors' insurance had total income less than the Massachusetts assistance standard and did not receive public assistance. Some of them would have been disqualified for public assistance because they had more assets than public assistance permitted or because they had adult children who could contribute to their support. According to the study made by the Social Security Administration, those who had below-assistance incomes and whose other resources would not

---

[1] *Benefit Levels in Veterans' Programs: A Study of Possible Criteria and Standards for Use in Determining Benefit Levels*, Staff Report V, President's Commission on Veterans' Pensions (84th Cong., 2d sess.) (Washington, D.C.: Government Printing Office, 1956), pp. 55–56.

have disqualified them for assistance if they had applied for it constituted from 13 to 18 per cent of the different types of beneficiaries.[2]

The situation may be much different today, and may vary in the different states, but the 1946 facts are still suggestive. How many persons receiving old age, survivors', and disability insurance are eligible for public assistance today and are not receiving assistance? Why? Here are some significant facts we do not know. This is likely to be an important subject for investigation as a co-operative federal-state research project.

There are still widespread inadequacies in the coverage and level of benefits in state workmen's compensation[3] and state unemployment insurance. They are not up to the level that the proponents of such legislation originally had in mind when they introduced it. Both state programs are inadequate and need substantial revision and improvement. Only eleven states have dependents' benefits in their state unemployment insurance and only fifteen states have such features in the temporary disability provisions of their state workmen's compensation laws. While both programs are in need of revision, workmen's compensation, especially, needs basic overhauling. It is the worst social insurance program in the United States. Some crusading spirits are needed to revise and improve these laws if they are to more fully accomplish their purpose.

## HOSPITAL AND NURSING INSURANCE

Our existing social insurance programs can be greatly strengthened and broadened and thus can help to minimize dependency. One of the most important next steps in improving our social welfare programs is the provision of hospital and nursing insurance to social security beneficiaries who are aged, disabled, or widowed. Most aged persons in the country do not have hospital insurance coverage. While such protection has been increasing in recent years, there is no indication that present voluntary arrangements can fully meet this problem. The reason is that the aged have substantially lower incomes when they retire, and they use more hospital care than the younger persons. Adequate protection to the aged usually increases costs beyond the ability of most individuals to pay or requires curtailment of service. Neither is desirable.

One suggestion for solving this problem is to provide hospital and nursing insurance to the nearly fifteen million persons who are receiving social security benefits or who are eligible to receive them if they retire.

This could be done by increasing the insurance contribution about one-fourth of one per cent on the employer and one-fourth of one per cent on the employee. By introducing employer sharing of costs and distributing

---

[2] "Nonrelief Income of Retired Insurance Beneficiaries in Boston," *Social Security Bulletin*, Vol. XI (September, 1948), pp. 17–18.

[3] See Alfred M. Skolnik, "Trends in Workmen's Compensation: Coverage, Benefits, and Costs," *Social Security Bulletin*, Vol. XXI (August, 1958), pp. 4–16.

the cost over an individual's entire working lifetime, the financial problem can be eased.[4]

## HEALTH NEEDS

Hospital and nursing insurance for social security beneficiaries, however, is only one part of a much larger problem. Greater emphasis should be given and more resources allocated to meeting the health needs of people who become sick or disabled.

Scientific and social advances in medical and hospital care and public health techniques during the last fifty years have made it possible to raise the health standards of our states and nation to new and unprecedented levels. Every individual, regardless of race, creed, color, national origin, or economic or social status, or whether he lives on the farm or in the city, should be entitled to receive all the benefits of modern medical, hospital, and public health services, regardless of his financial ability at the time of illness. Continued support should be given for improved and expanded national, state, and local medical, hospital, and public health services; expanded group practice; and the development of more adequate programs of hospital, medical, and nursing-home care for the chronically ill.

Only a small proportion of the nation's population has health insurance protection covering comprehensive care. Comprehensive insurance plans are necessary, including diagnostic services, out-patient care, nursing services, and mental health services.

The restriction in the social security program limiting permanent total disability insurance benefits to persons age fifty or over should be eliminated. There is no sound justification for this arbitrary limitation. A disabled individual aged thirty-five or forty should have this same insurance protection. If the need for assistance is going to be reduced, the insurance method should be made to apply where it has demonstrated its appropriate use.

Our nation has developed the insurance principle to the extent that a large proportion of the population working for a living is covered for wage-loss benefits due to sickness or disability. In 1956, about 25 per cent of all income loss due to short-time sickness or disability was compensated through cash sickness insurance programs or sick-leave plans. This proportion has increased from 16 per cent in 1948.[5] However, much remains to be done to extend this insurance still further. Many persons employed in small businesses and service occupations are still excluded from this protection. Only four states have insurance protection against short-term

---

[4] See Wilbur J. Cohen, "The Forand Bill: Hospital Insurance for the Aged," *American Journal of Nursing*, Vol. LVIII (May, 1958), pp. 698–702.

[5] "Growth in Protection against Income Loss from Short-Term Sickness, 1948–56," *Social Security Bulletin*, Vol. XXI (January, 1958), p. 19.

sickness and disability of a non-occupational character, and there is only one federal law for this purpose, a law covering only railroad employees. Further extension of the social insurance principle is desirable.

Since the enactment of the national Mental Health Act of 1946, a national policy has been adopted of expanding and strengthening mental health programs necessary for the full emotional and mental well-being of every individual. There is a need to expand the number of community child guidance and adult out-patient programs as well as community and state treatment, care, and educational programs for the mentally retarded. There is also the need to enlarge state treatment services for the mentally ill and the severely emotionally disturbed, especially for the growing number of young people who require this help; to promote an extensive program to provide public schools with skilled personnel to deal with emotionally ill children; to increase trained personnel and training programs; to provide more adequate follow-up and rehabilitation services; and to greatly strengthen research programs.

The citizens of our country have repeatedly demonstrated that they are aware of the need for these improved and broadened programs. They have also recognized that such programs represent a wise investment in the future well-being of their families and friends, an investment that will result in savings of thousands of dollars to the taxpayer. In recent years, great strides have been made towards achieving a broad, effective, and well-balanced mental health program, despite the short-sighted attempts of budget cutters in some states to cut back on meeting the needs of the mentally ill. Vigorous effort and leadership must be continued in this field.

## NEEDS OF CHILDREN AND YOUTH

Programs for children and youth have not been improved sufficiently to provide for the growing number of children and our rapidly advancing knowledge about them. The future of our nation depends on the opportunities which children and youth are given to develop their maximum individual potentialities, and to understand the meaning of, and to participate in the building of, a democratic community. Programs and services for all children should be broadened and expanded and should be more adequately supported financially by voluntary contributions and by state, local, and federal governments. Counseling and vocational training services needed by youth in the transition from school to work should be enlarged and constructive employment opportunities expanded under conditions that will safeguard the health and welfare of children.

Special attention should be given to the needs of the socially and economically disadvantaged, the children who drop out of school, the emotionally disturbed, and the mentally and physically handicapped. Existing programs of health, education, and welfare for all children and youth must be strengthened and adequate state facilities developed to retrain delinquent and socially maladjusted youth. Full support should be given to strengthening local courts responsible for children and youth and young adults in order to obtain adequate personnel and services. Local government, voluntary agencies, and citizen groups must all co-operate in the expansion and building of those programs needed by our children and youth in our complex, fast-moving economy. Government must take those steps which will strengthen the family unit and parents in meeting their full responsibilities. We must strive with dedication, vigor, and imagination for the fulfilment of the great potential of our children and youth.

## NEEDS OF THE AGED

The needs of our growing aging population are not being met. Society must provide for its increasing number of older people an environment in which they may lead normal and satisfying lives. It is the duty of responsive and responsible government to join with private agencies to assure that our senior citizens have the physical, mental, and financial capacity to give meaning to their added years of life.

Measures to broaden and strengthen job-finding services and to improve the economic status of older people should be taken. States should consider enacting legislation abolishing age discrimination in employment. To meet the health problems of the aging, facilities and personnel need to be increased and funds provided to purchase health services. Public and private programs are needed to meet the special housing, educational, and recreational needs of an older population. Each state should establish a permanent state commission on aging with an adequate budget to conduct research on the needs of older people, to co-ordinate existing state and local programs and to provide consulting services to local organizations.

It is now recognized that the federal social security program (old age, survivors', and disability insurance) is a necessary and proper function of government and should be broadened and expanded to provide protection for everyone. Those groups which have opposed social security now appear to be taking the position of attempting to delay any proposed action, to suggest it be studied more carefully, or to warn about the increased costs. In addition, those opposed or unsympathetic to the principle of social security take refuge behind the idea that benefits were originally designed to provide a "floor of protection," which is sometimes interpreted to mean benefits as low as they can be kept.

The aged, the disabled, and widows and orphans should, through public and private insurance, be provided with income adequate to maintain dignity, health, and the opportunity for happiness and comfort. This means that old age insurance benefits must be increased substantially. The average monthly primary benefit awarded in August, 1957, was $75. With the recent 7 per cent increase, the average should be a little over $80 in 1959.

As our next objective, a 20–25 per cent increase would seem desirable, so that the average primary benefit awarded in the future will not be less than about $100 a month.

## PREVENTION AND REHABILITATION

Greater emphasis must be given to programs of prevention and rehabilitation. Social welfare needs must be met whenever and however they arise. People in the United States have shown that they wish to support both voluntary and public measures to help meet their own needs and those of their neighbors. But we are not providing enough emphasis, or funds, or personnel to prevent dependency or to rehabilitate persons.

Rehabilitation and employment programs for the physically and emotionally handicapped should be extended and improved to help them achieve a maximum degree of self-care and self-sufficiency and, thereby, to permit them to lead happy and useful lives. A number of states, however, are not appropriating the full amount required to obtain the funds allotted to them under the Vocational Rehabilitation Act. Hence, there are many disabled persons whose rehabilitation is postponed or denied because of lack of funds and personnel. Our immediate goal should be the full use in every state of federal funds available to support the state programs, the establishment of more community facilities for rehabilitation services, and the training of additional professional personnel in those fields concerned with rehabilitation and employment. Additional state and federal funds should be sought for this purpose. But state and federal funds available under the Vocational Rehabilitation Act are not—and will not—be sufficient in the foreseeable future to rehabilitate all those who need such services. Consequently, additional financial support to the state vocational rehabilitation agencies should be obtained from the disability insurance program.

Consideration also should be given to placing the responsibility for the state administration of vocational rehabilitation in an agency interested in rehabilitation rather than in education departments, as at present.

We are also not allocating sufficient funds for research in the causes of dependency. The 1956 amendments to the Social Security Act provided for grants for this purpose but appropriations have not been made. It is important that this program be implemented at the earliest opportunity.

## ELIMINATING POVERTY

The many economic analyses of our actual and potential productivity and financial ability lead to an important conclusion. Stated simply, and without qualifications, it is this: Want and poverty can and should be abolished in the United States in our lifetime.

On the basis of the estimates made by the Twentieth Century Fund, expenditures for consumption goods in 1950 would have had to be increased only 6 per cent (about $12 billion) to have permitted "the small minority of sub-standard families and individuals to achieve a 'health and decency' standard of living without any modification in the living standards of the vast majority whose incomes were more than adequate to maintain such standards." By 1960, they estimate that (at 1950 prices) the increase would only need to be about 4 per cent (about $10 billion).[6]

Depending upon where the standard is set, want or poverty could be abolished in this country at a cost of about $10 billion a year. This sum would have been considered a fantastically large amount just a few years ago. Undoubtedly, it is a fantastic amount yet to many persons. But, in terms of what the nation is spending on missiles and defense, it is no longer fantastic. Moreover, if the economy is going to increase $10 billion to $25 billion a year, cumulatively, in the future it may be possible to start thinking about how to eradicate poverty without taking anything away from anyone.

Although there are a number of national and state studies under way in this area, intensive studies are needed of ways to eliminate poverty in each state and in depressed areas.

The many economic and social surveys made in Great Britain before the war convinced William Beveridge that abolition of want "was easily within the economic resources of the community; want was a needless scandal due to not taking the trouble to prevent it."[7] But he also pointed out:

> . . . Want is one only of five giants on the road of reconstruction and in some ways the easiest to attack. The others are Disease, Ignorance, Squalor and Idleness.[8]

To attack all five of these giants is a formidable task. But it can be done if a co-ordinated plan is designed for the future. Such a plan should be developed for the nation and for each state.

One of the important components of such a plan is a well-rounded and expanding permanent program for the training of personnel. The 1956 social security amendments marked an important milestone in public welfare in that Congress for the first time recognized the importance of training programs in public assistance. Congress previously had authorized training funds for child welfare, public health, and vocational rehabilitation. Funds have never been appropriated to implement the public assistance training program. If Congress provides funds for this purpose, state agencies should make a sustained effort to put an effective training pro-

---

[6] J. Frederick Dewhurst and Associates, *America's Needs and Resources: A New Survey* (New York: Twentieth Century Fund, 1955), p. 931.

[7] *Social Insurance and Allied Services* (New York: Macmillan Co., 1942), p. 166.

[8] *Ibid.*, p. 6.

gram into operation. An over-all program for meeting manpower needs in health, education, and welfare is essential.

## THE TASKS AHEAD

Each year, it is unfortunately true, federal, state, and local social welfare legislation becomes more complex. The financing becomes more involved and diffused. The administrative tasks become more difficult. As we have gone along, the easier tasks have been done first. This was only reasonable. But each year more difficult problems are tackled. The financial problems relating to health are far more complex than those relating to old age. When we begin to rehabilitate 100,000 disabled persons a year, we begin to handle cases more than twice as difficult as those we handled when we rehabilitated 50,000. To help strengthen family life is a real challenge, but a very vital one.

The tasks ahead will be more difficult than in the past and will involve more complex knowledge and skills relating to financial, administrative, and sociological factors. Administration of medical-care plans, the solution of the problems of juvenile delinquency and the aging of the population, and the social rehabilitation of the family are responsibilities of many units of our society. If everyone else in society were doing his job fully and effectively, social welfare agencies would not have to handle as many different tasks as they now do.

Social welfare agencies must be willing to pave the way to do the hard jobs others are unprepared or unwilling to do. If it were a perfect world, public welfare departments would not need to administer medical-care programs for the needy. This might be the responsibility of state health departments if they had the ability and courage to undertake to administer them. Perhaps some day they will, but, in the meantime, public welfare must fill the gap. This requires a knowledge of many financial, administrative, and medical elements which will require trained personnel. There will be many headaches, and much midnight oil will be used to solve some of the medical problems ahead.

But social welfare personnel have never shied away from the difficult tasks. During the depression they tackled a host of problems where both the angels and the public administration experts feared to tread. Whatever the task ahead, social workers must rise to the occasion.

To gear social welfare programs to a changing economy, social welfare responsibilities must be seen as a whole, in terms of both the immediate tasks and those emerging in the decade ahead. To achieve this, there must be continuity of administrative, legislative, research, and community action to improve social welfare programs.

Administration, legislation, research, and community action are not separate functions to be kept isolated from each other. As social welfare matures, we will more closely interrelate these functions. The responsibility of good administration is to blend all these elements into a harmonious working arrangement on both a short-time and a long-time basis.

Social welfare administration is not a "one-shot" proposition. Good administration involves a sound and long-range research program, the development of long-range legislative proposals as knowledge and experience evolve, and effective, long-range community action to appraise and interpret the program. As many people and groups as possible must be involved in every aspect of policy formulation and community organization of social welfare services.

If the service aspects of programs are to be developed during the coming years, then we must begin to develop research to evaluate these services. This is a much more difficult assignment than just a statistical analysis of assistance payments. Services to families, to children, to the aged; and health, rehabilitation, housing, community, court, and juvenile delinquency services—all these require definition, appraisal, and review. Some pioneering is needed in these areas. A variety of professional skills is required. While administrative research is essential and useful, longer-range research must be developed in those areas in which very little is known.

The process of social legislation is an evolutionary one which never stops. There are some organized groups in our society who considered the social security legislation of 1950, 1952, 1954, and 1956 so far-reaching that it was not necessary to have social security legislation in 1958. They are worried about the fact that there have been five important and successive changes in this program in an election year. But these changes are not really a cause for criticism or alarm; they should be a source of pride in the social conscience of our nation, in the constructive contribution of our two-party system, in the working of our representative democracy, and in the ability of the economy to meet the challenge.

If I were asked to make a prophecy and to try to pierce the future, I would say that, in all likelihood, there will be other important improvements in social welfare legislation in 1960, 1962, and in the years to come. In effect, we are but making up during the period 1950–65 for our inability, or unwillingness, to move forward during 1940–50.

## CONTROVERSIAL ISSUES

Social welfare problems are and will continue to be controversial. There are still many persons in social work who tend to be afraid to deal with questions just because they are "controversial." Every fundamental feature of our major social institutions once was controversial. Fifty years ago the proposal for insurance of bank deposits was believed by most bankers to mean the breakdown of responsibility in our banking system. Twenty years ago the old age insurance program was called administratively unfeasible in Congress and was attacked on the grounds that it would drive private pension plans out of existence. In 1956, when disability insurance was being considered by Congress, various medical groups attacked the proposal and even asked the President to veto the social security bill because of its inclusion.

There were many persons in influential positions in government and business who opposed social security legislation in 1956 and 1958. There were others who said legislation would not be enacted. But, throughout the stormy legislative weather, social welfare personnel kept their faith and their courage. They were a vital and essential force in achieving the 1956 and 1958 legislation over very powerful opposition.

Social workers should not evade responsibility for social action because of controversy. We must respect other points of view and marshal our knowledge, experience, and facts. Social legislation is born in controversy, and social workers must be willing to be criticized for their views and recommendations. However, they must be sure to have the facts to guide them and must continuously engage in research and re-evaluation to keep up with changing conditions.

Although we recognize controversy as part of our daily work, we must ever be tolerant of differing points of view. None of us has the sole clue to truth. We change our points of view, and so do others. We must be willing to work with others who have different points of view. In our democracy we try to emphasize the positive by finding those areas at any given time in which there is growing evidence of agreement.

We can afford to improve our social welfare programs. Our national income is growing and there is every indication that it will continue to grow in the immediate years ahead. There is strong evidence that in a few years the gross national product will be in excess of $600 billion and that real family income will be higher than it is today. We must readjust our sights to the steady growth of our economy. We must eradicate the depression psychology of a restrictive economy. We must plan our programs in a changing setting of increased ability to pay for our security, our welfare, and our social needs.

Naturally, at any given time there are financial limits to program changes. There is the all-important factor of method and timing. But the contributory social insurance system has demonstrated its effectiveness and, as wages and productivity and earnings increase, we should be able to revise and expand the program in harmony with our ability to pay.[9]

One of the strengths of our unemployment insurance and our OASDI programs is that long-range financing is possible. Moreover, by relating

---

[9] For those who may still have some doubts about our ability to afford improvements in our OASDI program, see chap. xiii in John J. Corson and John W. McConnell, *Economic Needs of Older People* (New York: Twentieth Century Fund, 1956). This chapter, entitled "How Well Can We Provide for the Aged?" reviews the measures of our economic capacity, and the relationship of the dependent population to our working population.

the contributions and benefits to earnings, the system receives increased income as earnings increase. In addition, employees have indicated their willingness to increase their contributions to the OASDI system for important improvements.

## CONCLUSION

The historian J. B. Bury, of Cambridge, spent many years studying the records of mankind. He came to the conclusion that there were two great discoveries in the history of thought. The first came in the fifth century B.C. when the Greeks found that man himself was the wonder of the world—"A wonder-working force in the world—a conqueror of the beasts of the field, the fowl of the air, the wind of the sea, and the patient earth."

The second great stage in human evolution was reached when mankind became conscious of what could yet be done when, as Charles Beard has said, "the idea of progress broke in upon the belief in the vicious circle of contentment with status." It was only with the Renaissance that the soil was prepared in which the seeds of progress could germinate.

It is only about three hundred years since the idea of progress has been circulating. For many years it was an idea discussed by philosophers and writers. But today it is an idea, or an objective, that has captured the imagination of men and women everywhere. Throughout the world, even among peoples who cannot read or write, the belief in progress, today, now, here in this world, is a force which is changing the face of the globe. It has uprooted governments, changed age-old practices, and given hope and incentive to people in rural villages, huts, and far-distant lands.

The proper development of our human resources, with our rapidly expanding population, requires additional public and private expenditures. This is an inescapable fact that many people fail to face. In a growing and expanding economy, we can afford these expenditures which are an investment that will maintain and strengthen the social and economic health and welfare of the nation, the state, and the community. The denial of opportunities to any individual, or their restriction to the privileged few, for economic or other reasons results in the loss of sorely needed talents and abilities. Moreover, it results in long-range increases in social and economic costs and large-scale social neglect, attributable to lack of vision and investment in meeting the needs of individuals and families.

Social work believes that a government responsive to the needs of people must imaginatively plan, provide for, and support those institutions and services required to extend such opportunities to all people—those who are well and normal and those who may have special needs and problems because of special circumstances—the dependent child, the aging and the aged, the physically handicapped, those who are, or may become, physically or mentally ill, and the indigent.

There are those who say that governmental action destroys initiative and incentive. They solemnly say this is a matter of principle. However, as Abraham Lincoln has said, "The legitimate object of government is 'to do for the people what needs to be done, but which they cannot, by individual effort, do at all, or do so well for themselves.' "[10]

Social work operates on the belief in the idea of progress: that there can be a better life for all; that want can be abolished and poverty eradicated; that many human problems are capable of solution by the use of knowledge, by education, imagination, and research, and by the intelligent use of our resources. These are great tasks, and it is a thrilling experience to be associated with a profession and a movement dedicated to these great objectives.

# 63. A SALUTE TO 25 YEARS OF SOCIAL SECURITY

EVELINE M. BURNS,
*Public Welfare,*
January, 1960.

THIS SESSION CELEBRATES the first quarter century of the Social Security Act. What will be celebrated 25 years from now? Prophesy is always dangerous, yet I suggest it is not too difficult to see, however dimly, something of the shape of the future in the realm of social security. I venture to say that just as the last quarter-century will go down in history as the age in which America came to grips with the problem of income security, so the next historical period will be known as the one in which the country came to grips with the problem of medical care and with the even more difficult challenge of the prevention of dependency and economic insecurity.

### Insurance Improvements Prophesied

Not that there will be nothing to do in the realm of income maintenance measures. Astounding progress has been made since 1935, but rounding out and completing of income-maintenance programs continues, as well as grappling with the task of keeping them in step with generally rising standards of living. By 1985, I hope, the gaps in coverage of risks will be filled in. The age limit now operative in the federal permanent disability insurance program will be eliminated; all workers, and not merely those in four states and in the railroad industry, will be able to claim disability insurance benefits when they are temporarily sick. The period for which

---

[10] A fragment in Lincoln's papers, quoted in *Complete Works of Abraham Lincoln,* ed. John G. Nicolay and John Hay (12 vols.; 2d printing from the plates of the Gettysburg edition; New York: Francis D. Tandy Co., 1905), Vol. II, p. 182.

unemployed workers can draw benefits will have been lengthened, and a system of automatic extension of benefit duration, when the general level of unemployment rises above some agreed level, may even have become permanent.

The years ahead will undoubtedly see too a broadening of the coverage of the social insurance programs. There are still several million workers, apart from self-employed medical men whose exclusion is their own silly fault, who need coverage by OASDI, but who are now excluded, many of whom will surely be brought under coverage in the not too distant future. Even more remains to be done about coverage in unemployment insurance, disability insurance and workmen's compensation. Workers in small firms and agricultural employees are notable examples of categories who still lack these types of income security.

### Benefits Must Be in Line with Economy

The problem of keeping social security benefits in line with rising costs of living and, even more challenging, with rising general levels of prosperity, will surely occupy much attention. There are indeed several problems and not one. There is the fact that even today the levels of benefits on some social insurance programs are difficult to defend if the purpose is to assure true income security when income is interrupted.

Unemployment insurance benefits, for instance, not only replace a very small percentage of income loss due to unemployment, but the percentage is even smaller than it was when the programs were first introduced 25 years ago. All the social insurance programs are in danger of becoming less liberal, in terms of the percentage of wages which the benefits represent, because this is a period of secular price increases and the policy of fixing dollar limits to both the maximum payments and to the amount of taxable earnings inevitably results in a downward pressure on benefits when wages and prices are increasing.

In the next quarter century it is hoped that these dollar maximums will be replaced by maximums related to some index of wages so that they will automatically rise as wages and prices increase. Such a method of defining maximum benefits and maximum taxable earnings would help also in keeping benefits more in line with rising levels of national income, at least to the extent that increases in productivity are reflected in increased earnings.

But still remaining will be the problem of the benefit levels of those who, at any time, have already retired and continue to live in a period of generally rising standards of living. The question of whether or not the already retired should share in the general increase in economic well-being enjoyed by the population as a whole will have to be dealt with.

### PA Will Always Be Needed

Some major changes in the public assistance programs are also to be expected. While the maturing of the OASDI system and the improvements in the other social insurance programs will undoubtedly reduce the relative importance of public assistance as a source of income security, it will still remain an important safeguard for large numbers of people.

There will always be some social insurance beneficiaries with needs in excess of what can be supplied by the insurance benefit. And there will always be some people who are not eligible for social insurance or who have exhausted the benefits to which they are entitled (in the case of the short-period benefits such as unemployment insurance), and there will be others the cause of whose lack of income does not fall into one of the "risk boxes" on the basis of which the social insurance system is organized. Notable among these are the millions whose need for income is due to family breakdown for causes other than the death of the breadwinner. Thus what happens or does not happen in public assistance will still be of major concern to a sizable segment of the population.

### Children Are Penalized

Surely it is not too much to hope that public assistance will experience major changes in the next quarter century. The level of living of those dependent on these programs is pretty disgraceful for a country as rich as this one. And it is particularly shocking that the needy group which is treated in the most niggardly way in most states, the ADC category, is the one which contains the largest proportion of children, the citizens of the future for whom deep concern and affection is constantly proclaimed. Even though the cost of maintaining a child may be less than that of an adult, the difference cannot be as great as is implied in the differential contained in the federal matching formula. I cannot believe that this disgraceful discriminatory treatment of children will be tolerated much longer. Nor can I believe that, 25 years from now, the nation will be as complacent as it now is about the living standards of the 54 percent of its children who are members of families with three or more children, a shockingly large proportion of which have money incomes of less than half the City Worker's Family Budget.[1] In certain cities some of these families are even now being subsidized by public assistance. But is this the best solution? Sooner or later will it not be necessary to contemplate some system of children's allowances to ensure that no child is penalized merely because of the number of his brothers and sisters?

### Categories, Financing, Residence

It seems not unreasonable too, to expect that the categorical approach, a pattern congealed by the Social Security Act in 1935 and for reasons which at the time were probably sound, will give way during the next 25 years to a policy which no longer differentiates between people on the

---

[1] U.S. Department of Labor, Bureau of Labor Statistics, *Family Budget of City Worker* (Washington, D.C.: U.S. Government Printing Office.)

basis of the cause of their need. Although some states may still decide
that they wish to retain two or more of the categories for local or historical reasons, I suspect that by the time of American Public Welfare Association's next celebration, and probably much before, federal policy will
provide for a single matching grant for all public assistance recipients dif-
ferentiating perhaps only between adults and children, though one may
hope on a more realistic basis than now.

Undoubtedly too, there will be changes in the financing of public assistance. The variable grant now introduced on a limited basis must be more
widely extended if the poorer states are ever to be able to provide adequately for their needy people. And while some other changes in the
matching formulae may be seen, I do not think one has to be a very experienced prophet to prophesy that the over-all federal share is unlikely
to be smaller than it now is. Also seen may be some new federal standards,
notably relating to residence requirements.

### Medical Care, New Area of Need

All of this, however, is in the nature of unfinished business, improving
and rounding out policies which have been in the process of implementation over the last 25 years. The exciting developments of the next 25 years
will move into new areas of human need. Outstanding among these, and
ripe for early action, is the problem of medical care.

The amazing developments in medical and engineering sciences of the
last quarter century have revolutionized the problem of medical care. On
the one hand they have made good medical care, including prevention
and rehabilitation, much more worth having, so that the demand for medical services has expanded tremendously, and in many quarters medical
care has been added to the good things of life to which people think they
have a "right."

On the other hand, these developments have greatly increased the cost
of care, and this cost has been further raised by the adoption of policies
such as hospitalization insurance, which have encouraged greater use of
one of the most expensive and sharply rising cost items, care in hospitals.

Serious as is the problem of securing access to modern medical care and
even more of paying for it, for the population as a whole, it is far more
acute for the growing group of the aged whose medical needs are far
greater than those of younger age groups and whose financial resources
are more restricted. Already the burden of medical care for the aged is
falling heavily upon public welfare agencies and is casting its shadow on
the sizable group of citizens who are approaching old age and who realize
that their savings may melt away overnight in the event of a serious illness.

At the same time knowledge is slowly growing, despite the distorting
efforts of the American Medical Association, that there are other ways of
organizing and financing medical care and health services in general and
that such methods can be devised so as to assure good quality care, so as

not to interfere with the relations between patient and doctor and so as not to lead to serious abuse of the system. The fact is even becoming more widely known that medical men themselves in other countries regard such systems as the British National Health Service as preferable to previous arrangements, even from the pecuniary point of view.

### Government Will Be Involved

In such circumstances, it is not being overly bold to prophesy that 25 years from now government will be deeply involved in the organizing and financing of medical care. Whether or not by then medical care will be a free public service is more doubtful, though I am convinced that this will happen in the end. But surely medical care for the aged will be added before too long to the benefits available to OASDI beneficiaries, and I cannot believe that within 25 years many people will not be asking why a policy that is good for those whose productive life is ended is not good also for children, who are the producers of the future.

Certainly the next quarter century will see many efforts to ward off the inevitable coming of a national health service by schemes for public subsidies to private insurance plans, by expanding medical care services to a more broadly defined group of "indigent" people, and by increasing support from public funds of medical education and research and construction of medical facilities. For the fact remains that the doctors are fighting a losing battle and it is only a question of *when* and *how* adequate medical care will be assured all citizens regardless of their personal ability to pay for it.

### Preventing Dependency of Top Importance

Second only in importance and in public interest to medical care will be a second new area of public need which seems likely to be a preoccupation of the next quarter century. I refer to the need to prevent dependency and I call it a new need only because, so far, relatively little attention has been devoted to it. The elevation to primary importance of policies devoted to restoring people to self-support and self-care and preventing family breakdown was begun with the social security amendments of 1956. Their effective implementation will be a major challenge for the years ahead.

But prevention of dependency is a function not only for the great public welfare agencies whose growth and vitality have been one of the most exciting developments of the 25 years now being celebrated. In addition to work with individuals who are already in need or in danger of becoming so through family disintegration, it is necessary to envisage a complex of programs and policies embracing more adequate public housing, physical and vocational rehabilitation, better employment counseling, measures to upgrade workers, to move people from areas of limited opportunity to those which are expanding, removal of various types of discrimination and the like.

\* \* \* \* \*

## Must Be Clear about Goals . . .

In my effort to peer into the future, although I have been very positive about developments in some areas, I have also frequently used the words "I hope" in regard to others. For while I am convinced that in time this nation, as an intelligent democracy, will act in response to the needs I have delineated, the speed of action and the efficacy and economy of measures will in large part depend on how far all of us who are committed to public welfare are prepared to fight for our beliefs, see clearly where we want to go, know how best to get there, and have counted and are ready to pay the cost.

## . . . And Ready to Fight

A willingness to fight for the policies one believes in means not only taking up new issues and causes but also a preparedness to fight again and again without undue discouragement, the battles that one thought were already won. Attacks upon individual programs occur again and again, as is happening now with ADC. Attacks on established national policy are even more serious and disturbing, and must not be allowed to pass unchallenged. It seems almost inconceivable that, a quarter of a century after the passage of the Social Security Act, a group of prominent voluntary agency executives could assert in a report to the Mayor of New York this very year that welfare in the American way meant that

. . . in our society those in need are expected to solve their own problems by self-help, through the resources of the family, by neighborly assistance, or, when all such individual efforts fail, by assistance from voluntary organizations. . . . Before undertaking to establish a new public welfare service it should be ascertained that voluntary effort is unequal to the task and is unable to perform it with assistance from government.

Perhaps it is too much to hope that in the short space of 25 years opposition to the policies established by the Social Security Act in 1935, and reaffirmed and strengthened by every successive amendment, will have died away. . . .

\* \* \* \* \*

## Know Where Each Road Leads

Unless we have given thought to the implications of various alternative ways of attaining our objective we may be tempted to grasp at an alleged solution only to find that we have still further entrenched the opponents of the truly effective program. We may grasp at public subsidies to private insurance companies as a relatively easy way of extending medical care to new groups of the population who could not afford to purchase health insurance on a business basis. But we will not do so if we are clear that the only satisfactory solution is one that covers the entire population (which even subsidized private insurance is unlikely to do), and if we are convinced that the only acceptable program is one that provides on a service, not an indemnity basis, and does not contain incentives for the overuse of certain forms of care such as hospitalization. These conditions are unlikely to be met by private insurance unless the public subsidies are accompanied by so many standards that the private companies may well feel that there is little advantage to themselves to be gained by participation, and the public may well ask whether in such circumstances it would not be more economical and effective to run the program as a public service.

But if we see the problem and the desirable solution in these terms, then we shall also realize that a policy of subsidies, however much it may seem for the short run to buy off the opposition, in the long run will make attainment of our goal even more difficult, for we shall be fostering a powerful vested interest opposition which will have much to lose and will fight hard against any change.

### Face Up to Costs

Knowledge of where we want to go in our future policies and of the possible ways of getting there implies also that we have faced up to the costs, not alone in money, of attaining our goals. I suspect that if we truly wish to see a comprehensive public assistance program, based solely on need as an eligibility condition and paying monthly allowances of which we in rich America need not be ashamed, we shall have to contemplate some sacrifices that we have not yet been willing to make.

We may well have to subordinate our present views of states rights to the need for federal standards in regard to residence requirements and perhaps other conditions as well—so too, in unemployment insurance, where progress toward a more adequate system seems unlikely without the enactment of additional federal standards.

We must be ready to face the fact that more adequate payments to the needy who reside in the poorer states (many of whom come to the richer states later on to man our factories and other undertakings) can be secured only if those of us who live in the richer states are prepared to envisage some interstate redistributions of income at our expense.

\*   \*   \*   \*   \*

# DISCUSSION QUESTIONS

1. "Social *Insurance* is a misnomer. The payments are merely promises of the government which it can repudiate." Discuss.

2. "The American social security programs do not represent a rational system. They are rather a bundle of piecemeal legislation lacking consistency and unity." Discuss.

3. "The American social security programs are still in their evolutionary stage." Indicate the probable lines of their future development.

4. Discuss the relative advantages and disadvantages of state versus federal responsibility for various social security programs.

5. "Social assistance is a progression from poor relief in the direction of social insurance, while social insurance is a progression from private insurance in the direction of social assistance." Discuss the applications of these trends to the American situation.

6. "There is very little logic in the present methods of financing social security." Explain the reasons for the present methods and how you would change them.

7. Should the United States aim at a social security program whose object is to provide protection from the cradle to the grave? Discuss your reasons.

# SELECTED REFERENCES

ALTMEYER, ARTHUR J. "The Future of Social Security in America," *Social Service Review* (September, 1953), pp. 251–68.

BEVERIDGE, WILLIAM. *The Pillars of Security*. New York: The Macmillan Co., 1943.

——— Social Insurance and Allied Services, New York: The Macmillan Co., 1942.

BRANDEIS, ELIZABETH. "Centralization and Democracy," *Survey Graphic* (December, 1942).

FAIRLESS, BENJAMIN. *Man's Search for Security*. New York: United States Steel Corporation, 1949.

GLUECK, SHELDON (ed.). *The Welfare State and the National Welfare*. Cambridge, Mass.: Addison-Wesley Press, 1952.

MATTESON, WILLIAM J. *What Will Social Security Mean to You*. Great Barrington, Mass., 1956.

MERRIAM, IDA C. "Merriam Trends in Public Welfare and Their Implications," *American Economic Review* (May, 1957), pp. 470–82.

INTERNATIONAL LABOUR OFFICE. *Approaches to Social Security: An International Survey*. Montreal, 1942.

NATIONAL ASSOCIATION OF SOCIAL WORKERS. *Goals of Public Social Policy.* New York, 1959.

ROCKEFELLER BROTHERS FUND, INC. *The Challenge to America: Its Economic and Social Aspects.* New York: Doubleday & Co., Inc., 1958.

SCHULTZ, THEODORE W. "Investment in Man: An Economist's View," *Social Service Review* (June, 1959), pp. 109–117.

STOKES, DILLARD. *Social Security: Fact and Fancy.* Chicago: Henry Regnery Co., 1956.

TENBROEK, JACOBUS. "The 1956 Amendments to the Social Security Act After the New Look—The First Thought," *Journal of Public Law* (Spring, 1957), pp. 123–62.

WILLCOX, ALANSON W. "Patterns of Social Legislation: Reflections on the Welfare State," *Journal of Public Law*, Vol. VI (Spring, 1957), pp. 3–24.

WILLIAMSON, W. RULON. "Social Security—'Magic' or Muddle?" *Tax Review*, Vol. XII (August, 1951).

# Recent Developments: 1960 Social Security Legislation

## 64. THE SOCIAL SECURITY AMENDMENTS OF 1960: An Analysis of the Provisions of the Legislation and Its Potentialities

WILBUR J. COHEN and
WILLIAM HABER,
1960.

THE SOCIAL SECURITY amendments of 1960 contain modest but important improvements in the social security program. The congressional debate was often marked by sharp ideological differences, especially on the proposed methods of dealing with medical care for the aged. The final changes, however, were largely noncontroversial in character and were adopted with bipartisan and wide support.

In the 25th anniversary year of the Social Security Act the Congress examined proposals relating to every title of the Act. As a result of this consideration, Congress developed legislation which made changes and improvements in nearly all of the programs in the Act.

The major issue before the Congress in the 1960 legislation was how to extend medical services to the aged. In both the House and Senate the controversy was over establishing some type of contributory insurance plan for medical services for the aged. The Forand bill, utilizing the contributory social security approach, was defeated in the House Committee on Ways and Means. The Anderson-Kennedy amendment, utilizing the same approach, was defeated in the Senate. Likewise, the Javits amendment providing for federal grants to the states for subsidizing voluntary health plans for the aged, supported by President Eisenhower and Vice-President Nixon, was defeated in the Senate.

The evidence presented to the Congressional Committees indicated that the cost of adequate medical care for older people was increasing. The Congress concluded that these costs derive, to a large extent, from the fact that impressive improvements have been made in medicines and medical technology, which assist in diagnosis and treatment, and from improved hospital and other facilities and their wider availability to the public. The knowledge that these costs, although unpredictable, are often very heavy, especially for older men and women living on reduced retirement incomes, became a matter of grave concern to the Congress.

As a result, the legislation provides for a program of federal assistance to the states for an expanded program of medical care for persons aged 65 and over. Under this plan the federal share of existing old-age assistance plans will be increased to encourage states to strengthen their medical programs for these people or to initiate new programs. In addition, federal funds will be made available, on a liberalized matching formula, to assist the states in aiding those aged persons, many of them otherwise self-sufficient, who need help only in meeting the costs of medical care.

In addition to these changes the new legislation improves and expands the old-age, survivors, and disability insurance program. On a selective and limited basis it extends coverage and improves certain benefits. This is done without increasing the contribution rates.

Some features of the unemployment insurance program are improved. For the first time in 25 years the contribution rate levied by the federal government for administration and loans to the states is increased. This will enable the federal loan fund to be built up to $550 million instead of $200 million. Coverage is also broadened somewhat.

The authorization for federal grants for maternal and child health services, crippled children services, and child welfare services is increased to $25 million annually for each program.

The exemption of earned income in the aid to the blind plan is increased and the continued approval of the Missouri and Pennsylvania blind assistance plans is extended to June 30, 1964.

### OLD-AGE, SURVIVORS, AND DISABILITY INSURANCE (OASDI) IMPROVEMENTS

**The Disability Insurance Program**

*1. Removal of Age 50 Eligibility Requirement.* An estimated 250,000 people—disabled insured workers under age 50 and their dependents—will qualify for benefits through removal of the age 50 qualification for benefits.

*2. Trial Work Period.* The law strengthens the rehabilitation aspects of the disability program by providing a 12-month period of trial work, during which benefits are continued for all disabled workers who attempt to return to work, rather than limiting this trial work period to those under the formal federal-state vocational rehabilitation plan.

*3. Waiting Period.* The law provides that the disabled worker who regains his ability to work and then within five years again becomes disabled will not be required to wait through a second six-month waiting period before his benefits will be resumed, as was required previously.

### Liberalized Insured Status Requirement

The new law liberalizes the fully insured status requirement by making eligible for benefits persons who have one quarter of coverage for every three calendar quarters elapsing after 1950 (or age 21) and before the year of attaining retirement age (65 for men, 62 for women), disability, or death. The old law required one quarter of coverage for each two quarters so elapsing. (No change was made in the requirement that a person must have a minimum of six quarters of coverage or 40 quarters of coverage to achieve permanent status.) As a result of this change, a person reaching retirement age in 1960 would need to have only 12 quarters of coverage to be insured; whereas, previously, he would need 18 or 19 quarters of coverage. About 400,000 people—workers, dependents, and survivors— will be eligible for benefits as a result of this change.

### Improved Benefit Protection for Dependents and Survivors of Insured Workers

The new law will increase the benefits payable to children in certain cases and would provide benefits for certain wives, widows, widowers, and children of insured workers who are not now eligible for benefits.

*1. Survivors of Workers Who Died before 1940.* Survivors of workers who died before 1940, and who had at least six quarters of coverage, would qualify for benefit payments. About 25,000 people, most of them widows aged 75 or over, would be made eligible for benefits for the first time by this change.

*2. Increase in Children's Benefits.* The benefits payable to the children of deceased workers which under the old law were 75 per cent of the worker's benefit for the first child, plus 50 per cent for each additional child will be made 75 per cent for all children, subject to the family maximum of $254 a month, or 80 per cent of the worker's average monthly wage if less. About 400,000 children would get some increase in benefits as a result of this change.

### Liberalized Retirement Test

A new principle is incorporated in the retirement test. Under the old law a beneficiary under age 72 lost one month's benefit for every $80 (or fraction thereof) by which his annual earnings exceeded $1,200. Under the new law, a beneficiary can earn up to $300 additional (above the $1,200) and can receive benefits equal to one half of such additional earnings. Any earnings above $1,500 will result in a reduction of benefits of $1.00 for each $1.00 of earnings. The change is generally more favorable to retired persons who work and introduces an incentive element into the retirement test between $1,200 and $1,500.

### Increased Coverage

The coverage of the program would be extended to additional people —parents who work for their sons and daughters in a trade or business, workers in Guam and American Samoa, American citizens employed in the United States by foreign governments and international organizations, and certain policemen and firemen under retirement systems.

Another opportunity would be provided for an estimated 60,000 ministers to be covered under the program. If the states take advantage of the opportunity offered them, nearly 2½ million employees of state and local governments could obtain coverage for certain past years on a retroactive basis. Other provisions would facilitate coverage for some of the noncovered people employed in positions covered by state or local retirement systems and for the 100,000 noncovered employees of certain nonprofit organizations.

### Investment of the Trust Funds

The law makes certain changes in the investment provisions relating to the Federal Old-Age and Survivors Insurance Trust Fund and Federal Disability Insurance Trust Fund so as to make interest earnings on new government obligations purchased for the trust funds more nearly equivalent to the rate of return being received by people who buy government obligations in the open market.

These changes make for more equitable treatment of the trust funds and are generally in line with the recommendations of the Advisory Council on Social Security Financing.

### Technical and Minor Substantive Changes

The new law makes a number of amendments of a technical nature. These provisions will correct several technical flaws in the law, make for more equitable treatment of people, and simplify and improve the operation of the program. One of the important changes is a revision in the method of computing the average monthly wage for benefit purposes.

### Financing and Actuarial Status of the Trust Funds

The improvements provided in the new law in the old-age, survivors, and disability insurance program will not necessitate an increase in social security taxes to keep the program actuarially sound. Both trust funds will remain in approximate actuarial balance.

### Scope of Advisory Council on Social Security Financing

The social security amendments of 1956 authorized the establishment of periodic Advisory Councils to study and report on the financing of OASDI. The new law provides that the Council to be appointed in 1963 is to make findings and recommendations with respect to extension of coverage, adequacy of benefits, and all aspects of the OASDI program in addition to those relating to financing. Under this amendment the Council can consider medical care proposals.

## THE MATERNAL AND CHILD WELFARE PROGRAMS

The new law provides that the authorization for annual appropriations for the maternal and child health services program be increased from $21.5 million to $25 million; the crippled children's services from $20 million to $25 million; and the child welfare program from $17 million to $25 million. A new authorization for research and demonstration projects in the child welfare services program permits grants to public and other nonprofit institutions and agencies for this purpose.

## IMPROVEMENTS IN UNEMPLOYMENT INSURANCE

The changes made in the legislation improve and extend the federal-state program of unemployment insurance. The changes, which were noncontroversial, include:

1. An increase in the net federal unemployment tax (the tax that may not be offset by a credit for taxes paid under a state program) from three-tenths to four-tenths of 1 per cent on the first $3,000 of annual covered wages.

2. A provision that the proceeds of this higher federal tax after covering the administrative expenses of the employment security program will be available to build up a larger fund for loans to states whose reserves may become depleted. The loan fund is increased from a maximum of $200 million to $550 million or four-tenths of 1 per cent of total wages subject to state unemployment taxes, whichever is higher.

3. Improvements in the arrangements for financing the administrative costs of the program by building up a revolving fund of $250 million for such expenditures.

4. Tightening of the conditions relating to eligibility for and repayment of loans.

5. Extension of the coverage of unemployment insurance to some 60,000 to 70,000 additional employees such as those working in Federal Reserve banks, federal credit unions, and commercial and industrial activities of nonprofit institutions.

6. Provision that Puerto Rico will be treated as a state for the purposes of the unemployment insurance program.

## CHANGES IN AID TO THE BLIND PROGRAM

### Increase in the Income Exemption

Effective July 1, 1962, a state agency, in determining need for blind assistance, must disregard the first $85 of earned income per month plus one half of earned income in excess of $85. Until July 1, 1962, a state is permitted to disregard the first $85 per month and one half of the excess or to continue to apply the $50 per month exemption in the old law.

### Missouri and Pennsylvania Plans

Special legislation providing for the approval of the Missouri and Pennsylvania blind assistance plans expire June 30, 1961. This temporary provision is extended to June 30, 1964.

## MEDICAL SERVICES TO THE AGED

The new legislation makes three basic changes in the existing old-age assistance provisions (title I) of the Social Security Act to encourage the states to improve and extend medical services to the aged:

1. Increases federal funds to the states for medical services for the 2.4 million aged persons now receiving old-age assistance.
2. Authorizes federal grants to the states for payment of part or all of the medical services of such aged persons who, at one time or another, according to the state may be in need of assistance in paying their medical expenses.
3. Instructs the Secretary of Health, Education, and Welfare to develop guides or recommended standards for the use of the states in evaluating and improving their programs of medical services for the aged.

After extended debate Congress designed a federal-state matching program based upon principles of federal-state cooperation. This program is established under title I of the Social Security Act, thereby providing additional matching funds to the states to: (1) establish a new program or improve their existing medical care program for those on the old-age assistance rolls, and (2) add a new program designed to furnish medical assistance to those needy elderly citizens who are not eligible for old-age assistance but who are financially unable to pay for the medical and hospital care needed to preserve their health and prolong their life. This two-fold plan would thus cover all medically needy aged 65 or over, whether or not they are eligible for old-age assistance, or whether or not they are eligible for the benefits under the social security or any other retirement program. It accomplishes this objective within the framework of a federal-state program with broad authority allowed to the states as to the programs they will institute, improve, and administer in meeting the health needs of the aged when illness occurs or continues.

## MEDICAL CARE FOR THE AGED
## RECEIVING OLD-AGE ASSISTANCE

### Purpose

Title I provides federal funds to the states for medical services to aged individuals who are determined to be needy by the states. States provide needy aged persons with "money payments" for medical services and also provide "vendor payments" to the suppliers of medical care (for instance, doctors, hospitals, and nurses). Congress found that these provisions vary greatly. Some states have relatively adequate provisions for the medical care of needy aged persons; others have little or no provision. The increased federal financial provisions in the new law are designed to encourage the states to extend comprehensive medical services to all needy persons receiving monthly assistance payments. Participation in the federal-state program is completely optional with the states, with each state determining the extent and character of its own program, including the standards of eligibility and the nature and scope of benefits.

### Effect of the Legislation

Prior to the 1960 legislation the federal government made available to the states funds for medical services to needy aged persons, but federal financial participation was limited to a stated statutory proportion of average assistance expenditures up to $65 per month.

To encourage all states to develop a comprehensive medical care program, additional federal funds will be available to the states, effective October 1, 1960, as follows: A provision is added to the existing law to provide for federal financial participation in expenditures to vendors for medical services of up to $12 per month in addition to the existing $65 maximum provision. In effect, the federal maximum is raised from an average of $65 to $77 a month. Where the state average payment is over $65 per month, the federal share in respect to such medical-services costs as bring the average over $65 would be a minimum of 50 per cent and a maximum of 80 per cent, depending upon each state's per capita income.

The payments under this program would be made directly to providers of medical services.

### Eligibility

Each state has the responsibility of determining the standard of eligibility for the medical care it provides aged persons. For aged persons receiving money payments, the state must take into consideration any income and resources of the individual.

### Scope of Medical Services

There is no federal limitation on medical services provided under the bill. Each state may determine for itself the scope of medical services to be provided in its program.

### Federal Matching

The bill provides for an increase in federal funds for medical services. The formula, as outlined above, would result in federal funds in addition to those presently provided. Additional federal funds may be obtained only for medical services, within the $12 per recipient maximum for payments, made directly to providers of the medical services. States have the option of transferring part or all of the money payments now made for medical services to vendor payments.

## MEDICAL ASSISTANCE FOR THE AGED
## NOT RECEIVING OLD-AGE ASSISTANCE

### Purpose

The new law amends existing title I to make it clear that states may extend their assistance to cover the medically needy. The states would have a financial incentive to establish such programs where they do not exist or to extend such programs where they are not adequate in coverage or comprehensive in the scope of benefits.

A state desiring to establish a program for assisting low-income individuals in meeting their medical expenses would submit an amendment of its old-age assistance plan which, if found by the Secretary of Health, Education, and Welfare to fulfill the requirements specified in this title, would be approved for federal matching. A number of the plan requirements are substantially the same as those in the present public assistance titles. Other plan requirements are directed specifically to accomplishing the purposes of the new title, to assist aged persons who are able to meet their expenses other than their medical needs.

A state would have broad latitude in determining eligibility for benefits under the program as well as the scope and nature of the services to be provided within the limitations prescribed. Thus, each state would determine the tests for eligibility and the medical services to be provided under the state program within the limitations described below. Federal financial participation would be governed by the establishment of an approved plan subject to the criteria and limitations prescribed in the law.

### Eligibility

Benefits under a state program may be provided only for persons 65 years of age or over to the extent they are able to pay the cost of their medical expenses. Under this program, it will be possible for states to provide medical services to individuals on the basis of an eligibility requirement that is more liberal than that in effect for the states' old-age assistance programs. The state plan could not be approved if it includes any residence requirement which excludes any individual applying for medical assistance for the aged who resides in the state.

Section 1 of the Social Security Act is amended to provide that one of the objectives of the title is to furnish medical assistance to individuals who are not recipients of old-age assistance but whose income and resources are insufficient to meet the costs of necessary medical services.

It would cover all medically needy aged 65 or over; it would cover every such person including those under the social security system, railroad retirement system, civil service retirement system, or any other public or private retirement system whether such person is retired or still working, subject only to the participation in the program by the state of which they are resident; it would cover the widows of such workers as well as their dependents who meet the age 65 requirement and are unable to provide for their medical care. There are many individuals who have not worked under the social security program or any other retirement program for a sufficient time to ever become eligible for retirement benefits; any or all of these groups would be able to receive medical assistance under the state health plan.

A state may, if it wishes, disregard in whole or part the existence of any income or resources of an individual for medical assistance. An individual who applies for medical assistance may be deemed eligible by the state notwithstanding the fact he has a child who may be financially able to pay all or part of his care, or that he owns or has an equity in a homestead, or that he has some life insurance with a cash value, or that he is receiving an old-age insurance benefit, annuity, or retirement benefit. The state has wide latitude to establish the standard of need for medical assistance as long as it is a reasonable standard consistent with the objectives of the title. In establishing such a standard a state must comply with all other applicable provisions of section 2 of the Social Security Act, as amended by the new law.

This is based on the grounds that an aged individual who has adjusted his living standard to a low income, but who still has income and resources above the level applicable for old-age assistance, might be unable to deal with his medical expenses. The Congress intends that states should set reasonable outer limits on the resources an individual may hold and still be found eligible for medical services. Individuals who are recipients of old-age assistance in any month would not be eligible for participation in the medical assistance program in that month.

### Scope of Benefits

The scope of medical benefits and services provided will be determined by the states. The federal government, however, will participate under the matching formula in any program which provides any or all of the following services, provided both institutional and noninstitutional services are available: (1) Inpatient hospital services; (2) skilled nursing-home services; (3) physicians' services; (4) outpatient hospital services; (5) home health care services; (6) private-duty nursing services; (7) physical therapy and related services; (8) dental services; (9) laboratory and X-ray services; (10) prescribed drugs, eye glasses, dentures, and prosthetic devices; (11) diagnostic, screening, and preventive services; and (12) any other medical care or remedial care recognized under state law.

The description of the care, services, and supplies provided with federal financial participation which may be provided for recipients of medical assistance for the aged is intended to be as broad in scope as the medical and other remedial care which may be provided as old-age assistance under title I of the existing law with federal financial participation. The various types of care and services have been enumerated primarily for informational purposes. A state may, if it wishes, include medical services provided by osteopaths, chiropractors, and optometrists and remedial services provided by Christian Science practitioners.

The medical provisions permit the states to utilize, at their option, existing voluntary health insurance plans if they wish. For instance, a state may make payments to Blue Cross, Blue Shield, or group practice prepayment plans for any medical services. Moreover, a state may utilize one or more of these plans in one or more communities. It is not necessary for the voluntary plan to be statewide in operation as long as the state, on behalf of individuals, provides for the payment, on a statewide basis, of the medical services covered in the state plan. A state may, if it wishes, pay for such services on a premium, fee for service, salary, or per capita basis, or any reasonable combination of such methods.

The "eligibility" conditions and the scope of medical services provided must be statewide in operation and must be available to all persons in the state in similar circumstances. But the state may select more than one method to carry out these policies. For instance, it may insure part of hospitalization costs through a Blue Cross plan by paying the premium therefor; and, if the state wishes, any part of the hospital cost not met through such insurance might be paid in part or whole by the state welfare agency. The state welfare agency could arrange through the state health department and a state visiting nurse agency to pay for visiting nurse services. All of these alternatives are available to a state provided it makes available the same content of medical service to all persons it has determined to be eligible under the income standards it has selected itself.

### Federal Matching

The federal government will share with the states in the cost of the new medical assistance program in accordance with the matching formula prescribed by the new law. The federal share of the cost will be determined in the same general manner as previously provided for the portion of the old-age assistance payments between $30 and $65 per month; that is, the federal share will depend upon the per capita income of the state as related to the national average, but with a range from 50 to 80 per cent. For Puerto Rico, Guam, and the Virgin Islands the matching will be on a 50–50 basis. There is no maximum upon the dollar amount of federal participation in the new program. Appropriation requirements, therefore, would depend upon the programs developed by the states. Thus, the total cost would depend upon the scope of services offered and the number of persons found eligible by the states under the respective state plans.

The federal government will participate in the cost of administering these programs on a dollar-for-dollar basis, as is now true in the four public assistance programs.

In recognition of the fact that some states might be able to take advantage of the federal funds for this program very quickly, Congress set the effective date for the new program as October 1, 1960.

### Plan Requirements

There are ten plan requirements which a state must meet to obtain federal funds and which apply to both old-age assistance and medical assistance for the aged. Nine of these are identical with those in the previous law. The state plan must:

1. Provide that it will be in effect in all political subdivisions and be mandatory upon those subdivisions if administered by them.
2. Provide for financial participation by the state.
3. Provide for establishment or designation of a single state agency to administer or supervise administration of the plan.
4. Provide for giving claimants a fair hearing if their claims are denied or not acted upon with reasonable promptness.
5. Provide methods of administration found necessary for the proper and efficient operation of the plan—these must include a merit system for personnel.
6. Provide for making of necessary reports to the Secretary.
7. Provide safeguards against use and disclosure of information concerning applicants for and recipients of assistance, except for purposes directly connected with the administration of the plan.
8. Provide all individuals wishing to do so an opportunity to apply for assistance, and provide that assistance will be furnished with reasonable promptness to those who are eligible.
9. Provide, if the plan includes assistance for or on behalf of individuals in private or public institutions, for the establishment or designation of a state authority or authorities to be responsible for establishing and maintaining standards for such institutions.

The new plan provision is one which requires that a state plan must include reasonable standards, consistent with the objectives of title I, for determining the eligibility of individuals for old-age assistance or medical assistance and the extent of such assistance.

The amended law retains the provisions included in the law in 1939 that the state plan for old-age assistance must provide for taking into consideration any other income and resources of an individual in determining his need for old-age assistance. This requirement is omitted for medical assistance to the aged.

There are four new plan requirements for the medical assistance for the aged. The state plan must:

1. Provide for inclusion of some institutional and some noninstitutional care.
2. Prohibit enrollment fees, premiums, and similar charges as a condition of eligibility.

3. Include provisions, to the extent required by the Secretary's regulations, for furnishing assistance to residents of the state who are temporarily absent therefrom.

4. Provide that property liens will not be imposed on account of benefits received under the plan during a recipient's lifetime and limit recovery of benefits paid from the recipient's estate after the death of any surviving spouse.

The Act provides that nothing in the amended title I is to be construed to permit a state to have in effect with respect to any period more than one state plan approved under such title.

## MEDICAL GUIDES AND RECOMMENDATIONS

As recommended by the Advisory Council on Public Assistance, appointed pursuant to the social security amendments of 1958, the law instructs the Secretary of Health, Education, and Welfare to develop guides or recommended standards for the information of the states as to the level, content, and quality of medical care for the public assistance medical programs. He would also prepare such guides and standards for use in the new programs of medical assistance for the medically needy aged. It is expected that the Secretary will appoint an Advisory Committee on Public Assistance Medical Care with whom he will consult on the medical assistance program. In these ways it is expected that the additional federal funds made available in this bill will be channeled as rapidly as possible into an improvement in and extension of medical services to needy aged persons. Under existing provisions of law the Secretary has authority to make any recommendations for changes in the program should any changes become apparent in the administration of the program. These provisions should ensure the development of an effective and efficient program adapted to the needs of the aged and to the differences among the states.

According to Senator Robert S. Kerr, the author of the plan, it is hoped and expected that states will make every effort to take advantage of the new legislation on October 1. Those states which do not have sufficient legislative authority or appropriations to take advantage of it were encouraged by him to do so as rapidly as possible. The Secretary was requested to make a report to the Congress by March 15, 1962, as to the steps taken by the states to carry out the purposes of the legislation. Such report shall include whether the states have utilized the additional funds to extend and improve their medical program for needy individuals and the Secretary's recommendations for obtaining the proper level, content, and quality of medical care in those states which he finds have not done so.

The Secretary was also requested to make a study of all the medical resources available to meet the needs of public assistance recipients and to report his finding to the Congress. According to the House Committee report:

The information is of vital importance to the Congress in considering the problems of medical care needed by the low-income people of the Nation. The committee expects the Department will obtain the cooperation of the states and various other public and voluntary agencies and organizations in making the study.

## NUMBERS OF PERSONS AFFECTED AND COSTS

Each year, after all state plans are in full operation, the Department of Health, Education, and Welfare estimates one-half to 1 million persons may become ill and require medical services that could result in payments under this title.

In the first year after enactment of the law, when relatively few states will probably have had an opportunity to develop comprehensive plans (although it is expected that all states now not having comprehensive medical programs for their old-age assistance recipients will adopt or extend such programs), an estimated additional $60 million in federal funds would be expended for medical assistance for the aged. In addition, increased federal funds for matching vendor medical-care payments in respect to the 2.4 million old-age assistance recipients are estimated at about $140 million. Thus, under both programs combined, the additional federal cost would total about $200 million. The Department estimated that the states and localities would participate to the extent of about $60 million. The combined federal, state, and local funds involved might be around $260 million.

With respect to costs after the new programs have been in effect for several years, it must be considered that the old-age assistance roll is decreasing slowly, but that states with no vendor medical payments now (or with small payments of this type) will probably develop quite comprehensive medical-care programs for the old-age assistance recipients. The increased federal funds for matching the vendor medical-care payments of old-age assistance recipients are estimated at about $175 million annually in the long run. In addition, an estimated $165 million in federal funds for medical services for the aged may be provided in a full year of operation after the states have had the opportunity to develop these programs (and this figure could even be much higher if all states had relatively well-developed and comprehensive plans). Thus, under both programs combined, the annual federal cost would total about $340 million. The state and local funds would be in the neighborhood of $170 million. The combined total thus would be about $500 million.

## CONCLUSION

The 1960 legislation does not compare in scope or significance with the social security amendments of 1950, 1954, 1956, or 1958. By rejecting the contributory social insurance approach for meeting medical care costs for the aged and instead extending the public assistance approach, the Congress disregarded the principles it has reiterated on several occasions. However, it should be recalled that this also occurred in 1950 when Congress rejected disability insurance and enacted disability assistance, only to return to disability insurance as the basic program in 1956.

If major reliance is placed on the public assistance approach for meeting medical care needs of the aged, it is likely that the potential cost may be in the neighborhood of $1.5 to 2.5 billion annually from general revenues. It is reasonably certain that the states will not be able to meet their share of such costs, hence the potential cost will not be realized and the problem will not be adequately met. The issue still remains, then: What additional measures should be adopted to make public assistance medical care a supplementary or second line of defense instead of a primary resource?

The congressional debate indicated that there was bipartisan support for some additional federal action to deal more effectively with the problem of medical care for the aged. It is likely, therefore, that the next session of the Congress will see some additional legislation enacted which is not based upon the public assistance approach.

Many states cannot take full advantage of the 1960 legislation without new legislative authorization and appropriations. Consideration will no doubt be given in some states to the calling of special sessions of the state legislatures to implement the new legislation. Other states which have administrative authority to implement the new legislation in part or in whole should make every attempt to do so and will no doubt take some steps in this direction.

The 1960 legislation does introduce some important new principles: The abolition of any residence requirement for medical assistance, the federal financial share for medical assistance without any dollar maximum, and the incentive principle in the retirement test in OASDI. Moreover, the abolition of the age 50 limitation in the disability insurance program is a notable achievement. Four years previously the disability insurance program was enacted in a most controversial and close debate. The program was enacted in the Senate in 1956 with only one vote to spare. Yet, despite the initial opposition of the medical societies, insurance companies, and employer groups to its enactment, the administration of the program has been successful. Its extension in 1960 is ample testimony to the fact that each step in the evolution of social legislation is won the hard way, over tremendous opposition and criticism. Then, when enacted, it eventually becomes the accepted way of dealing with the problem and soon gets to be supported by most of those who originally opposed it.

The 1960 legislation is thus another step in the process of social legislation which will continue.

# Index

*This book has been set on the Linotype in 10 point Janson and Caledonia Bold, leaded 2 points, and 9 point Janson, leaded 1 point. Chapter numbers and titles are in 14 point Caledonia Bold and 24 point Alternate Gothic; article titles are in 18 point Gothic No. 2. The size of the type page is 27 by 47 picas.*